MATCH HOLDERS

100 Years of Ingenuity

Denis B. Alsford

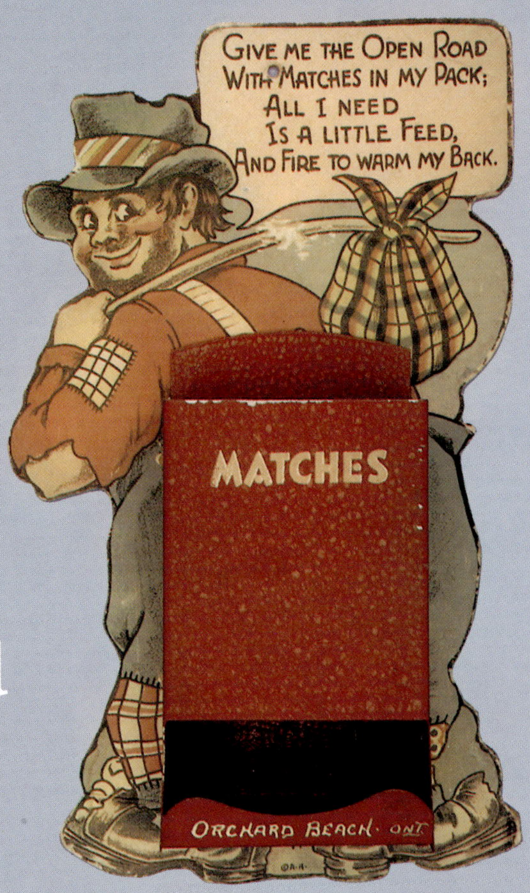

with Price Guide

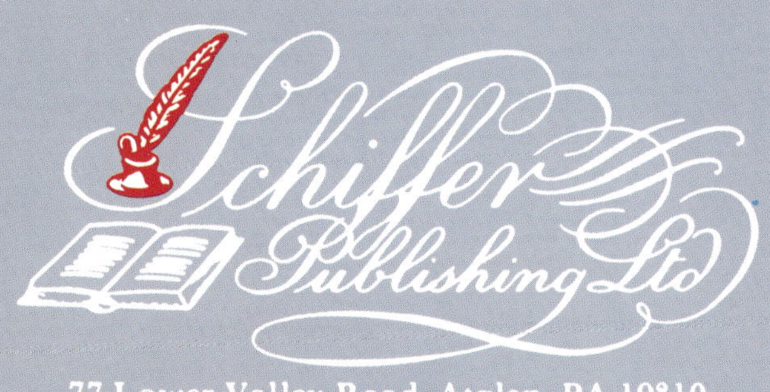

77 Lower Valley Road, Atglen, PA 19310

Acknowledgments

Without the support and encouragement of my wife over a period of fifteen years, throughout the process of collecting and the writing of this book, this publication would not have been possible. I am also deeply indebted to my son Stephen for his patience in reviewing the original manuscript, making countless corrections and helpful suggestions.

Stanley G. Aston of Barking, Essex, has permitted me to use a number of his illustrations, painstakingly copied from the Design Registers at the Public Records Office in London. Stanley has spent many patient hours copying each drawing in pencil, and then redrawing them in pen and ink at home. Through his numerous articles in the *Newsletter of the British Match Label & Booklet Society* he has made public a wealth of knowledge. He has shared his extensive knowledge with me, and without his help, much of the information herein would not have been available.

To Ed Wright go my heartfelt thanks for taking a week out of his busy life to accompany me and the collection to Pennsylvania for the photography; also for his constant encouragement and interest.

I would like to thank the following people and institutions for permission to use match holders from their collections: Jack Leaske of Ottawa, Ontario, for 476, 643 and 650. The National Museum of Science & Technology, Ottawa, Ontario, for 619 left and 620. Jake Graydon Smith of Ottawa, Ontario, for 216, 241, and 251 top. George Sparacio of Malaga, New Jersey, for 65 center, 83, 87, 112, 114, 118, 148, 149, 286, 287 and 288. From the Earle Stone family collection: 108, 199, 267, 268, 270, 271, 272, 284, 285, 289, 327, 328, 330, 331, 411 and 412.

Edward J. Wright of Ajax, Ontario, for 6, 65 left, 132 right, 235, 422 right, 426, 428 left, 436, 437 and 449.

I also wish to express my gratitude for permission to use illustrations from the following sources: Stanley G. Aston: 24, 28 left, 32, 34, 38, 304, 306, 309, 360, 413, 470, 510, 600, 601, 625, 626, 627, 628, 629 and 630. Controller of Her Majesty's Stationery Office: 28 right, 40, 70, 74, 142, 614, 617, and 618, Paul Jung: 213, 348, and 621. Painting The Town Inc: 689. Public Archives Canada: 86. Reproduced by permission of Punch: 15. United States Department of Commerce. Patent and Trademark Office: 79, 82, 223, 294, 297, 310, 324, 325 left, 326, 383, 384, 397, 446, 448, 469, 472, 474, 487, 488, 491, 492, 505, 506, 511, 615, 616, 634, 635, 640, 648, 651, 653, 657, and 659 top. United States Fish and Wildlife Service: 214 and 215. University of Reading, Rural History Centre: 75. From the collection of the late E. R. Wheatley-Hubbard of Warminster, Wiltshire: 622.

Finally a word of thanks to Peter Schiffer for his guidance, encouragement and trust, and to my editor and a fine photographer Jeffrey B. Snyder.

Library of Congress Catalog Number: 94-65852

Printed in China.
ISBN: 0-88740-633-5

Published by Schiffer Publishing, Ltd.
77 Lower Valley Road
Atglen, PA 19310
Please write for a free catalog.
This book may be purchased from the publisher.
Please include $2.95 postage.
Try your bookstore first.

We are interested in hearing from authors
with book ideas on related subjects.

Contents

Preamble

Soon after I had started to collect match holders, a hobby that my wife and I shared, it became apparent that very little had been published on the subject. As time went on and the collection grew, I began to find a little information here, and a little there, but not much.

It soon became obvious that I was collecting curios: undocumented pieces of Victorian and Edwardian nostalgia, about which few dealers knew anything. Nor could I find other fellow collectors locally with whom I could compare notes or share information. But the collecting bug had bitten, and I determined to seek out information that would give more meaning to my hobby, or rather, my obsession.

Slowly I began to assemble pieces of information, and with persistence, perseverance and perhaps a tinge of insanity, I found one or two other collectors around the world who were willing to correspond with me, and other resources that ultimately provided a wealth of documentary evidence.

By constantly re-examining my collection with the aid of a jeweler's loop, I discovered details that I had previously missed, and I began to understand how match holders were constructed.

Some match holders are marked with patent dates or other forms of registered marks, in addition to other marks that are traceable in official records and published sources.

From the patent records of Canada, Great Britain and the United States which are available in all three national capitals, and with some of the records available in some major institutions, it is possible to piece together a significant body of related information, including not only the details of a particular patent, but also some history and the extent of the product range of a company, or even the wide field of interest of a specific inventor.

In the U.S. Patent Index, published annually, it is possible to look under the heading of "match" and quickly find the items of interest. A survey of the Invention Patent index from the years 1858 to 1908 shows that over eight hundred match holders were the subject of inventions. It may be speculated that up until the 1930s there were probably well over twelve hundred such inventions. The United States Design Patents index reveals an additional two hundred Design Patents issued between 1856 and 1930.

Trade and mail order catalogues are a further invaluable resource. The Winterthur Museum collection of such catalogues has been recorded on microfiche, and is available in numerous institutions. A number of trade and mail order company catalogues have been reprinted. Such catalogues provide illustrations, dates, prices of the day, and occasionally manufacturers' names.

In the antique markets of Britain and North America match holders from those areas are obviously predominant, but this provides a false impression of the overall development of the phenomenon, to which the rest of Europe and Asia have provided a significant contribution. Thus a further obstacle to research is language, and available published resources in English relating to those areas.

As my information bank grew, my curios began to take on some real meaning; many have become quite well documented artifacts with a life and history of their own. With one or two exceptions, each piece started out in my collection as an undocumented relic of the past. Perhaps half are still undocumented; many of those may be undocumentable, but much research still remains to be done.

I intend to continue my research and add to the body of information so far assembled. But all of the research, however satisfying it may be to me on a personal basis, is a wasted effort if its results are not imparted to others who may have a similar interest.

The data base that I have assembled goes beyond the name of the manufacturer, the date of manufacture, and retail prices of the time. It revives memories of people, places, events, businesses, and a host of other matters perhaps trivial to some but intriguing to others such as myself. It opens up aspects of the past that have been long forgotten, all sorts of unsuspected slices of human history. Some of this I have tried to convey in this book.

When a body of discrete pieces of information has been assembled, it needs a certain amount of synthesis and interpretation to bring order out of chaos. Yet there always seem to be gaps in the information, and so conclusions are often less than satisfying, no more than hypotheses. I have found that the more information I accumulate, the less I seem to know! But, for all that, there comes a time when the information should be packaged and passed on, despite the deficiencies, in the hope of providing a foundation of knowledge for others, who will enlarge and improve what is already known.

All but about twenty-five examples illustrated in the book are from my own collection (which is by no means the most extensive in existence, but it is fairly diversified). The examples include some that I believe are rather exceptional, and others that are far from being the best or the most aesthetically pleasing. Although, in the minds of some collectors, some examples might be classified as junk, they are nevertheless examples that demonstrate the diversity of a phenomenon.

My hope here is to demonstrate that, from a collection of curios, with the right approach and some dedication, it is possible to build a meaningful body of information on a specific subject—in this case, match holders; the same methodology may be applied to other types of collections.

Why have I chosen to refer to these pieces of a historical past as match holders, when many other terms are, or have been, used? In Britain the term "Vesta boxes" is commonly used; but the boxes were made for other forms of match than the wax vesta. In the United States patent records, terms such as "match safe", "match box", "match case" and "match receptacle" are used for the same form of box regardless of its type. I have used "match holder" as a generic term for any device in which it was intended to relocate any of the various forms of match once they had passed from the match vendor to the purchaser.

Chapter I
Introduction

The friction match has been a mixed blessing to society. On the one hand it removed a lot of drudgery from peoples' lives, provided employment for a significant number, and in the subject under discussion here has provided convenience and in some cases, pleasure. On the other hand it has been the cause of considerable misery as a result of fires, helped to perpetuate dreadful working conditions, and caused fearsome, if not fatal, health problems.

Its appearance in the 1830s as an apparently minor tool of daily life has led to the match being more or less disregarded as an item of any historical significance. However, its impact has been far greater than is generally realized.

A long-sought-after means of instantaneous light eluded man for centuries until John Walker, a chemist living in Stockton-on-Tees in northern England, accidentally discovered the secret and went on to make the first friction matches. Previously, in Europe and most other areas of the civilized world, the flint and steel method was the norm for producing flame. A lengthy, painful and haphazard method, often attempted under poor circumstances, success in obtaining a flame was not guaranteed. Other methods were tried but found wanting: using friction to generate heat between two pieces of wood, a magnifying glass to concentrate the sun's rays to a point, as well as other chemical processes and devices.

Early matches were in the form of flat splints, about eight centimeters long by about half a centimeter wide and a millimeter thick. They were tipped with a mixture of chlorate of potash, sugar and some form of gum. When dipped into a phial of sulphuric acid and withdrawn, the splint burst into flame. This form of match was in use early in the l9th century, but was unreliable and the acid proved dangerous.

The shape of this match was retained by Walker in 1826 when he first produced his friction matches, tipped with a mixture of chlorate of potash, sulphide of antimony, gum arabic and water. The tip was placed within a folded piece of sandpaper and withdrawn sharply to produce ignition. He made and sold them in batches of one hundred for one shilling, plus twopence for a tin box container. He recorded the sales in his Day Book, in which the matches are called "Sulphurata Hyperoxygenata Frict."

Walker failed to patent his invention and so his matches were copied by others until he quit making them around 1830. Although the match industry had begun in a small way, eventually it was to spawn large business empires in Europe and North America.

Walker's flat splints were discarded by the copiers in favour of shorter rectangular or round stems, which at that time were called 'Lucifers', a term that became generic throughout the century.

In the early to middle Victorian period, the east end of London became a major center of match production, with numerous small businesses springing up. Many were little more than domestic businesses. Conditions of work were appalling, with young children and women employed in cramped and totally unsanitary spaces.

Large cities in continental Europe simultaneously developed their match industries in much the same manner, and by 1832 white phosphorus was first used on match heads in Austria and Germany, its use quickly spreading to Britain. This resulted in more reliability for ignition but introduced the dreaded disease known as 'phossy jaw', the destruction of facial and bone tissue, which caused severe disfigurement at least, and all too frequently death, to those who produced matches. It was to be almost eighty years before this scourge to human life was eradicated, despite the fact that alternative advances in the chemistry of matches had been made long before, and the continued suffering could have been avoided if governments had taken appropriate action.

Although the early phosphorus matches were unreliable, often difficult to ignite, or too easily ignited by accident if not carefully handled and protected, they quickly became cheap to purchase: one penny a box, and affordable to most people.

In the United States the first patent issued for a friction match was granted to Alonzo D. Phillips of Springfield, Massachusetts, in October l836. As in Europe there were many small American match manufacturing businesses that had sprung up. But it seems that the manufacture of match holders did not develop until the mid to late 1850s.

It has been said that the match was one of the greatest inventions for women. In most households it was a woman who was first out of bed, often when it was still dark and cold. The match permitted her to obtain instant light for a candle, rather than struggle in unfavorable conditions with flint and steel. The candle could then provide ignition for other sources of light or heat.

Men could carry a box of matches and light their pipes, cigars, and later cigarettes, outdoors. Where flame was required periodically in the work-place, the match could provide this without loss of time that other methods required. Boxes of matches, or special containers to hold matches, could be put in several convenient locations about the home, place of work, or centers of social gathering such as bars, clubs and hotels, wherever they were required.

Because the standard of living was very low for most people, social unrest was commonplace in Victorian times. Organized groups of workers called 'Trade Unions' were formed to force owners to improve working conditions. The first working women to form a Trade Union were the "matchgirls" employed by Bryant & May, the major British match manufacturer. They went out on strike in July 1888, after forming the Union of Women Match Makers.

By about 1860, the noxious white phosphorus had been replaced by innocuous red phosphorus and matches became safer and more reliable; moreover, the safety match had been introduced from Sweden. The principle behind the safety match was the separation of the chemicals. The head retained a mixture of chlorate of potash and sulphide of antimony; but the red phosphorus was mixed with sand and applied to the outside of the box. Friction was still required, but ignition could not be achieved without the chemicals on the head of the match and the outside of the box being brought in contact. Nonetheless, the "strike anywhere" matches remained popular, and in fact are still available today in a modified form, in which only the tip of the head is "alive", not the complete head.

There were numerous other forms of match introduced over the years, but all were essentially derived from Walker's original invention, and their popularity rose and fell with the times. Perhaps the most interesting development has been the wax vesta (the name being derived from the Roman goddess of hearth and fire). First invented as early as l832, it is still made today, particularly in Italy. Chemically the heads are the same as the "strike anywhere" and safety matches, but the stem is made up of cotton threads encased in wax: in effect, a miniature candle. Earlier forms are typically about five centimeters long, while later forms are seldom more than three to four centimeters.

From the time that matches were first sold, in shops or by street vendors, the manufacturers put them up in thin wood chip or cardboard boxes, as they are still sold today. The sizes of the boxes have varied according to the type of match being offered. Some other forms, such as cylindrical or cheap tin boxes, have come and gone, but in substance the rectangular box has changed very little.

The early boxes of matches were cheap and convenient, but provided little protection from accidental ignition in the home or in the pocket, and lacked aesthetic appeal for the more affluent members of society. Therefore it was not long before special fancy containers were being produced, providing better protection and novel designs, in an age when novelty was superseding necessity in social circles.

This trend developed in Europe in the 1830s, and did not catch on in North America until after the middle of the 19th century. The inventive and ingenious European craftsmen created a wealth of decorative match holders, intended primarily for use in the home. Meanwhile, mass production methods increased efficiency in the workplace, which kept prices down and helped to create a market that included the middle classes.

Pocket boxes were slower to develop, probably due largely to the fact that matches carried upon the person were subject to considerable movement, thus creating sufficient friction to cause ignition more readily, with disastrous results. At this time snuff-taking was popular, and the addition of a striking plate to a snuff box converted it to a match box; this was probably the most common form of pocket match box. Boxes made specifically for carrying matches in the pocket are quite rare prior to the mid 1850s.

The greater reliability and safety of matches, by about 1860, encouraged production of specialized boxes to hold matches, and reduced the need to provide a lid for those holders that hung on the wall or stood on some convenient horizontal surface. Lids were still required for pocket boxes, however. Mass production, fueled by the Victorian desire for novelties and knick-knacks around the home, led to the growth of the match holder industry in Europe and North America.

The development of match holders not only reflects the development of the match, but also the changing art styles of the period between about 1840 and 1930. Their styles also reflect or document social change and practices, historical events, local and national business interests, and places of popular appeal.

A significant introduction in the history of the match is the invention of the book match. This form of match has come to dominate the North American market since it was introduced there just before the turn of the century. Easy to manufacture and very cheap to produce, it became a useful and effective medium for advertising. As an advertising 'gimmick', matchbooks have been given away by businesses to promote their products or services. One United States company alone today manufactures almost four billion matchbooks each year, most of which are given away. In 1902 the Diamond Match Company made ten million matchbooks for the Pabst Brewing Company bearing the brewer's name; they were given away for promotional purposes.

In Europe matchbooks were less popular. In Britain this may be partly explained by the match tax system, which prevented businesses from giving them away as advertisements. In 1927 the British budget imposed a tax of twelve shillings (approximately three dollars at that time) per 1000 books, each containg twenty matches, a considerable sum in those days.

The invention of the matchbook is credited to Joshua Pusey, an American patent attorney. This claim, however, is arguable. His Invention Patent was issued on September 27, 1892 for a "Flexible Match," in the form of a strip of matches that remained joined to each other (at the end opposite the head) by a broad band, which also separated the first strip from a second strip of matches below. The broad band was folded, thus creating two rows of matches, like the pages of a book. The striker was to be located in between the two "pages". Pusey originally filed his application for the patent on August 6, 1889, but did not complete the application at that time, waiting until March 17, 1892, before he renewed and completed it. After another delay he sold the invention to the Diamond Match Company of America in l894, although it was another two years before they relocated the striker to the outside of the cover and commenced production

In Germany, Paul Lorenz applied for a patent for a similar invention on March 17, 1892 (the same day as Pusey re-applied), which was granted in 1893. Lorenz was a match manufacturer and immediately went into production, marketing his bookmatches under the name of "Pyroca", a name that is known to have been registered as a trademark in Britain in 1893. So the production of bookmatches began in Germany some three years before it did in the United States.

Some confusion arises over the dates of the patents. In the United States the date given to a patent is that of the day of issue, that is, September 27, 1892 for Pusey's invention. In Germany the date given to a patent is that of the date it was filed, that is March 17, 1892 for Lorenz. If the same had been true in the United States, then it could be claimed that Pusey's completed application was dated the same as that of Lorenz, or that his original incomplete application of August 1889 should stand as the original invention.

However, the idea of a strip of tear-off matches, albeit without the striking surface as part of the package and not in book form, was in use by 1850 in Europe on a form of match known as a "Fusee". Wooden block and comb matches had been made in the United States for many years, whereby the stems of the splints were joined at the base. So what was new in the two 1892 inventions was really only the cover.

This form of match also spawned special holders for the books, mostly in pocket boxes, but also for stand-alone holders; these are discussed later in the text.

Essentially there are three main types of match holder: wall holders, stand-alone holders, and pocket holders. Within these three types are a variety of subcategories, and occasionally one piece may fit two of the main types.

Quite often a match holder may be combined with some other function; for example, match holders were frequently combined with cigar cutters, which is reasonably logical. But other combinations almost defy logic; for example, the inclusion of a compass, or the combination of a pin cushion, mouse trap and match holder. Examples exist of match holders that also hold stamps, coins, whistles, tickets, corkscrews, candles, dice, pen knives, pencils, or toothpicks. Examples of some of these are illustrated in this book.

The variety of match holders is vast. Collections in excess of 4,000 are known to exist, but it would be possible to collect well in excess of 10,000 and still not have an example of every one produced. The term "unique" cannot safely be applied to any example, although there is the occasional piece that was made by an amateur craftsman for his own amusement, and many one-off pieces were made in the trenches in World War I.

The variety of materials used covers a wide spectrum. Precious and base metal examples are common. Precious and semi-precious stones have been used. Other inorganic materials appear, particularly glass and ceramics. Organic materials such as wood, leather, the early plastics, and paper products abound. Some unusual materials such as champagne corks, sea bean pods, and even the pincer of a lobster are also in evidence.

It is impossible to present in a single volume illustrations of all the known examples; but an attempt has been made to illustrate the variety, history and major types of these relics with a selection chosen from a small, diverse collection of about eight hundred.

It is against the background of the appalling social conditions of the times, and many fatalities resulting from accidents and from the diseases caused by the noxious chemicals used in the manufacture of matches, that the history of the match holder unfolds. It came into use as a novel form of expression of the wealth and lifestyles of the more affluent and privileged members of society, before eventually becoming a commonplace item in almost every household. What follows hopefully demonstrates this phenomenon.

Chapter II
Early Protective Match Holders

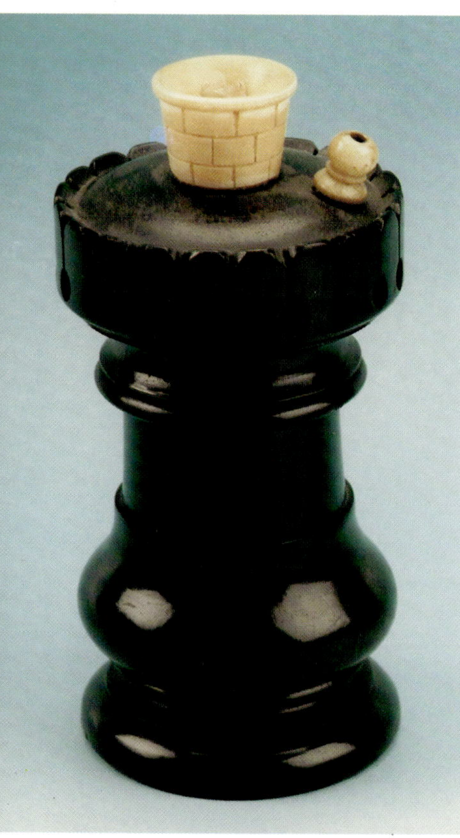

Fig. 1 Britain. Lignum vitae, wood. Berry type. c.1835. H - 9cms.

Samuel Jones, a chemist of the aptly named "Light-house" at 201 in the Strand, London, first started to produce "Lucifer" matches in about 1830, and was quickly followed by others, so that within a few years these unpredictable matches became readily available to the public. It was not long before special boxes were being produced into which the matches were transferred, in part to provide some additional protection for the purchasers of these matches, and in part as a decorative element in the home.

The time period of these early boxes was from about 1830 until about 1860, when the innocuous form of red phosphorus and the invention of the safety match made matches less hazardous. After about 1860, wall holders and stand-alone holders began to be produced without lids, pocket boxes were safer to carry, and the market, previously confined almost exclusively to Europe, began to open up in the United States. There is no definitive cut-off point in time to mark the end of the early period; until the turn of the century, match holders continued to be produced with lids, but more for aesthetic reasons than as a safety measure.

The match not only provided a quick and simple means of lighting a candle, but served as a means of lighting a tobacco pipe and for melting sealing wax for letters. It is perhaps not surprising that most match holders were likely to be found on a desk, on hand for the master of the household at his leisure or in the performance of his personal, domestic or business activities.

As an object for use at the desk, the box commonly included a sconce for a small candle, and a small socket for a match. The candle could supply sufficient light for writing a letter; a match in the small socket was intended for use to melt sealing wax, or it could have been used to hold the match while lighting a pipe. Many of these boxes were quite heavy and no doubt proved useful as paperweights.

Among the first known manufacturers of these boxes was Henry Berry of London. Since the early 1820s he had been producing Instantaneous Light Boxes in wood, which held some match splints and a bottle of sulphuric acid, and he was left with a stock of these boxes when the friction match was introduced. They were mostly made of *lignum vitae,* and it was a simple process to remove the central cylinder that held the bottle of acid, recess the underside of the base and glue a piece of sandpaper in that location to provide friction, and add a small socket to hold the stem of a match. An example of this type of box is shown in **Fig. 1.** It is unmarked, although Berry is known to have marked many of his boxes "Berry & Co.London", or "Berry's Patent", or "H.B. & H.W.". H.W. was Henry Webster, who succeeded Berry when he died in 1841, and who continued to use Berry's name. Berry's patent did not relate to his match holders.

A more complex box that displays Berry's ingenuity is shown in **Fig. 2**. In this the lid incorporated a spring-loaded striking device in the form of two plates: the upper plate was fixed and included a match socket; the lower plate was activated by a spiral spring which pressed the surfaces of the two plates together. The surfaces of these plates were covered with sandpaper, so that when the lower plate was pulled down (to permit a match to be inserted in the gap) and then released, it gripped the match, which could then be ignited by withdrawing it.

Berry also made simple cylindrical wooden boxes incorporating a match socket, with slip-on or screw-on lids. The top of such a box is seen in **Fig. 3**, and clearly shows one of the Berry marks, incorporating a crown.

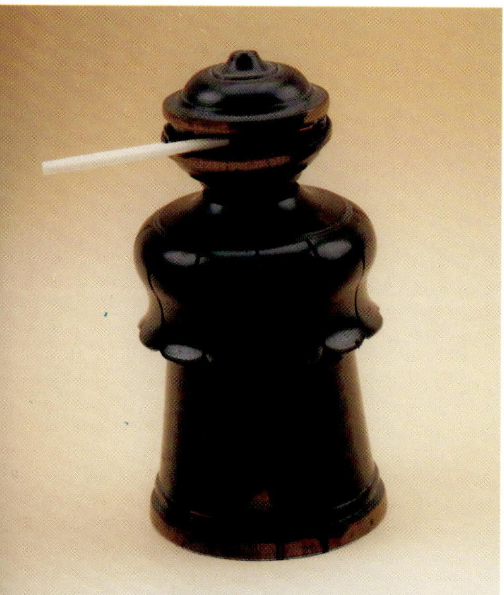

Fig. 2 Britain. Wood, with spring loaded top for striker. Berry type. c.1840s. H - 9.9cms.

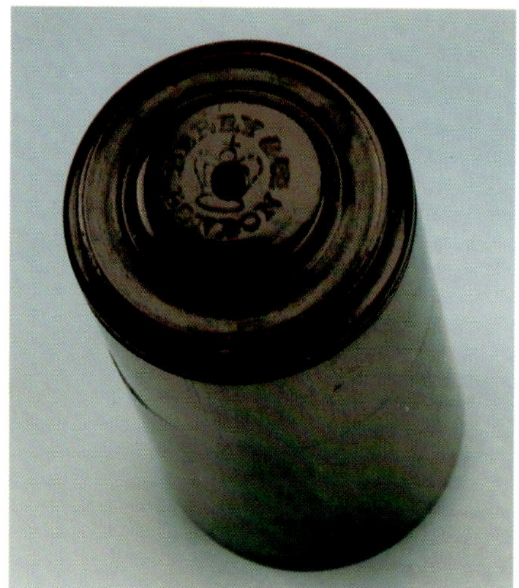

Fig. 3 Britain. Wood. Made by Berry & Co. c.1845. H - 6.5cms.

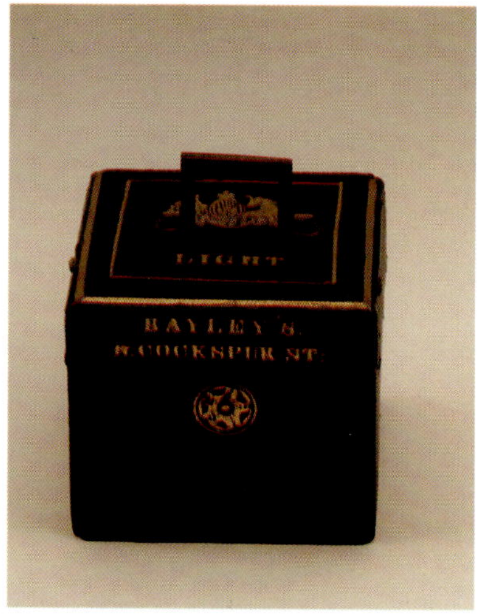

Fig. 4 Britain. Tin plate, leather. Berry type, travelling box. c.1860. H - 3.6cms.

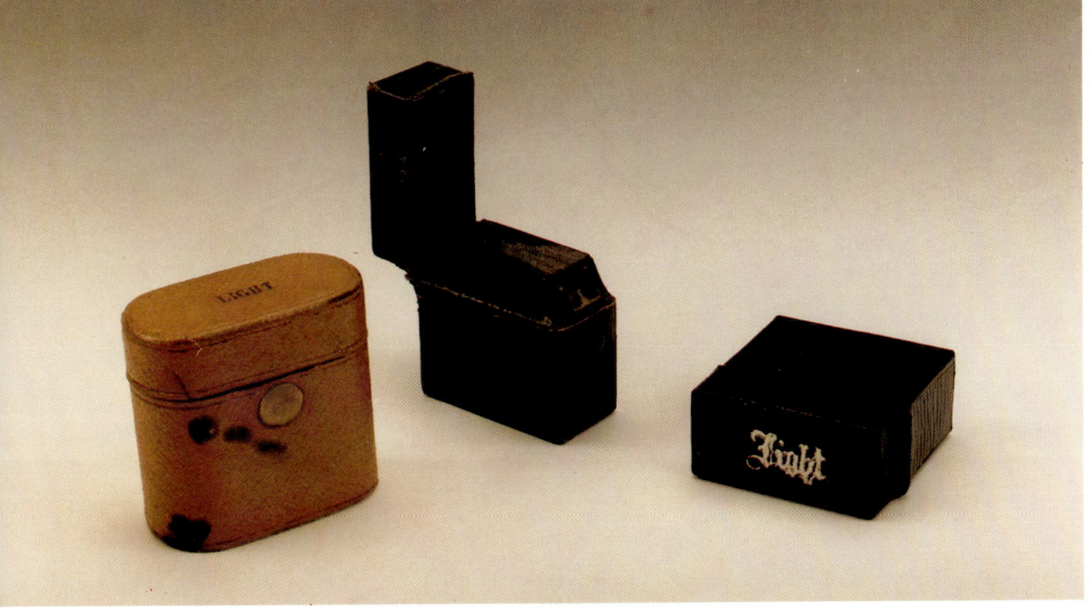

Fig. 5 Britain. Tin plate, leather. Travelling boxes, makers unknown, but in Berry style. Late 19th, early 20th century. H -5cms.

Tinplate boxes covered in leather or leatherette marked with one or the other of the Berry marks may also be found. They had hinged lids, and inside the match holder was a hinged plate roughened for friction and often provided with a match socket. They were the subject of a Useful Registered Design in 1844 by Alexander Coombs of London, which suggests that those boxes bearing Berry marks were made by his successor Webster, sometime after 1844. An unmarked box of this type is shown in **Fig. 4**. Impressed in gold on the lid is the word "LIGHT", but "VESTA" is also known to have been used.

Henry Webster continued to make these boxes for many years, as did others, and they may commonly be found as a pair combined with one marked "INK". They remained popular as a part of the accoutrements of travelling cases for gentlemen until at least 1918, with some variations occurring in shape, but always marked "Light" and "Ink." Three later models are shown in **Fig. 5**.

Not all of the Berry types of match holders were marked, and it is known that some were made by other manufacturers.

A simple domed box with a match socket in **Fig. 6**, made of wood, is marked "Watts & Co. 17 Strand". George Frederick Watts traded as a chemist at various London addresses from c.1830, turning to the manufacture of matches in about 1832. His business premises were at 17 Strand from 1834 until 1840, which adequately dates the example. But it is not known if Watts actually made the box, or if it was made for him by another company.

In Germany in about 1840, Ernst Georg Zimmermann moved from Berlin, a major centre of cast-iron products, to Hanau, about fourteen miles east of Frankfurt-on-Main, to set up an iron foundry producing small artistic items such as buttons and brooches. Soon, however, he began to extend his range of products to include match holders. The company expanded into brass and bronze casting, and added marble products to its line, all by about 1850. It exported worldwide and exhibited at International Exhibitions around the world, including the Chicago World's Fair in 1893. The business is still in existence today, although working only in marble. It is most unfortunate that in World War II it suffered the same fate as many others, when most of its records were destroyed.

The quality of Zimmermann's sand-molded, cast-iron products is perhaps unsurpassed in its field; they exhibit great detail, imagination and variety, particularly in their match holders.

Zimmermann's company appear to have marked all of its match holders. The pieces prior to 1850 were marked with the impressed wording "Verlag Bei E.G.Zimerman in Hanau." After 1850 it used an elliptical escutcheon with the same wording, but the surname was spelt "Zimmermann." An example of the latter form may be seen in Fig. 17.

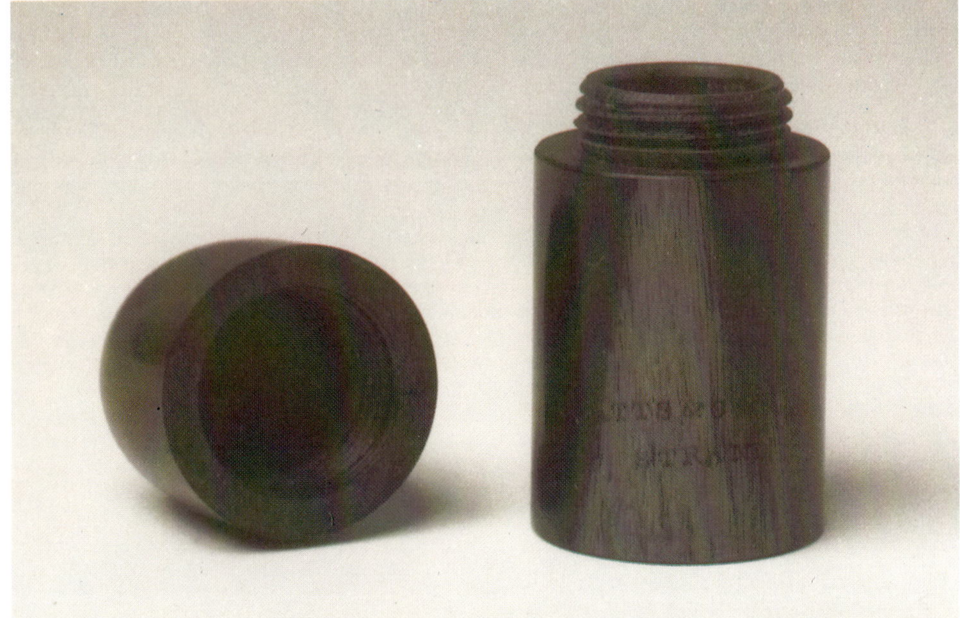

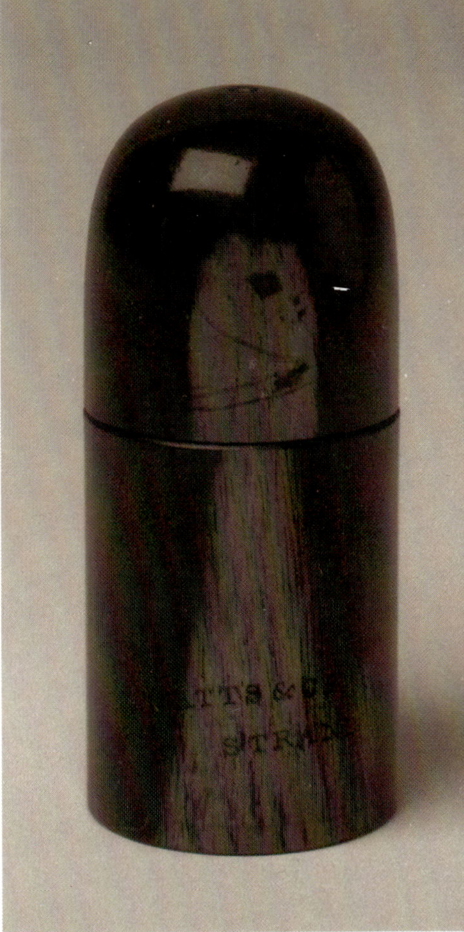

Fig. 6 Britain. Wood. Made for G. F. Watts of London. 1834-1840. H - 5.5cms.

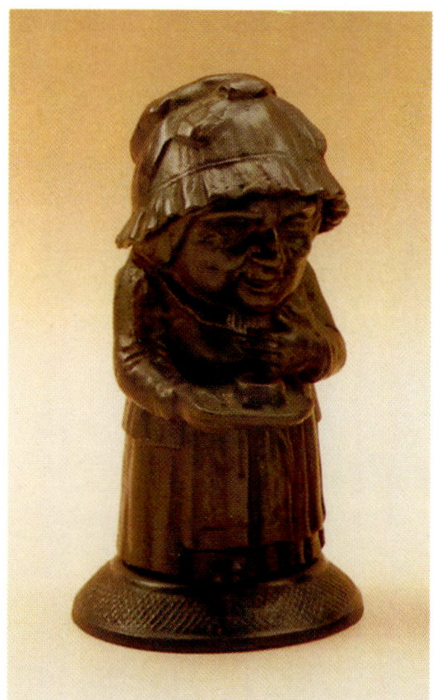

Fig. 7 Germany. Cast iron. Made by E. G. Zimmermann. c.1845. H -9.8cms.

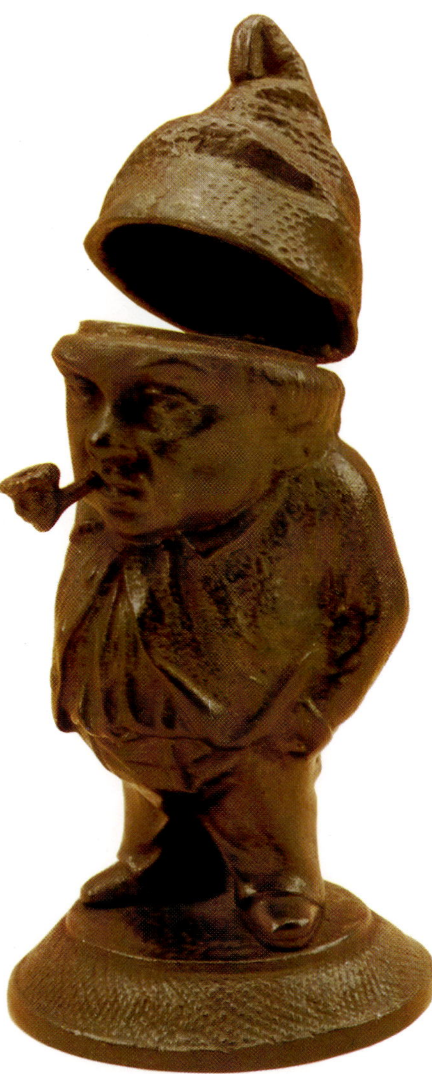

Fig. 8 Germany. Cast iron and brass. Made by E. G. Zimmermann. c.1845. H - 11.5cms.

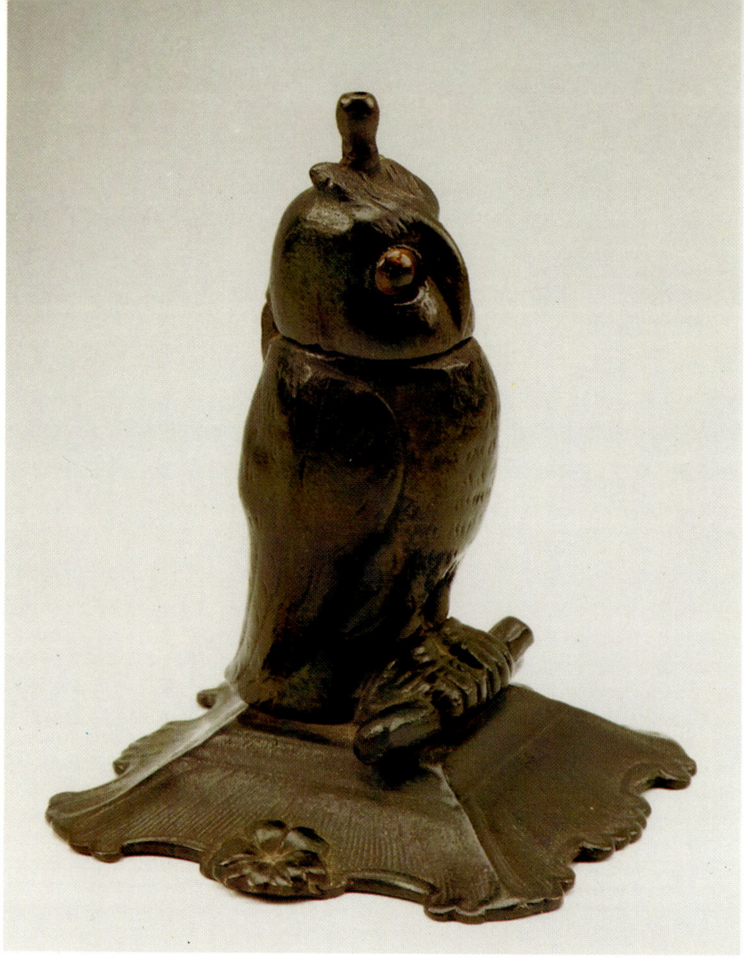

Fig. 9 Germany. Cast iron and glass. Made by E. G. Zimmermann. c.1845. H - 8.4cms.

Among its earlier pieces, made prior to 1850, are two human figures of great charm, the faces imbued with considerable character. The female figure, in **Fig. 7**, is standing holding a candle stick, which acts as a match socket. Her mop hat is hinged at the back to permit access to the matches stored inside the body, and the base is roughened for friction, with the company name impressed on the underside. The male figure, in **Fig. 8**, is standing smoking a pipe. The pipe is a separate piece cast in brass and with a face on the front of the bowl; this too serves as a match socket. The hat is hinged at the back, as is shown, and the base is identical to that of the female. They are both cast in four parts: the body and head as one part; the base, the hat and the match sockets as separate parts.

A third early piece is in the form of a long-eared owl with glass eyes, as seen in **Fig. 9**. The head is hinged at the back to provide access to the matches, and has a match socket mounted on top. The figure is mounted on a rectangular base, the location of the striker, and the company name is impressed on the underside.

Export to Britain appears to have been a major target of Zimmermann's manufactures. This becomes evident in its series of London street figures produced in the 1850s. At least seven are known. Illustrated here are, a policeman in **Fig. 10**, a female crossing sweeper in **Fig. 11**, and a chimney sweep and a shoeshine boy in **Fig. 12**. A second version of a shoeshine boy has been documented, and there are also figures of a male road sweeper and a female flower seller. Each of these figures is mounted on an oval base designed to represent a sidewalk, the top front edge roughened for friction. Beside the figure is a 'bollard'.

Bollards were posts alleged to have been made from the barrels of cannons taken at the battle of Waterloo; they were located at street corners or entrances to alleyways to prevent access or encroachment by horse-drawn vehicles, and were a common sight in London even in my own youth. In the match holders, the top section of the post is hinged to give access to the matches in the barrel, and has a match socket in the top.

There are also three other figures recorded, mounted on a different form of base. One is in the form of a man delivering a sack of coal, the sack acting as the match holder. The second, shown in **Fig. 13**, probably represents John Bull, holding an umbrella behind his back and with a small dog beside him. The head is hinged at the back for access to the matches held inside the body. The third figure has what are probably political overtones. It is the figure of a monk, holding aloft in his right hand what might normally be expected to be a torch, but which is almost certainly a bunch of flowers. The flowers are provided with a match socket at the top. The hat is hinged at the back for access to the match compartment, and the striker is located on the base. Illustrated in **Fig. 14**, the face, with its beard, moustache and aquiline nose is almost certainly that of Napoleon III. Was the monastic disguise and the bunch of flowers some reference to Napoleon III's dealings with Rome perhaps?

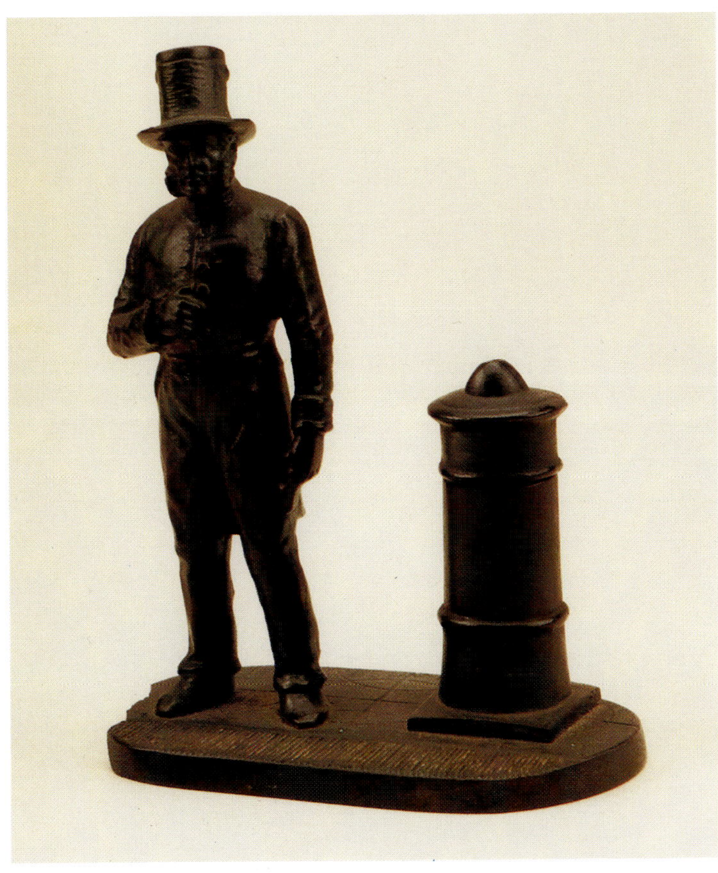

Fig. 10 Germany. Cast iron. Made by E. G. Zimmermann. A London policeman. c.1850. H - 11.8cms.

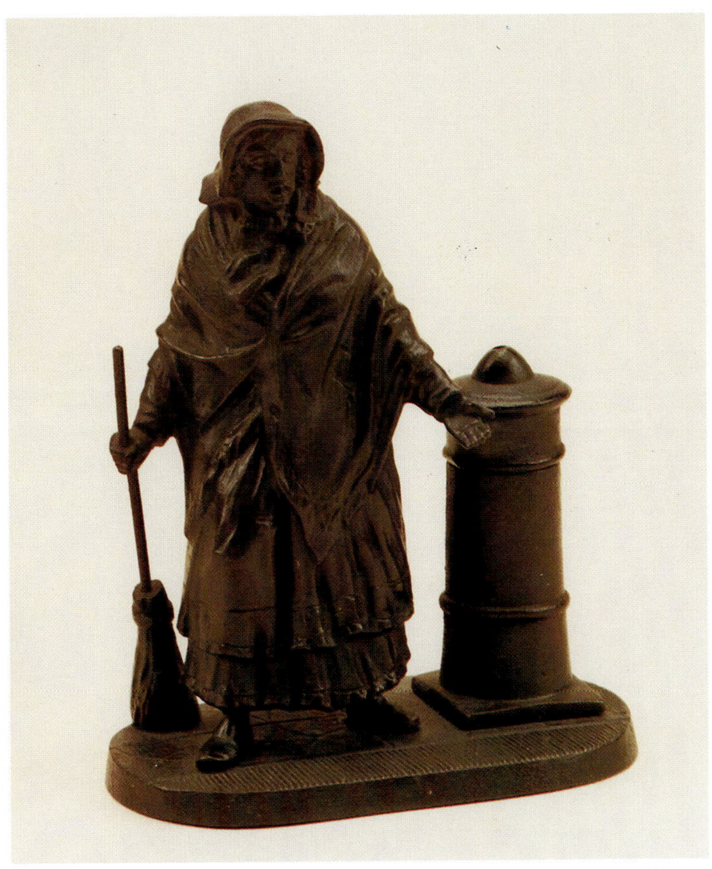

Fig. II Germany. Cast iron. Made by E. G. Zimmermann. A London crossing sweeper. c.1850. H - 11.2cms.

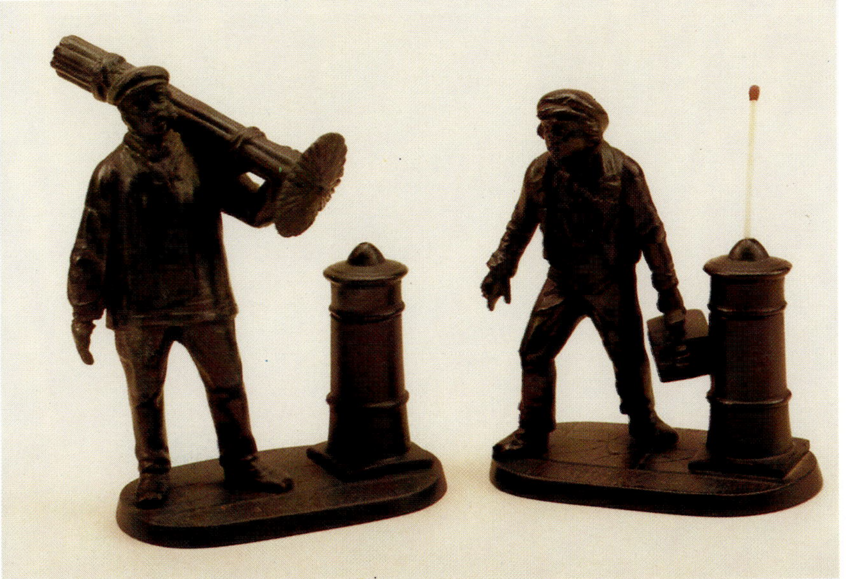

Fig. 12 Germany. Cast iron. Made by E. G. Zimmermann. A chimney sweep and a shoe shine boy. c.1850. H - 12.3cms.

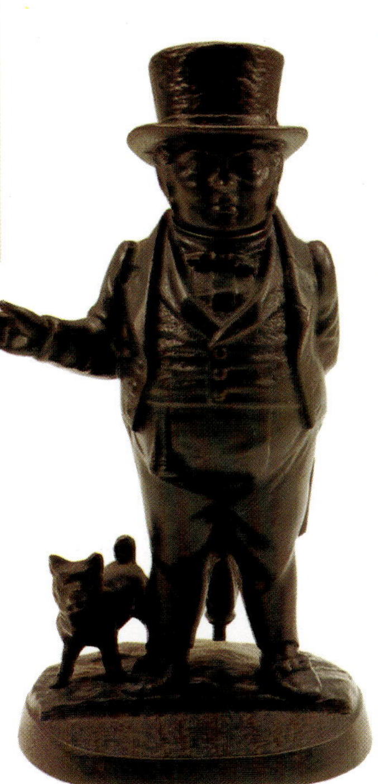

Fig. 14 Germany. Cast iron. Made by E.G. Zimmermann. Napoleon III. c. 1850. H - 12.2 cms.

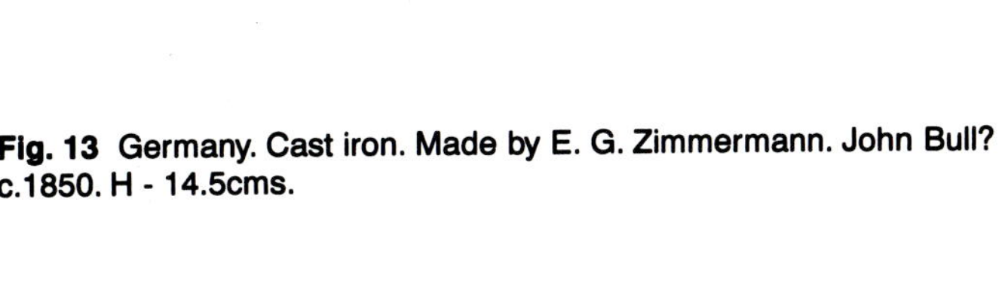

Fig. 13 Germany. Cast iron. Made by E. G. Zimmermann. John Bull? c.1850. H - 14.5cms.

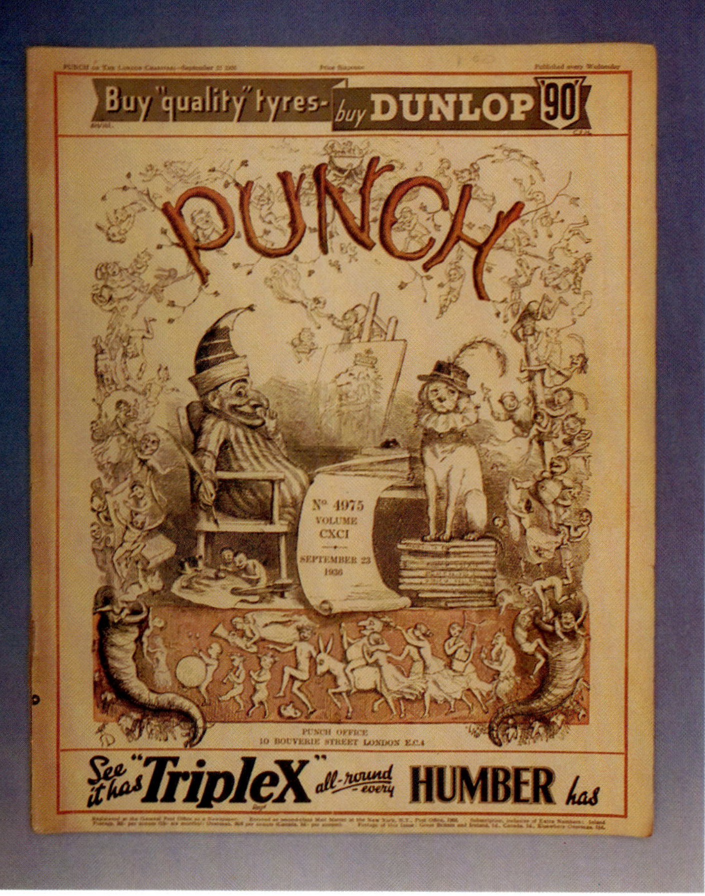

Fig. 15 The front cover of "Punch", published from 1844 until 1950, which was the inspiration for the figures in Fig. 16.

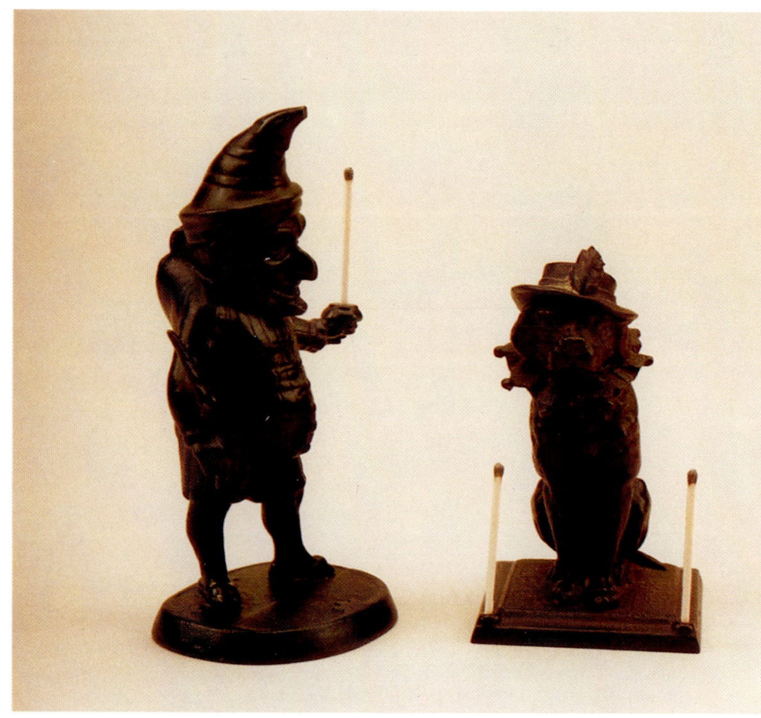

Fig. 16 Germany. Cast iron. Made by E. G. Zimmermann. Left: Mr Punch, and right: Toby. c.1850. H - 14.3cms

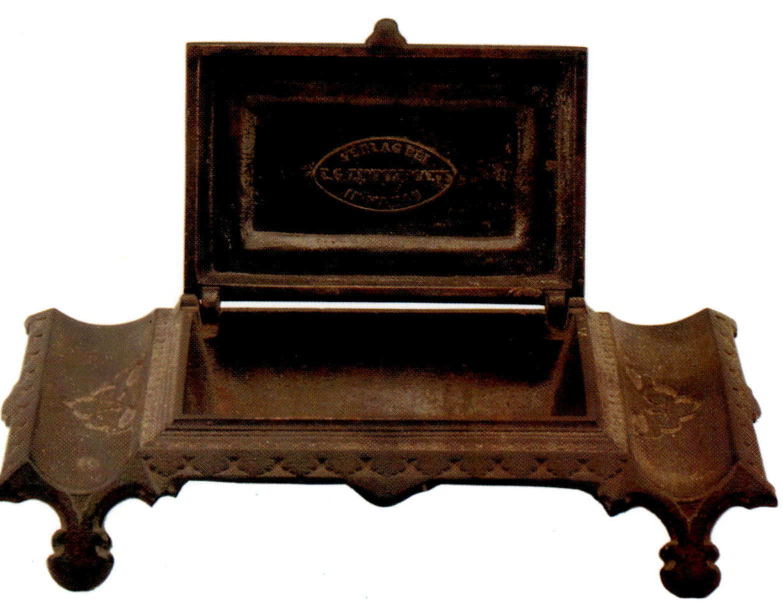

Fig. 17 Germany. Cast iron. Made by E. G. Zimmermann. The Zimmermann mark shown on the lid. c.1855. L - 14.8cms.

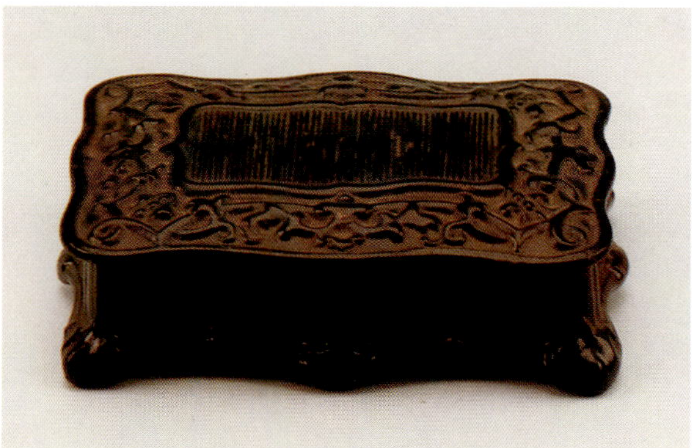

Fig. 18 Germany. Cast iron. Made by E. G. Zimmermann. c.1860. L -9.8cms.

Fig. I9 Germany? Cast iron. Maker unknown. c.1860. L - 13.6cms.

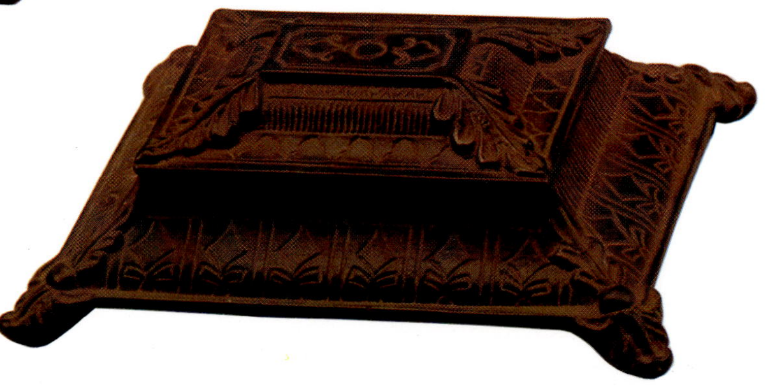

The British weekly publication "Punch" was the inspiration for another pair of Zimmermann figures, Mr. Punch and his dog Toby. "Punch" was first published in 1841 and continued in publication until 1992. In 1844 artist Richard Doyle designed what was to become the magazine's front cover until 1950. This, seen in **Fig. 15**, shows Punch seated and holding a quill pen in his right hand, with an inkwell on the table in front of him; Toby is seated on a pile of books. The Zimmermann figures of Punch and Toby, in **Fig. 16**, have Toby almost identical to the cover depiction, while Punch is shown standing, holding the quill pen in the same hand at about the same angle, and with the inkwell in his other hand.

In the traditional puppet theatre performance, Toby was usually a small live dog, and for a while the theatre was even called "Punch and Toby" rather than "Punch and Judy". The character Punch was a vicious thug who carried a club with which he beat his baby, his wife, a policeman, a clown, an alligator, the hangman, and any other character that the puppeteer chose to include in the performance. The puppet Punch never carried a pen; but in the publication he held a pen, which, as is known, is mightier than the sword (or in this case, the club).

Again the hats of both figures are hinged for access to the matches. A match socket is located in Punch's inkwell, and there is a match socket at both of the front corners of the Toby base.

It is known that there is at least one other Zimmermann figure, in the form of a one-armed man standing beside a tree stump, wearing a battered top hat and carrying a bag over his right arm. It is possible that there are others not yet recorded. As a group these figures reflect upon the close ties that existed at that time between Germany and Britain. They also demonstrate the skill of the German craftsmen.

At least two of the figures were copied long after Zimmermann ceased to produce them. Mr. Punch was the subject of a British Registered Design in 1896, taken out by Mallett & Sons, silversmiths of Bath, Somerset (now in the county of Avon), and was also reproduced as a gas fixture, which has been seen in the United States but may well have been made in Europe. Both representations are identical to the Zimmermann piece, except for the base. The Birmingham company Pearson-Page, which manufactured a variety of novelty brassware items, shows in its 1927 catalogue one of the shoeshine boys as a paperweight and as an ashtray.

Of a more mundane character are two match holders by Zimmermann in the form of caskets. They probably fall within the time scale of the early protective boxes; that is, before about 1860. One, in **Fig. 17 ,** is set upon four legs which raise it well clear of the surface upon which it stands. At each end is a groove, probably intended to hold a cigar. The lid is hinged longitudinally, the upper surface roughened for friction. The inside of the box, wherein the Zimmermann mark is found, is curved to simplify removal of a match. The underside of the box body is marked with a mold number, which is consistent with similar numbers found on many of the figures. The second casket, in **Fig. 18**, is raised clear of the surface upon which it stands only fractionally by extending the corners slightly downwards. The lid, also hinged longitudinally, has the striking surface on top surrounded by an ornate border. On the underside of the box body is a second striking patch. The inside is provided with the usual Zimmermann mark. The box has a painted black finish which may have been added later.

An unmarked cast-iron casket of similar form to those of Zimmermann was almost certainly made in Europe, probably Germany, and is shown in **Fig. I9**. The legs splay out and have a stylized floral design that runs from the base of each leg up to the platform on top of the lid. Around the rim of the box body is the striker, and there is a second area that could be used as a striker incorporated into the design on the lid. The box is a well made and finished item that compares favorably with those of Zimmermann.

The figure of a chatelaine, in **Figs. 20 and 21**, is marked "Verlag Bei A,M.... Berlin". The name is not clear, but may be "Meyer". Almost a caricature, this cast-iron figure has a bunch of keys at her waist, is wearing a mop cap and an apron, with her hands behind her back holding a shoe. With a rather haughty expression on her face, and a tipped-up nose, she appears ready to deliver an admonition. The head is hinged at the back for access to the matches stored in the body, and the striker runs around the edge of the base.

Another caricaturish figure, shown in **Fig. 22**, is cast in brass, in the form of a country gentleman. The straw hat is hinged to reveal the match compartment, and the striker is in the form of concentric circles located on the base. He is apparently smiling, but the modelling does not meet the standards of the Zimmermann pieces. The match socket is formed by the right hand, and as may be seen, the match is held out at an angle from the body rather than upright as in most of the figures. Presumably the figure was used to hold the folded sheet of paper of a letter together, with the match over the place where the sealing wax was intended to be deposited, which no doubt made the operation simpler. The figure has a gilt lacquer finish, but no marks to indicate its place of origin.

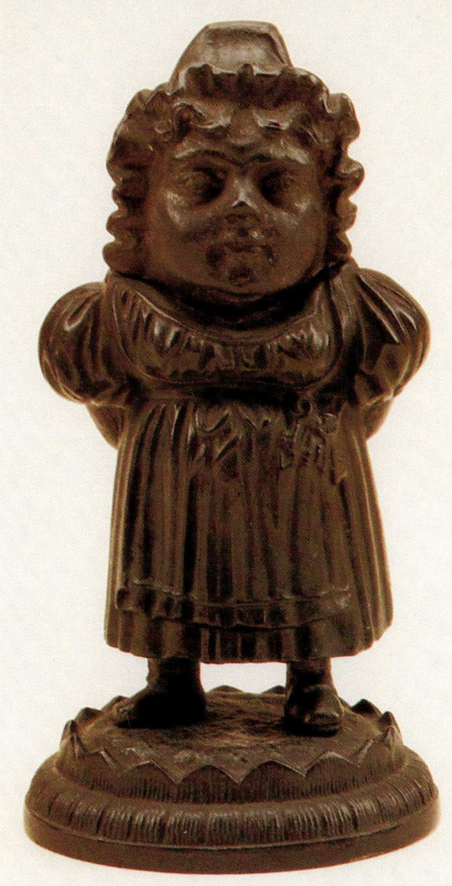

Fig. 20 Germany. Cast iron. Made by A. Meyer(?), Berlin. c.1850. H - 11.6cms.

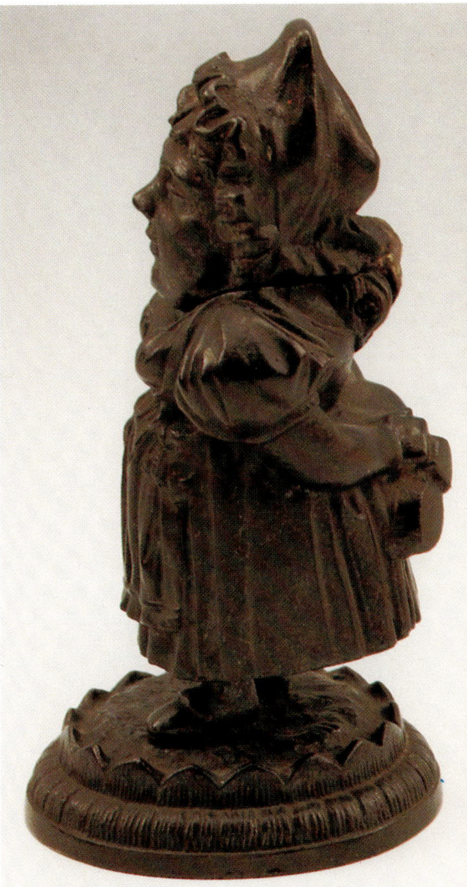

Fig. 21 As Fig. 20.

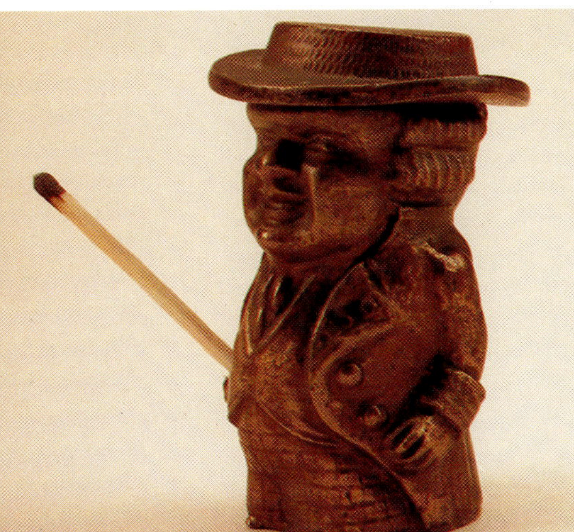

Fig. 22 Britain? Cast brass. c.1850. H - 7cms.

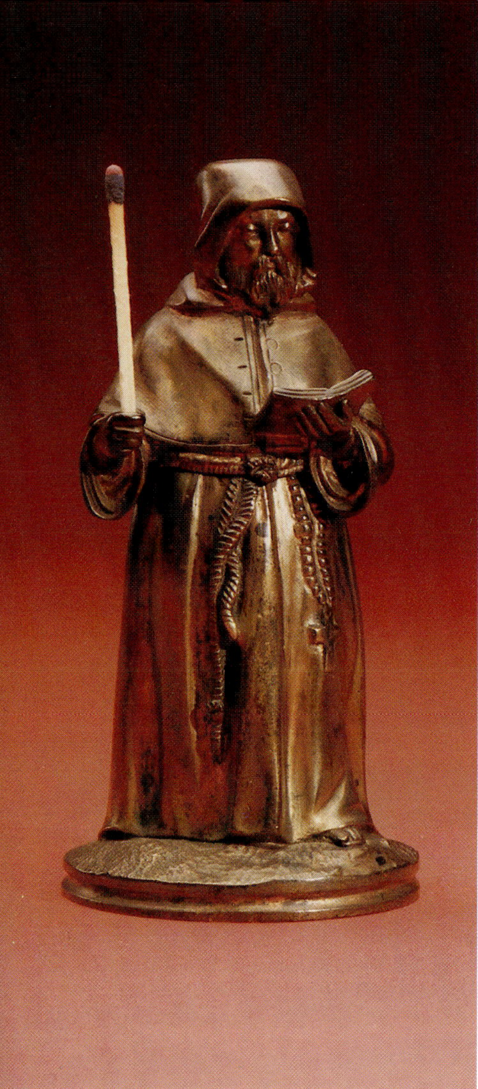

Fig. 23 Europe. Cast brass. c.1855. H - 13.1cms.

What is perhaps the most outstanding figure of all is also made of cast brass, as seen in **Fig. 23**. It is a superb rendering of a monk, wearing a hooded cape over his habit. At his waist is an ornate rope with tasseled ends, and apparently hanging from the rope in a loop is a cross. The toes of one foot peep out from beneath the habit and reveal the sole of a sandal. Beneath the hood is a bearded and moustached face, the eyes downcast to look at the book held in the left hand. The right arm is bent at the elbow and extended forward to form a fist, with a hole extending down into the fist serving as a match socket. The body is hinged at the back of the waist to provide access to the match compartment, and the upper part of the base is dappled to simulate a rough walking surface, part of which, at one side, is cross-hatched as a striker. The modelling is very sensitive with fine detail, and it has a gilt lacquer finish. To complete the figure and almost bring it to life, a match placed in the socket in the hand simulates a candle, by whose light the monk may read his book. This phenomenon of using the match in the socket to complete a figure is uncommon, occuring in only a few examples, some others of which are mentioned later in the book. Unfortunately it is unmarked, but it is assumed to be European.

Birmingham, dubbed the City of a Thousand Trades, was a major center in Britain for the production of brass match holders. The first recorded example was produced by Thomas Wharton about 1846. He registered an Ornamental Design in August 1846 that he called an "Ornamental Design for the Albert Matchbox." The drawing filed with the registration does not show the interior of the box, **Fig. 24 left**, which suggests that it was simply an empty box. Yet the known extant end products contain a fitting for a spring loaded candle, or taper. It seems likely that Wharton acquired the rights to the interior fitting from an earlier Useful Design, **Fig. 24 right**, registered in May 1845 by Augustus Septimus Braithwaite of London, for a "Portable Taper Holder", which corresponds precisely to the interior fitting of the Wharton box. Braithwaite's design is recorded as having been transferred, but not to whom it was transferred.

An example of the above bearing Wharton's name on a plate with the Diamond Registration Mark, set in an elaborate crest, is shown in **Fig. 25**. The top of the slip-on lid is provided with a disc impressed with a crown encircled by the words "THE ALBERT MATCHBOX", which may have served to impress a mark on sealing wax. This box was suitable either for standing on a desk, or for being carried in the pocket as a traveller's portable light. This is the only brass box for matches attributable to Thomas Wharton, but he is known to have also produced papier maché work.

By 1850 three Birmingham brass founders are known to have been producing match holders: the family business of the Dowlers, established by 1780; the Harcourt Brothers, William and Joseph, whose father had established their business by 1818; and Allen & Moore, of whom little is known. All three registered designs and invention patents for their boxes, and the last two exhibited at the Great Exhibition of 1851 in London.

On June 25, 1850, Thomas Dowler (believed to be the son of the founder) registered a Useful Design, shown in **Fig. 28, left**. This cylindrical box had a slip-on lid with a spring-loaded match socket on top. The socket was connected by a rod that passed through the top of the lid to a plate on the inside, the rod having a spiral spring that held the plate up to the underside of the lid. In the edge of the lid was a hole into which the match was placed after the plate had been depressed; once the match was in position the plate was released to grip the match which was then sharply withdrawn, being ignited by the roughened surface of the plate. An example is shown in **Fig. 26** with a match *in situ*. The top of the lid (**Fig. 27**, also with a match *in situ*), was impressed with the registration number and the date. Also impressed on the lid, the smaller version with straight sides as shown, were the words "DOWLER'S NOCTURNAL VESTA MATCH BOX". Larger versions with a flared base had the impressed words "DOWLER'S NOCTURNAL SPRING IGNITING MATCH BOX". All had an additional striking area on the underside of the base, in the form of concentric circles.

The Dowler nocturnal box had a fault in its design. As a match was withdrawn from the side of the box for ignition, it was possible for particles of the ignited chemicals to drop down into the box past the striker disc; there is no doubt that this did occur, with a nasty surprise for the user. In 1853, probably after Thomas had retired or died, his son George redesigned the box, placing a fixed diaphragm below the movable striking plate. George applied for and was granted an invention patent for this improvement in June of 1853; the drawing of the patent is shown in **Fig. 28, right**. His specifications state:

> "The diaphragm or partition prevents any detached and ignited portions of the composition on the match from falling into and igniting the matches in the box."

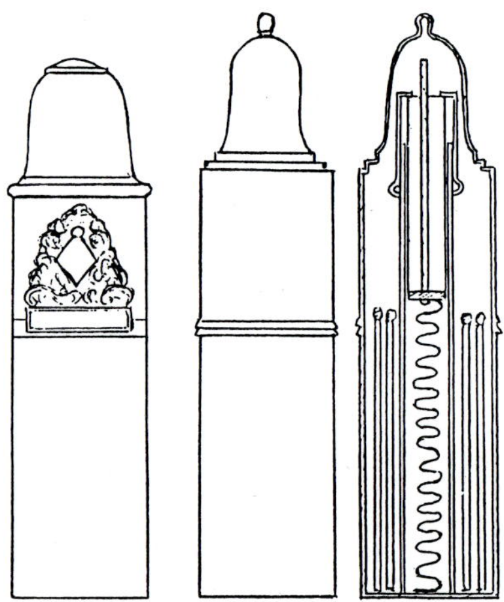

Fig. 24 Left: Ornamental Design by Thomas Wharton of 1846. Right: Useful Designs by Augustus S. Braithwaite of 1845.

No extant examples of this second version of the Dowler box have been recorded to date. The company remained in business until about the middle of the 1870s, turning to manufacturing matches and tin boxes to hold them in the 1860s.

The sides of the Dowler nocturnal boxes had designs in geometric and stylized floral patterns, which were produced by removing the background in a series of incised parallel vertical lines, and the designs were picked out in green, yellow, red or blue enamel.

A large series of boxes bearing this form of design are to be found, but lack any manufacturers marks; they have long been attributed to Dowler. **Fig. 29** shows four examples. However, it has recently been found that the technique for producing this form of design was also being used by Allen & Moore, and was recorded in the "Official Descriptive and Illustrated Catalogue of the Great Exhibition of 1851" as a part of W. C. Aitken's descriptive text relating to Allen & Moore, as follows:

> "The ornamentation is effected by coating the brass with a transparent varnish or lacquer of various colours, which is cut through in a series of lines, displaying floral or scroll devices by means of an embossing machine. This machine somewhat resembles a pantograph;—a cylinder of steel upon which the pattern is engraved is placed so as to act against the end of a long rod, the other extremity of which cuts away the lacquer on the brass box. Thus in an ingenious manner the pattern on the steel cylinder is reproduced upon the match box. Cigar-cases and taper-stands, with magazines or receptacles to hold matches, cigars, and tapers, are now produced in immense numbers by the same process of manufacture."

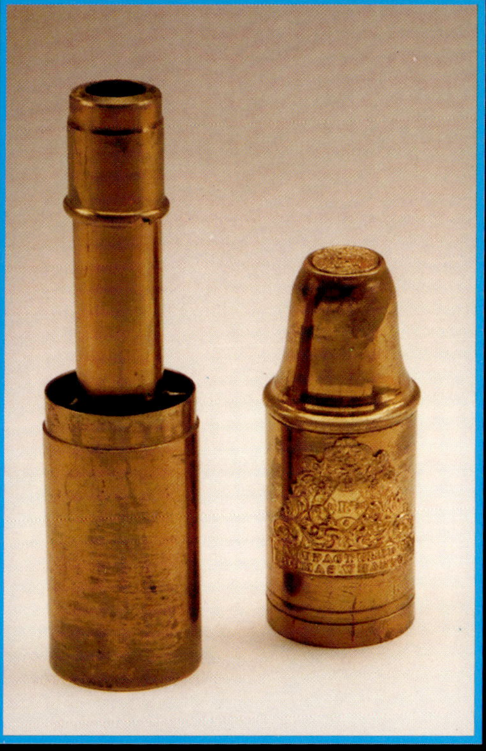

Fig. 25 Britain. Brass. Thomas Wharton's "Albert Matchbox" c. 1847. H - 10.1cms.

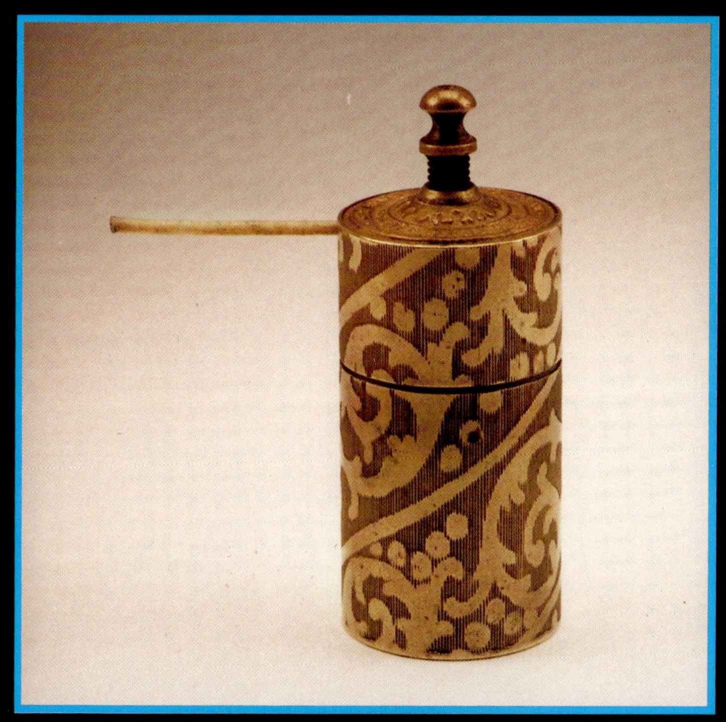

Fig. 26 Britain. Brass. "Dowler's Nocturnal Vesta Match Box". c.1850. H - 8.1cms.

Fig. 27 As Fig. 26, top of lid.

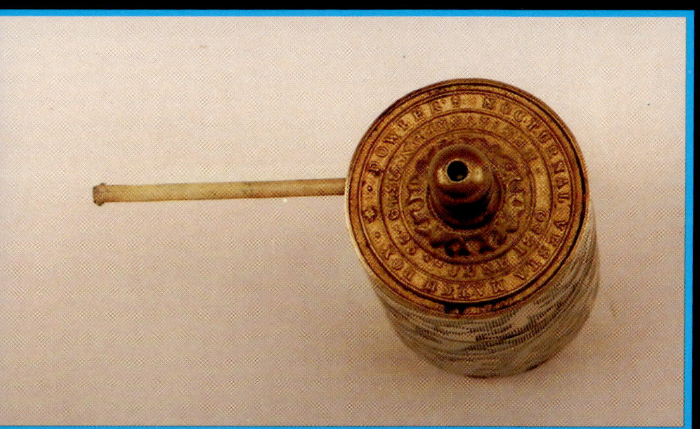

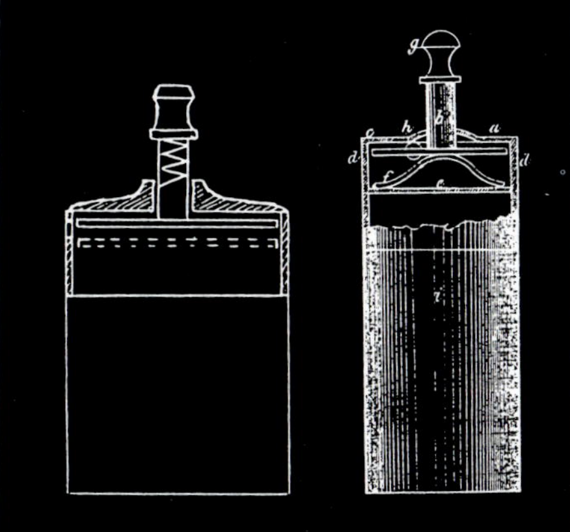

Fig. 28 Left: Useful Design by Thomas Dowler of 1850. Right: Invention Patent by George Dowler of 1853.

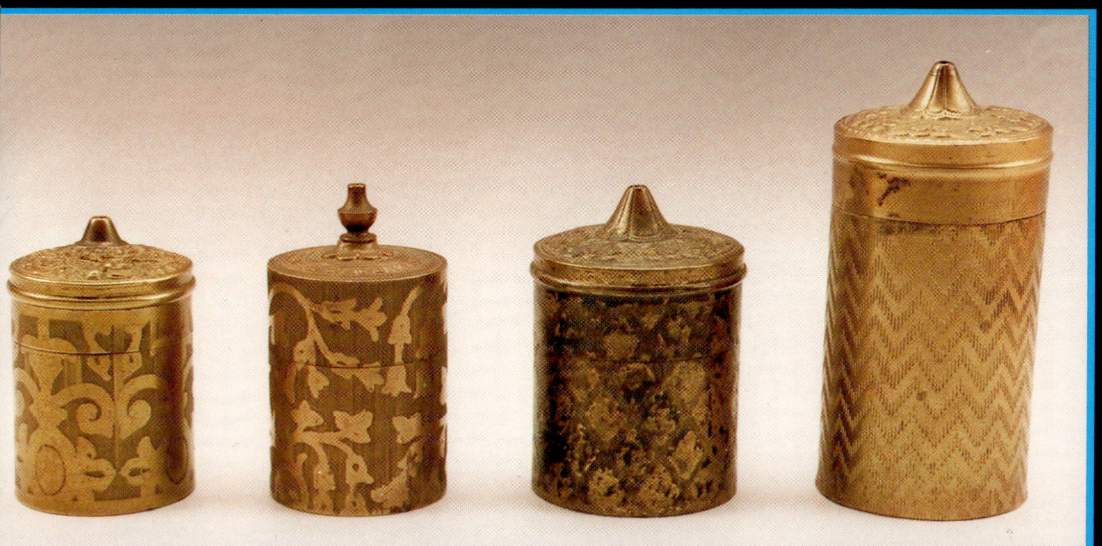

Fig. 29 Britain. Brass. A series of boxes by Dowler's or Allen & Moore. Early 1850s. H(maximum) - 9.5cms.

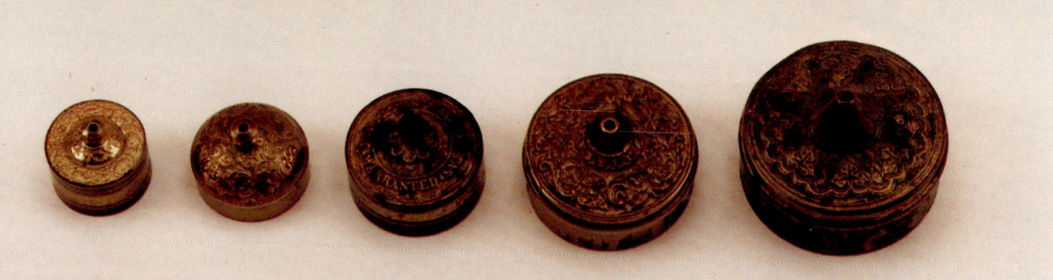

Fig. 30 Britain. Brass. Lids of boxes by Dowler's or Allen & Moore. Early 1850s. D(maximum) - 4.6cms.

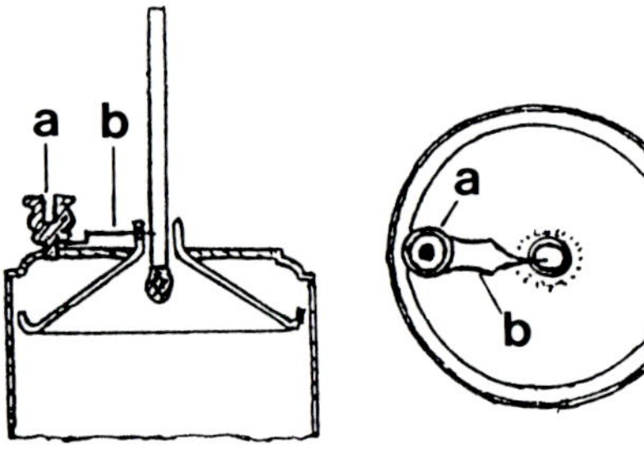

Fig. 32 Useful Design by Allen & Moore of 1850. a - match socket. b - striker strip.

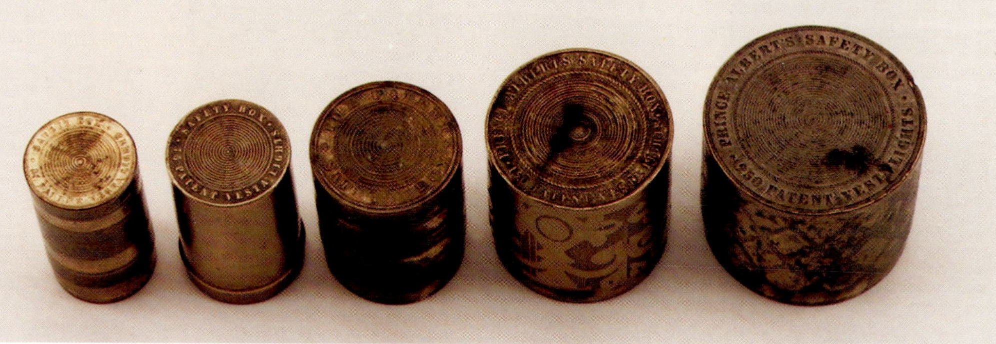

Fig. 31 Bases of boxes in Fig. 30.

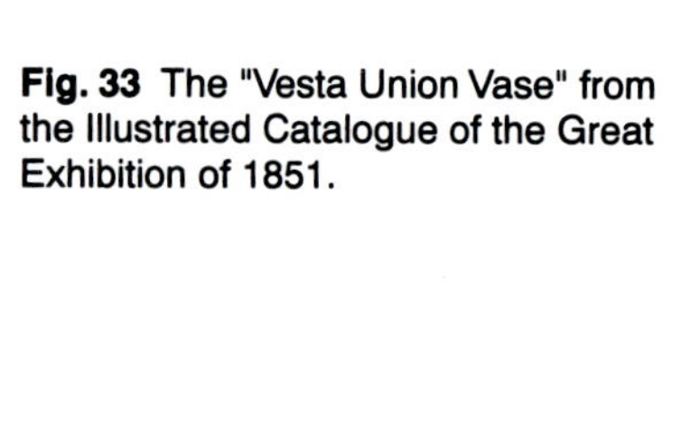

Fig. 33 The "Vesta Union Vase" from the Illustrated Catalogue of the Great Exhibition of 1851.

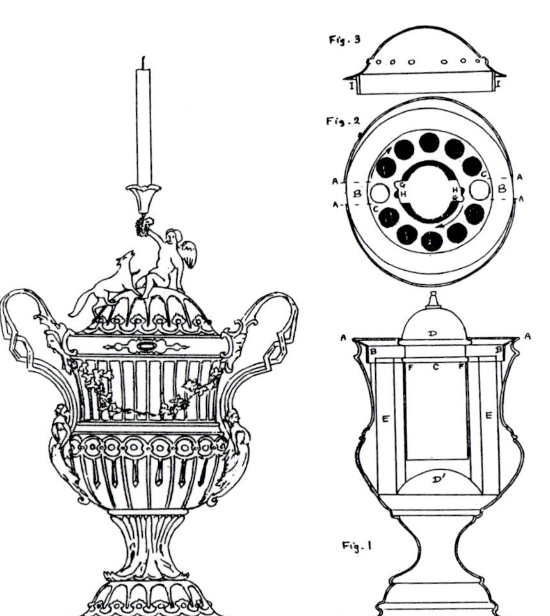

Fig. 34 Left: Ornamental Design; and Right: Useful Design, by the Harcourt's of 1851, for the "Vesta Union Vase".

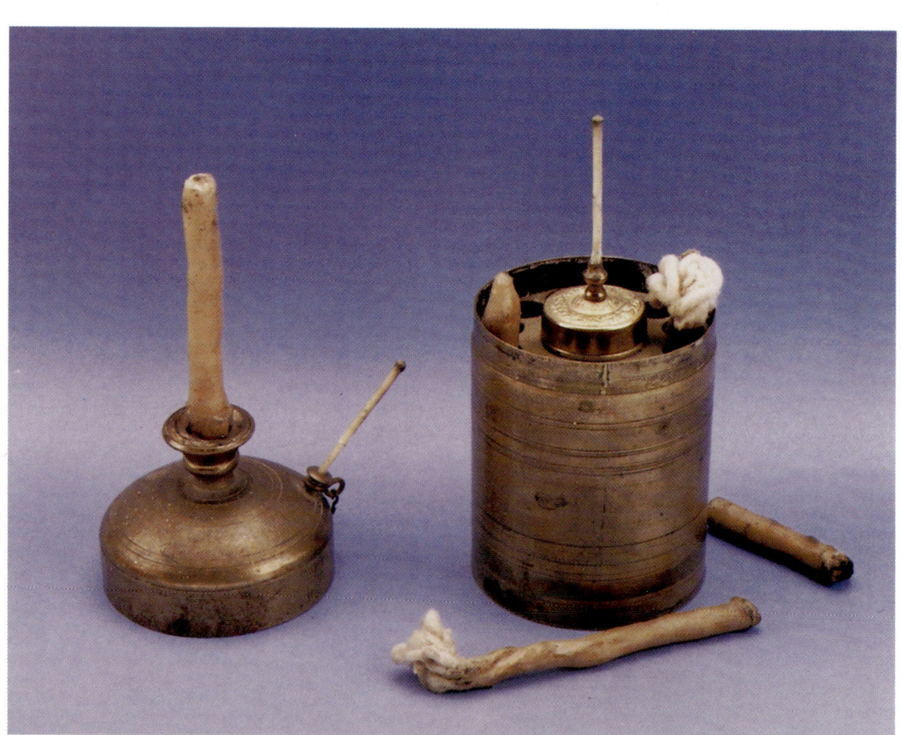

Fig. 35 Britain. Brass. Harcourt's box of the type incorporated into the "Vesta Union Vase". c.1851. H - 11.4cms.

This clearly describes the technique as used by Allen & Moore, which also fits the marked Dowler boxes, with both companies using brass tubing for the bodies of their boxes. It is therefore assumed that the unmarked boxes could have been produced by either company. No extant boxes are known to have been marked by Allen & Moore, and it is therefore impossible to check other techniques of manufacture to provide a basis of comparison and possible attribution.

The lids of these unmarked boxes, seen in **Fig. 30,** show considerable variety in design and match socket styles, and the corresponding bases in **Fig. 31** all follow a very similar style, each one indicating the number of matches the box would hold, from fifty up to two hundred and fifty. Smaller boxes to hold twenty-five matches were unmarked.

Allen & Moore also registered a Useful Design in 1850 for a cylindrical box that was potentially even more dangerous than the earlier Dowler box, but for which no examples have been recorded. A copy of the design illustration is shown in **Fig. 32**, which clearly indicates that it was intended that the matches should be placed in the box with the heads down. To extract a match the box was inverted; the match was slipped through the conical hole in the lid, to be gripped by the fingers and withdrawn, causing the chemical composition on the head to be ignited by the metal strip "b" held in place by a match socket "a", and with the tip of the strip entering the hole in the side of the cone hole. The risk of accidents occuring with this box were far greater than those in the Dowler box. If Allen & Moore became aware of this before they started to mass produce them for sale to an unsuspecting public, this would account for the apparent lack of extant examples.

The third Birmingham company, the Harcourt Brothers, was perhaps the most prolific producers of cylindrical brass match holders. It held several registered designs and some invention patents relating to the boxes, which assist in identifying its products, only one of which is known to have been marked with the company name.

At the Great Exhibition of 1851 three of its products were selected for inclusion in "The Art Journal Illustrated Catalogue", published in 1851 and showing "the most interesting and the most suggestive, of the various objects exhibited." This included a bronze vase, shown in **Fig. 33**, the subject of two registered designs. **Fig. 34** shows the two designs. That on the left is an Ornamental Design of April 10, 1851 for "A vase to hold matches, tapers, &c. as well as to form a taper stand", and only shows the exterior of the vase. The illustration at the right was a Useful Design registered on April 12, 1851 as "The Vesta Union Vase; for holding a match box, tapers, segars and so forth;" it shows the interior fittings, with a cross section of the match and taper holder above the vase.

The match box in the vase interior was also made and sold as a separate item, an example of which is shown in **Fig. 35** and includes some of the original tapers. The interior of this large domed box includes a second smaller match holder with a lid furnished with a match socket. The box is soldered to the disc, which is perforated to hold the tapers; the disc in turn is soldered to the inside of the main box body. The base plate of the small inner box, normally provided with a concentric circle striking area, has been fitted with a plate that is incongruously stamped "WARRENTED 3 MINUTES. SAFETY EGG BOILER," the lettering appearing in reverse and intended to be read from the underside. A second known example of the box has exactly the same base plate, and it is assumed that the craftsman used any available base of the correct size that was at hand at the time to finish the box, knowing that the base would not be exposed.

Although the box bears no maker's marks, there is little doubt that it was a Harcourt product. On the basis of the domed lid, two smaller boxes with domed lids are tentatively attributed to the Harcourts. The smaller piece in **Fig. 36** has a cross-hatched striker on the base and was intended to hold twenty-five Vesta matches, but is otherwise plain. The larger piece to hold seventy-five Vesta matches, in **Fig. 37**, has no body design. The lid and base are shown second from the left in Figs. 30 and 31.

In February of 1851, the Harcourts were issued a Useful Registered Design, essentially for a striker fitted externally, but no extant examples of this piece have been recorded either. The design is shown in **Fig. 38**, and includes an impressed design on the body, an example of which is shown in **Fig. 39**. On the lid are impressed the words "50 PATENT WAX VESTAS. WARRENTED." and the base has a concentric circle striker and impressed wording around it: "PATENT VESTA LIGHT BOX: IMPROVED SAFETY".

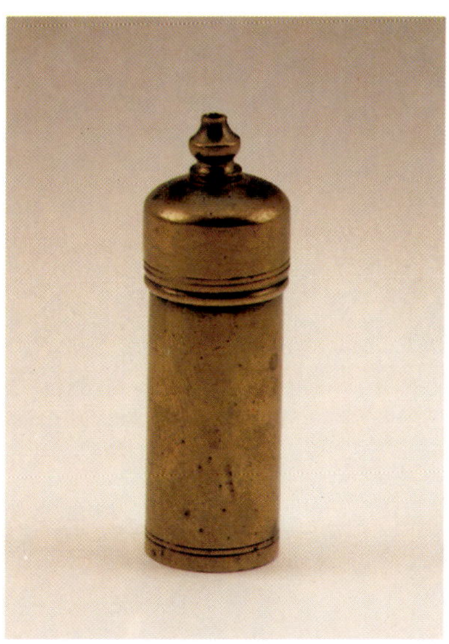

Fig. 36 Britain. Brass. Probably made by the Harcourt's. To hold 25 wax vesta matches. c.1851. H - 5.7cms.

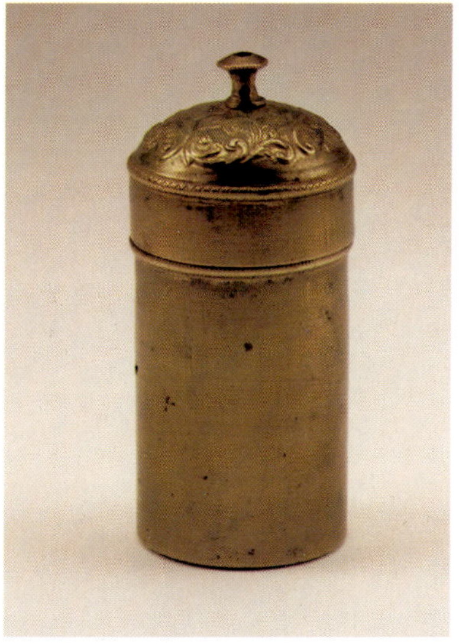

Fig. 37 Britain. Brass. Probably made by the Harcourt's. To hold 75 wax vesta matches. c.1851. H - 6cms.

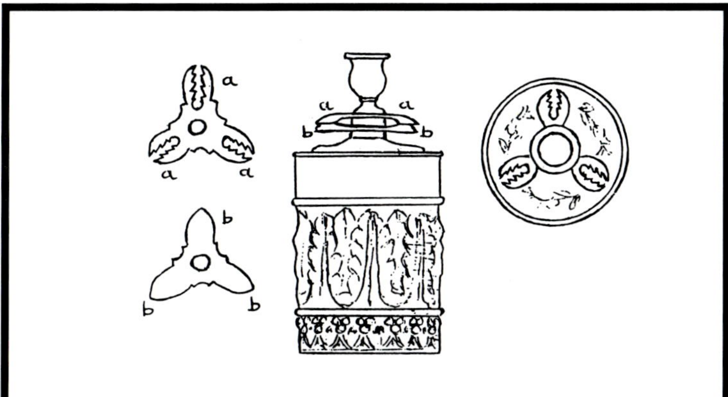

Fig. 38 Useful Design by the Harcourt's of 1851. Body design same as in Fig. 39.

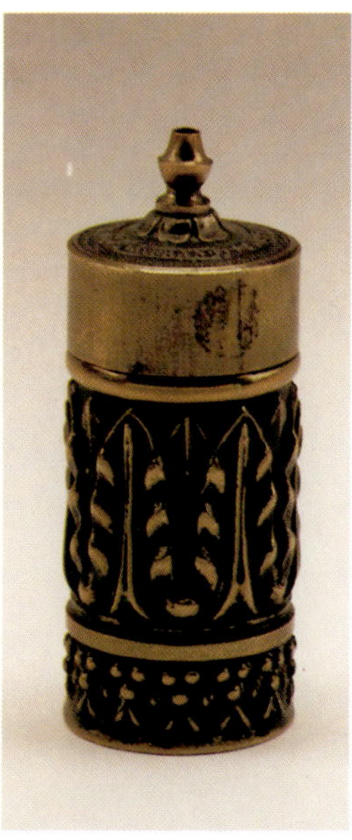

Fig. 39 Britain. Brass. Made by the Harcourt's to the design in Fig. 38. c.1852. H - 6.2cms.

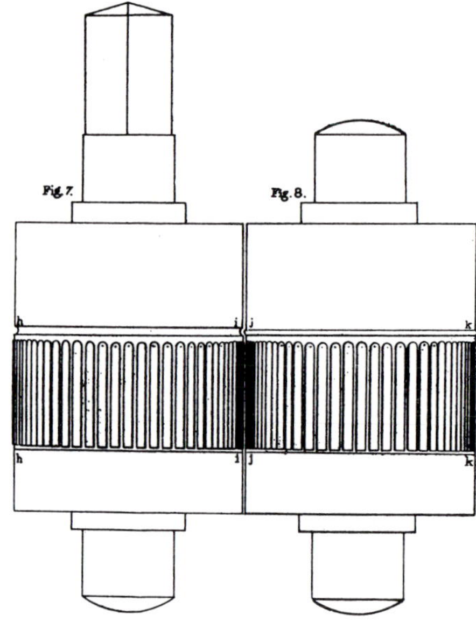

Fig. 40 Part of Invention Patent by the Harcourt's of 1852 for rollers to produce designs on box bodies.

The method used by the Harcourts to make the flared bases and body sides was the subject of a four part invention patent of October 1852. The first two parts related to the bases; these were made either by spinning the cylindrical body in a lathe and applying pressure to the bottom with a smooth tool to flare the base outwards, or by stamping the base out of a sheet of brass in a die, trimming off the residual metal, and soldering it to the body. The former method could be used with bodies made from tubing; the latter method was used on box bodies made from sheet brass. The third part of the patent related to forming bodies which were to have impressed designs from sheet brass. This is perhaps best described by the Harcourts in their specifications:

> "Thirdly, for raising or forming the ornament on or around such boxes, by producing the sunken design and counterpart on the periphery or surface of rollers, which being put in motion, and the strips of metal pushed between, will come out with the design formed upon them."

The fourth part of the patent related to the application of china and glass parts. The relevant part of the patent drawings are shown in **Fig. 40**.

A box made according to this patent, with a flared base soldered to a sheet brass body impressed by rollers, is shown in **Fig. 41**. The lid is equipped with a candle sconce, and with a match socket holding a wax vesta match contemporary with the box. The top is impressed with the Royal Arms and the wording "BY ROYAL LETTERS PATENT" and "VESTA". The disc inserted into the base is provided with a concentric circle striker.

A cylinder box made from tubing shown in **Fig. 42** is attributed to the Harcourts on the basis of the design on the lid, identical to the design on the lid of the inner box in Fig. 35. The base of the box has the usual concentric circle striker, with the wording around: "SAFETY BOX. 50 PATENT VESTA LIGHTS". It contains a number of the original wax vesta matches. The sides have incised lines separating bands of black and gold lacquer.

Boxes of a similar type are part of a desk set shown in **Fig. 43**, which highlights the intended use of these boxes as a source of light, and of heat for melting sealing wax. The desk set has a papier maché base with a drawer. On top is a cut-glass inkwell with a brass pen-holder. Behind the inkwell is a spring-loaded letter balance, with a scale marked in ounces on one side and pennyweights on the other. On either side of the inkwell is a match holder, the lids with a candle sconce and match socket, the bases with a cross-hatched striker. The match holders sit in flared bases that are fixed to the paper maché base.

The match holders and flared bases are attributed to the Harcourts, and there is no reason to doubt, if they made those items, that they probably made the other brass fittings as well. The paper maché was probably also made in Birmingham, which was a major center for that type of material.

Obviously intended for the same purpose as the pair of match holders above is a larger brass box shown in **Fig. 44.** The body is made from brass tubing, decorated with a band of gold lacquer in the center and some traces of black lacquer on the wider bands; near the bottom is a raised bead which is the seating for a flared base. The base disc has the concentric circle striker, with the wording around "PRINCE ALBERT'S SAFETY BOX: 150 PATENT VESTA LIGHTS". The lid has an impressed design of holly leaves and berries surrounded by a band of stylized foliage; in the center is a candle sconce of more robust form than for pieces previously described.

A similar box soldered into a flared base, and with a similar lid pattern is shown in **Fig. 45**. The body, made from sheet brass, is impressed with five different panels representing mixed flowers, leaves and fruit. On the inside is a tin disc, soldered to the body about 7mm from the bottom to prevent the matches from dropping too far into the box. The flared base has a band of impressed ivy leaves, and on the underside is a large disc with the concentric circle striker, shown in **Fig. 46**. The lid is surmounted by a candle sconce and two match sockets; the second match socket also served as an anchor for the chain of a candle snuffer, now missing except for the first link of the chain. This match holder was intended for use as an independent item, not as a part of a desk set.

A number of brass boxes were produced fitted with finger rings to facilitate transport of the boxes from place to place. All are probably by the same maker and are attributed to the Harcourts. Two are shown in **Fig. 47**, the smaller one at the left missing two match sockets, and that to the right with a single match socket to which a candle snuffer is attached by a chain. The bases of both are made from sheet tin plate, and they lack strikers. It is speculated that the strikers may have been in the form of a piece of sandpaper glued to the underside of the base.

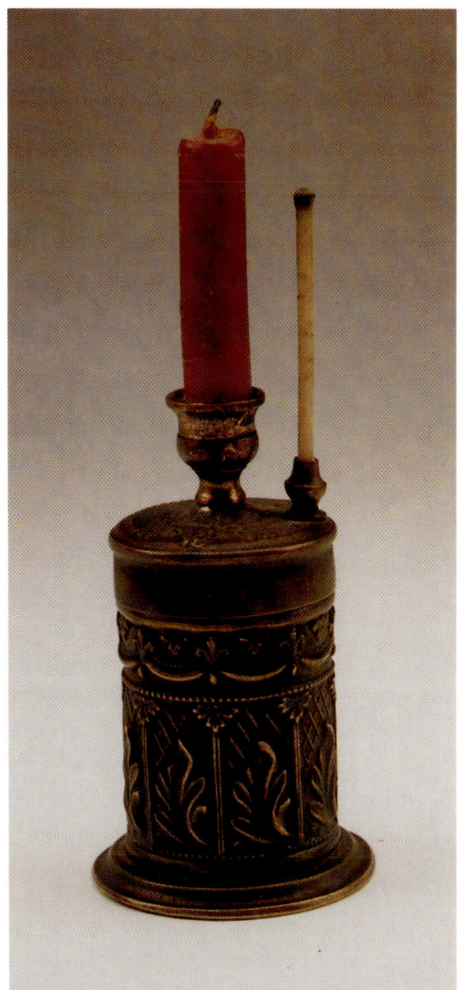

Fig. 41 Britain. Brass. Made by the Harcourt's. c.1851. H(of box) - 6.9cms.

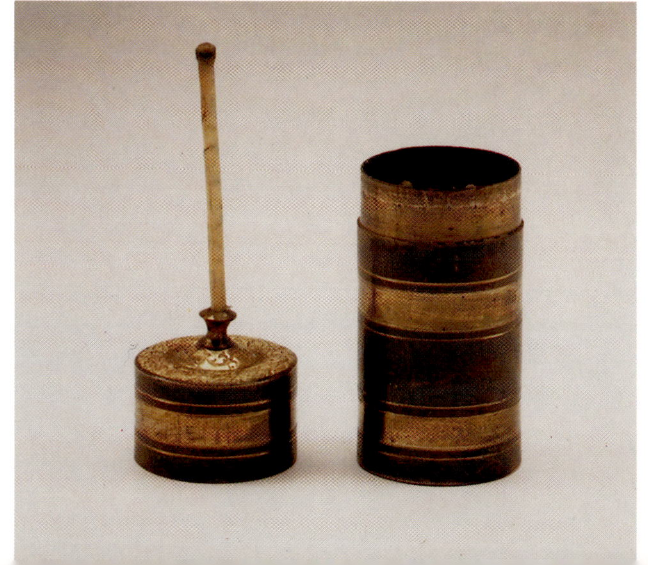

Fig. 42 Britain. Brass. Made by Harcourt's. With original wax vesta match. c.1851. H - 5.8cms.

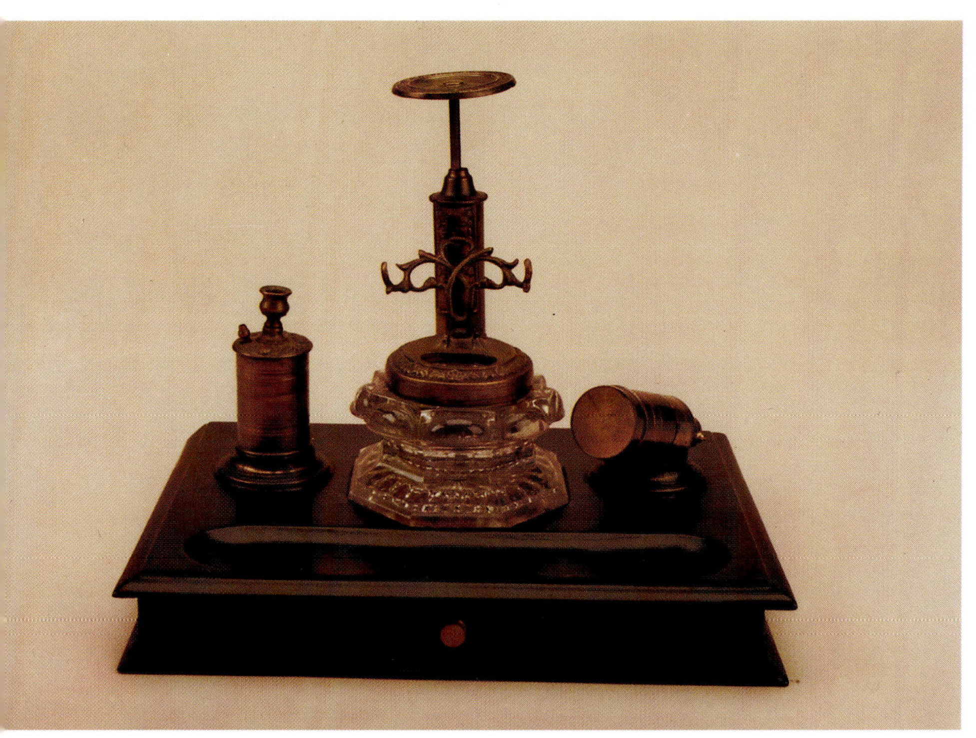

Fig. 43 Britain. Brass, glass and papier mache. Desk set. Brass elements probably all by the Harcourt's. c.1852. H - 21cms.

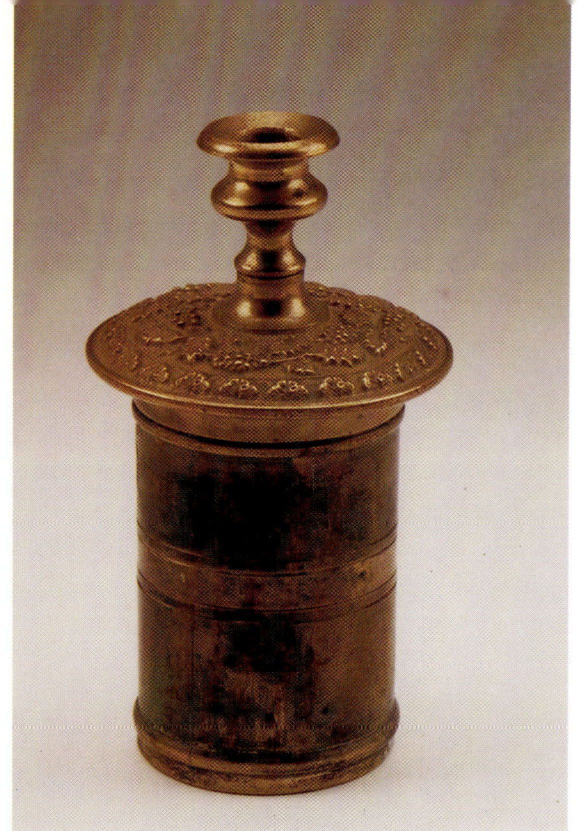

Fig. 44 Britain. Brass. Made by the Harcourt's to sit in a base, possibly as part of a desk set. c.1852. H - 9.5cms.

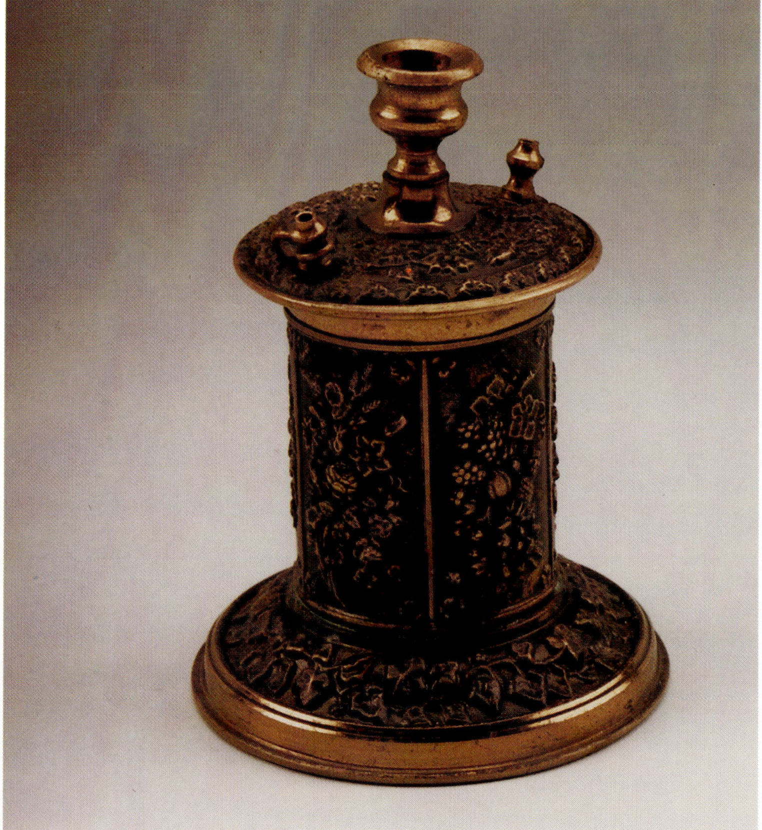

Fig. 45 Britain. Brass. Made by the Harcourt's, the body soldered to the base. c.1852. H - 9.9cms.

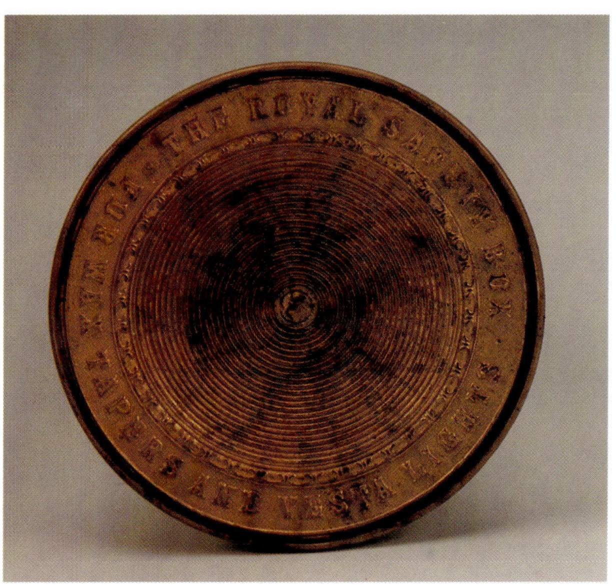

Fig. 46 Underside of base of Fig. 45. D - 7.1cms.

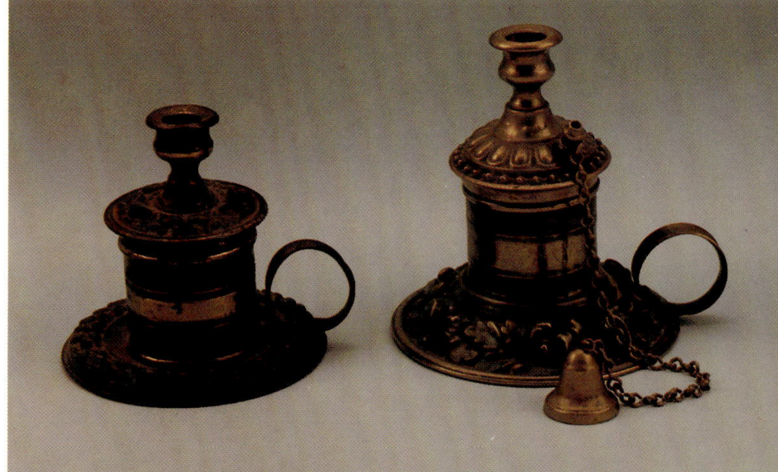

Fig. 47 Britain. Brass. Made by the Harcourt's. c.1852. Left: H -6.1cms. Right: H - 7.5cms.

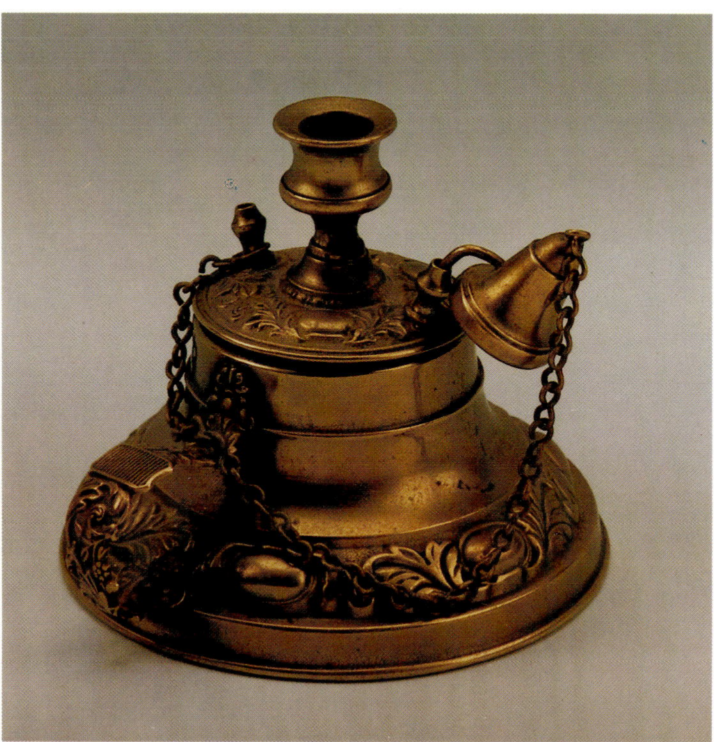

Fig. 48 Britain. Brass. Made by the Harcourt's. c.1852. H -6.5cms.

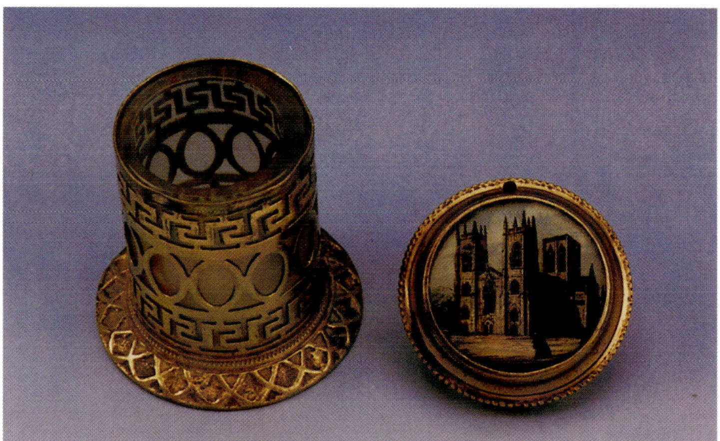

Fig. 50 Britain. Brass, glass, leather. c.1855. H - 6.3cms.

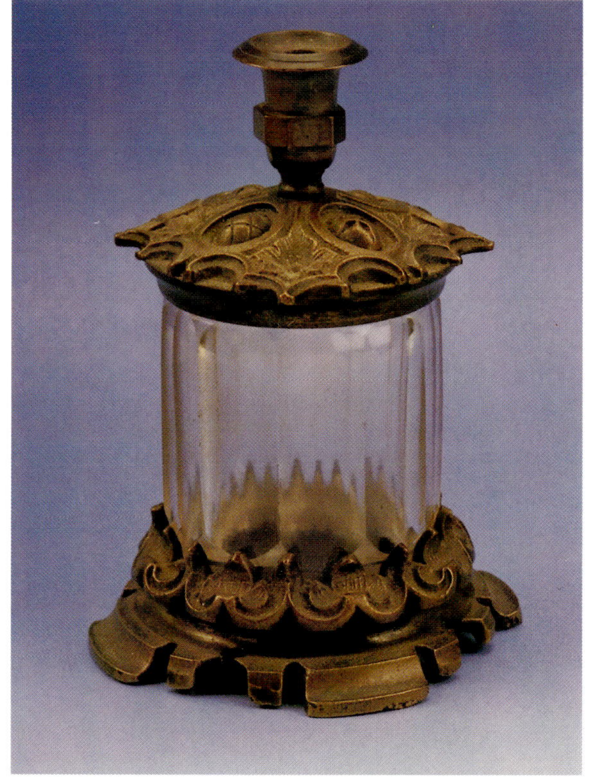

Fig. 51 Britain. Brass, glass. c.1855. H - 8.9cms.

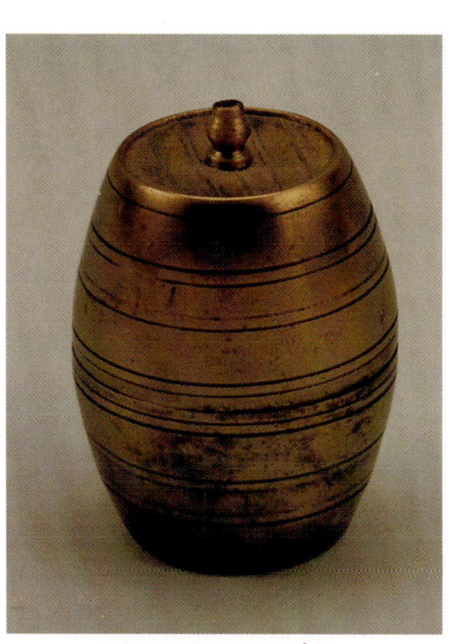

Fig. 49 Britain. Brass. Made by Dowler's, the Harcourt's or Allen & Moore's. c.1851. H - 5.4cms.

A third version shown in **Fig. 48** is far more ornate, with a bell-shaped body. The lid has a candle sconce and two match sockets, to one of which is attached a chain holding a snuffer fitted with a bent arm that conveniently fits only one of the sockets. The base has the same impressed design as the piece shown on the right in Fig. 47, and the lid has a very similar impressed design. The ornate finger ring has an impressed floral design with a rectangular striking panel in its centre. It is finished overall in gold lacquer, except for the tin base.

The variety of the brass match holders made by William and Joseph Harcourt is substantial, and they were obviously the most prolific of the three identified manufacturers. Of the three, they appear to have been the only ones producing the main bodies in a thin-gauge flat sheet form, rolled and bent to form a cylinder, then expertly soldered at the join. These bodies were produced in different sizes, and were interchangeable with lids and bases of different designs, thus increasing the variety available to the public.

Made by one of the three main brass match holder manufacturers of Birmingham is a novelty piece in the form of a barrel, shown in **Fig. 49**. The slip-on lid is one half of the box, the top simulating the planks that form the top of a barrel, and provided with a match socket. The lower half forms the main body of the box and has an angled strip fitted around the inside at the top, to keep the matches upright and prevent them from creating difficulties in closing the box. The base has a concentric circle striker with the wording around it "SAFETY BARREL: FOR PATENT VESTA LIGHTS". The sides have incised lines forming wide and narrow bands, and there are small traces of red lacquer. Four such boxes were recorded by Miller Christy in the Bryant & May catalogue (l928), said to be of various sizes, and "with bands of green, red and gold."

It is evident that Birmingham was a major center for the production of these brass boxes, of which many examples have survived. They were all made between 1850 and about 1855, or perhaps a little later; the Harcourts went out of business between 1855 and 1860. It is unfortunate that so few were provided with maker's marks, which has necessitated speculation and attributions based upon the patent records and comparative study.

The three pieces next to be described are of unknown origin, but are included here because of the brass content and some vague similarities to the form of the preceding pieces. They may have been made in Birmingham, but there is no recorded evidence to support such an attribution.

A series of match holders was produced in the form illustrated in **Fig. 50**. The body sides of this example are of pierced sheet brass, soldered at the join. Inside the body is a glass vessel of uneven thickness, the exterior with a ground translucent finish. The base appears to have been cast, its underside provided with a concentric circle striker. The cast brass, flared lid is provided with a match socket in the rim; the top of the lid is fitted with a glass disc, beneath which is a finely painted illustration of York Minster's west front and forecourt, backed with a piece of leather, and held in place by a brass ring.

Others in the series are said to have a fabric lining around the glass cylinder. Illustrations of Windsor Castle, Chester Cathedral, the Palace of Westminster and Liverpool Town Hall have been recorded.

The example in **Fig. 51** is of similar form and has a cast brass base and lid surmounted by a candle sconce. The body is of glass with eleven flat polished faces, glued into the base. There is no obvious striker, but the underside of the base bears a mark that indicates the former presence of a striker.

The third brass example, in **Fig. 52**, suggests some classical or ecclesiastical form, the finial providing the location for a match socket. The base is recessed for the striker, which is missing.

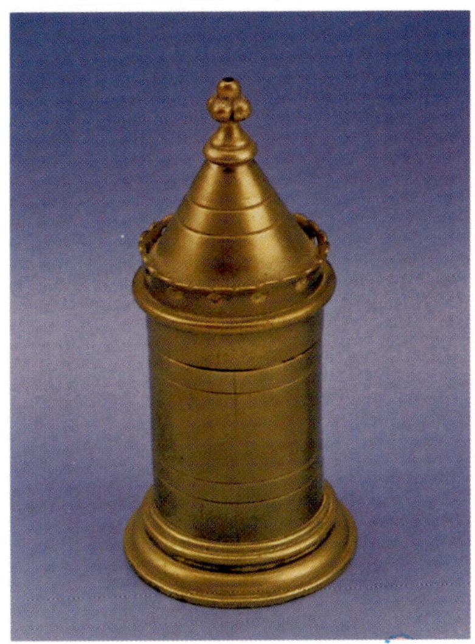

Fig. 52 Britain. Brass. c.1855. H - 10.7cms.

Early protective match holders made of wood were produced in Scotland. Mauchline, a small town in Ayrshire, was renowned for its small wooden wares. Today, these wares are commonly called 'Mauchline ware', often without foundation since their style was copied by European workers, particularly in France, and sold at lower prices.

Among the many small items skillfully crafted in Mauchline were match holders. One of the leading and most prolific producers, and the longest lasting company, was that of William and Andrew Smith. None of the examples shown here are marked with their name, and it is possible that one or more other companies made match holders; but the techniques used, and the forms of the designs, are consistent with their products, and they are therefore all tentatively attributed to the Smiths.

Under the leadership of their father, the Smith brothers were trading by 1823, making razor strops and snuff boxes for which they were highly regarded. But they were quick to diversify into other items, and the family was particularly inventive.

Their tartan designs on boxes were originally painted by hand, but in 1853, Andrew's son, also called William, invented and patented a machine for "Improvements in Ruling Ornamental Figures." This was a multi-pen device, later modified to use wheels or rollers, which printed intricate designs (specifically tartans) directly onto wood, paper or cloth. The machine was fitted with sixteen pens, and could repeat patterns, if need be, in different colors.

By 1845 the Smiths had already perfected a method of transferring black ink line illustrations to their manufactures. The engraved plates were made by various companies in Britain, and were used to print the designs onto Japanese paper. Their boxes were given two or three coats of varnish; then the print was varnished and placed ink side down onto the box and left to dry. When dry, the paper was rubbed off with a damp cloth, leaving the ink drawing on the box. Another coat of varnish was then applied.

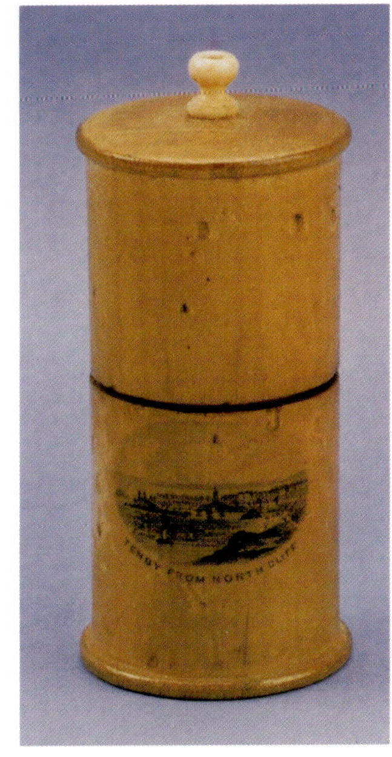

Fig. 53 Scotland. Sycamore wood, ivory. Made by William & Andrew Smith. c.1860. 7.2cms.

The Smiths had about five hundred illustrations of English, Scottish and Welsh scenes and noteworthy buildings from cities and from tourist and seaside resorts, plus a great number of similar subjects in other European countries, the United States, Australia, and India. Their products were exported to these countries, and it is amusing to think that many British travellers returned home with souvenirs of the places they had visited, probably without realizing that the souvenir had been made in the British Isles.

Of the several forms of match holder that the Smiths produced, the most common is probably the cylinder. The example in **Fig. 53** has a slip-on lid, fitted with a bone or ivory match socket, and the base is recessed for a sandpaper striking surface. The oval black transfer design is "Tenby From North Cliff," a coastal resort in South Wales.

A second transfer ware box is in the form of a barrel, with a deep slip-on lid, the top drilled for a socket, now missing. The base is recessed for a sandpaper striker. The example in **Fig. 54** has two oval illustrations of the cathedral city of Winchester in Hampshire, England, with the "City Cross, Winchester" on the side shown, and "College Chapel, Winchester." on the reverse.

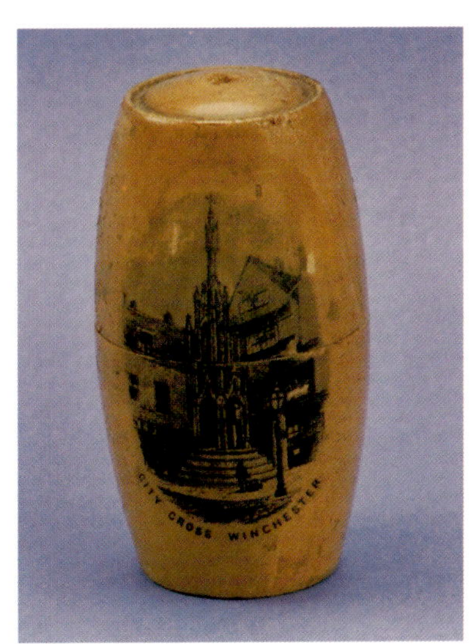

Fig. 54 Scotland. Sycamore wood. Made by William & Andrew Smith. c.1860. H - 6.2cms.

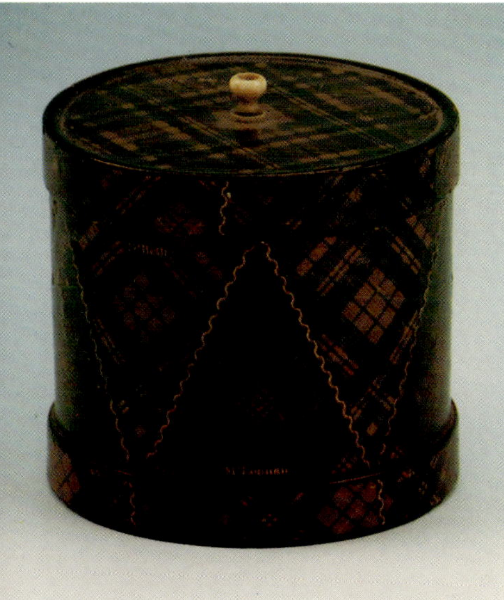

Fig. 55 Scotland. Sycamore wood, paper, ivory. Made by William & Andrew Smith. Represents a drum. c.1860. H - 5.5cms.

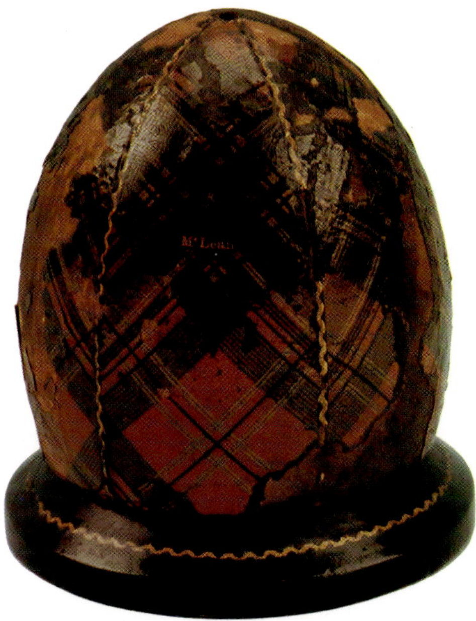

Fig. 56 Scotland. Sycamore wood. Made by William & Andrew Smith. c.1860. H - 6.7cms.

The tartan designs were printed on paper and glued to the surface of the boxes, after black lines were painted where the joins in the paper were to occur. This disguised any imperfections at the joins which would otherwise have appeared as white lines, formed by the sycamore wood showing through. Covering some of the shapes of these small boxes demanded great skill and concentration.

The broad cylinder in **Fig. 55** represents a drum, with gold lines covering the edges of the triangular panels to represent the strings used to adjust the tension on the skin head. The central panel is labelled "McLennan," that to the left "McBeth". The top has a McBeth tartan, with a centrally located bone or ivory match socket. The base is recessed and sanded for friction. On the underside of the lid, written in pencil, is "2/-", which may have been the original price of two shillings.

Another novelty shape in the form of an egg is shown in **Fig. 56**; its tartan is marked "McLean." The match socket (missing) was located at the top, and the egg is mounted on a black base with a zigzag gold line around the edge. The base is recessed for a sanded striker.

A match holder in the form of a hand bell was also produced; the same shape was also used for a tape measure.

Pocket match holders were included in the Smiths' wide range of products, usually of oval cross section. **Fig. 57** is an upright type with a slip-on lid set with a shallow bone or ivory match socket; the base is recessed for a sanded striker. The tartan is not identified. The example in **Fig. 58** has a sliding drawer, with the bone or ivory match socket set in the side and protruding through to the inside of the box to act as a stop to prevent the drawer from being pulled out from the main body. The tartan is identified on the lid as "Prince Charlie", and an illustration of a pair of classical figures printed on paper has been applied over the tartan. The blind end has been recessed for a sanded striker.

All of these boxes were produced with tartan and transfer design forms of decoration, and were being made by 1860 and probably until late in the l9th century. It is impossible to date the examples positively, but they are included here because they fit into the period under review.

The Smith company began to decline in the face of fierce foreign competition around the turn of the century; it turned to cheaper forms of decoration, examples of which are shown later. But it was not until a fire destroyed the works in 1933, and William Smith III retired, that the company faded badly. It closed at the outbreak of World War II.

In southern England, the adjacent towns of Tonbridge and Tunbridge Wells were renowned for their wooden products of furniture and small articles, which were referred to as "Tonbridge Ware" long before the towns became famous for their intricate mosaic work, which has taken over the name. Until recently the mosaic work was referred to as 'end grain mosaic', but it is now known to include side grain cut pieces in the multiple layered blocks of sticks that were used to produce the repeat patterns on their wares.

Fig. 59 is a sketch of a block of sticks, each stick approximately 1mm by 1mm square, glued together to form a pattern when viewed from the end. Each stick was cut from a sheet of veneer, either with or across the grain; this provided two slightly different shades of color from the same sheet. A slice cut from the end of the block could form a single panel of up to several hundred tesserae (the individual rectangles of the mosaic); or, butted together side by side, they could form a larger panel.

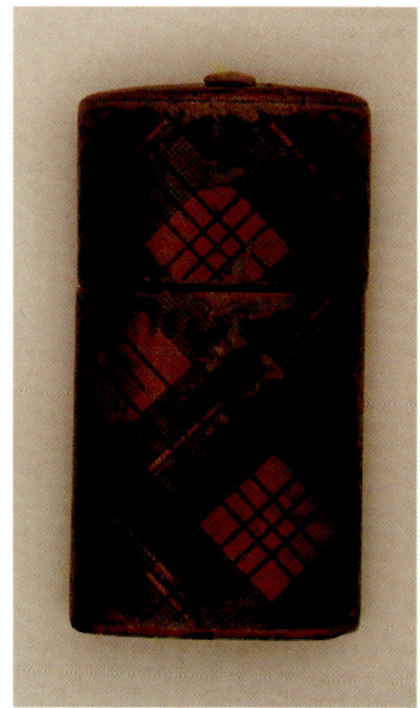

Fig. 57 Scotland. Sycamore wood, ivory. Made by William & Andrew Smith. c.1860. H - 5.9cms.

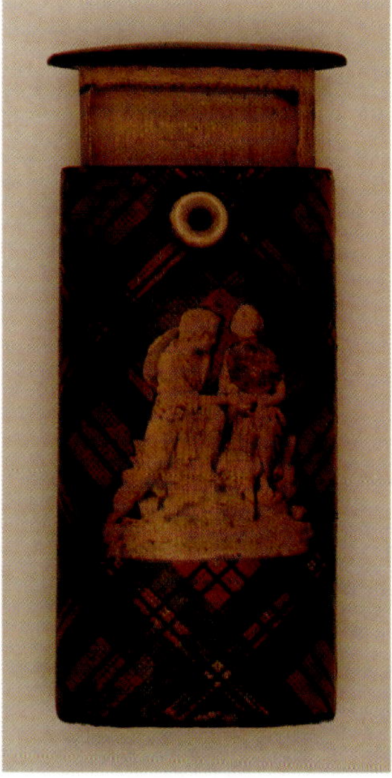

Fig. 58 Scotland. Sycamore wood, ivory. Made by William & Andrew Smith. c.1860. L - 5.9cms.

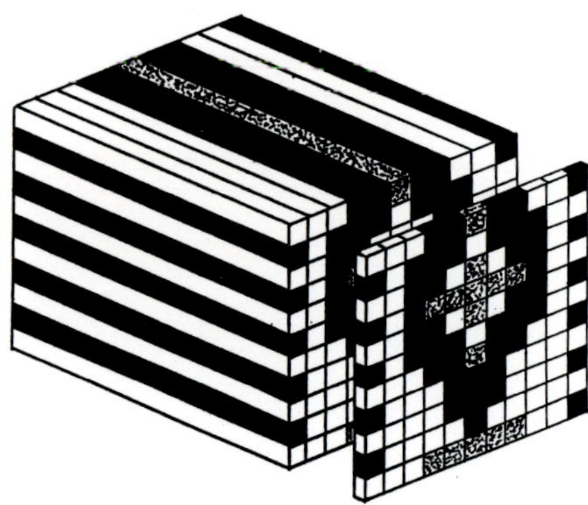

Fig. 59 Sketch of a block of splints forming a pattern, with a slice removed, to show how the Tonbridge ware mosaic designs are prepared.

Simple geometric patterns were the most common form of design; but floral, anthropomorphic, architectural and even landscape designs of considerable size and complexity were produced, to decorate anything from chairs and tables to napkin rings and other small items, including two or three types of match holders.

One form of match holder produced in the early period that is distinctive of Tonbridge ware is shown in **Fig. 60**. The octagonal body is provided with repeat designs on each panel, no doubt cut from the same block; each panel has approximately five hundred tesserae. An enlarged view of one panel is shown in **Fig. 61**. The inside of the body has a cylindrical compartment to hold a candle. The slip-on lid is decorated in a mixture of triangles, diamonds and rectangles—some in solid form, others made in the multiple stick technique. The centrally located candle sconce is made in the multiple stick technique, using larger sticks, before being turned at the center and trimmed to an octagon at the top; it is screwed into the lid. An ivory match socket is also present. The top of the lid is shown in **Fig. 62**. The base is a single piece, round, and screws on to the body; it is recessed inside to hold wafers for sealing letters. The underside has a concentric circle striker.

The Tunbridge craftsmen added other types of match holders to their product lines later in the century.

In Italy's Bay of Naples, probably mostly at Sorrento, the same type of mosaic work was produced. It has been suggested that Italian craftsmen went to Britain to teach the art to the craftsmen in Tonbridge, but there is no real evidence to support this theory. However it is not uncommon to find examples of the work of Italian craftsmen attributed to Tonbridge. For comparison, an example of Sorrento workmanship using the same form of mosaic work may be seen in Figs. 339 and 340.

A glass match holder of unknown origin, with a very loose-fitting, slip-on lid, is shown in **Fig. 63**. The central part of the body has nine sides, and the base and lid have numerous facets. There is a match socket located in the hexagonal knob on the lid, and the striker is a series of sixteen ground-out lines, in the form of a star, on the underside of the base. A similar piece was the subject of an Ornamental Design registered in 1847, shown in Fig. 601.

A finely cast brass figure of a small, long-haired dog is shown in **Fig. 64**. The dog is seated on a cushion, with a tassel at each corner and a small diamond-shaped patch roughened for friction. The head of the dog is hinged at the back, just below the collar, for access to the matches stored in the body. There are traces of gold lacquer on the cushion, but the figure has been treated to resemble bronze, and is mounted on a black stone base. Its origins are unknown, but it is perhaps a product of Germany.

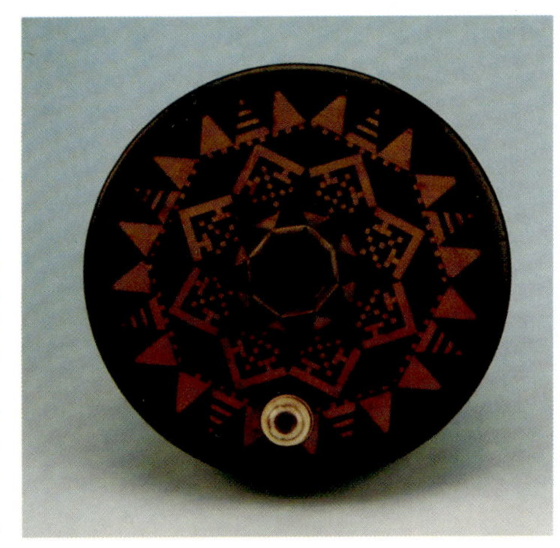

Fig. 62 Top of lid of Fig. 60.

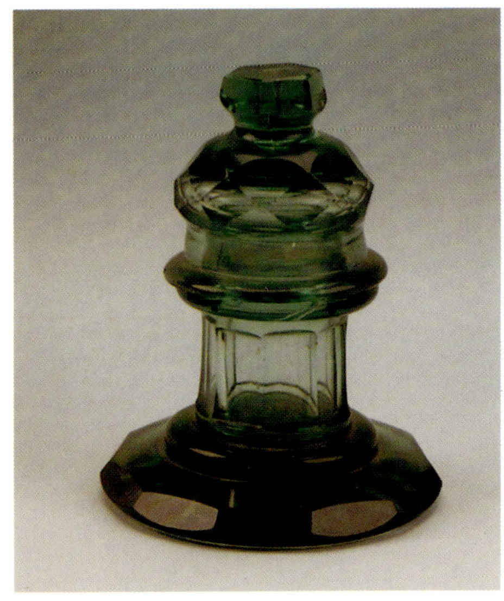

Fig. 63 Probably Britain. Glass. c.1850. H - 8.8cms.

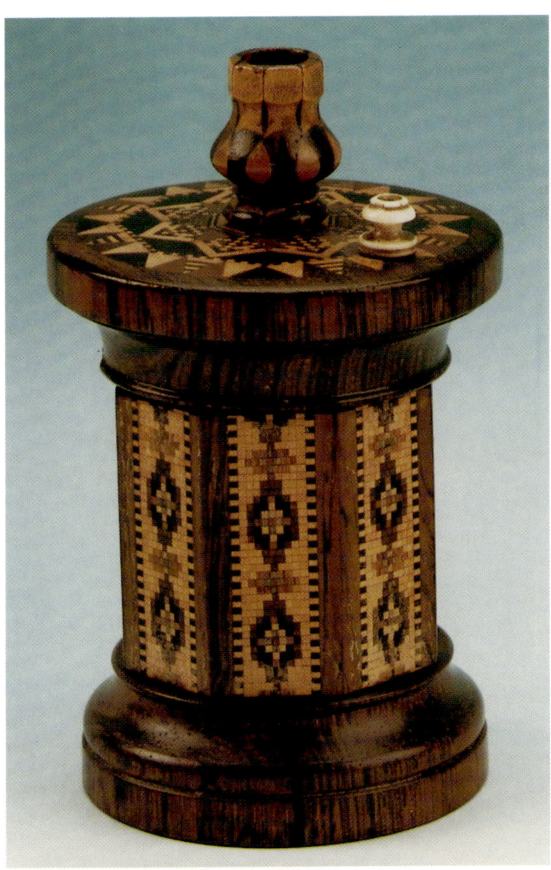

Fig. 60 Britain. Tonbridge. Wood, ivory. Match holder, with central tube inside the body to hold a candle, and a removable base to hold seals. c.1860. H - 10cms.

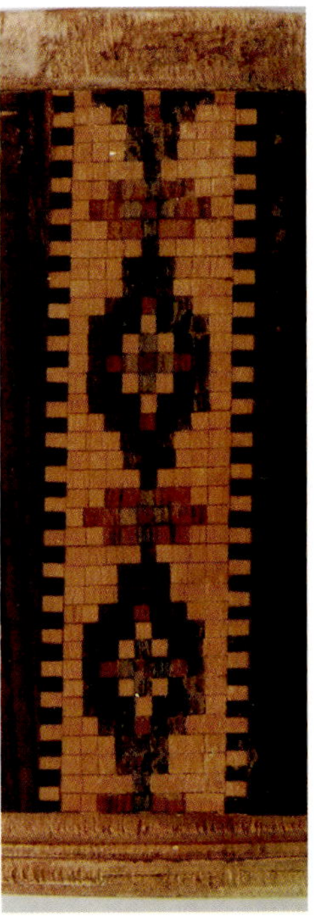

Fig. 61 Enlargement of one face of body of Fig. 60 - with almost 500 tesserae.

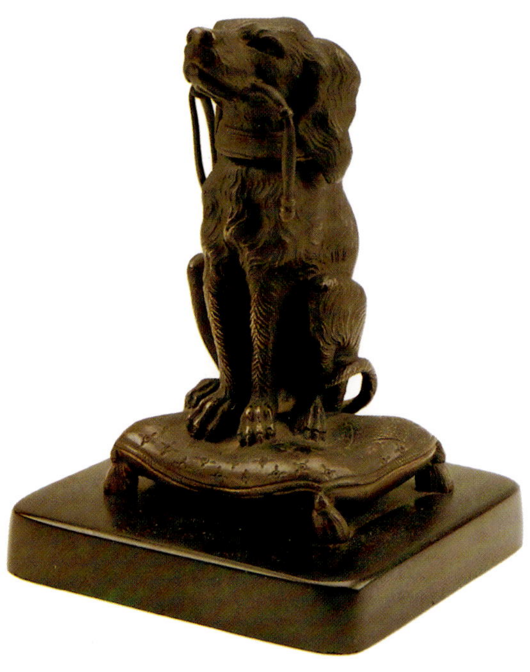

Fig. 64 German? Cast brass, stone. c.1850s. H - 12.2cms.

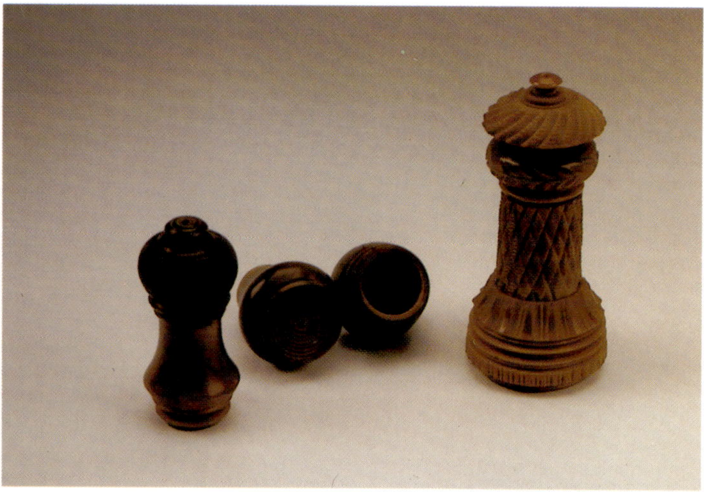

Fig. 65 Britain. Vegetable ivory. c.1850s. Left: H - 5.4cms Right: H - 8.2cms.

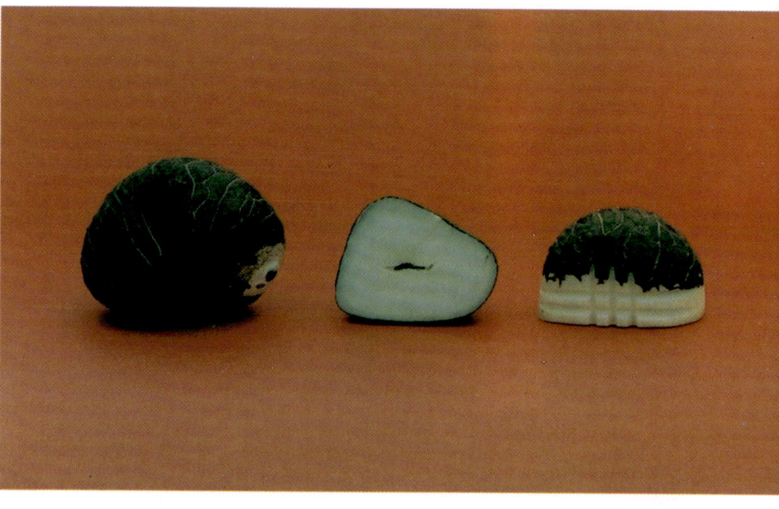

Fig. 66 Vegetable ivory. Left: the seed of the Phytelephas macrocarpa. Centre: cross section through seed showing fissure. Right: part of outside removed and worked with a file.

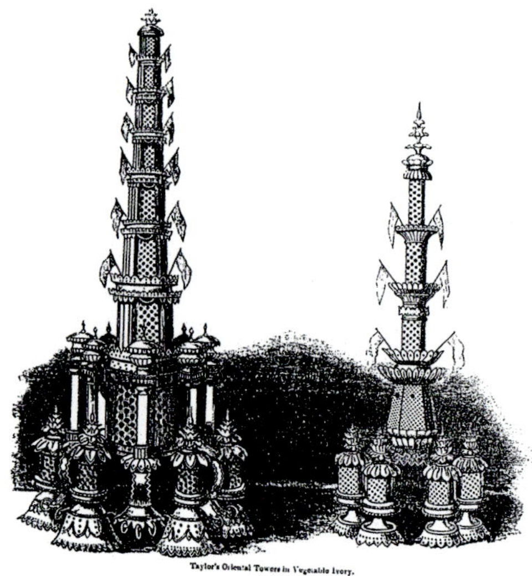

Fig. 67 Illustration from the "Official Descriptive Catalogue of the Great Exhibition of 1851" of the oriental tower made from over 1000 vegetable ivory nuts (seeds) by Benjamin Taylor of London.

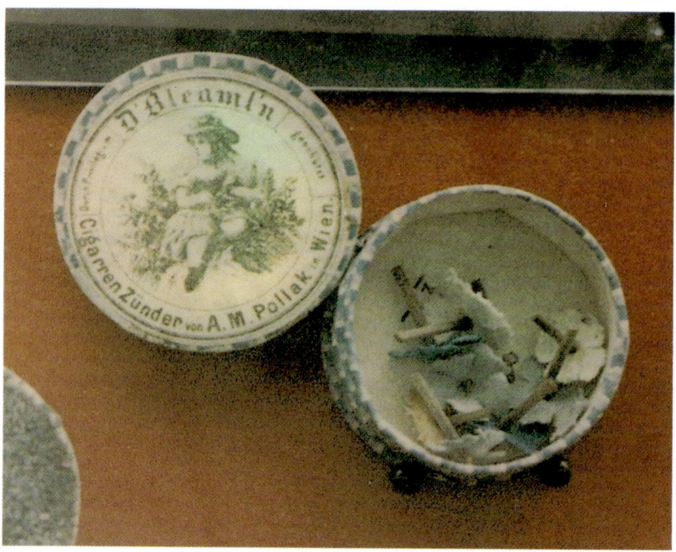

Fig. 68 Austria. Cigar tips made by A. M. Pollak of Vienna. c.1845.

In complete contrast to the foregoing are match holders made from vegetable ivory, three examples of which are shown in **Fig. 65**. Vegetable ivory is the endosperm part of the seeds of the palm *Phytelephas macrocarpa.* It is possible to find the seeds today, probably by the name of *Tagua nuts.* Usually about four to five centimeters long and three to four centimeters wide, they have a thin, brown, skin cover over a milky white body, which indeed does have the appearance of ivory. Through the center of the nut runs an irregularly shaped fissure. An example of a complete nut, and the two halves of another nut (one half showing the fissure, the other half worked with a file) are shown in **Fig. 66.**

The nut can be easily sawn, filed, and turned in a lathe, and may be dyed. The imperfections in the nut did not prevent Victorian craftsmen from making quite extensive use of it for buttons, jewelery, and a range of small decorative items, as well as (by joining the nuts together) large decorative items.

In the "Official Descriptive and Illustrated Catalogue of the Great Exhibition of 1851," Benjamin Taylor of Clerkenwell provided an illustration, shown in **Fig. 67**, of "An Oriental tower, with minarets composed of upwards of 1,000 pieces, manufactured out of the corozo, or vegetable ivory nut, the produce of New Granada." It is possible that the match holders illustrated were examples of the "Sundry fancy articles" to which Taylor also referred, that to the right in Fig. 65 being made from three nuts, the others each made from two nuts.

Two forms of match, manufactured in Austria and Germany in the early 1840s, were specifically intended for cigar smokers, and were referred to as cigar tips or cigar caps, depending upon the form. The cigar tips, in **Fig. 68**, have short stems, about 1.5cm in length, with a brightly colored head of igniting composition, the head surrounded by a five petal linen flower in a bright color. The stem was pushed into the tip of the cigar and then ignited. The cigar caps, in **Fig. 69**, were small cones of paper, usually pink, with a small knob of igniting composition on the tip; they fitted over the tip of the cigar, and were then ignited.

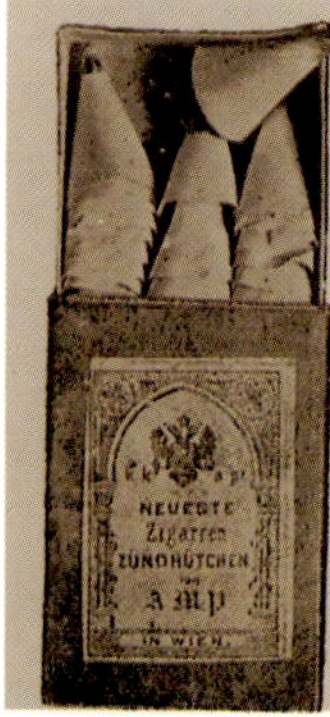

Fig. 69 Austria. Cigar caps made by A. M. Pollak of Vienna. c.1845.

In Britain, cigar tips were the subject of a patent issued to Jarvis Palmer of London in 1849, using a wire stem with a large head of igniting composition. Two of his patent drawings are shown in **Fig. 70**.

These small speciality matches for cigars probably led to the manufacture in Britain of one of the earliest recorded pocket match holders made of silver; it is shown in **Fig. 71**. The hallmarks show that it was made in Birmingham by Francis Clark in 1849. It has two compartments: the larger one for matches, but too small for the ordinary matches of the day, and the small compartment, probably intended for the remnants of spent matches, and provided with a steel striker set in the lid.

By 1853 Alfred Taylor, another Birmingham silversmith, appears to have been making silver pocket boxes with two compartments on a regular basis, but with the lids hinged longitudinally, as shown in **Fig. 72**. They were longer than the Clark example, the larger compartment being of sufficient size to take a small wax vesta match; the smaller compartment had the same type of striker as Clark's, but also incorporated a cigar tip cutter. **Fig. 73** shows the top of the lids of the Taylor box, with an engine-turned design and, engraved in an elaborate escutcheon, the crest of the Berry family of Scotland. The box no doubt originally belonged to John Berry, a prominent advocate.

Late in the period under review here (1830 - 1860), the first ceramic match holders began to appear. Edward Loysel, an engineer of London, held a number of patents for domestic items such as a mill for grinding tea or coffee, a coffee urn, a tea pot and, in 1861, a match holder. The text of his patent stated:

> "My invention consists in forming match boxes or cases of porcelain, parian, china, or other earthenware, and making a portion of the external part of the article with a roughened surface on which the matches may be rubbed for the purpose of igniting same. These match boxes or cases may be of any convenient form or design that the taste of the manufacturer may dictate, and they may be provided, if desired, with lids or covers to protect the matches when they are placed in the boxes."

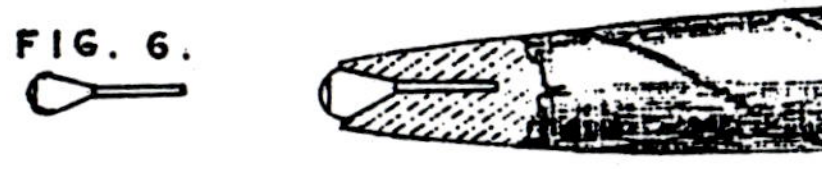

Fig. 70 Part of Invention Patent of 1849 for cigar tips, by Jarvis Palmer of London.

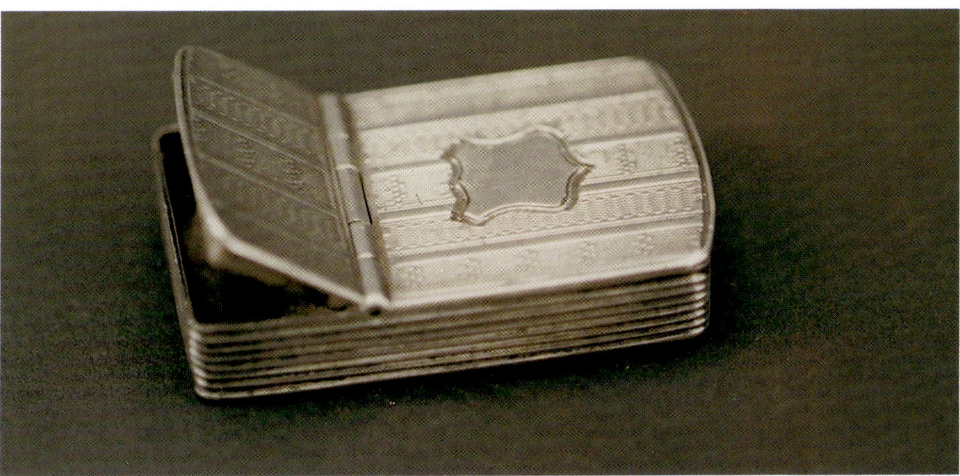

Fig. 71 Britain. Silver iron. For cigar tips. Made by Francis Clark of Birmingham. 1849 L - 4.3cms.

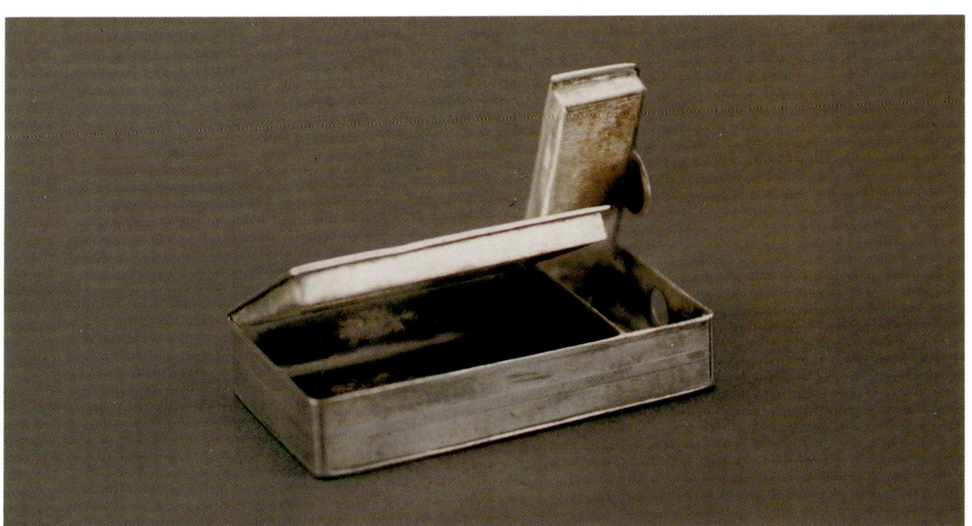

Fig. 72 Britain. Silver, iron. Match box and cigar cutter. Made by Alfred Taylor of Birmingham. 1854. L - 5.7cms.

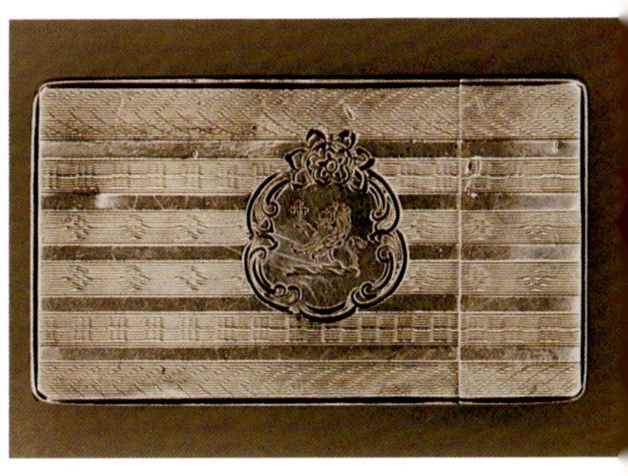

Fig. 73 As Fig. 72: the crest of the Berry family of Scotland.

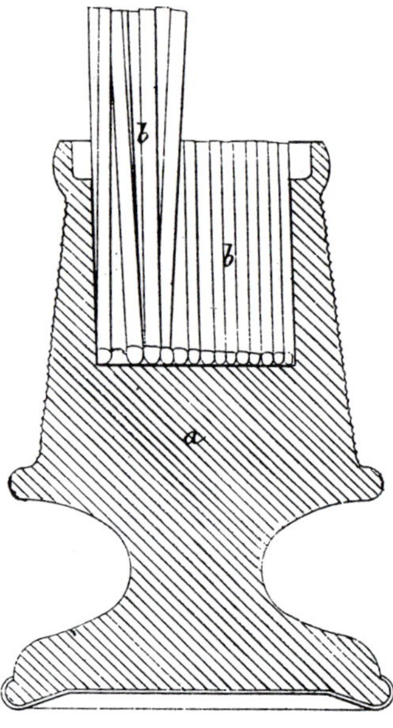

Fig. 74 Drawing from Invention Patent of 1861 by Edward Loysel, showing ribbed or threaded striker.

The "roughened surface" to which he referred was in the form of parallel grooves, as may be seen in one of his patent drawings, shown in **Fig. 74.**

One version of the end product was made at Sèvres, France, then imported into Britain where it was advertised in "The Ironmonger" of March 31, 1863, along with the illustration in **Fig. 75**, which showed that it sold retail:

"For kitchen use, without saucer or lid, 10d.
Extra large size, ls.3d.
For library, bed or sitting rooms, offices, hotels, plain white, with saucer at foot and lid, as illustrated, 2s.6d.
Ditto, decorated with fillets in colors, 3s.6d.
Ditto, with fillets of gold, 4s.
Ditto, with artistic designs in gold and colors, 4s.6d.
Ditto, extra rich, 5s."

Seven reasons for purchasing "This elegant invention" were also given:

"1.- The corrugated unglazed surface of the Sèvres China cannot wear out by usage, therefore the ignitor, unless broken, will always be efficient, and last forever.
2.- There is no more waste of matches in a series of unsuccessful attempts to ignite them.
3.- Persons tempers will be no more tried, especially in the dark.
4.- There will be no more occasion to deface the walls by striking matches upon them.
5.- The saucer at foot is most useful for half burnt matches and cigar ash.
6.- It is invaluable for sealing letters in the library, office, or hotel.
7.- It is undeniably a tasteful ornament to any room of a gentleman's house."

A second smaller version, probably made in Birmingham, was incorporated into a brass cylindrical box, similar in appearance to some of the Harcourt boxes. The lid section reaches down to the base, forming the box sides, and has a match socket on top, surrounded by two bands of an impressed floral design, with the wording between the lines "LOYSEL'S PATENT LUCIFER MATCH IGNITOR". The ceramic holder within the brass cylinder has the same wording with the Royal Coat of Arms printed on the inside; the external surface is provided with the grooved striker.

Loysel's ribbed holders seemingly faded from the scene for a number of years, but reappeared about 1880 in various styles, usually without a lid. They may have continued to be produced in France, and an example is shown in **Fig. 76** that probably dates from the last quarter of the century.

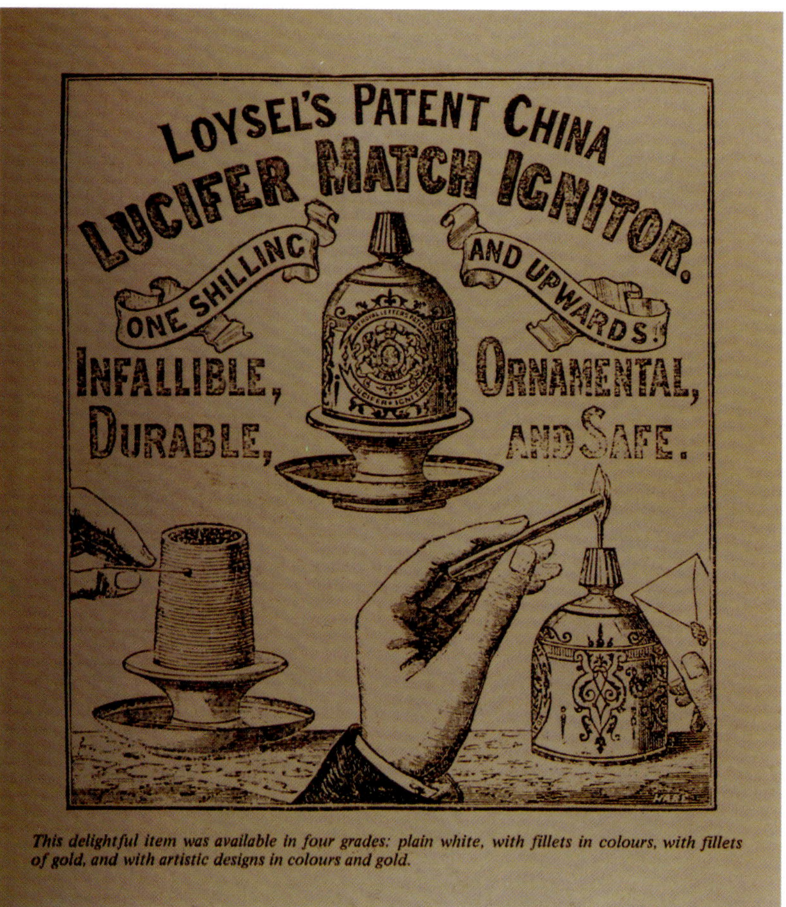

This delightful item was available in four grades: plain white, with fillets in colours, with fillets of gold, and with artistic designs in colours and gold.

Fig. 75 An advert from The Ironmonger of March 31, 1863, showing Loysel's patent produced at Sevres, France.

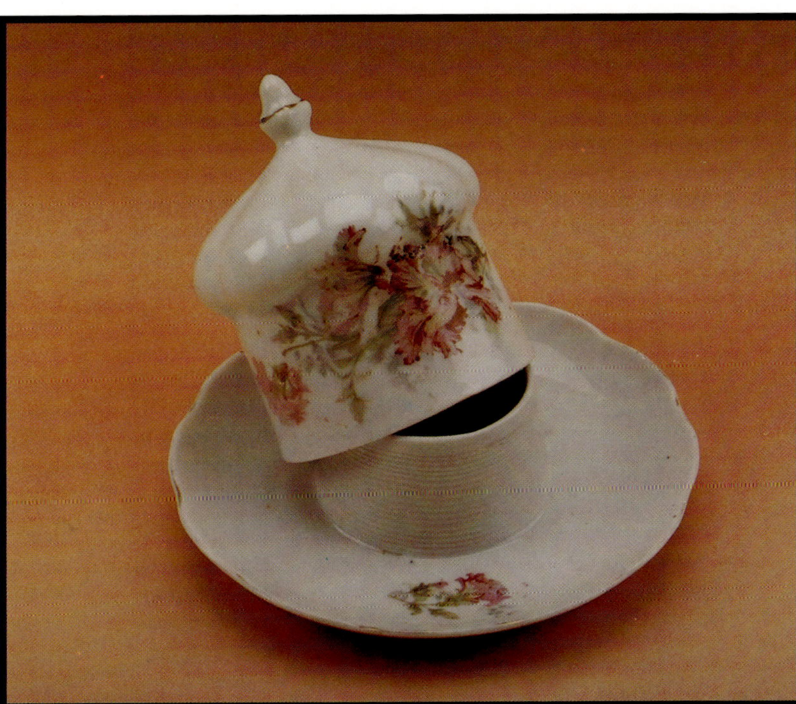

Fig. 76 French? Ceramic. After Loysel's patent. c.1880s.

Although match holders that could be referred to as "protective" continued to be made until late in the l9th century, by the late 1850s and early 1860s the match had been improved and was less subject to unintentional ignition. At this time holders without lids, of wall-hanging and stand-alone types, began to appear, and pocket holders became commonplace. The United States began to manufacture various forms of match holder, and the British match manufacturers Bryant & May began to make their presence felt in the production of inexpensive holders for the masses.

Inventiveness and ingenuity did not decline, but new materials, particularly the early plastics and plated base metals that resembled silver, combined with improved efficiency, mass production techniques, and the increased love and demand of the Victorians for novelty, led to the proliferation of match holders as an item of common usage.

MATCH SOCKETS AND THE "GO-TO-BED" MISNOMER.

The term 'go-to-bed' lights has been applied to match holders provided with a match socket, implying that the devices were designed for use in the bedroom. There is no contemporary evidence to support this theory, or perhaps more accurately, this romanticized story.

The "story" suggests that the boxes were placed beside the bed. The person getting ready for bed would place a candle stick that had been carried to the bedroom, with the candle lighted, on a piece of furniture well removed from the bed (thus reducing the risk of setting fire to the drapes surrounding the bed). When ready to climb into bed, the person would light a match from the holder beside the bed, fix it into the socket, go across to the candle and extinguish that flame, returning to the bed by the light of the match. The match was presumably extinguished once actually in bed.

This is an untenable hypothesis. There is no reason why the person, once ready for bed, should not collect the candle stick, carry it to the bed, and extinguish the flame at that point in time, thus avoiding the risks. No contemporary written source has been found to support the theory of the "go-to-bed" light; the term first appears in the literature in 1970 in a small book on smoking antiques.

It is possible that the theory is founded on the Dowler "Nocturnal Match Box", shown in Fig. 26, with the use of the word "Nocturnal" implying a night time use. This may in fact be true, but it is more likely that the box was kept beside the bed with a match located in the hole in the side, conveniently ready for use in the dark. But this would then be a "get-out-of-bed" light!

Also there are the Harcourt boxes provided with a finger ring for carrying from one place to another, shown in Figs. 47 and 48. They might serve for use in the bedroom, but equally as a mobile device to be carried from a sitting room to another place in the house where a letter could be written in seclusion. However, there is ample evidence to show that this type of device was used at a desk or a writing table as a means of providing heat to melt sealing wax when sealing a letter.

The advertisement for Loysel's device in Fig. 75 clearly and unambiguously indicates the intended use of the match socket, while the desk set shown in Fig. 43 provides evidence that the brass boxes were a part of the accoutrements used in writing. It is therefore safe to assume that the primary function of the match socket was to melt sealing wax.

Sockets continued to be placed on many match holders until well into the 20th century. The purpose may have changed on some of these later examples. On pocket match holders they may have been intended to hold the match while lighting a pipe or cigar; some may have been included solely for amusement. Others were probably intended to complete the figure, as in the example of the monk in Fig. 23. Lastly, some may have been used for what is perceived as the original purpose, to melt sealing wax.

Chapter III
Pocket Match Holders

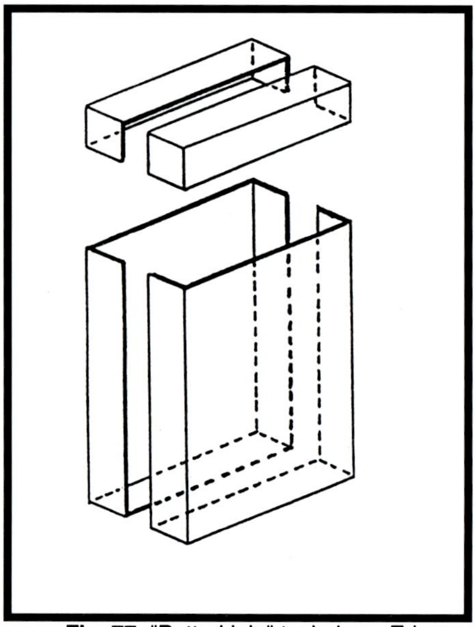

PART 1: INTRODUCTION AND MANUFACTURING TECHNIQUES

Many collectors of match holders specialize in the small pocket type, or even in one particular form of the type. Their small size is conducive to economy of space in which to keep the collection.

Their popularity as an item for use did not begin in earnest until about 1870, although, as has already been seen, some were produced prior to that date. In fact, probably the earliest form of pocket box was a snuff box, converted to a match holder by the addition of a striker. By the turn of the 20th century this popularity reached its zenith, maintaining the peak until about 1915, when the introduction of the cigarette lighter and the book match caused a decline. They eventually petered out to a trickle in the 1930s.

The range of shapes and materials is enormous, and what follows is but a glimpse of the phenomenon, less than the tip of the iceberg. No claim is made to the effect that all types are represented in this volume.

Trying to design a format that succinctly covers every category has proved impossible, for one piece may fall into two or three categories. Therefore it has been arbitrarily decided to present the boxes under nine headings, each as a separate part as follows:

Fig. 77 "Butted join" technique. Edges soldered together.

2. Boxes of precious and semi-precious materials.
3. Base metals boxes.
4. Novelty boxes.
5. Three-piece boxes.
6. Trick or puzzle boxes.
7. The "Candle-in-the-box".
8. Organic boxes.
9. Match book and book match holders.
10. Re-usable product boxes.

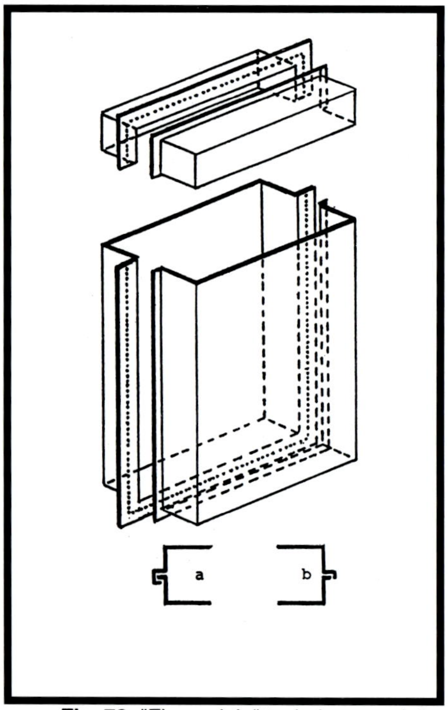

Many collectors will immediately protest that some important categories have been left out—such as commemorative, souvenir, complimentary, advertising, and combination types. But these are covered in one or other of the nine parts above, rightly or wrongly, in an endeavor to simplify the subject. In fact, almost any pocket match holder could be regarded as a 'novelty', and many were shown in trade and mail-order catalogues under the heading of 'Novelties'.

The possibilities are endless.

Boxes made of metal were the most abundant, probably representing about 75% of the total output. Of these, the majority were manufactured using one of three techniques.

Fig. 78 "Flange join" technique. a - full wrap around join. b -seated join, edges soldered.

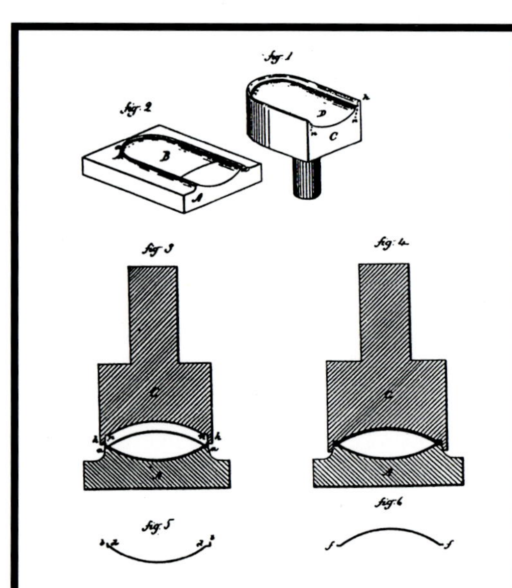

Fig. 79 Drawings from U.S. Invention Patent of 1874 by Chauncey Buckley of dies used to make full wrap around flanged join.

The most common technique, used around the world wherever the boxes were made, may be described as a 'butt join'. That is, the two halves of the main body and the lid were cast or die stamped, and joined by soldering, as shown in the diagram in **Fig. 77.** The result was a neat, smooth finish to the edges of the box, particularly desirable with precious or semi-precious metals, but also applied to boxes in base metals. With few exceptions, it was the preferred method for boxes made of silver and gold.

Considerable skill was called for in the soldering process, which required a higher standard of craftsmanship and was more time-consuming than the other two techniques, and was therefore more costly in labour. The other two techniques were more adaptable to mass production methods throughout most of the manufacturing process.

The second common technique was applied to boxes made with a main body and a lid, the sections being made in two halves, usually stamped out with dies. It may be described as a "flanged join" technique. Two forms of flange occurred and are illustrated by the diagram in **Fig. 78**.

An example of a match holder marked "C.Parker" is shown in **Fig. 80**. It bears dates of four patents all issued to Chauncey Buckley: the first in 1872 for a spectacle case using the flange; the second in 1874 for the lid catch and spring; the third for the dies as shown in **Fig. 79**; the fourth for a Canadian patent of 1873 combining his first and third U.S. patents. The end product is made of tin plate and somewhat poorly finished, with strikers formed from the joins at the top and bottom. It was illustrated in an 1879 catalogue by Metzler, Rothschild & Co., importers, of Chicago, Illinois, and described as "Nickel;" possibly the example may have had such a finish.

The third construction technique was for a three piece box, with the main body as one piece and the lid and base cap as separate pieces, as in the diagram in **Fig. 81**. The main body was usually stamped out of thin sheet tin-plate, and bent to form four sides with a butt join (either at the back edge, or on one side). To strengthen the box sides, a raised bead was provided near the top and bottom edges, also acting as a seating for the lid and base caps.

Again it was Chauncey Buckley, for the Charles Parker Co., who patented this method in the United States in 1880. One of the drawings from his patent is shown in **Fig. 82**. Parker produced these boxes in tin-plate, and also stamped the sides with advertising to a clients request, which may have been another first for the company.

The technique was used later by other companies, resulting in what is probably the most commonly found and inexpensive pocket match holders to be produced in the United States. Used largely for advertising and as souvenirs, this product gave rise to an intense rivalry between three companies in Newark, New Jersey, in the first decade of the 20th century. The same type of box was also produced in Britain up until at least 1922, probably copied from the United States examples and exhibiting some variations, but many of the United States boxes were imported into Britain.

The three techniques of manufacture mentioned above were far from being the only means of producing pocket match holders, as will be seen. Other materials do not lend themselves to these techniques, and given the ingenuity of Victorian craftsmen, other forms of box were inevitable.

Not all of the holders were intended to hold matches decanted from the store-bought cardboard or wood chip boxes. Some were to hold the box and its contents, while others were for book matches; boxes designed to fulfil two or more functions abounded.

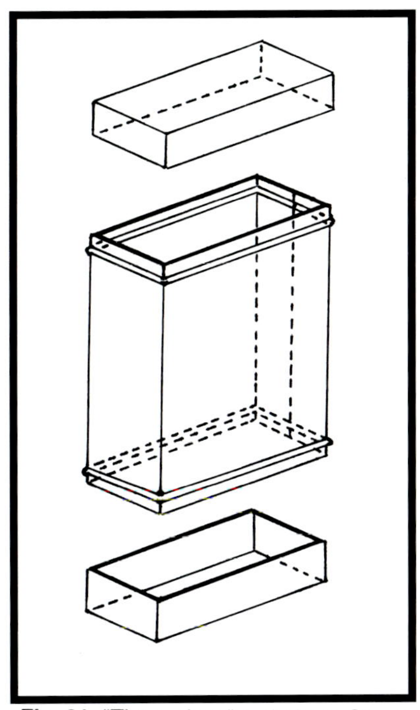

Fig. 81 "Three piece" technique. Sheet metal bent round to form the main body, with lid and base caps.

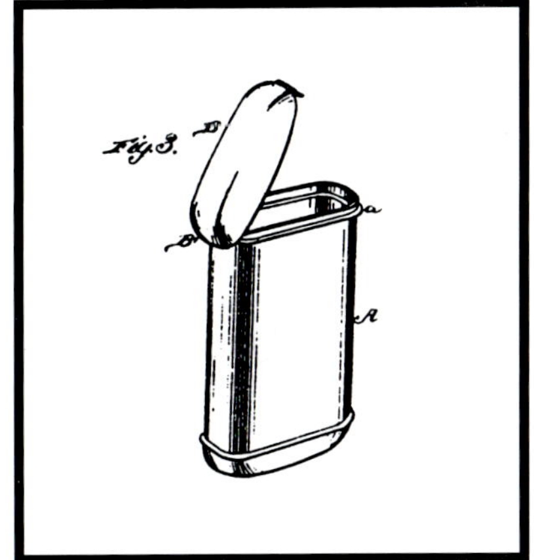

Fig. 82 Drawing from United States Invention Patent of 1880 by Chauncey Buckley of technique shown in Fig. 81.

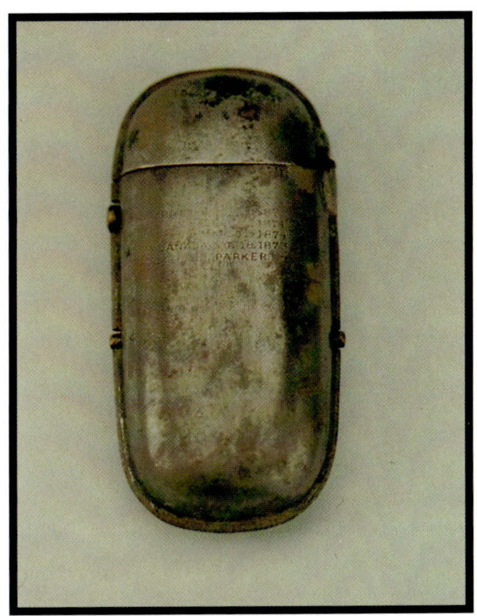

Fig. 80 United States. Tin plate. Made by Charles Parker Co. to Buckley's patents of 1872, 1873 and 1874. c.1874. H - 7.8cms.

PART 2: BOXES OF PRECIOUS AND SEMI-PRECIOUS MATERIALS

Fig. 83 United States. 14K gold, diamond, ruby, sapphire. c.1900. H - 6cms.

Gold and fine or sterling silver comprised the precious metals. But both metals were often embellished with other materials, such as precious and semi-precious stones, ivory and enamel. Boxes of these materials were, of course, the most expensive to buy at the time they were made, and the same often applies today.

The fineness of gold is measured in carats, 24 carats being the highest standard. But gold cannot be worked at that high standard and must be mixed with alloys; every one part of alloy reduces the carat value by one part, that is, 9 carat gold is l5 parts alloy. The highest standard normally used is 18 carat, or 6 parts alloy.

The cost of a relatively plain gold match holder in 1900 was anything from six to twenty times more expensive than a similar sterling silver match holder, depending upon the quality of the gold. They were made throughout Europe and North America, and to a lesser extent in Asia. They are a relatively rare find today, and it is likely that many have disappeared, melted down for the value of the gold.

Novelty shapes occurred, as is evident in the 1903-1904 catalogue of Streeters & Co. Ltd., of London, in which one in the form of a diamond, and a second in the form of a heart were illustrated.

The single example shown here, in Fig. **83,** was made in the United States around l900, but has no maker's mark. In 14 carat gold, the raised heart-shaped design is formed by two winged, ascending figures of cherubs encircling a diamond, a ruby and a sapphire. On the top of the lid at the hinge side is a ring for suspending the box from a watch chain, an unusual feature in a United States match holder, although a common feature on holders from Britain. The reverse side is plain.

Occasionally a match holder made from gold *and silver* is to be found, and **Figs. 84 and 85** illustrate the front and back of such a piece. It is both an item of precious metals, and a novelty item, in the form of a rolled, wrapped and addressed copy of the periodical *The Scientific American.* It was the subject of a United States Design Patent of 1890 issued to Adolph Thommen as assignor to Enos Richardson & Co., of Newark, New Jersey, who also had a showroom in New York City.

The rolled periodical is made of silver, and the wrapper of gold. The back of the wrapper has three enamelled seals in red, simulating sealing wax. The front has a representation of a blue l¢ stamp, a postmark in black of "San Francisco, 12, 6.P.M., 1892" and the engraved address is the "Hon. J.R. Thibaudau. Montreal, P.Q." The Hon. Joseph Rosaire Thibaudau was born in Cap Santé, Quebec, in 1837. He held various directorships and was a staunch Liberal, being called to the Canadian Senate in 1878. He died in 1910. His photograph is shown in **Fig. 86.** The match holder was no doubt given to him as a Christmas gift in 1892 by a friend, who either lived in or visited San Francisco; it was probably purchased at Haskell & Muegge, the Enos Richardson & Co. retail agent in that city.

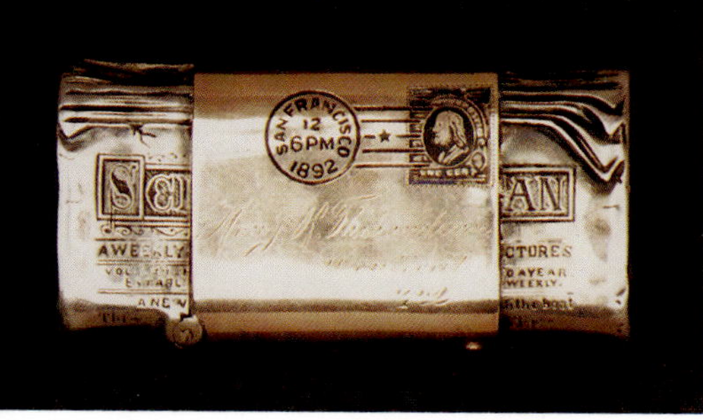

Fig. 84 United States. Gold, silver. Made by Enos Richardson & Co. to a Design Patent of 1890, in 1892. L - 5.6cms.

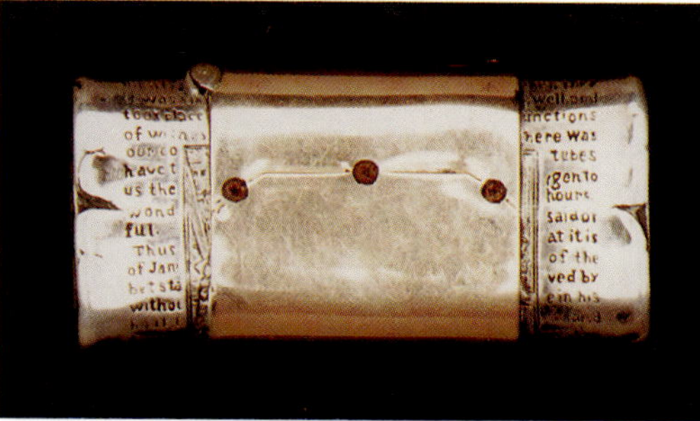

Fig. 85 As Fig. 84. Reverse.

Fig. 86 Photograph of the Hon. J. R. Thibaudau. Canadian Senator. The recipient of Fig. 84.

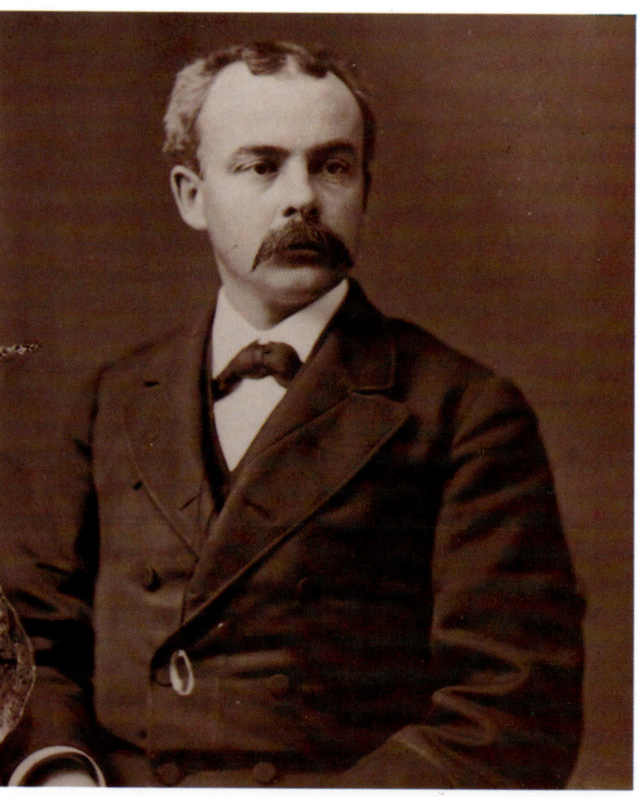

In December 1890, *The Scientific American* inserted a notice in their journal acknowledging "the compliment that has been offered us" by Messrs Benedict Bros. of New York in selecting their publication as a "representative non-political journal." This error in attribution was not rectified until November 1893, when the journal inserted a second notice giving credit to Enos Richardson & Co., repeating almost word for word their previous notice, without reference to the earlier mistake.

Enos Richardson & Co. advertised in *The Jewelers' Circular and Horological Review in 1892*, claiming the match holder as "The most successful Silver Novelty ever put on the market." The box was also offered by another New York importer and retailer in silverware in about 1891 for $7.00.

In Britain, Sampson Mordan & Co. of London, produced a box of typically British shape in 1914, with alternating vertical stripes of silver and gold, shown in **Fig. 87.** The striker, located along the bottom edge, is set with a saw tooth steel insert, a common practice in Britain, used to overcome the abrasive action of the match heads upon the soft silver. Attached to the suspension ring on the back edge is a silver charm in the form of one of the three wise monkeys, with its hand over its mouth.

Sampson Mordan and a partner set up in a small way in 1815 making silver and gold-cased pencils. They moved on to become perhaps the leading designers of high-quality specialized novelty items, displaying great flair and ingenuity. Mordan's earlier work concentrated on the production of writing accoutrements, but he also produced some of the finest enamelled match holders known. The business went into decline after World War I as other manufacturers began to produce similar pieces at lower prices. In World War II the factory was destroyed during the London blitz of 1941, which finally finished the company.

In typical British style is a silver box with applied panels of gold in the form of maple leaves at each corner, and a shield in the center of one side, against a background of engraved flowers on both sides. It is shown in **Fig. 88.** The box is hallmarked Chester, 1907, with the maker's initials "S & Bm." It was apparently made for the Canadian market, and this example is known to have been purchased from Ryrie Birks in Toronto for Wilfred Hicks, a pharmacist at the Sunnybrook Hospital in Toronto. Ryrie Bros. and Henry Birks & Sons had consolidated in Toronto in 1905, retaining the partnership until 1924. The box was intended for wax vesta matches; these were mainly made in Britain and elsewhere in Europe, but by 1895 the E. B. Eddy company in Hull, Quebec, had installed the necessary machinery and begun to produce wax vestas in Canada.

North American match holders were made to take the larger, wooden-stemmed, 'parlour' matches of the day which were made in North America, although wax vesta matches were being imported from Europe.

The most common shape for pocket match holders was rectangular, with rounded corners and edges. But generally speaking there are certain distinctive design elements that make it possible to differentiate easily between those made in Europe and those in North America.

The United States produced a significant percentage of their match holders in flamboyant and elaborate outlines, with heavily impressed designs. **Fig. 89** shows a range of popular shapes, taken from trade catalogues, that are typical and distinctive of the United States. Still, a great range in simpler styles was also produced. American silver boxes are only marked "STERLING," which in itself is not a guarantee of U.S. manufacture; some may be found with makers' marks or pattern numbers.

British boxes were more commonly of pure rectangular form, with engraved or engine-turned designs. Some are curved to fit the waist when put into the pocket of a waistcoat (a 'vest', in North America), and have been provided with a ring for suspension from a chain. They always have a set of hallmarks that indicate the assay office (which may not be the city of manufacture), the maker's initials, and a letter symbolizing the year. If legible, these marks reveal the date of manufacture. With good fortune, the maker's mark may be identifiable, though there is no known single source that lists all makers and their marks.

The main area of production in the United States was New England, with many small manufacturers in New York and New Jersey in particular. Three major manufacturers of a wide range of silverware produced significant numbers of pocket match holders between 1888 and 1910. No less than 156 different boxes are shown in the catalogues of the Gorham Manufacturing Co. (of 1888, 1896, 1902 and 1908); the Unger Bros. (of 1904); and Reed & Barton (of 1910). The 1901-1902 "Holiday Suggestions" catalogue of Unger Bros. shows another dozen, claiming "300 different styles in Match Boxes." Clearly, the production from these three companies alone was staggering.

Jabez Gorham was born in 1792; he set up in business by c. 1825, and establishing the Gorham Manufacturing Co. in Providence, Rhode Island four years before his death in 1869. The company ultimately became the Gorham Corporation (in 1961), having acquired a number of other companies on the way, and is still in business today. Gorham used a distinctive trademark derived from the British hallmark system. The mark was adopted in 1868 when Gorham abandoned the American coin silver standard of 900/1000 fine silver in favour of the British sterling silver standard of 925/1000.

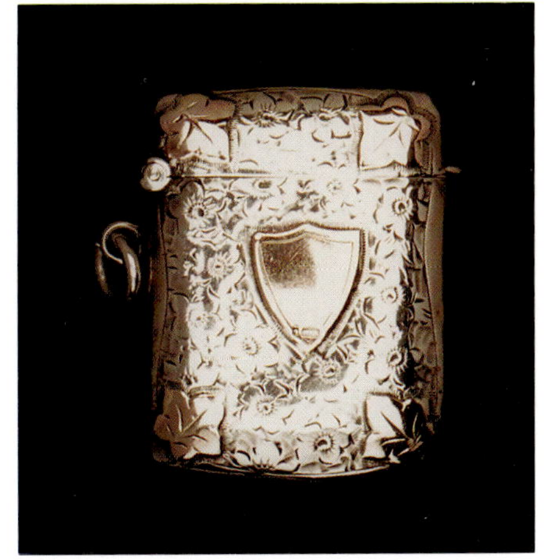

Fig. 88 Britain. Gold, silver. Marked "S & Bm", Chester, 1907. Made for the Canadian market. H - 4.5cms.

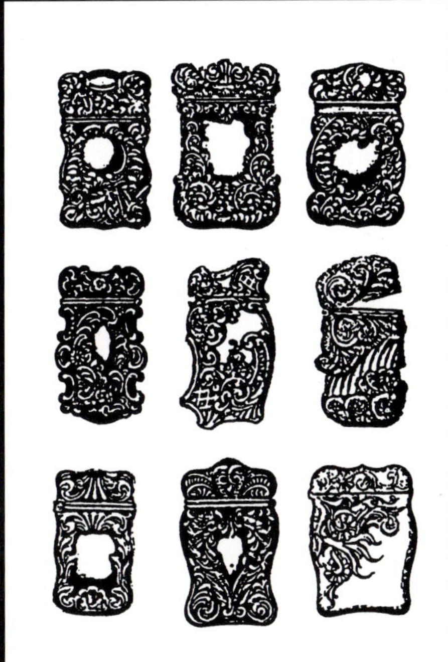

Fig. 89 Illustrations from trade catalogues of the typical United States flamboyant styles.

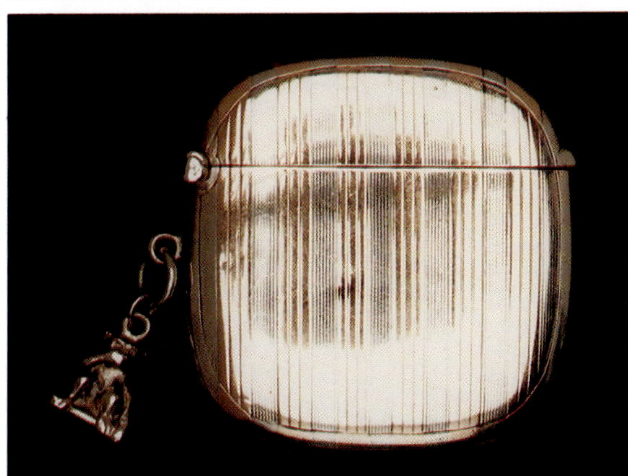

Fig. 87 Britain. Gold, silver, steel. Made by Sampson Mordan & Co.. 1914. H - 4.7cms.

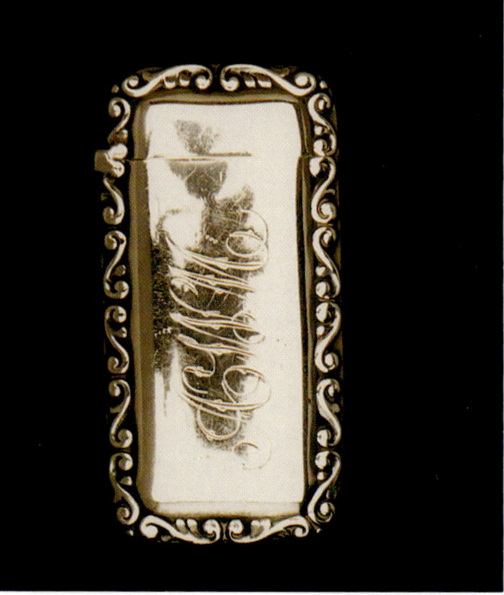

Fig. 90 United States. Silver. Made by the Gorham Mfg. Co. and marked 'Rosenthal' (a New York retailer) on the bezel. c.1910. H -5.8cms.

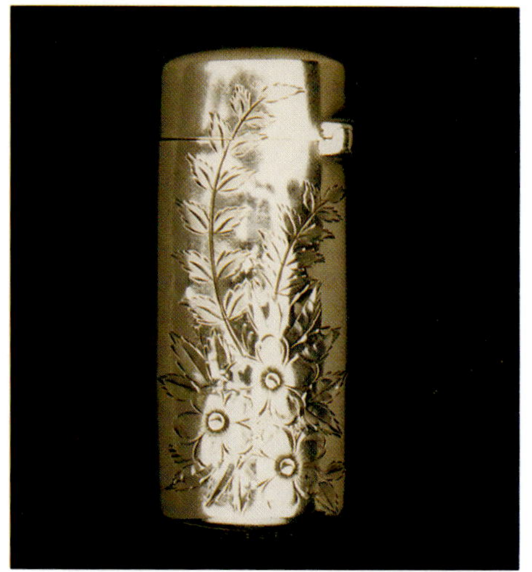

Fig. 91 United States. Silver. Made by the Gorham Mfg. Co.. c.1896. H - 6cms.

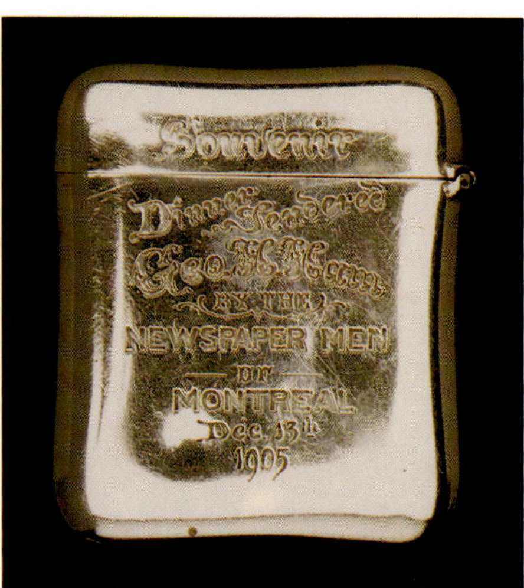

Fig. 92 United States. Silver. Made by the Gorham Mfg. Co.. Engraved souvenir of a presentation dinner. 1905. H - 5.9cms.

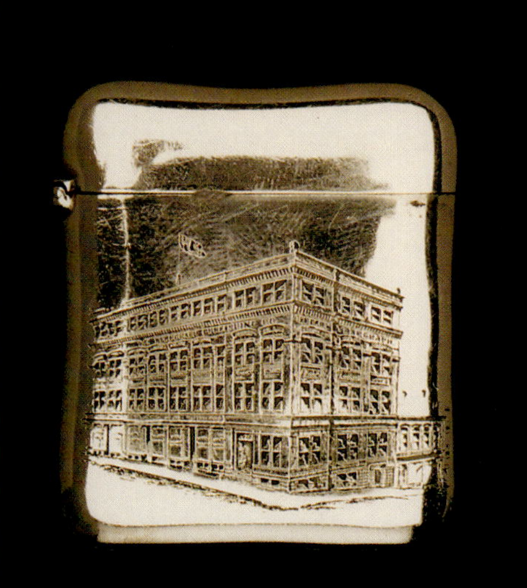

Fig. 93 Reverse of Fig. 92.

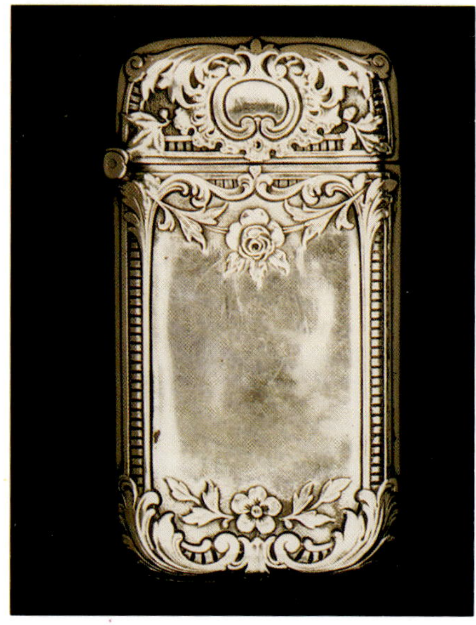

Fig. 94 United States. Silver. Made by the Gorham Mfg. Co.. Marked on bezel "PAT.1910". H - 7cms.

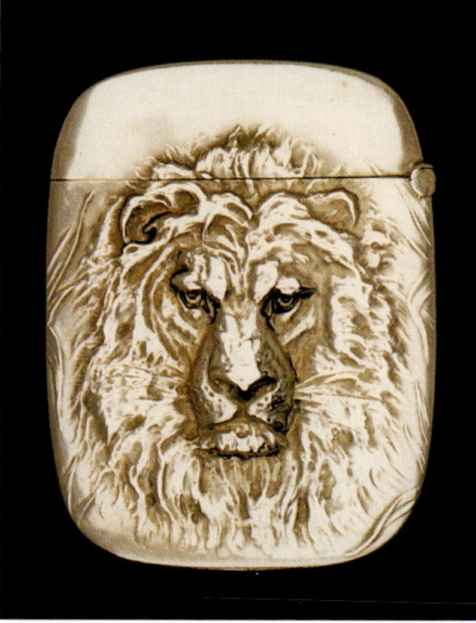

Fig. 95 United States. Silver. Probably made by Unger Bros. c.1904. H - 5.9cms.

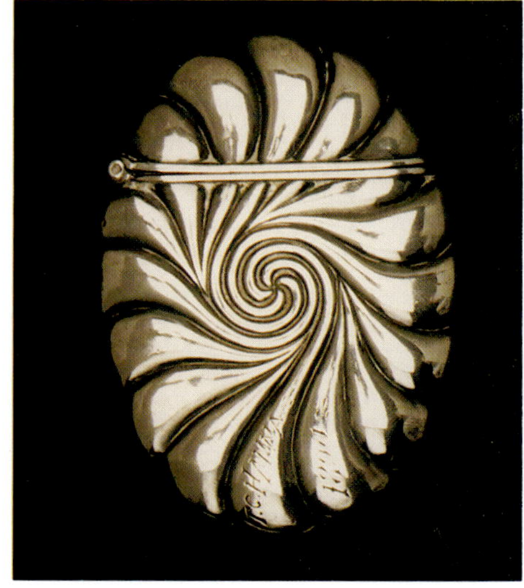

Fig. 96 United States. Silver. Made by LeRoy Fairchild & Co., to a Design Patent of 1890. H - 6.1cms.

Four examples of Gorham work are illustrated. The example in **Fig. 90** is marked on the bezel—the extension of the main body upwards beyond the seating, over which the lid fits—with the Gorham number "1055" and "Rosenthal". On the other side of the bezel is the Gorham trademark. The box is illustrated in the 1896 Gorham catalogue, and it is assumed that Rosenthal of New York retailed the item, adding its name to the bezel when it no doubt engraved the initials "AWM" on the side.

The example in **Fig. 91** is of an oval cross section, and has engraved floral designs on both sides. It bears the Gorham trademark on the bezel, but no catalogue number. It probably dates from c. 1890s.

The item shown in **Figs. 92 and 93** was made in 1905. It is marked "B5" on the bezel, and was originally plain on both sides; it was engraved for a special occasion, with the wording on one side "Souvenir. Dinner Tendered Geo. H. Hamm by the Newspaper Men of Montreal. Dec.13th.1905". The reverse side is engraved with a representation of the Telegraph Publishing Co. building in Montreal. George Hamm was a journalist who became the advertising manager of the Canadian Pacific Railway. The dinner was given to celebrate his return to health after a serious illness, and his return to Canada after a trip to Britain following the illness. The plain form of this box continued to be produced until at least 1911.

The fourth Gorham piece, shown in **Fig. 94,** is marked on the bezel "B3989" and "PAT.I910." It is not shown in the company's 1910-11 catalogue, nor has the patent heen found, but it was probably a Design Patent for use on a variety of other items.

An unmarked piece is shown in **Fig. 95.** It was almost certainly made by Unger Bros. of Newark, New Jersey. The same shape is shown in their catalogue of 1904, one with a plain finish, and two with embossed designs.

Between 1888 and 1892, thirteen Design Patents were issued to the New York silversmiths LeRoy Fairchild & Company. One of the designs of 1890 is shown in **Fig. 96** and is engraved "1890". All of the designs depicted boxes with irregular outlines.

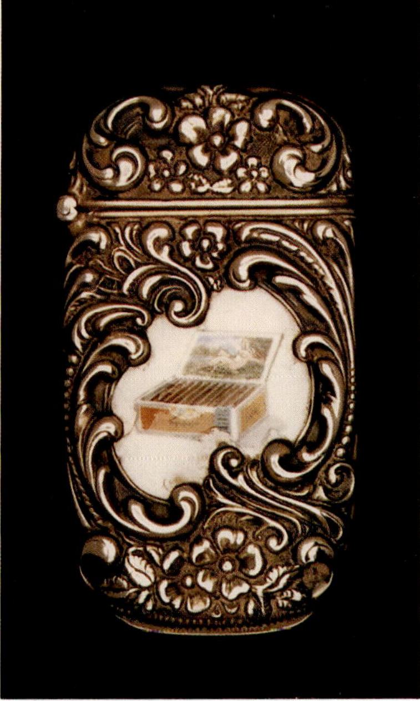

Fig. 97 United States. Silver, enamel. Made by Reeves & Sillcocks. c.1896 - 1904. H - 6.8cms.

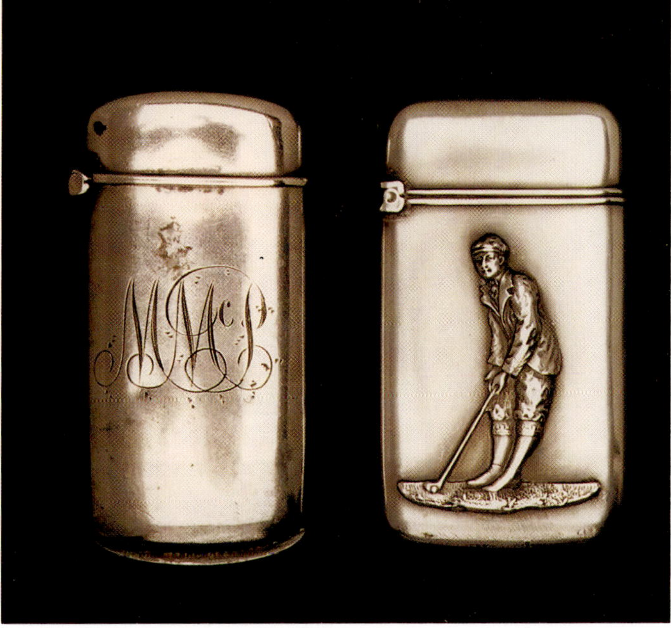

Fig. 98 United States. Silver. Left: made by Simmons Bro. & Co.. c.1900. H - 6.6cms. Right: c.1900. H - 6.2cms.

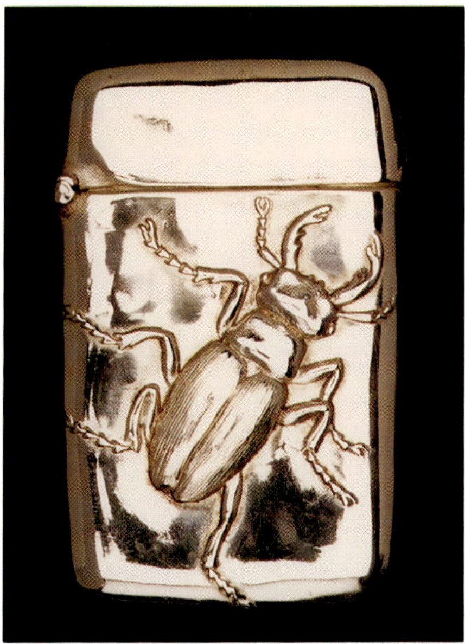

Fig. 99 United States. Silver. Made by Codding Bros. & Heilborn. c.1900. H - 7.1cms.

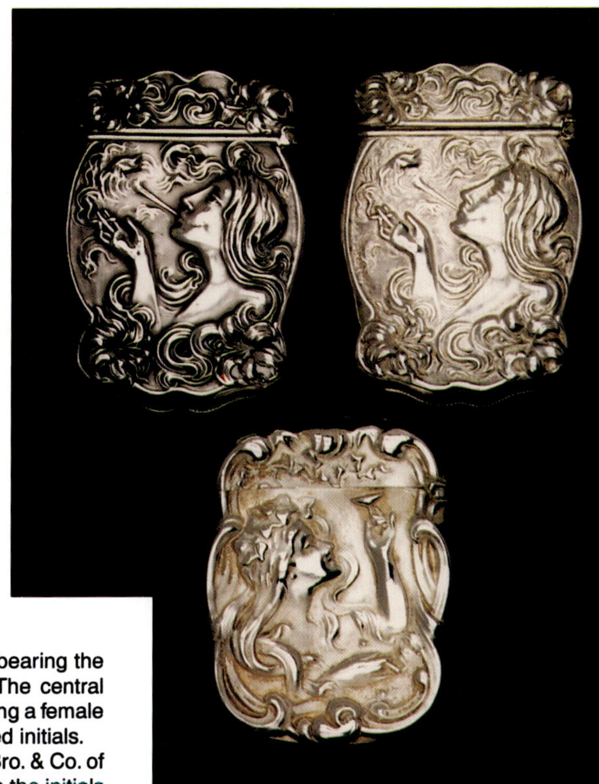

Fig. 100 United States. Top: made by the Bristol Silver Co., left in silver, right marked 'Silveroin'. Below: made by James E. Blake Co., marked 'Sterline'. c.1905. H - 6.2cms.

In Rococo style with heavily impressed design work is an example shown in **Fig. 97,** bearing the mark of Reeves & Sillcocks of New York, who were in business from c. 1896 to 1904. The central cartouche is embellished with an enamelled picture of a box of cigars, the lid open and showing a female nude in a sylvan setting. The cartouche on the reverse side is plain in order to take engraved initials.

Two examples are shown in **Fig. 98**. That to the left bears the trade mark of Simmons Bro. & Co. of Philadelphia, in business from 1840 until 1908. This simple and elegant box is engraved with the initials "M.Mc.P." and probably dates to c. l900. The box to the right is from about the same date. It has an applied figure of a golfer addressing his ball, and was no doubt intended as a gift for a devotee of the game.

A finely detailed male stag beetle is impressed on both sides of the box shown in **Fig. 99**. The box is marked with the maker's initials for Codding Bros. & Heilborn of North Attleboro, Massachusetts, and dates to c. 1900.

An interesting phenomenon, which appears to have started shortly after 1900, was the production of boxes that appear the same but are made of different metals. The examples in **Fig. 100** demonstrate this phenomena. The two examples at the top appear to be identical, and were probably stamped out using the same dies. Yet that to the left is marked "Sterling," while that to the right is marked "Silveroin." Silveroin is an alloy containing no silver; the trademark was used by the Bristol Silver Co. of Attleboro, Massachusetts, who made the boxes. The lower box is marked "SterlinE," a trademark of the James E. Blake Co., also of Attleboro. Blake registered his trademark in May 1902, claiming that he had used it since January 15. Blake undoubtedly made a version in silver too. The Nov-E-Line Mfg. Co. of New York, also produced look-alike silver novelties, using the names "Silvanir" and "Silverine," but it has not been established that they made match holders.

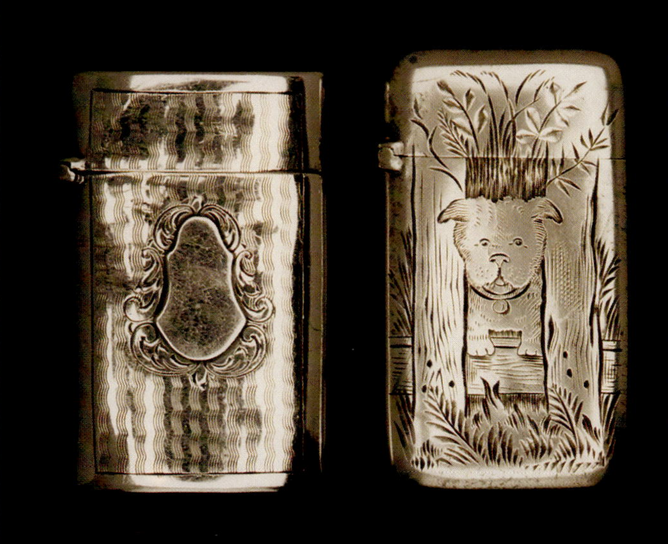

Fig. 101 United States. Silver. Left: c.1915 H - 6cms. Right: Made by Frank M. Whiting & Co.. c.1910. H - 6.2cms.

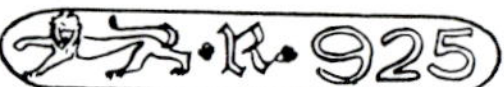

Fig. 102 Trade mark of Roden Bros. Ltd. of Toronto.

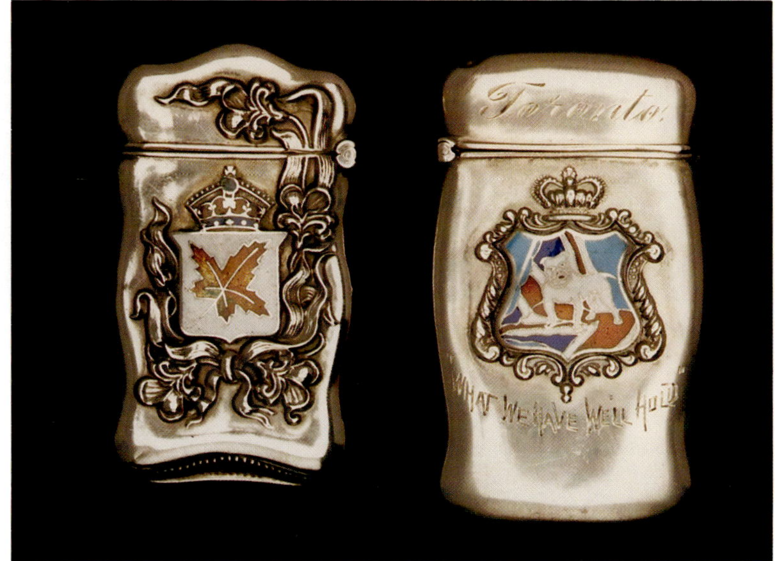

Fig. 103 Canada. Silver, enamel. Made by Roden Bros. Ltd. Left: c.1905. H - 6.1cms. Right: c.1910. H - 6.5cms.

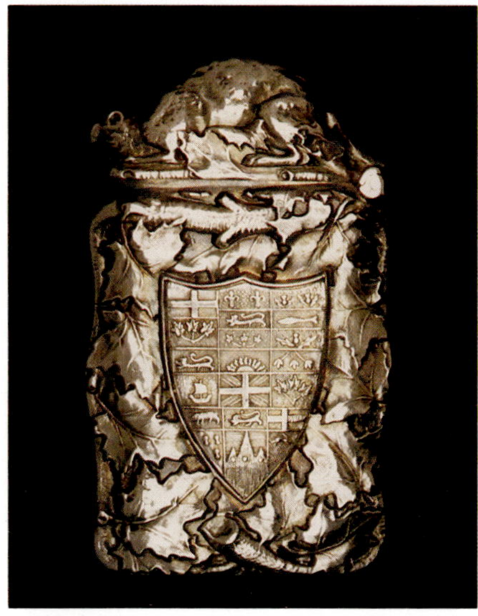

Fig. 104 Canada. Silver. c.1907. H - 6.4cms.

Fig. 105 Britain (for the Canadian market) and Canada. Silver. Made by Patterson & Sons Ltd. of Birmingham from 1912 to c.1916, and by Henry Birks & Sons Ltd. of Montreal, c.1917 to 1926. H -6.2cms.

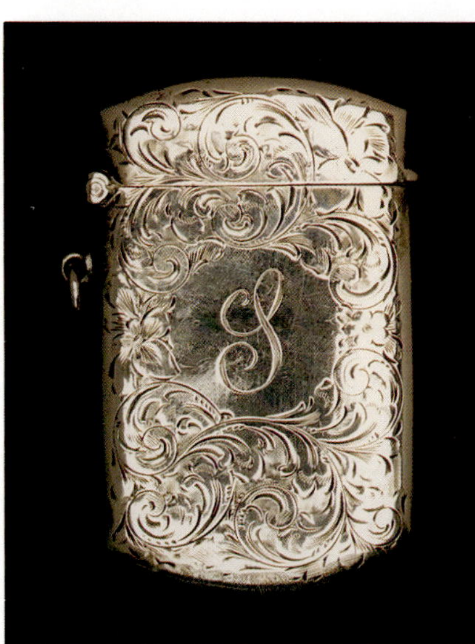

Obviously the intention was to provide novelties to suit all budgets; silver versions were available for those who could afford it, and the look-alike versions in cheaper metal for the less affluent. At about that time a silver box of that type would cost between $6.00 to $8.00 , and a plated version between $1.50 to $2.50.

Of somewhat unusual form for American pieces is the box illustrated in **Fig. 101 left**. Set in a panel of engine-turned design is an elaborate escutcheon framed against an engraved background. The box is curved to fit the waist, a feature more commonly found in British match holders. It is unmarked, other than the word "Sterling", and probably dates to c. 1915.

Illustrated in **Fig. 101 right** is a box engraved on one side with a charming dog peering through a fence. It bears the mark of Frank M. Whiting & Co., of North Attleboro, Massachusetts, and probably dates to c. 1910.

Canadian silversmiths produced very few match holders, and their styles reflect both United States and British influences. Roden Bros. Ltd. of Toronto manufactured a wide range of silverware including match holders, which they marked with their distinctive trademark shown in **Fig. 102**. This prominent Canadian company was in business from 1891 until 1922.

Typical of Roden Bros., in United States style, are two examples shown in **Fig. 103**. That to the left has an enamelled shield bearing a maple leaf surmounted by a crown. The reverse side has the same impressed Art Nouveau design, but the center is left plain for engraved initials. An identical box, but with the shield bearing the arms of Canada, was illustrated in a catalogue of 1904 issued by Henry Birks & Sons of Montreal and cost $1.70. The box to the right is similar in shape, but is slightly larger. One side has an impressed design around an enamelled shield depicting the British bulldog standing on the Union Jack; below are engraved the words "What We Have We'll Hold," and on the lid, "Toronto." The reverse side has an applied plaque in the form of a beaver on a log above a maple leaf. This is probably later, c. 1910.

The box in **Fig. 104** is unmarked, but must surely be Canadian, with a beaver lid, and maple leaf background enclosing the Dominion Coat of Arms (of Canada) on a shield. It is shown in a Henry Birks & Sons catalogue of 1908 at $2.25, as well as in the catalogues of T.Eaton Co. Ltd. of Toronto, from 1906 until 1908 at $2.00.

In the British style, and marked "Birks," is an example in **Fig. 105.** The engraved decoration is reminiscent of Birmingham designs, and (in a plain form) first appeared in the Henry Birks & Sons catalogue in 1912. The shape continued to be offered by Birks until 1926, rising in price from $2.25 to $6.50 in 1919, before dropping back to $5.25. These prices are in Canadian dollars.

The Birks records show that there were three styles of this type of box: plain, engraved and engine-turned. Until about 1916 they were apparently made by Patterson & Sons Ltd. of Birmingham, England. It is assumed that World War I difficulties prevented further imports across the Atlantic, and that Birks themselves started to produce them.

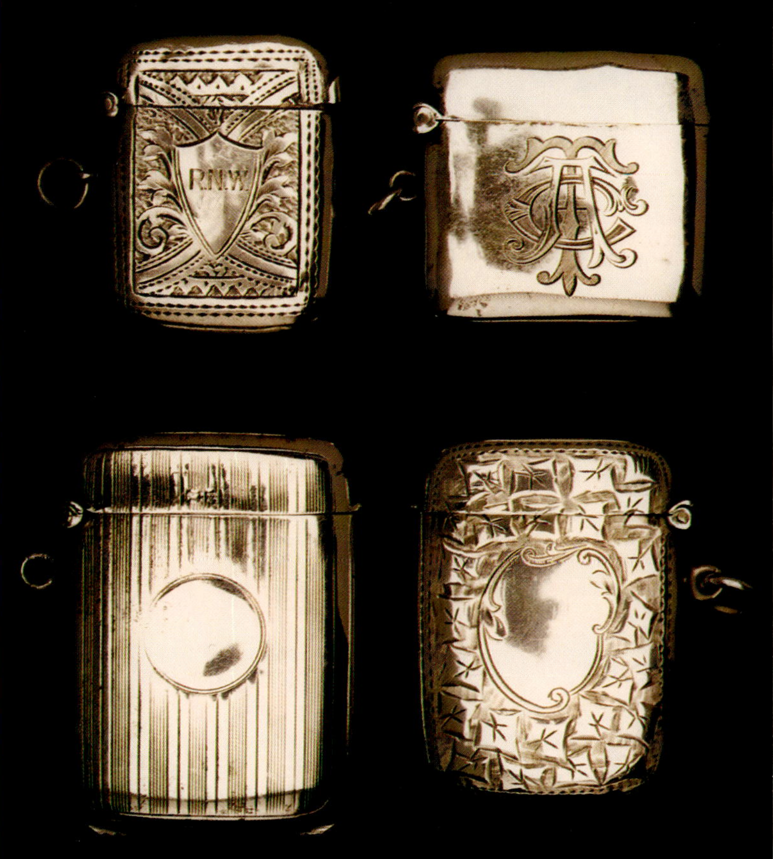

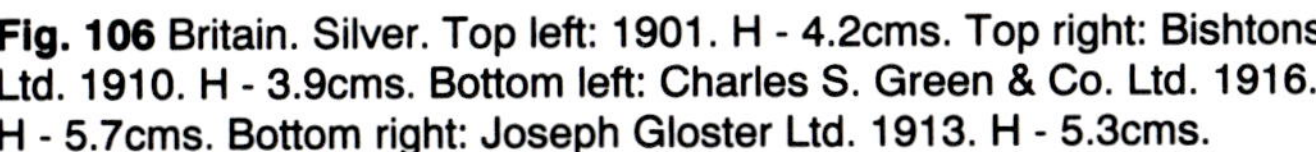

Fig. 106 Britain. Silver. Top left: 1901. H - 4.2cms. Top right: Bishtons Ltd. 1910. H - 3.9cms. Bottom left: Charles S. Green & Co. Ltd. 1916. H - 5.7cms. Bottom right: Joseph Gloster Ltd. 1913. H - 5.3cms.

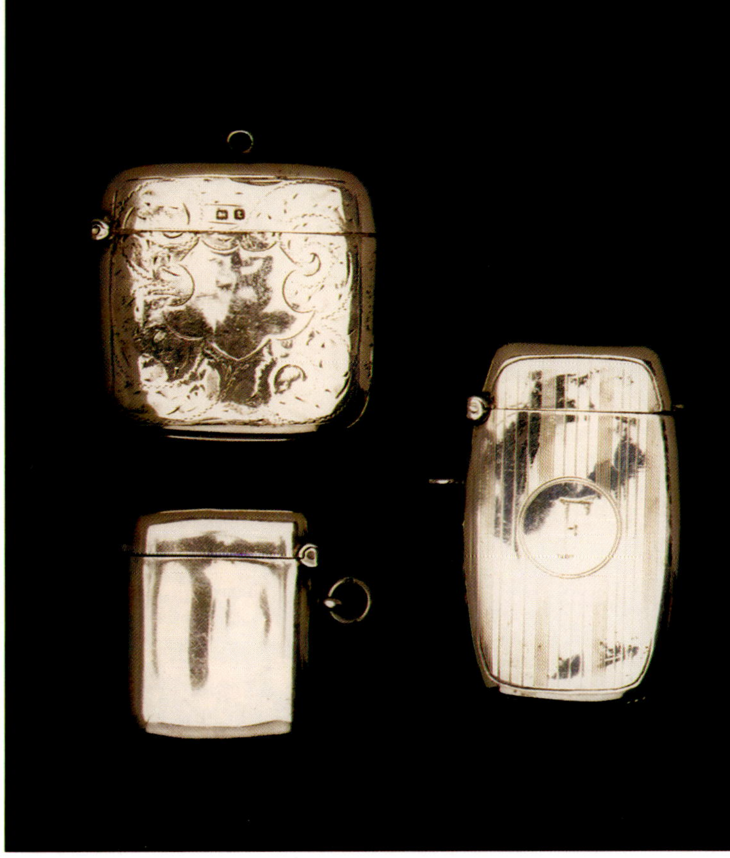

Fig. 107 Britain. Silver. Top left: 'S.M.L.'. 1918. H - 5.3cms. Right: William H. Haseler. 1920. H 6.3cms. Bottom left: William H. Haseler. 1926. H - 4.1cms.

Birmingham was a major center for the production of silverware, and in the two hundred years following 1773, almost 1500 manufacturers' punch marks were registered. Many of the companies were one- or two-man operations, and some specialized in one particular form of product, such as pipe mounts, tablewares, thimbles, and pencil cases. Only one company is recorded as specializing in match holders, but a number of companies made match holders along with other product lines. There were also a number of die makers, and "stampers," who made the parts and then shipped them to other companies to assemble and finish.

Many Birmingham makers engraved their boxes in a style that is almost exclusively Birmingham. Such a box is shown in **Fig. 106 top left,** intended for the small wax vesta matches, with a ring for suspension from a watch chain like so many of the British boxes had. The maker's mark is unreadable, but the box was assayed in Birmingham in 1901.

In **Fig. 106 top right** is a plain box with engraved initials on the front, and the date of March 7th, 1910 on the reverse. It was made by Bishtons Ltd., started by Thomas Bishton in 1889 and bought out in 1908 by Charles Westwood, who continued to use the original company name. In 1980 the company was still owned by the Westwood family. The striker, set into the base edge of the box, is a cylindrical piece of steel forming a channel, with raised punch dots along both edges—a practise that appears to have started about 1900.

The box at **Fig. 106 bottom left** was intended for larger matches. It has an engine-turned design, was curved to fit the waist, and has a steel striker. It was made in 1916 by Charles S. Green & Co. Ltd., another company still in existence in 1980.

Finally, at **Fig. 106 bottom right,** is a box made by Joseph Gloster Ltd., who specialized in cigarette cases, match boxes and small domestic wares. The company was established in 1880, finally going out of the silverware business in 1978. The ivy leaf design is perhaps the most typical and common Birmingham style, and many thousands of boxes must have been produced using the design. The striker along the bottom edge is silver and shows no signs of wear. The box, curved to fit the waist, is dated for 1913.

Fig. 107 shows another three Birmingham boxes. The box at the top left has the date letter for 1918, and an unidentified maker's mark of "S.M.L." It has a bold, scrolled floral design, is curved to fit the pocket, and the striker is silver. The other two boxes are by William Hare Haseler, renowned for his artistic flair, who formed his company in 1851. The box at the lower left is very small and plain, and was made in 1920. That to the right, made for standard wood-stemmed matches, has an engine-turned design and is an unusually elegant shape for Birmingham producers. It is dated for 1926.

A silver box with slabs of agate inlaid into the sides and lid is shown in **Fig. 108**. It was made by James Fenton in 1901. The Fenton company is known to have been in business from at least 1851 until 1911.

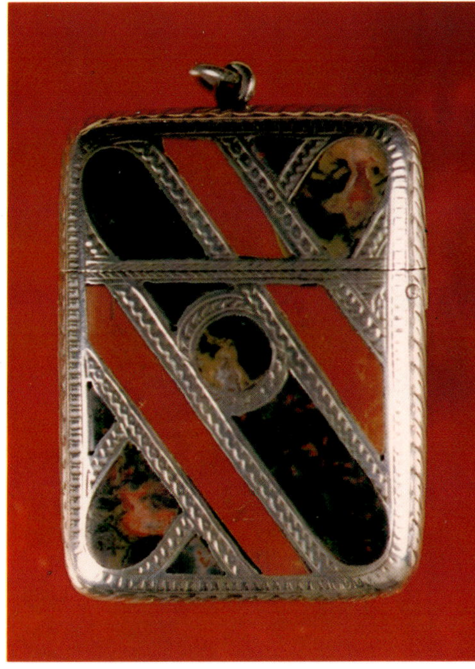

Fig. 108 Britain. Silver, agates. Made by James Fenton. 1901. H -4.9cms.

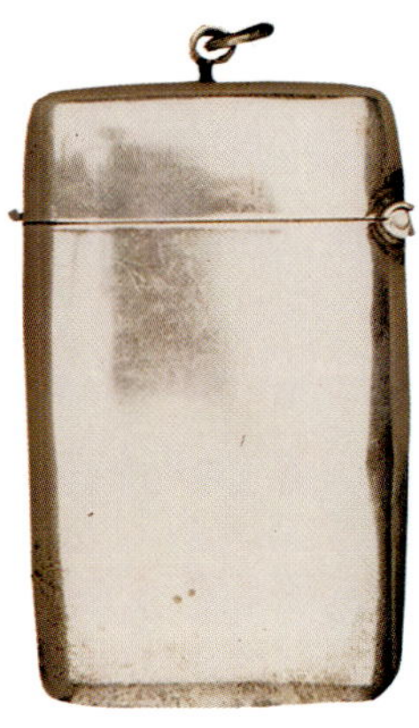

Fig. 109 Britain. Silver. 'S.M.L.'. 1910-11. H - 6.7cms.

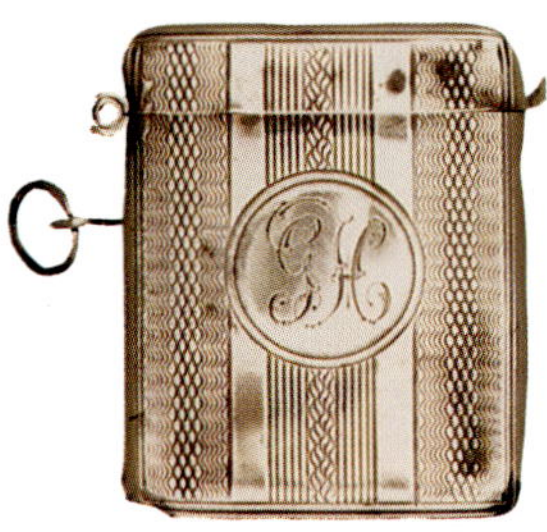

Fig. 110 Britain. Silver. William Neale & Sons Ltd. 1904-05. H -4.5cms.

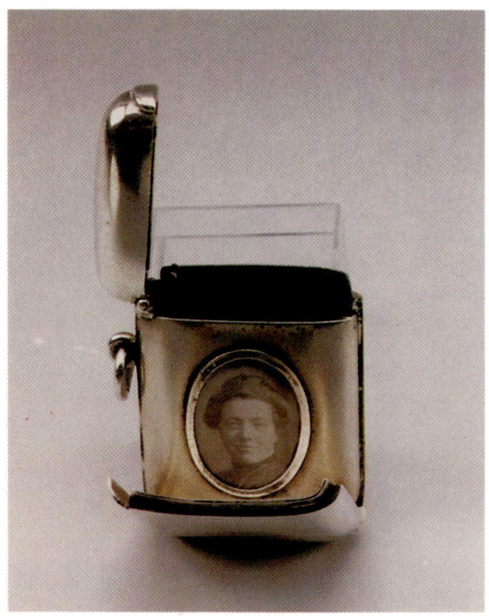

Fig. III Britain. Silver. William Neale & Sons Ltd., "Secret Photo Match-box." 1899-1900. H - 4.7cms.

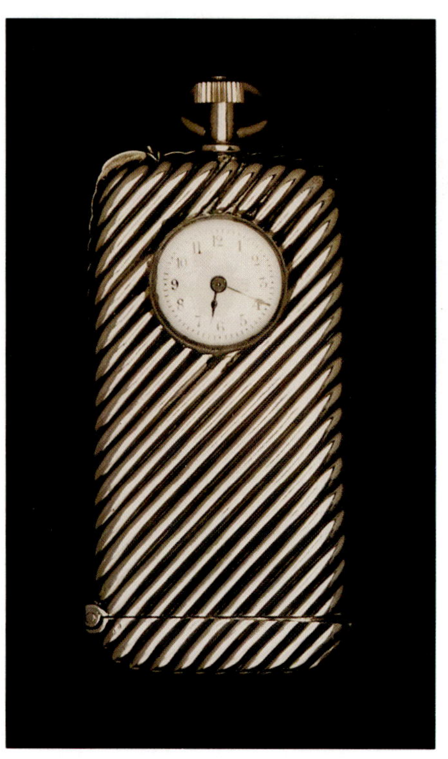

Fig. 112 Britain. Silver. Combination match holder, watch and sovereign holder. William Neale & Sons Ltd.. 1887. H - 8.5cms.

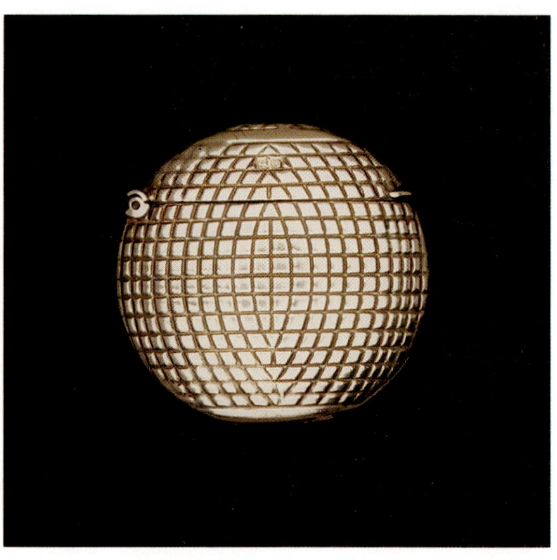

Fig. 113 Britain. Silver, steel. Sampson Mordan & Co.. 1906-1907. W - 4.6cms.

Fig. 109 shows another box marked "S.M.L.," but this one has the assay mark for Chester, and the date letter for 1910-1911. (The Chester date marks were registered from July to July). From 1854, silversmiths had been permitted to register at any Assay Office, and since long delays often occurred at the Birmingham Assay Office because of the high production in the city, it was not unusual for a Birmingham company to have its work assayed at Chester; "S.M.L." was no doubt one such company. It has also been suggested that the quality of some Birmingham companies had declined, inspiring some companies to use Chester marks in an effort to avoid the Birmingham stigma.

Another Birmingham company that used the Chester Assay Office was William Neale & Sons Ltd. Three examples of its work are shown here.

The first, in **Fig. 110,** has a date letter for 1904-1905, and has an engine-turned design. The second, in **Fig. 111**, is almost identical in size, but plain and with the date letter for I899-1900. Careful examination reveals a hinge along one side of the striker on the bottom edge, which is to permit the side to be opened once the lid has heen raised. Behind this hinged side is a frame for a photograph. The photograph is believed to be original. This type of match holder was advertised in I894 as the "Secret Photo Match-Box," made by Wilson & Gill of London. It was apparently quite a popular item, manufactured by several companies, and was also made of gun metal, two examples of which are shown in Fig. 128.

The third Neale piece, shown in **Fig. 112,** is a combination box to hold matches and sovereigns, with a built-in watch. It is dated 1887, and was the subject of a patent or registered design. It has the British hallmarks, and also import marks (possibly French) that probably relate to the watch. The upper back portion of the case opens by means of a press button catch to reveal the sovereign holder, which is hinged to gain access to the inside of the watch.

Sampson Mordan of London also sent pieces to Chester to be assayed. Did London, perhaps, suffer from the same problems of delays as Birmingham did, or was there some form of "reverse snobbery" occuring? It is speculated that some of Mordan's products were probably made by apprentices, possibly in thinner gauge silver, and therefore below the expected standard of Mordan. To hide this deficiency this work was assayed in Chester. An example with a Chester mark for I906-1907 is shown in **Fig. 113**. The design has been interpreted as representing the lines of longitude and latitude on the globe of the world. However, a similar piece marked in the form of a soccer ball has been seen, with the same marks: this example therefore probably represents a golf ball.

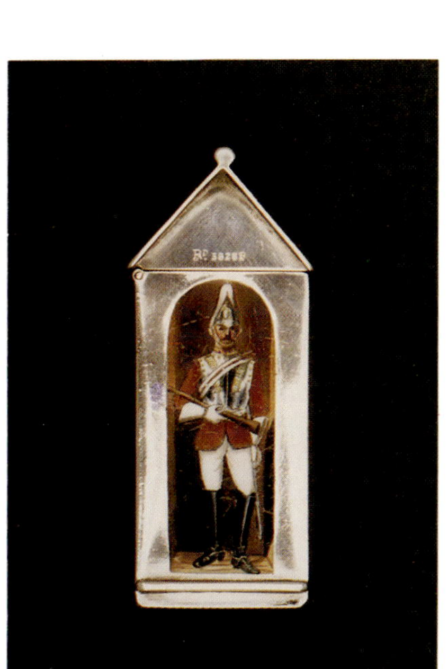

Fig. 114 Britain. Silver, enamel. Sampson Mordan & Co.. Made to a Registered Design of 1885. H - 6cms.

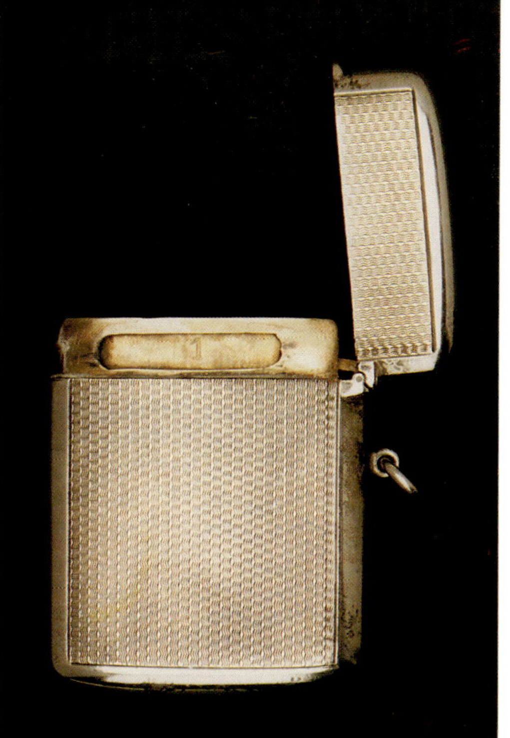

Fig. 115 Britain. Silver. "A & Co.Ltd". 1918. H - 6.5cms.

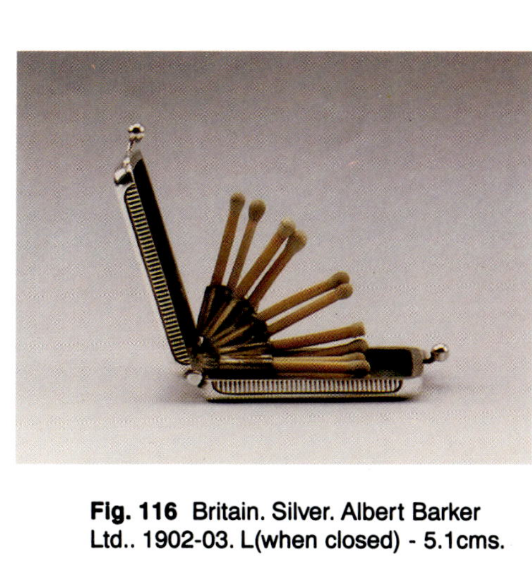

Fig. 116 Britain. Silver. Albert Barker Ltd.. 1902-03. L(when closed) - 5.1cms.

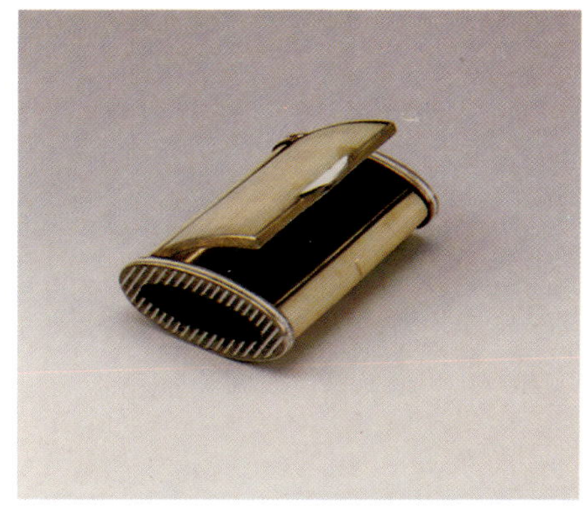

Fig. 117 Britain. Silver, ivory, enamel. T. Callow & Son. 1920. L - 5.3cms.

Among Sampson Mordan & Co.'s finest work, and a speciality of the company, were its enamelled match holders. The example in **Fig. 114** is one of a series (of which there are said to be twelve), all of guardsmen in sentry boxes. The roof is hinged at one side for the lid, and the striker is on the bottom. The bezel is hallmarked for London in 1885, and the front of the lid bears the Registered Number 38,283 of 1885. On one side it is stamped "Thornhill, Bond Street, W.," who were no doubt the retailers.

Throughout the last two decades of the 19th century the company produced an endless variety of rectangular match holders with hunting, coaching and sporting scenes, along with representations of visiting cards and railway tickets; there were also humorous or motto-bearing examples. But collectors should beware: some unscrupulous operators have taken perfectly good plain silver match boxes and enamelled them in the same styles, selling them as originals at the very high prices such boxes command today.

An unusually large pocket box is shown in **Fig. 115** bearing the London Assay Office mark, the maker's mark "A & Co.Ltd." (Asprey & Co. Ltd.), and the date letter for 1918. The box has an engine-turned design, and a bezel that is of exceptional depth. It is provided with a slot to take a strip of striking material from a box of safety matches. The bottom edge has the usual channel for striking ordinary friction matches.

A plain yet very elegant match holder, shown in **Fig. 116,** has an unusual feature. It holds twelve wax vesta matches, set into six pairs of sockets. The hinge appears to have ten knuckles, but only the two at each end form the knuckles of the hinge proper. The inner six are each provided with an external lug, set in a different position on each knuckle. When the box is opened the external lugs come into contact with the back edge of the box sides, one after the other the further the box is opened, causing the pairs of match sockets to present themselves like a fan. It was made in London by Albert Barker Ltd., and is dated for 1902-1903. The inside is marked "Barker's Patent Pathfinder. No.2205". No.2205 is a patent number for 1902, but Barker abandoned the patent, as it did with a later patent in the same year for cigar and cigarette cases.

In silver, ivory and enamel is a box of oval cross section with the lid hinged longitudinally, shown in **Fig. 117**. The silver acts as a frame for the ivory panels that are inlaid into the body and lid. The ends of the box and the lid catch are decorated in alternating lines of silver and enamel, with a steel striker set into one end. It was made by T. Callow & Sons of London in 1920.

Continental Europe produced some fine silver work, but examples are harder to find, and assay marks are usually difficult, if not impossible, to discern and interpret. The German example in **Fig. 118** is marked with the quarter moon and crown, with the fineness mark of 935. It has a suspension ring on the back edge and a finely enamelled picture of a female nude on one side. It is believed to be c. 1895.

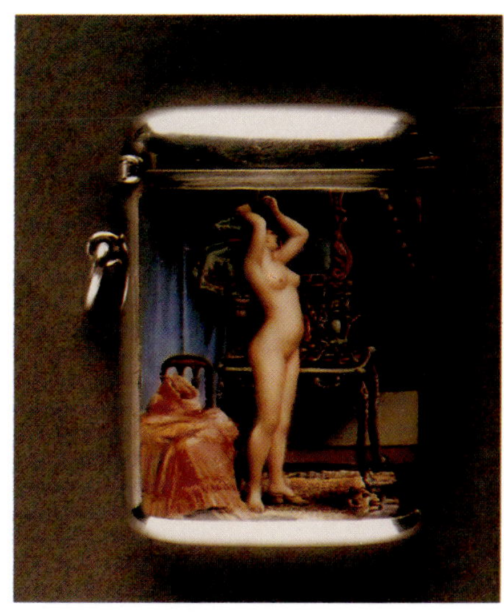

Fig. 118 German. Silver, enamel. c.1895. H - 5.4cms.

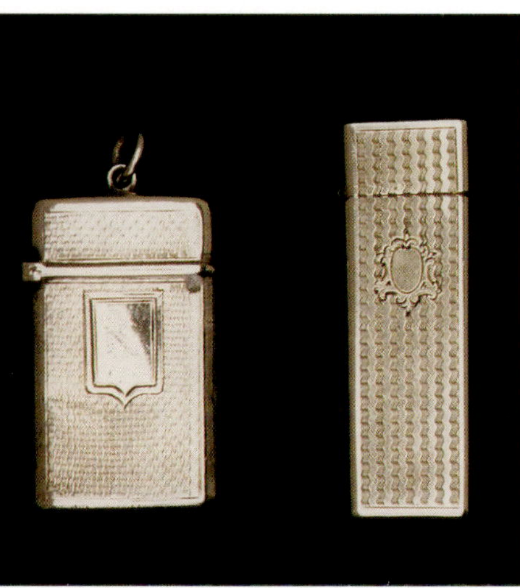

Fig. 119 France. Silver, steel. Left: 'A. Dubois'. c.1900. H -4.5cms. Right: 'O. G.'. c.1910. H - 5.2cms.

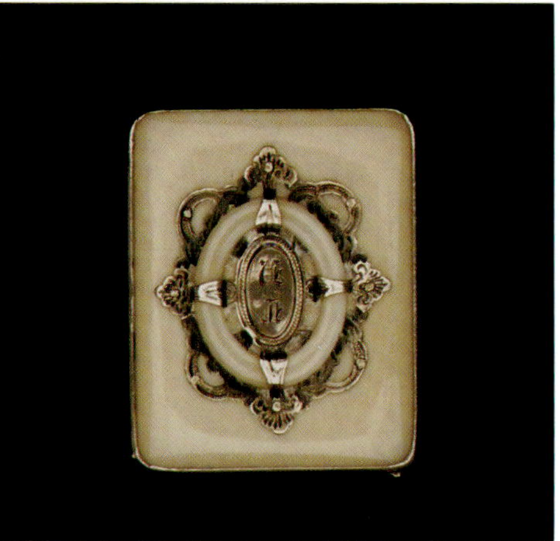

Fig. 120 France. Silver, ivory. c.1900. H - 4.1cms.

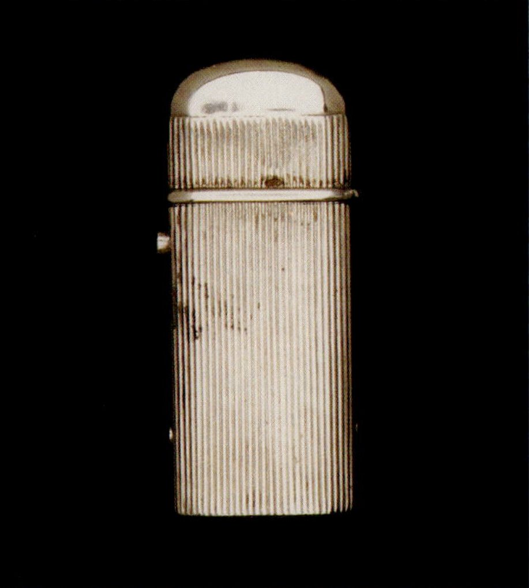

Fig. 121 Dutch. Silver. c.1900. H - 6cms.

The two silver boxes in **Fig. 119** are from France. The box at the left was no doubt intended for wax vesta matches. Provided with a suspension ring on top of the lid, this elegant box has an engine-turned design, and the base is fitted with a roughened steel insert for friction. On the bezel is the diamond-shaped maker's mark with what appears to be the name "A. Dubois" above another unidentified hall mark. This was probably made c. 1900. At the right is another box with an engine-turned design, also with a steel insert roughened for friction on the base. The lid is provided with a hole to hold a match, probably for a pipe or cigar smoker. The maker's diamond-shaped mark on the bezel has the letters "G" and "O" on opposite sides of a tree. It is probably c. 1910.

Also from France is another small box with ivory side panels. The side shown in **Fig. 120** has an additional ivory oval frame laid on an intricate silver backplate, which is held in place by the escutcheon in the center; this escutcheon has four arms, each bent over the ivory frame with the ends riveted through the backplate into the box side. This piece is an incredibly delicate and visually effective piece of workmanship. The striker is along the bottom edge. The front edge is marked with the small articles hallmark of a boar's head, which denotes a fineness of 800, but there is no maker's mark. This may well be from c. 1890.

Of Dutch origin, and shown in **Fig. 121,** is a simple box with a lid that springs open when the push-button on the front edge is pressed. Probably intended for the pipe or cigar smoker, the top of the lid has a socket to hold a match for lighting the tobacco. Both the lid and the body have a hallmark for small articles, and there is an unreadable mark on the bezel that is probably a maker's mark.

India is not well known for the production of match holders but it appears that the example shown in **Fig. 122** originates from that area. Makers did not mark their silver work, and it appears likely that the example may have a high copper content: it tarnishes rapidly like silver, exposing copper colored particles in places. The sides are impressed in a mixture of traditional-style figures and European-style floral designs; the recumbent figures at the top and bottom are applied from solid metal. There is a roughened surface on both sides as strikers.

Semi-precious stones were a popular adornment on match holders, set into the sides of the bodies and lids. The example in Fig. 108 shows pieces of agate, a form of quartz, set into a silver box. But other examples may be found of match holders using similar stones, or even glass, to form the sides of boxes, and offered as "agate" sided boxes. An example is shown in **Fig. 123;** the box sides are made from 'cornelian' ('carnelian') with bands of red and white, sometimes referred to as 'sardonyx'. The major commercial source of this stone is Brazil, but it is also found in a number of other places around the world. This form of agate is known to have been stained, and some forms may be color-enhanced by heating. This example, however, shows no signs of undergoing any form of treatment. The agate slabs are held in place by a plain band of plated brass. The lid, corrugated for friction, is released by a press-button.

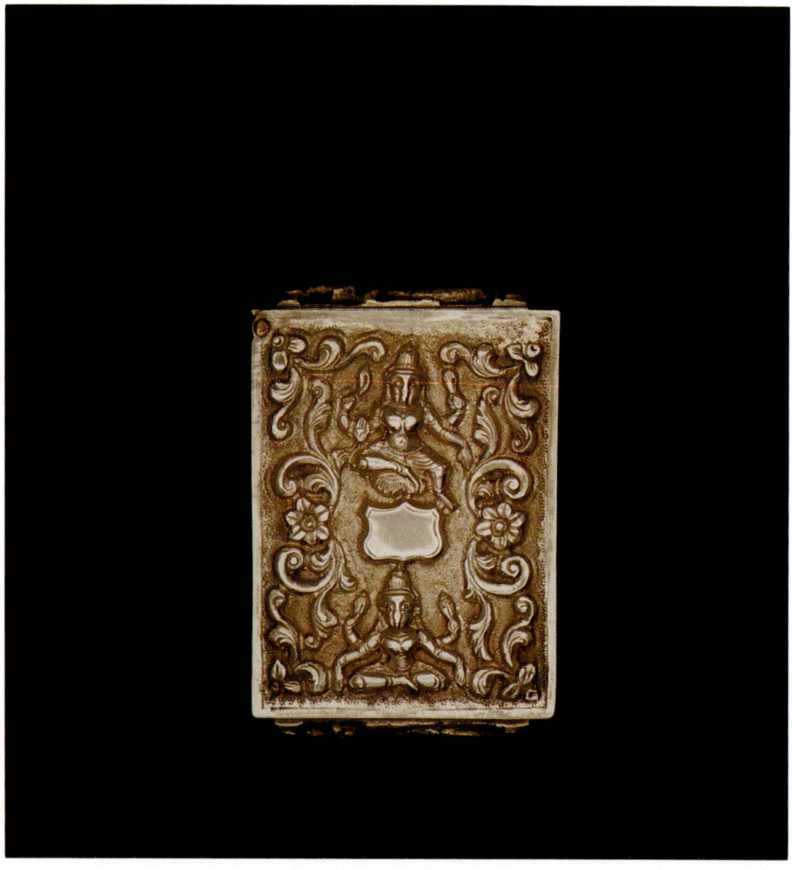

Fig. 122 India. Low grade silver. Date unknown. H - 6.2cms.

The slab sides of the example in **Fig. 124** are of 'tiger's eye' quartz, not agate, the dark veins originally created by a blue variety of asbestos called crocidolite'. This form of quartz is most commonly found in South Africa, and is sometimes dyed, which usually produces an unnatural color. The metal band separating and holding the slabs in place is of plated brass, embellished with a band of interwoven flowers and diamond design; it also acts as the striker.

The slab sides of the example in **Fig. 125** are made of glass, so-called 'aventurine' or 'goldstone' glass, created by the addition of cuprous oxide, which with subsequent treatment creates the spangled effect. The filigree metal band around the edge is probably plated brass. A piece of the glass, ground to form ridges, is set into the lid as the striker.

Moss agate was a popular stone used for the sides of this type of match holder, but some less attractive agates and no doubt other stones were artificially colored, and it is probably safer to consult a competent gemologist for a positive identification. It is believed that the three examples shown were made in Italy, probably around the turn of the century. None have been recorded with identifying marks.

The examples shown here only scratch the surface of the great variety that were available, and that collectors may still find today. There are further examples shown in Chapter III, Part 4 on novelty holders. A few have been reproduced. Others in a psueudo-American style have surfaced in recent years; they originate in Thailand. It is a matter of 'buyer beware'.

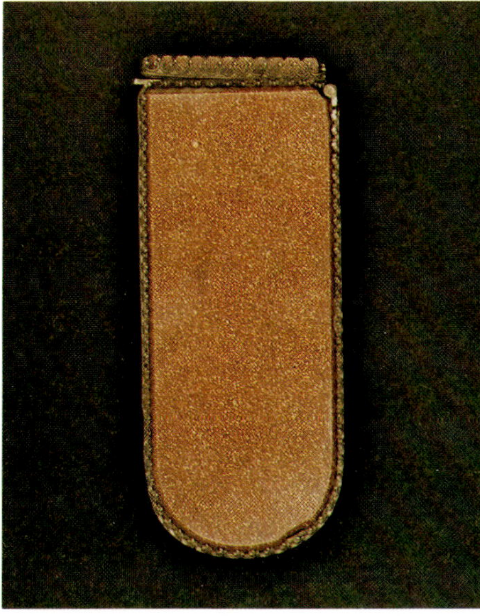

Fig. 125 Italy. Aventurine glass, plated brass. c.1900. H - 7cms.

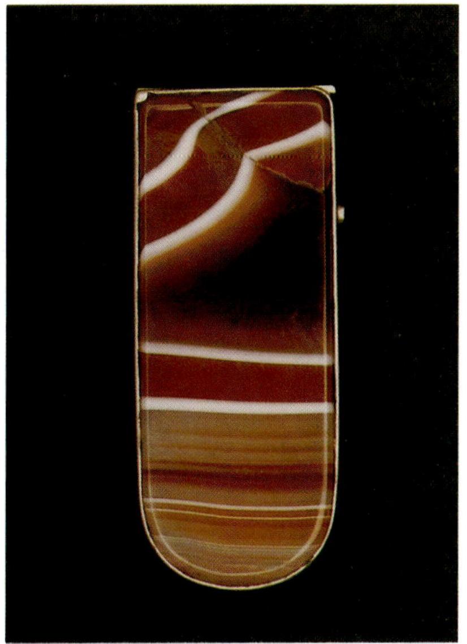

Fig. 123 Italy. Cornelian agate, plated brass. c.1900. H - 6.6cms.

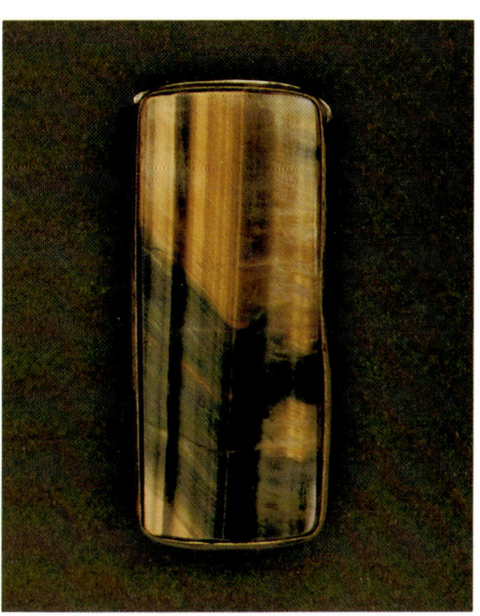

Fig. 124 Italy. Tiger's eye quartz, plated brass. c.1900. H -6.7cms.

PART 3: BASE METAL BOXES.

The term 'base metal' is applied here to those boxes made of aluminum, brass, copper, ferrous metals, pewter, and white and yellow metals.

Aluminum was first produced commercially in the late 1880s, with match holders appearing on the market by 1892. In an 1892 catalogue put out by George Zorn & Co., importers and manufacturers of Philadelphia, Pennsylvania, there is reference to aluminum as "The Wonderful Metal. As Rich in Luster as Silver and as Light as a Feather. The Metal of the Next Century. The Metal of the Future."

Thin sheet iron or steel that has been given a thin coat of tin should be called 'tin-plate', and not 'tin'. The tinning process is applied to reduce corrosion that would otherwise cause the thin metal sheet to break down rapidly.

White metal appears as a number of alloys, and occasionally was given a specific trade-name by a particular company, but is essentially non-ferrous.

Yellow metal is another non-ferrous alloy that usually gives the appearance of gold. 'Pinchbeck', an early 18th century invention, is one such alloy, occasionally used to describe a match holder, but there is no evidence to prove that Pinchbeck was ever used for these items—only analysis by a competent metallurgist could prove it.

Plating to simulate silver was commonplace, usually with nickel or silver. Nickel-plating occurred mostly on brass or tin-plate. On items in mint condition it may be difficult to establish the base metal; but this is easily resolved in most cases by using a magnet, which will be attracted by tin-plate, but not by brass or other non-ferrous metals. However, some caution should be exercised to ensure that the magnet is not being attracted by an internal component of the box, such as a lid spring; or that the lid and body are not of different metals, as is the case with the three-piece boxes dealt with in Part 5 of this chapter.

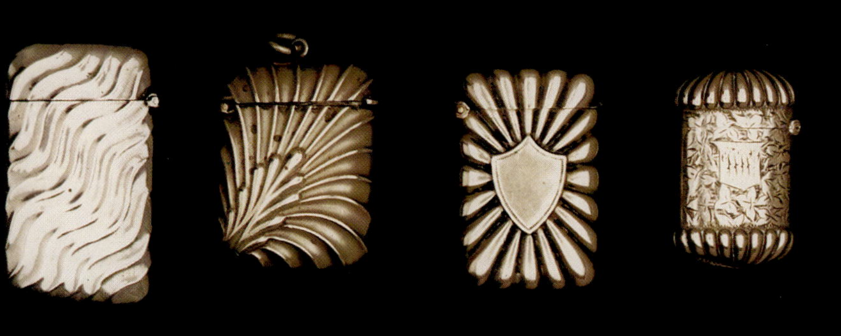

Fig. 126 Britain. Plated brass. Left: Made by the Albu Silver N.C.R. Co. to a Registered Design of 1889 by Jenkins William Evans. H - 6.3cms. Centre left: Made to a Registered Design of 1891 by Frederick W. Tomkinson. H - 5.2cms. Centre right: c.1890s. H 5.2cms. Right: c.1890s. H - 4.8cms.

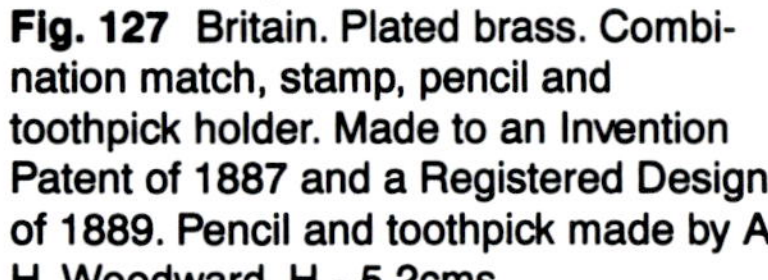

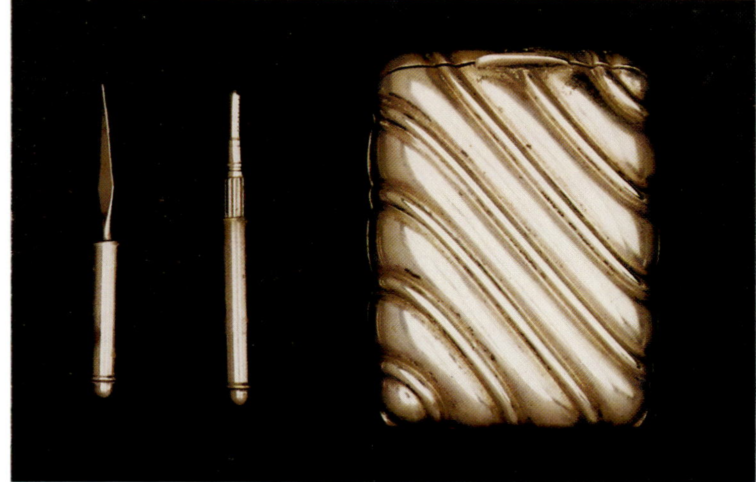

Fig. 127 Britain. Plated brass. Combination match, stamp, pencil and toothpick holder. Made to an Invention Patent of 1887 and a Registered Design of 1889. Pencil and toothpick made by A. H. Woodward. H - 5.2cms.

Many match holders of this type are immediately identifiable as to their country of origin by marks, or by shape and style of decoration. But there are plenty of borderline cases that lack diagnostic traits; then, to a large extent, identification may depend upon experience, detailed examination, and the pursuit of the contemporary literature. An overlap of manufacturing techniques, style and decorative elements occur between two or more countries, and designs influenced by other traditions occur all too frequently.

An attempt has been made here to group match holders by country of origin; but there is a significant number that remain a mystery, and they are referred to later as 'curios'. They are undocumented, and their features are not sufficiently distinctive to allow any attribution based on experience.

Starting with match holders manufactured in Britain, **Fig. 126** features four boxes exhibiting designs in which a form of fluting is present, a popular design element there.

The box at the far left has a Registered Design number for 1889, issued to Jenkin William Evans of Birmingham, a "Diesinker, Toolmaker, Stamper and Piercer." Evans established his company in 1880 and it is still in business today in the same location. He is known to have made the dies and stamped out the parts, before passing them on to another company to finish and market them. His design was for "Wavy hollow fluting for ornamentation of cigar, cigarette, match boxes and flasks." Made of plated brass, the bezel is marked "Albu Silver N.C.R.Co."

The box at center left has a Registered Design number for 1891, issued to Frederick W. Tomkinson, another Birmingham die-sinker; it too is of plated brass. Similar boxes to this were illustrated by Harrod's Stores Ltd. of London in their 1895 catalogue; silver-plated, the boxes sold at one shilling and seven pence each.

The remaining two boxes are also made of plated brass, and were no doubt made in Birmingham in the 1890s. The central section of the far right piece has a typical ivy leaf design commonly found on Birmingham pieces.

Another fluted, plated brass box is shown in **Fig. 127**. It is a combination box, with spaces for holding a pencil and toothpick (shown at the side), as well as a stamp compartment. It is marked inside "Rd.No.122107.Patent No.4709". The Registered Design for the form of the box was issued in 1889 to Albert Lines, a jeweler of Aston (near Birmingham). The patent was issued in 1887 to F.W.Powell, a wholesale manufacturing jeweler of London, for a box that incorporated a pencil, toothpick, stamp compartment *and* a sovereign holder, more accurately represented in the center of Fig. 129.

It is not clear who made the box in Fig. 127, but there was obviously some working agreement between Lines and Powell. However, the pencil within this box is stamped "A.H.W.", for A. H. Woodward, a Birmingham silversmith who specialized in the manufacture of pencil cases, and is known to have been in business between 1884 and 1907. It is assumed that he also made the toothpick.

Gunmetal boxes were popular items. Some were made in Britain, others may have been made in Germany and France. All of the known examples have a boss fixed onto the front edge of the lid as a thumb-push, set with a turquoise stone. They may also be found with semi-precious stones forming initials, and other forms of decoration on one of the sides.

The example at the left in **Fig. 128** is another of the 'Secret Photo Match Boxes'. The front side has an enamelled flag with vertical stripes bearing the initials N, W, A, R and C. On the same side is engraved "1st Place. Best Decorated Boat. Aug.3.03." The reverse side is engraved with the owner's initials.

In the center is a slightly larger box with the head of a stag, probably made of plated brass, attached to the side by means of three lugs that pass through into the inside of the box where they are turned over.

The gunmetal box at the right is in a rather corroded condition, but is yet another of the 'Secret Photo Match Boxes'. When the box was collected, the photograph appeared to be recent, of a young man. When the frame was removed another photograph was found behind the first one—a newspaper image of the British model Twiggie, a popular personality of the late 1960s and 70s in Britain.

In Canada, Henry Birks & Sons of Montreal were obviously importing gunmetal match and cigarette boxes by 1901, and in 1903 the secret photo match box appeared in their catalogue at $4.25. By 1904 the price had dropped to $3.50, and a year later was $3.35. Plain boxes were $1.00. In 1906 and 1907 the plain box was still being offered at $1.00; the secret photo box was not listed, but a new version with applied silver decorative elements and a shield was offered at $2.50. From this it is assumed that gunmetal boxes were probably only made in the first decade of the 20th century.

It is not known if the secret photo match boxes were ever the subject of an invention patent in Britain, but two patents were issued in the United States for the same idea. Battin & Co., of Newark, New Jersey, was issued a patent in 1896, and advertised the boxes as made of gold and silver, in the typical flamboyant style of the United States. A second patent was issued in 1899 to Evan H. Eastwood, also of Newark, but the cover over the photograph frame was hinged at the top of the box side, as opposed to the bottom edge.

The match holder in **Fig. 129 left** is of plated brass, made for wax vesta matches, with an engraved design in a Japanese style. It is marked "H.J. & Co.", and is probably c. 1905.

The box in **Fig. 129 center** was made according to the same patent as that in Fig. 127, but more accurately meets the patent drawings of F. W. Powell; it lacks only the cigar cutter of Powell's patent, but includes his sovereign holder and stamp compartment, which are located under the lid at the bottom. In this example the toothpick is missing; the pencil is present, but unmarked. The engraved design suggests that the box was made in Birmingham, and has a silver-plated finish. An advertisement of 1890 referred to them as "The Albert Combination Matchbox," finished in plain electro-plating; they sold at five shillings and sixpence. Mappin & Webb Ltd. of London offered them in 1900, made of silver, for one pound five shillings.

The brass box in **Fig. 129 right** is deeply embossed in Rococo style, and was probably made in Birmingham in the 1880s.

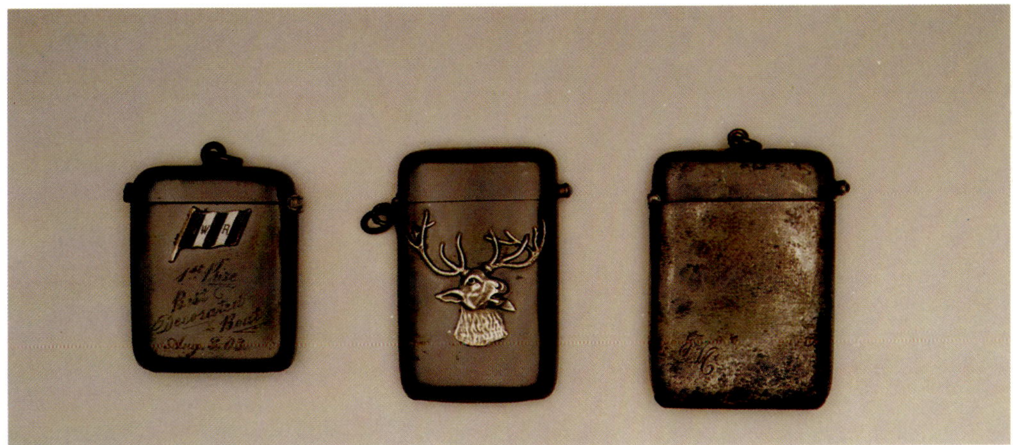

Fig. 128 Britain. Gun metal, enamel, plated brass. Left: "Secret photograph box", 1903. H - 5.5cms. Centre: c.1905. H - 6.1cms. Right: "Secret photograph box" c.1905. H - 6.5cms.

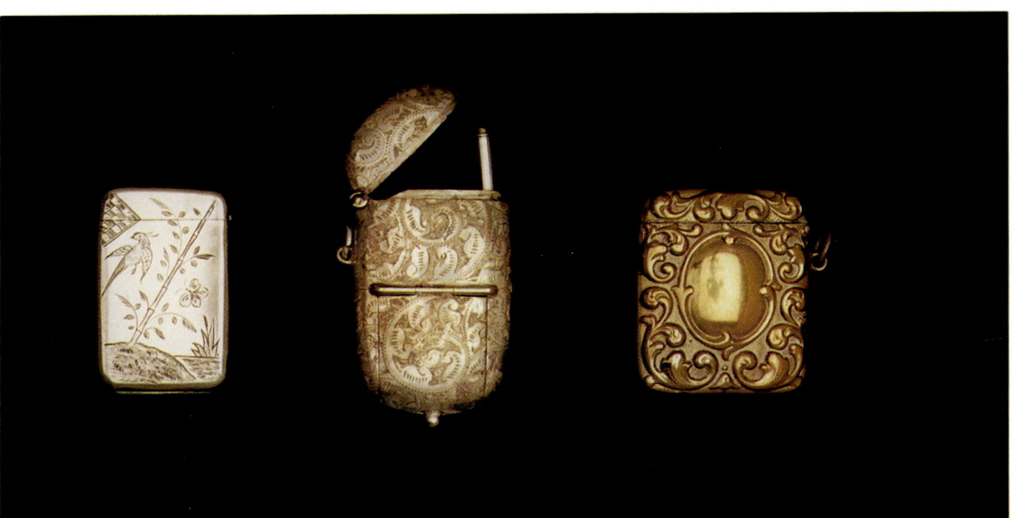

Fig. 129 Britain. Plated brass. Left: "H.J. & Co.". c.1905. Centre: combined match, stamp, sovereign, pencil toothpick case. Made to an Invention Patent of 1887. H - 6.6cms. Right: (not plated) c.1880s. H - 4.9cms.

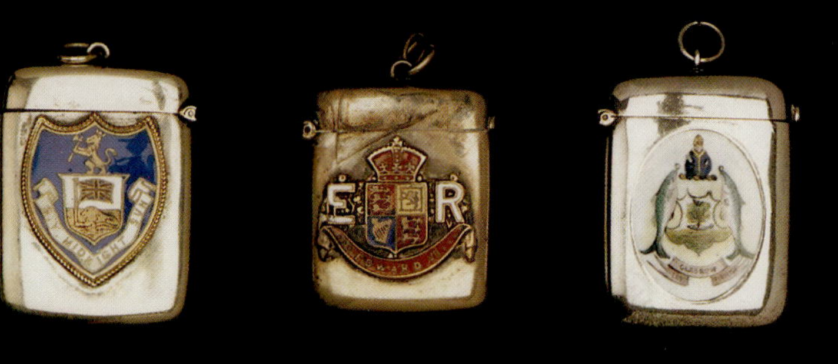

Fig. 130 Britain. Plated brass. Left: c.1902. H - 5.8cms. Centre: c.1905. H - 5.7cms. Right: c.1902. H 5.1cms.

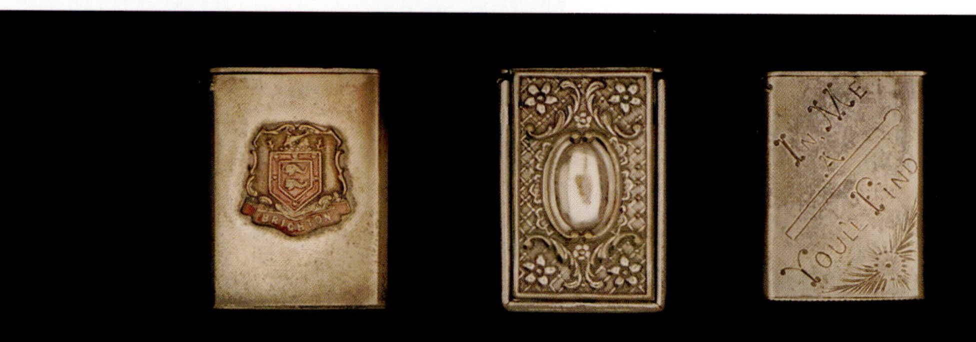

Fig. 131 Britain. Plated brass. Left: c.1910. H - 4.5cms. Centre: made to a Registered Design of 1900. H 4.4cms. Right: "AF & Co.", c.1910. H - 4.2cms.

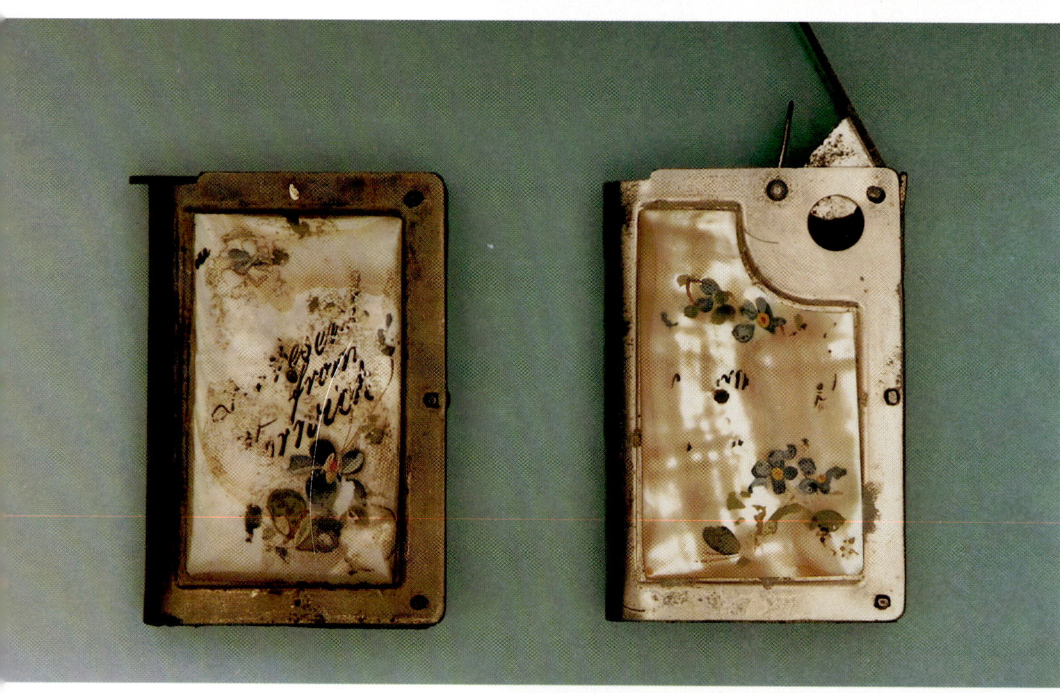

Fig. 132 Britain. Plated brass, shell. Both by same maker. Right with cigar cutter. c.1900s. H - 5.9cms.

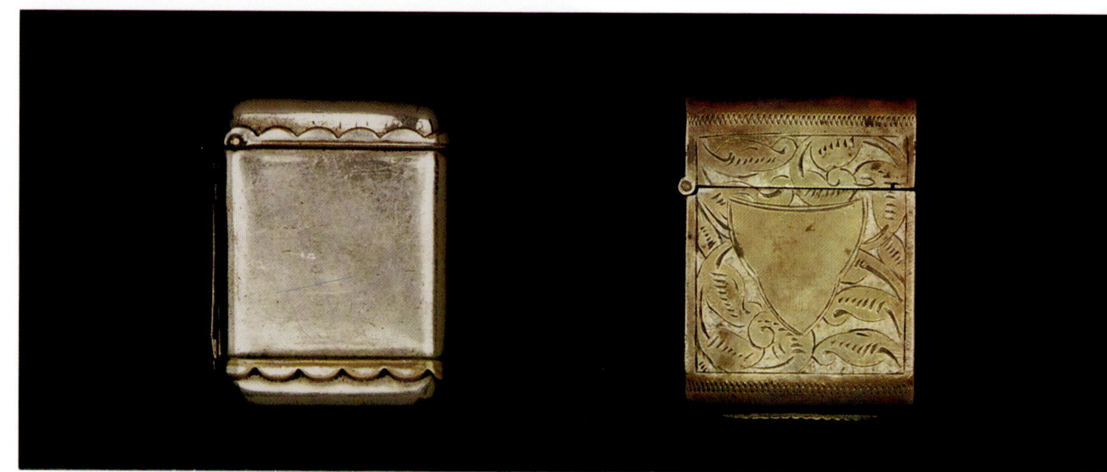

Fig. 133 Britain. Left: plated brass; made to a Registered Design of 1888. H - 4.3cms. Right: brass, c.1880s. H - 4.6cms.

The three boxes in **Fig. 130** have applied enamelled panels. That to the left has a shield and enamelled crest for the "S.Y. Midnight Sun" on a plated brass box. In the center is a silver-plated box, curved to fit the waist, with a crest for King Edward VII; it was probably made to commemorate his coronation. The box at the right is silver-plated with an enamelled version of the coat of arms for Glasgow set directly into a shallow oval depression in the box side. The language of heraldry is rooted in Greek and Latin, and descriptions of heraldic designs are very formal. The Arms of Glasgow are described thus:

> "Argent, on a mount in base vert an oak-tree proper, the stem at the base thereof surmounted by a salmon on its back also proper, with a signet-ring in its mouth or, in the top of the tree a red-breast, and in the sinister fess point an ancient bell, both also proper. Above this shield is placed a suitable helmet, with a mantling gules, doubled argent; and issuing from a wreath of the proper liveries is set for crest, the half-length figure of St. Kentigern affronté, vested and mitred, his right hand raised in the act of benediction, and having in his left hand a crosier, all proper. On a compartment below the shield are placed for supporters, two salmon proper, each holding in its mouth, a signet-ring or, and in an escroll entwined with the compartment this motto, 'Let Glasgow flourish'."

The enamelled crest seems to lack the 'ancient bell', but all other elements are there, although the two salmon may not be in the approved place.

The three boxes in **Fig. 131** all have flat lids, but are otherwise quite different. To the left is a plated brass box with the enamelled coat of arms for Brighton, Sussex. There is no reason to doubt the authenticity of this particular box, but this type of crest is known to have been applied to plain boxes in order to raise their price to unsuspecting collectors.

In the center is a plated brass box marked with a registered design number for 1900, issued to a patent agent in Birmingham, where the piece was no doubt made. The design was for a simple method of construction, with the edges and base produced from a single strip of channelling, with slots along the sides to hold lugs on the edges of the side plates. The side plates were no doubt produced with several designs available.

The plated brass box at the right is engraved on one side "In Me A Match You'll Find." A representation of a match replaces the word. Other examples with wording of a related nature occur, such as "A match for you at any time," "Help yourself," "Strike me," and others.

A series of boxes in plated brass, each decorated on one side with a mother-of-pearl panel painted with flowers and having a composite striker set into one short edge, are all by the same unidentified maker. Two forms are shown in **Fig. 132,** that to the left solely a match holder, and that to the right a box incorporating a cigar cutter in the lid. Another pair enclosing a candle are shown in Fig. 329. Most of the painted flowers and wording have rubbed off, and they may have been intended as cheap souvenirs for travellers, probably late in the l9th century.

The box at the left in **Fig. 133** is of plated brass with a Registered Design number for 1888, which (although not checked) was no doubt for the method of construction. It is similar to the three-piece box construction shown in Fig. 81. Here, however, the lid and base elements sit inside the raised bead, and the join along the back edge is held together by a separate striker plate. The box at the right is of brass, poorly made, with a crudely executed Birmingham-style design, which is probably where it was made in the 1880s.

The box in **Fig. 134** is made of copper, in the form of a bale tied with rope, possibly representing a sail. On one side is a rectangular panel applied to the surface, embossed with a sailing ship and the words "This article is warrented to be made of copper from the ship Foudroyant." The *Foudroyant* was launched at Plymouth, England, in 1798 and became the flagship of Lord Nelson for a few months in 1800. She had a brief active career spanning about twelve years, eventually becoming a gunnery training ship in 1861. She was sold to a German ship-breaker in 1892, but after a public outcry in Britain, was bought back, refitted as close as possible to her original state, and began an exhibition tour around Britain. In a gale off Blackpool in June 1897 she broke her moorings and was driven ashore; she survived this, only to be severely damaged by another gale later in the year. Her hull was sold for scrap, the copper cladding being turned into garden seats, medals and other articles, all marked with her name. A larger silver-plated version of the *Foudroyant* match box was made, with different wording on the plaque. The bezel is marked with a trade mark in the form of an anchor.

The plain, thick, plated brass box in **Fig. 135** conceals a roller blind of yellow silk in the lid. The lid is marked "Jobson's Pat," but a search has so far not revealed the patent. The silk ribbon has a printed text that states "Permanent Cyclist's Lighting-Up Time Table. (Runs for ever) G. Jobson. Boston Rd., Horncastle. (Copyright)" Above this is a calendar, with the lighting-up times next to each recorded date. The patent is probably for the textual content of the calendar, and not related to the box, which was probably made in Birmingham in the first decade of the 20th century.

In brass is a slim oval cross-section box with a seal, bearing the letter "R" at the base (no doubt intended for creating an impression on sealing wax), shown in **Fig. 136**. It was the subject of a Registered Design of 1912, issued to John Walker & Co. Ltd., of London, and presumably made by them.

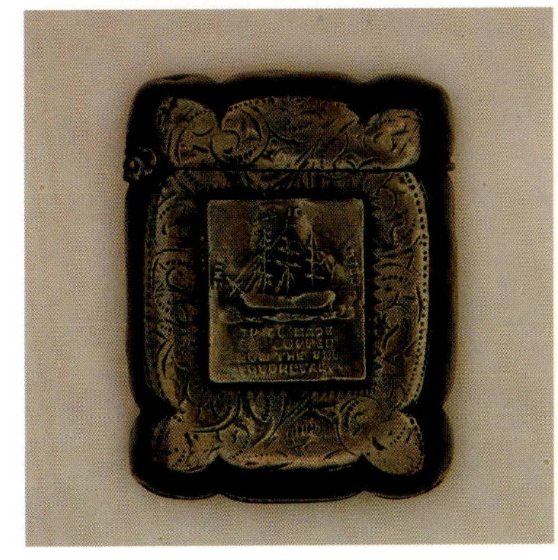

Fig. 134 Britain. Copper. c.1898. H - 4.9cms.

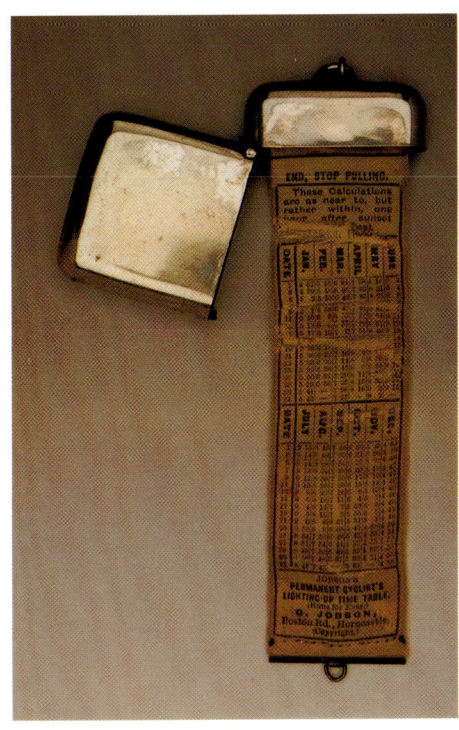

Fig. 135 Britain. Plated brass, silk. Ribbon patented. c.1910. H(of box when closed) - 6cms. L(of ribbon) - 11.7cms.

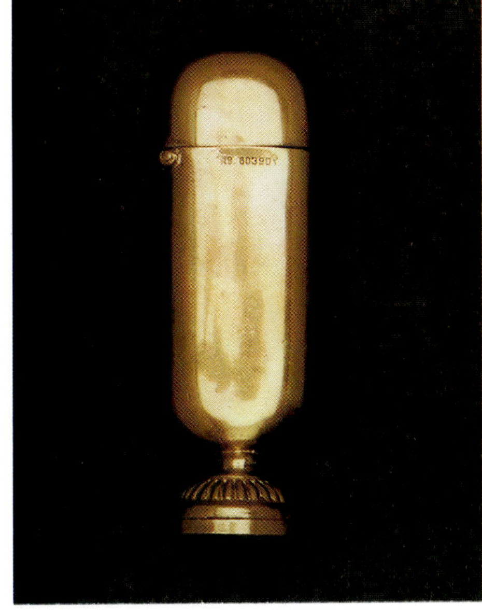

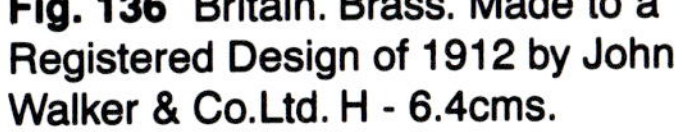

Fig. 136 Britain. Brass. Made to a Registered Design of 1912 by John Walker & Co.Ltd. H - 6.4cms.

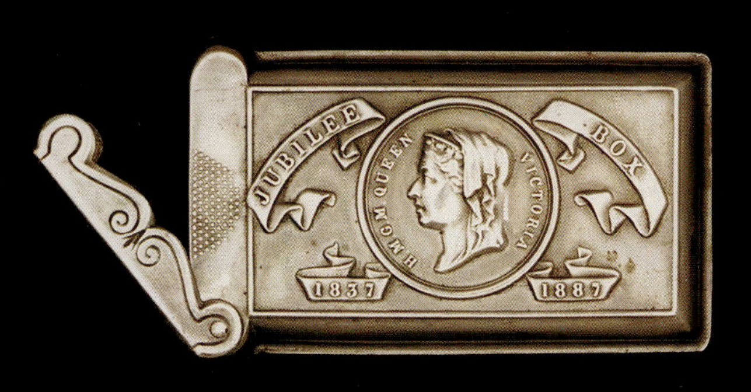

Fig. 137 Britain. Plated brass. Probably made by Perry & Co. Ltd. 1887. H - 6.2cms.

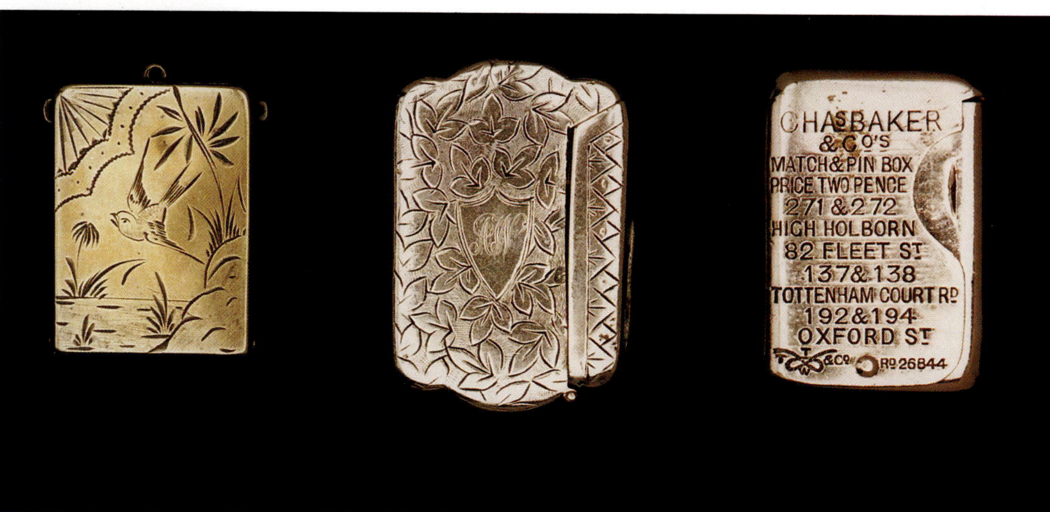

Fig. 138 Britain. Brass and plated brass. Left: patented, c. 1885. H - 4cms. Centre: patented 1887 by Samuel Basnett. H - 4.9cms. Right: Made by Thomas Turner & Co. to a Registered Design of 1885. H - 4.6cms.

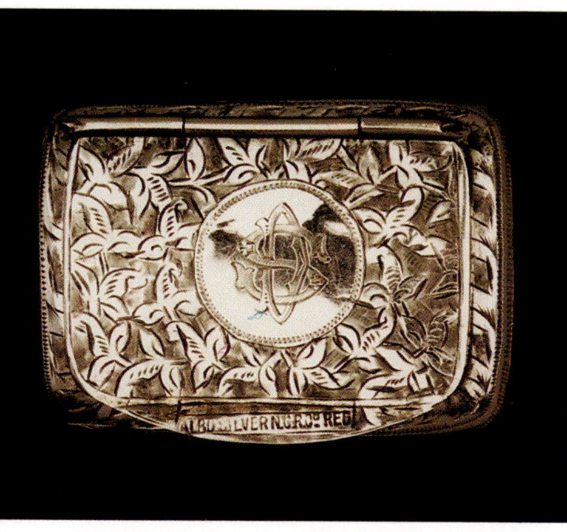

Fig. 139 Britain. Plated brass. Made by the Albu Silver N.R.C. Co. c.1900. L - 5.3cms.

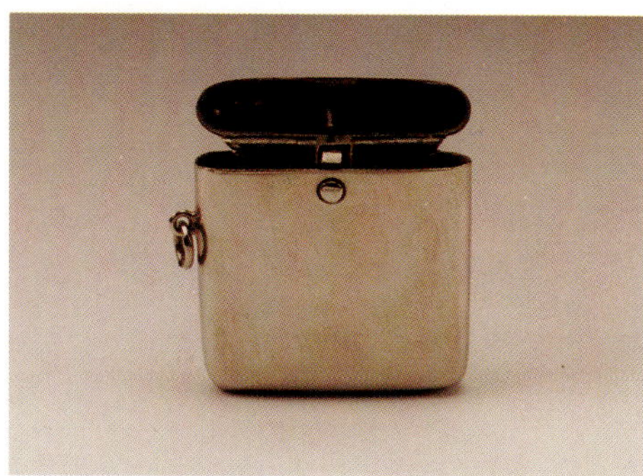

Fig. 140 Britain. Plated brass. Marked "Rd.No.704. Patent" Probably 1884. H - 4.9cms.

The box shown in **Fig. 137** is of thin plated brass, the main body made in two halves with out-turned flanges that have been soldered together. In the same material, the lid is formed as a channel, the sides in scroll form and the top corrugated for friction. The lid does not rely upon a spring to hold it closed, but on a triangular patch of punch dots on either side at the top of the body to grip the inside edges of the lid. The box was one of thousands of items made to commemorate the Golden Jubilee of Queen Victoria in 1887, and is marked "JUBILEE BOX". It was made for, and probably by, Perry & Co. Ltd., the well-known steel pen makers of London and Birmingham, whose name and trademark are impressed on the reverse.

The boxes in **Fig. 138** open in a different manner to more conventional match holders. That to the left is made of brass, engraved on one side with a Japanese inspired design. It is hinged at the bottom, and may be opened by pressing the lugs on each side near the top, permitting the box to spring open. The front side is fitted internally with a 'pocket' to hold the matches in place. It has a patent number, but no date, and is probably from the 1890s.

The box in **Fig. 138 center** is silver-plated, and made to a patent of 1887 issued to Samuel Basnett, a Birmingham silversmith, for "Boxes for pens, matches, address cards, &c." The box has an inner compartment attached to the lid located at the side, and hinged on the lower edge, which is sheathed by the outer cover of the box. It has the typical Birmingham engraved ivy leaf design.

In **Fig. 138 right** is a box of somewhat similar form: an inner box in a sheath, but hinged at the centre of the bottom edge. It is made of plated brass. It was the subject of a Registered Design of 1885, issued to Thomas Burns and James S. Dumbell, partners in the company of Thomas Turner & Co., of Wolverhampton, manufacturers of "locks and fancy metal goods". The company trademark and the Registered Number can be seen at the bottom of the box. There is advertising copy on both sides, showing that the box was sold (for two pence) to hold matches or pins for Charles Baker & Co., a gentleman's clothing outfitters with three addresses in London.

The box exemplified in **Fig. 139**, of silver plating on brass, is sometimes referred to as a "snuff box" type because the lid is hinged longitudinally. The overall shape is conventionally British, and the top has the engraved ivy leaf design. It is marked "Albu Silver N.C.R. Co." and was probably made between c. 1895 and 1905.

An unusual match holder, made of undecorated plated brass, is shown in **Fig. 140**. The lid is hinged longitudinally and released by a press-button on the front side. On the inside, the box is divided into two compartments by a column that supports a lateral plate at the bottom, which in turn supports the matches. The central column encloses a spring, so that when the press-button is pressed to release the catch, the central column is pushed up, applying pressure to a bracket soldered to the inside of the lid and springing it open, at the same time raising the lateral plate attached to the base of the column, thereby raising the matches clear of the rim of the box. The back of the box is stamped "Rd.No.704.Patent." This is confusing, because it is not clear if the 704 refers to a Registered Design, which would be for 1884, or if the number refers to an invention patent. In the British system, a patent number (but not the year) was marked on an item, and the patent numbers were repeated each year.

Of later vintage are two examples in **Fig. 141** made of plated brass, hinged longitudinally, and with heraldic devices soldered on the lids. They were the subject of an invention patent and a registered design. The invention patent, was issued to Philip G.Marr of London in 1926, states:

> "This invention relates to holders or carriers for match-striking surfaces and of the type adapted to receive one or more replaceable striking surfaces obtained, for example, from the shell of an ordinary match box."

The relevant drawings from the patent are shown in **Fig. 142**, with the invention applied to the top of the lid. The end product positioned the invention on the underside of the box, and is marked "Centre-Bar," "British Made," and with the patent and design numbers. The Registered Design has not been traced.

An inexpensive box in **Fig. 143** is made of plated brass, is of oval cross section, and has a sliding drawer with a composite striker at the end. The celluloid wrapped paper label bears advertising on one side "With Compts. from Your Old Pal, Wally Broad. THE FOX, TEYNHAM, KENT;" the reverse shows a photograph of 'mine host'. This is probably from the early 1920s.

The examples in **Fig. 144** are made of plated brass, with twin compartments, the lids hinged across the top of the box, and similar to the box shown in Fig. 71. The box at the left is plain, and has an external striker along one long edge. That to the right has an engine-turned design on the top and bottom; the smaller compartment is provided with a hole in one side and a cigar cutter fixed in the lid, and the seating for a steel striker, now missing. They are probably both c. 1855 to 1865.

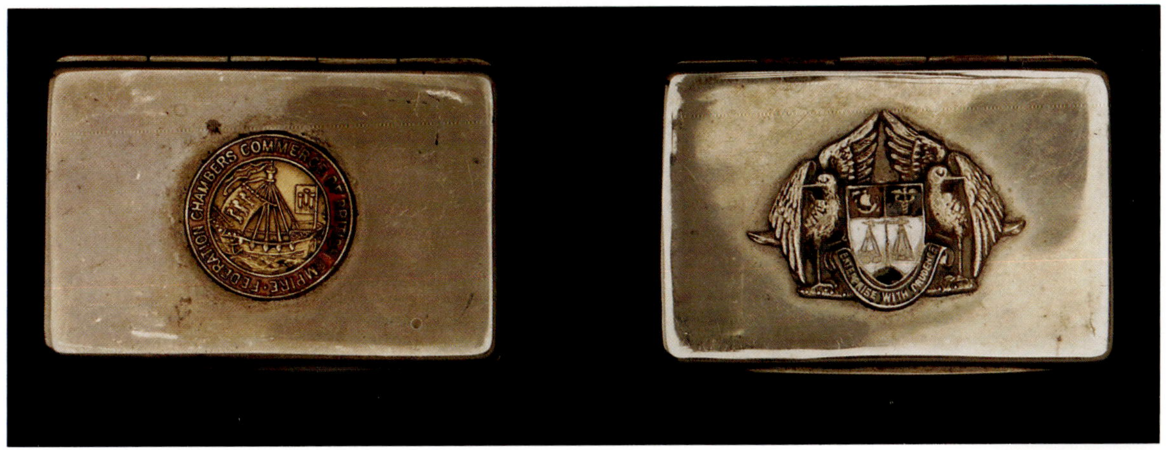

Fig. 141 Britain. Plated brass, enamel. Made to an Invention Patent of 1926 (see Fig. 142), and a Registered Design of 1927. L - 6.1cms.

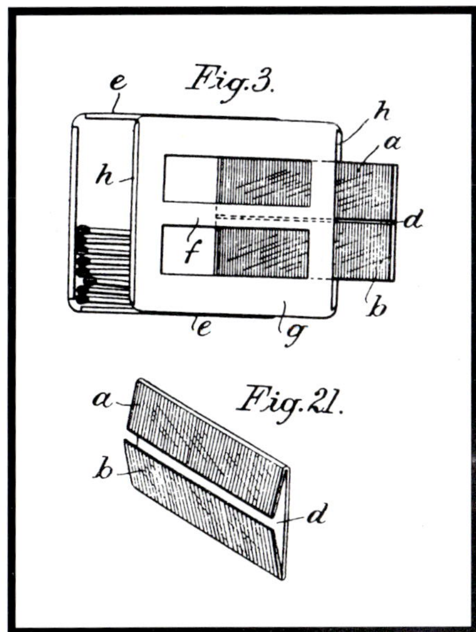

Fig. 142 Part of patent drawings of Invention Patent of 1926 used on the underside of the boxes in Fig. 141.

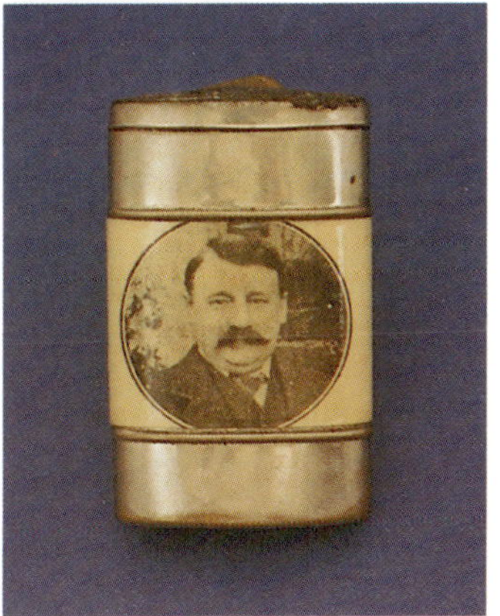

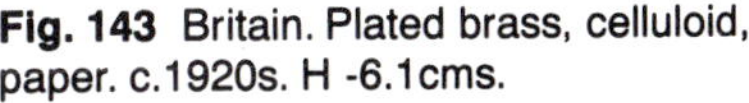

Fig. 143 Britain. Plated brass, celluloid, paper. c.1920s. H -6.1cms.

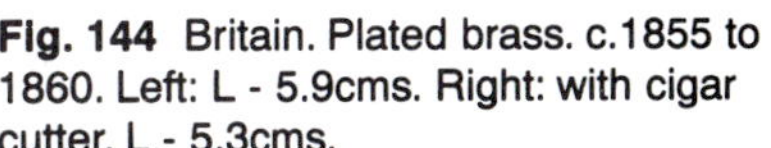

Fig. 144 Britain. Plated brass. c.1855 to 1860. Left: L - 5.9cms. Right: with cigar cutter. L - 5.3cms.

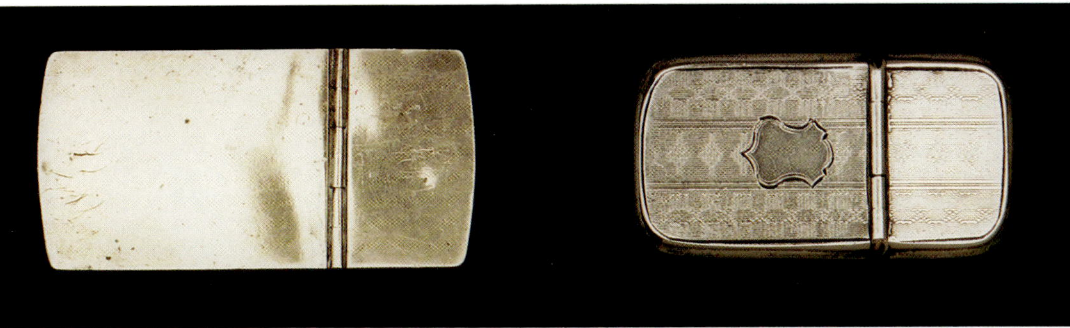

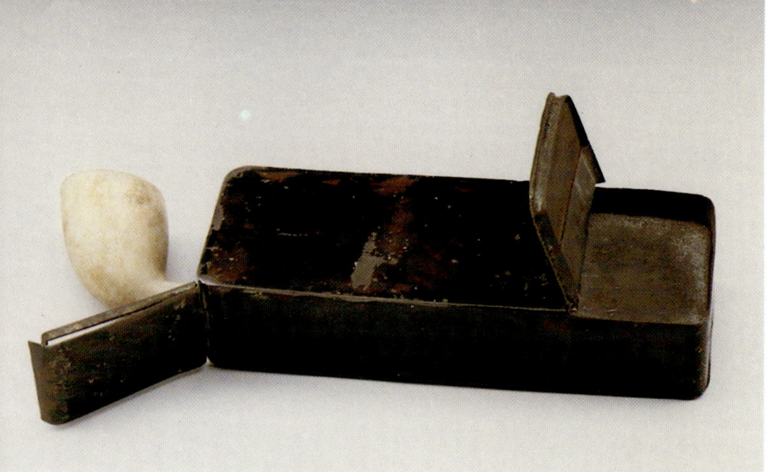

Fig. 145 Britain? Tin plate (with clay pipe). c.1860. L - 12.8cms.

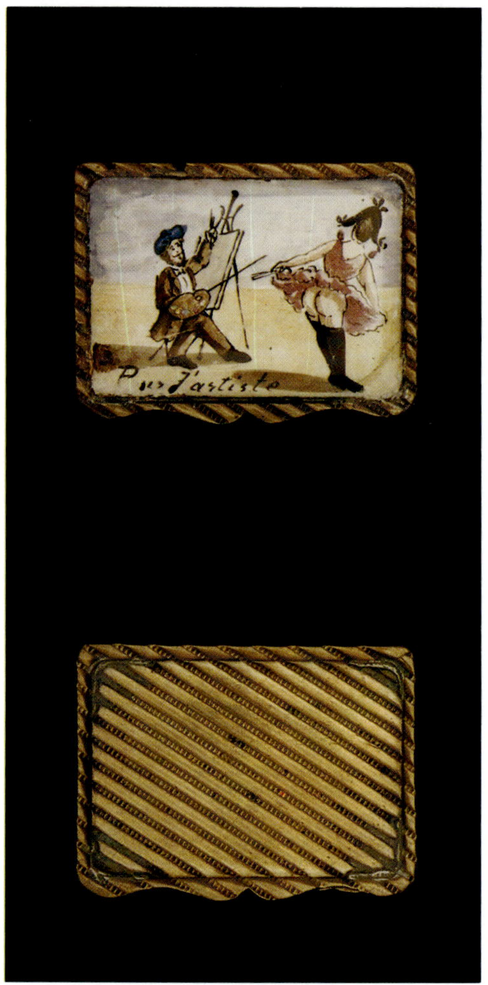

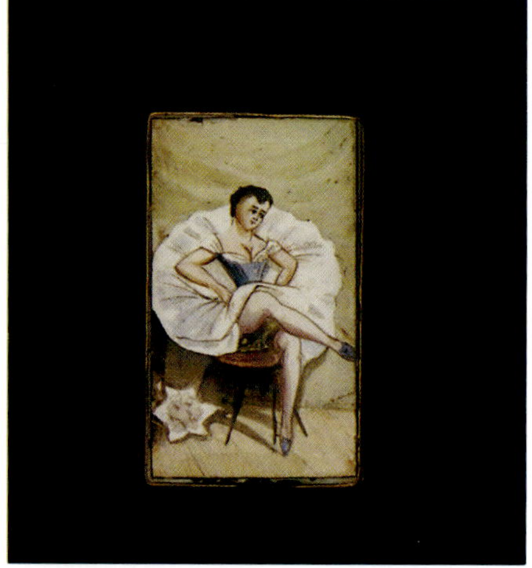

Fig. 146 France. Brass, enamel. c.1890s. H - 4.1cms.

Fig. 147 France. Brass, enamel. c.1890s. Top: W - 4.5cms. Lower: enamelled plate missing. W - 4.5cms.

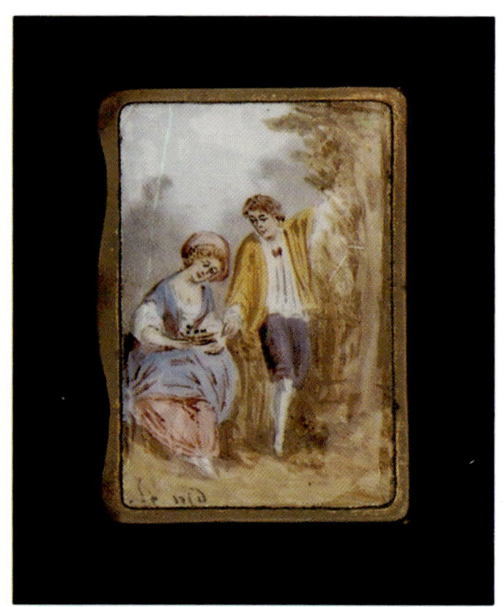

Fig. 148 France. Brass, enamel. Made for Cie Des Allumettes Chemiques. c.1890s. H - 5cms.

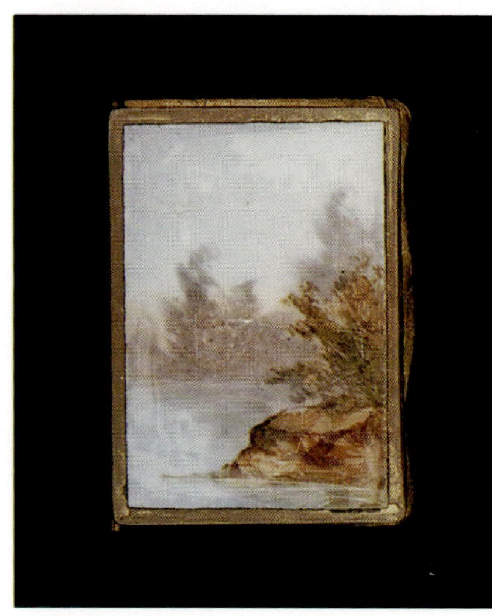

Fig. 149 Reverse of Fig. 148.

In complete contrast is a combination box in tin plate to hold tobacco, a clay pipe, and matches, shown in **Fig. 145**. It has a painted red and black mottled finish, and originally had a rectangular plate (for engraved initials) soldered to the lid of the tobacco compartment, which is located on the underside in the illustration. This box was probably intended for an outdoor worker or a travelling man, enabling him to carry his fragile pipe safely along with the other necessary supplies. It is believed to date from c. 1860.

Continental Europe produced its share of the market, some in quite distinctive styles that are typical of a particular country.

In France, a wide range of brass boxes with enamelled images was produced. Many exhibited scantily clad females, with erotic scenes being common; occasionally the inside of the lid depicts more graphic subject matter, hidden from the eyes of those who may be offended. But country scenes were also used. Many boxes were enamelled on all six sides. There were several different shaped boxes, from a simple rectangular form, to an upright version similar to the North American mailbox with a sloped lid at the top; most were hinged longitudinally. They are all believed to have been made late in the l9th century and, possibly, just after the turn of the century.

A very simple rectangular box in **Fig. 146** depicts a seated ballet dancer with a disgruntled expression on her face.

The most common form is shown in **Fig. 147**, the lower example missing its enamelled plate, but showing how the plate, which was made separately, was soldered to the lid of the box. The upper example is provided with a saucy illustration titled *Pour l'artiste*, and was no doubt one of a series of such illustrations. The sheet brass used for the box has a design pressed into the exposed surface forming diagonal lines, with the reverse side smooth; the front edge has additional raised lines running vertically for the striker. The wavy front edge of the lid is a common element in many boxes of this type.

In the same form, the example in **Figs. 148 and 149** is enamelled on both sides and three edges, the fourth edge sanded for friction; the exposed brass has a smooth gilt finish. The lid has a lady and gentleman in a garden setting, the underside a lakeside scene. Both ends are marked in the brass "15" in a circle, and "Paris", against an enamelled background of pink at one end and blue at the other. The back edge is marked "CHAUSSEE D'ANTIN 66" against a dark blue background; this mark is believed to be the address of Cie Des Allumettes Chemiques, for whom the box was probably made.

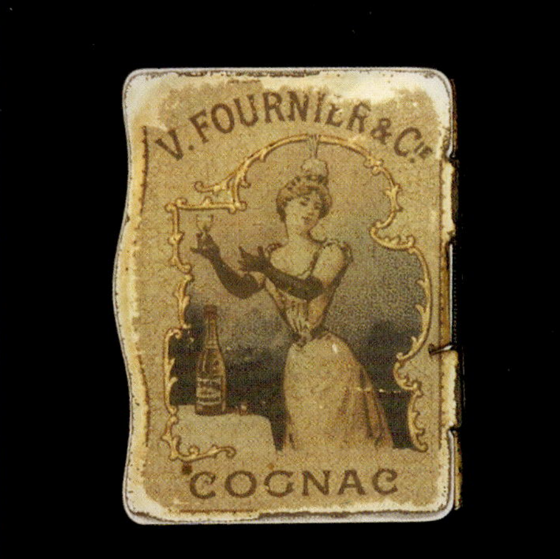

Fig. 150 France. Tin plate. Made by Breger & Nettre. c.1900-1910. H - 5cms.

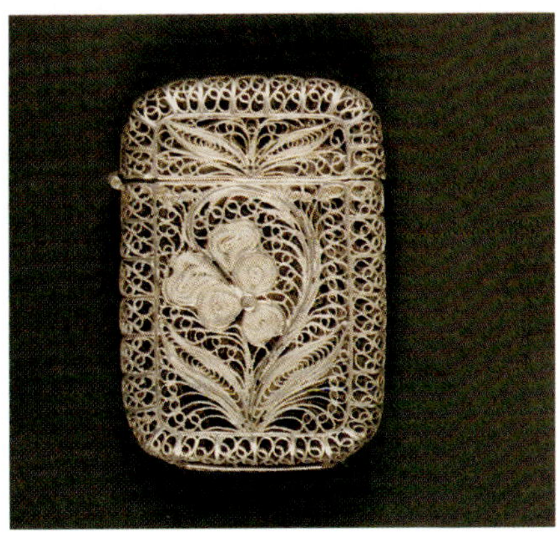

Fig. 152 Italy. Plated brass? c.1890s. H - 4.7cms.

Fig. 153 Russia. Brass, cloisonne enamel. c.1900. H - 5cms.

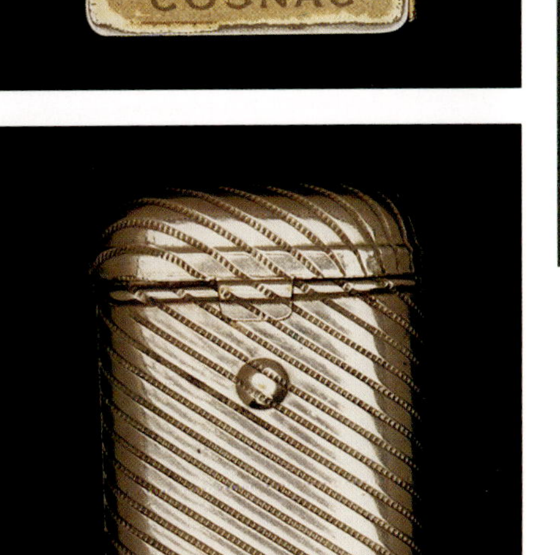

Fig. 151 France. Plated brass. Made to a registered design. c.1900. H - 6.6cms.

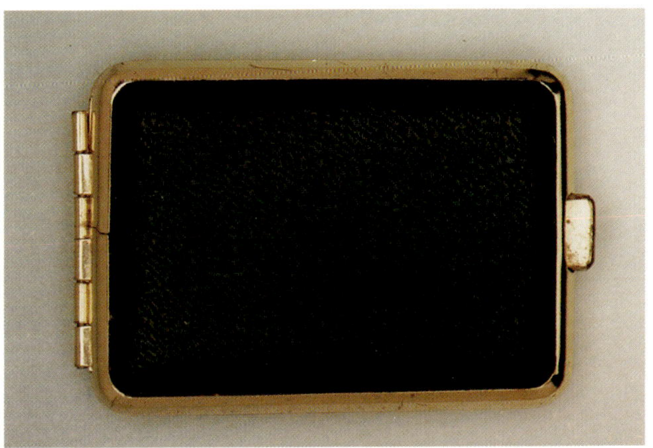

Fig. 154 German. Brass plated tin plate, leather. c.1960. L -6.8cms.

Made of tin plate in the same form is an example in **Fig. 150**. It has lithographed design work on each side and edge, advertising the cognac of V. Fournier & Cie. On the underside is printed "IMP.BREGER & JAVAI.BREGER & NETTRE Succrs. PARIS," believed to be the manufacturers. The striker, on the underside, is a rectangular patch of punch dot holes forming a grater. This probably dates from the first decade of the 20th century.

In quite a different style is the example in **Fig. 151**. It is made of thin-gauge plated brass, the metal having the same design and manufacturing technique as that in Fig. 147. It is made in two halves, the join around the edge overlapplng and soldered together. The lid is stamped out of one piece, hinged along the back edge, and stamped on the top "MODELE DEPOSE," which indicates a registered design. It is probably c.l900 to l910.

The example in **Fig. 152** is probably from Italy, c. 1900, in silvered metal filigree. These dainty but fragile boxes were also made in gilded metal, with various floral designs, probably for ladies. The striker is located along the bottom edge.

An example of Russian workmanship may be seen in **Fig. 153,** dating from c. 1900. The cloisonné enamel against a gilt finish on brass is typically Russian; similar designs on a range of domestic wares, particularly spoons, may be found.

From Germany, of recent manufacture (c. 1960), and shown in **Fig. 154,** is a match holder made of brass-plated sheet steel, with green leather covers. The box opens in two equal halves, with the inside of one half fitted with a plastic pocket to hold the matches, inset with an elliptical tablet roughened for friction.

In North America, Canada relied largely upon its neighbour to the south, or imports from Europe, to meet its needs in this field. But a few Canadian pieces are to be found, and two examples are shown here.

The first, in **Fig. 155**, is distinctly British in style and is marked "E.P.N.S." (electro-plated nickel silver), on brass, with an enamelled emblem attached on one side by means of lugs. The emblem represents the Dominion Arms, with the emblems of the Canadian Provinces, prior to 1905, surmounted by a crown. The maker's mark of "R.H." in a distinctive cartouche is stamped on the outside of the lid, and is the mark of Canadian Jewelers Ltd., of Montreal.

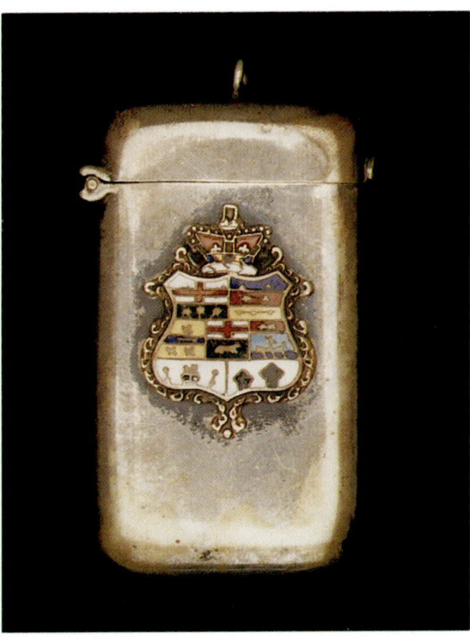

Fig. 155 Canada. Brass, electro-plated nickel silver, enamel. Made by Canadian Jewelers Ltd. c.1905. H 6.7cms.

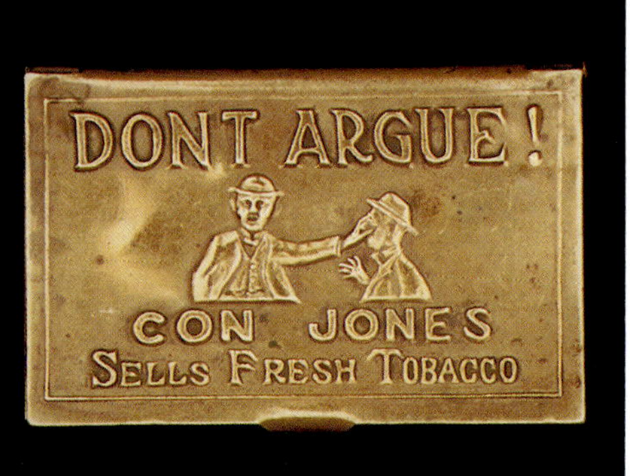

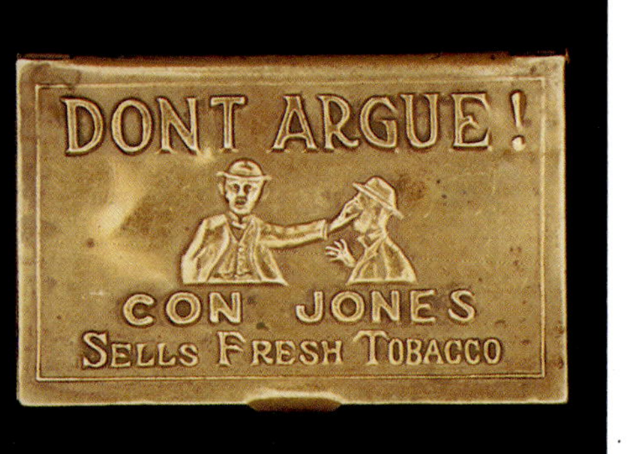

Fig. 156 Canada. Brass. Made by Caron Bros. c.1920. W - 5.5cms.

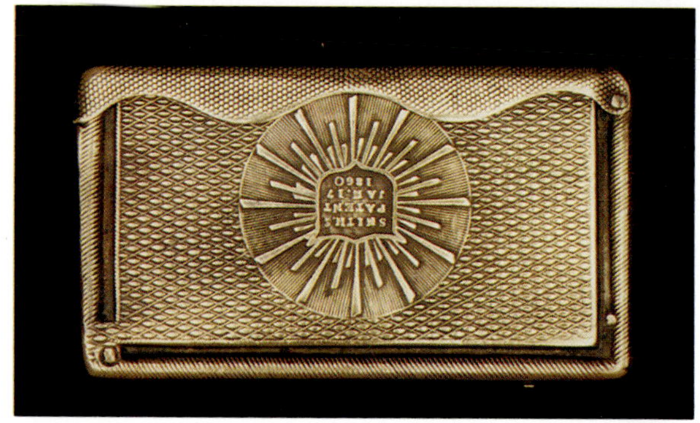

Fig. 157 United States. Brass. Made to an Invention Patent of 1860 by Albert M. Smith. L - 6.3cms.

An unusual brass box is shown in **Fig. 156**; it too was made in Montreal, by Caron Bros., who were manufacturing jewelers until about 1920 before diversifying into other forms of manufacturing. The box was made for a Vancouver business man, Con Jones, who started the Brunswick Pool Rooms between 1905 and 1910; that business continued in one form or another until well into the 1930s, at a number of different addresses. In 1919 he began to sell cigars in his bowling alley and pool room, eventually opening two tobacco stores, which suggests that the box may be as late as the early 1920s.

The United States provides a wide range of styles, although it was perhaps a little later than its European counterparts in entering the field. The Design Patent records show that the first pocket match holder was issued in 1857 for a simple sliding drawer box, and it was not until 1879 that another was issued. In the Invention Patent records, the first patent issued was in 1858, for a box that would present one match at a time, and ignite the match as it was withdrawn from the box. This was a recurring theme in match holders of all types, and gives the impression that it amounted almost to an obsession in the United States among the patentees of match holders.

It is not clear how many of these inventions ever reached the production stage, but it appears likely that many were doomed to remain dreams in the inventors' minds. Some inventions were incredibly complex, and probably far too expensive to manufacture as a competitive item in a market that was also directed towards lowering production costs.

The example shown in **Fig. 157** was patented in 1860 by Albert M. Smith of New York City. His specifications and drawings show that the box held a single line of matches, probably about ten, ejected singly by means of a lever on one edge of the box, and ignited as they were ejected. The patent also included a cigar cutter, operated by raising and lowering the lid, which had a knife set into the end. The actual product did indeed provide the means for ejecting the match, but it then had to be struck along a striker set into one end. The cigar cutter was abandoned. Made of brass, this box bears Smith's name and the patent date in the shield, as shown, and it is assumed that he was the maker. An illustration of the box has been found in a catalogue put out in 1886 by the U.S.Trick and Novelty Co. of Palatine, Illinois. The text to the illustration states "Our 50 cent pocket match safe reduced to 25 cents." It also says that it is "silver plated," and was available from L.A.L. Smith & Co. of Palatine, who were the proprietors of the U.S. Trick and Novelty Co. Were Albert M. and L.A.L. Smith related?

Charles Scofield of Vineland, New Jersey obtained a patent for a box to hold matches and stamps or tickets, issued on December 25, 1877; the box is shown in **Fig. 158**. The book-shaped cover is made of plated brass, and the inner body, pivoted at one corner to swing outwards, is made of tin-plate, with brass edges to form the striker. The spine is stamped with the patent date, Scofield's name and his home town. The 1875-6 Hammitt's Directory of South Jersey lists "C.Scofield & Co., Vineland Machine Works," where it is assumed the boxes were made.

Francis S. Dangerfield, from Auburn, New York, held two U.S. Invention Patents and one Canadian patent. The first was filed in 1879, the second in 1880 for an improved version of his first patent. The Canadian patent was filed in 1881 and was the same as his 1880 U.S. patent. The end product is shown in **Fig. 159.** The example substantially meets his specifications for a box that ejects one match at a time, igniting the match as it does so; but in this case a cigar cutter has been added to the box, which was not a part of the patent. It is made of tin plate, and marked on one side under the rim of the lid "MANUFACTURED BY HARVEY D. BLAKESEE. BUFFALO, N.Y." and on the exposed part of the same side "DANGERFIELD'S IGNITING MATCH CASE" plus all three patent dates.

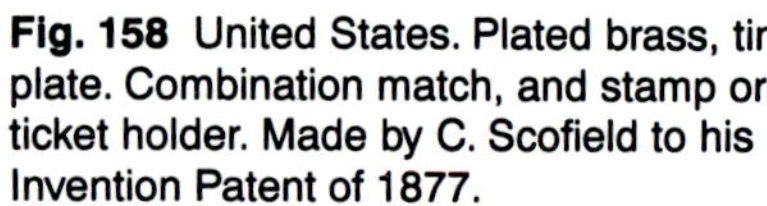

Fig. 158 United States. Plated brass, tin plate. Combination match, and stamp or ticket holder. Made by C. Scofield to his Invention Patent of 1877.

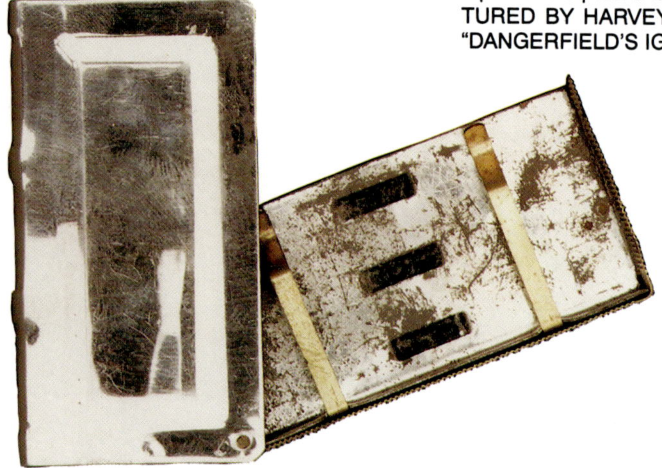

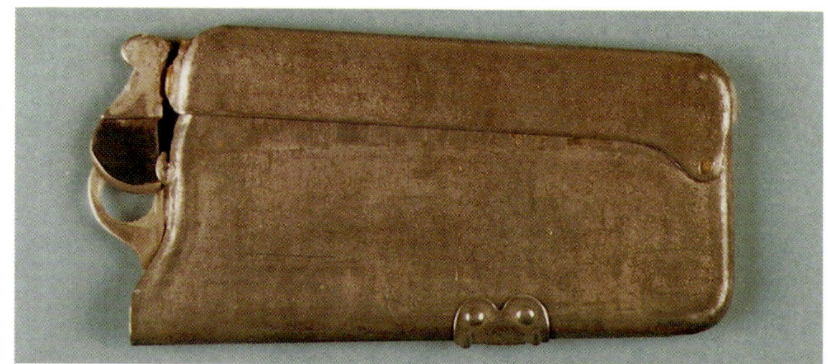

Fig. 159 United States. Tin plate. Made by Harvey D. Blakeslee to an Invention Patent of 1880 by Francis S. Dangerfield. L - 8.9cms.

Between Smith's 1860 Invention Patent and Dangerfield's of 1880, several other pocket match holders are known to have been patented and produced, but the next example illustrated here, shown in **Fig. 160**, was issued in 1882 to Arthur P. Yates of Syracuse, New York, for a "Combined pocket-case and cigar-clipper". Yates provided two options in his patent drawings, but it is believed that only the version shown was produced; it does not bear a maker's name. Made of plated brass and with a steel cigar cutter, it gives access to the matches by means of the lid, which is at the bottom in the illustration. The box is shown in a catalogue put out by Peck & Snyder of New York in]886, with the caption "The only practical combined pocket match safe and cigar clipper. Made of white metal and finely embossed, the neatest and best article in the market. Price per dozen, $4.50. Each, 50 cents." The illustration showed two holes of different sizes to take the tip of cigars.

Another combined match holder and cigar cutter is shown in **Fig. 161**. It was the subject of one of four invention patents issued in 1885 to William M. Ducker of New York City, all displaying variations of the same theme. The box is made of plated brass, with the steel cutter fixed to the hinge pin and passing between two cones set in either side of the lid, cutting off the tip of the cigar as the lid is closed. Ducker had his own company and no doubt made this box.

A box made with a "flanged joln" technique, as described in Part 1 of this chapter, was the subject of a patent issued to John Lines as assignor to the Scovill Manufacturing Co. of Waterbury, Connecticut in 1884. It is shown in **Fig. 162 left**. Essentially, his claim was for the method of hinging the lid. It is made of brass with a gilt finish, the bezel riveted to the main body and stamped with the patent date. These boxes were made for many years with various raised surface designs in floral and geometric patterns. The example in **Fig. 162 right** has a gilt lacquer finish, but the bezel is formed by extending the height of the body sides; it is unmarked. This is perhaps a later version made by Scovill, and was illustrated in a 1908 catalogue of the Simmons Hardware Co., of St.Louis, Missouri, for $4.75 per dozen.

Very similar boxes were shown in the George Zorn & Co. catalogue of 1892, in 'Old Silver' at $1.00 per dozen, and in 'Old Gold' at $1.10 per dozen. However, they appear to be slightly smaller and with a different shaped bezel, and may have been made by another company. George Zorn & Co. was located in Philadelphia, Pennsylvania, trading in domestic and imported pipes and smokers' articles, and in its 1892 catalogue showed some forty-three 'Plain and Fancy Pocket Match Safes', mostly full size, several of which are referred to herein.

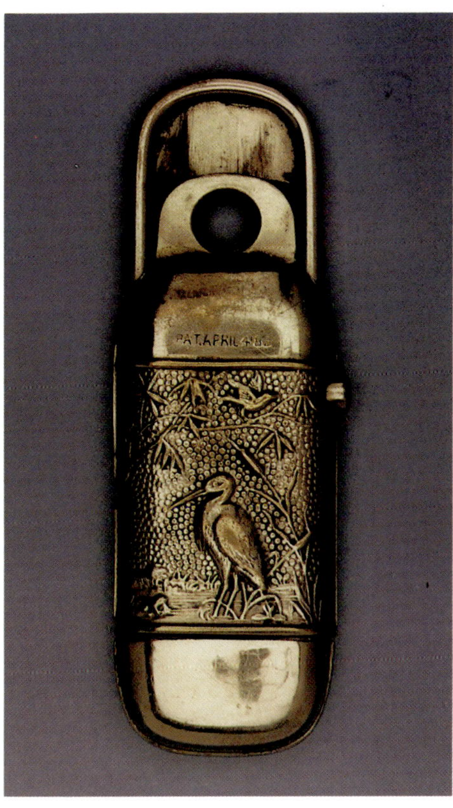

Fig. 160 United States. Plated brass, steel. Made to an Invention Patent of 1882 by Arthur P. Yates. H - 9.2cms.

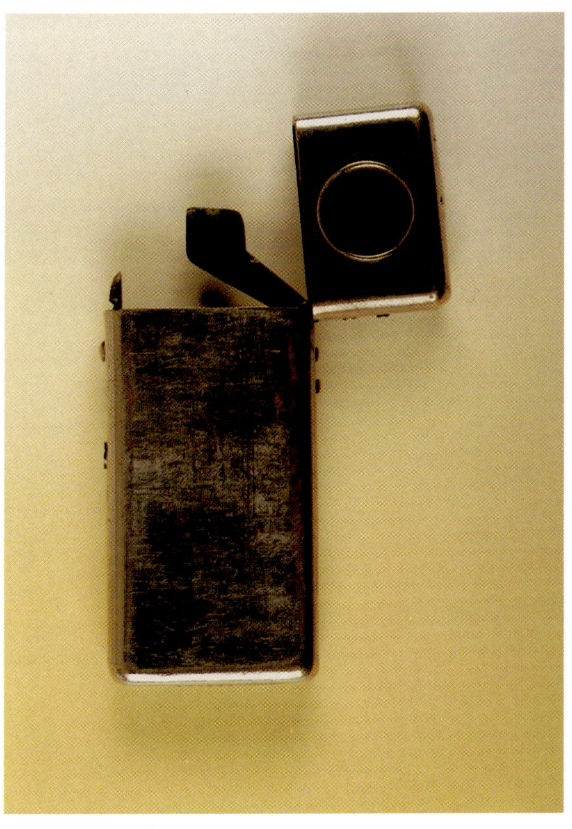

Fig. 161 United States. Plated brass, steel. Made by William M. Ducker to his Invention Patent of 1885. H - 8cms.

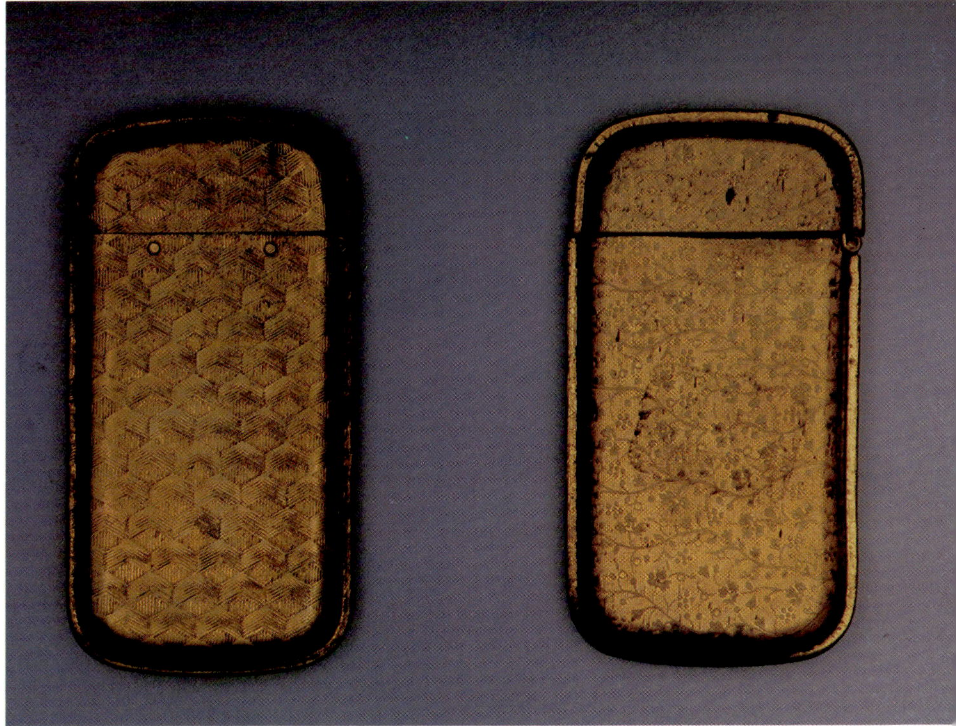

Fig. 162 United States. Brass. Left: Made by the Scovill Mfg.Co., to an Invention Patent of 1884 by John Lines. H - 7.6cms. Right: probably by the same company, but c.1908. H - 7.5cms.

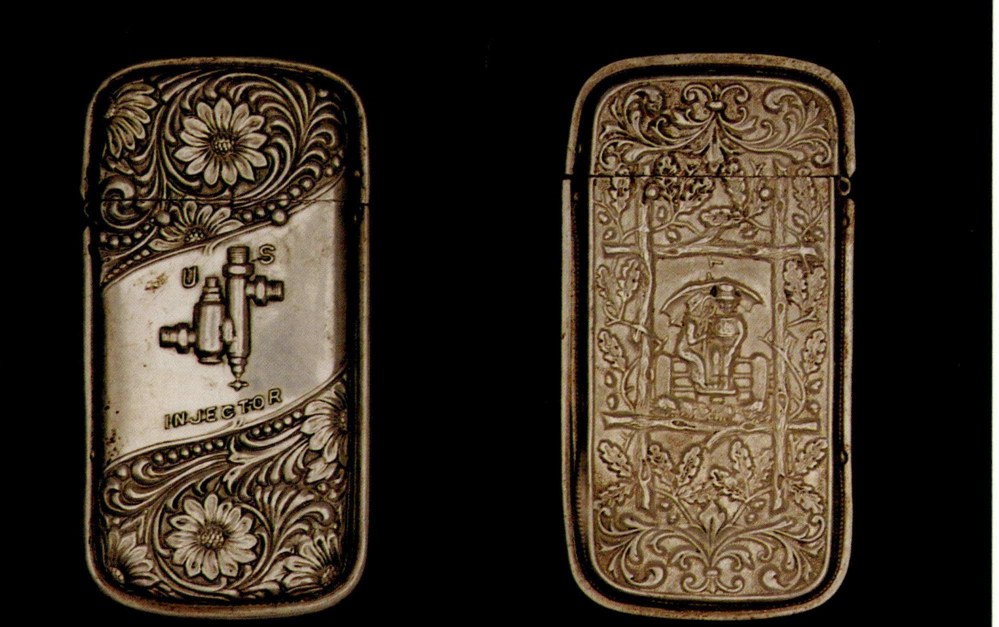

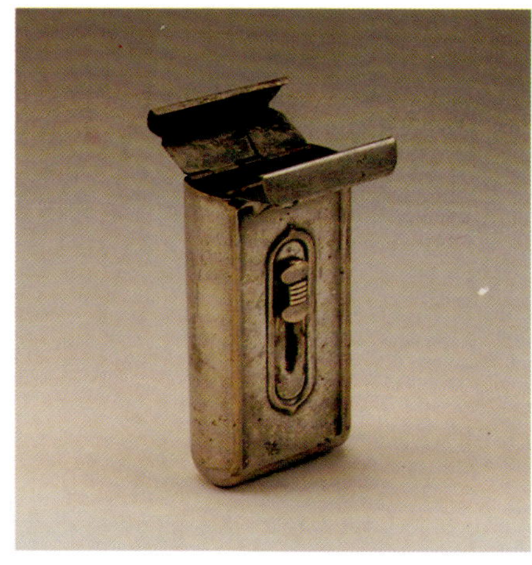

Fig. 164 United States. Plated brass. c.1892-1896. H - 6.4cms.

Fig. 163 United States. Aluminum. Left: made by the N.J. Aluminum Co.. c.1900. H - 7.6cms. Right: c.1892. H - 7.6cms.

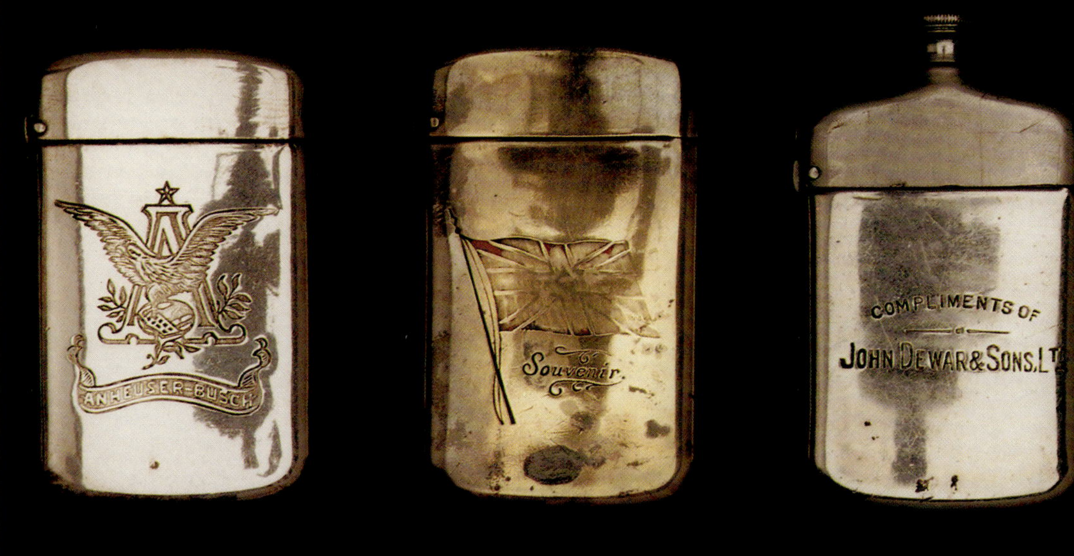

Fig. 166 United States. Plated brass. Made by William Schimper & Co., to an Invention Patent of 1897 by Ernest Oldenbusch. H(left) - 6.5cms., (right) - 6.8cms.

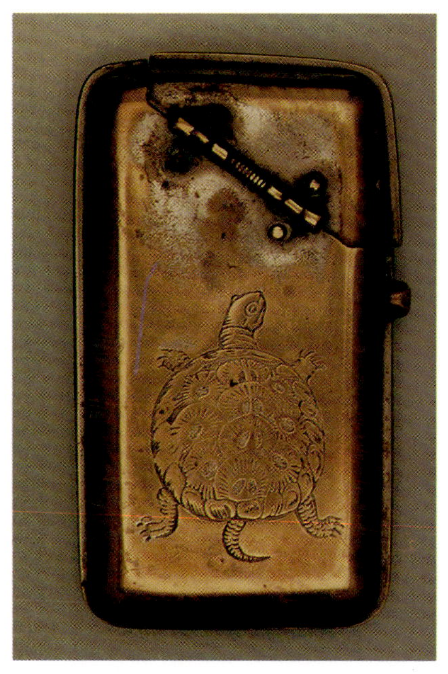

Fig. 165 United States. Plated brass. c.1892. H - 7.3cms.

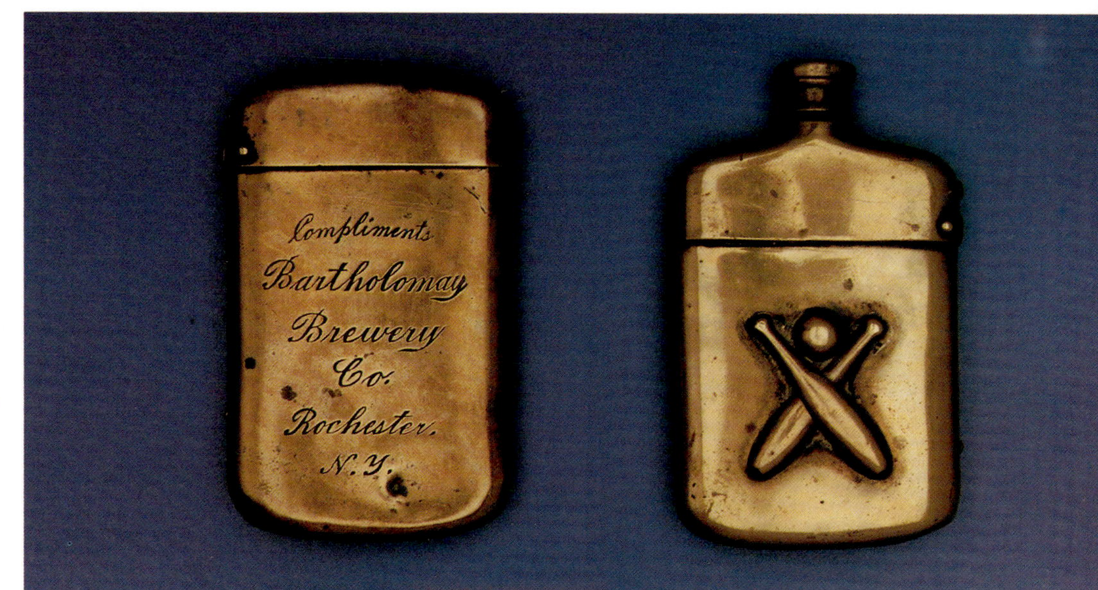

Fig. 167 United States. Brass (probably originally plated). Probably made under license to Schimper examples as in Fig. 166. Left: by Barstow & Williams, pre 1904. H - 6.4cms. Right: H -6.5cms.

Two match holders made of aluminum and with flanged joins are shown in **Fig. 163**. That to the left is marked on the bezel "N.J.Aluminum Co., Newark, N.J.," who began to make novelties in 1895, and ceased operations as an independent company in 1908. That to the right is unmarked and was also apparently made in tinware with nickel-plated and oxidized finishes. In Zorn's catalogue, the aluminum version sold at $2.00 per dozen or $22.00 per gross, and the tinware version at $1.50 per dozen or $16.50 per gross. They were also shown in a catalogue by Hobbs Hardware of London, Ontario, in about 1898.

The example in **Fig. 164** is made of nickel-plated brass, with a pair of lids that are opened by means of a sliding button on one side, the action lifting the matches in the box above the edge of the opening. These too were shown in the Zorn catalogue, at $1.25 per dozen or $13.50 per gross, and in the 1895-96 mail-order catalogue of Montgomery Ward & Co. of Chicago at 14¢ each or $1.50 per dozen.

In nickel-plated brass, with lids on each side that open diagonally, is the holder in **Fig. 165**. The two halves of the holder have flanged edges, but are without return lips, and the flanges are soldered together to form the join. The tortoise design appears on three boxes in the Zorn catalogue, each with a quite different form of lid, but otherwise of the same construction; no doubt all were made by the same company and around the same date of c. 1892.

Ernest Oldenbusch held a number of patents, including several for match holders, as an assignor to William Schimper & Co. of Hoboken, New Jersey. Three boxes in **Fig. 166** are marked on the bezel with an Oldenbusch patent date for 1897 and with the company name, all of nickel-plated brass. The patent was for the lid hinge arrangement. The example at the right is in the form of a spirit flask. They appear to have been used mostly for advertising or as souvenirs, but plain versions did occur and were shown in a 1902 Sears, Roebuck & Co. mail-order catalogue at 9¢ each for the rectangular type, and 18¢ each for the flask.

Fig. 167 shows two further examples of the same type. That to the left, in plated brass, is marked on the bezel "Barstow & Williams," a company which started about 1880 by manufacturing jewelry, adding silver novelties about 1888; Williams left in 1904 and the company became N. Barstow & Co.. The example on the right is unmarked, but the reverse side is engraved "COMPLIMENTS OF DOUGLAS PAVILION, CHICAGO." They appear to be made to the Oldenbusch patent, and it is assumed they were made under license to Schimper.

August Goertz of Newark, New Jersey, was in the business of manufacturing novelties, particularly handbag or purse frame parts, by 1884, when he filed his first patent. But it was not until 1892 that he filed a patent for a 'Stamp and Match Box'. This was also the last patent that he was to file personally, other patents being filed by his assignors until well into the 1930s.

Two versions of his 1892 patent are shown in **Fig. 168.** The version at the left conforms to his patent, with a pair of lids on the top of the box, the smaller covering the stamp compartment, the larger for the matches, and marked with the patent date. The two examples at the right also bear the same patent date, but they do not meet the patent drawings or specifications. The lid houses a stamp compartment covered by its own lid, the whole thing sliding on the main body. A third version has been seen with a hinged lid, with the stamp compartment inside the main body, and marked with the wrong patent date, of "Oct. 14" instead of "Oct. 11". All three versions have the same size main body with the striker located on the base in the form of a rectangular patch of corrugations. Goertz appears to have been careless with patent dates marked on his products, with two other known mistakes recorded later.

From about 1895 until at least 1918 Benno vom Eigen filed all of the Goertz patents, and was probably employed by Goertz as an engineer in the company. The match box of his first patent, in 1900, is shown in **Fig. 169.** It is an unusual form, the two halves being held together by the hinge pin, which is made of flat spring steel, twisted in tension, and held in place at each end to force the two halves of the box together. The scooped out section at the front allows a match to be pulled out of the box without opening the box. It is made of nickel-plated tinware, and is marked on the inside with the patent date and "H.B.H. & Co. N.Y.", which is H. B. Hardenburg & Co., who presumably made these boxes under license from Goertz.

Fig. 168 United States. Brass, plated. Match and stamp boxes. Made by Aug. Goertz & Co. to his Invention Patent of 1892. Left: L -7cms. Right: 6.9cms.

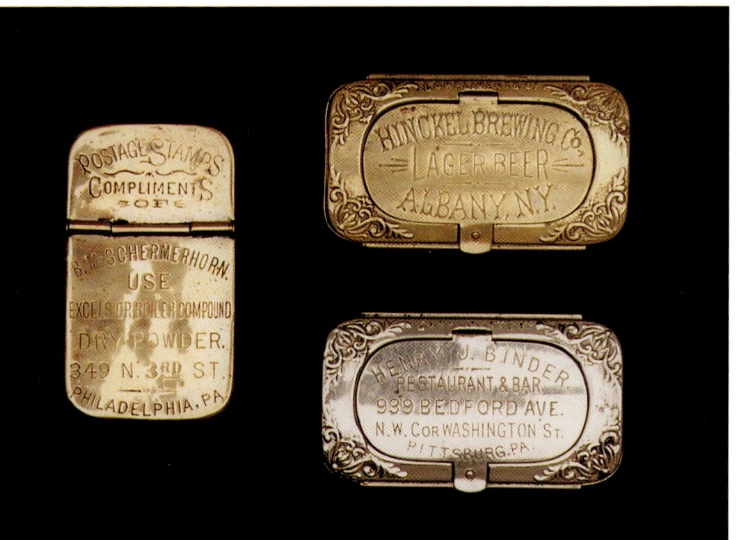

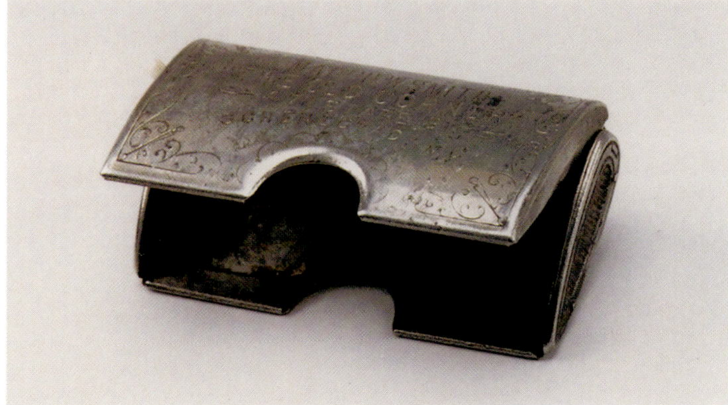

Fig. 169 United States. Plated tin plate. Made by H. B. Hardenburg & Co., to an Invention Patent of 1900 issued to Benno vom Eigen of Aug. Goertz & Co.. Probably made under license. L - 6.7cms.

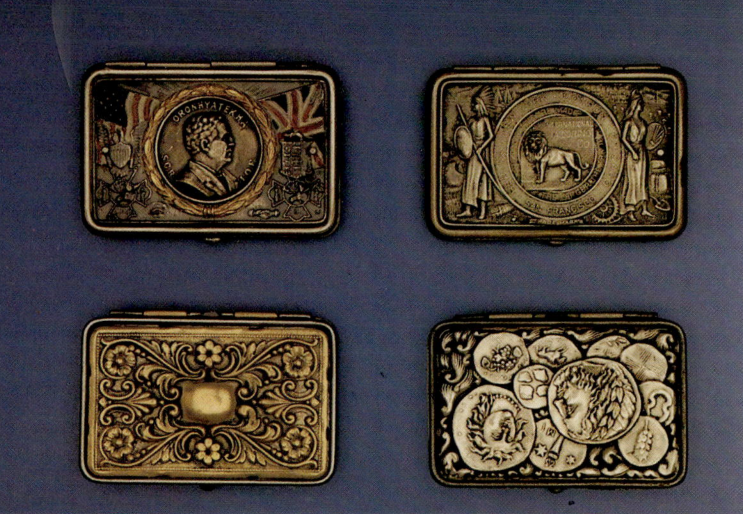

Fig. 170 United States. Plated brass. Top: left enamelled. Made by Aug. Goertz & Co., to an Invention Patent of 1904 by Benno vom Eigen. L - 6.2cms. Lower: probably made by Aug. Goertz & Co. pre 1904? L - 6.1cms.

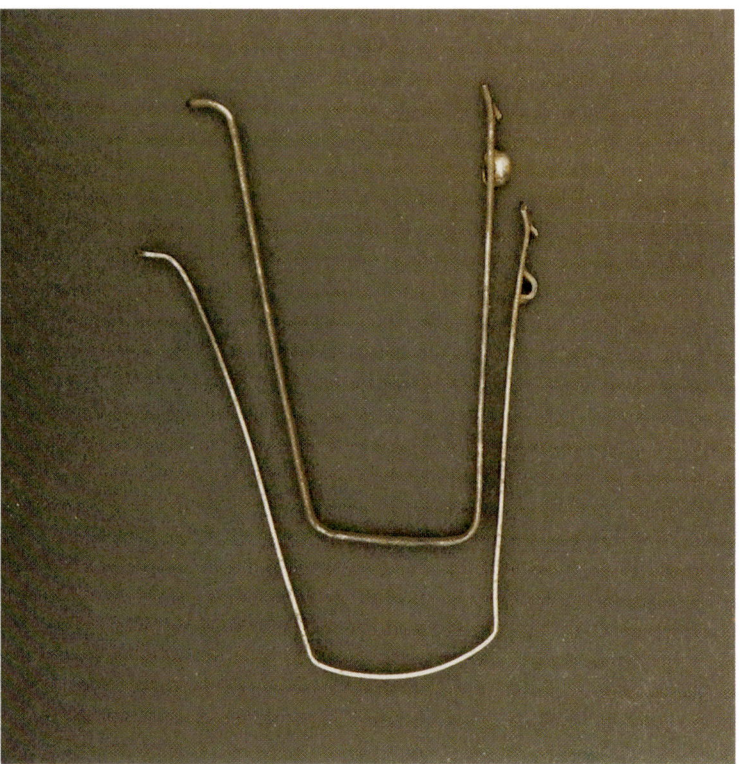

Fig. 172 United States. Steel. Springs from boxes in Fig. 171. Inner: with thumb push added (from box at right). Outer: the Ashworth patent, with thumb push formed by part of spring (from box at left).

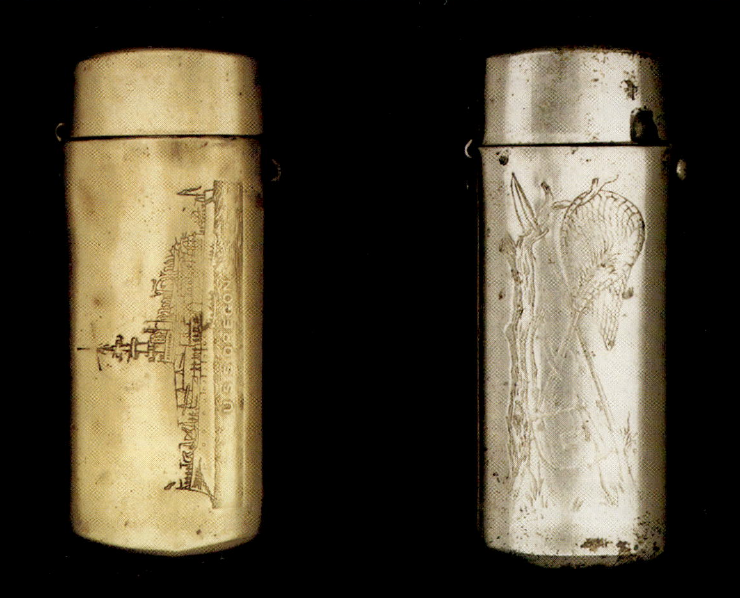

Fig. 171 United States. Brass, plated. Left: Made by the Waterbury Mfg. Co., to an Invention Patent of 1897 by Richard J. Ashworth. H - 7.2cms. Right: Made from c.1892 to 1913. H - 7.4cms.

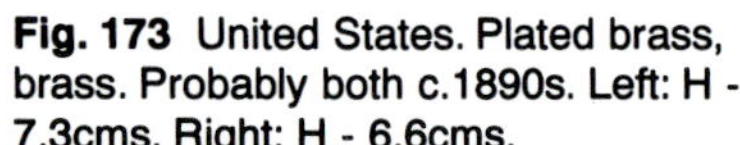

Fig. 173 United States. Plated brass, brass. Probably both c.1890s. Left: H - 7.3cms. Right: H - 6.6cms.

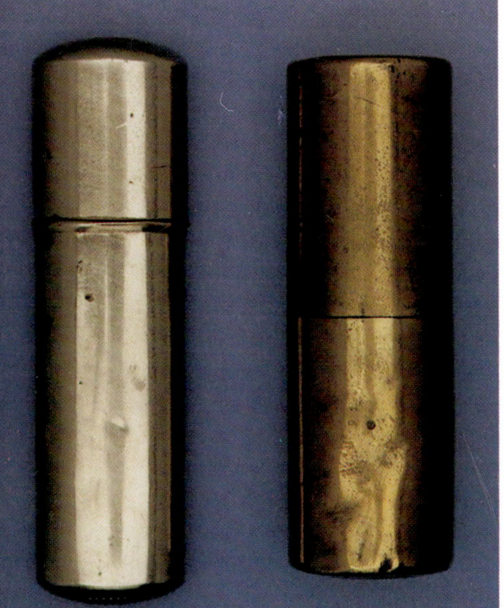

The four boxes in **Fig. 170** superficially appear to be made by the same manufacturer, but only the top two are marked; the lower two lack marks and have some very minor technical differences. Vom Eigen was issued with two patents relating to this type of box, in March and May of 1904. They are all hinged longitudinally.

The box at the upper left is marked with a patent date for January 1904, another vom Eigen patent but for a totally different type of box—the second known example of a Goertz mistake. The box was made in 1907 and must have been a special order for Goertz. It has a nickel-plated brass body and lid, as do all four boxes, but the plate attached to the lid is in silver with enamelled decoration. This must have been a most unusual feature on an otherwise inexpensive box.

The plate was made to commemorate the death of Oronhyatekha, a remarkable Mohawk born on the Six Nations Reserve near Brantford, Ontario, and given the Anglicized name of Peter Martin. He spent three years at Oxford University, returning to Canada to complete his medical degree at the University of Toronto. He later joined the Independent Order of Foresters, going on to become elected as the Supreme Chief Ranger in 1881, guiding the order from a membership of four hundred and on the brink of bankruptcy, to a membership of more than a quarter of a million and a fund of eleven million dollars. At his death it was said of him, "As an Indian he was, perhaps, the greatest man of his race."

The underside of the box is impressed with an image of the Temple Building in Toronto, the headquarters of the Independent Order of Foresters. Each end has a striker for friction matches; inside the lid, exposed through a rectangular hole, is a piece of safety match striker, held in place by the top plate.

The box in **Fig. 170 top right** is provided with a top plate embossed with advertising for the International Tailoring Co. It is marked inside with a patent date for March 1904, the earlier of the two correct patents relating to this type of box.

The two boxes in **Fig. 170 bottom** are unmarked and show minor differences in construction details, with the striker located along the back edge, and the front plate attached by means of lugs set into slots in the lid. It is assumed that these boxes were made by Goertz, possibly before the two vom Eigen patents of 1904.

Of oval cross-section are two boxes in **Fig. 171** that are very similar in appearance. That to the left has a patent date for 1897, but that to the right was being produced by c. 1892 and continued to be made until well into the l900s. The patented example was made by the Waterbury Manufacturing Co. of Connecticut, to a patent issued to Richard J. Ashworth for the internal spring. The form of the spring was a common element in oval boxes, the push-button on the front edge being made from a separate piece, usually in brass. The Ashworth design had the push button made directly from the spring, thus eliminating the necessity of making a separate piece and then fixing it to the spring. Examples of the springs are shown in **Fig. 172.**

The Waterbury box has an engraving of the *U.S.S. Oregon,* a battleship built in San Francisco in 1897, and sent the following year to join the U.S. Fleet in the Caribbean to help in the Spanish-American war. The only available route was around the Horn, so the *Oregon* took close to three months before it could get on station. It was this journey that tipped the scales in the United States in favor of building the Panama Canal, thus reducing significantly the sea voyage from coast to coast.

Several variations of oval boxes with springs bearing a separate button were produced, and appear in the Zorn catalogue at 60¢ per dozen or $6.00 per gross; in the Montgomery Ward & Co. catalogue of 1895-96 at 5¢ each or 50¢ per dozen; and in two hardware company catalogues in 1908 and 1913 at $1.20 per dozen. These were all made of brass, often nickel-plated, and with a variety of engraved designs.

Examples of two unmarked, plain, simple boxes with slip-on lids may be seen in **Fig. 173**. That to the left is of oval cross-section, made of nickel-plated brass. They were shown in the Zorn catalogue at 35¢ per dozen or $4.00 per gross, and a larger version at 5¢ more. The box at the right is of round cross-section in plain brass, but has not been traced. Both types are probably from the 1890s.

The example in **Fig. 174** is a combined "Match-safe and Lamp," the subject of a patent issued to Charles Jacobi of Ransom, Illinois, in 1878. It is unmarked but probably made by Jacobi, from two brass tubes soldered together: the smaller tube for the matches, the larger for the lamp. It has a wick, almost filling the section, and held in place by a screw-on plate; the wick was fueled with coal oil. The base of this section is roughened for friction. Both lids are of the slip-on type.

The waterproof match holder in **Fig. 175** was first produced in 1900 and is still being made in the 1990s, which must be an almost unprecedented record for an invention. The invention patent was issued to Webster L. Marble of Gladstone, Michigan, who had his own company specializing in items for the outdoor enthusiast. His patent specifications stated:

> "Lumbermen, hunters, sportsmen, and all who have occasion to live an outdoor life are frequently subjected to great inconvenience and even hardship by having their matches get wet. The ordinary pocket match safe is not water-tight and will not long prevent the entrance of moisture, especially if the wearer accidentally falls into a stream or lake. The need of an absolutely impervious match-box has long been appreciated, and my invention aims to meet this need".

His invention succeeded, probably beyond his wildest dreams, for it was made bearing his name until at least 1939, and is still being made in Hong Kong today and imported into North America. A modern example may be seen in Fig. 685.

His design may have been inspired by a shotgun shell, which it resembles, but the end product underwent some minor changes, probably to reduce manufacturing costs, and some models include a ring for attachment to a belt or clip, which was not an original part of the patent. It was, and still is, sold throughout North America; the following table traces its sale over the years, mostly from Canadian sources:

1910—Hudson's Bay Co., Winnipeg	50¢ each
1927—Sears, Roebuck & Co., Chicago	48¢ each
1930—Marshall-Wells Co.Ltd., Winnipeg	$12.60/doz.
1932—Caverhill, Learmont & Co. Ltd., Montreal	$14.40/ doz.
1939—Marble Arms & Mfg. Co., Gladstone	60¢ each
1992—Scout Camping Centre, Ottawa	$3.10 each

Webster L. Marble was raised to the outdoor life, until at age forty-four in 1898, he established his business of manufacturing axes, knives, the waterproof match holder, and other items for use by recreational and professional woodsmen. He had over twenty patents, and the company grew rapidly, quickly gaining national recognition for the quality of its products—a reputation that lasted until well after his death in 1930. His designs were copied, and other companies made identical products, leading to a steady decline for Marble's company, from which it never fully recovered. Webster Marble's waterproof match holder reflects the life of the company.

Park Sherman Co., of Springfield, Illinois produced a similar waterproof match holder, also made of plated brass, and shown in **Fig. 176**. It is marked "Everdry," but apart from the company name there is no indication of the date, and examples have not been found in any catalogues. They may well have been produced in the first two decades of this century. Probably not patentable because of Marble's patent, they were sufficiently different to avoid any court action.

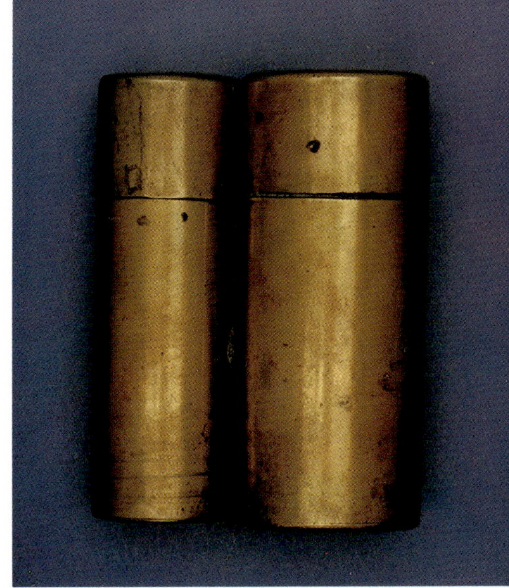

Fig. 174 United States. Brass, cotton. Lamp and match holder. Made by Charles Jacobi to his Invention Patent of 1878. H - 5.9cms.

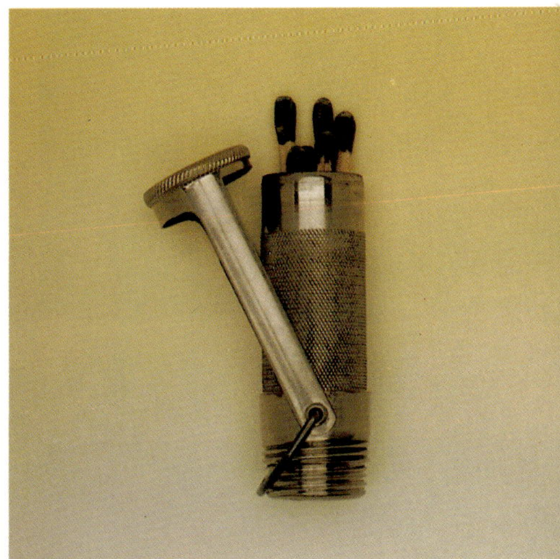

Fig. 175 United States. Plated brass. Waterproof. Made by Webster L. Marble to his patent of 1900, until at least 1932. Made today in Hong Kong. H - 6.7cms.

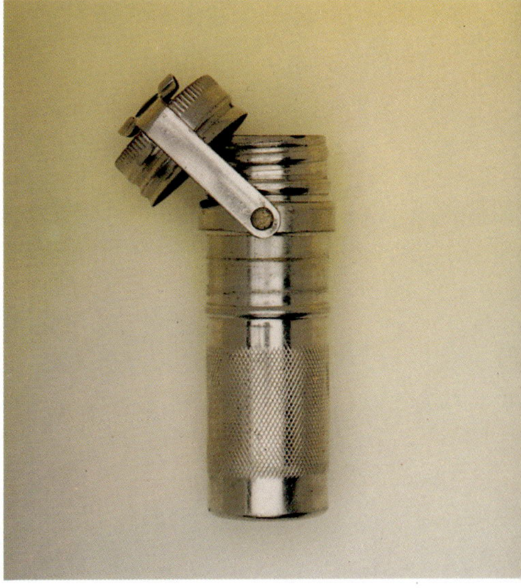

Fig. 176 United States. Plated brass. Waterproof. Made by the Park Sherman Co. probably post 1917. H - 7cms.

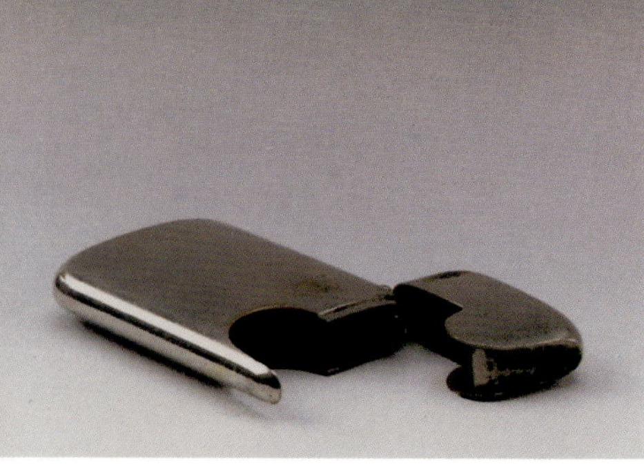

Fig. 177 United States. Plated brass. Made to an Invention Patent of 1900 by Thomas A. Bell. H - 6.4cms.

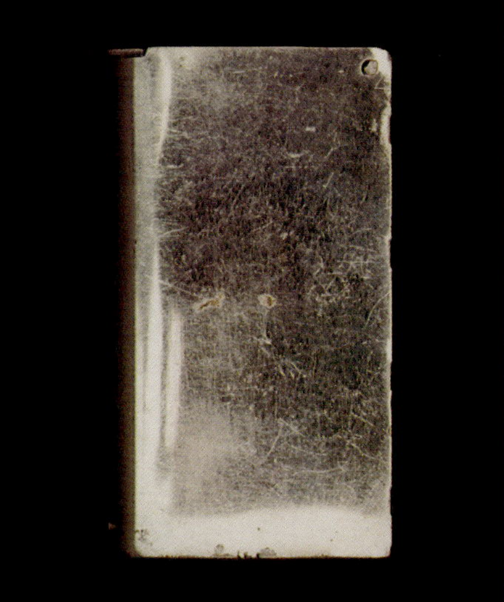

Fig. 178 United States. Plated tin plate. Marked "BeBe". c.1900. H - 5.9cms.

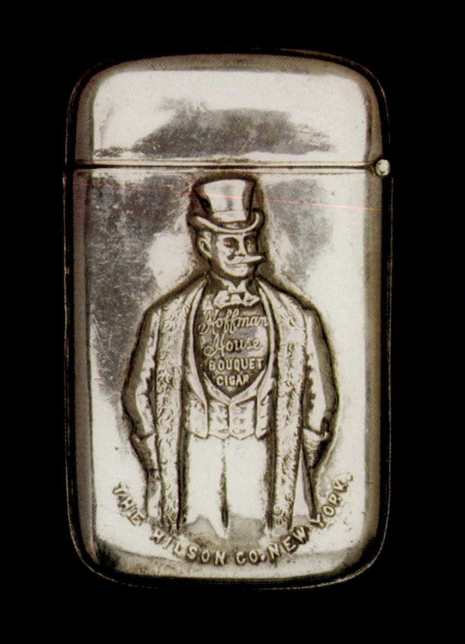

Fig. 180 United States. Plated brass. Possibly by Whitehead & Hoag Co. c.1900. H - 6.6cms.

Fig. 181 United States. Brass; plated brass. Top: c.1900. H -7.2cms. Lower: c.1895. H - 7.3cms.

In 1900, Thomas Addison Bell of Birmingham, Alabama, was issued a patent for a match box that would ignite a match as it was withdrawn. His patent drawings included three versions of the lid arrangement, an example of which is shown in **Fig. 177**. The box is made of nickel-plated brass and marked with the patent date, but no maker's name. The matches were placed in the box with the heads down. To remove a match the lid had to be opened and the stem of a match gripped and partially withdrawn before the lid was closed upon the head; upon withdrawal the head of the match passed between two striking surfaces located on the front edge of the lid and the inside edge of the box body. This has been tried and found to be difficult, with the head of the match, or particles of the igniting compound, dropping back into the box, which is potentially dangerous.

The match holder in **Fig. 178** is made of plated tinware. It has a flat lid at the top, marked on the front edge "BeBe" in an oval. The striker on the bottom edge is of some chemical composition intended for use with safety or strike-anywhere matches. It probably dates from c. 1900.

The two boxes in **Fig. 179** are made with a flange join technique as shown in Fig. 78.b. Both are marked "W & H. Newark, N.J." for the Whitehead & Hoag Co., and made of nickel-plated brass. They were mostly used for advertising the central panel on both sides bearing wording, and designs of products or a company building. They were probably made just before the turn of the century, after which time the company concentrated on its celluloid covered boxes, as shown in Part 5 of this chapter. The lids of these boxes were used in their early three piece boxes, and an example may be seen in Fig. 293.a.

The box in **Fig. 180** is unmarked but otherwise conforms precisely with the previous two, and may therefore have been made by Whitehead & Hoag.

The four examples in **Fig. 181** are also very similar, but slightly longer, and possess other very minor differences in certain elements. None has a maker's mark; all are of brass or nickel-plated. No patents have been found for any parts of these boxes, and there may have been one or two other companies making them before and after the Whitehead & Hoag versions were produced. They covered a range of markets, from advertising to souvenirs, commemoratives and retail outlets. The lower box was shown in a catalogue of Otto Young & Co. of Chicago, Illinois in 1895, in which it was said to be silver-plated at 60¢ each.

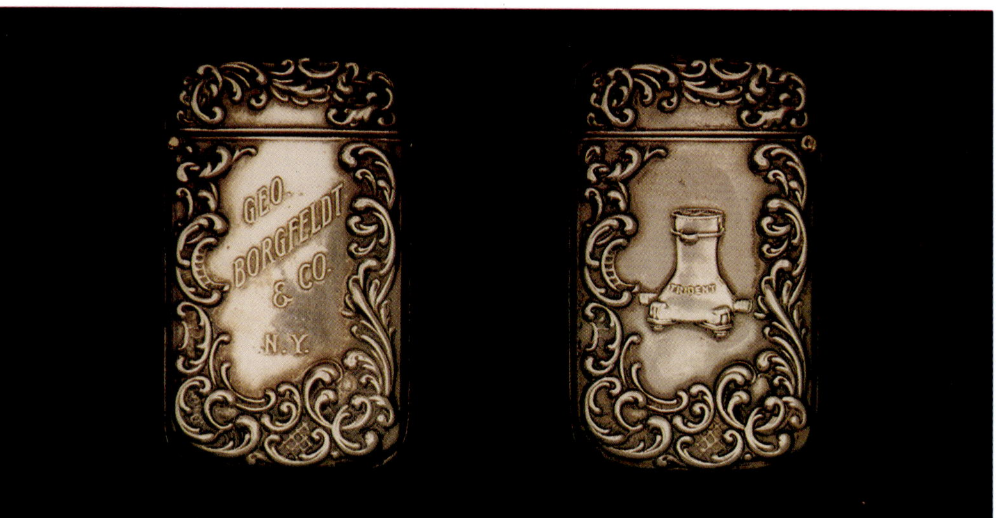

Fig. 179 United States. Plated brass. Made by Whitehead & Hoag Co. c.1900. H - 6.6cms.

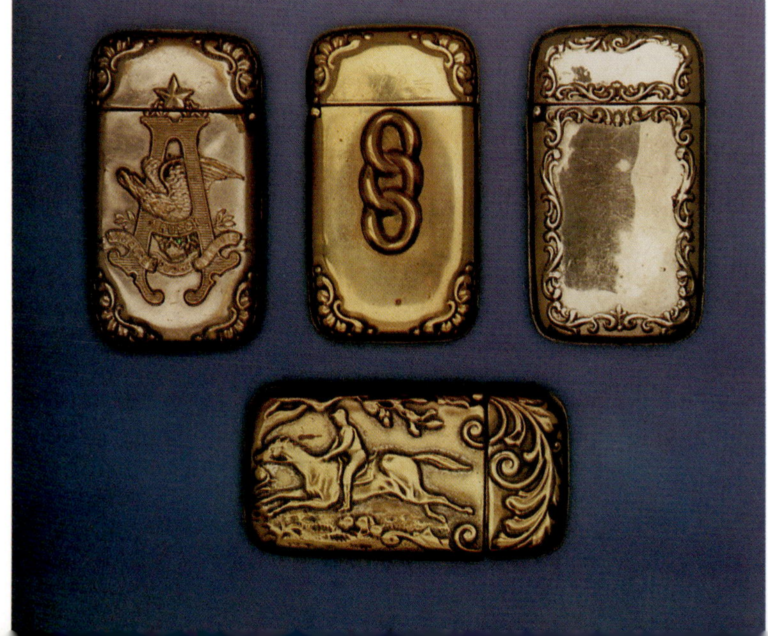

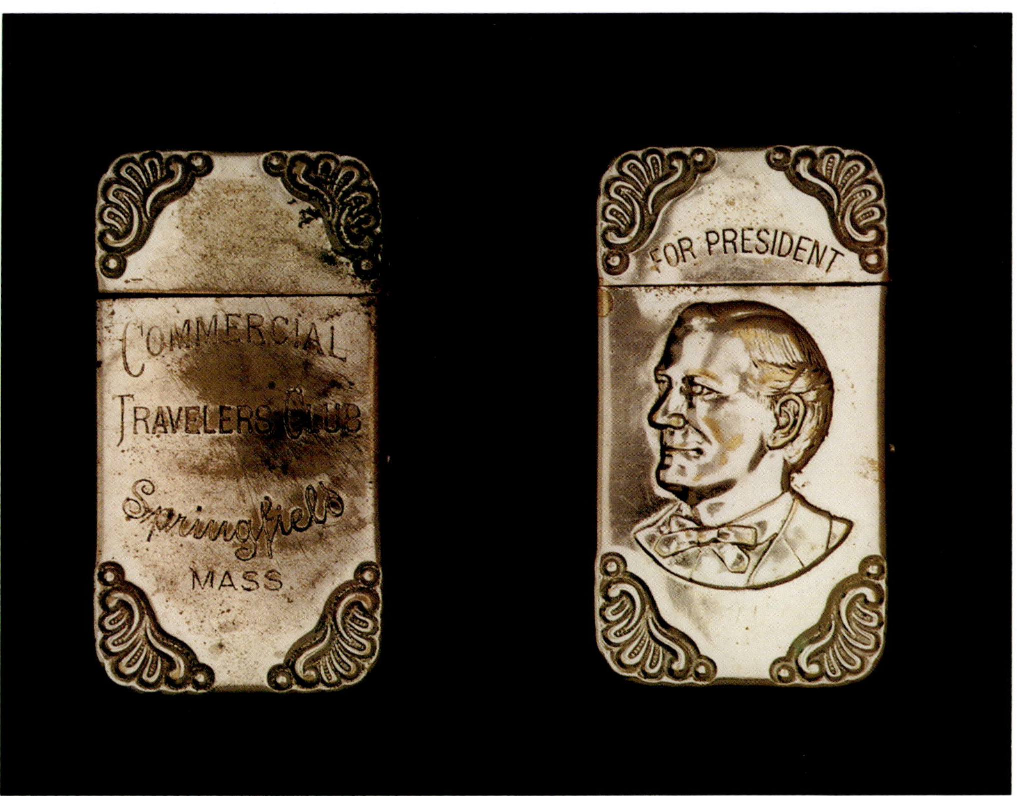

Fig. 182 United States. Plated brass. c.1897. H - 7.2cms.

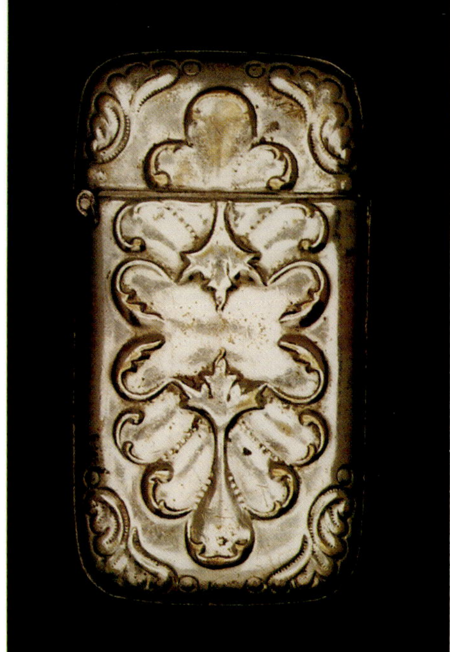

Fig. 183 United States. Plated brass. c.1900. H - 7.3cms.

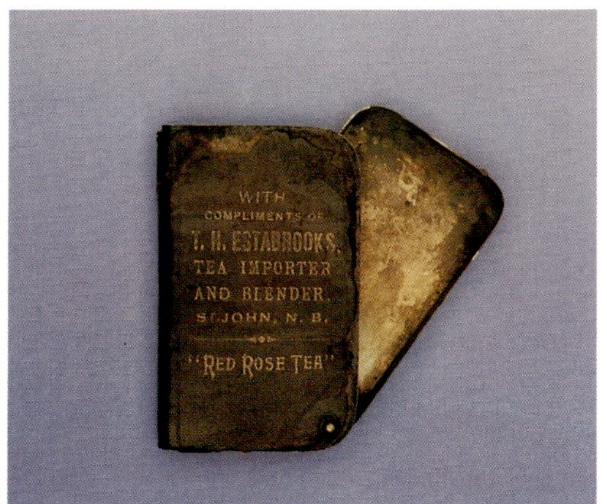

Fig. 185 United States. Brass, tin plate, leather. c.1905. H -6.2cms.

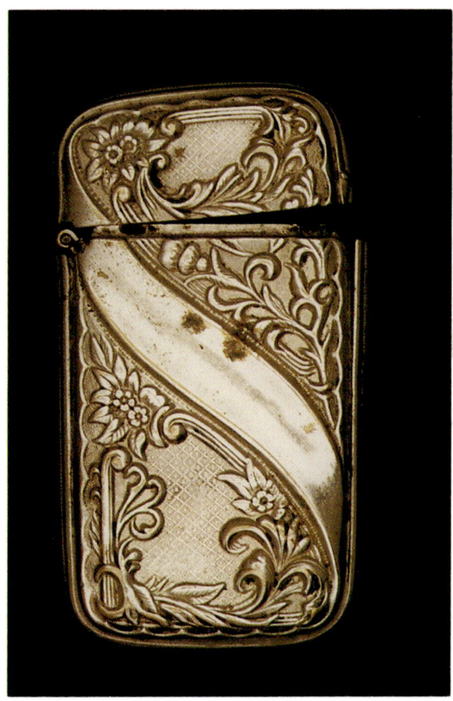

Fig. 184 United States. Plated brass. c.1894. H - 7.3cms.

The two match holders in **Fig. 182** are of poor quality, in nickel-plated brass. Obviously made by the same company, both can be accurately dated. The example at left is a souvenir of a "Clambake, August 6, 1897," and that to the right is inscribed "For President" and bears the head and shoulders of William Jennings Bryan, the Democratic nominee for the 1897 Federal Election (which he lost to William McKinley).

An even cheaper version of the two previous groups, in plated brass and unmarked, may be seen in **Fig. 183.** The join is formed by flanges with no return edges, butted together and soldered. It is probably c. 1900.

The example in **Fig. 184** is of nickel-plated brass, the two halves of the body and lid butted together, and joined by means of a strip soldered around the edges, the strip roughened for friction. It was shown in the Montgomery Ward & Co. catalogues of 1894 and 1895 at 20¢ each or $2.00 per dozen.

In a quite different style is an example in **Fig. 185** made to look like a book, the covers of red leather over tin plate. The match compartment is in the form of a tray, pivoted in one corner to swing out, and made of brass. It was probably made in the United States and exported to Canada. It is marked in red lettering "WITH COMPLIMENTS OF T.H. ESTABROOKS, TEA IMPORTER AND BLENDER. ST.JOHN, N.B. 'RED ROSE TEA'." It was probably made between 1900 and 1910. Theodore H. Estabrooks was a bookkeeper until about 1898, when he started his own tea importing and blending business. He created Red Rose tea in 1899, and it is still being produced today; if television advertising is to be believed, people from all over the world come to Canada "just for the tea." Estabrooks advertised every week in The Canadian Grocer from 1902 until at least 1908, with a different advertisement every week. By 1910 he had branches in five Canadian cities; in 1959 the family business was taken over.

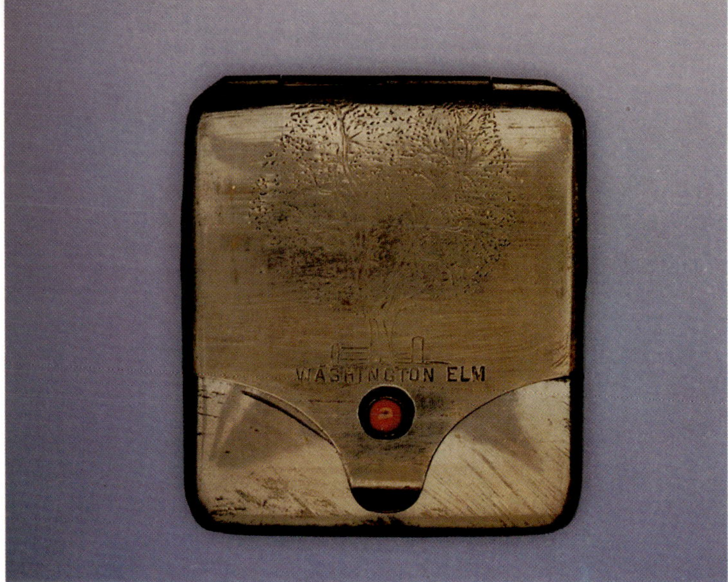

Fig. 186 United States. Brass, glass. Made by L. F. Grammes & Sons. 1908. H - 6.1cms.

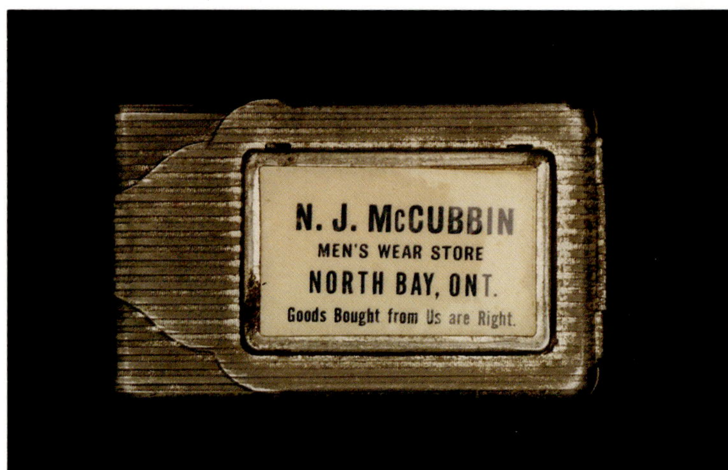

Fig. 187 United States. Tin plate, celluloid. Post 1906. L -6.7cms.

In brass with a bronzed finish, in what may be termed a 'satchel style', is the example in **Fig. 186**. The front flap lid is held closed by a red 'jewel' knob, and is engraved with a tree and the words "WASHINGTON ELM" below. The back is engraved with a representation of a lapel pin with the word "SOUVENIR," supporting a medallion, and below this the words "CAMBRIDGE COMMANDERY FIELD DAY, JUNE 24, 1908." It was made by L.F.Grammes & Sons of Allentown, Pennsylvania, who offered them in its 1909 catalogue at $52.00 per gross without advertising, "nicely polished and nickel plated. Suitable for paper and ordinary matches." The striker in the form of a strip of prepared paper is located inside the lid, and held in place by a pair of lugs formed by the edge of the lid being bent over.

The 'satchel style' example in **Fig. 187** is made of tin plate with a nickel-plated finish, on a ribbed surface that is adequate to serve as the striker. A frame to hold advertising matter is attached by lugs to the lid; in the example this is for a men's wear store in North Bay, Ontario, that opened in 1906. It holds a single line of matches. A larger version has also been seen, but neither has any makers mark. It is believed that it was made in the United States, but almost identical pieces have been marked "Germany." They probably date from about l910.

The two examples in **Fig. 188** are marked on the bezel "Silver soldered", and are silver-plated. That to the left also bears the mark of Maltby, Stevens & Curtiss, of Wallingford, Connecticut, who manufactured flatware between 1890 and 1896, before being taken over by the Watrous Manufacturing Co. The example at the right has no maker's mark, but the lid is engraved "Xms.88."

Also marked "Silver soldered," and probably silver-plated, are another two boxes in **Fig. 189**. The example at the right is marked "R. Wallace & Sons" of Wallingford, Connecticut; this company produced a wide range of match holders from the early 1880s. They were silversmiths and they may well have produced their boxes in silver and in plated versions to reach a wider spectrum of the population. The example to the left may also have been made by them, but does not bear a maker's mark.

The match holder in **Fig. l90** is marked "Pairpoint Mfg.Co." of New Bedford, Massachusetts, who traded under that name only from 1880 to 1900. It too manufactured a range of these boxes, and this one has a model number of "5003" marked on the bezel, and is silver-plated.

We see again the typically United States flamboyant style in the two examples in **Fig. 191**. They were made by the Bristol Silver Co., and are marked "Silveroin." The yacht represented in the example on the left may possibly be the *The Vigilant*, winner of the America's Cup in 1894, while the example at the right depicts a golfer; both images have rococo style surrounds.

In the same style is the example in **Fig. 192**. It is marked "German silver," an alloy of mostly copper, nickel and zinc; this name was dropped by most companies in World War I in favor of the term 'nickel silver'. This is probably c. 1900.

Probably silver-plated is an example of the Art Nouveau style, depicting a nude female emerging from a flower, shown in **Fig. 193**. It is unmarked and probably dates from c. 1910.

In nickel-plated brass, the example in **Fig. 194** has impressed swirls and fluting, and a broad plain band with the representation of a scorpion. This was probably intended as a birth sign for November; presumably others were made bearing the other signs of the Zodiac. It is unmarked and probably dates from the 1890s.

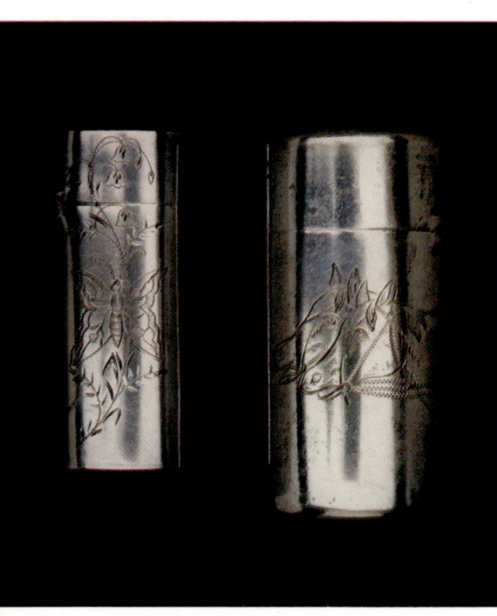

Fig. 188 United States. Silver plated. Left: made by Maltby, Stevens & Curtis. c.1890 to 1896. H - 5.8cms. Right: 1888. H -6.8cms.

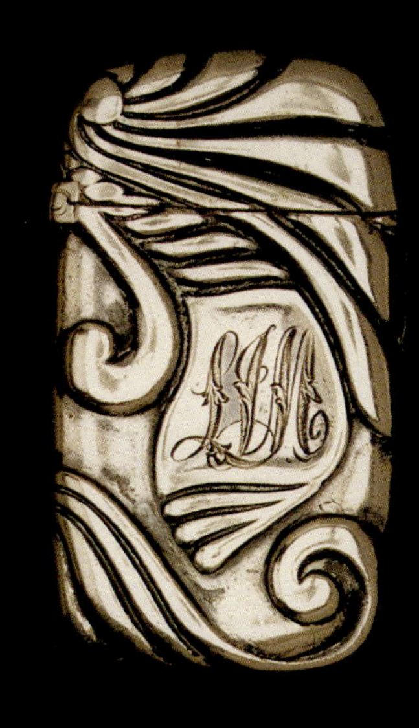

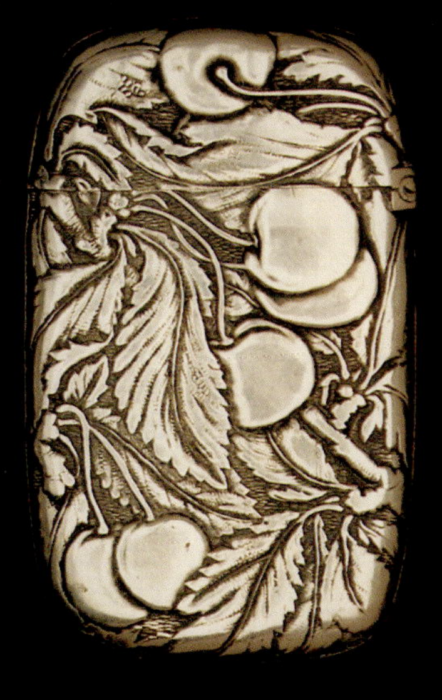

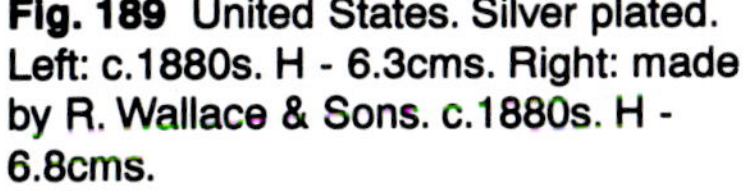

Fig. 189 United States. Silver plated. Left: c.1880s. H - 6.3cms. Right: made by R. Wallace & Sons. c.1880s. H - 6.8cms.

Fig. 193 United States. Silver plated. c.1910. H - 6.7cms.

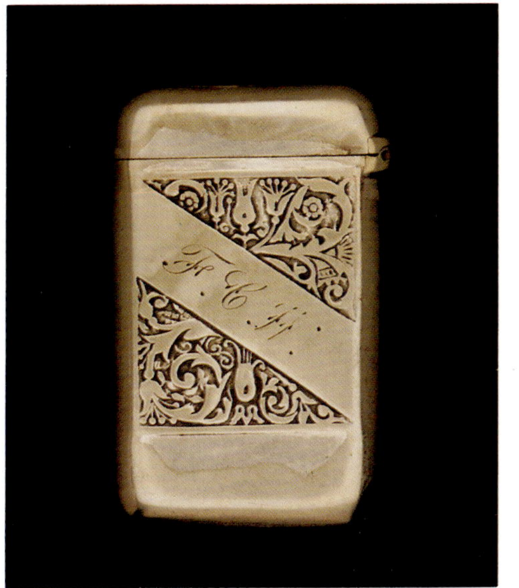

Fig. 190 United States. Silver plated. Made by Pairpoint Mfg. Co.. Between 1880 and 1900. H - 5.9cms.

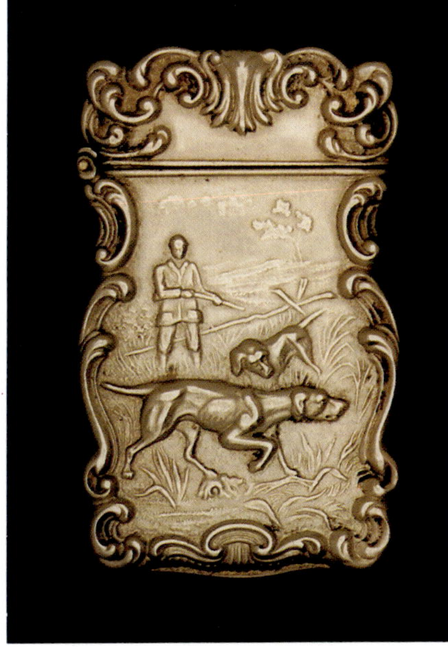

Fig. 192 United States. German or nickel silver. c.1900. H -6.7cms.

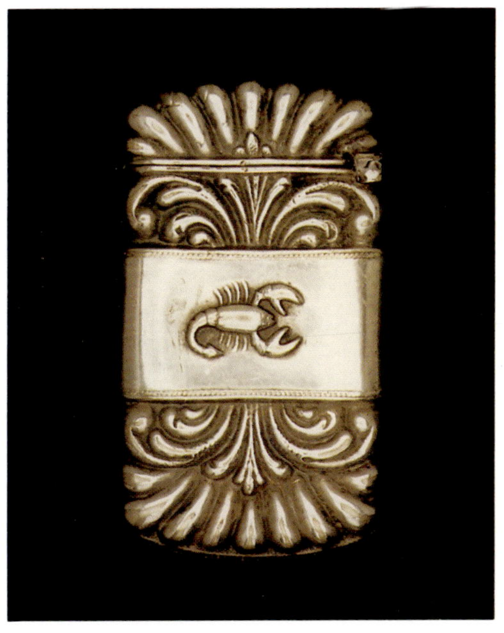

Fig. 194 United States. Plated brass. c.1890s. H - 6.4cms.

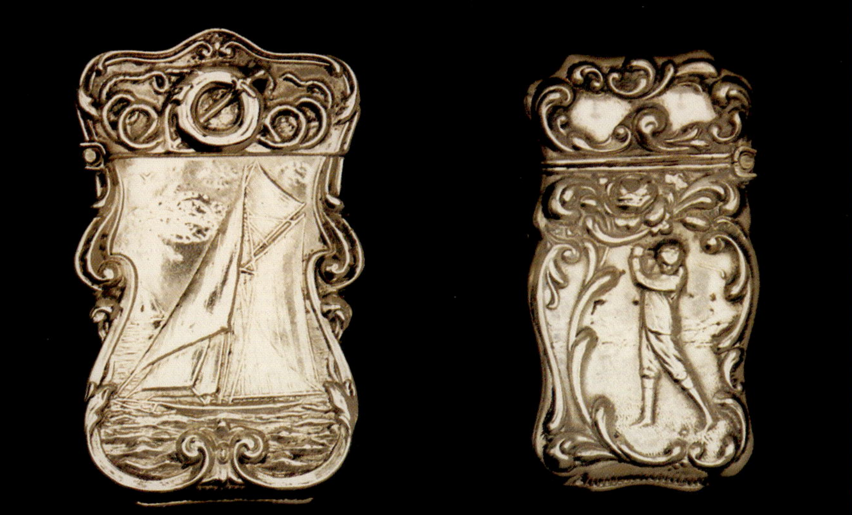

Fig. 191 United States. Alloy, marked "Silveroin". Made by the Bristol Silver Co. c.1905. Left: H - 6.4cms. Right: H - 5.9cms.

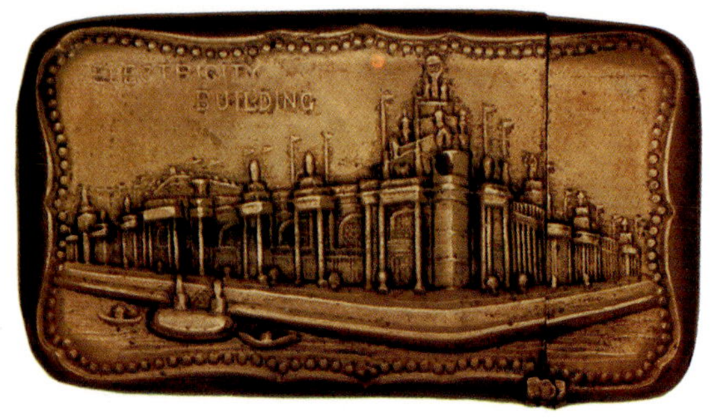

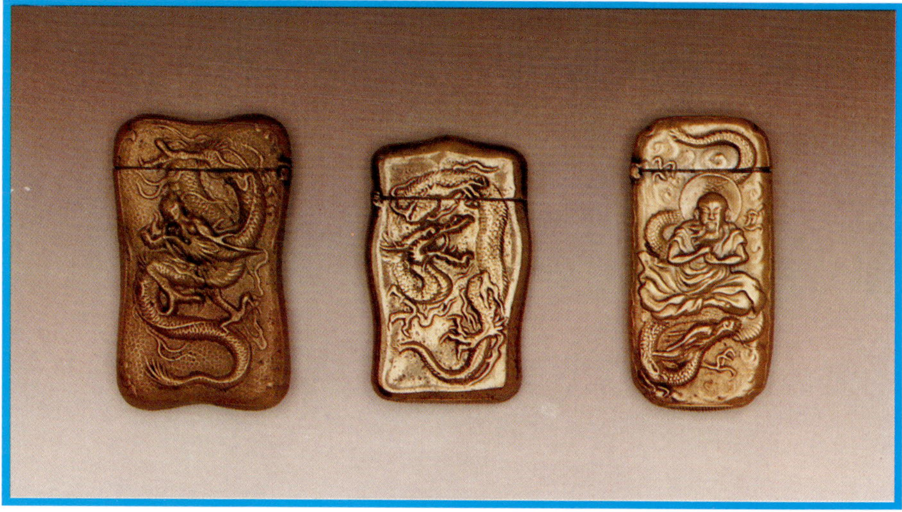

Fig. 196 Japan. Brass. c.1900. Left: H - 6.9cms. Centre: H -6.2cms. Right: 6.7cms.

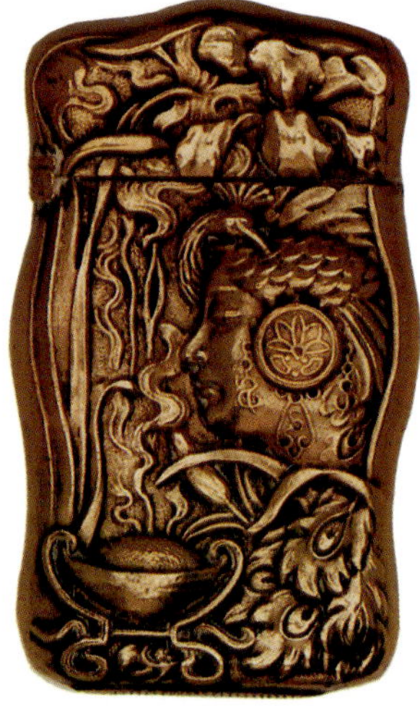

Fig. 195 United States. Brass. Probably made by Barstow & Williams. c.1904. Top: H - 6.7cms. Lower: 6.3cms.

Almost without exception, the production of pocket match holders in the United States was confined to the northeastern states, with no more than two hundred miles separating those companies farthest removed from one another.

Oriental art greatly influenced art forms and designs in Europe and the United States in the I9th century, inciuding match holders in the last quarter of the century. But the influence was not all one way, and the Japanese were particularly adept at copying the work of other nations in whose markets they competed. The results of copying can be seen in some match holders.

The two boxes shown in **Fig. 195** are made of brass, and were collected in the belief that they were of Japanese origin, since they exhibited several technical similarities to Japanese boxes. Both were made for the St.Louis World's Fair of 1904, and the lower example has what was perceived as a decidedly Oriental flavor. However, a second example with an identical design and made of silver has been seen, and was marked as "Barstow & Williams" of Providence, Rhode Island; it is therefore assumed that the brass example here was also made by that company.

This discovery led to a re-assessment of a number of similar brass boxes, leading to the attribution of the upper brass box to the United States, probably also made by Barstow & Williams.

The dragon was a favorite subject of Japanese art and mythology and three examples are shown in **Fig. 196.** The undulating outlines of two suggest United States influence. At least a dozen variations of boxes depicting dragons have been recorded.

A well-known Japanese myth of the rabbit and the malicious badger is depicted on the example in **Fig. 197.** The rabbit, incensed by the badger who had killed a human friend, eventually persuaded the badger to go fishing in a clay boat, with the rabbit close by in a wooden boat. The boat dissolved in the water leaving the badger floundering, and the rabbit struck the badger with his oar until he drowned.

The example in **Fig. 198** shows one of the seven gods of Good Luck, Ebisu, the patron of work, typically depicted with a fishing rod and a fish.

A particularly fine example in brass, in **Fig. I99,** depicts flying cranes, another popular Japanese theme. A second box depicting cranes is shown in **Fig. 200,** along with further brass boxes providing evidence of the variety of themes: in the center of the top row, a box combined with a compass (depicted in a hanging box); at top right, a lady painting a long scroll, the reverse side with a lady holding a basket of flowers and Mount Fuji (another favorite subject) in the background. The lower row shows (at left) a hexagonal weave basketry bird cage, with bird, and (center) a smaller basket of fruit with mice; the box at lower right shows what appears to be a fruit-bearing plant supported by a tripod, with a bird in the background—its reverse side has five butterflies.

It is believed that all of these boxes were made in the first decade of this century, but there is no supporting evidence for this dating.

In quite a different style, and probably from the late 1880s or early 1890s, is a box in the form of a book, with both sides shown in **Figs. 201 and 202**. It is made of brass with a patinated copper finish. Both sides have applied copper figures decorated with thin sheet gold, and some gilding. Fig. 201 represents a priest with a begging bowl, and Fig. 202 roving street peddlers selling tea. The box opens on the side opposite to that which a person from the West would expect, and the striker is located on a patch on the inside of the lid.

Craftsmen who specialized in making Samurai swords were forced to cease this art form in about 1870, and turned their attention to the manufacture of domestic items. The S*hakudo*, originally a part of the elaborate handle of a Samurai sword, lent itself nicely to forming match holders; examples may be found occasionally. The box in Figs. 201 and 202 may have been made by one of these craftsmen.

Probably from the 1920s is a box made of tin plate, shown in **Fig. 203**. Hinged along one side edge, the box opens in two equal halves, each half provided with an internal pocket for matches; one pocket is corrugated for friction, the other with slots to hold a piece of safety match striking surface. The interior is painted black and marked "MADE IN JAPAN". The exterior on one side only has a stylized scene of Mount Fuji against a black background. The front and back panels are set into a frame that has been plated.

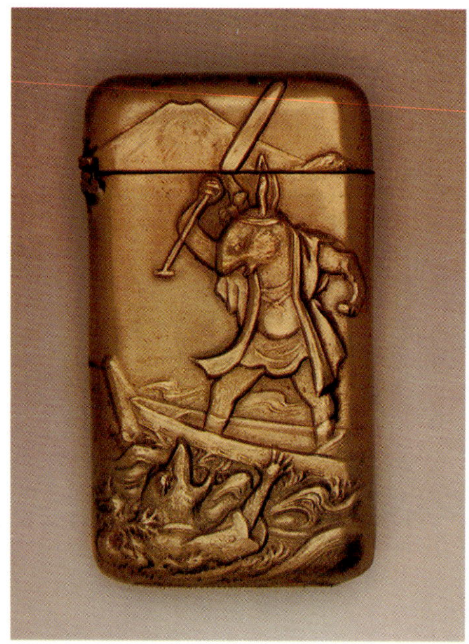

Fig. 197 Japan. Brass. c.1900. H - 6.6cms.

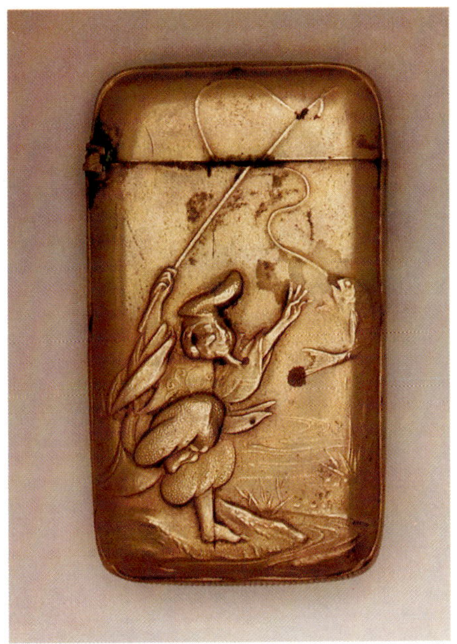

Fig. 198 Japan. Brass. c.1900. H - 6.6cms.

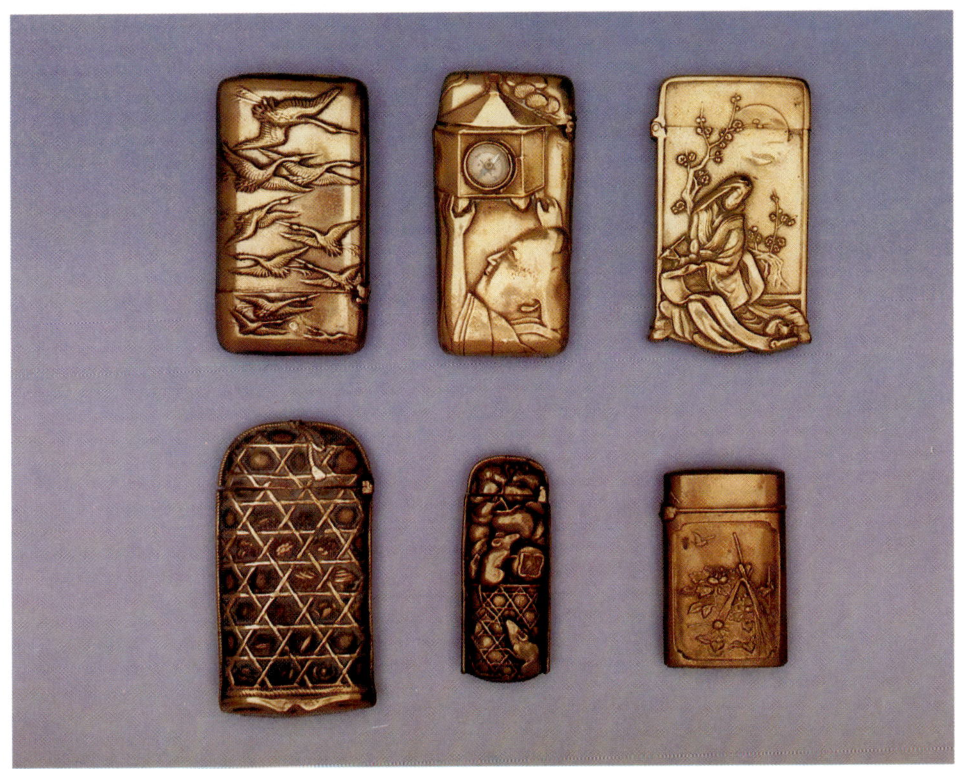

Fig. 200 Japan. Brass. c.1900. Lower left: H - 6.7cms. Lower right: H - 4.6cms.

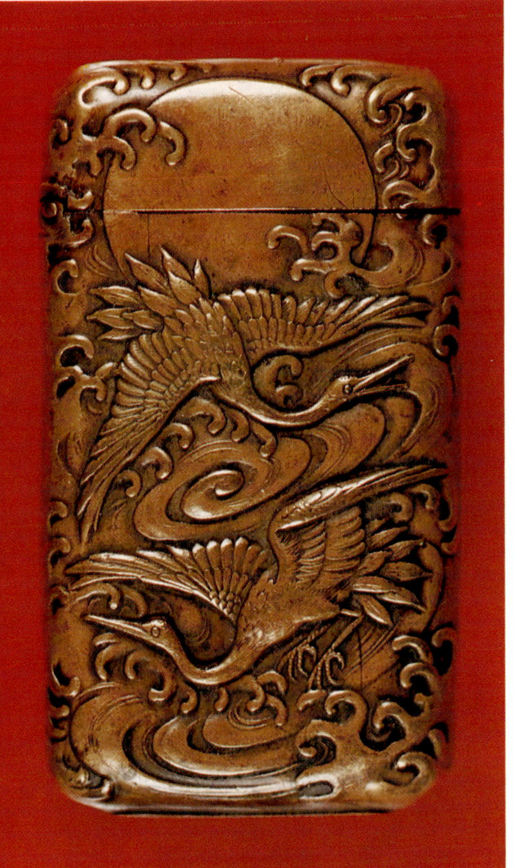

Fig. I99 Japan. Brass. c.1900. H - 6.5cms.

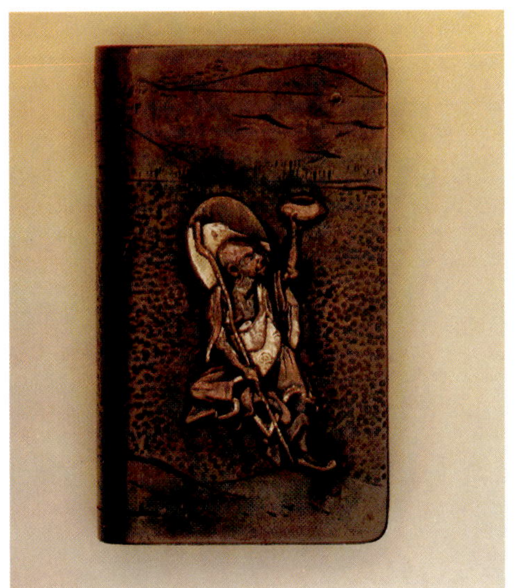

Fig. 201 Japan. Brass, gold inlay. Late l9th century. H - 5.9cms.

Fig. 202 Reverse of Fig. 201.

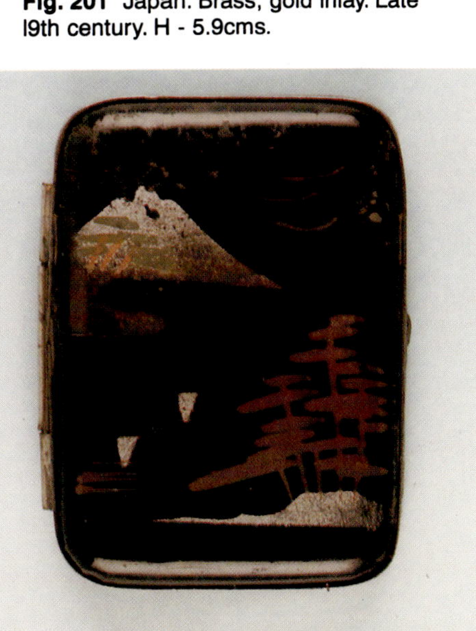

Fig. 203 Japan. Tin plate. c.1920s. H - 6cms.

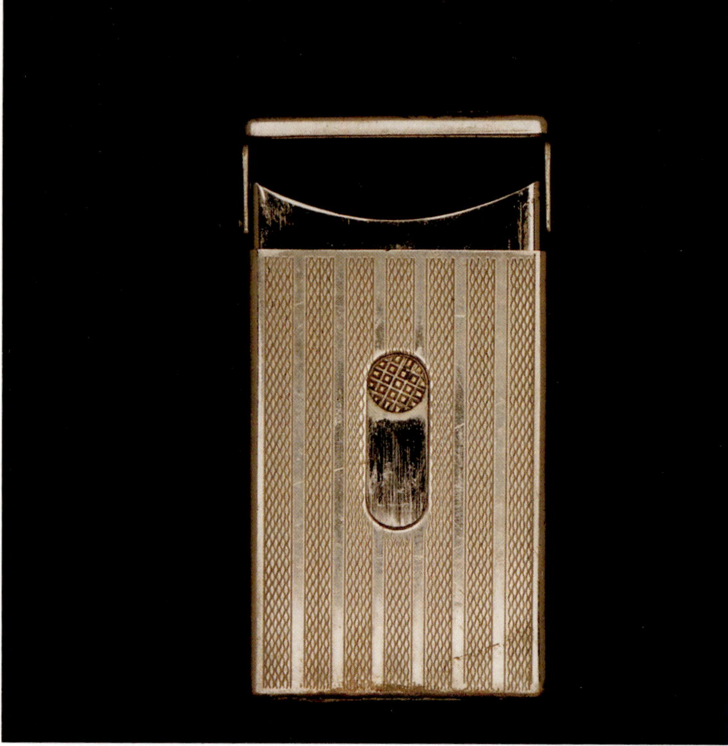

Fig. 204 United States? Plated brass. Marked "D.R.Pa." c.1920s. H - 6.2cms.

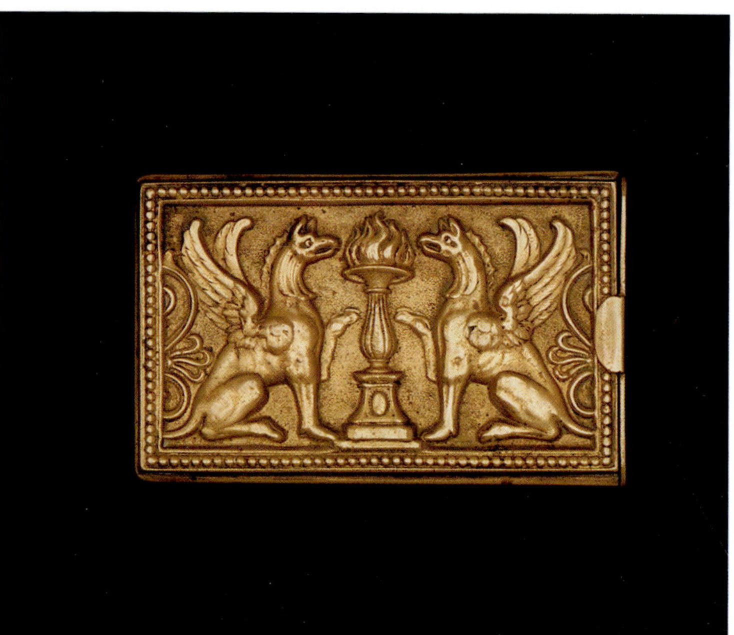

Fig. 206 Europe. Brass. c.1890s. L - 6.2cms.

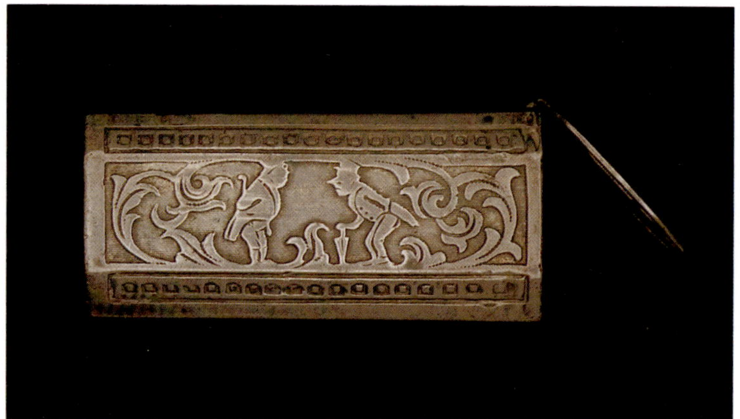

Fig. 205 Europe. Pewter. c.1880s. H - 6.1cms.

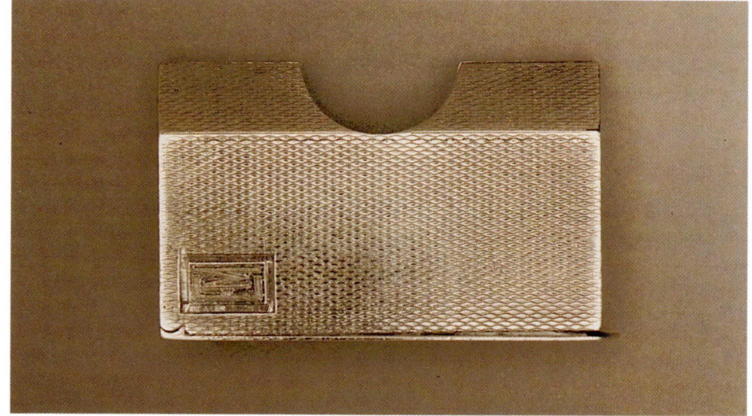

Fig. 207 Unidentified. Marked "Silver". L - 5.9cms.

Although the preceding discussion has dealt with examples that can for one reason or another be identified with some certainty, based upon the documentary or built-in evidence, there are some that remain as 'curios', undocumented, mostly unmarked, and the subject of speculation or opinion as to their origins. Some purists may regard these as of no consequence; but, given time, more experience, and prolonged research, these too may be documented eventually. Each, in its own right, is a three-dimensional archival source, waiting to reveal its secrets.

The first such 'curio' example in **Fig. 204** is made of plated brass. It has a slide button on one side which pushes up an interior compartment along with the lid, which swings aside when fully raised. Strikers of a composition suitable for friction and safety matches are set into the top and bottom edges. A mark is hidden on one edge of the interior compartment—"D.R.Pa."—which suggests a Pennsylvania company, and it may date from c. 1920.

The match holder in **Fig. 205** is of white metal, possibly pewter. The design and shape suggest a continental European origin, from about 1880.

In brass with heavily embossed designs, the example in **Fig. 206** is a well made box with slots on each side into which may be slipped striking surfaces from a box of matches. This too has the feel of continental Europe. When collected it held some small candle matches of the type referred to in Part 7 of this chapter. It possibly dates from the 1890s.

Although marked "silver," the box in **Fig. 207** is probably not of sterling fineness. It is scooped out along the top edge to facilitate the removal of one match at a time, and the bottom edge is hinged at one end to permit filling with matches and replacement of a striking surface in a slot located inside. This may possibly be from the United States from c. 1920.

The three boxes in **Fig. 208** are of brass, two of them plated, and of the standard "flip-top" type. The lower piece is engraved with what appears to be a happy lion in a setting that would be totally alien to a lion in its natural habitat.

The two brass boxes in **Fig. 209** are hinged longitudinally. The top box has a panel of some plastic material bearing a scene set against an iridescent blue background; the panel is set into the lid and held in place by four rivets. The lower box is possibly hand-made, with small pieces of turquoise set into a black substance, and a brass swastika; the striker is a piece of sandpaper glued to the inside of the lid. This is probably from India. The swastika is of the form adopted by the Nazi regime in the 1930s, but the symbol is ancient. It has been theorized that it originated from tying two sticks together as a cross, which, when thrown and rolled on its edge, broke the arms and thus formed the swastika.

Probably silver-plated, the example in **Fig. 210** is simple and elegant, and incorporates a cigar cutter set into the base.

Fig. 211 is an example for which only quite recently has some documentation been discovered. It is a waterproof box, the lid being opened by pushing the switch on the top from one side to the other, which releases the lid to lift up and be swung to one side. It is made of plated brass, and marked on one of the lid arms "Pat.Oct.1912." A search of British, Canadian and United States patents has not revealed the source. The side of the box is engraved with the name and service number of a gunner in the Canadian Field Artillery who was with the Canadian Expeditionary Force in France in 1916. These boxes were offered by Henry Birks & Sons of Montreal in their catalogues of 1916-17 at $1.00 each, where described as "silver plated," and one illustration shows the box with a serviceman's name and number. A handwritten annotation in the 1917 catalogue shows they were made by "Ballow," but this company has not yet been identified.

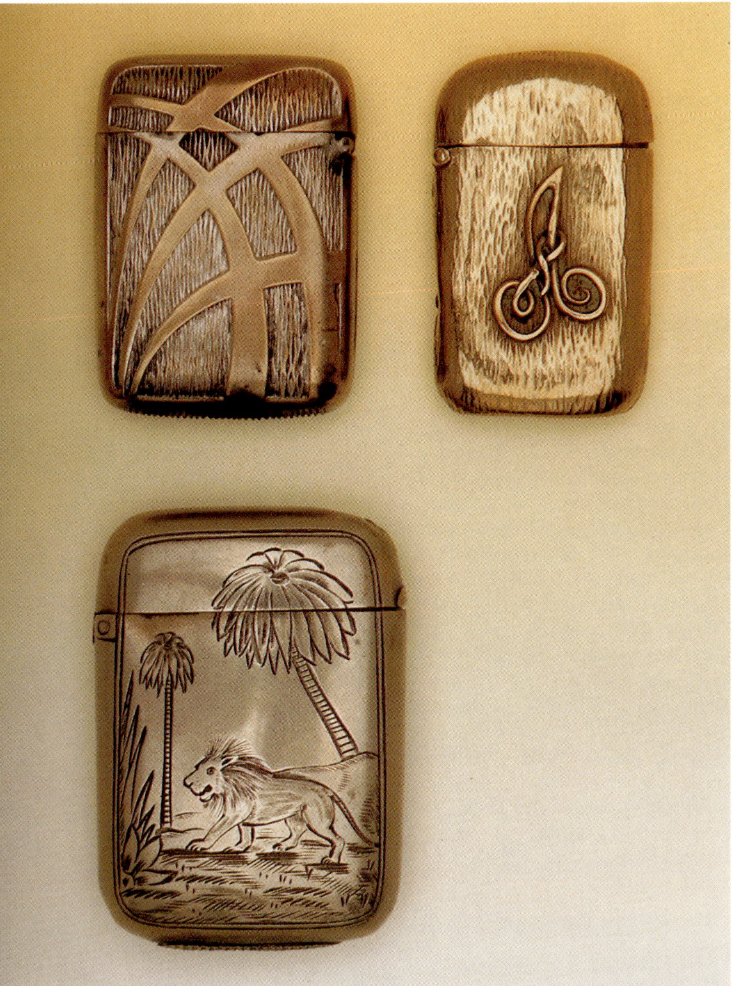

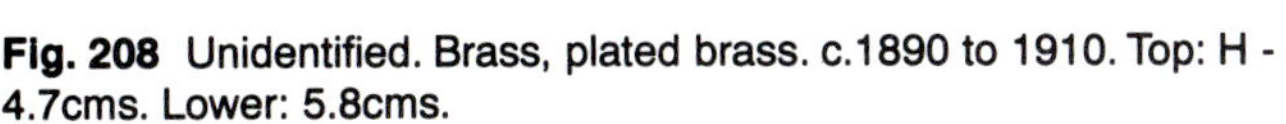

Fig. 208 Unidentified. Brass, plated brass. c.1890 to 1910. Top: H - 4.7cms. Lower: 5.8cms.

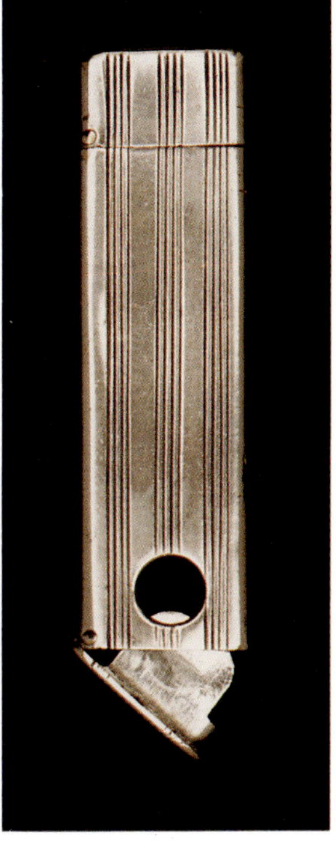

Fig. 209 Top: brass, celluloid; H - 4.4cms. Lower: India; brass, turquoise; W - 5.3cms.

Fig. 210 Possibly French. Plated brass? With cigar cutter. H -7cms.

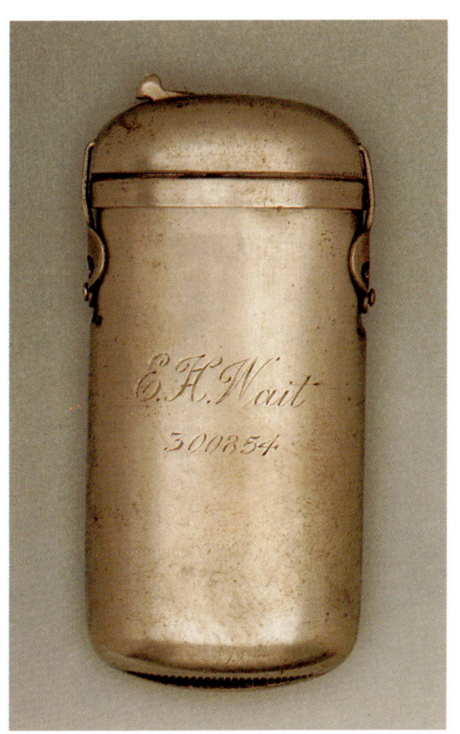

Fig. 211 Possibly Canada. Silver plated. Waterproof. Made by Ballow? Patented 1912. H - 8.1cms.

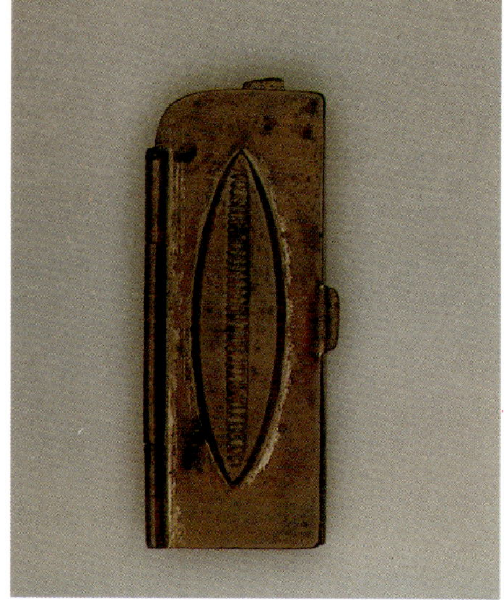

Fig. 212 Possibly United States. Plated copper. From a cigar case shown in Fig. 213. c. 1892. L - 5.4cms.

The final example was until only a few days ago (at the time of writing) one of the curios. Shown in **Fig. 212**, it is made of copper with traces of some form of silver plating. Its odd shape suggested that it had been removed from some parent body, but for several years it remained a mystery. **Fig. 213**, found in Zorn's catalogue of 1892, shows the match holder as a part of a ciger case (the elusive parent body), although this still does not identify the maker.

There is little point in pretending that this survey is any more than brief. Serious collectors will be quick to pinpoint the absence of this type or that style, or will refer to better examples in their own collections. This is in no way denied, but the intent here is to introduce the reader to a subject that has previously had very limited attention, and demonstrate how much may be learned from arduous research.

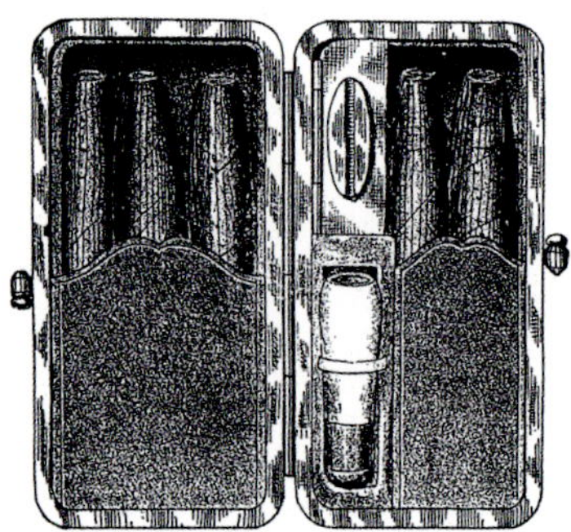

Fig. 213 Illustration from George Zorn's catalogue of 1892, showing the match holder in Fig. 212.

PART 4: NOVELTY BOXES.

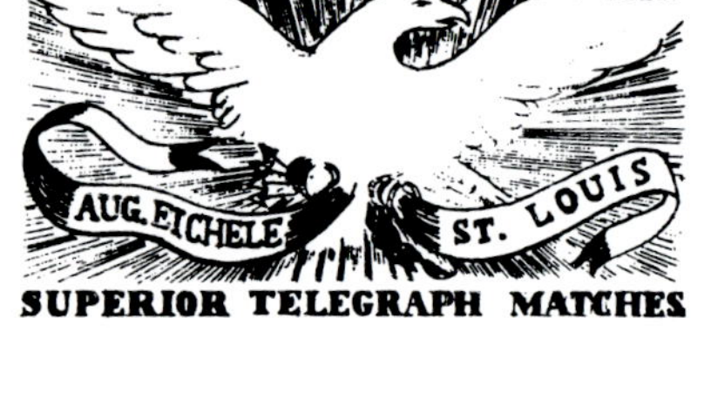

Fig. 214 Illustration of a label from a box of matches found in the cargo hold of the "Bertrand". United States. 1865.

In 1864 the *Bertrand* was described as "a nice trim little steamer, neat but not gaudy, and sits upon the water like a duck." It left St.Louis on March 18, 1886 for its first working trip on the Missouri River, bound for the gold country of Fort Benton, Montana, with a cargo of supplies for the region and a number of passengers. On April 1 it was about twenty-five miles north of Omaha when it hit a snag and sank. The passengers and deck cargo were saved, but the rest of the cargo went down with the steamer.

Over the years a number of abortive attempts were made to locate the *Bertrand* without success, and there were rumors as to the value of the cargo, including the presence of gold. The Missouri meantime changed its course, leaving the steamer some twenty feet below the surface, and when it was located in 1968 on the Desoto National Wildlife Refuge, federal property, it was three hundred and fifty feet from the Missouri in one direction and three thousand five hundred in another.

Excavations were carried out by archaeologists working for the U.S. Department of the Interior, and the varied cargo was recovered, including sixteen cases of boxed matches and some thirty match holders consigned by Campbells Dry Goods of St.Louis.

A drawing taken from the match box labels in **Fig. 214** shows that they were produced by Aug. Eichele of St.Louis, about whom very little is known. The company underwent a name change to "P. & Co." and is believed to have been taken over in the amalgamation of several companies that formed the Diamond Match Co. in the early 1880s.

An example of the match holder is shown in **Fig. 215**. Made of brass in rectangular form, the novelty aspect is expressed in the roll-top lid, an unusual feature in such a small box—although they were made of wood in Europe, but not until c. 1880. The striker is located at one end, but there are no marks to aid in identification. The length suggests that it may have originated in the United States to hold their slightly longer wood-stemmed matches. This example is very early for such a novelty form.

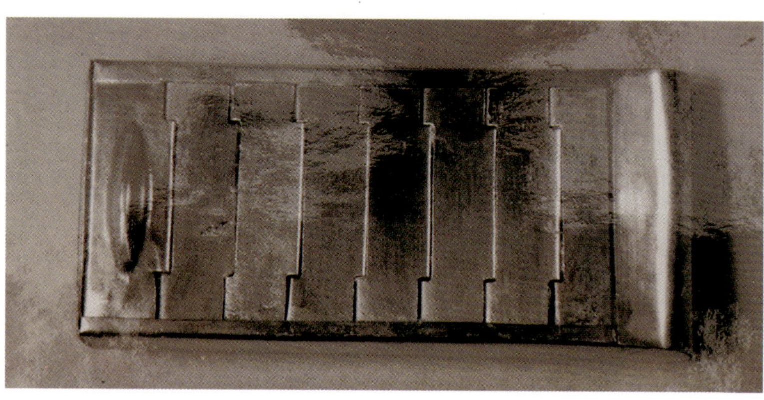

Fig. 215 United States? Brass. From the cargo of the "Bertrand". 1865. L - 7cms.

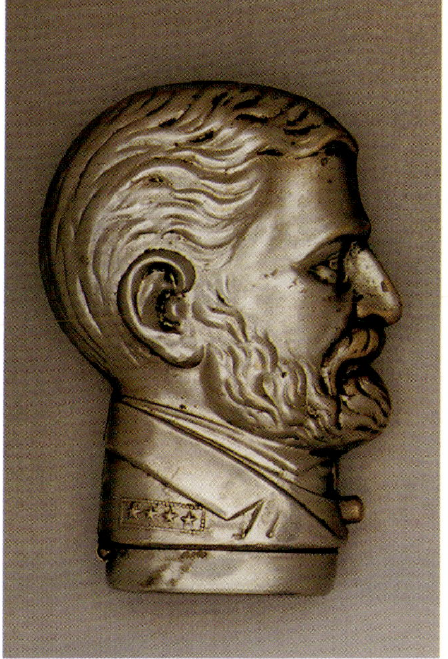

Fig. 216 United States. Plated brass. Head of Ulysses S. Grant. c.1890. H - 6.3cms.

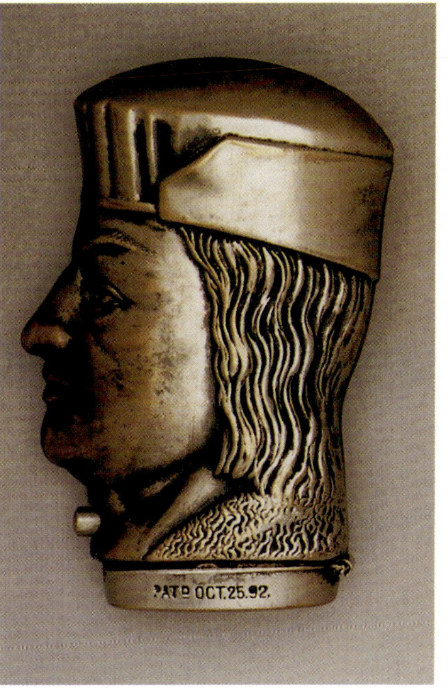

Fig. 217 United States. Plated brass. Head of Columbus. Made to a Design Patent of 1892, possibly by G. M. Thurnauer. H - 6.7cms.

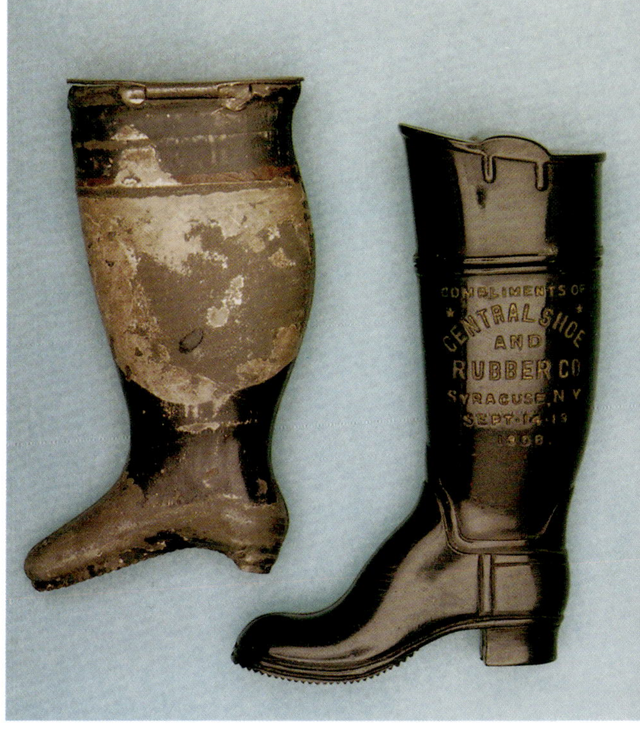

Fig. 218 United States. Left: tin plate; c.1880s; H - 6.6cms. Right: vulcanite; 1908; possibly made by Central Shoe and Rubber Co. H - 7.1cms.

The United States production of novelty boxes in forms other than that of rectangular or cylindrical shapes was far less than that of their European counterparts. However, the term 'novelty' was often applied to match holders in sales catalogues.

The representation of *The Scientific American* in silver and gold has been referred to and illustrated in Figs. 84 and 85, and some trick or puzzle boxes which may be regarded as novelties appear in Part 6 of this chapter. But other notable novelties were produced, as will be seen.

A series of heads of prominent people were made, including Ulysses S. Grant and Christopher Columbus, shown in **Figs. 216 and 217.** Others in this series include Grover Cleveland, Benjamin Harrison, William McKinley, George Peabody and Daniel Boone; there were probably others. They all appear to have been made by the same company. Columbus, Cleveland and Harrison were the subjects of Design Patents issued to Simon Zinn of New York, Columbus in 1892, the other two in 1888. Columbus was advertised in late 1892 by G.M. Thurnauer of New York City at $2.00 per dozen in oxidized silver and nickel plate, but it is not clear if that company made them or not. The lid spring is of the same type as that shown in Fig. 172.

The two boots in **Fig. 218** demonstrate an interesting change in styles and materials over a period of approximately twenty years. The boot at the left is said to be made of German silver, according to a catalogue of the late 1870s put out by William Demuth & Co. of New York, who manufactured and imported smokers' articles. This example is painted black with red and brown trim on a cream undercoating, now much eroded. The lid is hinged on the side; the striker is located on the sole. The boot at the right has a slip-on lid and is made of vulcanite, a mixture of rubber with 25% to 50% sulphur, heated and molded. It was a complimentary advertising piece, given to customers of the Central Shoe and Rubber Co. of Syracuse, New York, between September 14 and 19, 1908. It is possible that the company made the boot.

Bale patterns of the type shown in **Fig. 219** were a popular design on both sides of the Atlantic. The brass example is of United States origin, and they are also to be found with a nickel-plated finish, but they lack maker's marks. In Britain they were shown in the Harrod's Stores Ltd. catalogue of 1895 in silver, and were also made as cigarette and cigar cases, being referred to as the "New Bale Pattern."

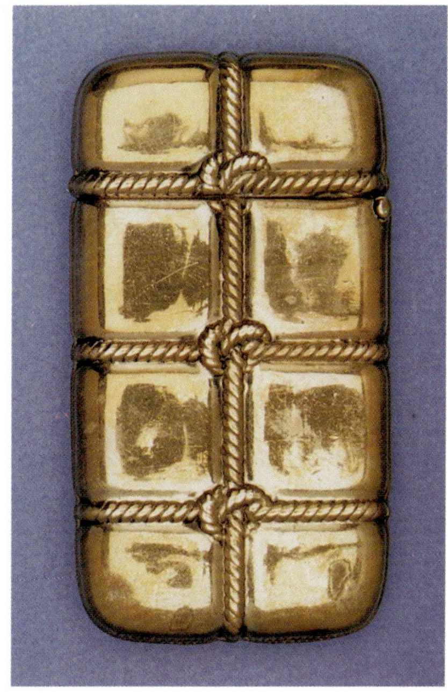

Fig. 219 United States. Brass. "Bale" pattern. c.1900. H - 7.2cms.

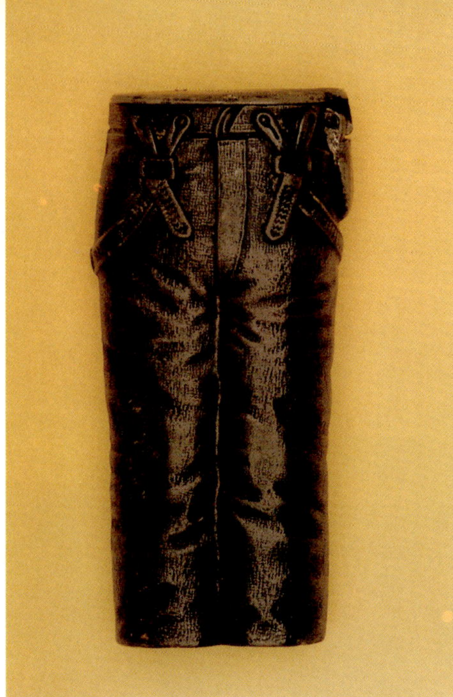

The item shown in **Fig. 220** was termed the "Pants Safe" in the Zorn catalogue, where it was offered at $1.75 per dozen or $19.50 per gross. It was the subject of a Design Patent in 1886. It appears to be made of some form of white metal, but is unmarked other than the patent date under the lid.

The match holders in **Fig. 221** represent a bunch of cigars and a cigar case respectively. That to the left is marked "G.Silver" and is probably of United States origin. The example at the right is nickel-plated, and the form of the striker and the ring for suspension suggest a British origin. They probably date from the 1890s.

In the form of a purse are three examples in **Fig. 222** made to an Invention Patent of 1883, issued to Edward J. Hauck, the son of the manufacturer. The larger version is inscribed "COMPLIMENTS of C.J.Hauck & Son. MANUFACTURERS OF Metal Novelties. BROOKLYN, E.D. NEW YORK." The patent drawings are shown in **Fig. 223**, demonstrating how the pair of lids opened, and a raised section within the box prevented the matches from obstructing the closure of the lids. An interesting feature of the patent is the catch, which Hauck describes thus: "Suitable fastening devices retain the lids in a closed position. In the example I have shown two balls for this purpose." Although Hauck did not mention the ball catch in his claims, it is possible that he had inadvertently invented it at this time.

These boxes were sold widely throughout North America, appearing in several catalogues, including Zorn's, which also showed four other versions of a similar nature probably made by Hauck. The larger version was offered for $1.65 per dozen or $18.00 per gross, while Montgomery Ward & Co. offered them in 1894-95 at 20¢ each or $2.20 per dozen.

Both of the smaller versions are marked "POSTAGE STAMPS," yet are provided with a striker on the base, from which arises a very speculative theory. Were these boxes the forerunners of the "His and Hers" phenomenon of more recent times? Perhaps the smaller version was intended for use by ladies to disguise the fact that they were carrying matches to light their cigarettes, at a time when it was frowned upon for a lady to smoke.

Fig. 220 United States. white metal. Made to a Design Patent of 1886 by August H. Wirz. H - 7.2cms.

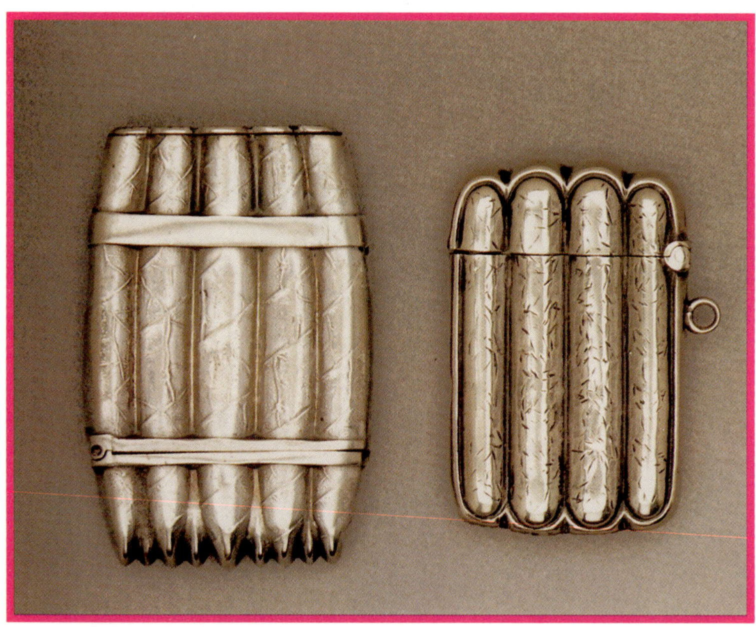

Fig. 221 United States. German or nickel silver, plated brass. c.1890s. Left: H - 5.9cms. Right: H - 5cms.

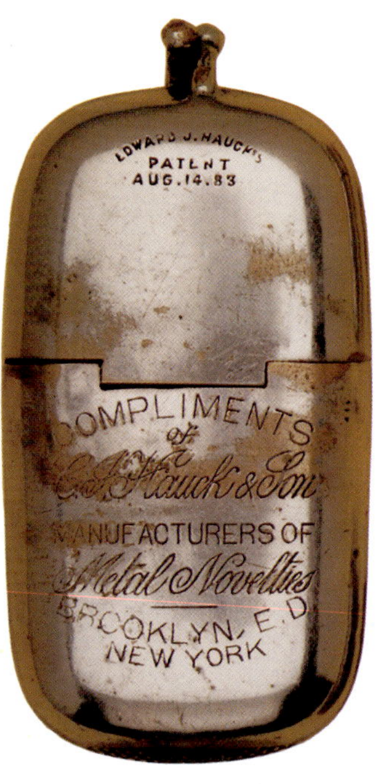

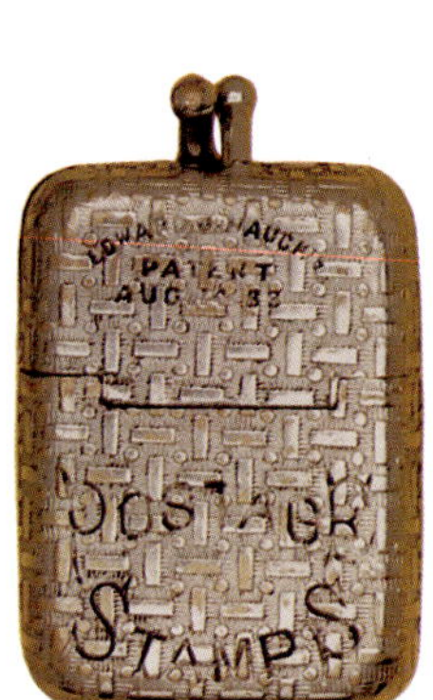

Fig. 222 United States. Plated brass. Made by C. J. Hauck & Son to an Invention Patent by Edward J. Hauck of 1883. Left: H - 8.3cms. Right: H - 4.6cms.

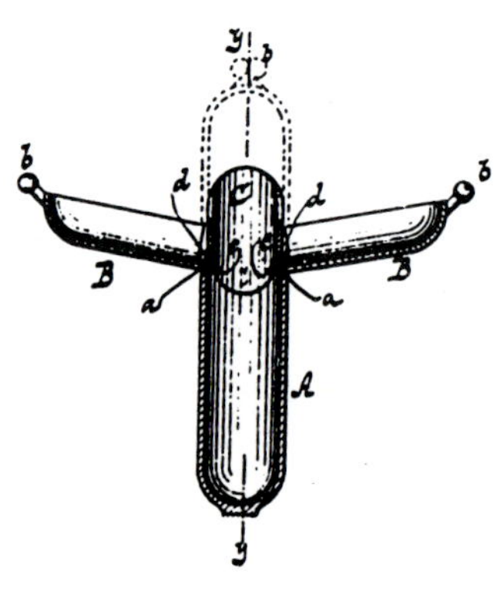

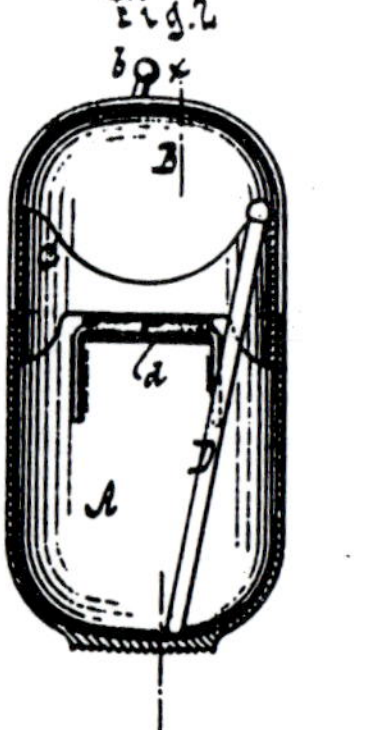

Fig. 223 Drawings from Invention Patent of 1883 by Edward J. Hauck for examples in Fig. 222.

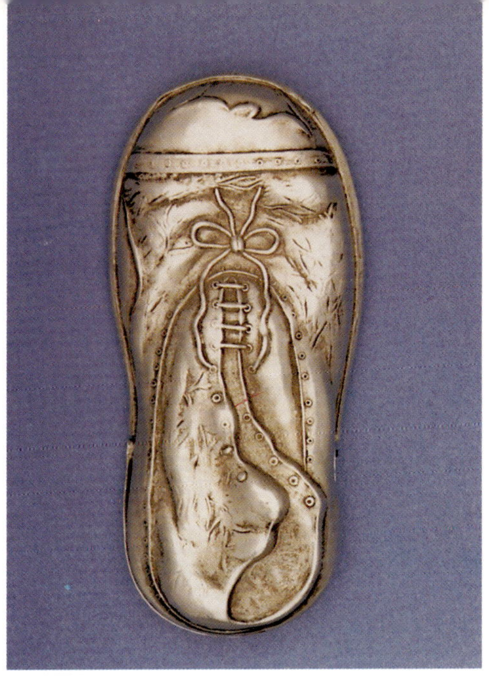

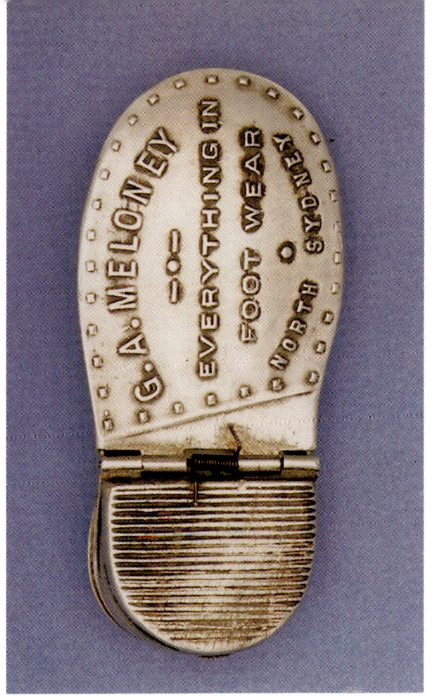

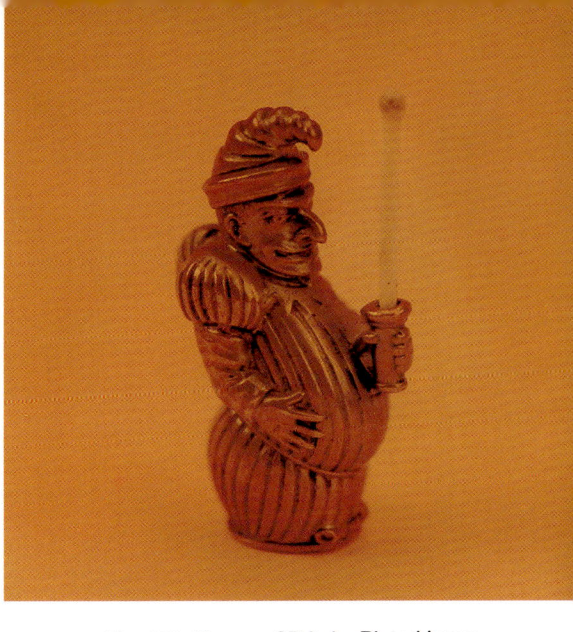

Fig. 226 Europe, ?Britain. Plated brass. c.1900. H - 5.5cms.

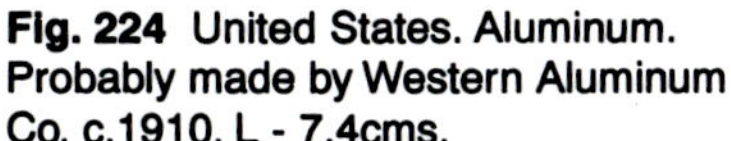

Fig. 224 United States. Aluminum. Probably made by Western Aluminum Co. c.1910. L - 7.4cms.

Fig. 225 Reverse of Fig. 224.

Aluminum match holders were not uncommon, but novelty forms were quite rare. The example in **Figs. 224 and 225**, in the form of an old scuffed shoe, is such a piece. It was illustrated in a catalogue of c. 1900 put out by the Western Aluminum Co. of Chicago, who presumably manufactured it as well, for $1.20 per dozen or $12.00 per gross. The example, however, has impressed wording on the sole: "G. A. MELONEY. EVERYTHING IN FOOTWEAR. NORTH SYDNEY." George Meloney had been a manager of a shoe department in a department store, branching out on his own in about 1909 with a shoe store in Sydney Mines, Nova Scotia, which burnt down the night before it opened. He then moved to North Sydney, opening in about 1910, and the business continued in operation until about 1978. The example must therefore date from after he opened in 1910, by which time some very minute changes had occurred, with only four laces showing instead of the five shown in the 1900 catalogue version. The heel is hinged for access to the matches, and is the location of the corrugated striker.

In Europe the ingenious craftsmen let their imaginations run riot in the production of novelty shapes. Well over two hundred different shapes have been listed by the author, not including the many variations of book, bottle and horseshoe forms, which are among the most common. A comprehensive list might well exceed five hundred. The examples shown here only scratch the surface, but hopefully indicate the vast range that may be found. It is unfortunate that so few are marked, but the major centres of production appear to have been Birmingham and Austria. Most were made between 1880 and 1900, but a silver horseshoe has been recorded as early as 1864, and some were made in the first decade of this century.

Punch was a popular figure, appearing in several forms of pocket box. The example in **Fig. 226** is perhaps the most common, with Punch holding a box which in fact is a match socket; socket and match combined represent the club that Punch typically carried, thus completing the figure. It is made of plated brass. The same version has been illustrated with an enamelled finish, but it is suspected that this may have been done at a much later date, to enhance the price to collectors. There is also a second version with a raised base.

The seated figure of Punch in **Fig. 227** shows him in a more benign mood. This box may have been made in Austria. A representation has been seen of the canvas puppet theatre with Punch and his dog Toby on stage, made of silver, and hallmarked for Birmingham, 1894, with a maker's mark of "D & C," which may have been Dukes & Clemmens.

Heads of prominent and fictional people were made. Ewart William Gladstone, four times Prime Minister of Great Britain, was represented by two heads, one in profile, the other shown in **Fig. 228** and made of plated brass. He was also represented in bust form in two silver-plated versions, one shown in **Fig. 229**. These may have been made on his death in 1898.

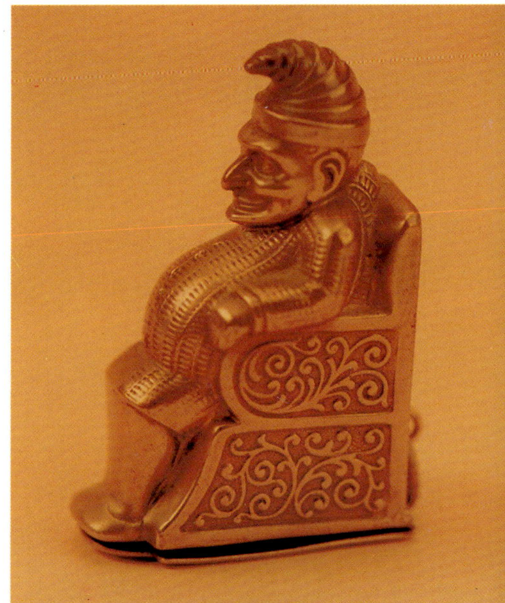

Fig. 227 Europe, ?Austria. Brass. c.1900. H - 6.1cms.

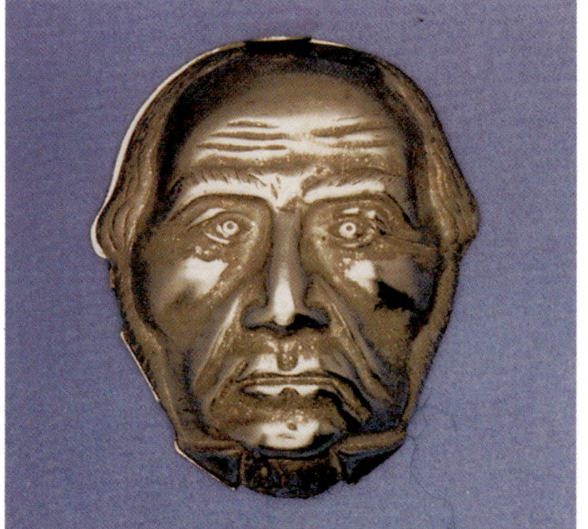

Fig. 228 Britain. Plated brass. William E. Gladstone. c. 1890. H - 4.8cms.

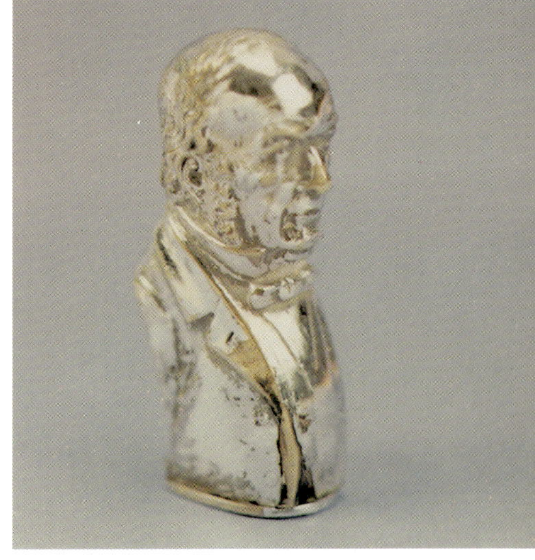

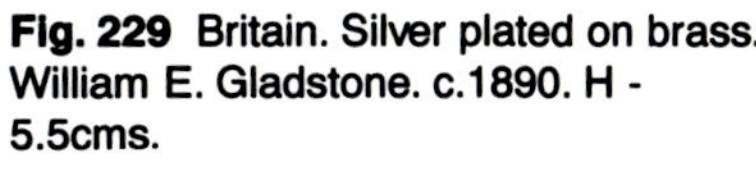

Fig. 229 Britain. Silver plated on brass. William E. Gladstone. c.1890. H - 5.5cms.

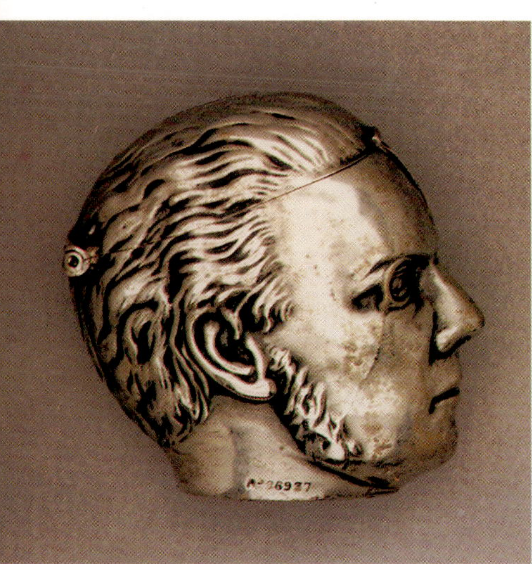

Fig. 230 Britain. Plated brass. Joseph Chamberlain. Made to a Registered Design of 1888 by Jenkins W. Evans. H - 4.8cms.

Another prominent politician was Joseph Chamberlain, shown in **Fig. 230**. The son of a London shoemaker, he moved to Birmingham as a young man to join a company owned by a relative, rising rapidly to make his fortune by his early forties. He then went into politics, becoming a very popular Mayor of Birmingham from 1873 until 1876, before moving on to national politics, serving under Gladstone as a Cabinet Minister. He married twice, each wife presenting him with a son; the second, Neville, was Britain's Prime Minister at the outbreak of World War II. Four years after Chamberlain became a Member of Parliament for Birmingham, Jenkin William Evans, a die-sinker, stamper and piercer started his own company in Birmingham; he was issued with a Registered Design in 1888 for the Chamberlain head as illustrated. Evans' company still exists today (at the same address), as do all of his dies, some of which are still being used. It is possible that Evans only stamped out the parts using his dies, then passed the parts to another company to assemble and market, a practice that he is known to have followed with other products.

A very popular fictional character is the subject of **Fig. 231**. It was acquired in North America and the dealer claimed that it represented W.C.Fields, the great comedian. But it is actually Ally Sloper, the subject of an early British comic paper, popular before Fields became well known, and the inspiration for Fields' characterization. The head is clearly marked with a British Registered Design number for 1888, issued to Frederick W. Tomkinson, a "trade die sinker" of Birmingham.

Ally Sloper was a fictional character created in 1867 by Charles Henry Ross, a writer of 'penny dreadfuls'. Ross sold the rights to the character in 1884 to the Dalziel Brothers, London publishers, who created a weekly comic paper "Ally Sloper's Half Holiday." William Giles Baxter provided the early topical front page cartoon, setting the standard for his successor W. F. Thomas, a contemporary example of which is shown in **Fig. 232**. The comic paper ceased publication in 1923.

The name Alexander Sloper, to give him his full title, was created at a time when an out-of-work man without money to pay the rent would "slope off" down the back alley to avoid the rent collector. Ally was usually depicted wearing a battered top hat, cut-away collar, cut-away coat, narrow trousers, large boots, and carrying a "gamp" (umbrella). He acquired money by devising nefarious schemes, mixed with the upper classes whenever he could, and disliked older women, small children and dogs. This could also describe the characters that Fields often portrayed in his sketches and movie films.

W. C. Fields started his theatrical career as a juggler, first appearing in 1900 and going on to become "The Greatest Eccentric Juggler in the World," without saying a word on stage. He travelled extensively, including trips to Britain, where he must almost certainly have seen "Ally Sloper's Half Holiday" before he signed up with the Ziegfeld Follies in 1915. He then changed his act, speaking in the numerous sketches that he wrote. His sketches reflected the inspiration he drew from Ally Sloper, including his style of dress. The similarities between Ally Sloper and the characters portrayed by Fields in his stage and film career go beyond those referred to here. Although Fields never acknowledged the fact, there can be little doubt about the connection.

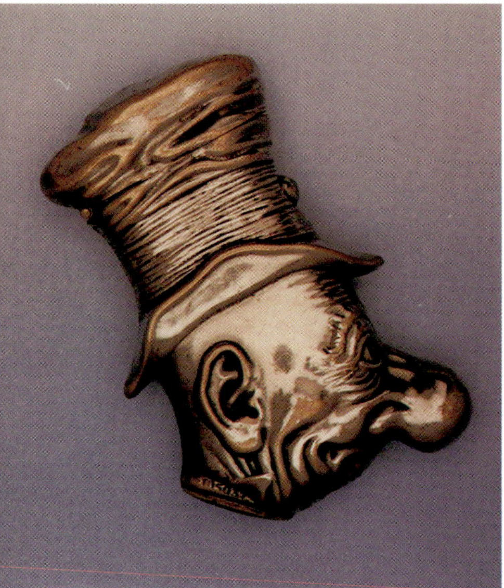

Fig. 231 Britain. Plated brass. Ally Sloper. Made to a Registered Design of 1888 by Frederick W. Tomkinson. H - 5.9cms.

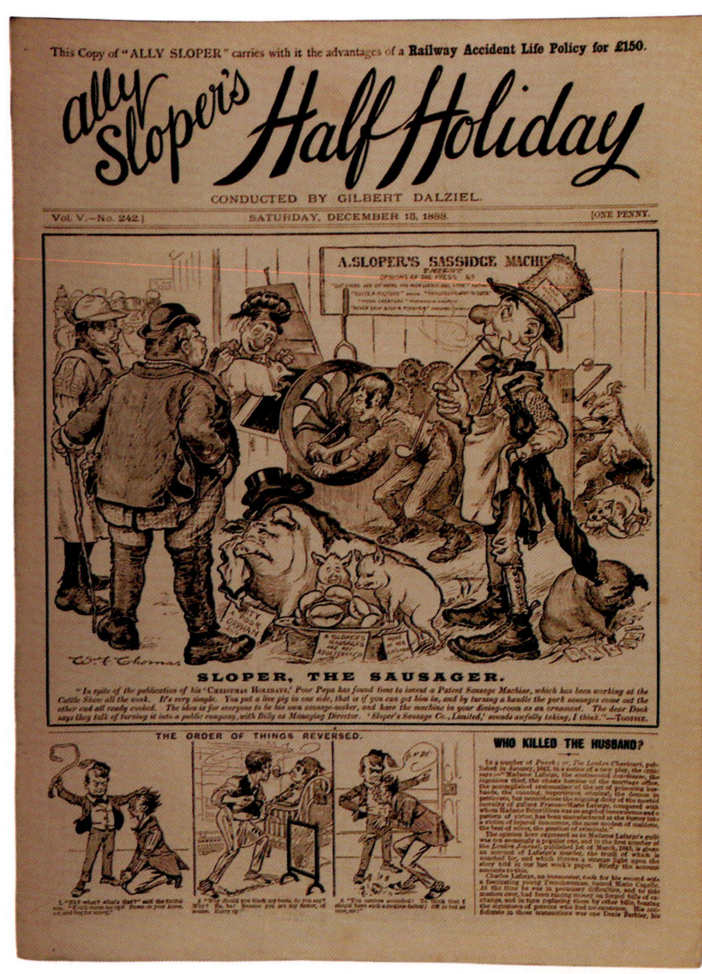

This Copy of "ALLY SLOPER" carries with it the advantages of a **Railway Accident Life Policy for £150.**

Ally Sloper's Half Holiday

CONDUCTED BY GILBERT DALZIEL.

Vol. V.—No. 242.] SATURDAY, DECEMBER 15, 1888. [ONE PENNY.

SLOPER, THE SAUSAGER.

"In spite of the publication of his 'Christmas Holidays,' Poor Papa has found time to invent a Patent Sausage Machine, which has been working at the Cattle Show all the week. It's very simple. You put a live pig in one side, that is if you can get him in, and by turning a handle the pork sausages come out the other end all ready cooked. The idea is for everyone to be his own sausage-maker, and have the machine in your dining-room as an ornament. The dear Dook says they talk of turning it into a public company, with Billy as Managing Director. 'Sloper's Sausage Co., Limited,' sounds awfully taking, I think."—Tootsie.

THE ORDER OF THINGS REVERSED.

WHO KILLED THE HUSBAND?

Fig. 232 "Ally Sloper's Half Holiday" of December 16, 1888, published weekly from 1884 until 1923. This edition contemporary with Fig. 231.

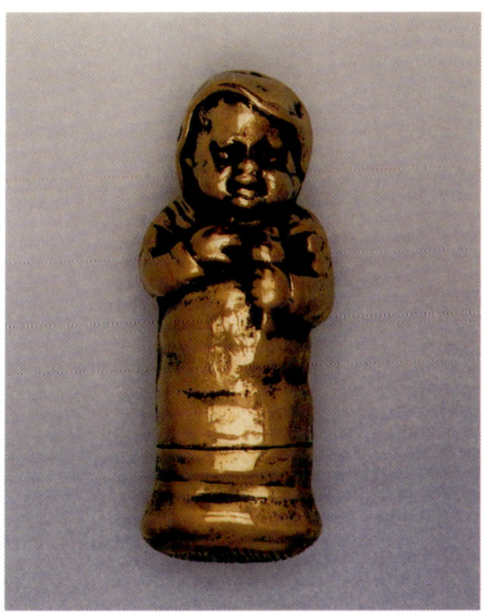

Fig. 233 Britain. Brass. c.1890s. H - 6.1cms.

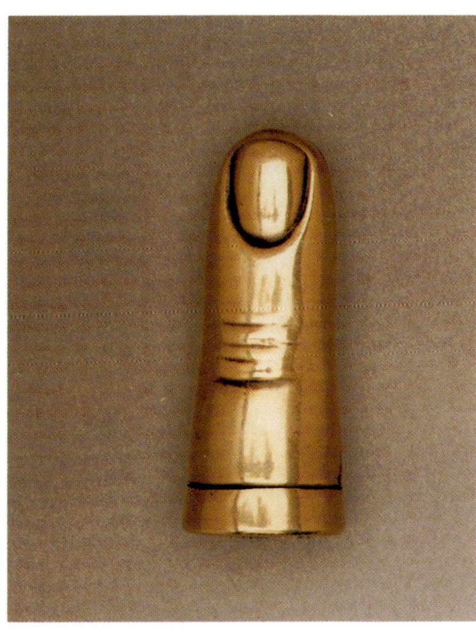

Fig. 235 Europe. Brass. c.1890s. H - 5cms.

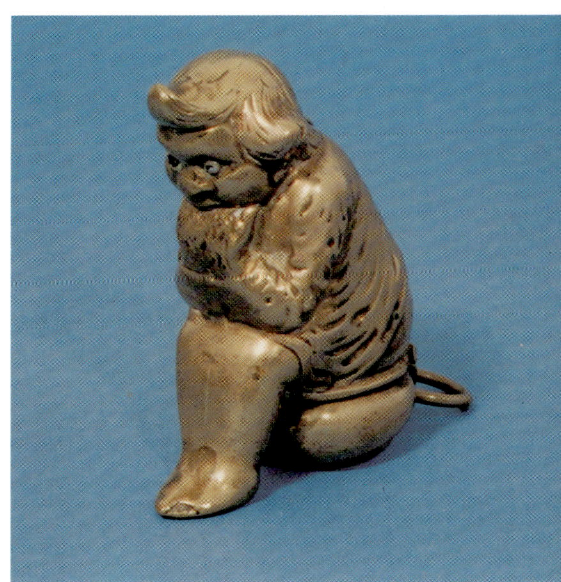

Fig. 237 Europe. Brass, glass. c.1890s. H - 4.5cms.

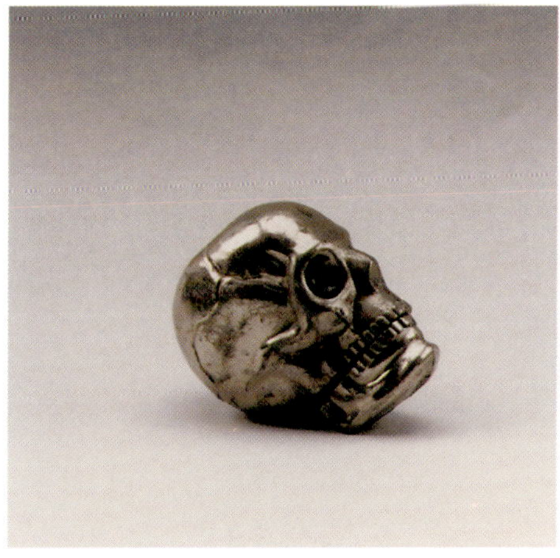

Fig. 234 Europe. White metal. Possibly a reproduction copied from a brass original. H - 4.5cms.

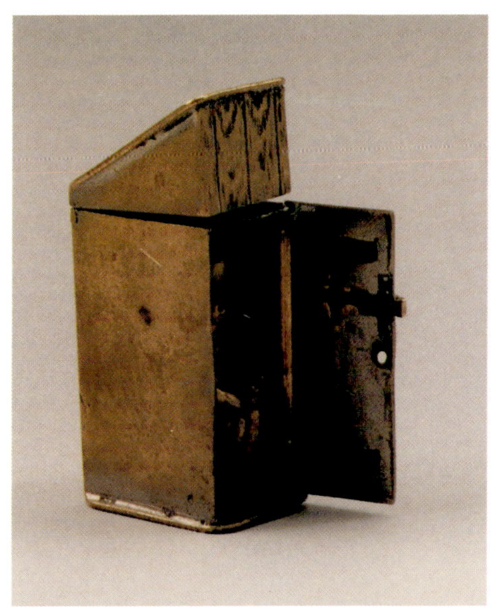

Fig. 236 Europe. Brass. c.1890s. H - 5cms.

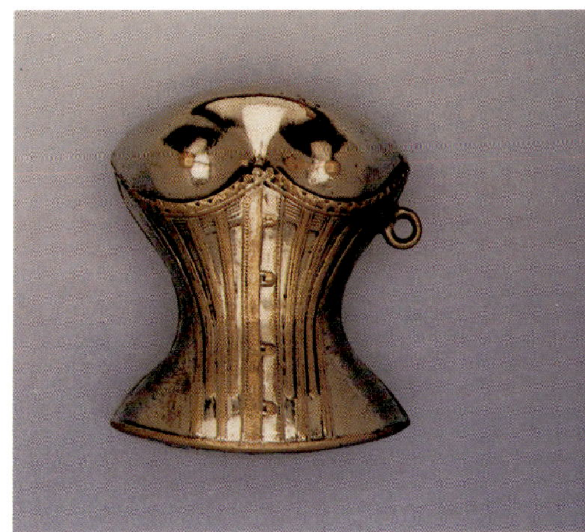

Fig. 238 Europe. Plated brass. c. 1890s. H - 4.2cms.

The baby in swaddling clothes shown in brass in Fig. **233** was also produced in silver by Sampson Mordan of London in 1881-82. The brass version does not show the same clarity of definition, and was probably copied from Sampson Mordan's original.

The skull in **Fig. 234** is cast in white metal and is probably a fake copied from an original in brass. Other novelty boxes are also known to have been copied, including a brass pig of the type shown in the center of Fig. 243, and silver versions of Punch and Toby. The latter were produced with hallmarks for the 1970s which are usually rubbed to make it impossible to decipher them.

Perhaps slightly bizarre is the single finger made of brass shown in **Fig. 235**. In a slightly risqué vein is the brass outhouse containing a seated man in a top hat in **Fig. 236**. In **Fig. 237** is a small child sitting on a 'potty', holding a towel which he is thrusting into his mouth with both hands, a look of extreme concentration on his face. The chamber pot is hinged for access to the matches and has a suspension ring attached to the back. It is made of brass. From the 'naughty nineties' is a nickel-plated bosom forming the lid of a box representing a corset, with a ring for suspension; it is shown in **Fig. 238**.

The 'man in the moon' box, as shown in **Fig. 239**, is missing its glass eyes. It lies conveniently on its back to hold a match in a socket formed by its mouth. This has been seen in brass, and the example here is plated brass. This too is said to have been the subject of modern copies.

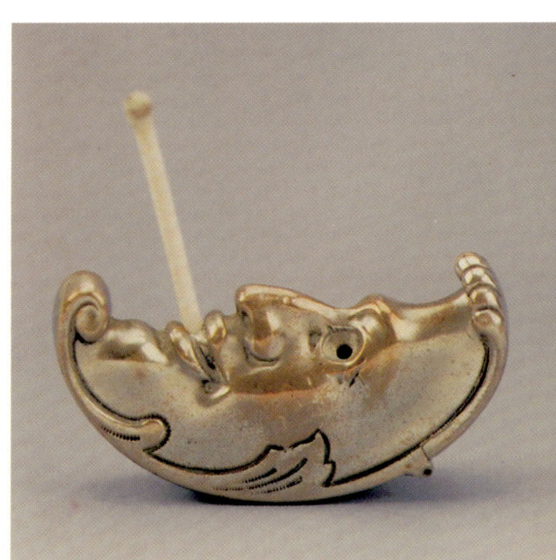

Fig. 239 Europe. Plated brass. Glass eyes missing. c.1890s. L -5.1cms.

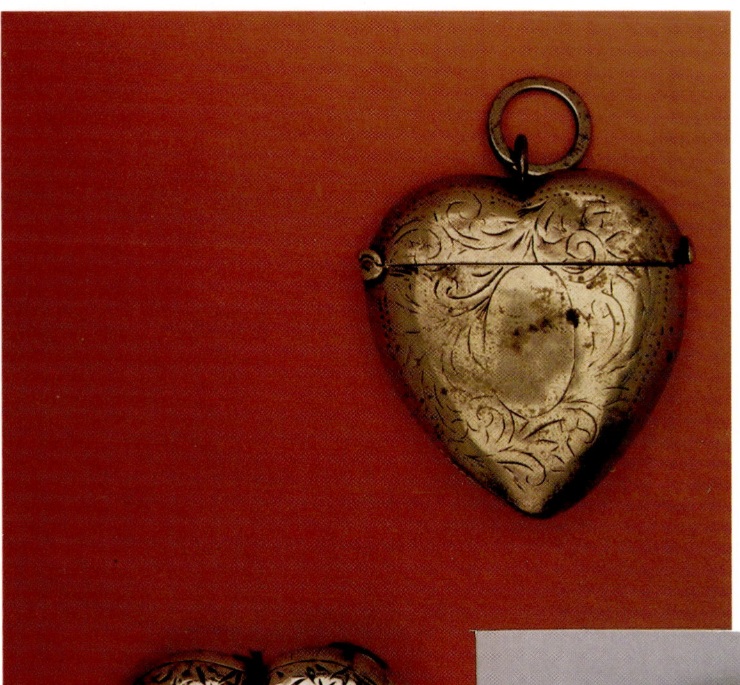

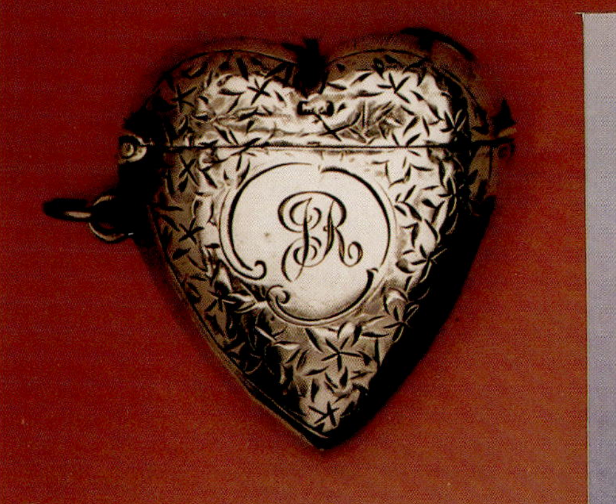

Fig. 240 Britain. Top: plated brass; c.1900; H - 5cms. Lower: silver; "S & Bm"; 1910. H - 4.7cms.

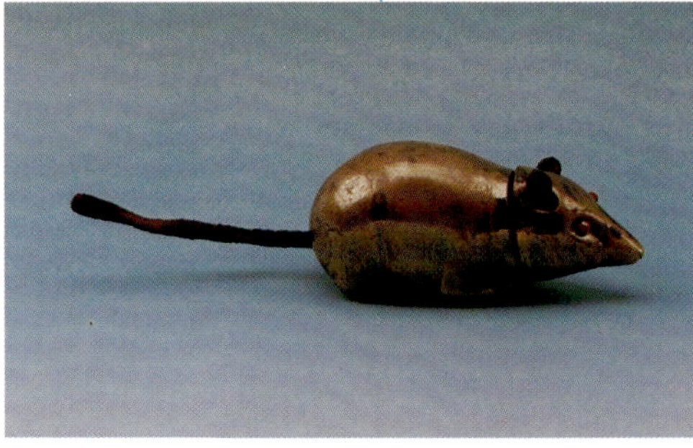

Fig. 243 Europe. Brass. c.1890s. Left: L - 6.1cms. Centre: H -4.5cms. Right: L - 5.1cms.

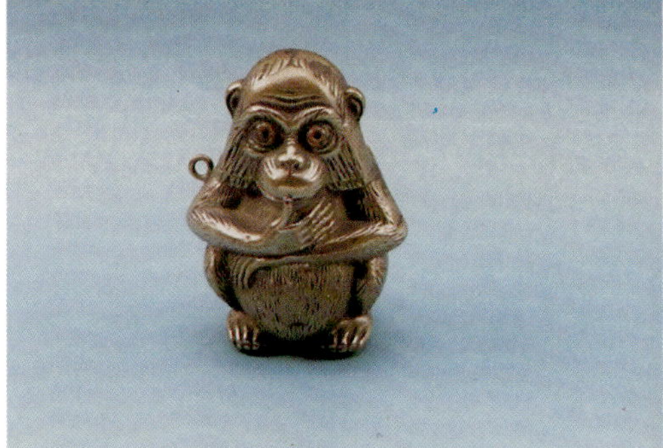

Fig. 244 Europe. Brass. c.1890s. Tail, eyes and ears, replacements. L (of body) - 5.5cms.

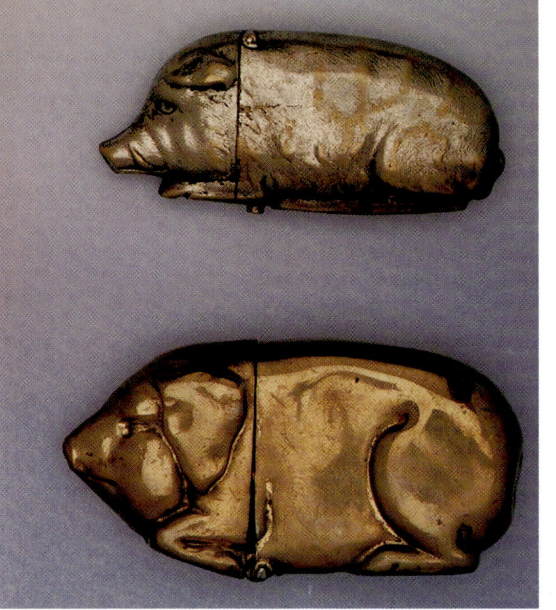

Fig. 242 Europe. Top: plated brass; c.1890s. L - 5.3cms. Lower: brass (tail missing); c.1890s. L - 6cms.

Fig. 245 Europe. Plated brass, glass. c.1890s. H - 5.5cms.

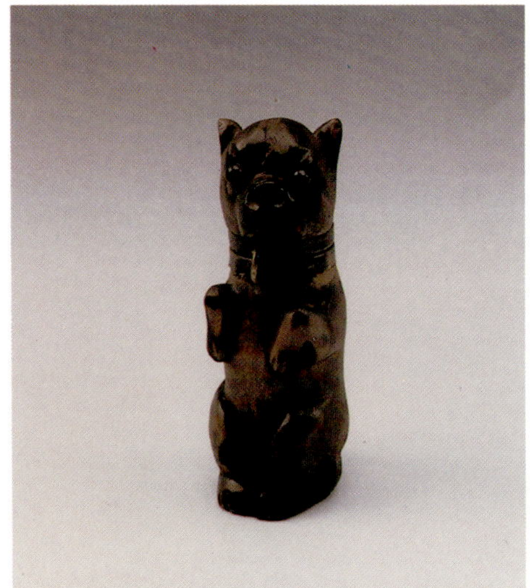

Fig. 241 Europe. Wood, brass, glass. c.1880s. H - 7.8cms.

Another body part that was quite popular was the heart, with two examples in **Fig. 240**. The example at the lower left is in silver, with hallmarks for Chester in 1910, the maker's mark of "S & Bm," and a background design of ivy leaves, which suggests a Birmingham origin. The same mark is recorded for the box in Fig. 88. The silver-plated box at the top right is unmarked, but is probably also of Birmingham origin. A gold box with a small enamelled heart in the center was illustrated in color in the catalogue of the London jewelry firm of Streeters & Co. Ltd., c.l900, and priced at five pounds.

Faunal representations abound. The dog is represented here in **Fig. 241** by an unusual example in wood, with a brass collar that acts as a seating for the head and the body; it is hinged at the back. It has glass eyes, and the striker on the base is formed by a cross-hatching technique. This example may be a little large for the pocket and may have been intended as an item to stand on the mantle-piece.

Porcine examples were a very popular form. Two in a rather two-dimensional aspect are shown in **Fig. 242**. The upper example, in nickel-plated brass, represents a wild boar, and was shown in the Zorn catalogue at $1.25 per dozen or $13.50 per gross. The lower example is in brass. Three-dimensional representations are shown in **Fig. 243**, all in brass, the center example holding a bag, and a subject of modern copies as mentioned previously.

A domestic mouse in brass with leather ears and tail, and glass eyes (replacements in the example) is shown in **Fig. 244**, and what is probably an orangutan, with suspension ring, in **Fig. 245**, made of plated brass.

Three examples in **Fig. 246** depict larger species. That to the left has an elephant surmounting a representation of a canine tooth in plated brass; it is also known to have been made with a lion on top. Top right is an elephant's head in brass with glass eyes and tusks of bone or ivory; the small ears suggest that it is an Indian elephant. A very small box in the form of a lion's head and made of plated brass is at the bottom right; a hole through the nose is probably intended for a suspension ring, and there are sockets for glass eyes.

Representations of two deer legs are shown in **Fig. 247**. The larger piece is made of plated brass and covered with hide. The smaller one is polished brass, but may originally have been plated and with a hide covering. Both are marked with back to back half-moons, the trade mark of G. Goliasch & Co., of Berlin, Germany.

The cockerel's head in **Fig. 248** is brass, with glass eyes and a suspension ring. It may be opened by squeezing the beak, thus releasing the lid on the base, which is also the location of the striker. The fierce-looking eagle in **Fig. 249** has red glass eyes and a suspension ring; it has a nickel-plated finish on brass.

The *carapace* of the turtle in **Fig. 250** is in some form of plastic, probably celluloid, set in a nickel-plated body, with good detailing. The underside, or *plastron*, forms the striker. The head, with small green glass eyes, is hinged on the underside for access to the matches. These are known to have been made by T. Johnson of London in 1881, and many were marked and sold by Walter Thornhill & Co. of New Bond Street.

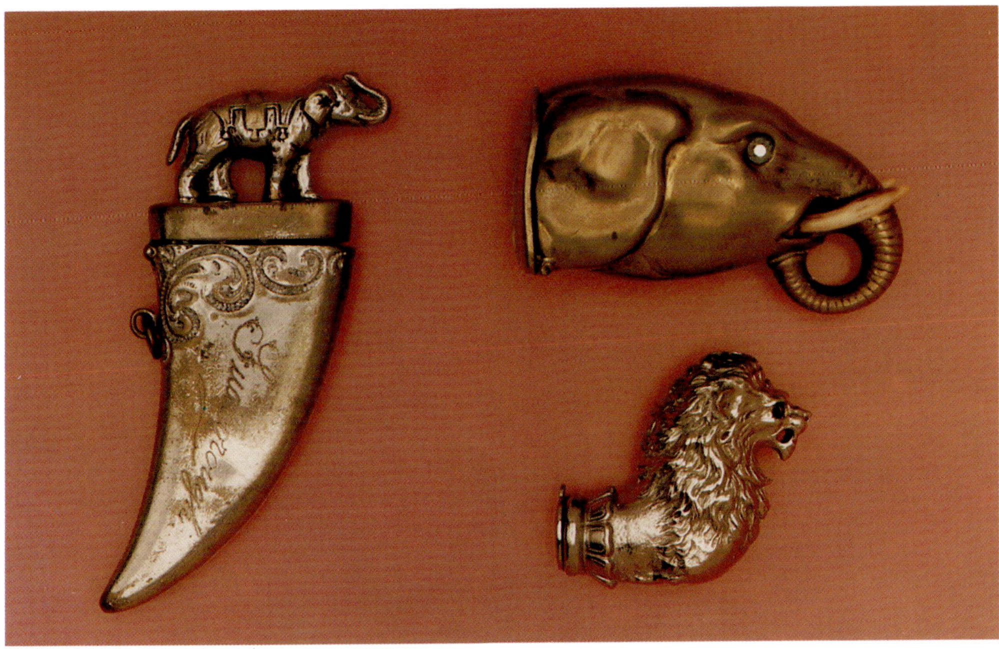

Fig. 246 Europe. Plated brass, brass, glass, bone. c.1890s. Left: H - 7.4cms. Right, top: L - 5.1cms. Right, lower: H - 3.1cms.

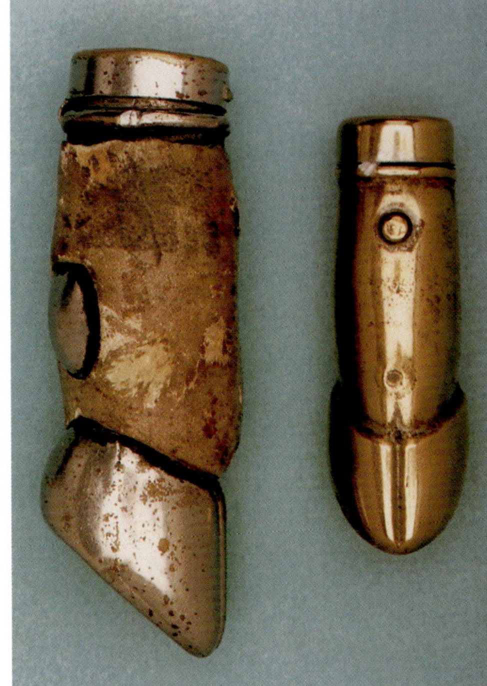

Fig. 247 Germany. Plated brass, skin. c.1890s. Left: H - 7.6cms. Right: made by G. Goliasch & Co. H - 5.7cms.

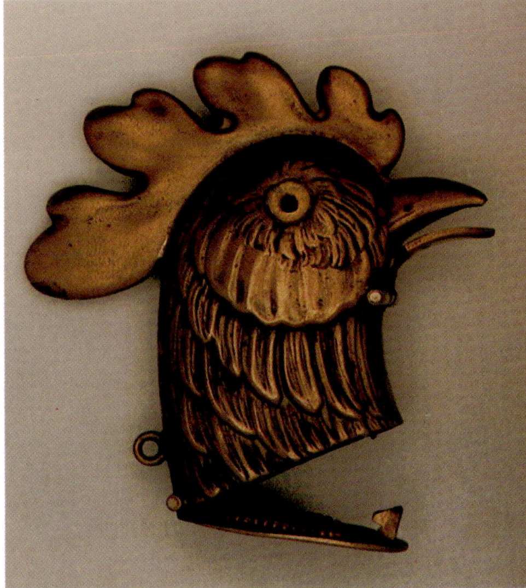

Fig. 248 Europe. Brass, glass. c.1890s. H - 5.1cms.

Fig. 249 Europe. Plated brass, glass. c.1890s. L - 6cms.

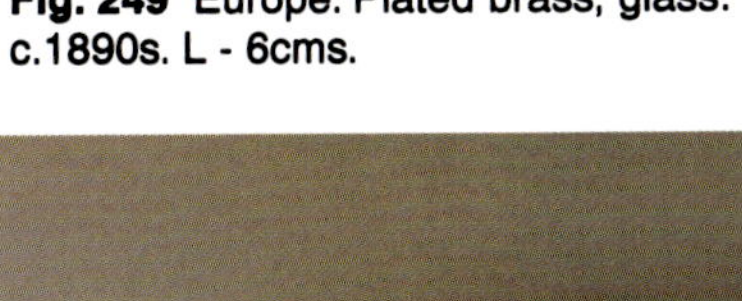

Fig. 250 Britain. Plated brass, ? celluloid, glass. c. 1881. L - 5.7cms.

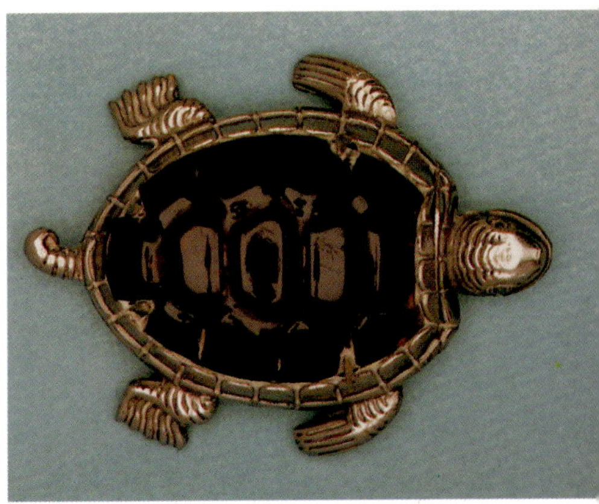

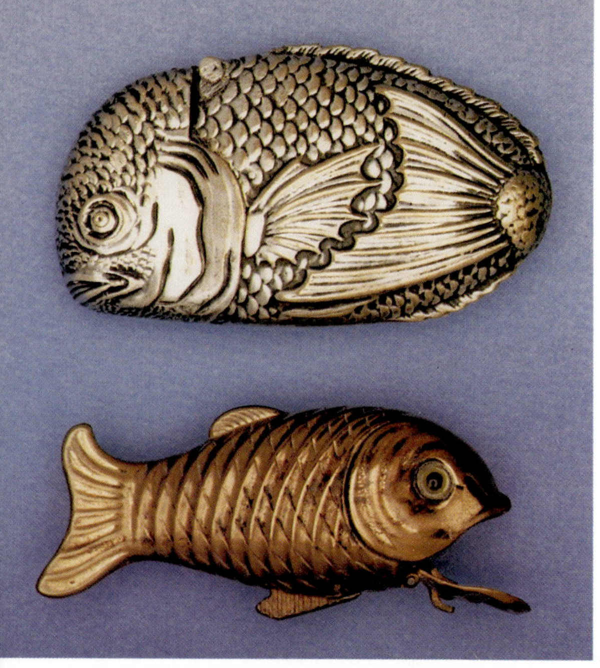

Fig. 251 Europe. Plated brass, brass, glass. c.1890s. Top: L -6.5cms. Lower: L - 5.9cms.

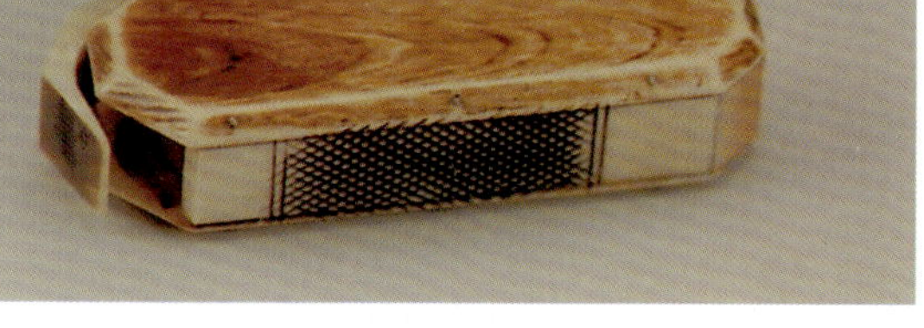

Fig. 252 Europe. Ivory. c.1890s. L - 6.2cms.

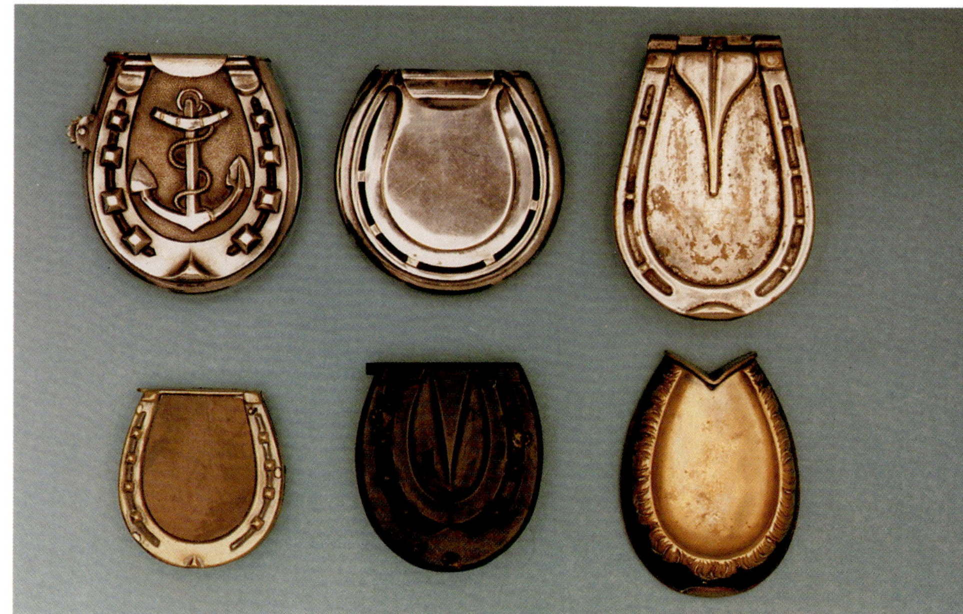

Fig. 255 Europe. Plated brass, brass, vulcanite, leather. c.1870s to 1900. Top right: made by G. Goliasch & Co. H - 6.4cms. Lower left: H - 4.1cms.

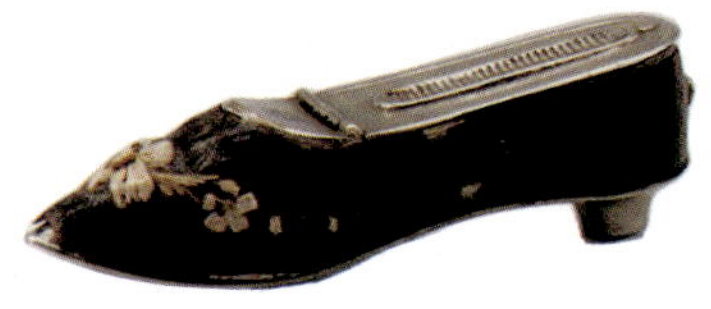

Fig. 253 Europe. Plated brass, leather, ?cotton. c.1890s. L -8.1cms.

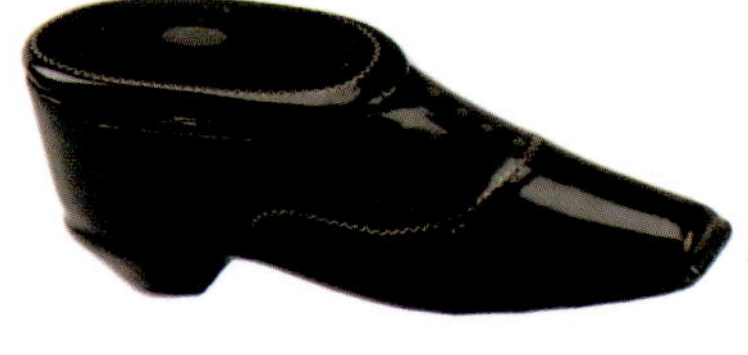

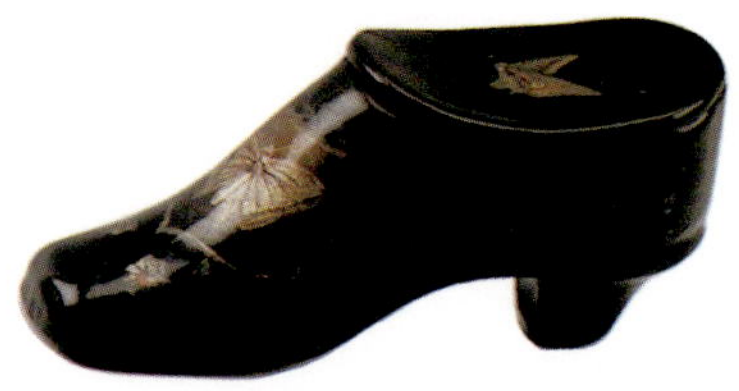

Fig. 254 Europe. Papier mache, pewter. c.1870s. Left: probably Britain; L - 8cms. Right: possibly France; L - 8.1cms.

The representations of fish shown in **Fig. 251** are probably of European origin. The upper example in nickelplated brass is almost identical to one of Japanese origin in patinated copper with some gilding. A third version was shown in the Zorn catalogue with an oxidized finish at $1.75 per dozen or $19.50 per gross, and yet another version appeared in an 1888 catalogue of the Busiest House In America, a Chicago company, in "Old Silver" at $2.00 each. Each version shows only very minor differences. The brass fish below has glass eyes and an articulated mouth, opened by pressing the lower fin.

In ivory and bordering on the macabre is a coffin shown in **Fig. 252**. It has acquired a nice patina from handling during its lifetime.

Shoes were quite popular forms for match holders. The example in **Fig. 253** is made of nickel-plated brass, covered with leather that is decorated with embroidered flowers. Bearing the striker, the lid on the top is released by a push-buttom at the back of the heel, and in front of the lid is an unidentified maker's mark. The two shoes in **Fig. 254** are made of papier maché. That to the left is inlaid with pewter to simulate buttons and seams, with an oval cartouche on the lid. That to the right has finely painted butterflies and flowers on the upper and lid. Both are sanded on the sole for friction.

Horseshoes and horse hooves were also favorites, as the examples in **Fig. 255** demonstrate. At top left is one with an apparent nautical flavor, yet the reverse has a Pointer dog against a background of field and trees. The shape and detail of the horseshoe are impressed work, but the anchor and dog motifs are soldered to the central panels. Around the rim is a tube for tinder cord, the cord becoming exposed when the lid is raised. The cord is pushed out by rotating the cogged wheel on the side, to be ignited by a match, and the smouldering end is used to light a pipe, finally being returned to the tube and extinguished by closing the lid. This holder is made of plated brass, but the type was being made in silver by a London company as early as 1864, and several other versions are known to exist.

The central match holder appears to open in the same manner as the previous piece, but the lid on the top opens only to reveal the striker. The lid for access to the matches is the front panel, which may be opened from the bottom edge with the thumb nail, and in so doing also opens the top lid. It is made of plated brass.

The example at top right, also in plated brass, represents the underside of a horse hoof, which is the lid of the box, opened by a push-button on the lower edge. It has the double half-moon mark of Goliasch & Co., of Berlin. The same design was used by this company for a candle holder and to hold other unspecified objects.

In the bottom row on the left is a brass horseshoe with leather panels. In the center is a vulcanite box; a similar box adorned with a photograph may be seen in Fig. 352. At the right, a representation of a horse hoof in brass, with a black plastic material around the edge to represent the actual hoof. These three boxes all have their lids at the top; none are marked.

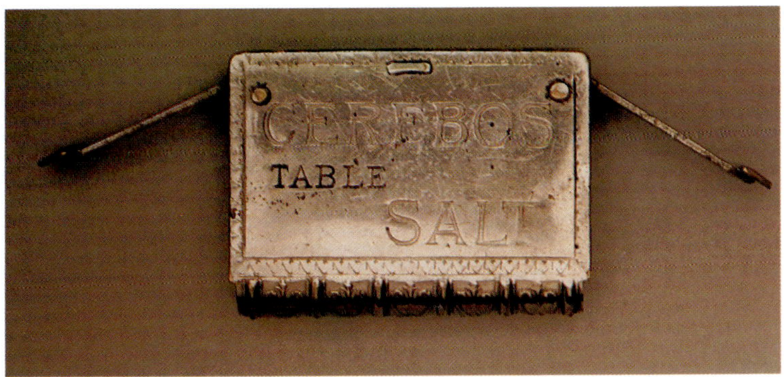

Fig. 256 Britain. Plated brass. Probably made by Buncher & Haseler, c.1880s, to a Registered Design of 1876. H - 4.4cms.

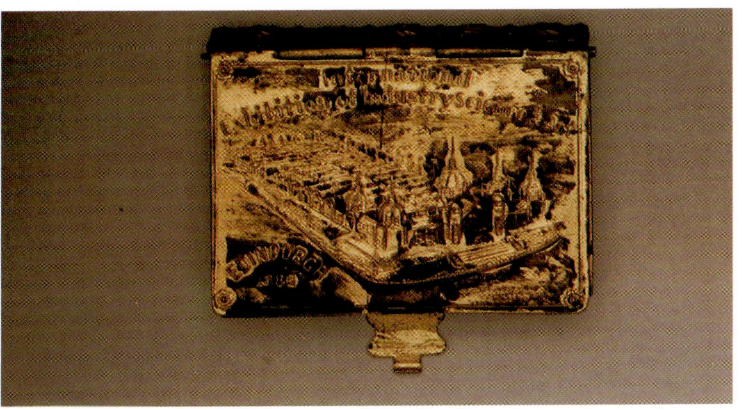

Fig. 257 Britain. Brass. Made to an Invention Patent of 1886 by Hezekiah Hewitt. L - 4.9cms.

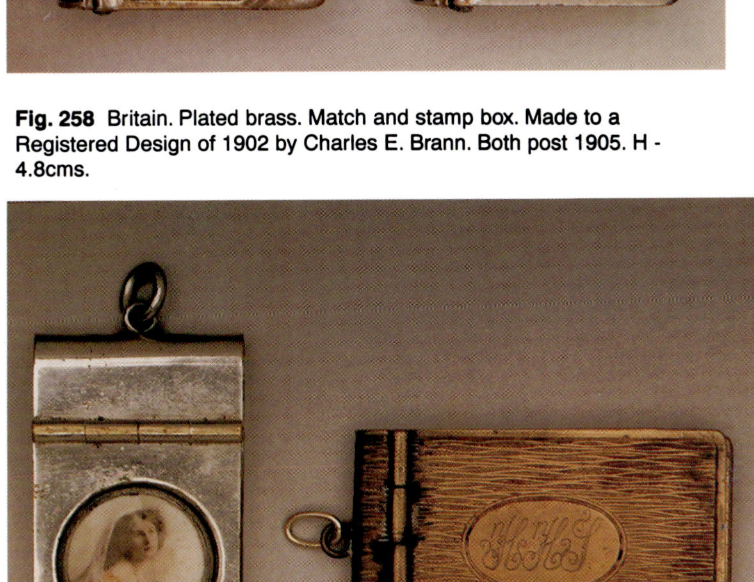

Fig. 258 Britain. Plated brass. Match and stamp box. Made to a Registered Design of 1902 by Charles E. Brann. Both post 1905. H - 4.8cms.

Fig. 259 Probably Britain. Plated brass, brass, celluloid. c.1900. L - 5.4cms.

Book forms are perhaps the most common shape of novelty match holders to be found; several more examples are to be seen in other parts of this chapter. The plated brass example in **Fig. 256** is unmarked, but was made to a Registered Ornamental Design of 1876 by Buncher & Haseler of Birmingham. The design protection only lasted for three years, so this example must be post-1879.

The gold-lacquered brass box in **Fig. 257** was the subject of an Invention Patent of 1886 issued to Hezekiah Hewitt, a steel pen and penholder manufacturer of Birmingham, for the "Manufacture of Metallic Boxes for Holding Steel Pens, Pins, Needles, and other Small Articles." The front cover acts as the lid, held closed by a clasp, and is impressed "International Exhibition of Industry Science & Art. EDINBURGH. 1886." The spine is impressed "VOL.II," and the back cover "D.LEONARDT & CO. BIRMINGHAM. UNIVERSAL PEN. WHOLESALE AGENTS, ORMISTON GLASS, EDINBURGH." The box was no doubt sold at the exhibition full of steel pen nibs, but the top and bottom edges are roughened for friction, and the box was evidently intended to be used for matches when the nibs had been exhausted. This is one of the earliest examples of a box with a secondary use once the original contents were gone; such boxes are the subject of Part 10 of this chapter.

The nickel-plated brass examples in **Fig. 258** were the subject of a Registered Design in 1902 issued to Charles E. Brann of London, a "Fancy Goods Merchant." They are combination boxes: one side opens for the matches, the other side to reveal a compartment for postage stamps. The example at the left is marked with the Registration Number and "C.E.B.," that to the right is unmarked and is probably therefore post-1905. They may be found with various designs, including the crest of the Isle of Man (three legs); others have red, blue or green enamelled covers. A second Registered Design of 1912 was identical except that the second side was constructed to hold sovereigns, a coin that went out of use a few years later when the pound note replaced the coin early in World War I.

The examples in **Fig. 259** represent ledger type books; both are unmarked. In the plated brass box at the left, the cover has a photograph of a lady, probably in her wedding gown, held under celluloid in a frame attached to the lid with a pair of lugs. The box to the right is of brass. Both are provided with suspension rings.

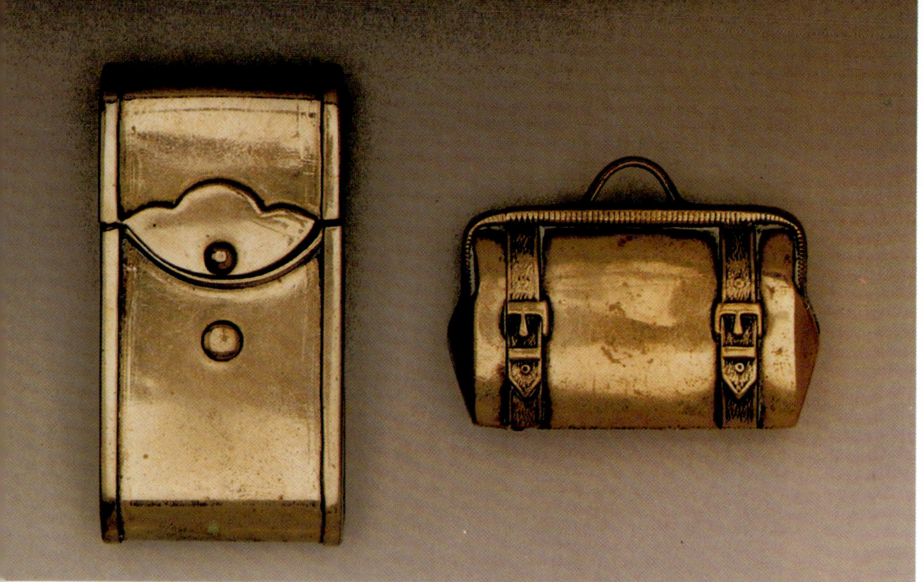

Fig. 260 Europe. Brass. c.1890s. Left: made by same company as shoe in Fig. 253; H - 6.3cms. Right: L - 4.8cms.

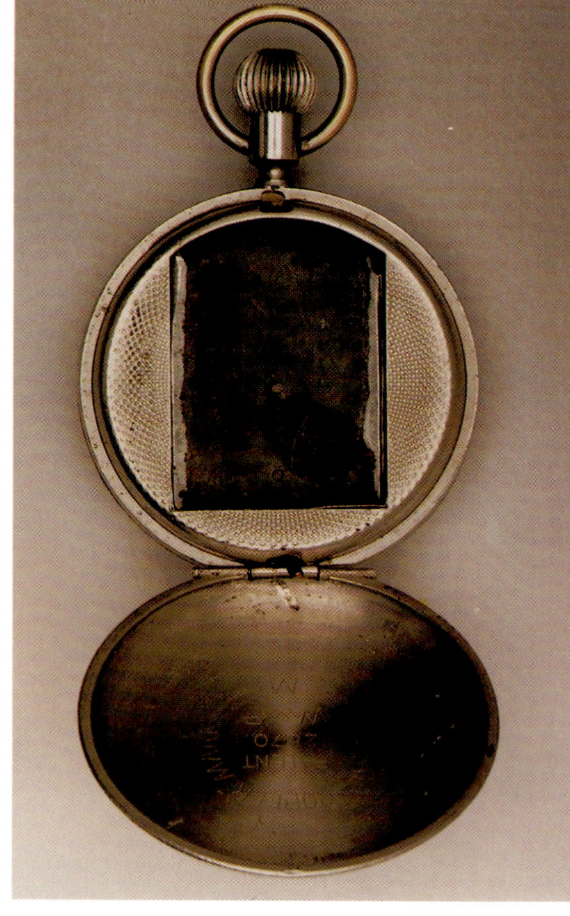

Fig. 263 Inside of back of Fig. 262.

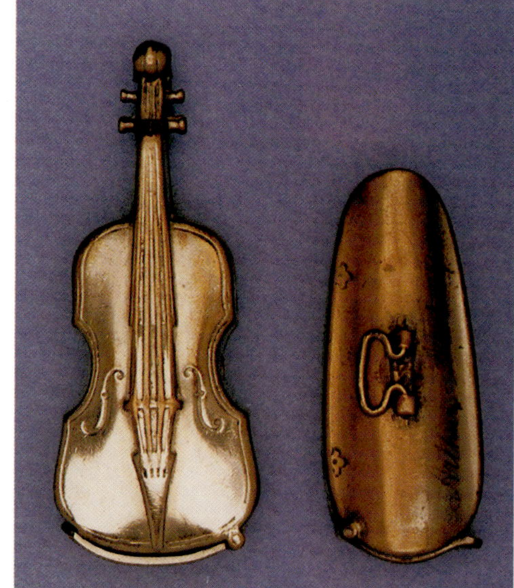
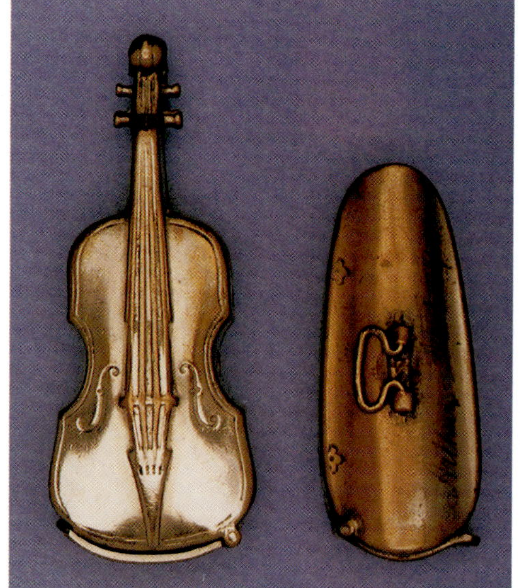

Fig. 261 Europe. Plated brass. c.1890s. Left: H - 6.5cms. Right: H - 4.9cms.

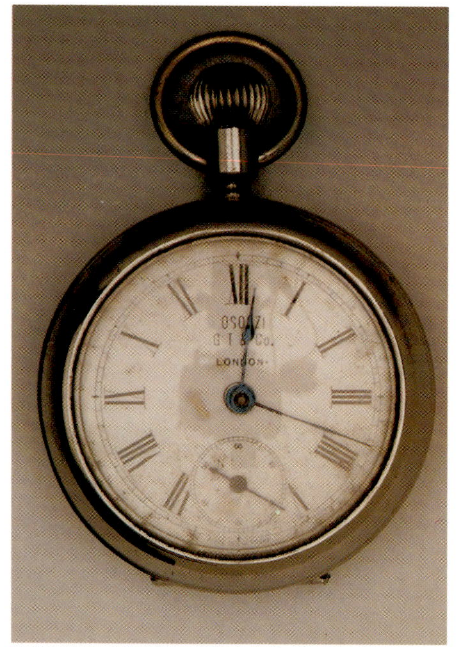

Fig. 262 Britain. Plated brass, tin plate, glass. Made to an Invention Patent of 1899 by Gregory A. Robinson. H - 7.5cms.

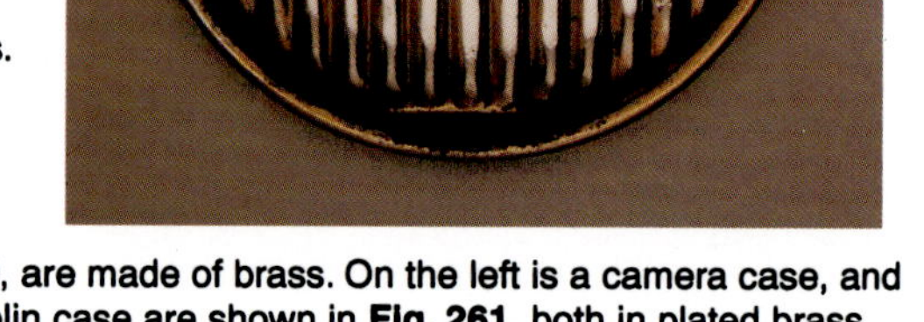

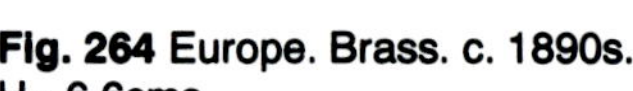

Fig. 264 Europe. Brass. c. 1890s. H - 6.6cms.

Two cases of very different use, in **Fig. 260**, are made of brass. On the left is a camera case, and on the right a "Gladstone" bag. A violin and a violin case are shown in **Fig. 261**, both in plated brass.

The pocket watch case in **Fig. 262** was no doubt made as a standard inexpensive watch case in plated brass to hold an inexpensive movement. The dial was made in Germany and is marked "Osoezi" (Oh so easy) and "G.T. & Co. London". The inside of the back cover, which is released by pressing the winder, is marked "W & P. M. TRADE 'POPLER' MARK. PATENT 2870," believed to be a Manchester company. The patent was issued in 1899 to Gregory A. Robinson of London, a "Fancy Importer," and was for a "Watch Case and Vesta Box Combined" in which the works may or may not be included. The match box, with its own lid, was attached to the inside of the case. The interior of the end product is shown in **Fig. 263**, the works replaced by a cavity lined with tin plate to hold the matches, and a surrounding cover to fill the rest of the void with an impressed design suitable for use as the striker.

Although the box in **Fig. 264** has the appearance of a pocket watch superficially, it was made specifically as a match holder. It is made of brass with a gold lacquer finish, the edge seamed as in Fig. 78.a.

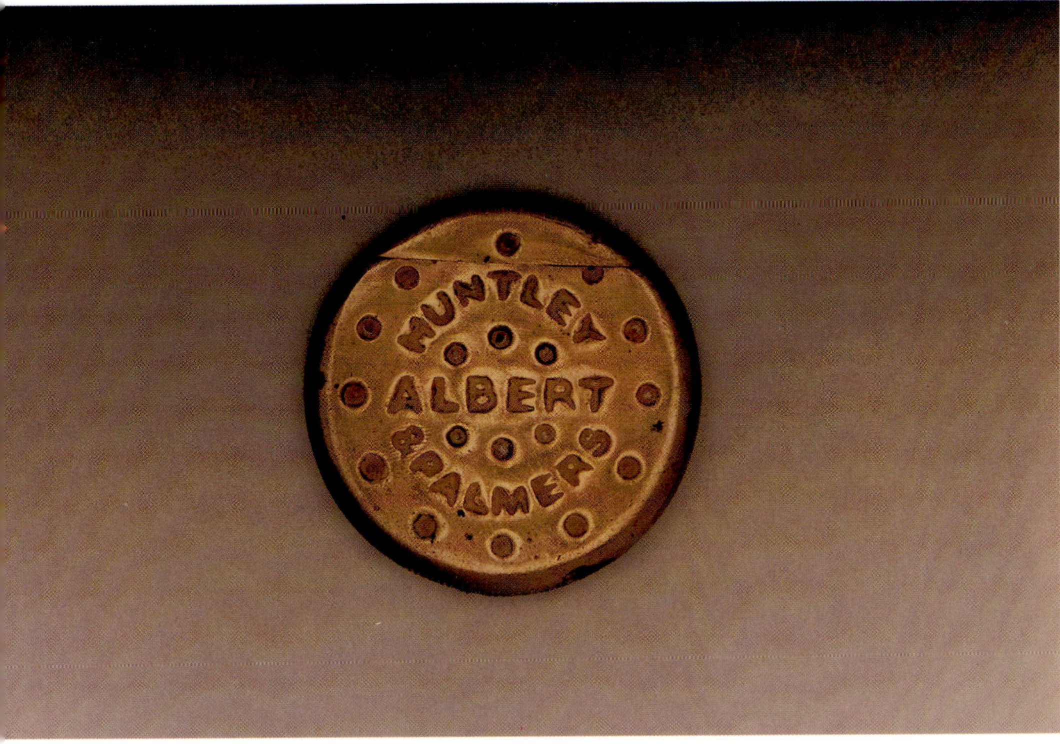

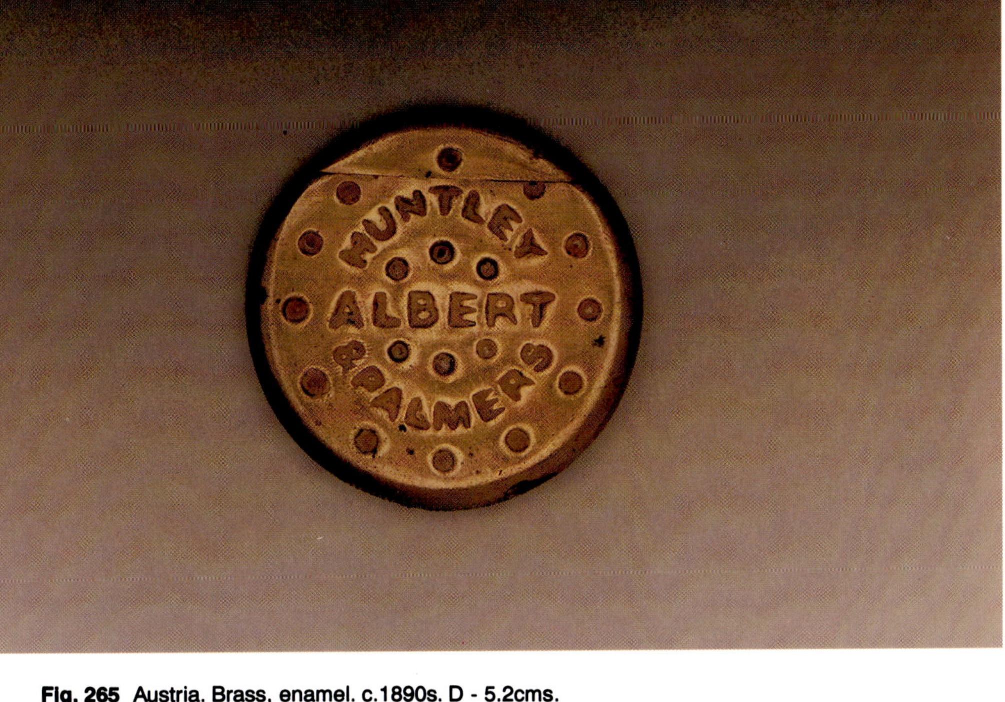

Fig. 265 Austria. Brass, enamel. c.1890s. D - 5.2cms.

Fig. 267 Austria. Plated brass. c.1890s. H - 6cms.

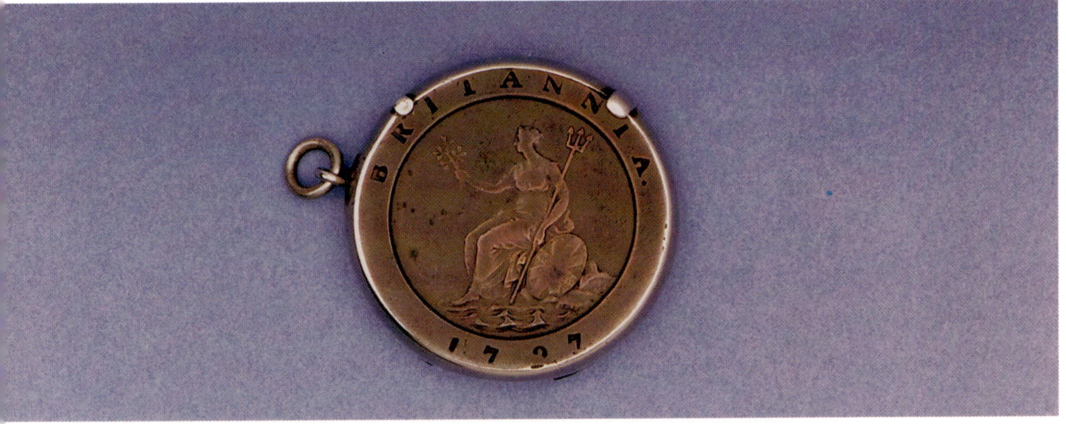

Fig. 266 Britain. Copper, plated brass. c. 1890s. D - 4.4cms.

Marked "MADE IN VIENNA," the box in **Fig. 265** is made of brass, enamelled to represent a biscuit. The box also bears the word "GESCHUTZI," indicating that it was the subject of a registered design or patent. This was one of several novelty boxes offered by Salmon & Gluckstein, London wholesalers of tobacco and sundries in 1899; the product line also included a pig and a bottle, priced from three to six pence each.

An unusual item shown in **Fig. 266** is made from a two penny piece known as the "Cartwheel penny." The coin was designed and made by Matthew Boulton, a prominent Birmingham silversmith with his own mint. A copper penny that weighed exactly one ounce and the two penny piece weighing two ounces were introduced at the same time in 1797, but the latter was less popular and only produced for a short period. The penny piece was produced for some years, although all of the coins were marked for 1797. The two penny piece in the example was cut in half, the front and back halves separated by a silver-plated rim with a lid and striker; the box is unmarked. A second example has been recorded marked "A. Barrett & Sons, 53-54 Piccadilly," a London company who may have been the makers. The reverse side of coin has the head of King George III.

It is probably almost inevitable that, with drinking and smoking closely linked as social habits, representations of drink-related match holders were commonplace. Beer is represented by the Bass & Co. Pale Ale bottle in **Fig. 267,** with the company's red triangle trademark (the first trademark registered in Britain on January 1, 1876), and Guinness's Stout bottle in **Fig. 268**. Both were made in Austria, of brass, were hinged below the neck at the back, and had the striker on the base.

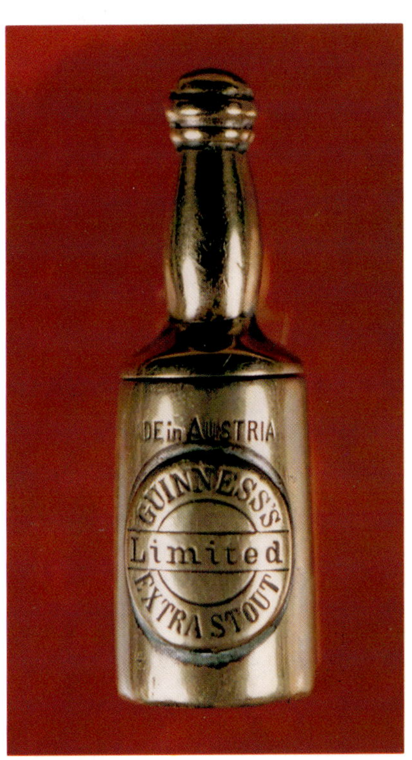

Fig. 268 Austria. Brass. c.1890s. H - 6cms.

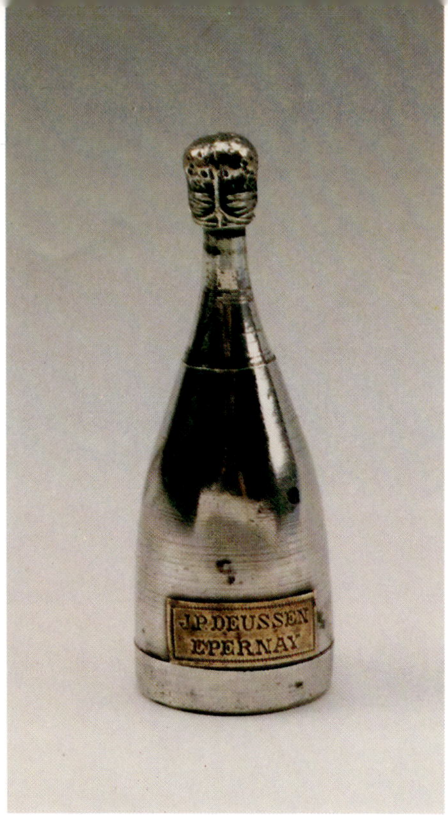

Fig. 269 Probably France. Plated brass, brass. c.1890s. H -7.1cms.

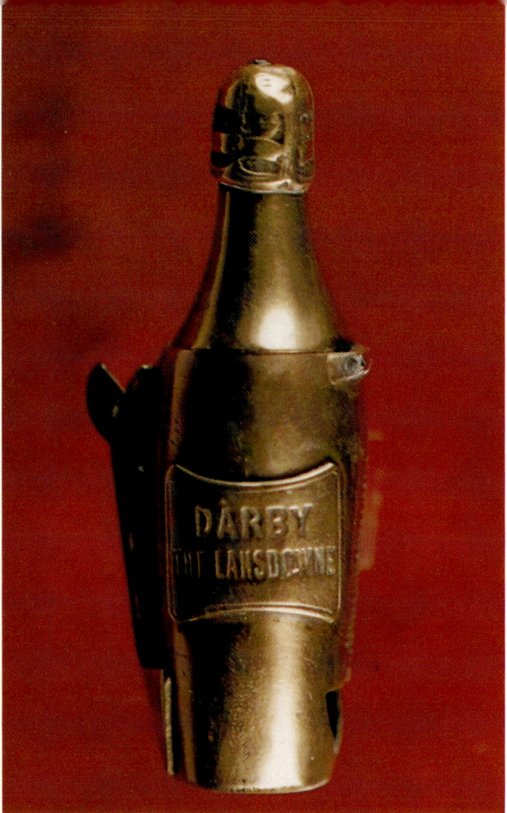

Fig. 271 Europe. Brass. With cigar cutter. c.1890s. H - 6.8cms.

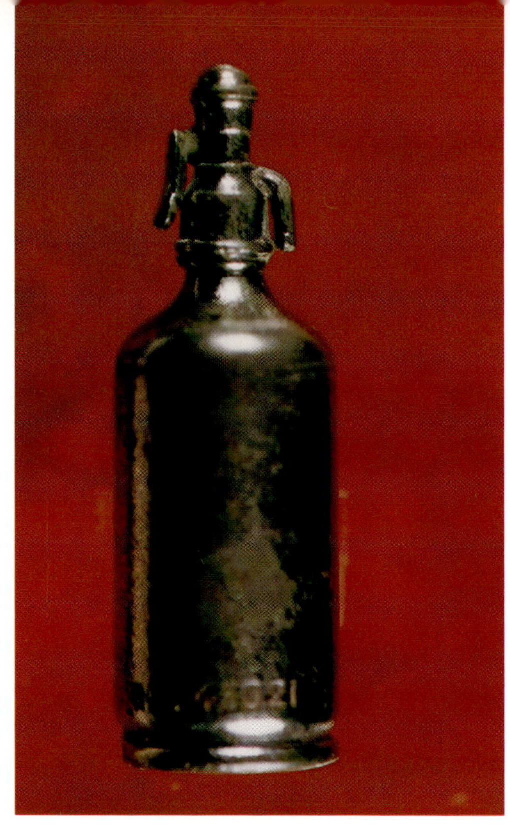

Fig. 272 Britain. Plated brass. Made to a Registered Design of 1894. H - 6.5cms.

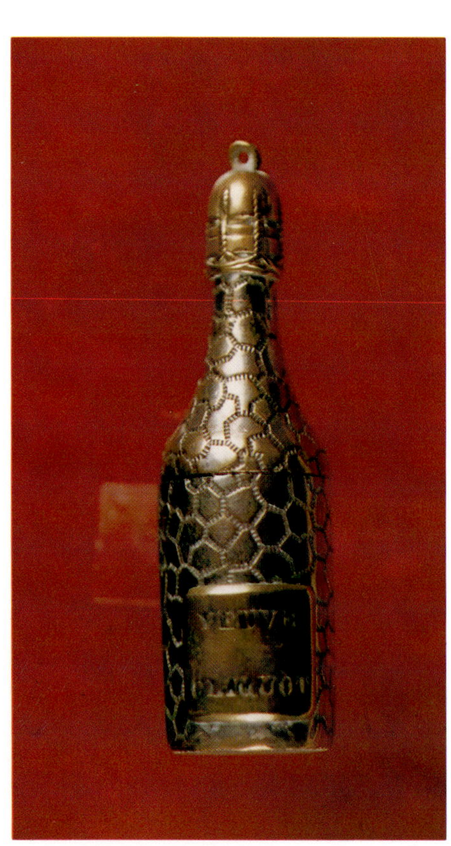

Fig. 270 Probably France. Brass. c.1890s. H - 6.5cms.

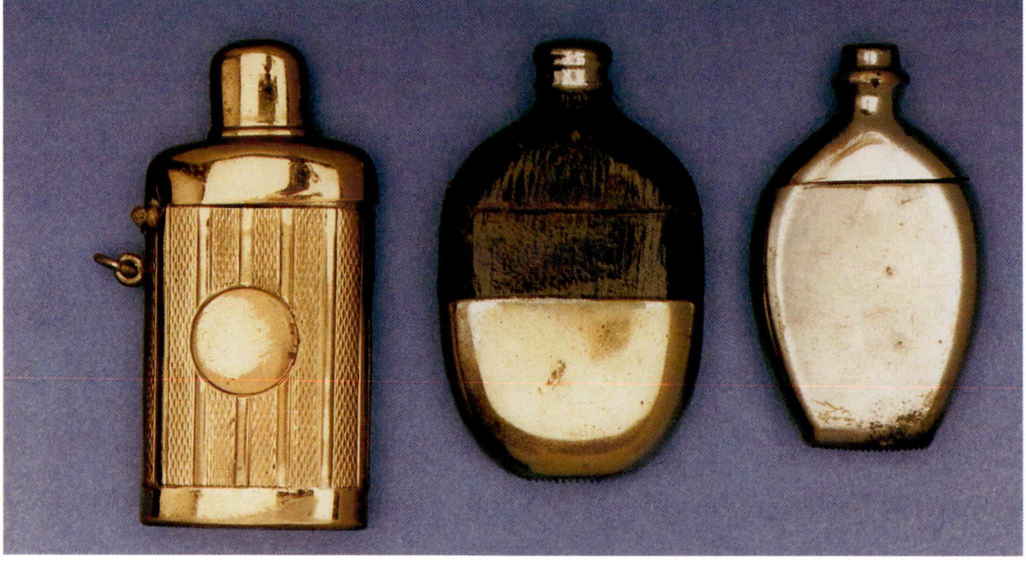

Fig. 273 Europe. Brass, plated brass, leather. c.1890s. Left: H -6.4cms. Centre: H - 5.9cms. Right: H - 5.3cms.

Champagne was well represented, with a silver-plated bottle featuring a brass label advertising "J.P.DEUSSEN. EPERNAY," the base hinged for access to the matches and with a concentric circle striker, in **Fig. 269. Fig. 270** shows a bottle of "VEUVE CLIQUOT." The match holder in **Fig. 271** reads "DARBY. THE LANDSDOWN;" a cigar cutter is incorporated into the bottom with its lever up the side, a feature found on several bottles. The last two are hinged just below the neck, and made of brass.

For those who liked their whisky or brandy diluted, there was a soda syphon, shown in **Fig. 272.** Made of nickel plated brass, it too opened just below the neck, and bears a Registered Number for 1894.

Fig. 273 shows three flasks of the 'dram', 'hip', 'pocket' or 'spirit' type. That at the left is in gold lacquered brass, the lid hinged at the side and with a suspension ring, and the top representing a cup. The box in the center is in nickel-plated brass, with the top half covered in black leather; the lower section represents the drinking cup. The box at the right, in nickel-plated brass, may represent a flat bottle, a similar version being shown in the Harrod's Stores Ltd. catalogue of 1895 for ten and a half pence.

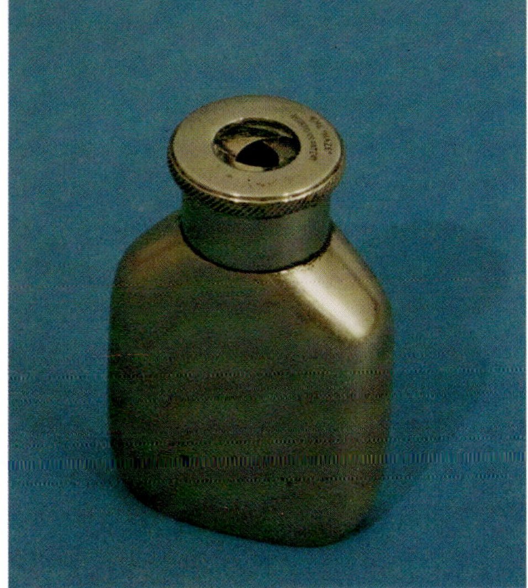

Fig. 274 Britain. Plated brass. Made to Invention Patents in Britain and France of 1895, by Thomas Morton. H - 5cms.

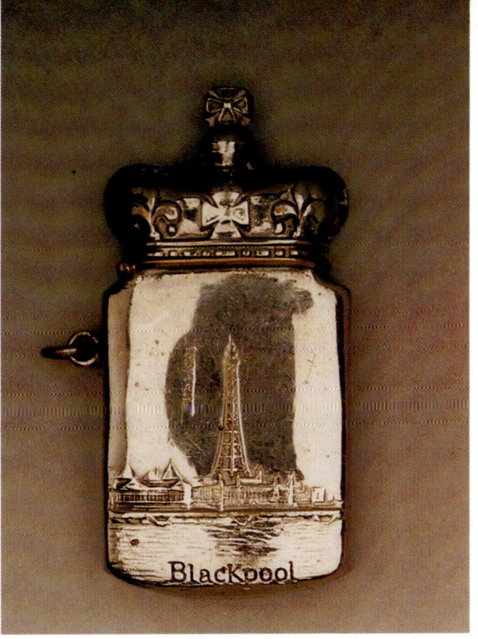

Fig. 276 Europe. Plated brass. c.1900. H - 6.6cms.

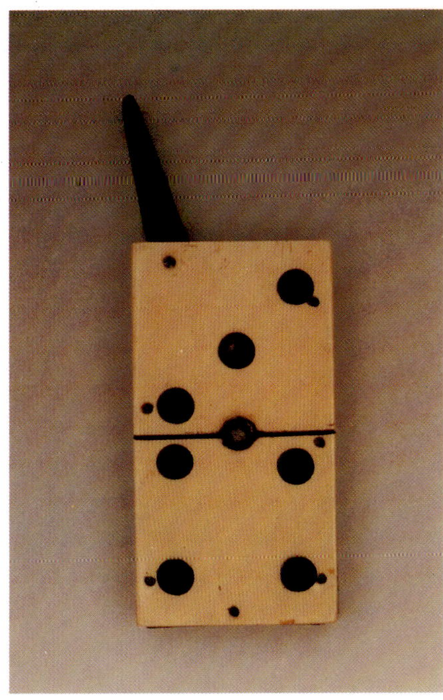

Fig. 278 Europe. Vulcanite, celluloid. c.1880s. H - 4.9cms.

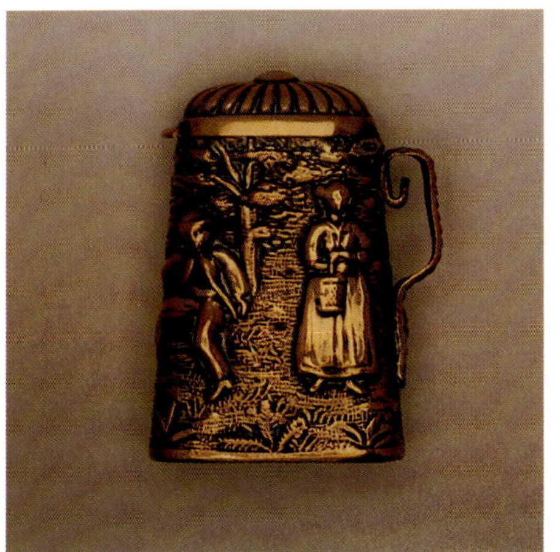

Fig. 275 Europe. Brass. c.1890s. H - 4.2cms.

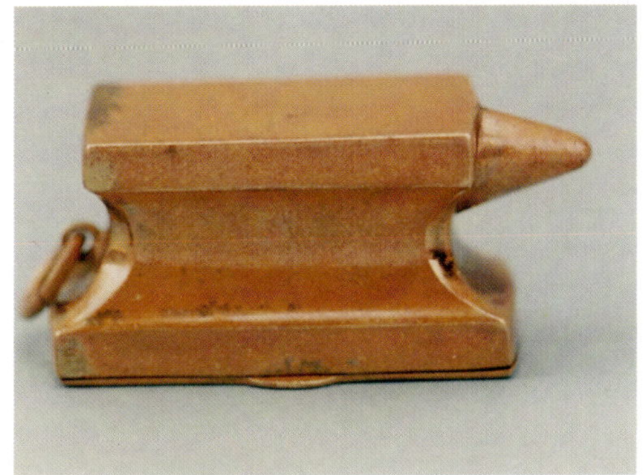

Fig. 277 Europe. Brass. c.1890s. L - 5.5cms.

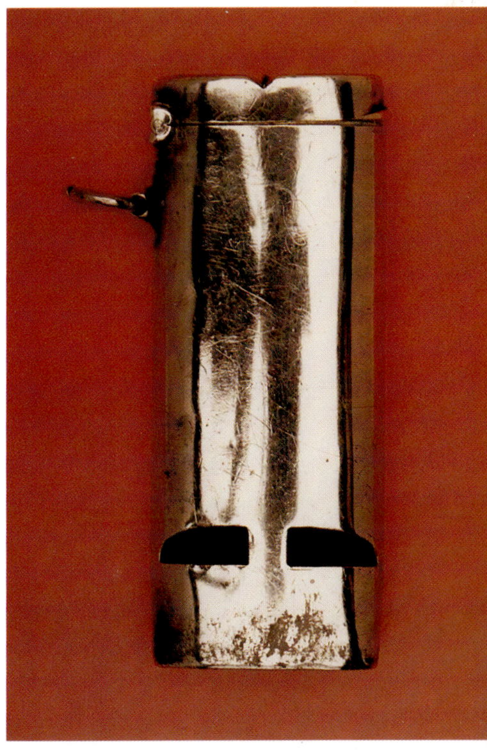

Fig. 279 Britain. Silver. Match holder and whistle. Made by the Goldsmiths & Silversmiths Co.Ltd., 1902. L - 7.7cms.

The flask or bottle in **Fig. 274** is in nickel-plated brass, and is marked on the top of the rim "THE MAZE. MORTON'S PATENT." The rim has a knurled edge which may be turned to open three plates (like the shutter of a camera) for access to the matches. The illustration shows the plates at the mid-way stage. One plate is marked "BREVETE.S.G.D.G." - Patent—that is, without government guarantee (of quality). Thomas Morton of Birmingham was a Stamper and Piercer; he patented his box in Britain and in France in 1895 and probably made them himself.

The brass beer stein in **Fig. 275** is decorated with impressed male and female figures set against a background of grass and trees, the same design on both sides. Although unmarked, it is assumed from the subject matter to be of Austrian or German origin.

A box with its lid in the form of a crown is shown in **Fig. 276.** The body has impressed designs illustrating the sea-front at the resort of Blackpool, the skyline dominated by the famous tower which was not completed until 1895, thereby dating this piece as post-1895. Made of nickel-plated brass, it is marked "FOREIGN," and was no doubt made as a cheap souvenir of the seaside town.

Some of the novelty boxes may perhaps have been intended to attract buyers by symbolizing their profession; thus the anvil in **Fig. 277,** perhaps for a blacksmith or an engineer. The box is made of brass, its base forming the lid for access to the matches.

The domino in **Fig. 278** has a main body and lid made of black vulcanite representing an ebony back, and a celluloid front depicting the ivory face. Examples may be found with different numbers of dots. Other versions produced included brass boxes, a silver and copper version marked for Birmingham in 1891-92, and a silver and enamelled version made by a London company in 1881-82.

In London it was common practice to hail a horse-drawn taxi by whistling, and a hotel or club doorman carried whistles for the purpose. Thus a whistle was a natural item to combine with a match holder, an example of which is shown in **Fig. 279.** It is made of silver with the striker formed from a piece of saw-toothed steel set into the lid, by the Goldsmiths & Silversmiths Co. Ltd., of London in 1902. The Harrod's Stores Ltd. catalogue of 1895 shows two similar whistles, both using the same 'cut', and obviously the same item, but one in the Cigars and Tobacco Department at twenty one shillings, and the other in the Jewellery Department (on the floor above) at twenty three shillings and six pence; the latter was described as a "Solid Silver Match Box with Cab Whistle."

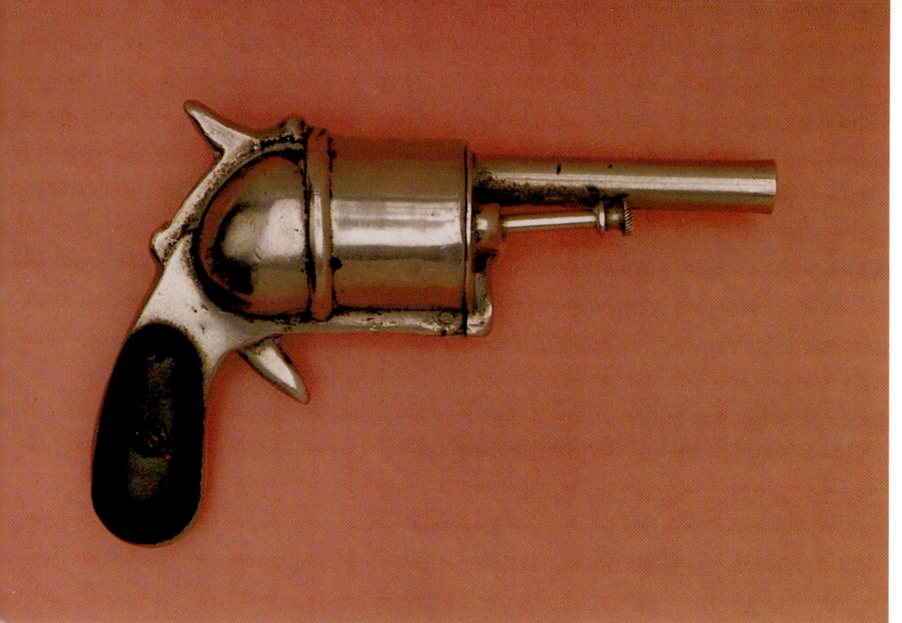

Fig. 280 Europe. Plated brass, vulcanite. c.1890s. L - 8.8cms.

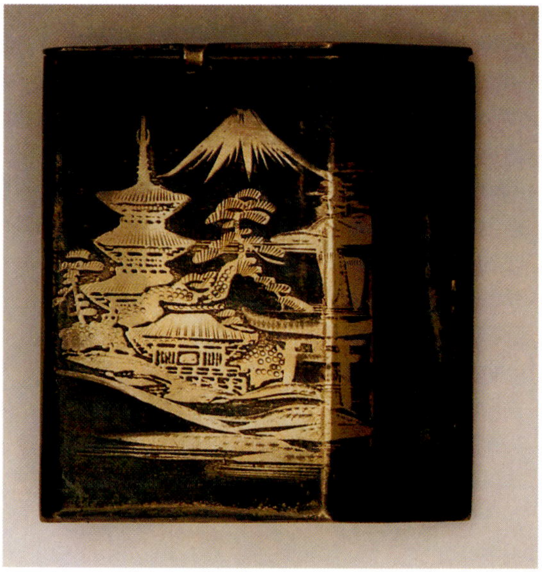

Fig. 283 Japan. Brass and gold inlay. c.1930s. H - 6.2cms.

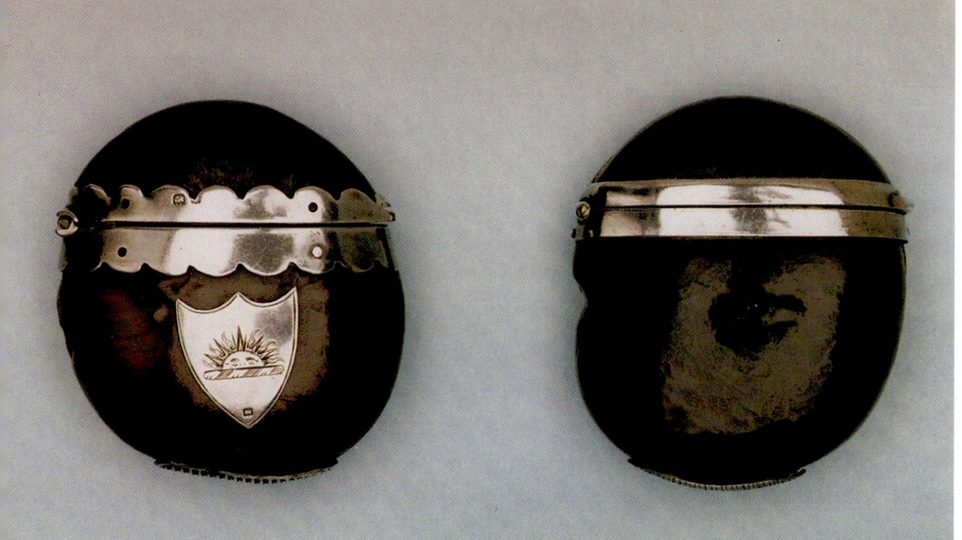

Fig. 281 Britain. The seed of the "Entada Scandens", silver, silver plate. Left: 1905; H - 5cms. Right: c.1905; H - 5.2cms.

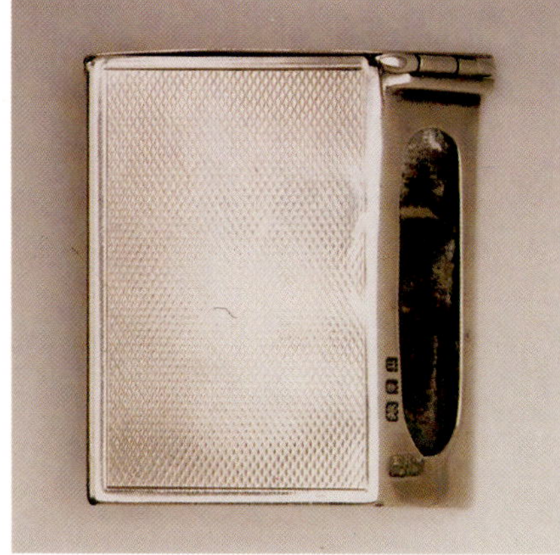

Fig. 282 Britain. Silver. 1935. H - 4.5cms.

The pistol in **Fig. 280** is hinged just below the barrel at the front of the chamber, which acts as the match compartment. The striker is located along the underside of the barrel. It is made of plated brass with vulcanite hand grips.

The examples in **Fig. 281** are included in the novelty category more for material than for shape. The bodies and lids are made from the seed of the *Entada Scandens, a* species of tree or vine that produces a very large seed pod of two to four feet long, and three to four inches across, containing many hard, polished, chestnut-colored seeds. The species grows widely in the tropics, and is particularly common in the Caribbean, where it is also known as the St. Thomas bean. It is perhaps best known as the sea bean, possibly from the fact that the seeds have been known to get into the Gulf Stream and float to the north-western coasts of Europe. It is also known as the nicker bean and the sword bean. Also used for snuff and jewel boxes, the bean has a segment cut off from the main part; the hard but brittle white inside layer is cleaned out, and the two parts are fitted with rims and a hinge, or a flat lid may be substituted for the top, and the striker and some decorative elements may be added. The example at the left has silver fittings, with hallmarks for Birmingham, 1905, and an inidentified maker "R.P." The example to the right has silver-plated fittings.

Of much later vintage, from a period when these small pocket match holders had all but disappeared, is a silver novelty match box holder in the form of a partially flattened box, shown in **Fig. 282.** The outer cover of a store-bought box of matches is removed, pressed to one side and inserted inside the silver box, which leaves the strikers of the internal box exposed through slots on both sides of the silver box. The matches are then transferred from the original box. The example is hallmarked for London, 1935, but the makers mark is unreadable.

A similar form of match box holder is shown in **Fig. 283,** but is of Japanese origin. It is made of brass with gilded decoration, almost inevitably with Mount Fuji as the background to the scene illustrated, and with three butterflies on the reverse. It probably dates from about the same time as the previous piece.

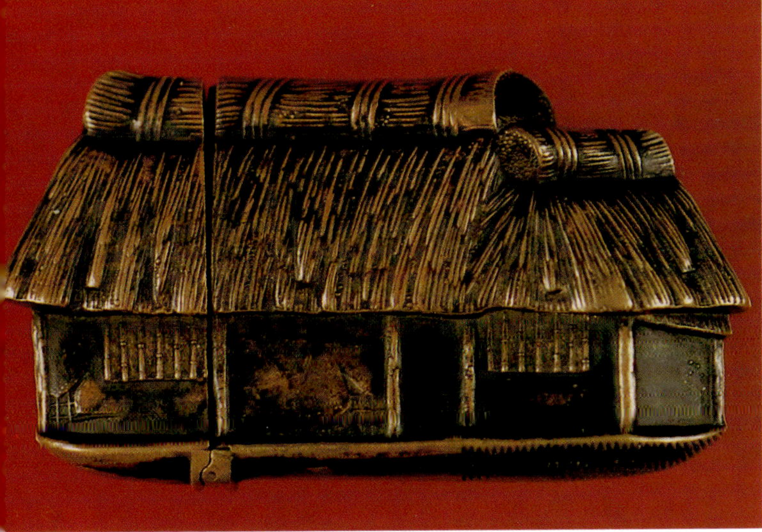

Fig. 284 Japan. Brass. c.1890s. L - 6.6cms.

Fig. 285 Reverse of Fig. 284.

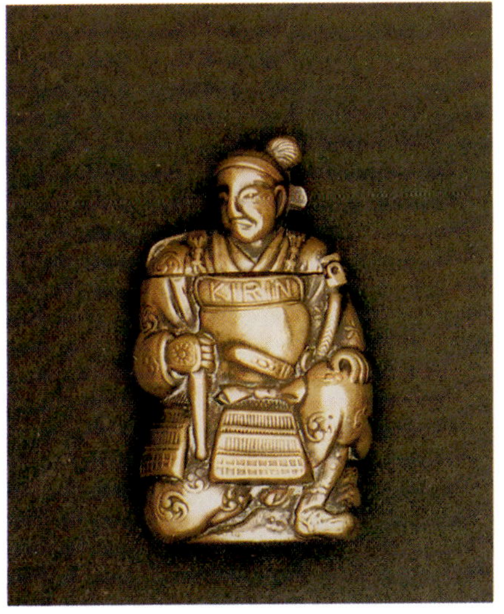

Fig. 286 Japan. Brass. post 1907. H - 4.7cms.

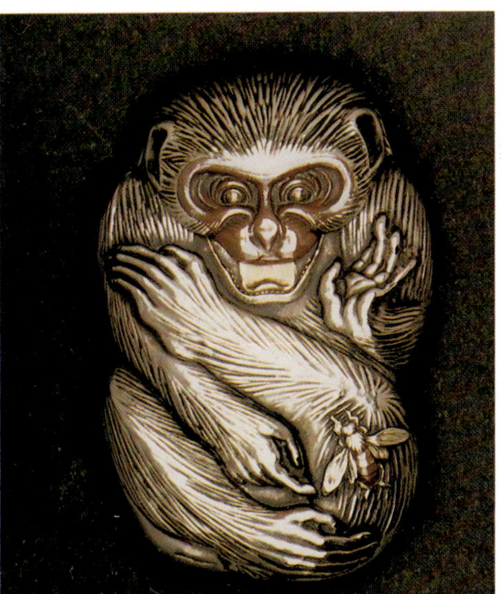

Fig. 288 Japan. ?Brass, ?copper, gold. c.1890s. H - 6.6cms.

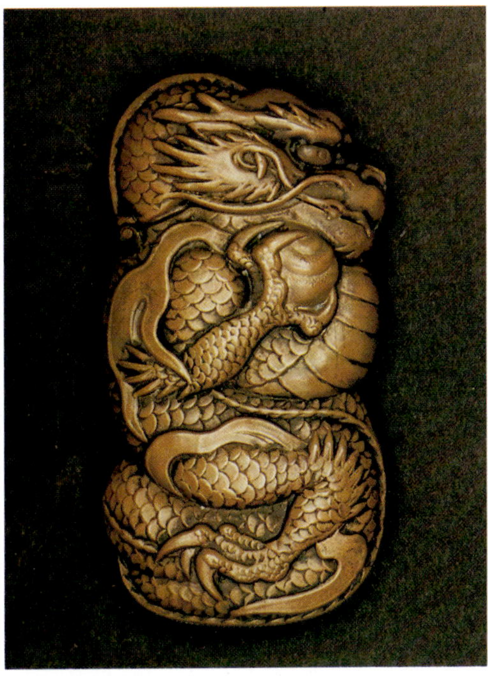

Fig. 287 Japan. Brass. c.1890s. H - 6.9cms.

The Japanese exhibited great imagination in their range of earlier novelty match holders, coupled with fine technical skill and an eye for detail that surpasses those of their European counterparts. Both sides of a Japanese farm house are shown in **Figs. 284 and 285,** in brass, exhibiting even greater detail when examined under a strong magnifying glass.

The example in **Fig. 286** is a Samurai warrior in armor, but without his helmet (which would only be worn going into battle). However, the breast plate bears the word "KIRIN," a Japanese brewery established in 1907. The holder is therefore an advertising item, which is believed to be unusual for a Japanese product of this type. Again there is great attention to detail.

The brass dragon in **Fig. 287** is clutching a sphere, probably representing a pearl, its head hinged at one side. While the monkey in **Fig. 288** (probably also brass) has a gold tongue and a two-tone brass color fly on its left leg, the head hinged at the back.

Shown in **Fig. 289** in copper is a fine stylized melon, with a species of fly just below the lid, and a leaf, both with gold plating. On the reverse is a lizard in silver and two more gold-plated leaves.

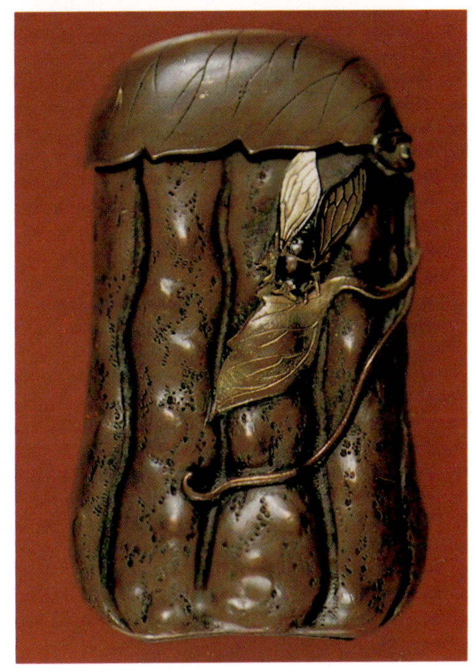

Fig. 289 Japan. Copper, gold plate, silver. c.1890s. H - 5.3cms.

46 A. A. VANTINE & CO.,

MATCH SAFES.

Pocket Match Safes.

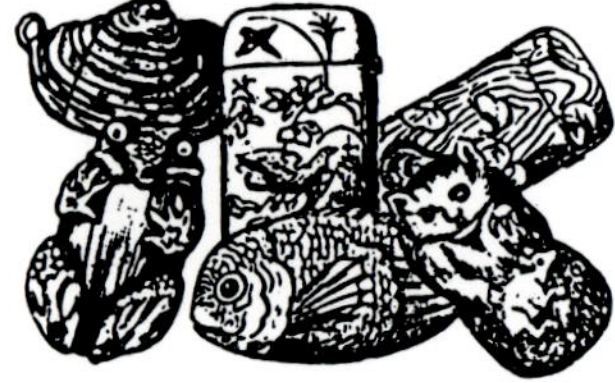

Fig. 290 Illustration of Japanese match holders from an 1895 catalogue of A. A. Vantine & Co..

There were numerous other forms of novelty match holders produced in Japan, those illustrated here being of exceptional quality; cats, toads and rabbits were also very popular subjects. **Fig. 290** is an illustration from a catalogue of 1895 by A.A.Vantine & Co. of New York, importers "From the Empires of Japan, China, India, Turkey, Persia and the East." A small frog was priced at 17¢, a larger frog at 35¢, the fish at 37¢, and the cat at 75¢. Rectangular boxes were priced from 30¢ to 42¢ each.

The final match holder shown in this section, **Fig. 291,** is marked "Sterling" and was made in Thailand—within the last two or three years! This, and several other match holders copying the earlier United States forms and styles of designs, are being imported into the United States and Britain, openly and honestly, all marked "Sterling." However, their original packaging and labels are being discarded, and they are being placed on the antique market to be sold as antiques. It is recommended that an article written by George Sparacio (see the bibliography for futher information) be read for further details, or that the buyer beware.

These examples of novelty-shaped match holders are only a small sampling of the extensive range from around the world. Further examples can be found in other parts of this chapter to illustrate other aspects of pocket match holders. There was something to satisfy all tastes and all pocketbooks. Match holders are evocative of their periods, amusing, entertaining, and often good reflection of social status, but at the same time were useful objects—particularly if you were a smoker.

The Victorian period craved novelty, and match holders provided craftsmen with an ideal forum for displaying their ingenuity and technical skills, particularly from the mid-1880s through to the pre-World War I period.

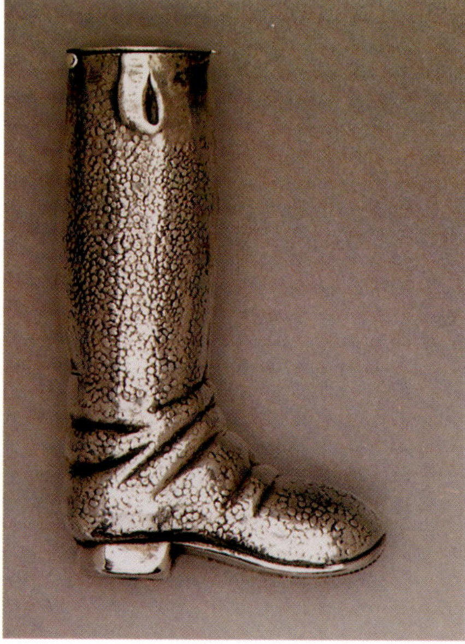

Fig. 291 Probably Thailand. Silver. c.1992.

PART 5: THREE-PIECE BOXES.

The technique of producing match holders with the sides and edges forming the main body as one piece, and the lid and base cap as separate pieces, is described in Part 1, with Figs.81 and 82 illustrating the method.

Following the Chauncey Buckley patent of 1880 and the first examples manufactured by the Charles Parker Co., of Meriden, Connecticut to that patent, other companies made similar boxes until 1900 or 1901, when the idea of wrapping the main body with metal plates, leather or celluloid covers made its appearance. Over the next ten to fifteen years an intense rivalry developed between three Newark, New Jersey companies; other companies in the United States became involved, and the idea also spread to Britain.

Used mostly as a form of advertising for commercial purposes, three-piece boxes also served as cheap souvenirs of events and places visited, often as complimentary gifts. They were inexpensive to produce; the covers could be made to order cheaply, in large or small quantities. Consequently they are probably the most common form of pocket match holder, with the greatest variety of decorative side panels, to be found today. They reflect the consumer goods of the day. They provide nostalgic reminders of companies long forgotten, or occasionally still in existence today. They mark occasions of local or national importance. Moreover, they remind us of how the world looked in the first decade of this century. They are, in effect, documents (albeit minor documents) of history.

The three rival Newark companies—The Whitehead & Hoag Co., Aug. Goertz & Co., and The J. E. Mergott Co.—vied with each other in attempts to reduce costs, improve the visual attractiveness, and invent and incorporate novel features into their products. They were competitors not only in their match holders, but also other novelty items they maufactured. Yet, in the match holder field, their products show such remarkable similarities that it is often difficult to distinguish between them. Fortunately some are marked with patent dates and, from the patent record and close examination of individual examples, it is possible to distinguish between each company's products in most cases, even those where no patent date is marked on the box.

The Whitehead & Hoag Co. was responsible for the invention of the pin-on political button, but made various other novelties using celluloid as the major material for carrying advertising matter. In 1900 the company applied for a patent for a method of printing on celluloid that would not rub off. Until then, the celluloid had been used to cover a piece of paper bearing the printed matter. The patent sought was not issued until June 6, 1905, but in the meantime the company used its new process notwithstanding.

The company had started in business before the middle of the 1890s, and before 1900 was making advertising match holders in metal, two of which are shown in Fig. 179. Its earliest recorded match holder with a wrap-around celluloid covered body appeared in 1903 and is shown in **Fig. 293.a.** It has the same lid and base cap as the examples in Fig. l79.

In about 1902 the form of the lid and base cap was altered to a plain version in plated brass. The body (as is the case in all three companies' products) was made of tin plate. Details of the components and construction of the Whitehead & Hoag boxes are shown in **Fig. 292.** None of its boxes is marked on the metal components, but the celluloid covers are marked with the company name and, after 1905, with the patent date. However, it also made covers for other manufacturers' products, so the company's name on a cover does not guarantee that the box was made by it. Distinctive diagnostic features are the pair of raised dimples on each edge of the base cap, and a single raised dimple on the front edge of the lid. No other company is known to have used these features.

The boxes shown in **Fig. 293 B, C and D** have the company name on the covers, but no patent date, and were made prior to mid-1905. The beautiful lady in D appears frequently on the reverse of advertising matter, in this case for the Whitehall Portland Cement Co., of Philadelphia.

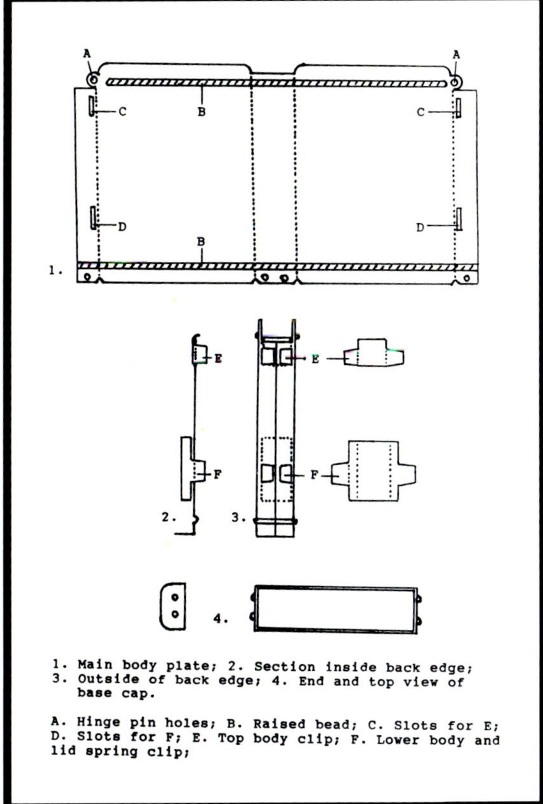

Fig. 292 Details of the components of the Whitehead & Hoag boxes.

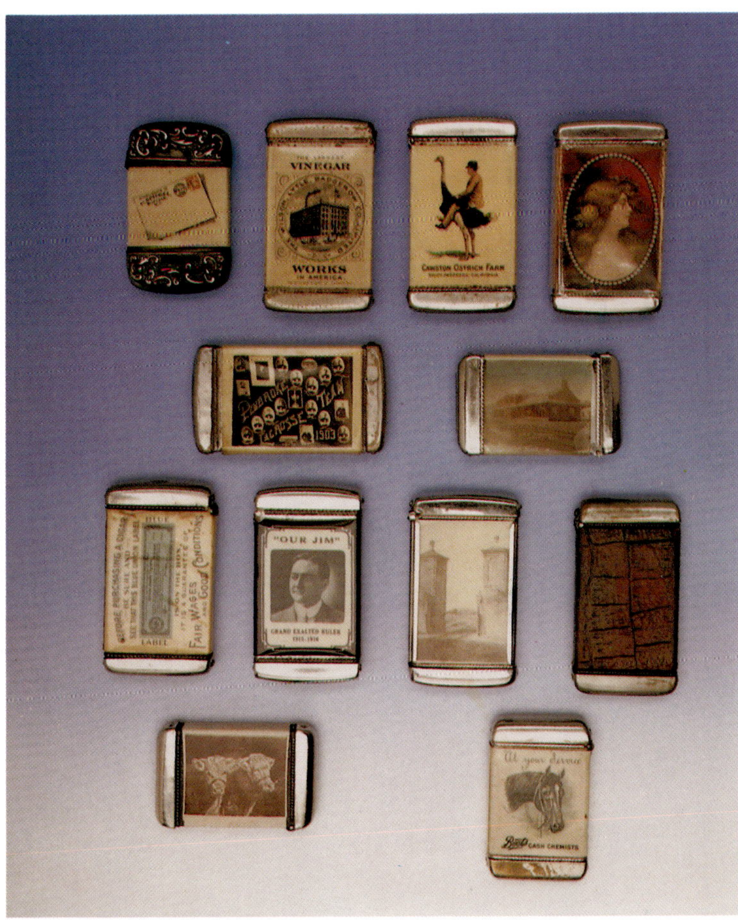

The boxes in **Fig. 293 E and F** have unmarked covers. E was a presentation gift at a celebration in Pembroke, Ontario for the town's championship lacrosse team of 1903; an enlarged photograph in the collection of a museum in Pembroke records all of the players' and officials' names. F is a souvenir of North Bay, Ontario.

Fig. 293 G and H are two boxes marked with the patent date on the cover. G advertises the Cigar Makers International Union of America. H is a complimentary souvenir given by "Deep Rock Water" to guests at a dinner and reception tendered to "James R. Nicholson, Grand Exalted Ruler of the Association of Massachusetts Elks" on February 15, 1916, which is evidence that this type of box was still being produced at that time.

An unusual Whitehead & Hoag box is shown in **Fig. 293 I;** its celluloid side panels are held in place by nickel-plated brass plates soldered to the edges. The unidentified photographic views on both sides are on paper under celluloid, which suggests that this box was made in about 1900 before the patent application relating to the printing process on celluloid.

The cover of the box **Fig. 293 J** is made of red leatherette simulating reptile skin. Since it bears no advertising, it may have been made for retail, rather than promotional purposes.

Fig. 293 K has advertising for H. Gilchrist, a livestock agent in Montreal, who was in business only from 1906 to 1908. The cover is marked "Woodburn Sons Co.Limited. Montreal," who acted as agents for Whitehead & Hoag from 1901 until at least 1909.

The box in **Fig. 293 L** was made for export to Britain, and the cover is marked "Made in U.S.A." The horse head design was used on a numher of these covers, which are marked (just below the neck) "Copyright 1901." This is not the date of the box, but of the illustration, which was presumably owned by Whitehead & Hoag. The advertising on the reverse is for Boots, a well-known chain of British chemists (called 'druggists', 'drugstores', or 'pharmacies' in North America) which still thrives today.

The Whitehead & Hoag Co. was probably the most prolific producer of this type of box, and its products were widespread around the world. In the first decade of this century it is known to have had offices in London (Fleet Street) and in Toronto, Ontario. It also had agents such as Woodburn's in Montreal, Canada, and Rae Munn & Gilbert in Melbourne, Australia, and may well have had other offices and agents in various cities throughout North America and in other countries. The company remained in business until the 1950s, when they were taken over by another great rival in the celluloid novelty business, Bastien Bros. of Rochester, New York, which has in turn been taken over by another company in the early 1990s. Regrettably, Bastien Bros. destroyed the Whitehead & Hoag records, although it is not known what such records may have contained.

Julius E. Mergott had established his novelty manufacturing business by 1882 when he was issued with his first patent, for a catch on a cigar box. Assignors to his company were still applying for invention and design patents well into the 1930s; five patents relating to the three-piece match holders were filed between 1903 and 1910.

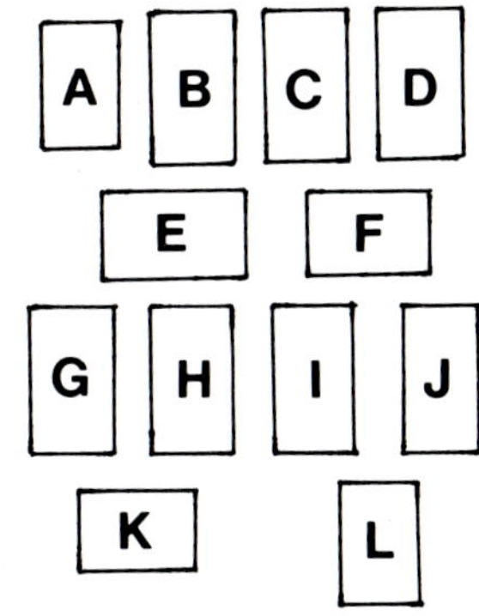

Fig. 293 United States. Tin plate, plated brass, celluloid, leather. Made by Whitehead & Hoag. A - 1903. B, C, D and F -between 1900 and 1905. E - 1903. G after 1905. H - 1916. I -probably c.1901. J - c.1901 to 1910. K - cover marked "Woodburn & Sons Co.Ltd. Montreal", 1906 to 1908. L - marked "Made in U.S.A.", for export to Britain, 1904 to 1909. Max. H - 7cms.; min. H - 5.8cms.

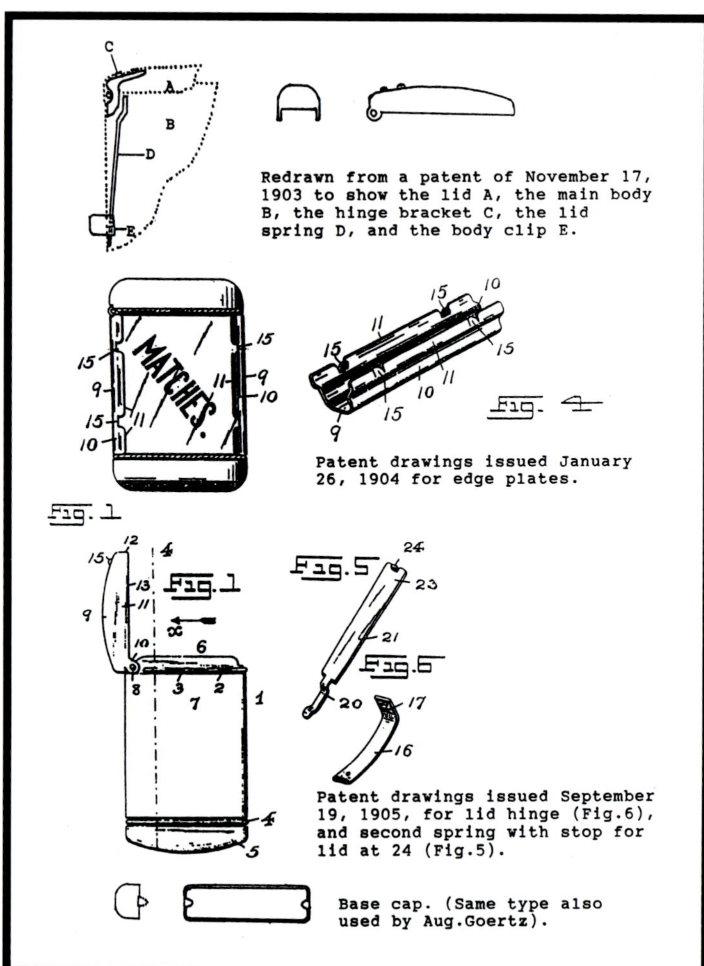

Fig. 294 Details of J. E. Mergott Co., boxes. Top: redrawn to show lid, hinge bracket and spring, from boxes patented in 1903. Centre: drawings from Invention Patent of 1905. Below: drawings from Invention Patent of 1904. Lower: sketch of base cap, also made by Aug. Goertz & Co..

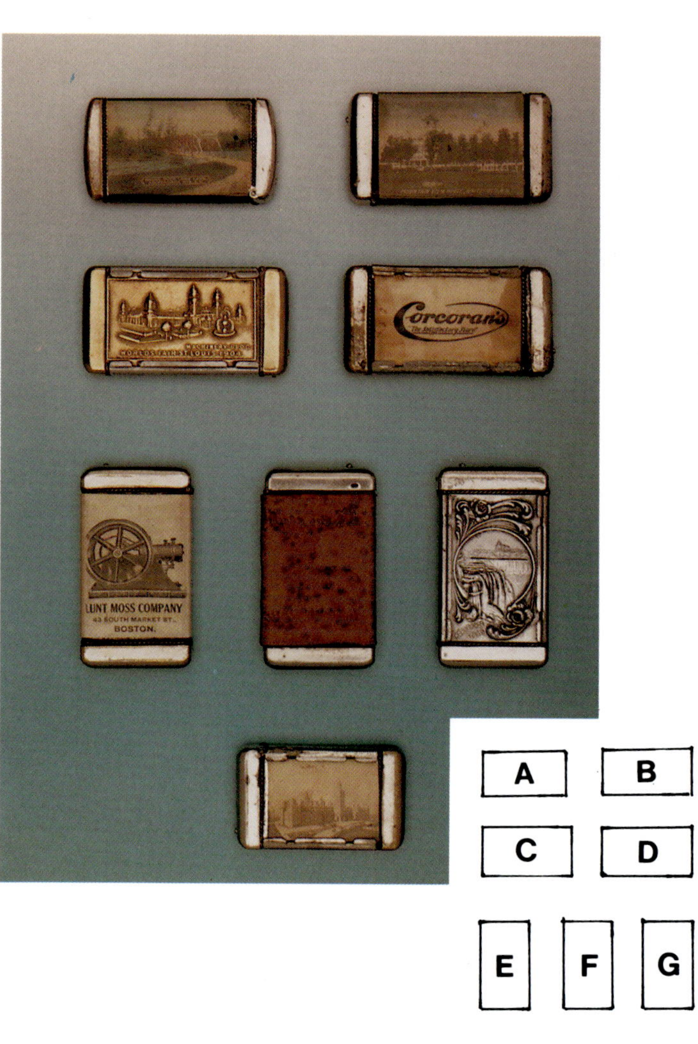

Fig. 295 United States. Tin plate, plated brass, aluminum, celluloid, leather. Made by J. E. Mergott Co.. A - pre 1903. B -pre 1905. C - 1904. D - pre 1905. E - c.1905, cover by Bastien Bros.. F - after 1910. G - after 1905. H - c.1903 to 1905. Max. H - 7.2cms; min. H - 5.9cms.

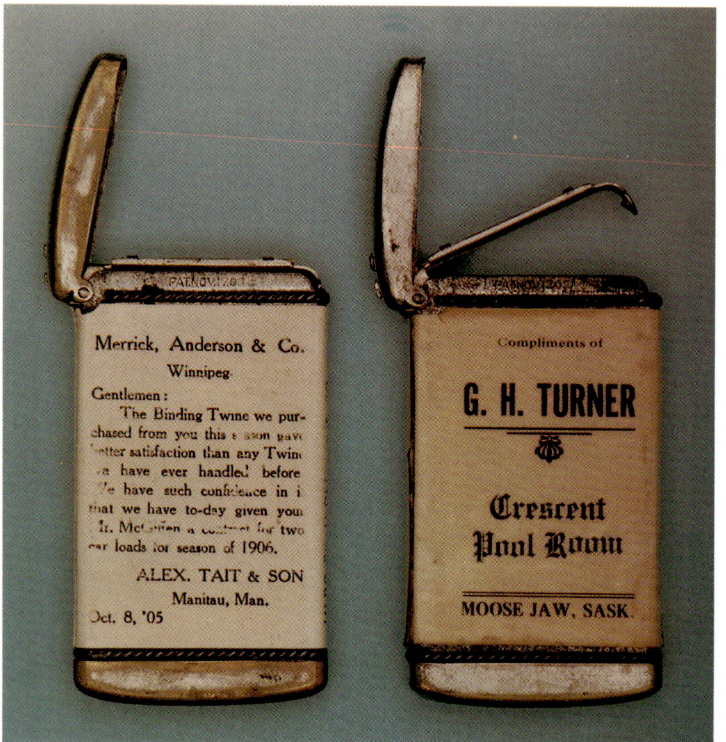

Fig. 296 United States. Tin plate, plated brass, celluloid. Trick boxes. Made by J. E. Mergott Co., to an Invention Patent of 1903. H - 6.8cms.

Fig. 294, taken mostly from three of Mergott's patents, illustrates the distinctive diagnostic features to be found in his match holders. In the uppermost drawings, the hinge bracket (C) and the lid with its hinge flanges on the side are two such features. The drawing below shows his design for edge plates which held the side plates in place, with two distinct notches created by the lugs (15) that pass through holes in the main body to be turned over on the inside, thus locking the face-plates in place. The third drawing illustrates a different hinge bracket and spring (16) which is riveted to the lid near the front edge, the return (17) catching on a small lug (at 24) on the inner body spring of Fig. 5, and retaining the lid in an upright position when opened. At the bottom of Fig. 294 are end and plan views of the base cap, which was common to both Mergott and Goertz boxes.

Several examples of Mergott boxes are shown in **Fig. 295.** Boxes A and B have wrap-around covers with colored photographs on paper under celluloid. Box A, unmarked and probably pre-1903, bears views of Long Lake in the Adirondack Mountains of New York State. Box B is marked "Patented" on the bezel, which relates to a patent issued in 1905; it has views of Whitefield, New Hampshire. Both were souvenirs, no doubt sold locally at Long Lake and Whitefield.

Box C is marked "PAT.APP.FOR", and exhihits features from two patents; both were filed in 1903, but one was not issued until Fall 1905, well after the 1904 World's Fair held in St.Louis, Missouri, from which this box is a souvenir. The lid, base cap and side plates are made of brass, the edge plates of aluminum.

Box D is an advertising item, with the same patent mark as on box C on one side of the bezel, but the other side is marked "N.J.Aluminum Co. Newark, N.J." The celluloid-covered side panels are held in place with aluminum edge panels, and it is assumed that the box was made by Mergott, and then passed to the New Jersey Aluminum Company to finish by supplying the celluloid panels, fixing them with aluminum edge plates that the company itself made, and then applying its name to the bezel.

Box E also is marked "PAT.APP.FOR" on the bezel, but has a wrap-around celluloid cover marked "Bastien Bros. Rochester. N.Y."—Whitehead & Hoag's rivals in the celluloid field.

The leather covered box F has a tooled impression of a stag with a fine set of antlers, and on the reverse the inscription "Bar Harbor.Me." has been rather poorly burned in. The bezel is marked "Patented," which refers to a patent of 1910 for a "trick or puzzle box." The trick or puzzle is how to open the box, and is simply solved by pressing the center of the side panel which releases a catch in the lid.

Box G is a souvenir of Niagara Falls, with impressed views from the U.S. side on nickel-plated brass plates. Marked "Patented" on the bezel, it must have been made after 1905. Box H is a smaller version, pre-1905, with celluloid-covered photographs of the Parliament Buildings in Ottawa, Ontario, on one side, and the Lady Aberdeen Bridge in Hull, Quebec (just across the Ottawa River from Ottawa) on the reverse side.

Both boxes in **Fig. 296** are marked "PAT.NOV.17.03," a Mergott patent for a trick or puzzle lid. This relates to an inner lid under the main lid; the inner lid springs open when the the front edge of the main body is pressed just below the front of the main lid. The example on the left shows the inner lid in the closed position; on the top of this inner lid is a small printed panel with the wording:

> "The finding of the hidden spring,
> Depends upon the side you press.
> A letter sent to us will bring
> The needful secret of success."

The celluloid cover is marked with the Whitehead & Hoag Co. name and a patent date for 1905. The advertising is in the form of a letter from a farmer to a Winnipeg, Manitoba, hardware company and dated "Oct. 8, '05." The box on the right shows the trick lid half opened. The celluloid wrapper is marked "The Canadian Art Works, Limited, Montreal, Que." and was produced as a complimentary item for a pool room in Moose Jaw, Saskatchewan.

From this it can be seen that Mergott made the boxes, but often used other sources for the covers—even their rivals Whitehead & Hoag. Some of Mergott's inventions suffered long delays before their patents were issued; this may have been the case because his written specifications always included a description of the box, which was not new, and which may have raised some doubts in the Patent Office Examiners' minds. It is somewhat suspicious that both Mergott and Goertz used the same attorney and witnesses for their patents, which in one case were almost identical, and that Goertz, who had filed after Mergott, was issued with his patent before Mergott.

August Goertz was in business by 1884 and until the late 1930s, producing a wide range of novelties in direct competition with Mergott. From just before 1900 until at least 1918, Benno vom Eigen, his assignor, filed many patents, inc]uding seven for match holders.

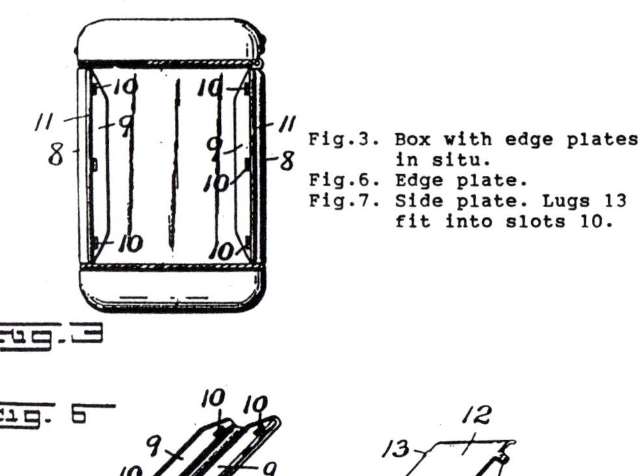

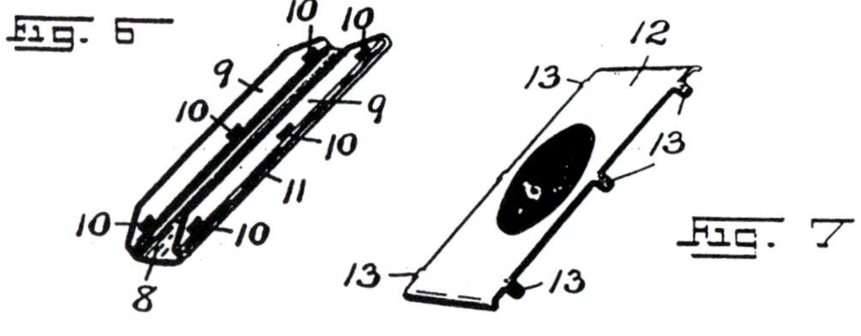

Fig. 297 Patent drawings of Invention Patent of 1904 for Aug. Goertz & Co.. Key: 8, 9, 11 - edge plates; 10 - slots in edge plates; 12 - side plates; 13 - lugs on side plates to pass through 10.

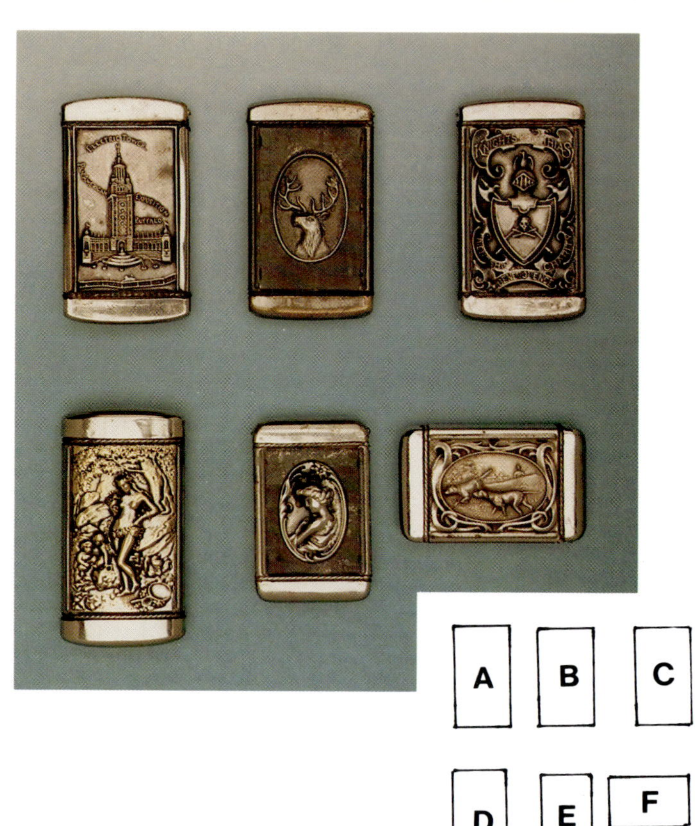

Fig. 298 United States. Tin plate, plated brass. Made by Aug. Goertz & Co.. A - 1901, H - 7.1cms. B - F - after 1904. D - oval cross section, H - 7.3cms; F - H. 5.8cms.

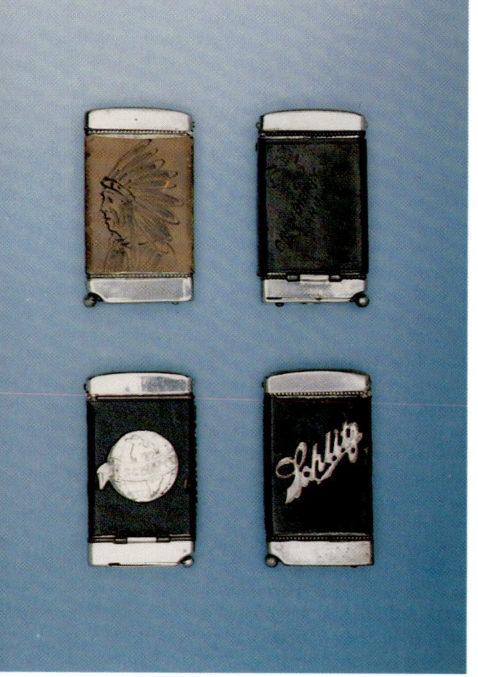

Fig. 299 United States. Tin plate, plated brass, leather. With cigar cutters. Made in Goertz style. Top: unmarked. Lower left: marked "Wm Schimper & Co.". Lower right: marked "H.B.Hardenburg & Co." H (of all) - 6.8cms.

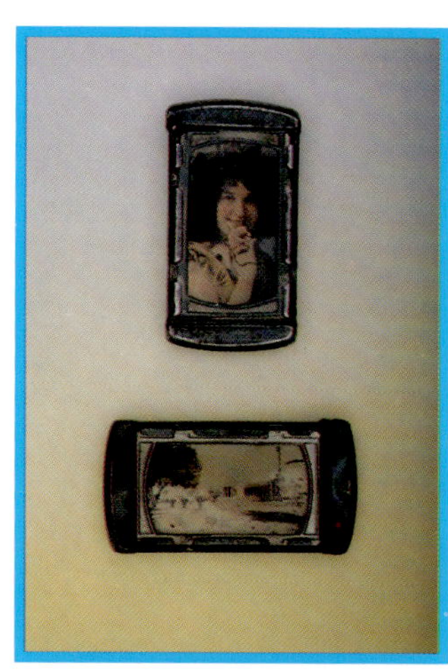

Fig. 300 United States. Tin plate, aluminum, paper, celluloid. Made by L. F. Grammes & Sons. c.1909. H - 6.8cms.

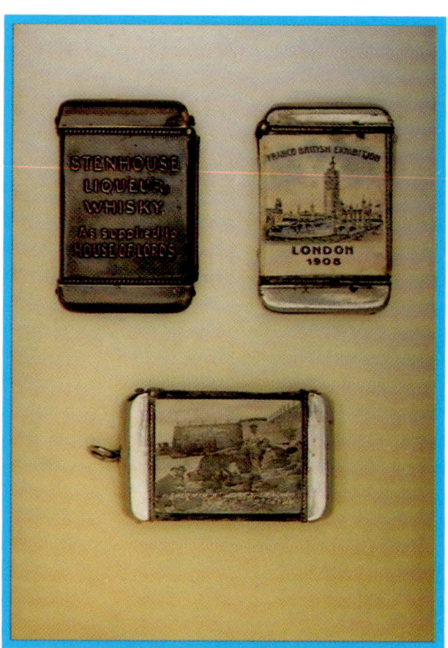

Fig. 301 Britain. Tin plate, plated brass, celluloid, leather. Top left: c.1910. Top right: 1908; cover marked "Made in Rhineland" to a Registered Design of 1904 by Charles E. Brann. Lower: made to Whitehead & Hoag pattern, c.1905. H - 5.9cms.

Of particular interest here is a match holder that was very similar to a Mergott patent, proposing a system of edge and side plates that were easy to assemble and inexpensive to produce. The relevant drawings from the patent are shown in **Fig. 297.** In this proposal, the side plates were provided with three lugs (13), on each side, which passed through the slots (10) in the edge plates and were turned over inside the box. The end product provided a neater finish to the box than Mergott's plan.

These boxes are almost identical to those of Mergott at first glance. However, many of the Goertz boxes bear his patent date on the bezel, the internal lid fittings are different, and there is the difference in the method of fixing the external plates; these things make attribution possible.

Fig. 298 shows six examples of Mergott boxes. Box A was made in 1901; the edge plates are soldered to the box, a time-consuming and skilled job, which prompted the invention of the elements designed to be fixed by lugs, thus speeding production and reducing the cost. The side plate of this example was for the Pan-American Exposition, held in Buffalo, New York in 1901, which conveniently dates the box. The plate on the reverse shows a female nude looking into a hand mirror while reclining in a rococo style chair.

The side plates that Goertz used could be "mixed and matched" to suit the taste of a client. The female nude was apparently one of his standards, for it is shown on a match holder in a Simmons Hardware Co. catalogue of 1908, and offered as one of a dozen having "Silver finish side plates, clinched to body" sold in a cardboard box, priced at $7.00 for the dozen.

An innovation is shown in box B in Fig. 298: a plain side plate is made with an oval cut out of the center; into this space was fitted any one of a number of designs, or it was filled with printed advertising matter or the owner's name. A smaller version using the same idea, with a smaller opening, is shown as box E. Although box F also has an oval central panel, this is part of the complete rectangular side panel; again several different designs were produced.

Box C is one of many with plates made for the numerous fraternal or friendly societies in the United States.

Box D is oval in cross section (whereas the others are rectangular). A lid at each end is provided with a striker, and hinged at the side. The main body join is in the center of one side. The bezel at one end is marked with the Goertz patent date of January 12, 1904, and the side and edge plates conform to that patent. The side plate shown has an impressed design of a female nude, accompanied by two children and a large feline, in a sylvan setting. The plate on the reverse side has an elaborate art nouveau border around an oval opening that was probably intended for printed matter, but could also have taken one of the inserts as for box B.

It can be seen that the Goertz products catered more to the retail trade, since the designs they bear are predominantly decorative, and less to the advertising market which his two main competitors appear to have targeted.

The examples in **Fig. 299** are all provided with a cigar cutter in a small box attached to the base of the main body. The two lower examples are marked inside the cigar cutter box: the one on the left "Wm.Schimper & Co. Hoboken, N.J." and that to the right "H.B.Hardenburg & Co. N.Y." Both have black leather covers with nickel-plated emblems for the Schlitz brewery of Milwaukee, Wisconsin. The two upper examples are unmarked, and have leather covers, the one to the right designed as a souvenir for Cranberry Lake, New York. In each example the striker is located on the top of the lid. All have elements that match those of the Goertz boxes. Their main body joins are located in the center of one side, produced in the same manner as the Goertz example in Fig. 298.D; but some differences occur in other elements, such as the raised beads. It is assumed that the two marked boxes were made by the company whose name appears on them. But did Goertz make the other two? No patent infringements are involved, and there is no apparent reason why other companies should not have made this type of box. Sears, Roebuck & Co. of Chicago offered this type of box in their mail-order catalogue of 1908 at 19¢ each, plus 2¢ for postage.

In Allentown, Pennsylvania, L. F. Grammes & Sons were making a similar form of three-piece box, referred to in their 1909 catalogue as "Advertising Novelties" at $28.70 per gross without advertising, or $38.80 per gross with advertising. Two examples are shown in **Fig. 300.** The raised lugs (to hold an aluminum frame) are stamped out of the tin-plate main body, and no edge plates are required. The lids and base cap are also made of tin-plate, rather than plated brass. The panels under the frames are celluloid-covered paper, the upper box bearing the name of the owner printed upon the reverse side, and the lower box (a souvenir) views of Riverside, California.

In Britain, at least four versions of this type of box are known; the idea was probably copied from Whitehead & Hoag, whose boxes were imported into the country and were no doubt marketed through the London office which the company had established by 1904. The boxes made for the British market, or made in Britain, were of the smaller version, suitable for the more popular wax vesta matches.

Three examples of these are shown in **Fig. 301.** That in the upper left has an antique copper finish; it lacks side and edge plates, the advertising being impressed directly into the main body. The back edge has a channel attached to take a piece of safety match striker material; the usual striker for ordinary friction matches is located on the underside of the base cap.

The box at top right has a celluloid wrap-around cover, with a Registered Design number for 1904 printed on one edge; this had been issued to Charles E. Brann of London, who also held a registered design for the stamp and match box shown in Fig. 258. The cover is also marked "Printed in Rhineland." Brann's registered design showed the Arms of Blackpool on one side and a view of the sea front on the other; but in fact he produced numerous different designs for covers, all bearing the same Registration Number. The example here relates to the Franco-British Exhibition of 1908 in London.

The lower box has a leather wrap-around cover, with a photograph of "Fishermen at Work, Sheringham" glued on one side. All three of these boxes exhibit minor differences in some elements, and are therefore believed to have been produced by different companies.

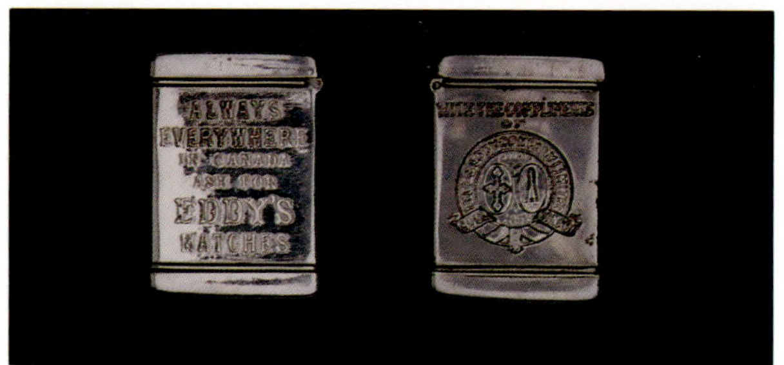

Fig. 302 Britain, made for export to Canada. Plated tin plate and brass. c. 1910. H - 6cms.

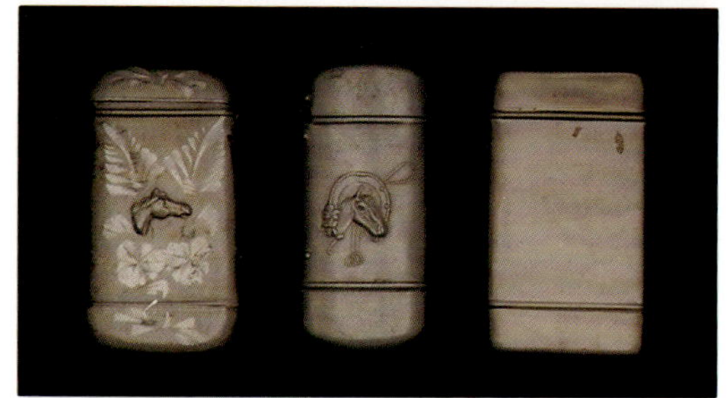

Fig. 303 United States. Aluminum. Left: made by E. A. Fargo Co. c.1903. Centre and right: probably made by Western Aluminum Co. c.1900. H - 6.9cms.

The two examples in **Fig. 302** are marked "Made in England," but were obviously made for the Canadian market, specifically Canada's largest match manufacturer, The E.B. Eddy Co. Ltd. of Hull, Quebec, now the Eddy Match Company of Pembroke, Ontario. They lack the side and edge plates, and the join is an overlapping seam up the back edge, but otherwise show many Whitehead & Hoag features. They were probably made around 1910, but at least four versions have been seen that exhibit minute differences in the details of the lettering and the Eddy trademark.

The final word on the British-made three-piece boxes goes to Buncher & Haseler of Birmingham, who placed an advertisement in the British trade journal "Tobacco" in 1922 that clearly shows this type of box. This probably represents the end of its lifetime.

A few examples of three-piece aluminum boxes made in the United States are shown in **Fig. 303.** They do not have edge and side plates, nor wrap-around covers. The thin-gauge aluminum created a flimsy carcass. The example at the left was made by The E. A. Fargo Co. of Attleboro, Massachusetts, and was advertised in The Jewelers' Circular-Weekly of 2 September, 1903, offered at $12.00 per gross or $1.20 per dozen. The other two boxes were probably made by the Western Aluminum Co. of Chicago. In a catalogue put out by the company around 1900 there appears a box of the same shape as that on the right, and with a design identical to that on the center box. They were priced at 80¢ per dozen or $9.00 per gross. The bases of these two boxes are held to the main body by means of impressed dots on both parts, located in corresponding positions to allow them to snap into place.

The three-piece box offers interesting insights into company histories and rivalries in addition to recording (on the side plates) the life and times of the first decade or so of this century.

PART 6: TRICK OR PUZZLE BOXES.

Match holders incorporating a secret means of opening them are not very common, but did appear in the United States and in Europe. Some examples, such as the "Secret Photo Match-Boxes" in Figs. 111 and 128, and the two Mergott boxes in Figs. 295 F and 296, have already been presented.

Most of the inspiration for these boxes probably stemmed from props devised by magicians for their performances; some of the ideas were used by magicians long before being adapted to match holders.

Probably the earliest example of a trick match holder is that of a box with concealed hinges, a principle shown in part of a British Invention patent of 1899 (in **Fig. 304**). The hinge pins are set inside the box (e), and the lid (c) fits closely into the main body of the box, with the lugs at each end provided with holes that correspond with the hinge pins. The lid is opened simply by applying pressure to its back edge. To prevent the matches from getting trapped by the lid and possibly igniting, a wall (g) is inserted, running the length of the box. There was an earlier invention patent for a box using the same principle in 1895, and two Registered Designs in 1898.

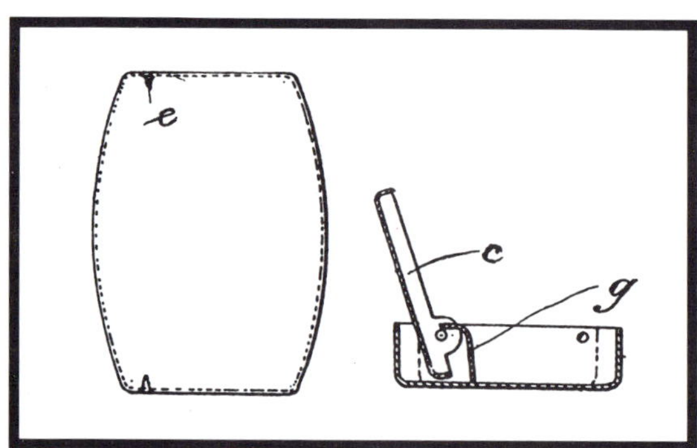

Fig. 304 British Invention Patent of 1899 by Alfred Pearce.

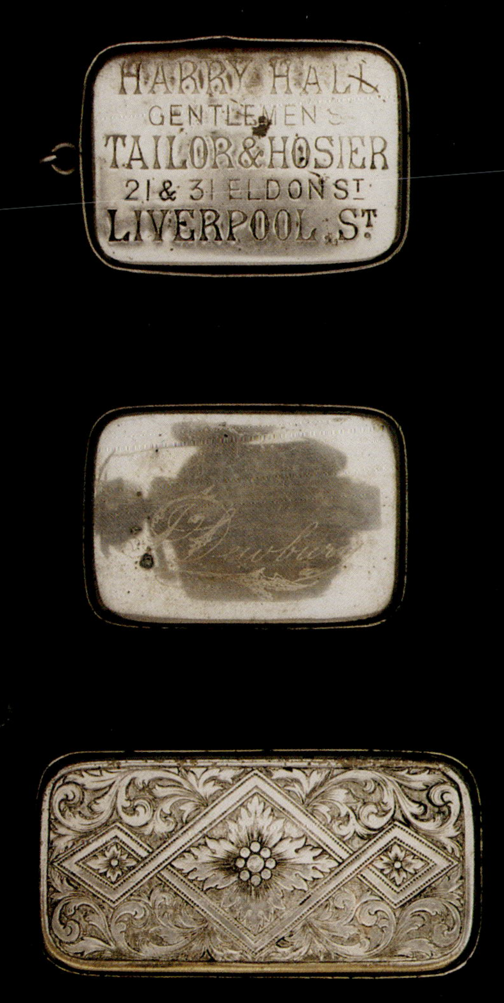

Fig. 305 British. Plated brass. Trick boxes using same method as Fig. 304. c.1895 to 1910. Top and centre: L - 5.1cms. Lower: marked "PAT.APPL'D FOR"; L - 6.9cms.

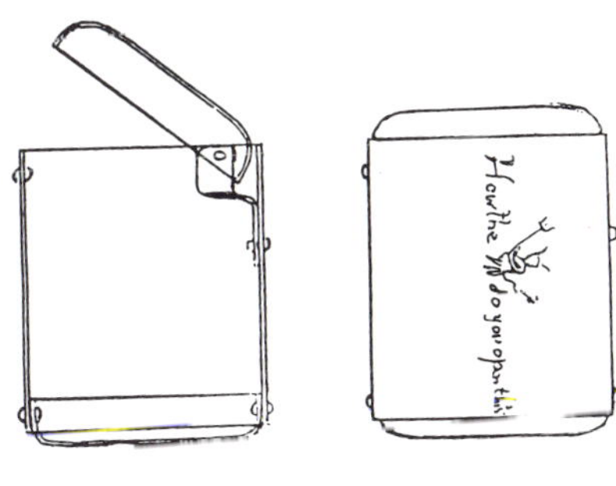

Fig. 306 Sketch of a box in the collection of Stanley G. Aston. Marked "Made in England. Prov.Patent." The patent was probably abandoned.

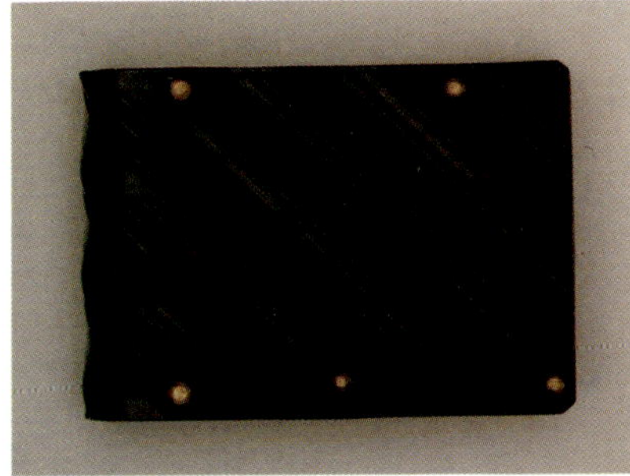

Fig. 307 Probably Germany. Vulcanite. c.1890s. L - 4.8cms.

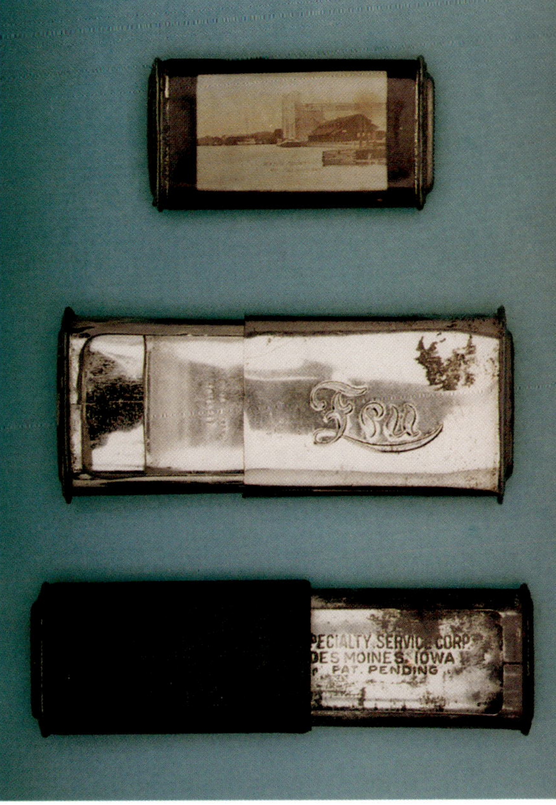

Fig. 308 Tin plate, leather, celluloid. "Magic drawer" boxes. Top and centre: made in Austria; c.1900; L - 6.5cms. Lower: made in the United States by the Speciality Service Corp., patent pending; c.1910; L - 6.9cms.

Alfred Taylor, a Birmingham silversmith, was probably the first to make a box incorporating this trick; it was hallmarked for 1864. Three later examples are shown in **Fig. 305**, all in plated brass, and in two sizes. The uppermost box advertises a gentleman's tailor in London, and is fitted with a suspension ring. An upright version was also made, and is illustrated in **Fig. 306.** It is inscribed on the side "How the (drawing of a devil) do you open this." They are otherwise unmarked.

In Professor Lewis Hoffman's book *Puzzles Old and New,* published in 1893, he illustrates this type of match holder which he refers to as the "Ne Plus Ultra"—the highest perfection, or peerless—match box. There is no explanation as to where he obtained this name.

A box in the form of a book, shown in **Fig. 307,** is in vulcanite and was probably made in Germany in the 1890s. The lid is at the opposite end to the spine, hinged at the rivet on the bottom right hand side. To open the lid, the top edge of the book is pressed between the two rivets, and at the same time the bottom edge must be pressed between the center and right hand rivets. The top edge curves to release the edge of the lid, and the pressure on the bottom edge applies pressure to a notch at the hinge of the lid, causing it to spring open.

The "Magic drawer box" was the subject of several invention patents in Europe and the United States, and was in vogue as early as 1877. At first try the box is easily opened to reveal the matches. Yet when it is closed and reopened, the matches have disappeared! The secret is a pair of drawers fitting very closely one within the other. The inner drawer contains the matches and may be pulled into the open position to reveal them. When the drawer is returned, the box is tilted slightly, causing a catch to engage at the back of the inner drawer, preventing it from being pulled out in tandem with the outer drawer.

Three examples of this are shown in **Fig. 308.** The upper box is in the closed position; it is marked on the inner drawer "MADE IN AUSTRIA. PATENTED," and the celluloid cover has illustrations of Prescott, Ontario on both sides. The middle box is partially opened and shows the inner drawer inside the outer drawer; one side is impressed "Feu," and it has the same marks as the previous piece. The lower box has both drawers fully open; it is marked "SPECIALITY SERVICE CORP. DES MOINES, IOWA. PAT.PENDING." and has a leather cover marked for an Adams, New York, bakery.

This type of box was invariably made of thin, sheet tin plate, and bears a striker at each end: one for friction matches, the other for safety matches.

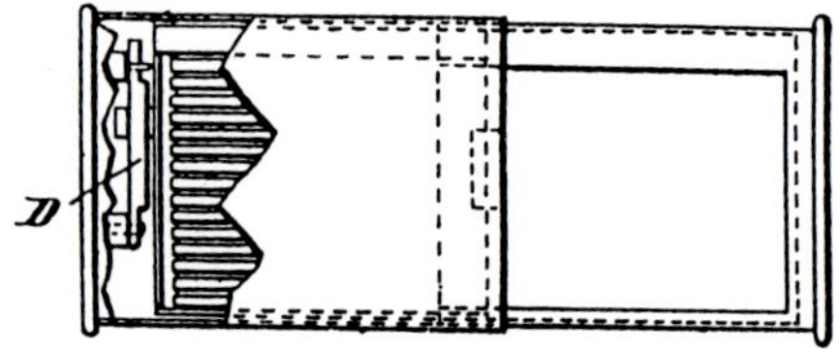

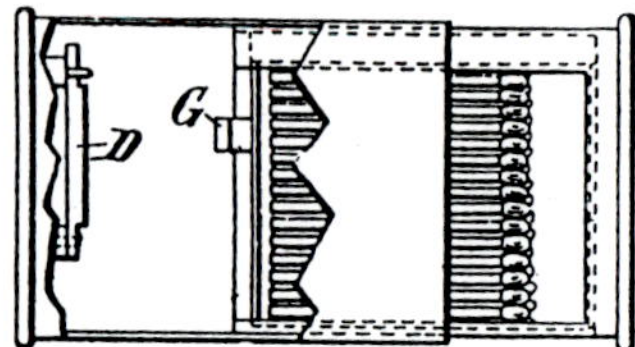

Fig. 309 British Invention Patent drawings of 1896 by Frederick M. B. Bertram and Gregory A. Robinson, for "Magic Drawer" box.

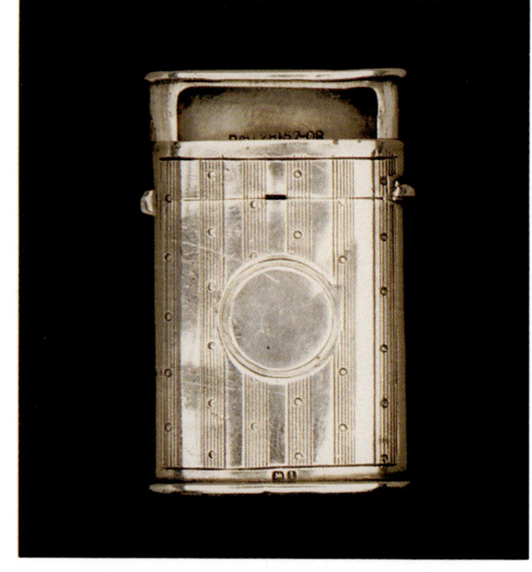

Fig. 311 Britain. Silver. Trick sliding drawer box. Made by Spurrier & Co.Ltd., in 1910, to an Invention Patent of 1908 by Judah Ahronsberg. H - 4.5cms.

Fig. 310 United States Invention Patent drawings of 1925 by Alexis F. Gillet, for hidden release mechanism at end of "Magic Drawer" box.

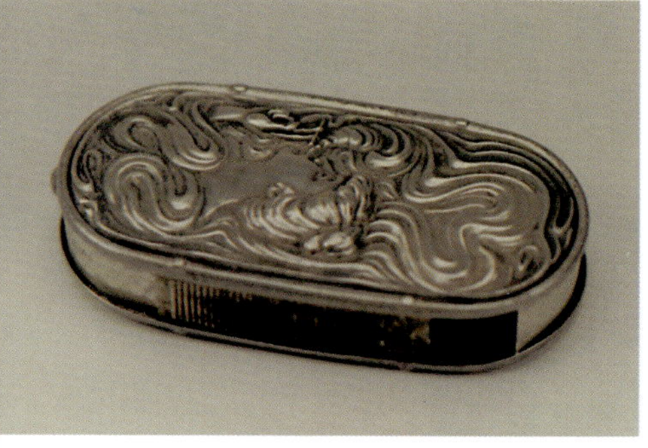

Fig. 312 United States. Plated tin plate. Both ends open by applying pressure to either side of the end plate and sliding the end plate behind the side plates in a channel. Marked "PATENTED". c.1910. L - 6.9cms.

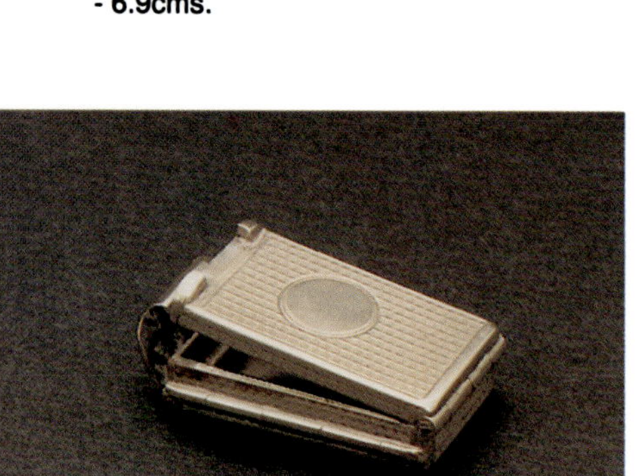

Fig. 313 Probably France. Plated brass. "False hinge" box. c.1900. L - 4.1cms.

In Britain two patents were issued in 1896 and 1897 to Frederick M. B. Bertram and Gregory Robinson (the inventor of the watch match box in Fig. 262) of London, the drawings of the 1896 patent shown in **Fig. 309.** In the United States, Alexis F. Gillet of Omaha, Nebraska, as assignor to the Jubilee Manufacturing Co., was issued a patent for the same type as late as 1925. The essential elements of the catch are shown in **Fig. 310.**

A larger version to hold a "small paper of tobacco" was being offered in 1877 by the Eureka Trick and Novelty Co. of New York, for 25¢ each. E.G.Rideout, also of New York, offered the same thing in 1881 at 30¢ each or $2.00 per dozen. The Sears, Roebuck & Co. (Chicago) mail-order catalogues of 1908 and 1909 offered the match box version at 15¢ each.

Another sliding-drawer box is shown in **Fig. 311,** but is quite different from the previous boxes. When closed it resembles a standard match holder with a lid at the top, hinged at the back edge, and with a projection on the front edge for opening with the thumb; the striker is located on the bottom edge in the traditional manner. The hinge and thumb projection are connected by a line that gives the appearance of the lid seating, all of which is false; the striker is in fact the opposite end of the internal drawer and must be pushed inwards to open the drawer. The illustration shows the box partly opened. The box is made of silver, hall-marked for Birmingham, dated for 1910, and with the maker's mark "S & Co.," which is probably Spurrier & Co. Ltd. It was the subject of an Invention Patent in 1908 issued to Judah Ahronsberg, a manufacturing jeweler of Birmingham.

Made of tin plate with a nickel-plated finish is a puzzle box that is marked "PATENT," and was probably made in the United States; it is shown in **Fig. 312.** Each end is provided with a flexible sliding panel, fitted into channels in the top and bottom plates, and with a knob in the center. The sliding panels may be opened by pressing either end of each panel inwards and pushing the knob to one side or the other, which causes the panel to pass behind the striker strip on the side of the box. Thus the box has four openings for access to the matches. The top panel shown has an impressed design in the Art Nouveau style of a woman smoking a cigarette. The opposite side panel has an oval opening in the center for some form of printed matter, either advertising or the owner's name.

The match holder in **Fig. 313** may be of French origin from the first decade of this century. It is made of nickel-plated brass with engine-turned design work. There is a false hinge along one side and genuine hinges at both ends. The catch is hinged (at the end shown to the left) with a very strong spring and, where it fits over the closed lid, gives the appearance of yet a fourth hinge. The striker is of corrugated metal set into the side and is held by another plate which makes that side appear very thick. It is so cleverly made that is difficult to spot how it is opened.

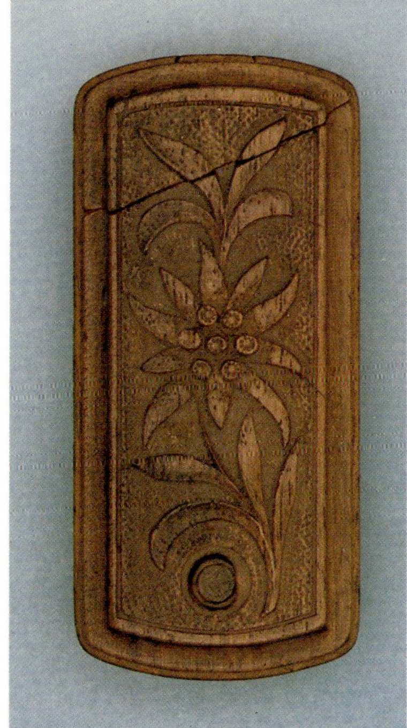

Fig. 314 Switzerland. Wood. c.1890s. L - 7.5cms.

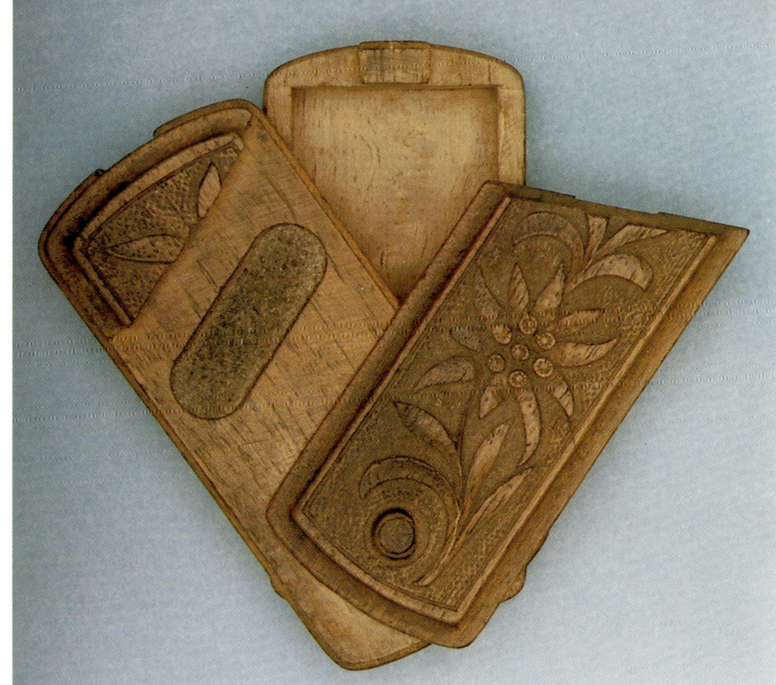

Fig. 315 As Fig. 314 opened.

The box shown in **Figs.314 and 315** is of wood, and originates in Switzerland. It is made in three parts: the main body, hollowed out to hold the matches; and a pair of interlocking lids, pivoted on a wooden pin. Once the upper lid section is swung aside, the lower lid section may be slid free of the dovetail tang that is part of the base, and then itself swung aside. However, in order to free the lower lid section from the tang, the box must first be inverted to release a hidden catch (usually in the form of a small ball) set in the pivot pin cavity. Fig. 315 shows the box in the open position, and the sanded striker located on the lower lid section.

The top side is carved in the representation of an Eidelweiss flower. This design is typical of these boxes during the last two decades of the l9th century, although some include a ribbon effect with the name of a town (such as "Luzern" or "St.Moritz") engraved into the surface. One has been seen with a paper label glued to the underside, printed with the wording "[?]. Buschard. Sculpture Suisse. Montreux." This may refer to the maker, but could just as well be the retailer.

What is believed to be a later version is shown in **Fig. 316.** It is slightly longer, made of a different wood, and has a stylized floral design that is well executed but lacks the delicate touches of the previous piece. It has the same trick method of opening. Written in pencil on the back of the main lid section is "Trygve Gundersen fra Helga Jackarty. April 1918". The first name and "fra" are Norwegian, but the box is presumably Swiss-made and perhaps dates from 1918.

No record has yet been found of these boxes being patented in Europe. However, two patents were taken out in the United States: the first by Myer Byall of Winterville, Mississippi in 1902, the second by Benoit Guerry, a citizen of France (who declared his intention to become a citizen of the U.S.) in 1909. Both have arrangements very similar to the hidden pivotal catch of the Swiss examples.

This type of box was offered in a catalogue put out by the well-known London toy store of W. & F. Hamley in 1882, where it was called "The Psycho Box." Two versions were offered: in wood at seven pence each, and in plated nickel silver at one shilling and six pence each. In the United States they were offered in 1886 as "The Magic Fusee Box" by the U.S. Trick Novelty Co. of Pallatine, Illinois, and by Peck & Snyder of New York, for 50¢ each in oak and for $1.00 each in brass. In 1896 Martinka & Co. of New York offered the two versions at the same price, but called them the "Sine Qua Non Match Box."

The wooden box in **Fig. 317** may or may not have been intended as a puzzle box: so beautifully hand-carved is it, that the sliding lid is almost impossible to detect. The striker on the bottom was produced by using a V-shaped gouge to cut parallel lines in one direction, and a second series at right angles to the first. The pieces of the imitation strap down the sides are let in to the box body, which is carved from a single piece. When I acquired the box, a piece of paper inside it (dated August 18, 1936) stated that the box originally belonged to Job Tower Souther, the great grandfather of the 1936 owner. This could date the box to as far back as the 1860s, assuming that the previous owners passed it on at twenty five year intervals.

There are other forms of trick or puzzle match holders, including a brass cylinder type in which the lid unscrews using a left hand thread, and a type of box that provides some doubtful humor insofar as the false press button conceals a needle which pricks the finger or thumb when pressed.

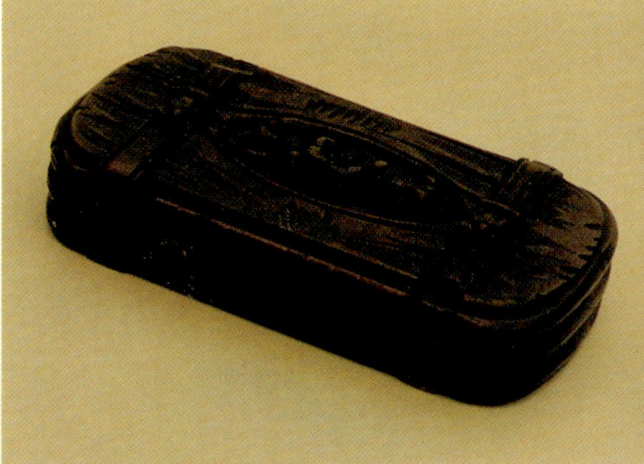

Fig. 317 Switzerland. Wood. Sliding lid. c.1860s. L - 7.9cms.

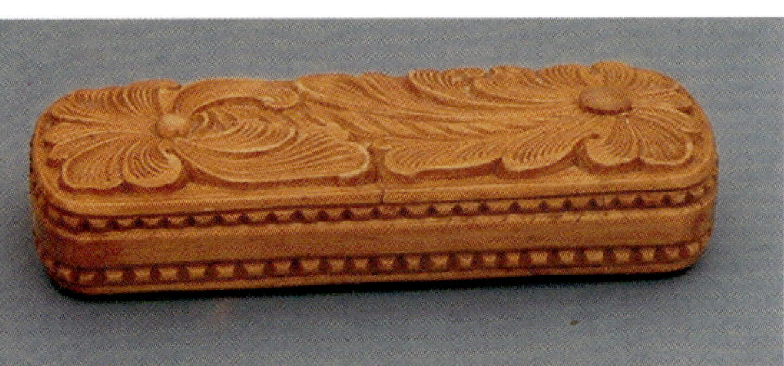

Fig. 316 Switzerland. Wood. c.1918. L - 9cms.

PART 7: THE "CANDLE-IN-THE-BOX"

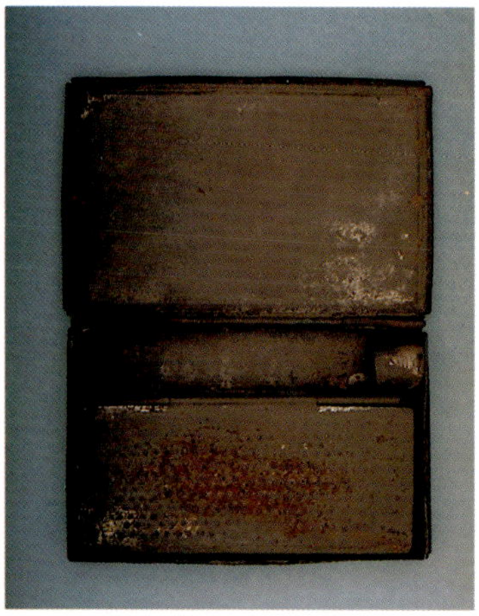

Fig. 318 British. Tin plate. Possibly made by Jones Bros.. c.1850s. L - 8cms.

Many of the early protective boxes of the stand-alone type were provided with a candle socket and, in some instances, a compartment inside the main body to hold a candle. Most were not intended to be carried in the pocket but by the early 1850s pocket boxes to hold a candle and a supply of matches were beginning to appear.

The travelling man would often lodge in an ill-lit establishment and require some light by which to read or write. A box that would fit easily into a pocket and that held the necessary materials to provide light was a considerable asset. Not all of the examples shown here were designed specifically for that purpose, but a good many were.

What appear to be the earliest were of tin plate, somewhat crudely made by hand, and finished with a coat of paint. Jones Bros. of London, who made lucifer matches, marketed some in such cheap boxes, although it is not known if they manufactured the boxes. A box once in the Bryant & May Museum of Fire-Making Appliances has a paper label glued to the inside of the lid, worded as follows:

> "Jones Brothers & Co.'s Royal Cossack Lucifers; 1/— This portable and elegant Case of Lucifers is strongly recommended for general use; having a wax taper, they suit the wants of the Traveller, Man of Business, and Gentlemen of Literary pursuits."

Two examples of this type of box may be seen in **Figs. 318 and 319,** which may well have been produced by Jones Brothers. Both are made of tin plate, the box in Fig. 318 painted green, the other with some minute traces of gold lacquer. Each is hinged longitudinally, with one end hinged to fold out holding, ready for use, a candle in a socket soldered to the inside. When folded away, the candle lies in its own channel at the back of the box. The rest of the inside of the box is partitioned off to hold a supply of matches; it has its own hinged lid, bearing the striker: in Fig. 318 a set of punched holes like those of a grater, and in Fig. 319 a strip of framed sandpaper.

Although described by Jones Brothers as "elegant," neither example can honestly be said to show much evidence of elegance, even taking into account their age and the amount of use they have probably had. However, they do demonstrate an early recognition of the need to satisfy the requirements of travellers.

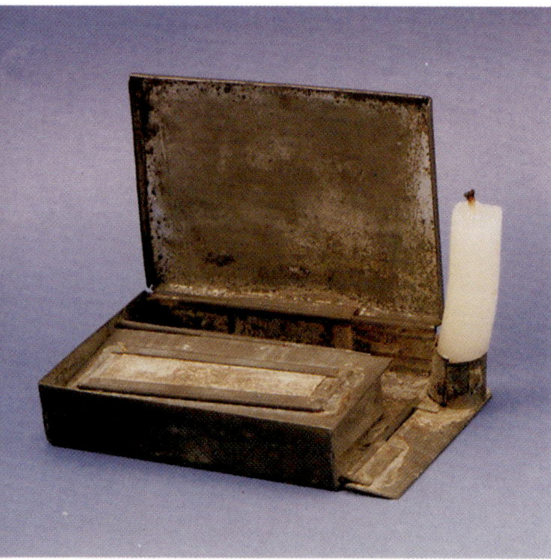

Fig. 319 British. Tin plate. Possibly made by Jones Bros.. c.1850s. L - 7.4cms.

In 1862 Thomas Johnson, a highly respected London silversmith, produced a similar box that was indeed elegant. Simple and compact, it included a match socket on the lid and a space for sealing wax. As with most silver boxes for holding matches, it had a gilt wash finish inside to inhibit the chemical from the matches reacting upon the otherwise exposed silver. It was sold as a "travelling accessory."

Pocket lanterns appeared that held matches and a candle, usually with a concealed hook from which it could be suspended, and hinged glass panels that opened up to create the sides of a lantern, or folded away when not in use. A small version is shown in **Fig. 320;** it has a single glass panel of beveled glass set in a frame hinged to one lid, and able to swing out to form one of three sides. Both sides of the box open; one side holds the glass and the candle on a movable arm, the other side opens for two-thirds of its width for access to the matches. The box is made of plated brass, with a framed panel of black leather set in each lid. The inside is highly polished to give good reflective capability. There is a striker on each long edge, one roughened for friction, the other to hold a strip of safety match striker. It is unmarked. However, a slightly larger version has been recorded, obviously made by the same company, and with a glass window system capable of forming a rectangle; this version is said to be German, c. 1870 to 1880.

Using the same principle as the Jones Brothers boxes, and shown in **Fig. 321,** is a box made in France by the "COMPAGNIE GENERALE DES ALLUMETTES CHIMIQUES", of Paris. Made of cardboard, it does not have an inner lid covering the matches, and the sanded striker is located along the front edge. The matches are quite different from those of today, made of cardboard, short, and each one is joined to its neighbor as in the later book matches; they evidence that the inventions of Pusey et al. were not entirely new. The example dates from the 1870s and, on the inside of the lid, reference is made to a French patent and one for "A L'ETRANGER"—for abroad.

A large series of cardboard boxes were produced that contained a complement of small wax tapers (candle matches), each provided with a chemically treated head for friction on the sanded surface located at one end of the box. The box drawer is pulled out by means of a cloth tab attached to the front edge of the drawer. Once ignited, the candle match may be inserted into a metal-rimmed socket set into the box near the back. Most boxes were made in France or Italy, and were known in continental Europe as "bougies de poche." They were popular from about 1880 until about 1905.

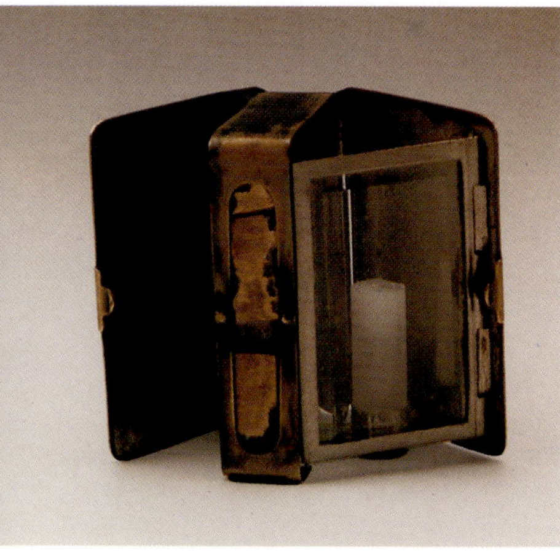

Fig. 320 Germany. Plated brass, leather, glass. Match holder and lantern. c.1870s or 1880s. H - 6.2cms.

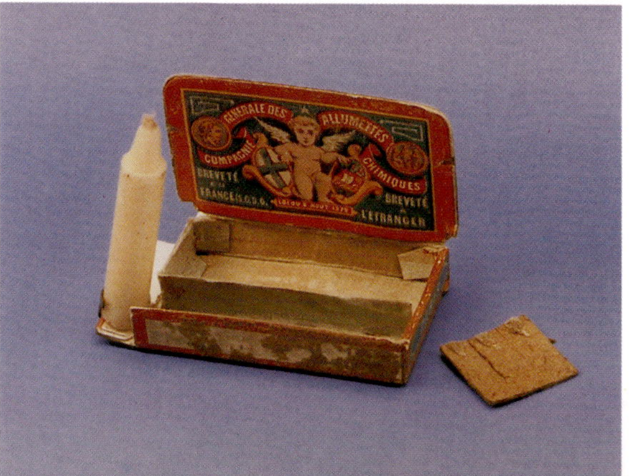

Fig. 321 France. Cardboard, tin. Patented. c.1870s. Made by Compagnie Generale Des Allumettes Chimiques. L - 6.7cms.

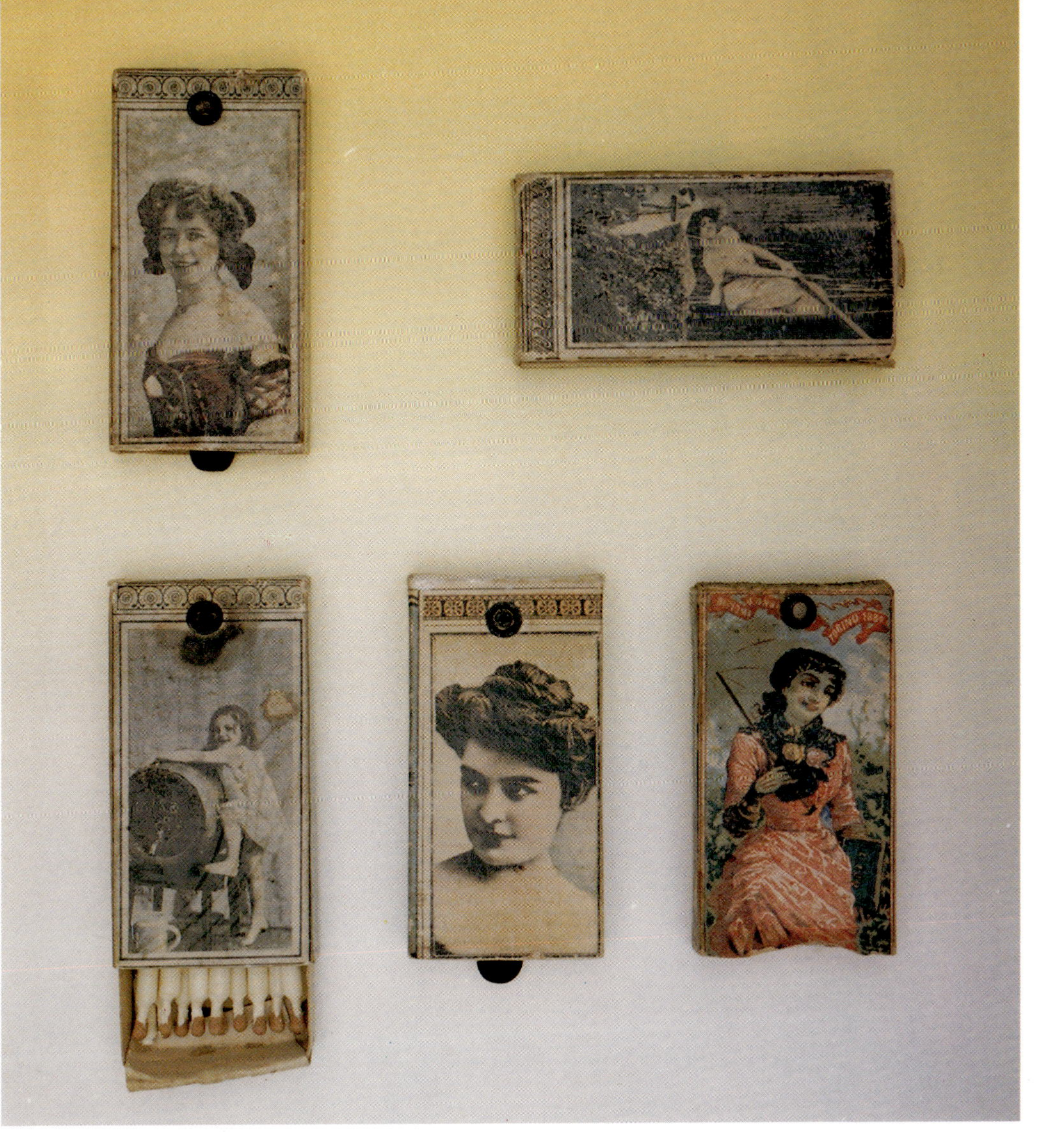

Fig. 322 France and Italy. "Bougies de poche". Cardboard. Lower right: made by Fabbriche Riunite di Flammiferi. c.1880s. H -7.8cms. Others made by Roche & Cie. at their factory in Belgium. Post 1900. L - 8cms.

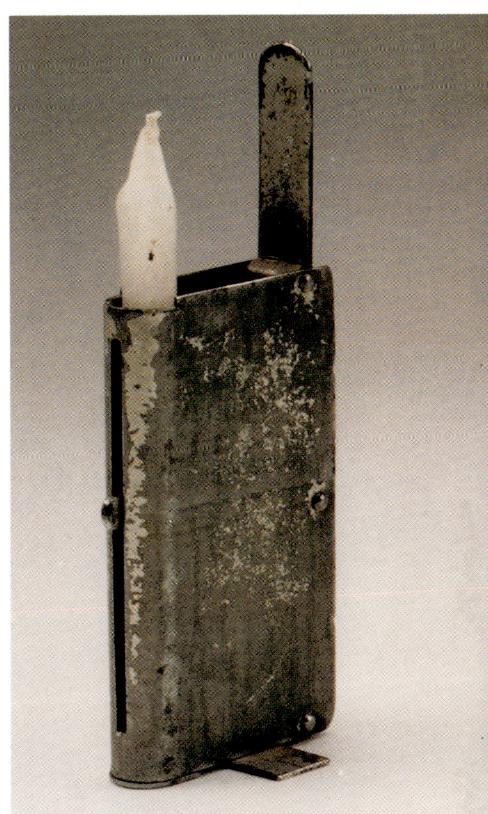

Fig. 323 United States. Plated tin plate. Made to an 1879 Invention Patent by Francis A. Farrell. H - 7cms.

Five examples are shown in **Fig. 322.** That at bottom right was made in Italy, and is marked "A.Dellacha" and "Riunite di Flammiferi"—two companies which combined in the 1870s. Their boxes are illustrated with paintings of beautiful ladies. The example is probably from the 1880s. The other four boxes were all made by Roche & Cie. of Paris and Marseille, at its factory in Ghent, Belgium. Well-known as match producers, the company was established in 1855. Its boxes of candle matches commonly displayed colored illustrations of beautiful ladies on one side, with some form of action photograph on the other side. The two top boxes are in fact the opposite sides of identical boxes. These four examples are all post-1900.

In the United States, Francis A. Farrell of Brooklyn, New York patented a combined match and candle holder in 1879, shown in **Fig. 323.** Book-shaped, and made of nickel-plated tin plate, the candle is in a tube inside the front edge, moved up and down by means of a lug attached to the candle socket. The back edge is the striker, and on the base is an additional plate, pivoted in the center to swivel around at right angles to the box body for stability when standing.

But Farrell's invention was far from the only combined candle and match holder in the United States. At least three others are known to have been produced prior to 1879, and are illustrated here from the patent drawings.

J. A. Whipple's invention of 1867, shown in **Fig. 324,** was manufactured in tin plate or brass. The candle socket was hinged to fold down and away inside one half, while the matches were contained in the other half.

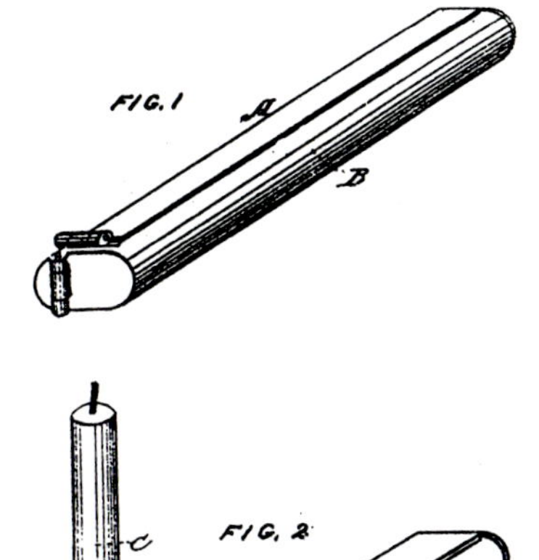

Fig. 324 United States Invention Patent drawings of 1867 by J. A. Whipple.

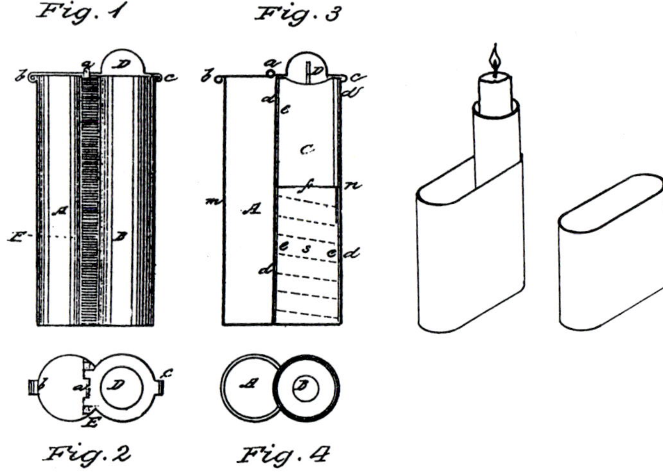

Fig. 325 Left: United States Invention Patent drawings of 1867 by C. R. Stickney. Right: sketch of the end product from an illustration in the A. Coulter & Co. catalogue of 1878.

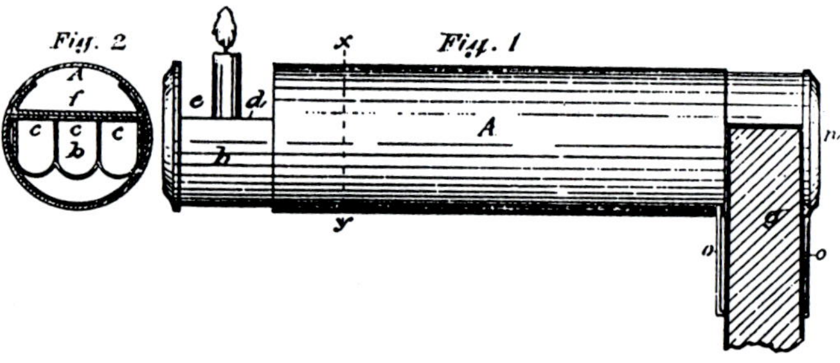

Fig. 326 United States Invention Patent drawings of 1874 by M. Goldman.

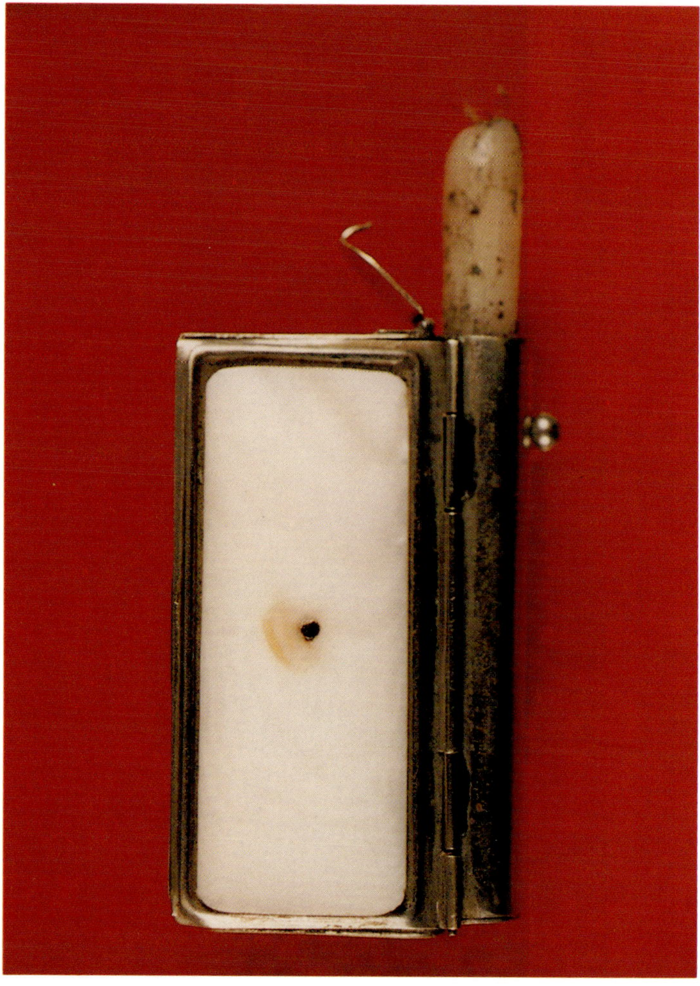

Fig. 328 As Fig. 327 open.

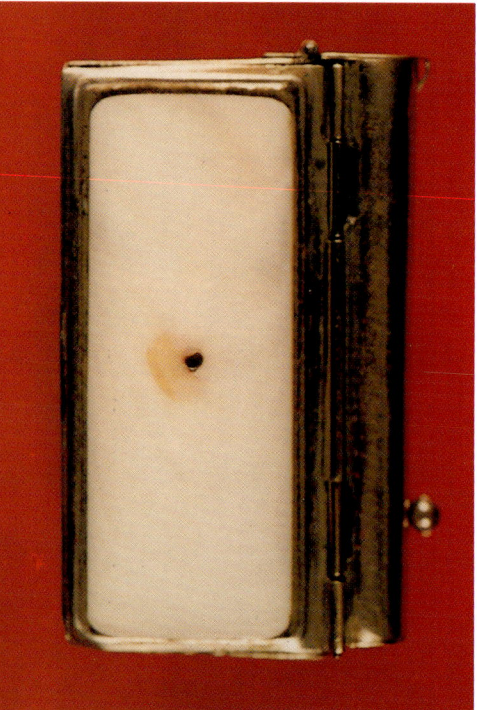

Fig. 327 United States. Brass, shell. c.1880s. H - 6.4cms.

The patent for C. R. Stickney's invention, shown in **Fig. 325,** was issued a month later in the same year. This too was probably made of tin plate or brass; but by the time that the end product was introduced it had undergone a significant change, retaining only the idea of the spring-loaded candle, and shown at the right of the illustration.

It was illustrated in an 1878 catalogue by A. Coulter & Co. of Chicago, wholesale dealers in "Staple Goods & Novelties" as "new" at $1.50 per dozen, with extra candles priced at 15¢ for a box of half a dozen. It was still claimed as being new by Peck & Snyder of New York in their catalogue of c. 1885, and was still the same price. The spring-loaded candle in Stickney's invention was *not new* in 1867, and corresponds with a part of the Birmingham manufacturer Wharton's box shown in Fig. 25, that in itself was a part of a Useful Design of 1845. Coulter's catalogue text for this box stated that it "represents the new combination Pocket Match Safe and Candle Holder" and that

> "It is one of the most useful inventions ever brought out, it is something that has long been needed and is already having a rapid sale. We have yet to see a person who has used them that would be without them for ten times the cost. AGENTS coin money with them."

In the written specifications for the M. Goldman patent of 1874, shown in **Fig. 326,** he states:

> "The object of my invention is to furnish a convenient and safe pocket-light that shall be capable of being readily attached to the arm of a chair, edge of a bedstead, or other suitable and convenient article."

The drawing shows the "convenient article" as 'g', and the plate 'n' is the end of a spring-loaded cylinder which pulls out and clamps the device to the furniture. In the end product, the plates "o" were eliminated, which made it a more convenient shape to fit in a pocket.

An unmarked book-shaped box resembling the Farrell example in some respects is shown in **Figs. 327 and 328.** The candle is moved up and down in the same manner. But there is a small separate lid over the candle that shares the same hinge location as the lid over the match compartment. One side of the box has a shell plate, attached by a single steel rivet; over the years this has caused corrosion stains. The box has no means of keeping it in the upright position. It probably dates to c. 1880.

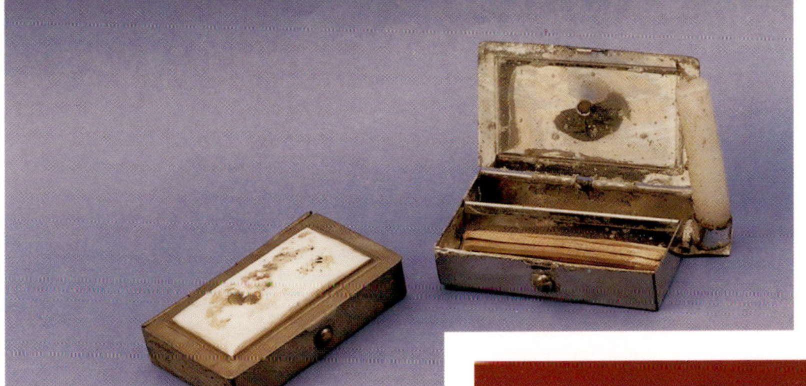

Fig. 329 Britain. Plated brass, tin plate, shell. c.1900s. L -5.9cms.

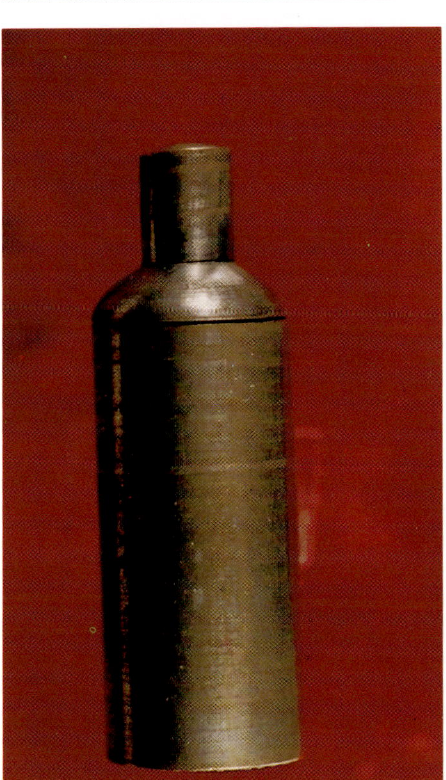

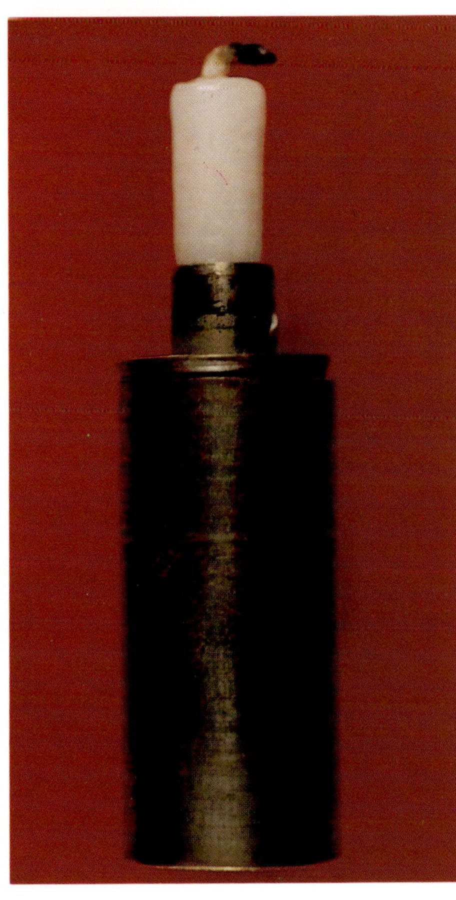

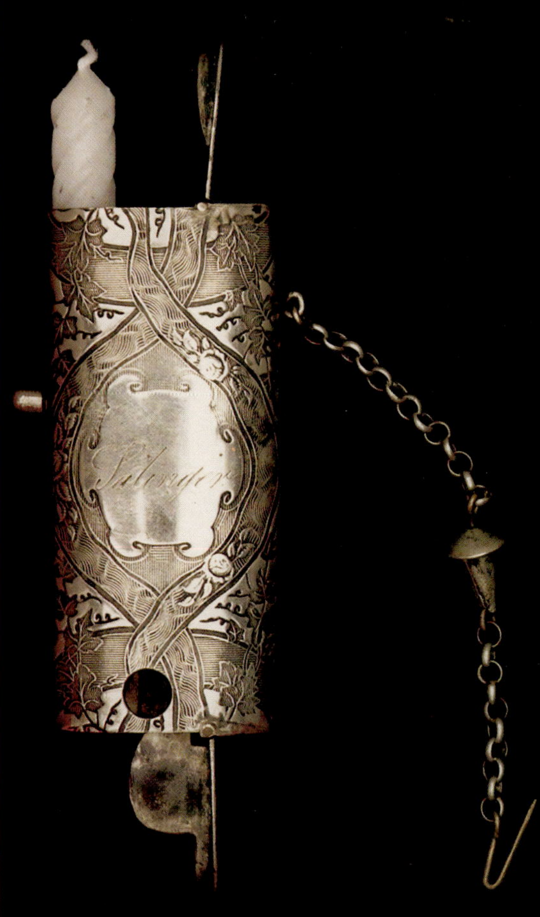

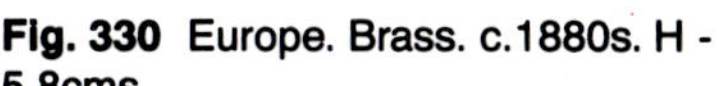

Fig. 330 Europe. Brass. c.1880s. H - 5.8cms.

Fig. 331 As Fig. 330, open.

Fig. 332 German. Silver plated? Combination match and candle holder, cigar cutter, with hanging chain. c.1880s. H - 6.9cms.

The two boxes shown in **Fig. 329** are made by the same company, in a style similar to those shown in Fig. 132; they are believed to be of British manufacture. The shell plates on the lid have lost most of their painted floral decoration and printed wording, but the boxes were probably intended as cheap souvenirs. The candle socket is attached to a small hinged section of the end, with the striker (of chemical compound suitable for both safety, and ordinary friction, matches) located at the opposite end. Although poorly made, these boxes were produced in several models as their makers strove to meet the needs of specific segments of the public.

A very simple and effective candle box, shown in **Figs. 330 and 331,** is in the form of a flask or bottle and is unmarked. It is probably of European origin from about the 1880s. The candle is held in the lid, and when the lid is closed, it is protected by a cylinder inside the box. The matches are stored between the inner cylinder and the outer wall of the main body. When the lid holding the candle is removed and inverted, the external lid section holding the candle is the right diameter to fit snugly into the central cylinder. The striker is located on the base.

The final example in this part, shown in **Fig. 332,** is equipped to serve five functions. Within its main body is a compartment for the matches. Inside the front edge is a tube housing the candle; the candle is set in a socket attached to a button for moving it up and down. Inside the back edge is a tube to hold a length of tinder cord. Inside the base is a cigar cutter with hinged lid and a hole in the side for the tip of the cigar. And attached to the back edge is a chain with a hook at the end to catch on the tinder cord, so that the tinder cord could be withdrawn to light with a match. The exposed end of the tinder cord at the bottom of the box would be used to pull it back into the tube and extinguish the flame. The box appears to be silver-plated; it has an unusual decorative design, with engraving on both cartouches of "Robert und George" and "Salinger." It is presumed to be of German origin from about the 1880s.

Many other designs for pocket candle boxes are to be found. Essentially, all were intended for use by the traveller in an era before gas and electric lighting became commonplace.

PART 8: ORGANIC BOXES.

Match holders made of organic material include those in wood, ivory, horn, leather, and the early natural plastics. Specific types of these materials are often difficult to identify, particularly the species of wood used; ivory, while probably always from the elephant, was also simulated in celluloid; horn has been reproduced in plastic, and treated to simulate tortoise shell; substitute leathers on a cloth base may cause a problem; and some of the early plastics, particularly gutta percha (if it was ever used for these small boxes) can also make positive identification challenging.

Wood was used quite extensively for pocket match holders. The Scottish woodenware makers and the manufacturers from Tonbridge, Kent (referred to in Chapter II) were pre-eminent in this field. But others also produced in this material.

As the business of William & Andrew Smith of Mauchline began to decline with the severe competition encountered from continental Europe in the last quarter of the l9th century and early in the twentieth century, they produced a form of match holder of the 'pencil box' type, an example of which is shown in **Figs. 333 to 336.** The illustrations show the layers of the box and how it was opened, but unlike the Swiss box of this type shown in Figs. 314 and 315, there was no trick method involved. The underside has a transfer design of the 'Old Man of the Mountains', a popular scenic attraction in the White Mountains of New Hampshire, and the box was no doubt sold locally as a souvenir.

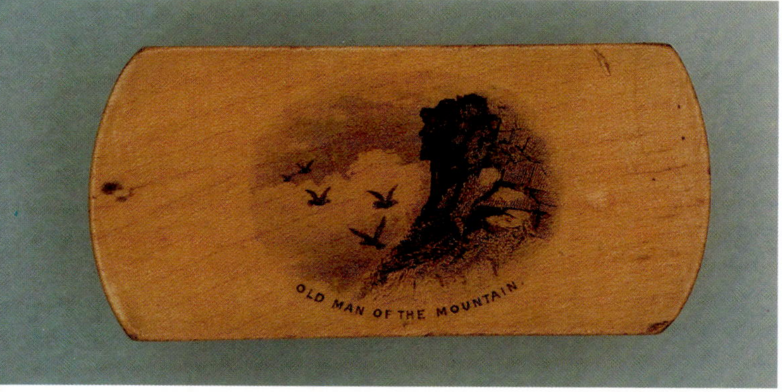

Fig. 333 Scotland. Sycamore. Made by William & Andrew Smith for the United States market. c.1900. L - 7.4cms.

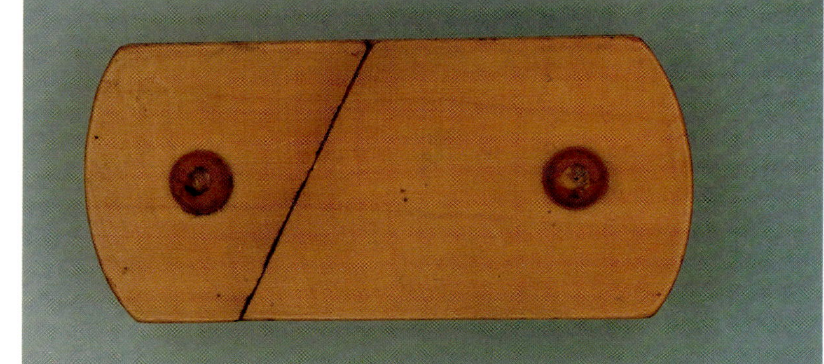

Fig. 335 As Fig. 333. Lid surface.

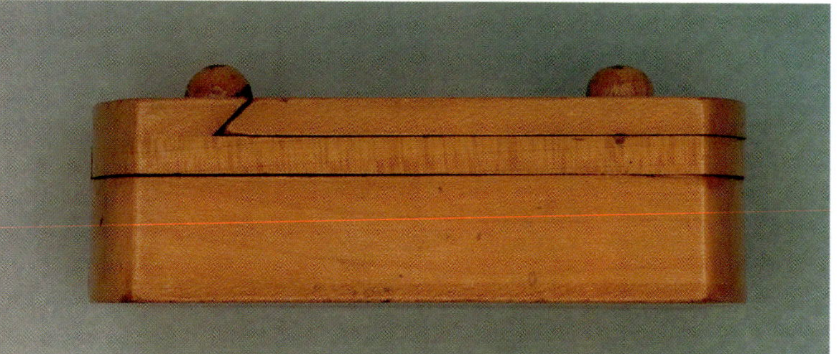

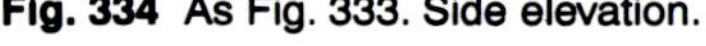

Fig. 334 As Fig. 333. Side elevation.

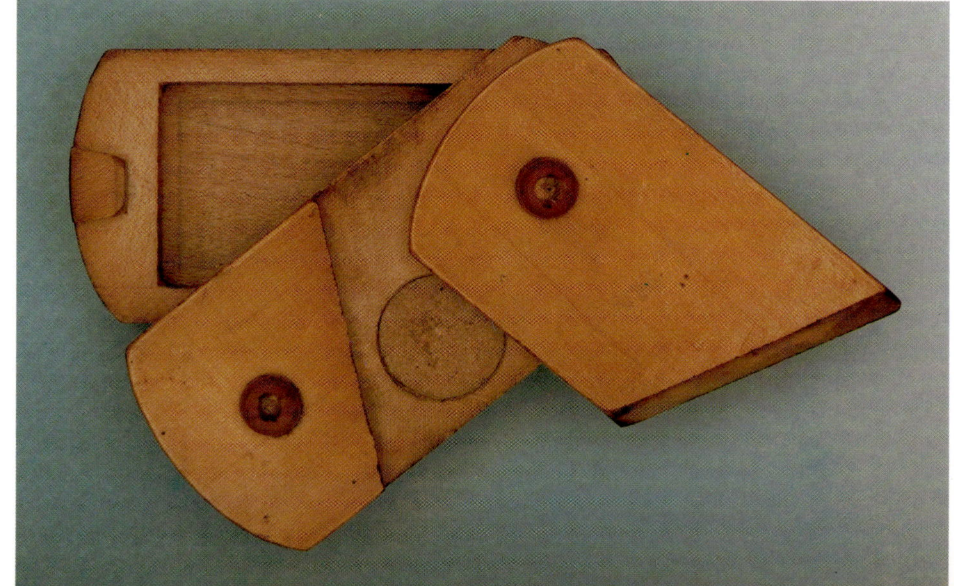

Fig. 336 As Fig. 333. Open.

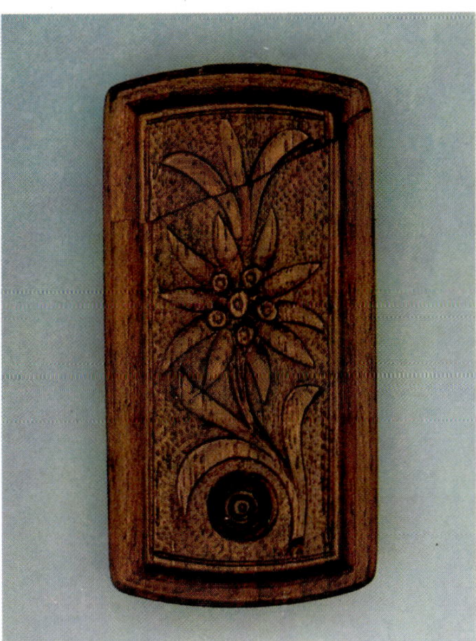

Fig. 337 Switzerland. Wood. c.1890s. L - 6.5cms.

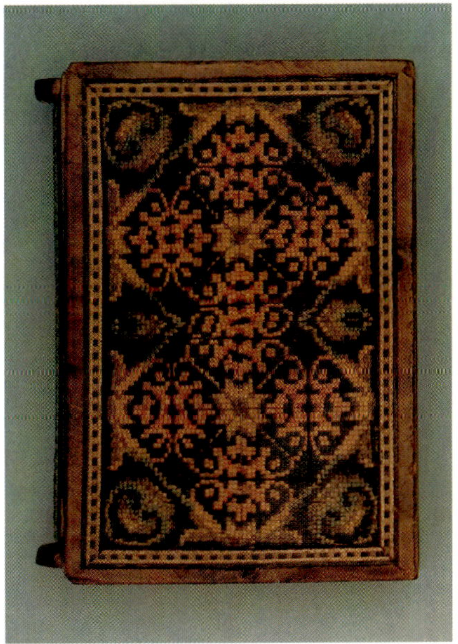

Fig. 338 Britain. Tonbridge. c.1920. H - 6.1cms.

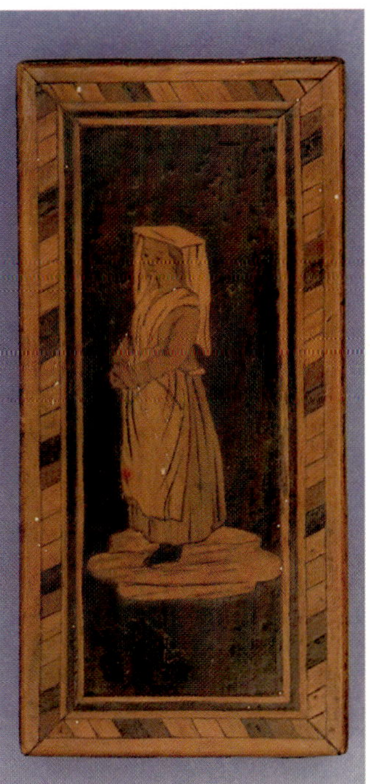

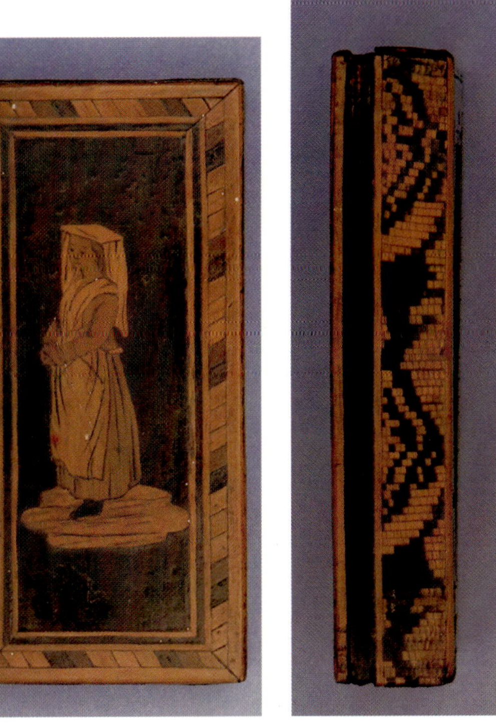

Fig. 339 Italy. Bay of Naples. Wood. c.1890s. H - 7.8cms.

Fig. 340 As Fig. 339. Edge view.

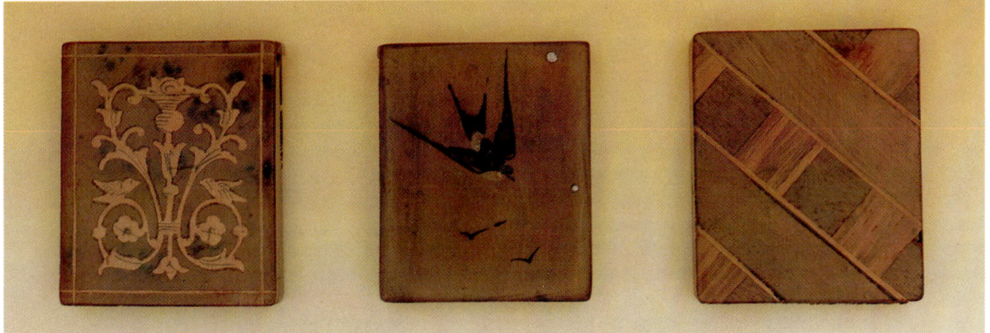

Fig. 341 Italy. Bay of Naples. Wood. c.1900s. Left: marquetry. Centre: painted. Right: inlay. H - 6cms.

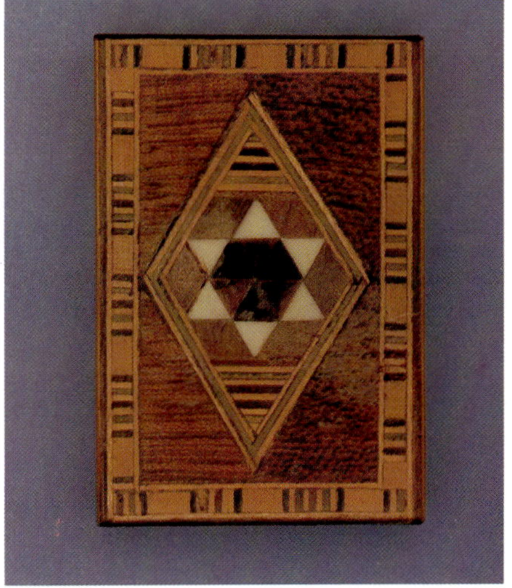

Fig. 342 Italy. Bay of Naples. Wood, shell. Inlay. c.1930s. H -5.4cms.

In the same form, in **Fig. 337,** is another Swiss box, a little smaller than the trick box, and also lacking the trick mechanism.

The ubiquitous book form boxes, with lids at the top and bottom, were also made in Mauchline and Tonbridge; the former's products are most commonly found bearing a black transfer design. An example of what is believed to be a Tonbridge mosaic-work box is shown in **Fig. 338.** Close examination reveals that some strange joins occur in the overall design, suggesting that the blocks of tesserae were cut in triangles, with the joins not precisely matched in color or alignment in places. It is speculated that this box may have been made between about 1915 and 1920 (or just after) as the quality of workmanship began to decline.

In Chapter II's discussion of early protective match holders, reference was made to a similar form of mosaic work produced in Italy (either Naples or Sorrento) that is occasionally mistaken for Tonbridge ware. An example of the Italian mosaic work is shown in **Figs.339 and 340.** This box has a sliding lid decorated with inlay work, as may be seen in Fig. 339; but the edge of the box (Fig. 336) has the tiny tesserae of the Tonbridge ware—in this case in black and light wood, but also known to have been produced in various colors. On the underside of the box a strip of sandpaper is glued into a recess as the striker, and is framed with mosaic work in a style and design similar to that of the lid. This box probably dates from around the turn of the century.

Three more examples of the Bay of Naples' wooden boxes are shown in **Fig. 341.** The lid is recessed into the sides at the top, and a sandpaper strip is glued into a recess in the base in each example. They exhibit three distinct styles of decoration popular in the region: at the left, marquetry; in the center, painted swallows; and at the right, another example of inlay work. They were probably all made in the first decade of this century.

The box in **Fig. 342** may also be from Sorrento or Naples, but the work is not well executed, with the glue being quite obvious and smeared in some places. The white pieces of tesserae appear to be made of shell. The design on the reverse side follows the same idea, and is also poorly finished. The box has a sliding drawer that appears to be made of balsa wood, with sandpaper glued to both ends as strikers. This probably dates from the 1930s.

Fig. 343 Ireland. Bog wood. c.1890s. H - 4.8cms.

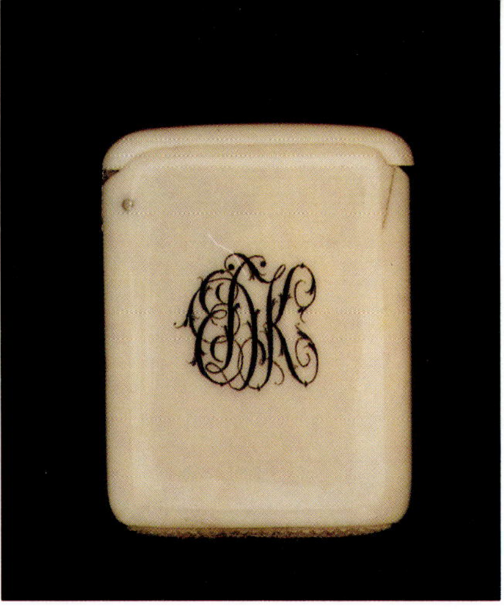

Fig. 346 Europe, possibly French. Ivory. c.1890s. H - 4.7cms.

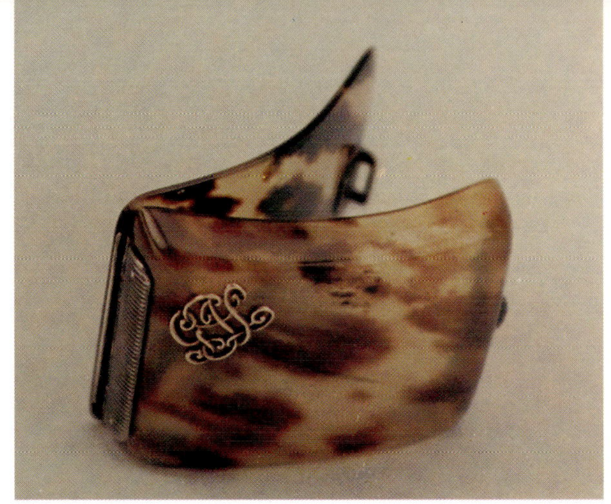

Fig. 347 Britain. Horn or tortoise shell, gold, silver. Marked "HA", 1892. L - 4.9cms.

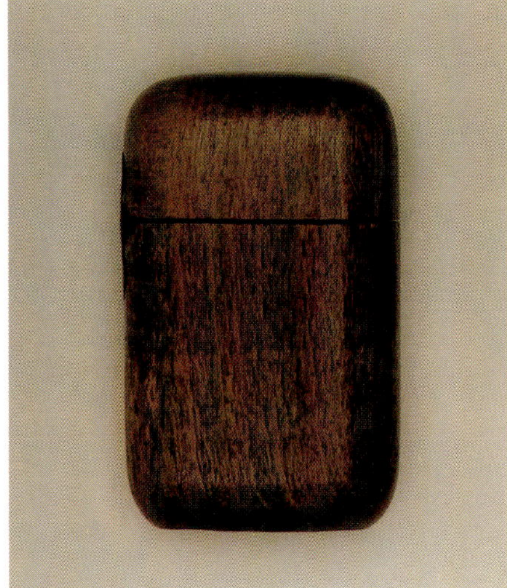

Fig. 344 Jerusalem. Olive wood, ?brass, iron. c.1890s. H - 5cms.

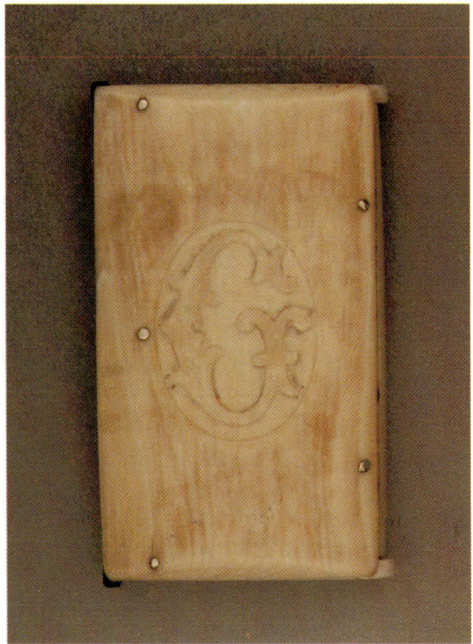

Fig. 345 Europe. Ivory, brass, composite. c.1880s. H - 5.9cms.

From Ireland is another book-shaped match holder, shown in **Fig. 343,** and made of what has been termed "bog wood" or "bog oak." Ireland is well known for its bogs, patches of ground saturated with water, from which the Irish cut out peat as a form of fuel for their fires. The bogs often contain logs and tree stumps which are preserved, turning black, and used for carving various ornaments. The example has a flat lid set into a recess between the sides; the front edge is a separate piece riveted into place and cross-hatched as a striker. The spine has lines representing the spine of a book, and both sides have clover leaves carved in relief into them. The box probably dates from the late 19th century.

Probably made from olive wood in Jerusalem, the example in **Fig. 344** is very simple. It has a neat brass strap hinge fixing the lid to the body by steel rivets. The striker is missing. The box is probably from c. 1890.

Match holders made of ivory were fashionable in the latter part of the l9th century, but are seldom marked and subsequently difficult to date. They are usually made by riveting strips of ivory together to form a box; but occasionally one may be found in which the body has been hollowed out from a single piece, or ivory side plates are attached to a metal frame or side panel.

The example in **Fig. 345** is in the shape of a book made by the ivory strip method. It has lids at both ends, and on the front edge is a strip of material that appears to be for striking safety matches, although experiments have failed to ignite that form of match. Also made in the strip method is the example in Fig. 252 in the shape of a coffin. Boxes made to represent crates, with the word "Fragile" on them, are also to be found occasionally.

An example of a match holder made by hollowing out the main body is shown in **Fig. 346.** The lid has a metal hinge, and the striker is carved out of the base with a cross-hatched design. It must have taken incredible skill and patience to hollow out this elegant box with the sides little more than 1 mm thick. Other boxes made using the same technique have been recorded as having deep, hollowed-out lids, and a catch activated by a press-stud.

Examples of metal-framed boxes with ivory side-plates may be seen in Figs.117 and 120. Others may be found in a purse form, hinged longitudinally.

Boxes made of horn or tortoise shell are quite rare, but a fine example in the latter material is shown in **Fig. 347.** It is curved to fit into the pocket of a waistcoat (vest in North America); the hinge and clasp are made of silver, hall-marked for London, 1892, and a makers mark of "HA." The owners initials are made of gold wire attached by two minute gold rivets. If carefully heated, horn and tortoise shell may be molded under pressure to permit bending and accept impressed decoration.

Plastic materials have been around for centuries in a natural form; amber, horn and tortoise shell are examples of vegetable and animal substances that may be worked and heat-shaped like today's synthetic plastics. Papier machê is in fact a man-made form of plastic material and was patented in 1772. Probably the earliest form of pocket match holder was a papier machê snuff box, converted to a match holder by the addition of a striker surface applied to one edge.

Bois Durci was probably the first true plastic, used for book-shaped match holders. The material was made from sawdust, mixed with blood and egg albumen or gelatine; the mixture was dried, placed in a mold, and compressed in a heated press. *Bois Durci* was patented in 1855 in Paris, but the end products were produced only through the 1860s until 1875. Consequently, examples of match holders in this material are very rare.

Gutta percha is another natural form of plastic which arrived on the scene in the mid-1840s. It originated in Southeast Asia, and is usually thought of as a derivative of rubber trees, but the species is different. A major drawback of the material is that it deteriorates quite rapidly when exposed to oxygen. Although match holders on sale today are quite often said to be of gutta percha, there is no proof they were ever made of this material, and many so-called gutta percha boxes are actually vulcanite.

Rubber was first imported into Britain in 1774, but found very limited use. It was not until 1840 that Charles Goodyear of the United States discovered the secret of producing a hard rubber that could be molded. By adding 25% to 50% sulphur to rubber and heating the mixture, the process known as vulcanizing was discovered; it was found that the material could be molded into almost any shape. This was the first natural substance to be chemically altered by man. It became known as vulcanite or ebonite, because of its resemblance to ebony.

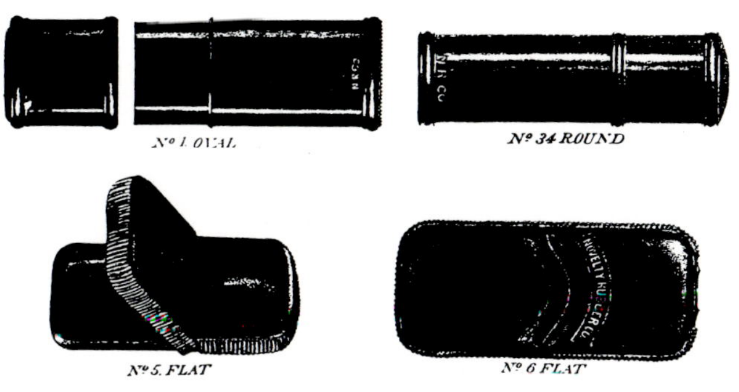

Fig. 348 Illustrations from a 1876 catalogue by the Novelty Rubber Co. of New York, of vulcanite match holders made by that company.

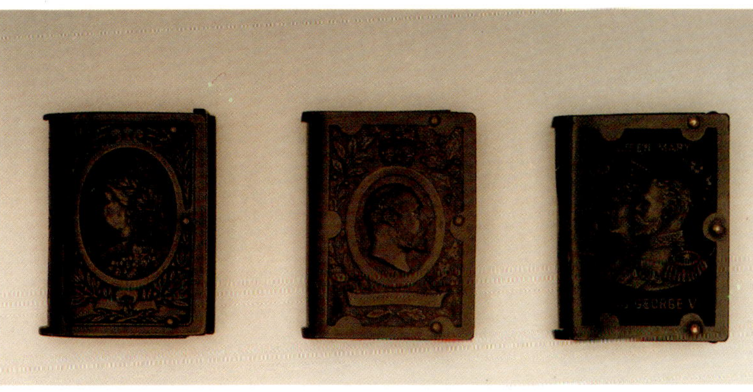

Fig. 350 Germany. Vulcanite. Left: probably 1897. Centre: 1901 or 1902. Right: 1910 or 1911. H - 5cms.

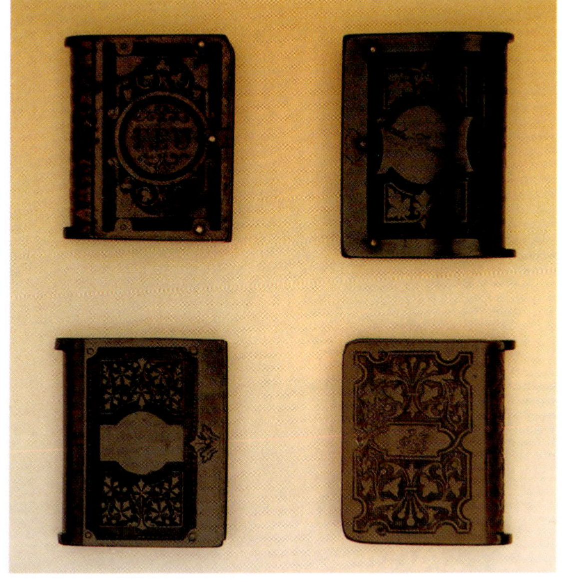

Fig. 349 Germany. Vulcanite. Top left: for Bryant & May, 1879, H - 4.6cms. Others: c. late 1870s to c. early 1900s. Top right: made by New York Hamburg G.W.Co. H - 5cms. Lower left: H - 4.7cms. Lower right: H - 4.6cms.

Fig. 351 Reverse of Fig. 350.

The first recorded use of vulcanite for match holders is difficult to establish; but in the United States, the Novelty Rubber Co. of New York was certainly making them as evidenced by **Fig. 348.** This illustration is from the company catalogue of 1876, and shows four different shapes of box, one of them made in four sizes.

In Europe it appears that they were probably first made in Germany, and were being exported to Britain by 1879, where they were shown in the 1879 Diary and Almanac of Bryant & May, and called "The VULCANITE," to hold wax vesta matches. An example of a Bryant & May box is shown at the upper left in **Fig. 349.** It has a laquered bronze finish on the smooth surfaces; however, the recessed background, both lids, and the front striker area have been left the dark brown of the material. The spine is marked "Bryant & May" and, in the round cartouche on the front, it is engraved "Feu".

The other three boxes in **Fig. 349** were made in Germany. That at the upper right is black; engraved across the escutcheon is "Made in Germany," and on the spine "New-York Hamburg. G.W.Co." This is probably the name of the manufacturer, the "G.W." standing for Gummi Werker, or rubber works. Hamburg had strong sea trade ties with the United States from the 18th century, and the company may have been jointly owned in Hamburg and New York. The reverse side of this box is marked "Feu". The remaining two boxes are both brown, and bear no maker's marks.

Three examples of a series, produced over a period of many years and decorated with the heads of British monarchs of the period, are shown in **Figs. 350 and 351.** From left to right, Fig. 350 shows Queen Victoria, King Edward VII, and King George V with Queen Mary. The reverse sides are shown in Fig. 351 in the same order. That of Victoria was probably made for her Diamond Jubilee of 1897, and the same box was marked "In Memoriam" on her death in 1901. The Edward VII box was probably made for his coronation in 1901 or 1902, and the George V/Queen Mary box was no doubt made in 1910 or 1911, after his accession to the throne. All are dark brown.

The two boxes in **Fig. 352** were made in Britain, probably by Charles Mackintosh & Co., established in Manchester as India Rubber Manufacturers in 1824, where they had their office, factory and showroom, and with a warehouse in London. The box at the bottom is horseshoe-shaped and has a photograph of Harrogate, Yorkshire, behind a celluloid sheet. Other scenic views, architectural structures, and famous or private persons are also to be found. The box above, in book form, has an oval metal-framed photograph under glass, of the Musselburgh Bridge, near Edinburgh, Scotland. The cover and spine are in an orange reptile-skin design form of vulcanite. The box has a single lid and the front edge a ribbed striker in brown vulcanite. The lower edge is a striker made of a chemical composition for safety matches

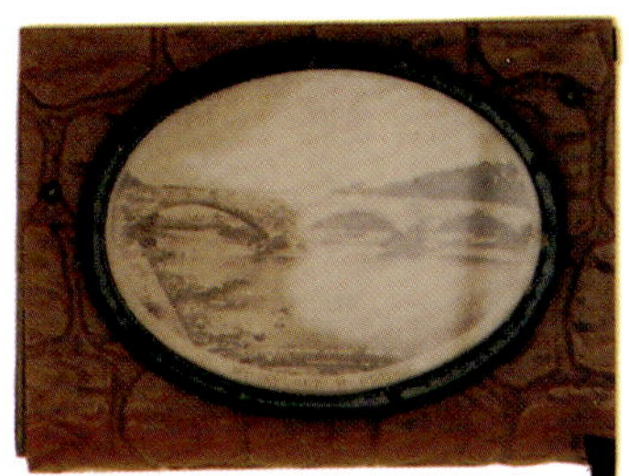

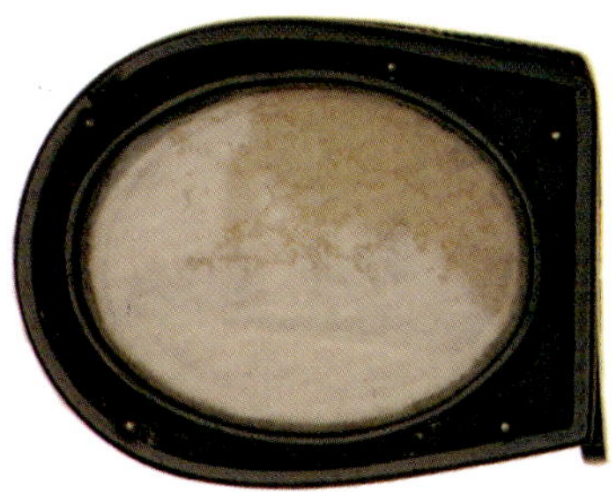

Fig. 352 Britain. Vulcanite, glass, tin plate. Possibly made by Charles Mackintosh & Co. c. 1900. Lower: L - 5.4cms. Upper: L - 5.3cms.

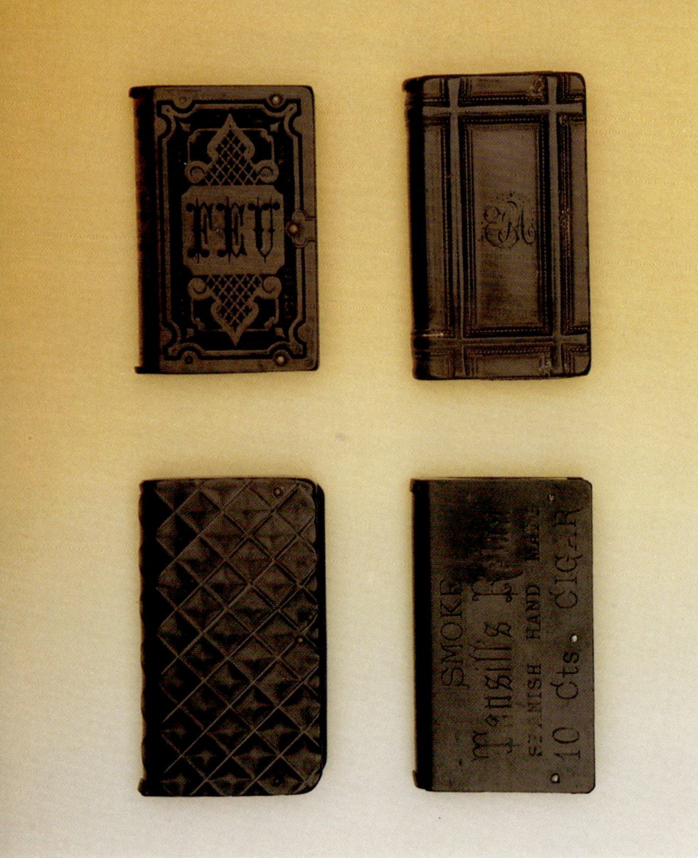

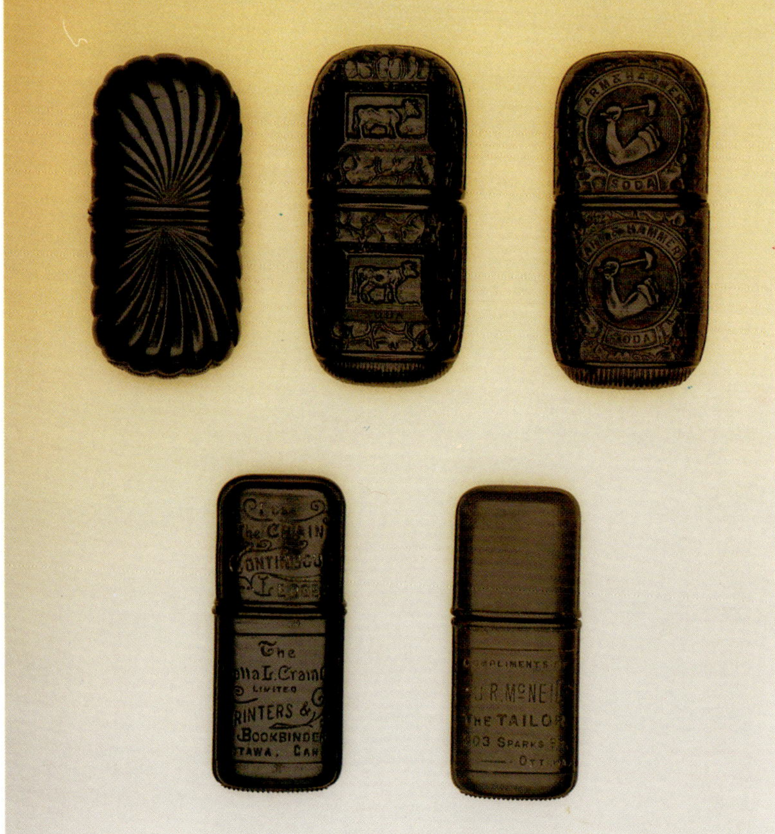

Fig. 353 Vulcanite. Top left: made by Hannov G. K. C. in Germany. H - 6.4cms. Top right: made in Germany. H - 6.9cms. Lower left: probably made in Germany. H - 7.1cms. All c.1870s to 1900. Lower right: made in the United States. c.1890s. H - 7cms.

Fig. 354 United States. Vulcanite. c.1900. H's - from 7.1 to 7.6cms.

Of the larger versions of vulcanite match holders in book form shown in **Fig. 353,** the example at top left is marked in the spine "Hannov G.K.C. Hannover". The G.K.C. is known to mean Gummi Kamm Co.—the Rubber Comb Co. The example at top right is unmarked, has a single lid, a ribbed striker on the front edge, and a second for safety matches on the base. The front panel has finely engraved initials. The lower left example has lids at both ends. Both are dark brown and are probably of German origin.

The example at bottom right was made in the United States. It is black, with lids at both ends, and is an advertising item. It is marked "R.W.TANSILL & CO. CHICAGO" on the spine, "SMOKE Tansill's Reina SPANISH HAND MADE 10 Cts CIGAR" on one side, and "SMOKE Tansill's Punch. AMERICA'S FINEST 5 Cts CIGAR" on the other side. These were shown in the Zorn catalogue of 1892 as "Rubber Match Safes. Plain Rubber. $0.75 per dozen; $8.00 per gross."

The vulcanite boxes in **Fig. 354** were made in the United States, probably between 1890 and 1910. At least two were said by the dealers to be bakelite, the first totally man-made plastic, invented and patented by Dr.Leo Baekeland in the United States in 1907. Analysis by a professional museum conservation analyst has shown that the boxes have a very high content of rubber and sulphur, consistent with vulcanite, but quite unlike bakelite.

The example at top left is purely decorative, the other four are advertising items. That in the top row, center, is for Cow Brand soda, and is marked on the bezel "Compliments of John Dwight & Co.;" the example in the top row, right, was made for Arm & Hammer Soda, and marked on the bezel "Compliments of Church & Co." These two companies ultimately merged to become Church & Dwight by 1908.

The two lower boxes are marked with advertising for companies in Ottawa, Ontario. That at the left is for the Rolla L. Crane Co. Ltd., printers and bookbinders, until quite recently still a family-run business. The box at the right is marked "J.R.McNeil. The Tailor;" McNeil's business was started in 1889 and closed shortly after he died in 1908.

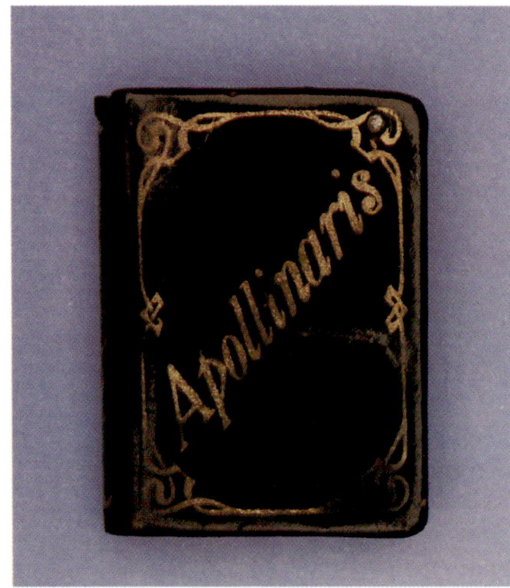

Fig. 355 Possibly Germany. Vulcanite, wood. c.1900. H - 4.9cms.

The vulcanite book-shaped box in **Fig. 355** has a single lid, and its front and lower edge is sanded for friction. Between the front edge and a strip of vulcanite set inside the box is a thin strip of wood which acts to hold the lid in the closed or open position, activated by a hidden spring. The outside of the box, painted black, has gold decorative elements and the word "Apollinaris" on both sides. As Apollinaris is a well-known German mineral water, it is assumed that the box was made in Germany.

Celluloid was invented by 1862, but the original formula was not very stable, and it was 1869 before the problems were corrected and patented in the United States. It was marketed under such names as Xylonite, Ivoride and Pyroxylin, and was also commonly known as French Ivory. It was highly flammable, so it seems strange to think that it should be used for match holders. Although cinegraphic and photographic film made of celluloid has proved to be unstable over a period of many years, due to self-destruction caused by its own nitric acid fumes, there have been no reports of this adverse property in relation to the many domestic wares made of celluloid. However, museum conservators recommend that this material be stored in a space with ample air circulation as a precautionary measure, and if possible separated from other materials which could be adversely affected.

The book-form example in **Fig. 356** has a celluloid cover that looks like ivory, but has vulcanite lids and front-edge striker. Printed on the side is "Haarlem" (Holland), and the box may therefore be of German origin. The domino box in Fig. 278 is another example of mixing these two materials in the same box.

Other boxes made partially or totally of plastics are referred to elsewhere in this and other chapters.

The match holder shown in **Fig. 357** is a rather elaborate book form, with a wooden frame covered in leather, and brass fittings and edges, the latter neatly roughened for friction. The front cover is impressed "Feu" in gold letters, and hinged to the back edge of the box by the leather covering. It is probably of French origin, from the last quarter of the 19th century.

The combined cigar and match case in **Fig. 358** opens at both ends when the internal central portion is slid backwards or forwards in the sleeve. It is leather-covered over tin plate and cardboard, with a beaded panel in a Berlin woolwork-style design. The pair of lids at one end spring open by means of elastic as the central portion is exposed, to reveal the deep cigar compartment; only one lid, however, is hinged to spring open at the opposite end to provide access to the matches, a fixed side forming a small compartment with its own internal lid, sanded on the outside for friction. The origin is unknown, but it is speculated that it may be from the United States, perhaps in the last decade of the 19th century.

Telescopic-style leather cases with full-depth, slip-on lids were popular in the last two decades of the l9th century. In the example in **Fig. 359** it is difficult to tell which is the top and which the bottom. A number of catalogues show this type of holder with the inner section at the top, where the striker is usually shown. The example here has the striker located at the opposite end, and it would seem more logical to open these holders by removing the outer cover from the top, thus keeping the matches inside the smaller section and thereby making it easier to replace the lid. Be that as it may, most of this type had domed ends, with the British ones often having the Royal Coat of Arms impressed on one side. Occasionally the outer rim had a silver fitting, while others had silver or plated escutcheons attached to one side. The example is plain with a steel striker.

In Zorn's 1892 catalogue an example was referred to as "London make" at $1.75 per dozen or $18.00 per gross. In the 1893 Montgomery Ward & Co. catalogue, they were offered at 20¢ each or $2.00 per dozen, and in 1894 William Demuth sold them for $1.75 per dozen.

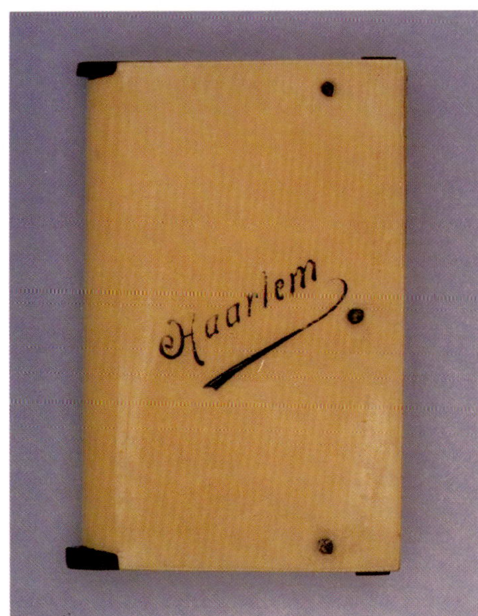

Fig. 356 Germany. Vulcanite, celluloid. c.1900. H - 6.3cms.

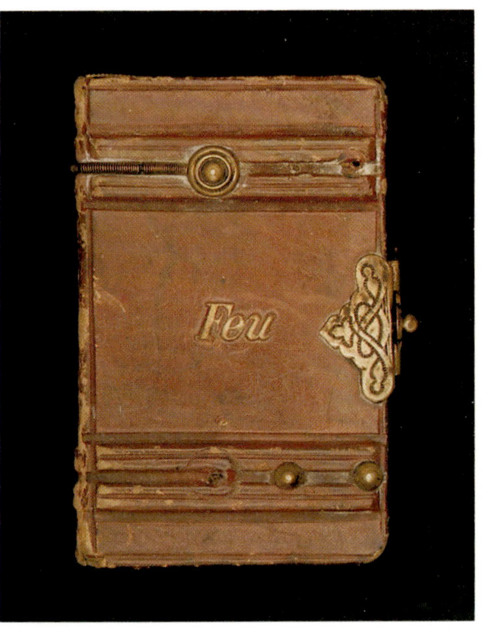

Fig. 357 France. Wood, leather, cloth, brass. c.1890s. H - 6.5cms.

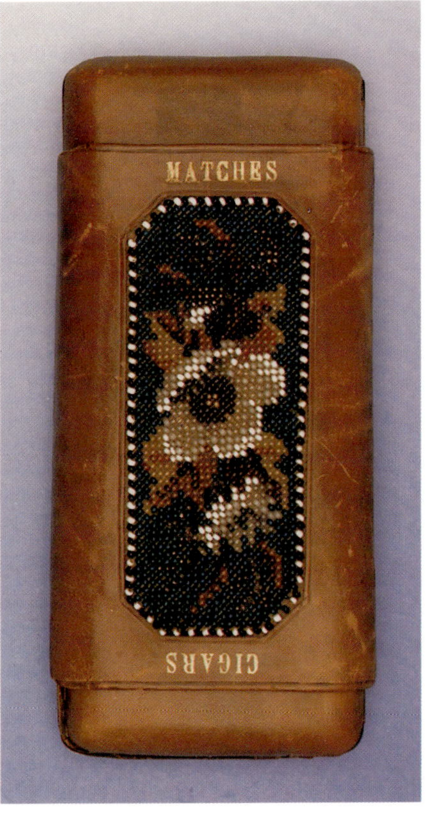

Fig. 358 United States? Leather, cardboard, tin plate, paper, beads. Cigar and match holder. c.1890s. H - 16cms.

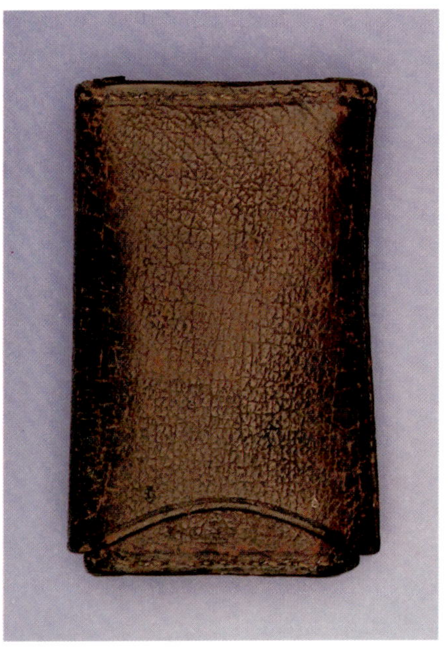

Fig. 359 Britain? Leather, iron. c.1890s. H - 6.3cms.

PART 9: MATCHBOX AND BOOK MATCH HOLDERS

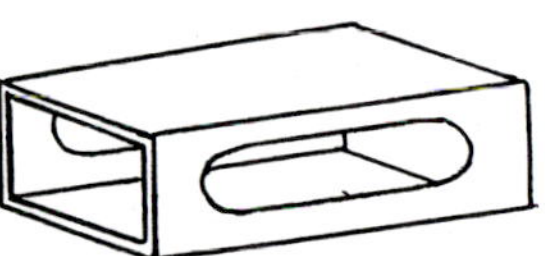

Fig. 360 Useful Design of 1873 by Bryant & May.

Soon after friction matches were first manufactured they were most commonly sold in boxes of thin chip wood with sliding trays, later made of cardboard, and are still sold in the same format. The sizes of these boxes became standard, leading to the development of covers to hold them. The same was true of book matches when they were introduced.

Providing a decorative cover to hold an existing box of matches, which could then be slipped into the pocket, or placed in a convenient location in the home, did not occur until 1873 when Bryant & May registered a Useful Design in Britain. The very simple design is shown in **Fig. 360.** It was described as "a case for containing a matchbox which is in occasional use in a secure manner" and noted that "the whole of this design is new." Bryant & May went on to produce numerous variations and designs, often in four sizes, up until at least the late 1930s. Some examples may be seen in Chapter IV, "The Match Manufacturers' Contribution."

Basically there were two forms of covers. Those with two sides and a spine, with the ends and one side open, are referred to by the specialist collectors as "grips." Those shown in the Bryant & May design in Fig. 360 are sometimes open at both ends, or have one end closed but with a hole for a finger to push out the matchbox tray. These are usually referred to as "slides." There were several variations on these two themes.

Apart from some of the Bryant & May examples, early versions of the slides appear to be scarce. A common type made in China, and usually so stamped, has cloisonné enamel designs. An example is shown in **Fig. 361;** its design is said to represent the blooming prunus or cherry, and is poorly executed, as are designs on many of these slides. The bodies are usually made of brass, and one end is closed except for a finger hole. These were imported into North America, and probably Britain as well, in great quantities in the 1920s and 1930s. They were shown in the 1925 catalogue of Henry Birks & Sons of Montreal at $1.25, or as part of a smoker's set (with matching ashtray and cigarette box) at $5.75, and again as a set in 1934 at $2.25.

Also marked "CHINA" is a slide for a smaller box of matches in **Fig. 362.** On top is a crude engraving of birds, and on the bottom of flowers. Soldered to the top is a cast animal with a certain naive charm. It is probably from about the same period as the previous example.

Again from the same period is a silver slide in **Fig. 363,** for a small hox of matches. It was made by Henry Birks & Sons of Montreal, and bears its name. Birks was offering this type of holder as early as 1918 at $2.50 each, and in 1921 for $5.00 each. In 1935, in the same size as the example, they were $1.00 each. Similar slides were offered by L. & C. Mayers Co. of New York in its catalogue of 1940 as part of a "Smokers Set" with four ash trays and four slides at $18.00 a set, or six ash trays and six slides at $21.70 a set, all in silver. In Britain, the Goldsmiths & Silversmiths Co. of London in 1932 offered 9 karat gold slides at six pounds, ten shillings for a large size, and three pounds, fifteen shillings for the small size, and silver slides from twelve to twenty-three shillings, plus a slide to take the large "Swan" vesta boxes in silver at three pounds, five shillings.

Grips seem to have first appeared just after the turn of the century. The examples in **Fig. 364** were made in the United States of aluminum. The edges of the thin-gauge metal are turned down on the open side to add strength to the box. The upper example was made as a souvenir for the Pan-American Exposition held at Buffalo in 1901. The lower example was made in 1907 by the N.J. Aluminum Co. of Newark, New Jersey.

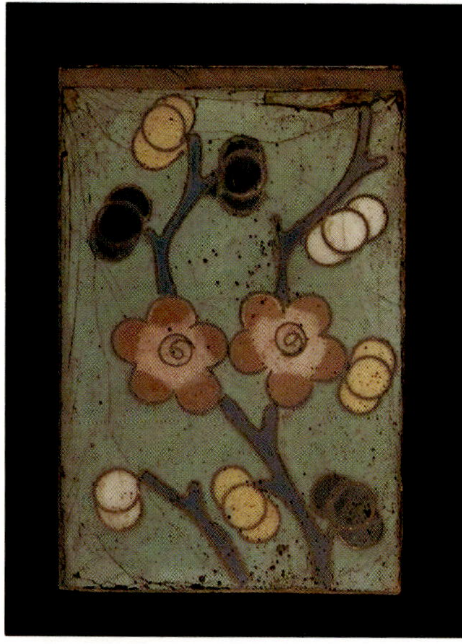

Fig. 361 China. Brass, enamel. 1920s and 1930s. L - 6cms.

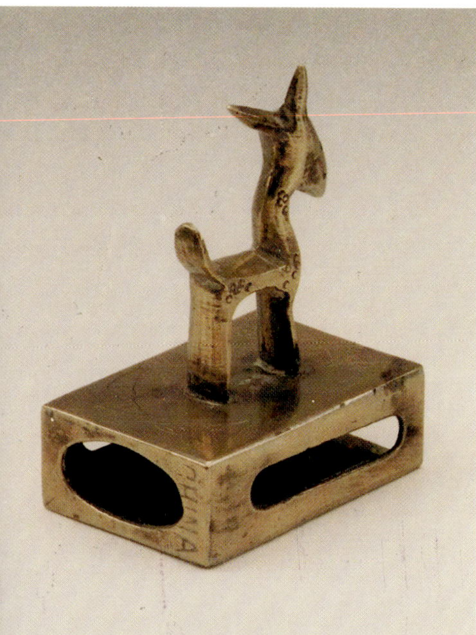

Fig. 362 China. Brass. 1920s and 1930s. H - 5.8cms.

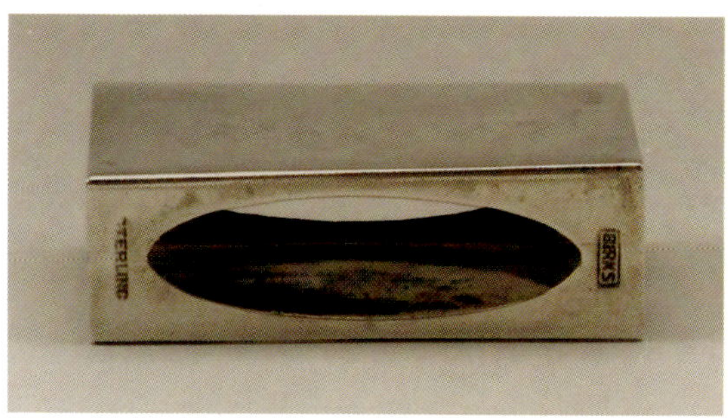

Fig. 363 Canada. Silver. Made by Henry Birks & Sons Ltd. 1918 to 1940. L - 4.6cms.

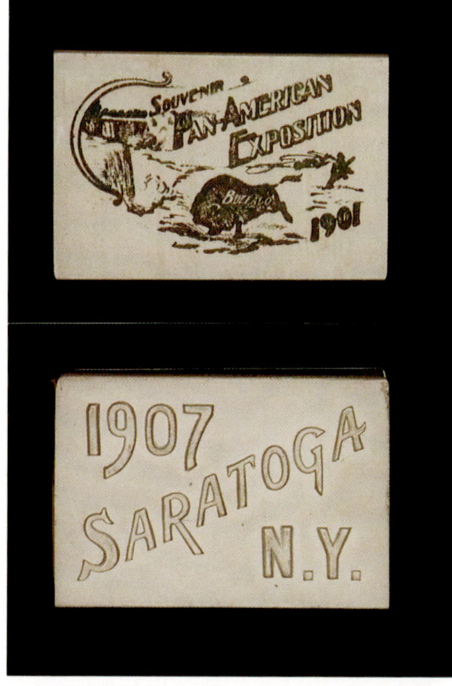

Fig. 364 United States. Aluminum. Top: 1901. Lower: made by the N. J. Aluminum Co. 1907. L - 4.3cms.

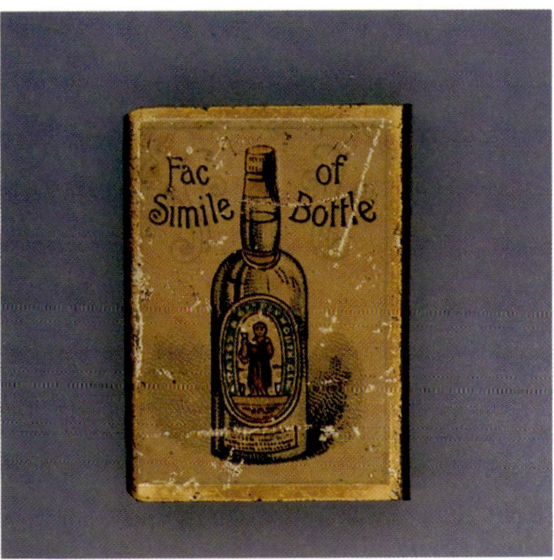

Fig. 365 Britain. Tin plate. Marked "Wedekind & Co. London. E.C.", wholesalers. Probably c.1910. L - 4.4cms.

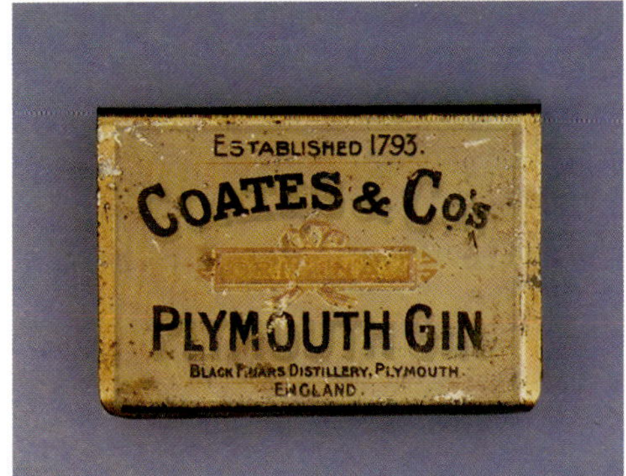

Fig. 366 As Fig. 365.

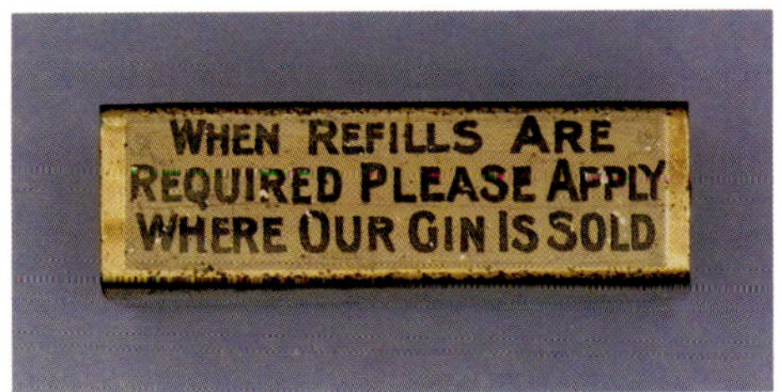

Fig. 367 As Fig. 365.

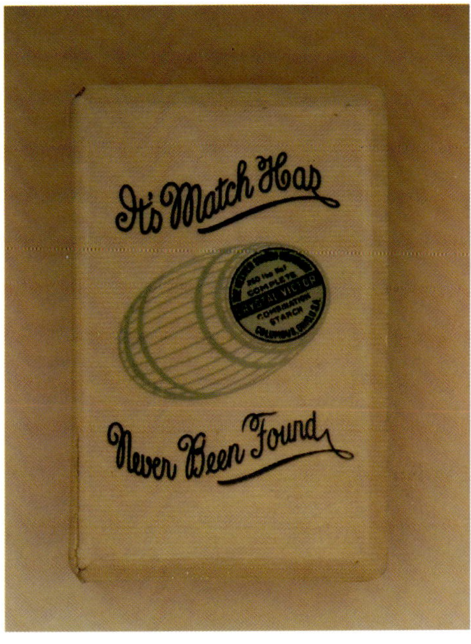

Fig. 368 United States. Celluloid. Made by the Whitehead & Hoag Co.. Between 1905 and 1922. H - 6.3cms.

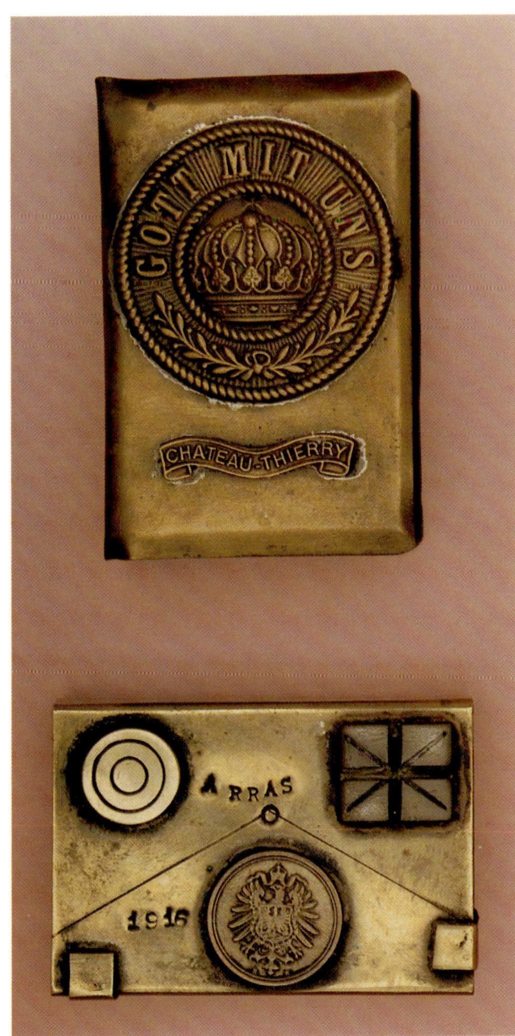

Fig. 369 Europe. Brass, copper, steel. Top: German. 1918. H -6.1cms. Lower: made in France. 1916. H - 5.6cms.

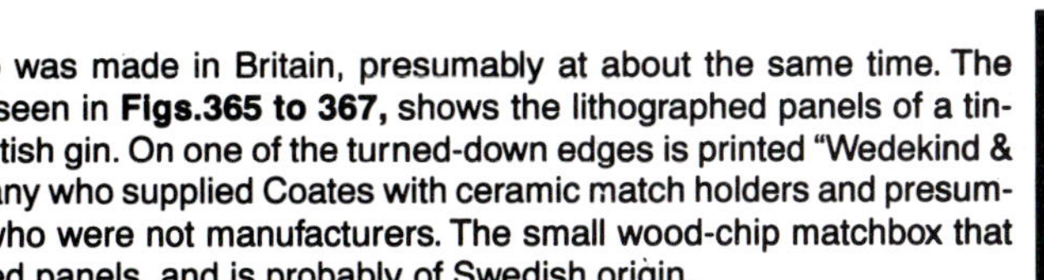

The same form and size of grip was made in Britain, presumably at about the same time. The example, various views of which are seen in **Figs.365 to 367,** shows the lithographed panels of a tin-plate grip advertising a well-known British gin. On one of the turned-down edges is printed "Wedekind & Co., London.E.C.," a wholesale company who supplied Coates with ceramic match holders and presumably other advertising novelties, but who were not manufacturers. The small wood-chip matchbox that came with the grip has identical printed panels, and is probably of Swedish origin.

It is perhaps not surprising to find that, with the expertise developed by Whitehead & Hoag in the use of celluloid for novelties, they produced grips made solely of celluloid. The example in **Fig. 368** bears the company name and patent date for 1905, and must have been made between 1905 and 1922. The advertising is for The Keever Starch Co. of Columbus, Ohio.

Two examples in brass of World War I grips are shown in **Fig. 369.** The upper one is German-made, with the words ""Gott Mit Uns" (God with us) and below this a ribbon marked "Chateau-Thierry," the French town briefly overrun by the German army in 1918 before the final counterattack pushed the German forces back, leading to the end of the war. The lower grip is what has been termed "trench art;" made by a soldier, probably from a shell case, it bears applied decorative items, including a German coin, and is stamped "Arras." The sides are supported by two narrow brass bands, soldered at one end and on one side edge. Arras was the scene of a massive, but inconclusive, battle in the Spring of 1917.

Grips made of tin plate and provided with a celluloid cover displaying design work were first produced in Britain in 1911, but did not become popular until the beginning of World War I. This type of grip does not appear to have been patented, although the technique of applying the celluloid covers may have been used on some other types of articles. Such grips occurred in the United States at a later date, and a second method of fixing the celluloid to the tin-plate cover was devised.

Fig. 370 shows the different methods. The British method, in the top two sketches, was more complex, with the celluloid covering the edges of the tin plate. The second United States method was simpler, but left the edge of the tin plate exposed on the outside edges. In the sketches, "A" represents the tin plate, and "B" the celluloid cover.

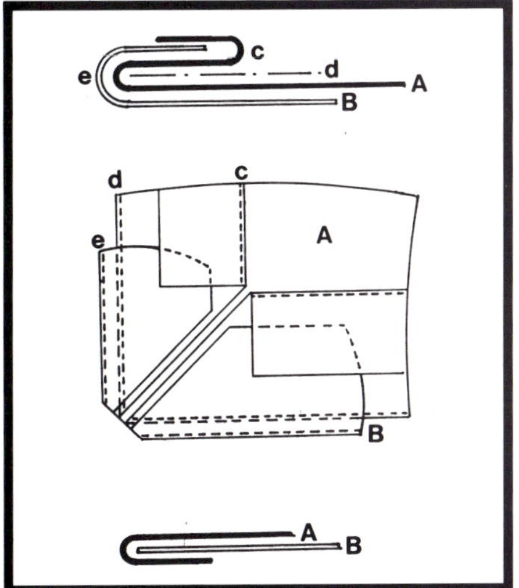

Fig. 370 Sketches of methods used to apply celluloid cover to grips. A - tin plate body. B - celluloid cover. c and d - folds in tin plate. e - fold in celluloid. Top and centre: Britain. Lower: United States.

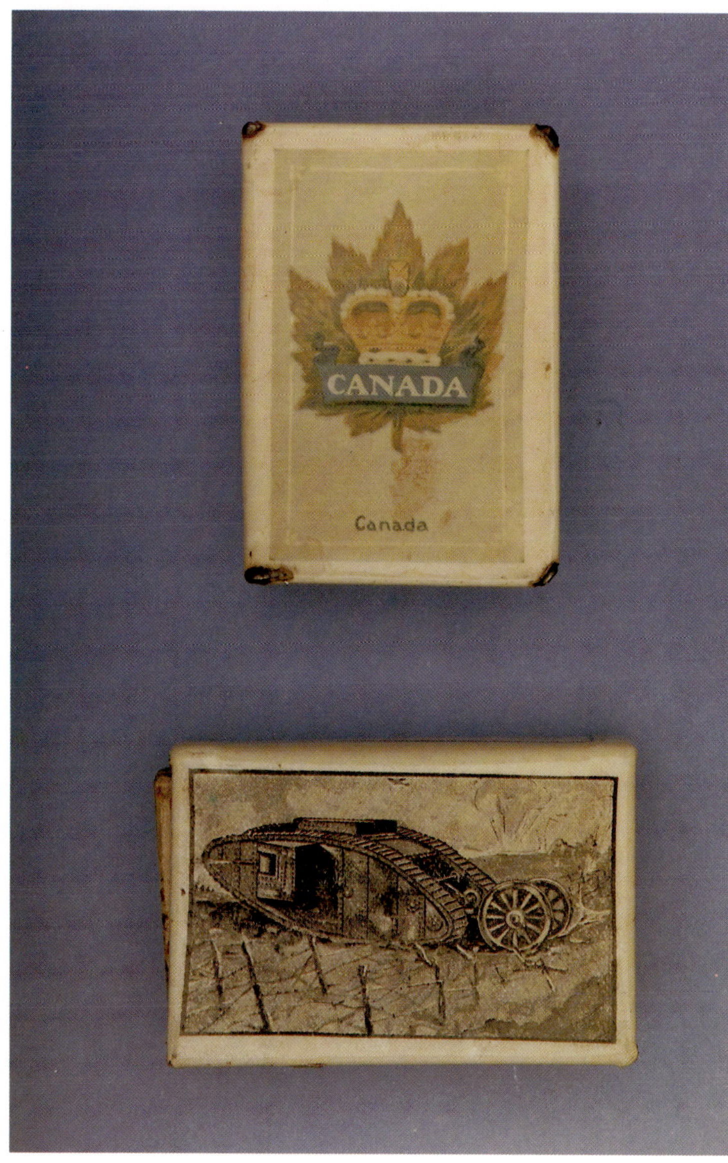

Fig. 371 Britain. Tin plate, celluloid. World War I. Top: H -5.9cms. Lower: made by Permo Co. H - 6cms.

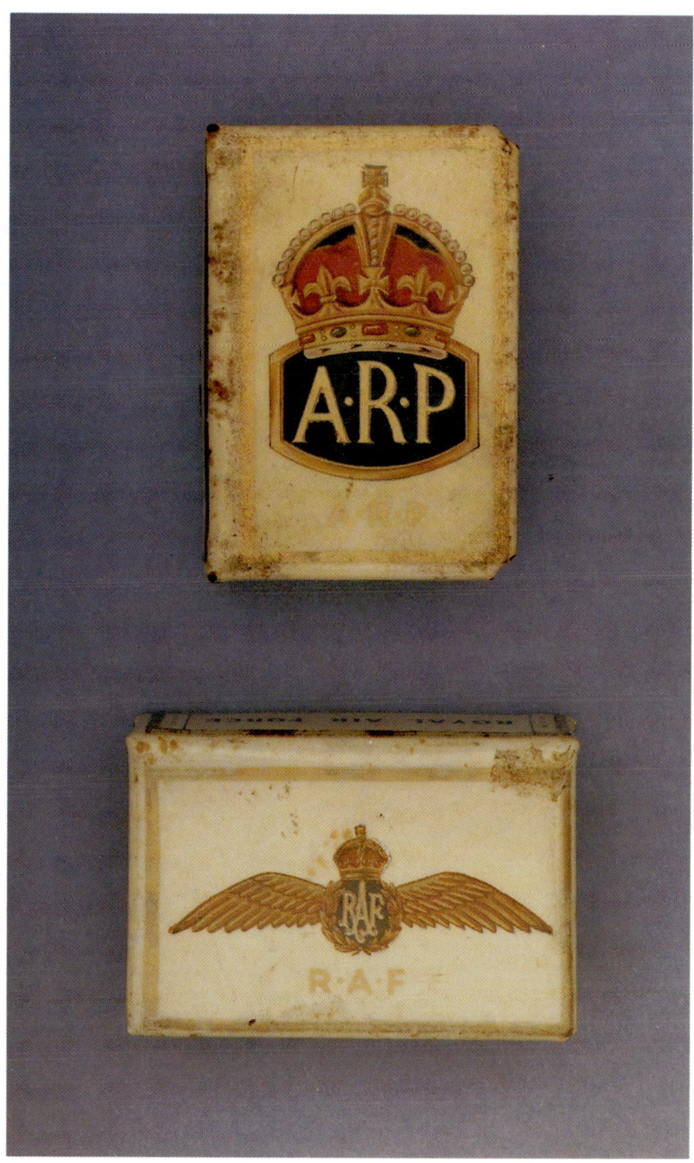

Fig. 373 Britain. Tin plate, celluloid. World War II. H - 5.8cms.

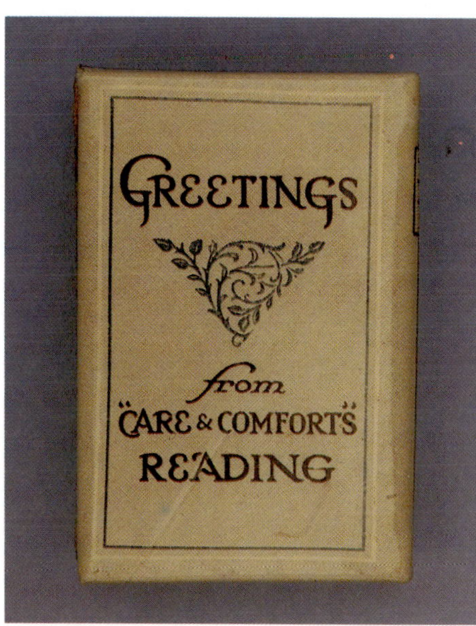

Fig. 372 Britain. Tin plate, celluloid. 1916. H - 6.1cms.

These grips were produced in Britain until at least 1954; hundreds of designs were made, using patriotic themes for both World Wars, advertising for products, services and hostelries, souvenirs of towns and cities, royalty and famous personalities, and some ribald humor. They were also to be found in Australia, Canada and New Zealand, and may have been made in Scandinavia, if not elsewhere in Europe.

The examples in **Fig. 371** are from World War I. That at the top records the "European War. Canadian Contingent" with the flags of the six allied nations on the reverse. That below illustrates a Mark I tank, with Lord Kitchener on the reverse. In **Fig. 372** is a grip sent as a gift at Christmas 1916 to soldiers from Reading, Berkshire.

In **Fig. 373** are two grips from World War II. The upper one has the badge of the A.R.P. (Air Raid Precautions) on both sides; the A.R.P. were mostly volunteer citizens who patrolled the streets, making sure that no lights could be seen in houses, reporting the location of bombs, and assisting in recovery operations. The lower grip has the badge of the Royal Air Force, the reverse with the famous 1940 Churchill quotation "Never in the field of human conflict was so much owed by so many to so few."

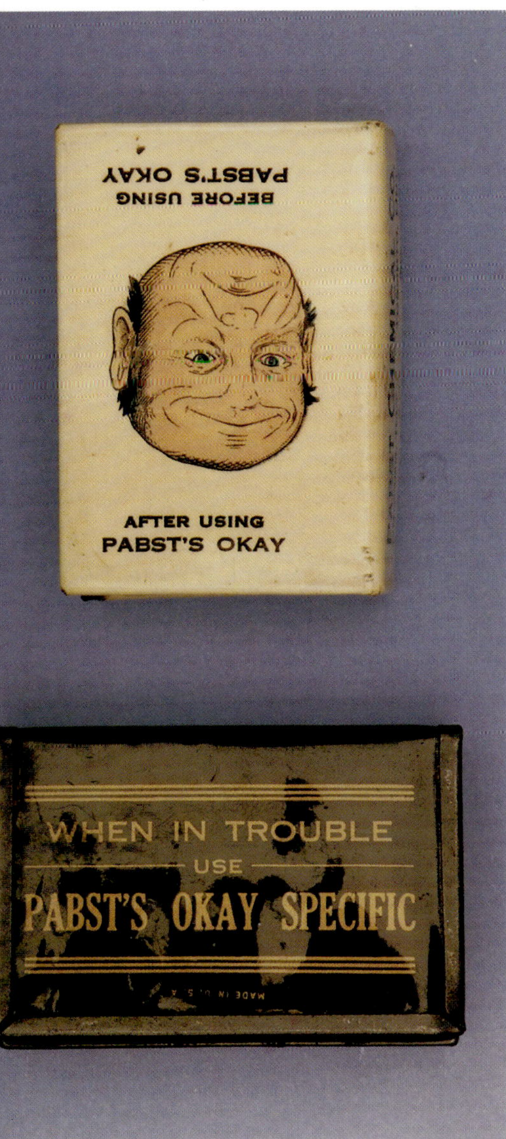

Fig. 374 United States. Tin plate, celluloid. Top: date uncertain. Lower: 1925. H - 6cms.

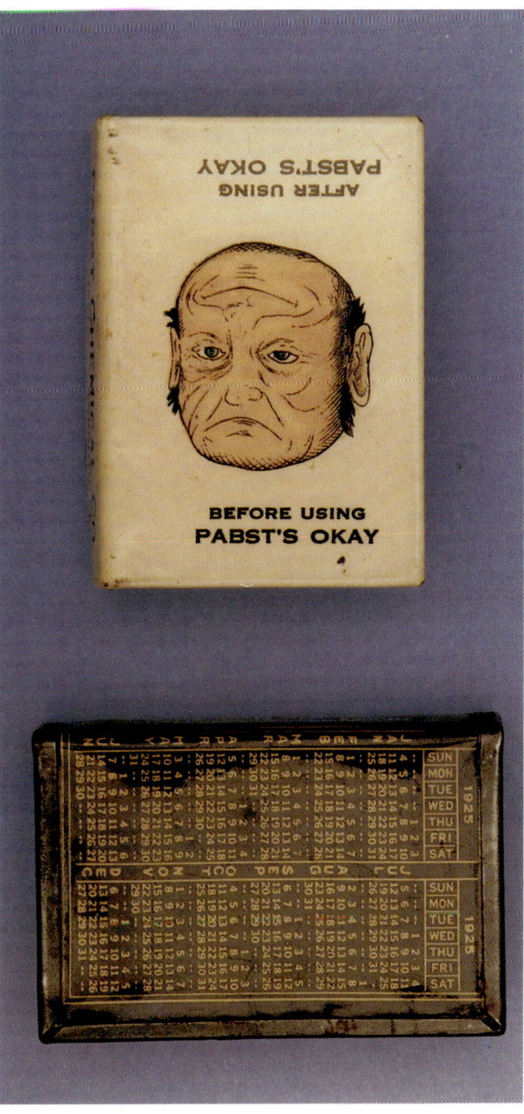

Fig. 375 As Fig. 374. Top: inverted. Lower: reverse side.

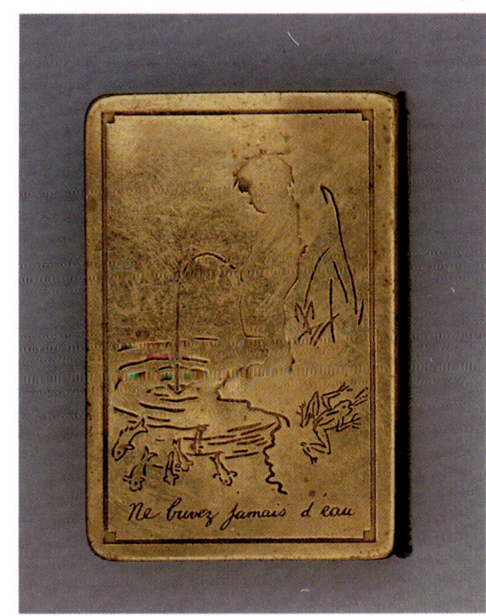

Fig. 376 United States. Brass. Made for the Canadian market. Probably 1930s. H - 5.7cms.

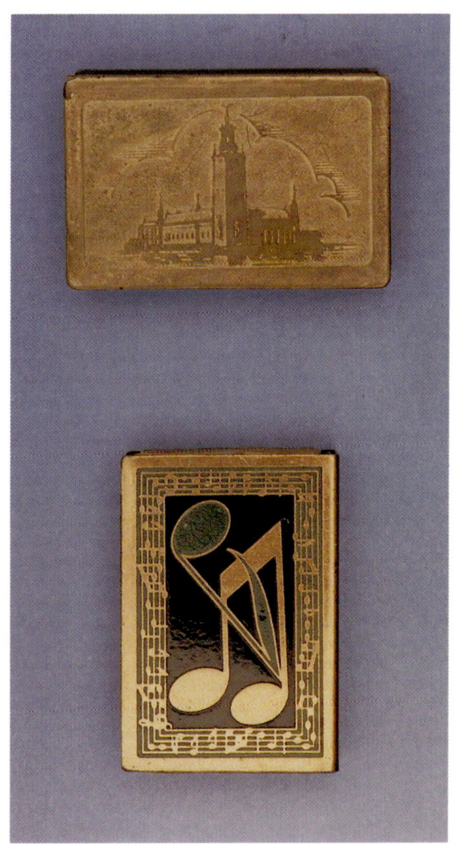

Fig. 377 Scandinavia. Brass. c.1930s. H - 4.2cms.

Figs.374 and 375 show both sides of two grips marked "Made in U.S.A.;" they were made for the Pabst Chemical Co. of Chicago, Illinois, to advertise its "Okay Specific," a patent medicine for curing social diseases, selling for three dollars a bottle. The upper grip was made in the British manner, the lower grip in the more common form found in the United States. The particular reversible face shown was used on many of these grips, and was quite common in Australia.

Manufactured in the United States is a brass grip made for the Taverne Wilfred Methot Limitée in Montreal, Quebec, shown in **Fig. 376.** The tavern stood in the same location in Montreal from 1918 until the 1960s. The grip is engraved with a risqué cartoon, of which many similar versions occurred on celluloid-covered grips, and which was particularly popular in Australia.

Grips for smaller boxes of matches were also popular and, by the late 1930s and early 1940s, were being produced with elaborately decorated sides. The two brass examples in **Fig. 377 are** probably from Scandinavia. The upper one depicts the "Stadshuset," the Stockholm City Hall that was completed in 1922, and was no doubt made in Sweden. The lower box has a musical theme, and on the reverse side is a man playing a guitar.

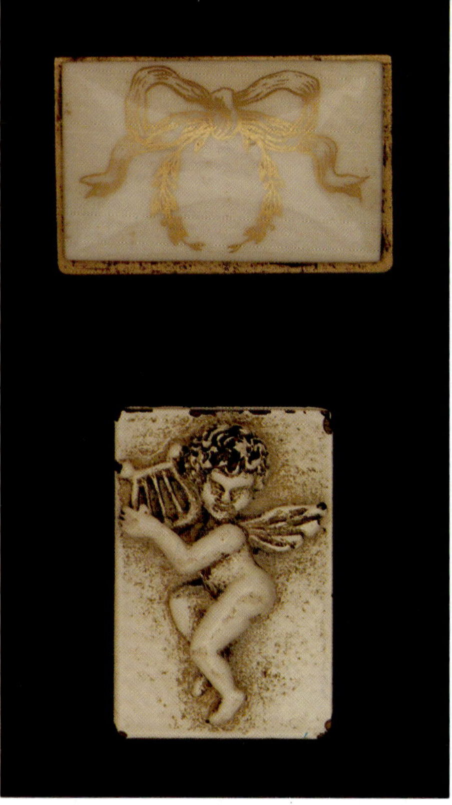

Fig. 378 Top: France. Brass; porcelain side made in Limoges. H -4.4cms. Lower: Origin unknown. Tin plate and ? H - 4.3cms. Probably 1930s.

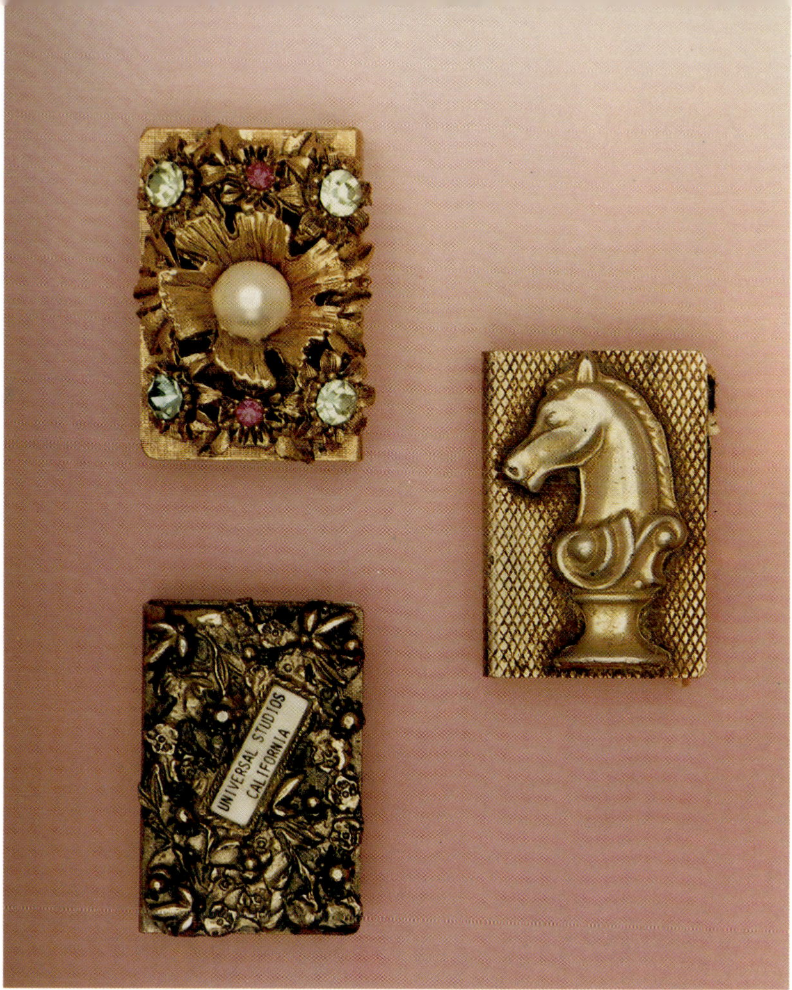

Fig. 379 United States. Tin plate bodies, other metals, glass. Probably 1940s. H - 4.3cms.

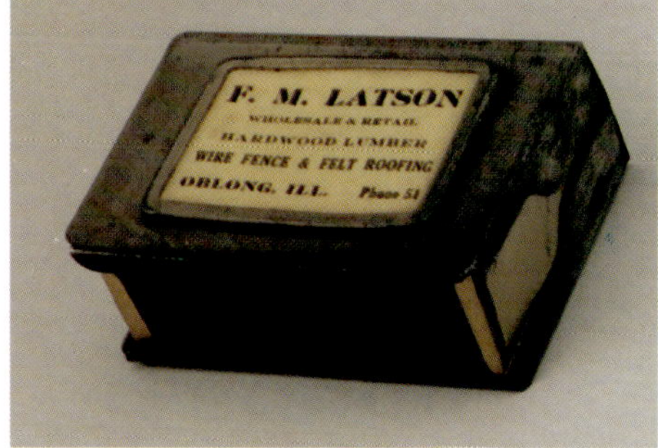

Fig. 380 United States. Tin plate, celluloid. Made by the Metal Speciality Mfg. Co. Probably from the 1920s. L - 5.7cms.

In **Fig. 378** the upper grip, in brass, has a porcelain panel glued to the side, which is marked on the back "Made in Limoges, France." The lower grip, made of tinplate, has a three dimensional angel enamelled overall in white, but is otherwise unmarked.

The three grips in **Fig. 379** are believed to have been made in the United States, and all have tinplate bodies. The top left example is decorated with imitation gems, while the lower grip was made for Universal Studios in California.

The tin matchbox holder in **Fig. 380** is technically not a grip; it was designed so that the matchbox could be slipped in and out of the cover with ease. It was the subject of a patent application, but no trace has been found of a patent being issued for this holder. It was made by the Metal Speciality Manufacturing Co. of Chicago. On the reverse side is marked "The Wind Shield", and there is a diagram of the entire matchbox partially pushed out of the holder, with an ignited match inserted into the wine glass-shaped opening in the end, to protect the flame from a wind. Attached to one side by lugs is a frame to hold advertising. This device probably dates from the 1920s.

Within a few years of the introduction of book matches to the market, specialized boxes to hold them began to appear. Harold A. Dodge of New Jersey was among the first to apply for an Invention Patent, in 1903. Before it was issued in January 1904, Mark O. Anthony of New York filed for a Design Patent for what appears to be an identical box. Some legal proceedings must have occurred, because the Anthony patent was withdrawn and the Dodge patent was re-issued in November 1904.

An end product was produced until at least 1919, as may be seen in **Fig. 381,** which is marked with the Dodge patent number. The maker's mark is for "A.R.T.Mfg.Co.N.Y." The initials of this company are those of the Directors surnames: Mark 0. Anthony, Samuel Robert, and Henry C. Traute. So it is assumed that Anthony and Dodge reached some mutually satisfactory agreement in their patent dispute. It seems beyond the bounds of coincidence that two Henry C. Traute's could be engaged in the book match industry; therefore this was presumably the same Traute employed by the Diamond Match Co., who is alleged to have been the marketing salesman behind the success of the book match, and who remained in that company's employ until the 1940s.

The example is made of brass, bearing the patent date and company mark, but it does not meet precisely the patent specifications. They were also made of silver, bearing the same marks; by 1915, the A.R.T.Mfg. Co. had become a part of the International Silver Co. of Merriden, Connecticut.

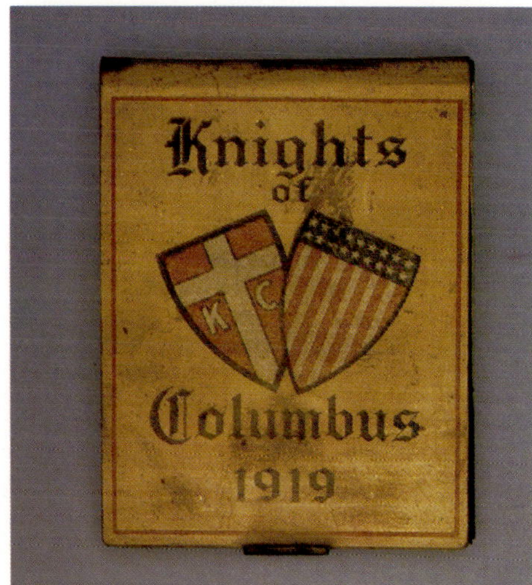

Fig. 381 United States. Brass. Made by A.R.T. Mfg. Co. in 1919 to an Invention Patent of 1904, by Harold A. Dodge. H - 5.6cms.

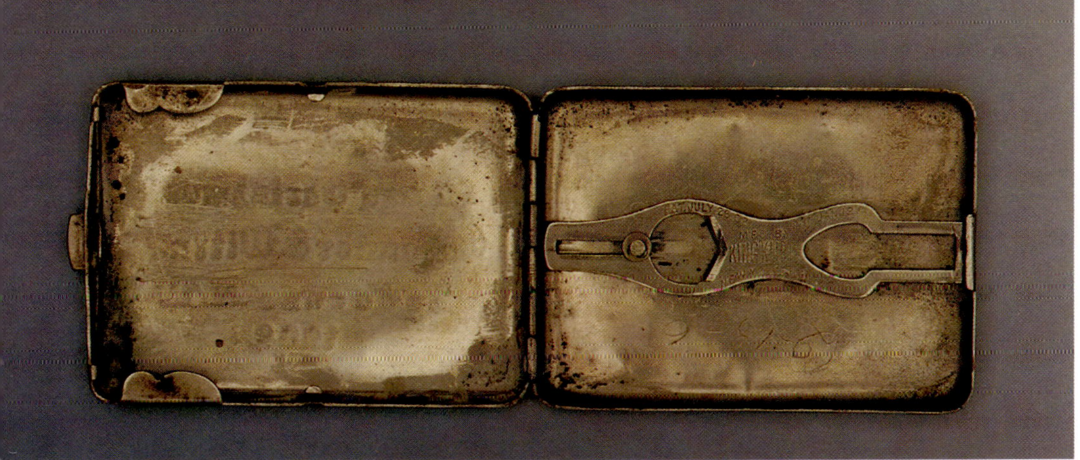

Fig. 382 United States. Plated brass. Combined book match holder and cigar cutter. Made by Kingklip Co. in 1909 to Invention Patents of 1904 and 1908. Shown open. L (closed) - 6.1cms.

Fig. 384 Drawing from 1904 Invention Patent by Benno vom Eigen, for catch in Fig. 382.

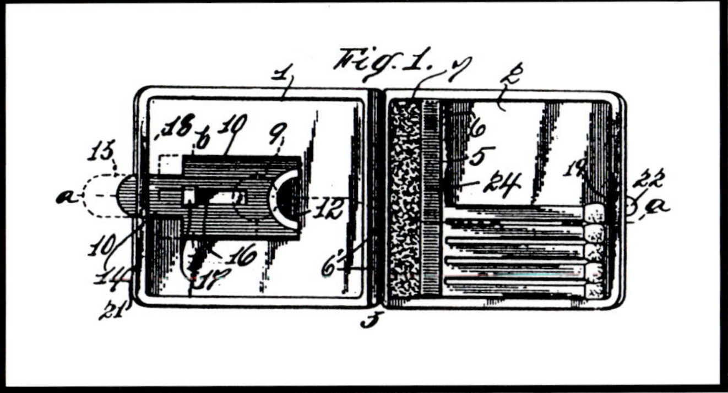

Fig. 383 Drawing from 1908 Invention Patent by Emanuel Ciner for Fig. 382.

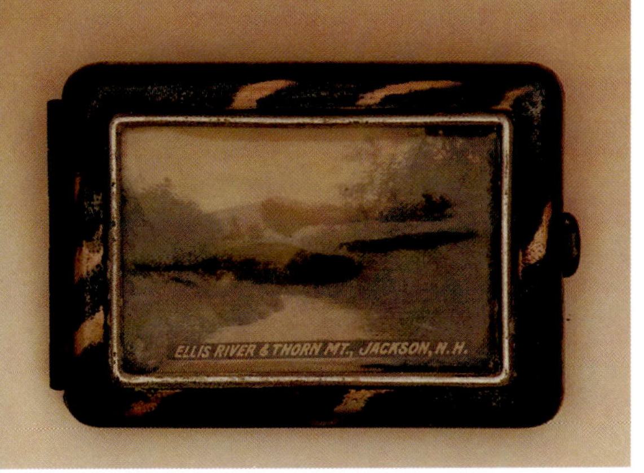

Fig. 385 United States. Tin plate, celluloid. Made by J. E. Mergott & Co. to an Invention Patent of 1912. L - 6.1cms.

In 1908 Emanuel Ciner of New York was issued with an Invention Patent for a combined match case and cigar cutter. An example of the end product is shown in **Fig. 382,** and Ciner's patent drawing in **Fig. 383,** which illustrates some differences. The box has the maker's mark of the Kingklip Co. of New York, and two patent dates. The second patent was issued to Benno vom Eigen of Aug. Goertz & Co. in January 1904, but does not relate to any part of the box. However, the box catch does not meet the Ciner patent, but does meet a vom Eigen patent of May 1904, as shown in **Fig. 384.** This is the third example of the careless use of patent dates by Goertz, for he must have given permission for the use of the patent to Kingklip.

It seems to have been the fate of the J.E.Mergott Co. of Newark, New Jersey, to have to wait a long time between a patent application and the issue of a patent (which normally took a few months). Seven Mergott applications took from well over one year up to three years before they were issued. The example in **Fig. 385** was no exception. The patent for it was filed in January 1911 and issued in July 1912. It is made of tin plate with an "antiqued" copper and black finish, the front with a rectangular frame holding a photograph of Ellis River and Thorn Mountain, New Hampshire, under celluloid. Other versions have been seen with the same finish, and an oval frame with advertising, or the front cover with advertising impressed directly into the metal.

The Elgin American Manufacturing Co. of Elgin, Illinois, produced an elegant book match holder, shown in **Fig. 386.** The example is marked "Gold Filled," the United States term for gold-plated. Ball catches are used to hold it closed. It is provided with a ring for suspension from a watch chain, an unusual feature for a United States box. Two versions were shown in a 1918 Carson Pirie Scott & Co. catalogue, in nickel silver for $7.50 each.

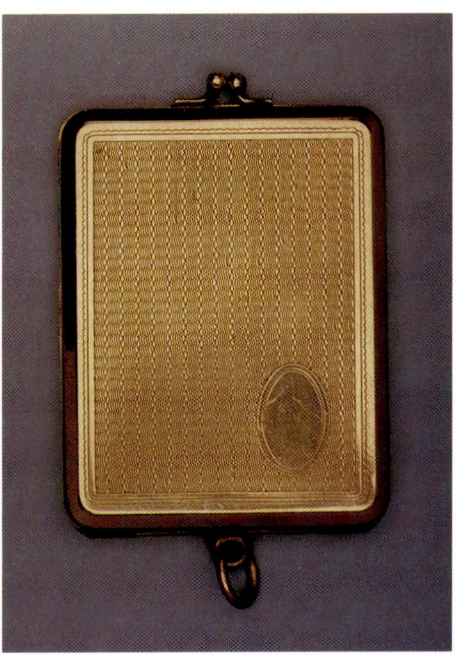

Fig. 386 United States. Gold filled. Made by the Elgin American Mfg. Co. c.1918. H - 6.5cms.

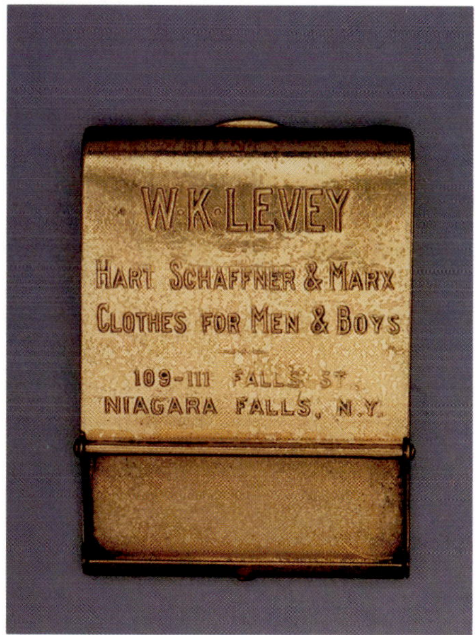

Fig. 387 United States. Brass. Made by the J. E. Mergott Co. between the date of application in September 1920 and the date of issue in April 1921 of a Design Patent. H - 5.8cms.

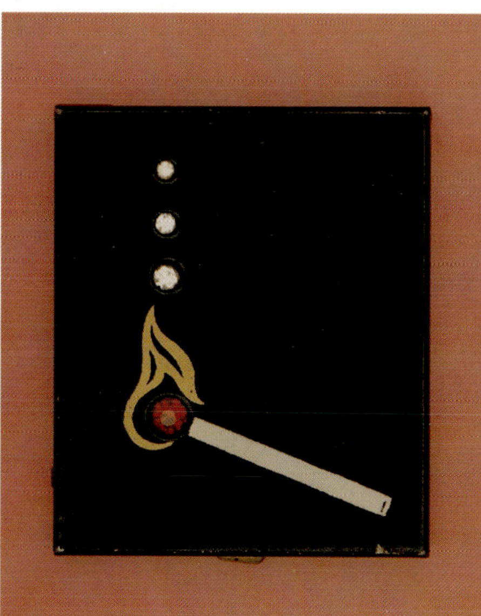

Fig. 389 Unknown origin. Tin plate, glass. Possible 1960s. H -5.6cms.

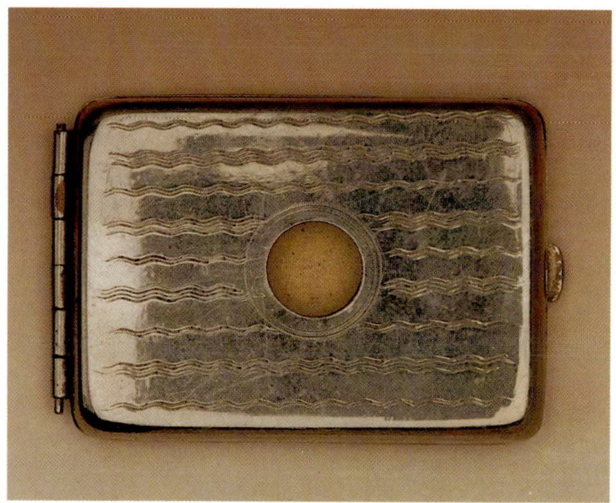

Fig. 388 Britain. Plated brass. c.1920s. L - 6.4cms.

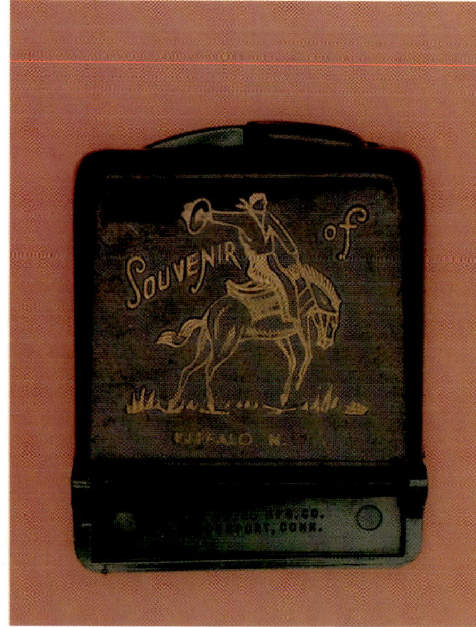

Fig. 390 United States. Bakalite. Made by the Vogel Mfg. Co. to an Invention Patent of 1933. H - 5.6cms.

The example in **Fig. 387** is made of brass and marked "The J.E.Mergott Co. Newark, N.J. Pat.Apl.For." This refers to a Design Patent applied for in September 1920 and issued in April 1921; the box must have been made between those dates. The Mergott assignor for the patent was Franz A. Fuller; it is assumed that Albert F. Fuller of earlier patents was the same person.

Marked "Made in England" is a book match holder, nickel-plated on brass, shown in **Fig. 388.** The front cover has a hole in the center to enable the user to see that matches are present. The inside has been treated with gilt wash, as were many British-made boxes, yet it is a cheap product and probably dates from c. 1920.

Of unknown origin, made of tin plate with glass brilliants set into the lid, is the box shown in **Fig. 389.** Although quite well constructed, it has sharp corners that would be rough on cloth, a problem that manufacturers of pocket-carried boxes were well aware of in the 1870s. This example may be as recent as the 1960s.

Max Vogel of Frankfurt-am-Main, Germany, was issued with a United States Invention Patent in 1933. Vogel had been established in Germany prior to World War I as a manufacturer of stapling machines. He visited the United States regularly and established an agency in Bridgeport, Connecticut, in 1921. He started to manufacture his staplers there in about 1933; at about the same time the Nazi goverment took over the German plant, so he emigrated to the United States. By 1939 he had moved into new and larger premises and the company was renamed Neva-Clog Products Inc., going from strength to strength. His 1933 Invention Patent went into production; an example is shown in **Fig. 390.** They have the patent number marked on them, and may be found marked "The Vogel Mfg.Co." or also "Neva-Clog." Vogel referred in his patent to making the cases "from a moulded material, [such] as bakelite," and the end product is probably made from bakelite.

In 1913 and 1914 the well-known silversmiths Webster & Co. of North Attleboro, Massachusetts, showed a dozen book match holders in their catalogues. There appears to be only two different types made of silver, but each type had a range of designs. They were offered by the dozen, one type at $49.50, the other at $58.50. In 1915 Shreve & Co. of San Francisco, California, offered a combined match holder and cigar cutter in 14 karat gold at $60.00 each.

Although book match holders must have been produced in great quantities, they are not commonly found today, nor do they appear to be a popular collector's item. In view of the popularity of the book match in North America, this is perhaps surprising.

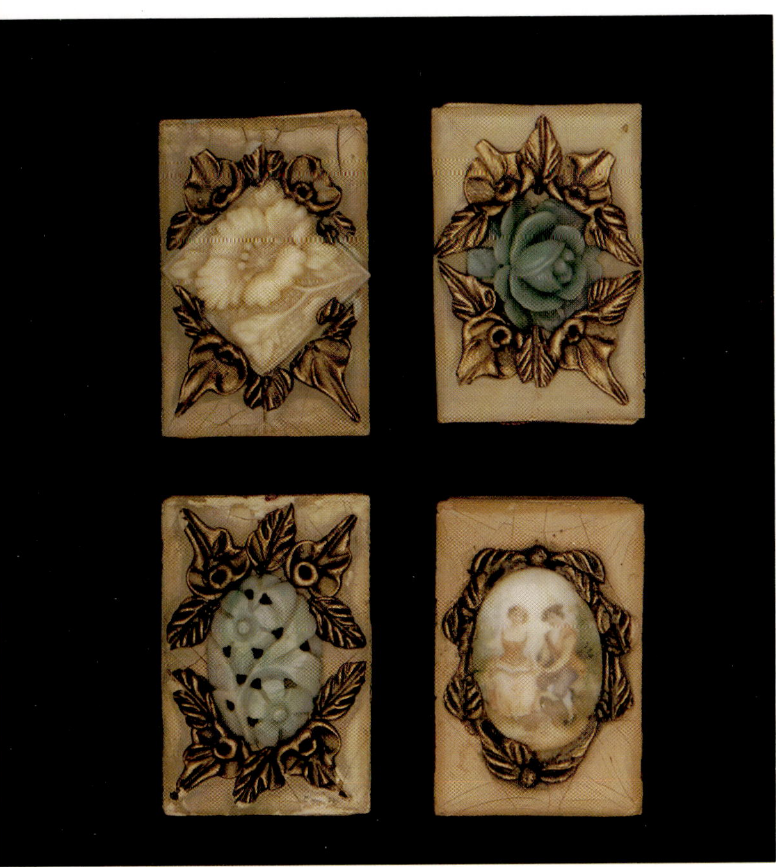

Fig. 391 Boxes of matches, probably Swedish, decorated with applied plastic(?) panels. Between 1927 and 1940. H - 4.1cms.

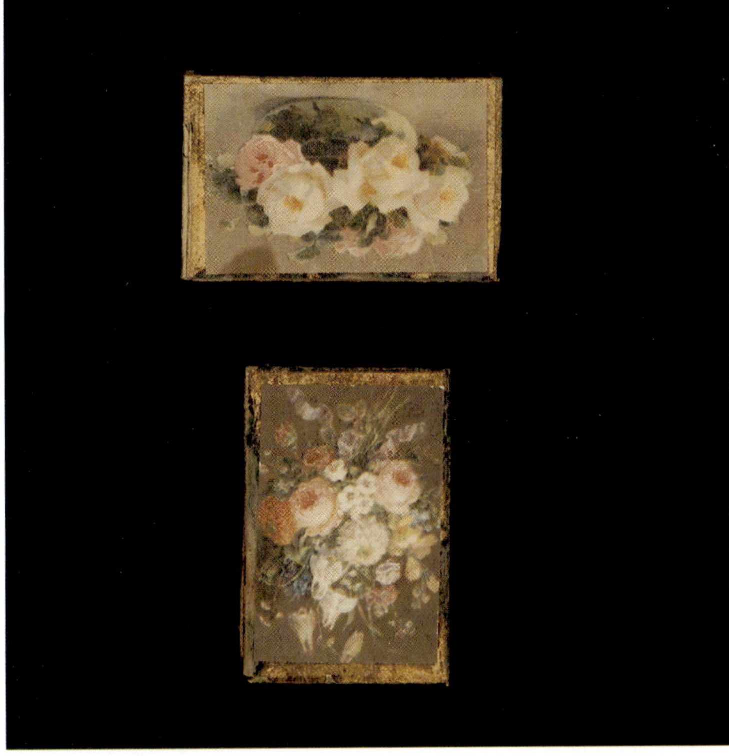

Fig. 392 Boxes of matches, probably Swedish, decorated with applied printed designs. Probably 1930s. H - 4.1cms.

There have been found small boxes of matches to which some form of plastic material, possibly a hard form of wax, has been attached in decorative shapes of various colors, and with what appears to be painted figures. Examples are shown in **Fig. 391.** On the back of one of the boxes is a 3/16¢ Canadian Excise stamp, which was used for imported matches between 1927 and 1940. The matches are probably Swedish. Examples of a cheaper version, possibly even homemade, with paper panels displaying flowers, are shown in **Fig. 392.** These may have been intended for use at a dinner party in place of the silver slides shown in Fig. 363, which is the excuse for mentioning them here.

PART 10: RE-USABLE PRODUCT BOXES

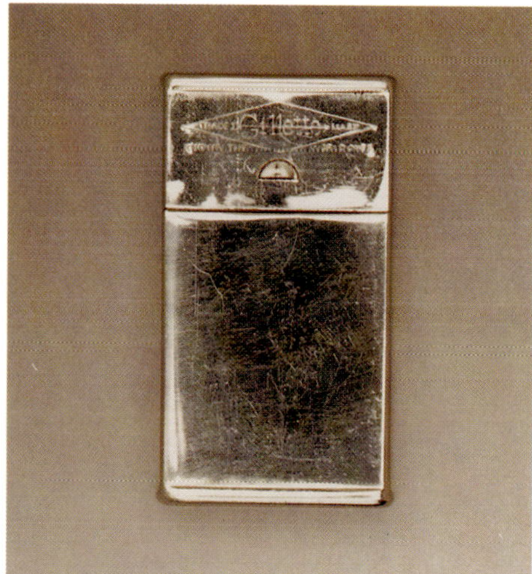

Fig. 393 United States. Nickel plated brass. Made to hold Gillette razor blades. In use by 1908. H - 4.9cms.

A number of companies marketed non-match products in boxes that were nonetheless provided with an area on the box in the form of a striker. Once the original product contents had been exhausted, the box could continue to be used as a pocket match holder, thus extending the lifetime of the advertising potential of the box, with regard to its original contents.

The evidence suggests that this idea may have started in the 1870s when Perry & Co., London pen nib makers, used a sliding lid tin-plate box presumably for selling their pen nibs, yet with a striker located at one end. This box, shown in Fig. 429, is marked with a United States patent date. Similarly, the Hewitt box shown in Fig. 257 was patented in 1886 and, although the patent does not specifically mention matches as one of the intended contents, the top and bottom edges were provided with strikers; the box bears advertising for pens.

The first known conclusive evidence of a box made to hold one product, but capable of use later as a match holder, is that of the Gillette razor blade boxes shown in **Fig. 393;** a striker is located on the bottom edge. King Gillette first patented his three-hole razor in 1902 and, by 1907, held patents for it in another twenty countries. In November 1908 a newspaper advertisement in the Ottawa Citizen, shown in **Fig. 394,** stated:

> "New Process Blades are put up in handsome nickel boxes, which hermetically seal themselves when closed—and which make convenient match-boxes when empty.

It is not known for how many years the Gillette company produced these boxes, but it is assumed to be for over twenty years. They are commonly found in North America and Europe.

Two companies produced cylindrical boxes to hold sticks of shaving soap, provided with a roughened base as a match striker, as shown in **Fig. 395.** The box at the left was made for, or by, The J.B.Williams Co. of Glastonbury, Connecticut, and bears a patent date for 1907, which relates to the hinge for the lid. The box at the right was made for Colgate & Co. Ltd., and has a screw-on lid. Both are made of thin nickel-plated brass. It is not known when the striker patches were introduced.

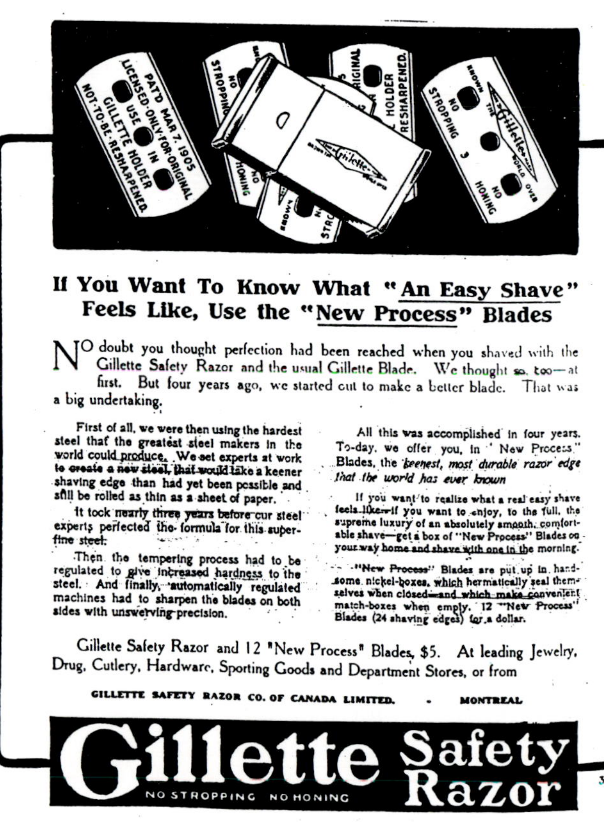

Fig. 394 Advertisement from the Ottawa Citizen of November 1908, showing razor blade box in Fig. 393.

Fig. 395 United States. Plated brass. Shaving stick holders. Left: for the J. B. Williams Co., after 1907. H - 8.8cms. Right: for Colgate & Co.Ltd. H - 5.9cms.

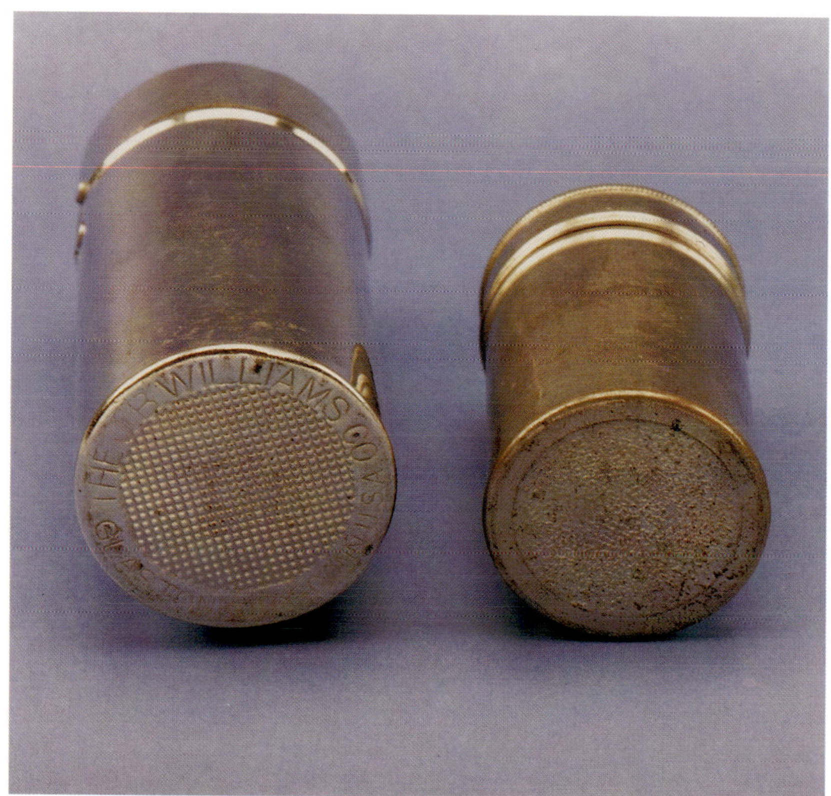

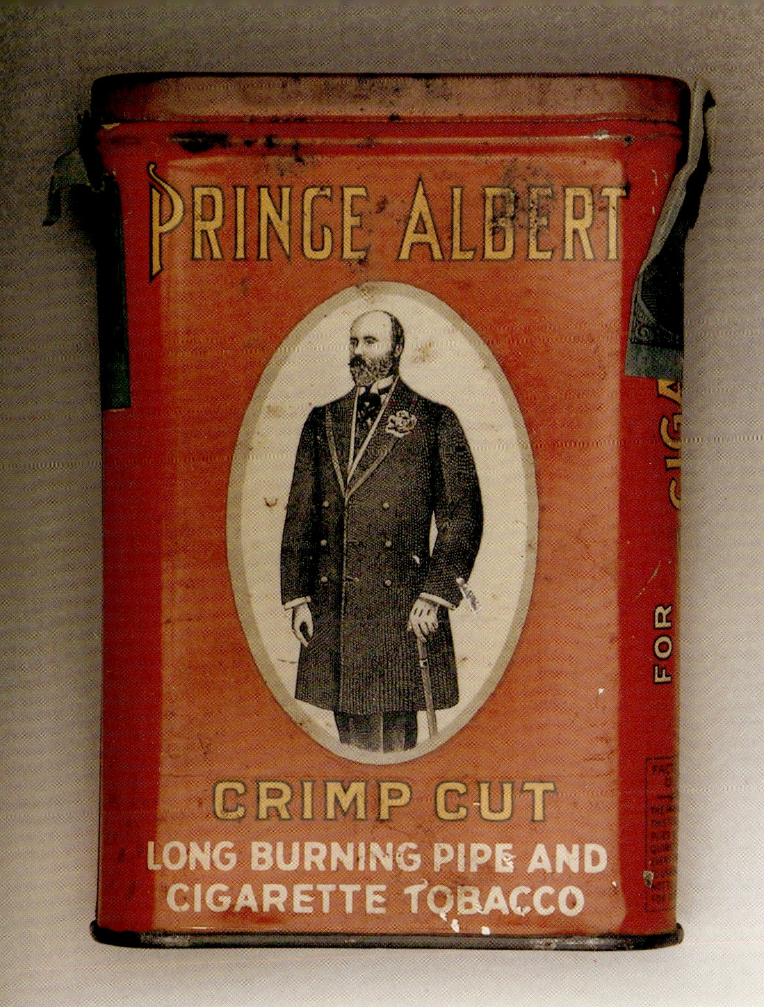

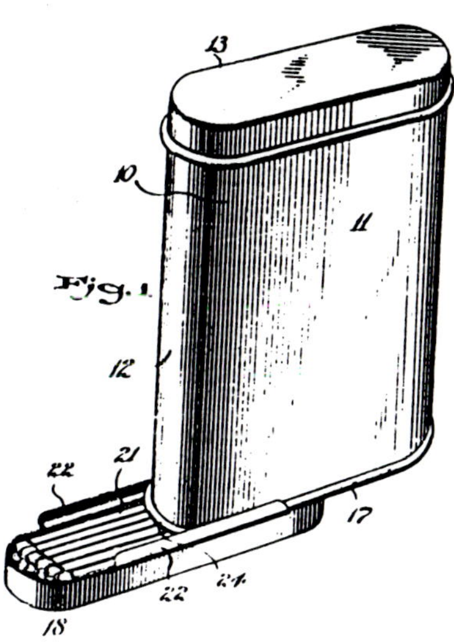

Fig. 397 Drawing from Invention Patent of 1916 by Hans Fritz Richter for match holder to fit base of tin in Fig. 396.

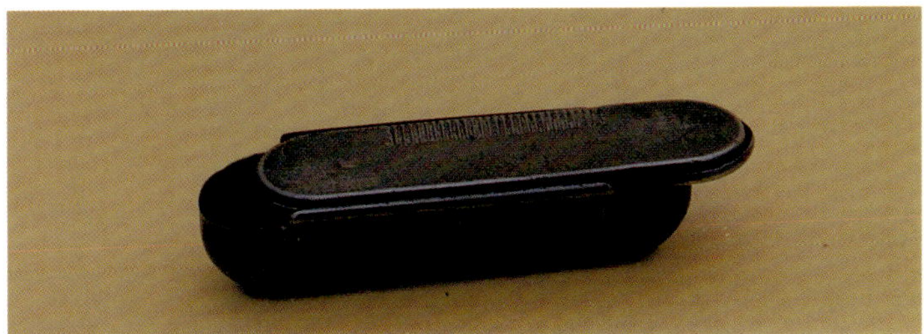

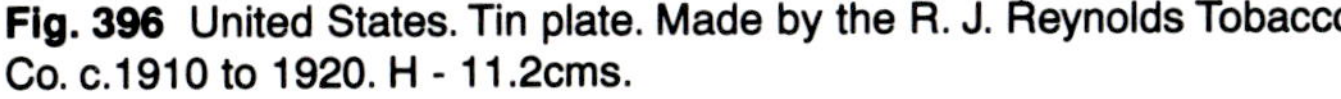

Fig. 396 United States. Tin plate. Made by the R. J. Reynolds Tobacco Co. c.1910 to 1920. H - 11.2cms.

Fig. 398 United States. Tin plate. Made by the R. J. Reynolds Tobacco Co. End product of the Richter patent in Fig. 397, to fit box in Fig. 396. L - 7.7cms.

Tin-plate boxes to hold two ounces of tobacco were made by many North American companies. Many included a corrugated striker patch on the base, but this was more as a convenience to a smoker, and the box was not intended to be re-used.

The R.J.Reynolds Tobacco Co. of Winston Salem, North Carolina, first produced its Prince Albert brand of tobacco in 1907, put up in cloth bags; it started to use two-ounce tins in 1909, very similar to that shown in **Fig. 396.** Strikers were not provided on the base of its tins. In 1916, however, Hans Fritz Richter, a German immigrant who had become the general superintendent of the company's tin box shop, invented a match holder that slipped on to the base of the box, as shown in his patent drawing in **Fig. 397.** The end product underwent some changes in shape, and a lid was added, produced from the base section of the two-ounce box; this is shown in **Fig. 398.** The finished item could be used either without its lid, attached to the base of the tobacco box, or with its lid as an independent pocket match holder. The underside of the base section is stamped "PRINCE ALBERT. THE NATIONAL JOY SMOKE," and was provided with a striker on both sides, plus the striker on the lid.

In the United States, smaller one-ounce tins may be found with a striker on the underside. The example in **Fig. 399** was made by the American Can Co. to serve Larus & Bro.Co. of Richmond, Virginia, as an Edgeworth Plug Slice tin-plate box.

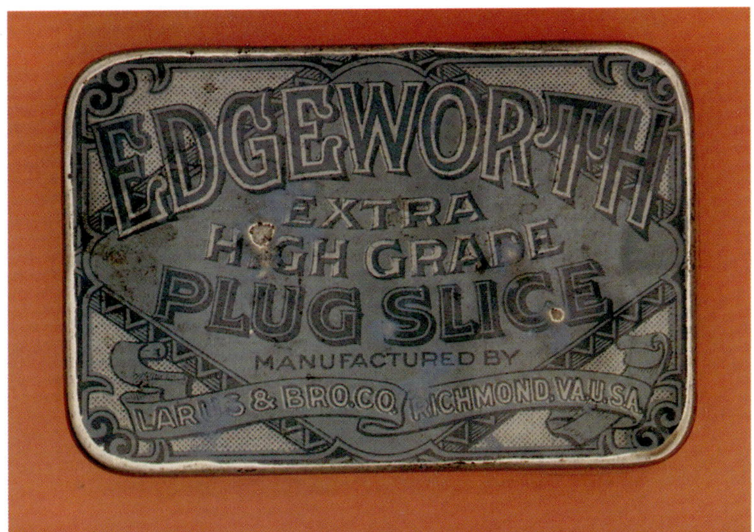

Fig. 399 United States. Tin plate. Made by the American Can Co. for Larus & Bro.Co. c.1920s. L - 8.2cms.

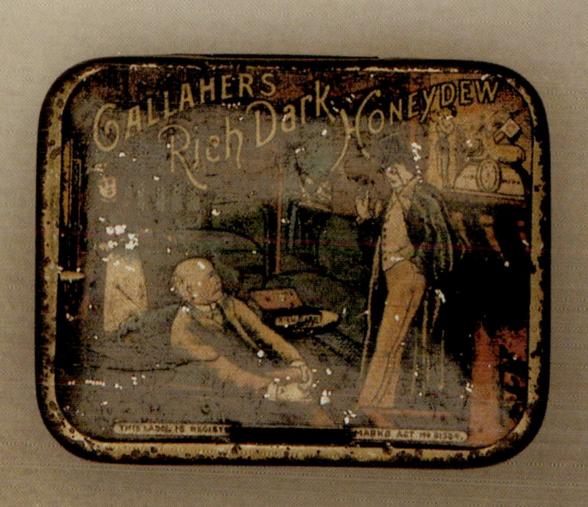

Fig. 400 Britain. Tin plate. Made for Gallaher Ltd. L - 6cms.

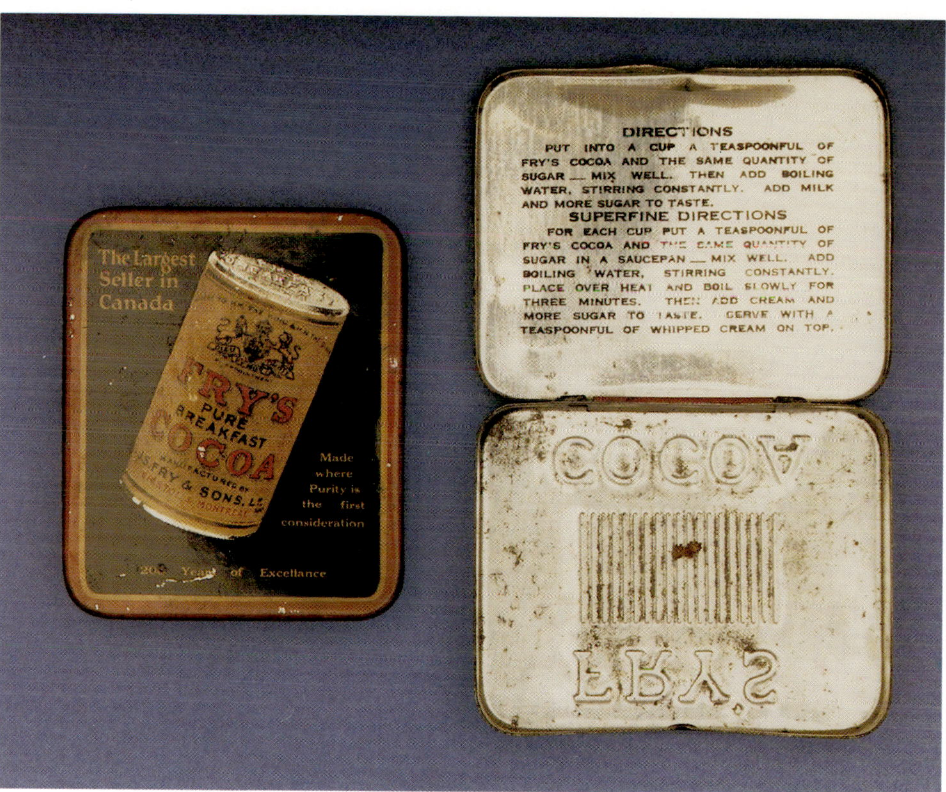

Fig. 402 Canada. Tin plate. Made by the A. R. Whittall Can Co.Ltd. for Fry's cocoa. c.1920s. L - 6.2cms.

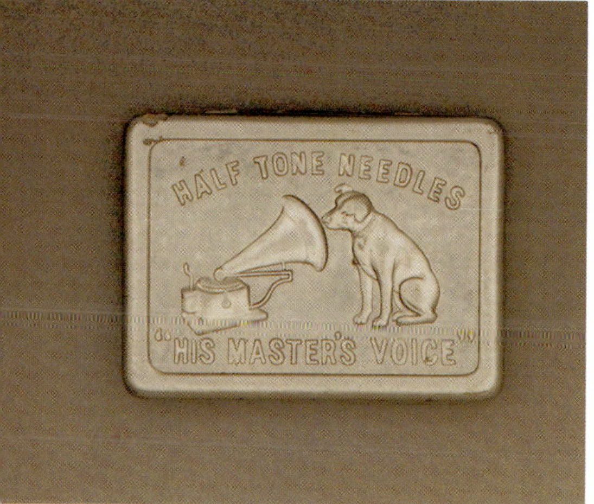

Fig. 401 Britain. Aluminum. Made for His Master's Voice gramophone needles. c.1920s. L - 4.7cms.

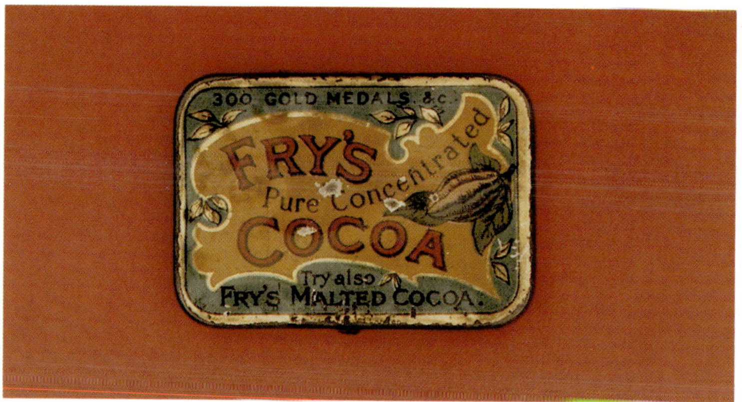

Fig. 403 Britain. Tin plate. Made for Fry's cocoa. c.1920s. L -4.7cms.

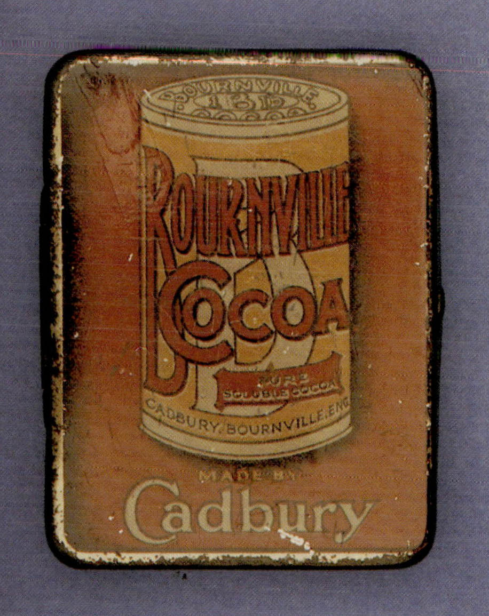

Fig. 404 Britain. Tin plate. Made for Cadbury's Bournville Cocoa. c.1920s. L - 6.4cms.

In Britain a number of small tobacco tins, probably half-ounce samples, were provided with corrugated strikers on their bases. An example made for Gallaher's Rich Dark Honeydew is shown in **Fig. 400.** The label on the box was registered in 1889, but the box was probably not made until after the turn of the century.

Made in Britain of aluminum is a small box intended to hold gramophone needles, shown in **Fig. 401.** The lid is impressed with the well-known trade mark of a gramophone and the dog 'Nipper'. Francis Barraud sold his painting of Nipper to The Gramophone Co. of London in 1899, and it appeared on the company's needle tins from about 1903, but the trademark was not registered until 1910 when the company became His Master's Voice. In the United States, Nipper is used as the trade mark of RCA. The box, with the striker on the bottom, was probably made in the 1920s

The three big British cocoa companies of Cadbury, Fry and Rowntree all produced good lithographed tins to hold enough of their product to make one cup of the beverage. The Fry's examples in **Fig. 402** show the outside of the lid, and the inside of the box with its instructions on how to make a cup of cocoa. It was made in Canada for the Canadian market by the A. R. Whittall Can Co. Ltd. of Montreal. The corrugated striker in the lower part of the box is a typical example of strikers to be found on most of the boxes dealt with in this part of the chapter.

The small Fry's cocoa box in **Fig. 403** was made in Britain, and is printed along the front edge of the lid "Support British Labour." The Cadbury Bournville Cocoa box in **Fig. 404** was also made in Britain and is almost identical in size to the box in Fig. 402. They all probably date from the 1920s.

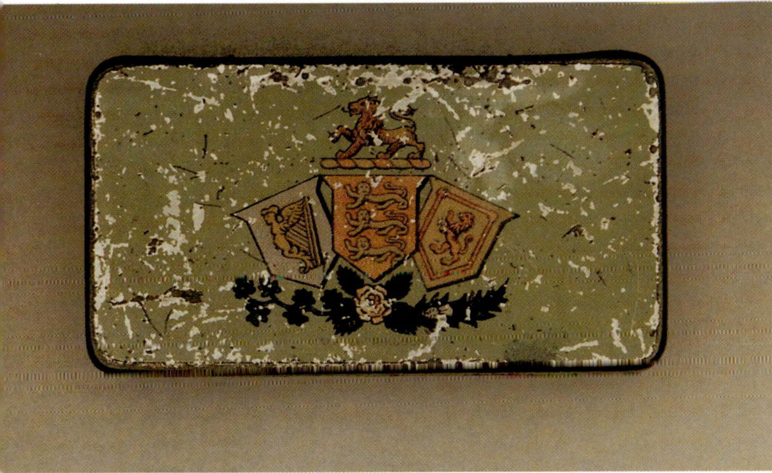

Fig. 405 Britain. Tin plate. Made for the United Kingdom Tea Co.Ltd. c.1920s. L - 7.4cms.

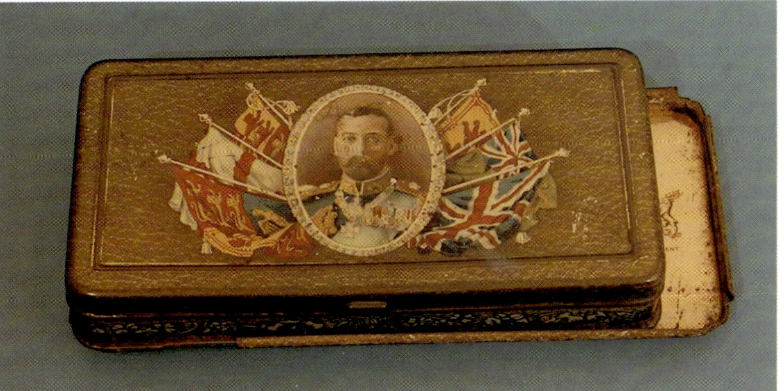

Fig. 406 Britain. Tin plate. Made for Rowntree & Co.Ltd. chocolates. c.1912. L - 15.6cms.

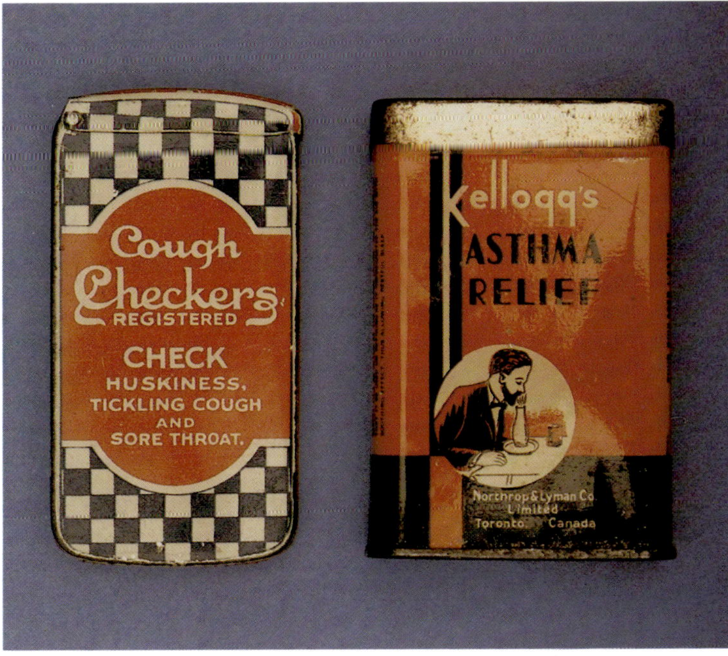

Fig. 407 Canada. Tin plate. Left: made in England for the Laurentian Laboratories Ltd. of Montreal. c.1930s. H - 7.5cms. Right: made for the Northrop & Lyman Co.Ltd.. After 1933. H -7.1cms.

Several British tea companies made sample boxes with strikers, a rather poor example of which is shown in **Fig. 405.** On the inside of the lid is printed "UNITED KINGDOM TEA Co.Ld. EMPIRE WAREHOUSES, LONDON. SAMPLE OF CHOICE BLEND No.7. PRICE 2/10 PER POUND, CARRIAGE PAID" (2/10 is two shillings and ten pence). This is also probably from the 1920s.

The tin-plate box in **Fig. 406** was probably produced at the time of the coronation of King George V in 1911, and almost certainly before 1924 when his beard had turned grey. The lid is hinged longitudinally and lithographed with a portrait of the King flanked by six flags. The bottom of the box is provided with a shallow slide tray that terminates 2 cm short of the end of the box, the remaining section of the base forming a pocket-platform for a striker. The inside of the tray is printed with the wording "ROWNTREE & CO.LTD. YORK. Cocoa & Chocolate Makers TO THEIR MAJESTIES THE KING & QUEEN," flanked by the two monarchs' coats of arms. Once the original chocolate contents had been consumed, the upper compartment was of sufficient size to hold up to about fify cigarettes, or perhaps two ounces of tobacco, and the lower tray compartment was capable of holding a supply of matches.

The pharmaceutical industry in Canada was responsible for at least two examples of tin-plate boxes, shown in **Fig. 407.** The box to the left is marked on one edge "CONTAINER MADE IN ENGLAND. No.15901." It was purposely made in the form of a flip-top match holder of traditional form, with the striker located along the bottom edge. It was for "Cough Checkers," made by the Laurentian Laboratories Ltd. of Montreal, Quebec, and the contents were registered under The Proprietary or Patent Medicine Act, in June 1929. Therefore, it is safe to assume that the box was made in the 1930s. The box on the right was for "Kellogg's Asthma Relief," an inhalant made by Northrop & Lyman Co. Ltd. of Toronto, Ontario. The company was established as wholesale dealers in patent medicines in 1877, and was producing "Dr.J.D.Kellogg's Asthma Remedy" by 1903. The tin, however, says that it was registered under The Proprietary or Patent Medicine Act in 1933, so the box must have been produced after that date.

A British pharmaceutical product "Phosferine" was advertised extensively as a nerve tonic in World War I and sold in bottles at that time. It was put up in phenol formaldehyde bakelite boxes, in a simple, traditional match holder form as shown in **Fig. 408,** probably in the 1930s.

Thus a cheap box, used for a brief period of time and normally discarded, was given a second useful life—an early example of recycling. As a match holder the box extended its usefulness as an advertising medium, and probably to a wider audience, although the exterior printing would no doubt have soon rubbed off with constant use. These boxes are easily overlooked by collectors, and dealers often do not realise that the box has had a secondary use.

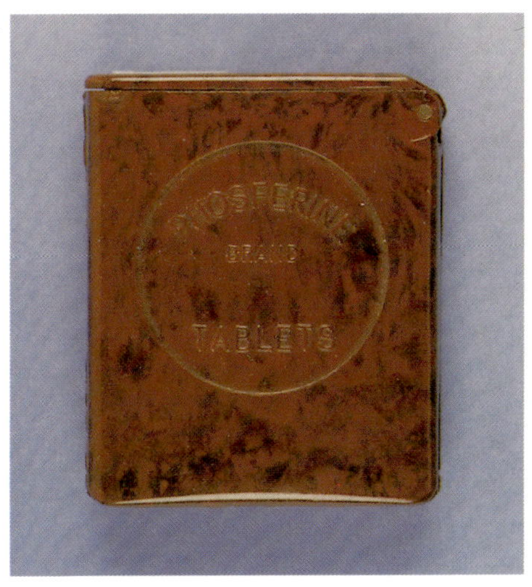

Fig. 408 Britain. Bakalite. Made in the form of a pocket match holder for Ashton & Parsons Ltd., Phosferine tablets. c.1930s. H -4.9cms.

Chapter IV
The Match Manufacturers Contribution

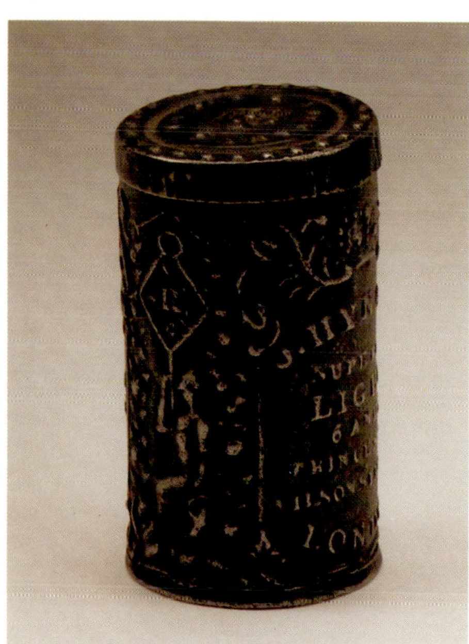

Fig. 409 Britain. Tin plate. Made to an Ornamental Design of 1844, by J. Hynam. H - 6.4cms.

A few match manufacturing companies made match holders themselved or contracted out to other companies to do so, and then provided or sold these match holders to retailers or directly to the public. They were a form of advertising since they always bore the company name, were usually quite inexpensive, and they covered the three main types: pocket, stand-alone and wall-hanging holders. Because of the significant contribution that the match manufacturers made to the development and popularization of match holders, their products are treated here as a separate group.

One of the first companies to produce inexpensive boxes in which their own matches were sold was that of John Hynam of Finsbury, London. He began making matches in 1838 and continued until he died in 1876, when another London company, the Bell & Black Match Co. Ltd., acquired the business.

Hynam registered some ten designs between 1841 and 1849, only three of them for match holders; it is assumed that he made these at his factory. An upright rectangular box, the subject of an Ornamental Design in late 1844, was an item he is known to have made in tin-plate; he also produced the same design on a cylindrical version shown in **Fig. 409.** Britannia is shown holding a staff surmounted by the diamond registration mark, and there is the impressed wording "MANUFACTORY FOR EVERY DESCRIPTION OF CHEMICAL LIGHTS. PERFUMED FUSEES &c.," and also Hynam's name and address. The workmanship is somewhat crude, and the designs and lettering are inclined to be indistinct. It lacks a definite striker, but it is believed that he applied a piece of sandpaper to the bottom for this purpose.

He also made a pocket box with two different designs, but they are not known to have been registered. One of them is shown in **Fig. 410,** with a pair of reversible faces and the captions "THE WEDDING DAY" with the couple smiling, and "THREE WEEKS AFTER MARRIAGE" with the couple scowling. The box may be opened with the smiling couple facing the user. The origins of this design may lie in the United States. At the Thomas Jefferson family home in Monticello, Virginia, reproductions of pressed glass cup-plates bear an almost identical design; they are said to be designs used by the Jefferson family, and the original plates would probably pre-date the Hynam design by about twenty years.

In 1848 Alexander S. Stocker of Wandsworth, Surrey, (now a suburb of London) was granted an Invention Patent for a matchbox with a sliding lid, both sides of which are shown in **Figs.411 and 412.** The box is made of thin brass and has a match socket in the center of the lid. Stocker did not make matches, but he supplied his boxes to match manufacturing companies, including Bryant & May, whose name and address may be seen impressed on some examples.

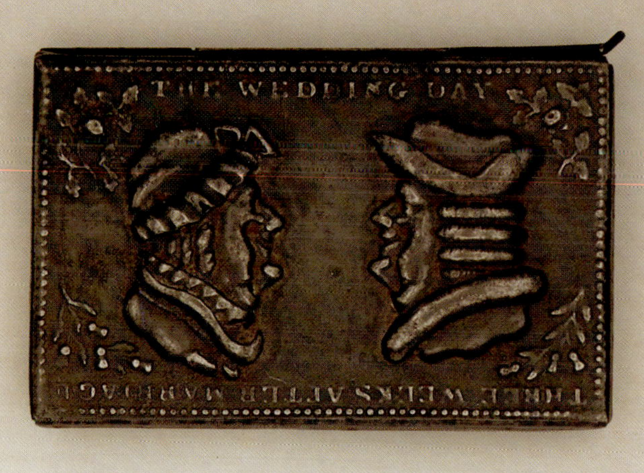

Fig. 410 Britain. Tin plate. Made by J. Hynam. c.1850. L - 7.1cms.

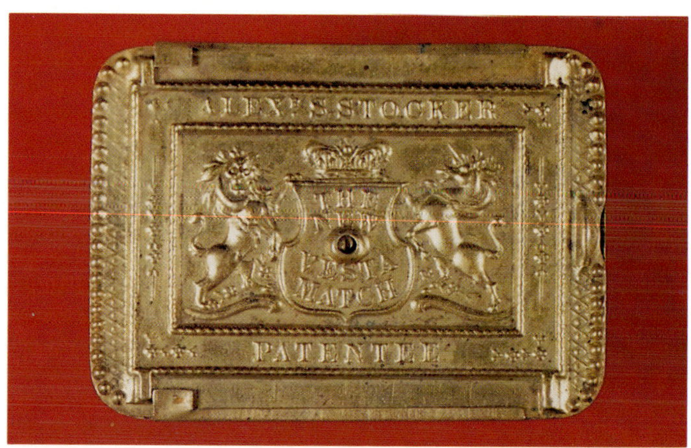

Fig. 411 Britain. Brass. Made to an Invention Patent of 1848 by Alexander S. Stocker. L - 6.4cms.

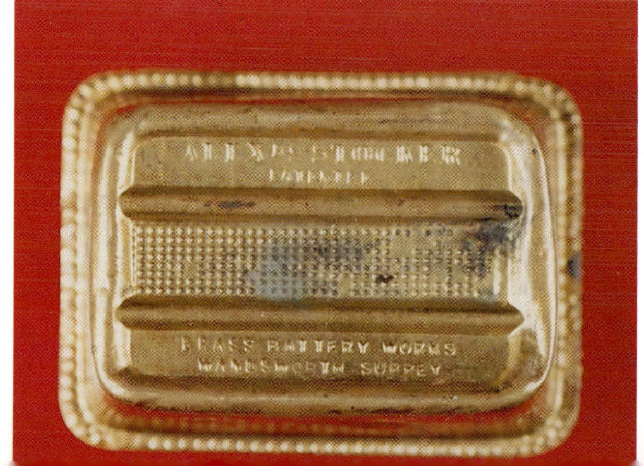

Fig. 412 As Fig. 411. Reverse side.

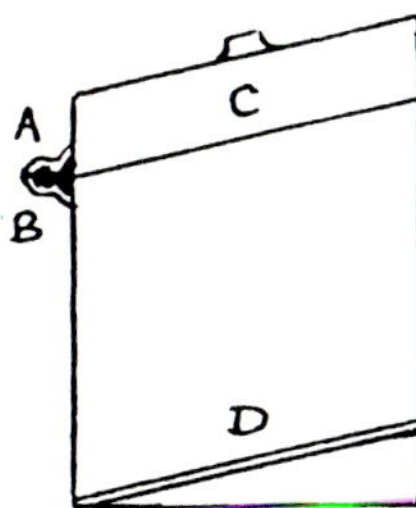

Fig. 413 Drawing from a Useful Design of 1851 registered to Samuel A. Bell and John Black for "The Matchless Matchbox".

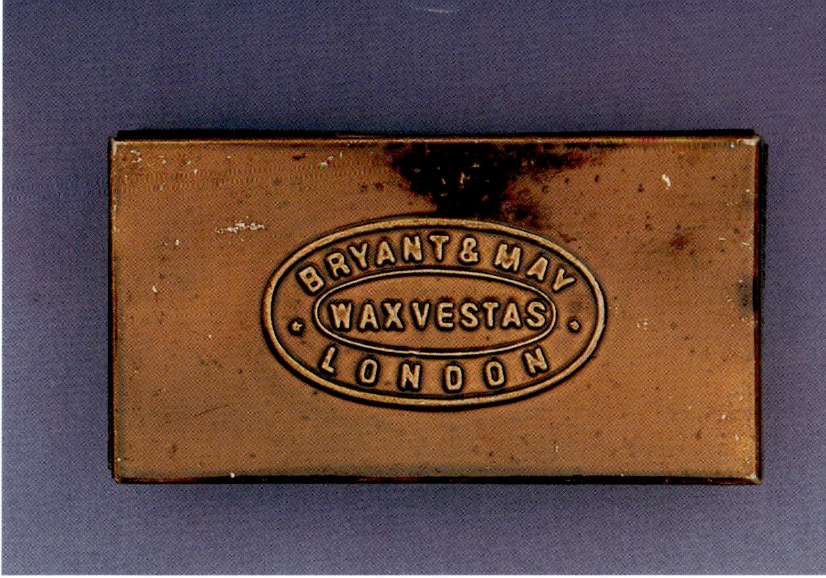

Fig. 415 Britain. Tin plate. Made by Bryant & May. Type made from c.1865 until c.1880s. L - 9.8cms.

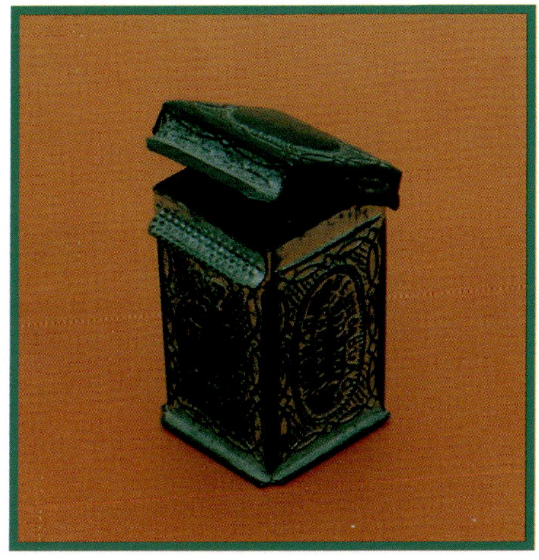

Fig. 414 Britain. Tin plate. Made for Bell & Black to the Useful Design in Fig. 413. 1851 to 1854. H - 5.7cms.

William Bryant and Francis May formed their partnership in 1843, trading as provision merchants in Tooley Street, Southwark (then Surrey, now a London borough). They began to trade in matches in 1850, importing them from Sweden, and re-packed them using Stocker's boxes.

Stocker's box was the forerunner of dozens, if not hundreds, of various forms of match holders and other items of hardware, which Bryant & May went on to use in their business after they moved into their own factory in Bow, London in 1861.

In May 1851 a Useful Provisional Design was registered to a Patent Agent, James Septimus Cockings; this was transferred at the time that full registration was made, in September 1851, to Samuel Alexander Bell and John Black, and was called "The Matchless Matchbox." A copy of one of the drawings from the registration is shown in **Fig. 413.**

Bell and Black were match manufacturers located in Bow Lane, Cheapside, London. They introduced an amended version of the design, as shown in the example in **Fig. 414,** although they probably did not make the boxes themselves. As may be seen from the original design, the box had a sloped inner base (D), with the lid (C) correspondingly sloped and a match socket on top. A projecting strip along the front edge (A) met another projecting strip (B) attached to the front of the box body. The two strips created a cavity along the front of the box in which a match could be placed when the lid was open; with the lid closed, the punch dots applied to the strip acted as a striker when the match was withdrawn.

Bell & Black changed the design by increasing the height of the box, replacing the sloping base and lid with horizontal elements, leaving out the match socket, and providing an additional striker on the base. However, they still used the registration mark, shown as the date impressed on a shield within a belt marked "BELL & BLACK. PATENTEES". The back panel of the box (not shown) is impressed "NEW PATENT GAS CAMPHORATED CONGREVE LIGHTS WITHOUT SULPHUR."

The same box was later used by Bryant & May with its Fairfield Works (Bow) address, which was not open until 1861, and without the registered date, which was no longer in force.

In 1855 Johan Lundstrom, Bryant & May's Swedish supplier, patented the safety match and sold the British rights to Francis May for one hundred pounds. Lundstrom continued to supply Bryant & May with the ordinary friction matches, and agreed to supply the safety matches. But only a very few cases of safety matches arrived in Britain over the next five years, and Bryant & May's unsuccessful efforts to goad Lundstrom into providing a constant and steady supply eventually pushed it into building its own factory to produce matches.

In the mid-1860s Bryant & May began to make its own tin plate matchboxes, with a japanned version in at least three different sizes among the first to appear. The company continued to produce these boxes for many years with minor variations occurring, including rounded corners, the addition of a match socket, and a seamed inset base. A later version is shown in **Fig. 415;** others produced by R.Bell & Co., shown in Fig. 441, were identical to the Bryant & May boxes. The ends are sanded for friction.

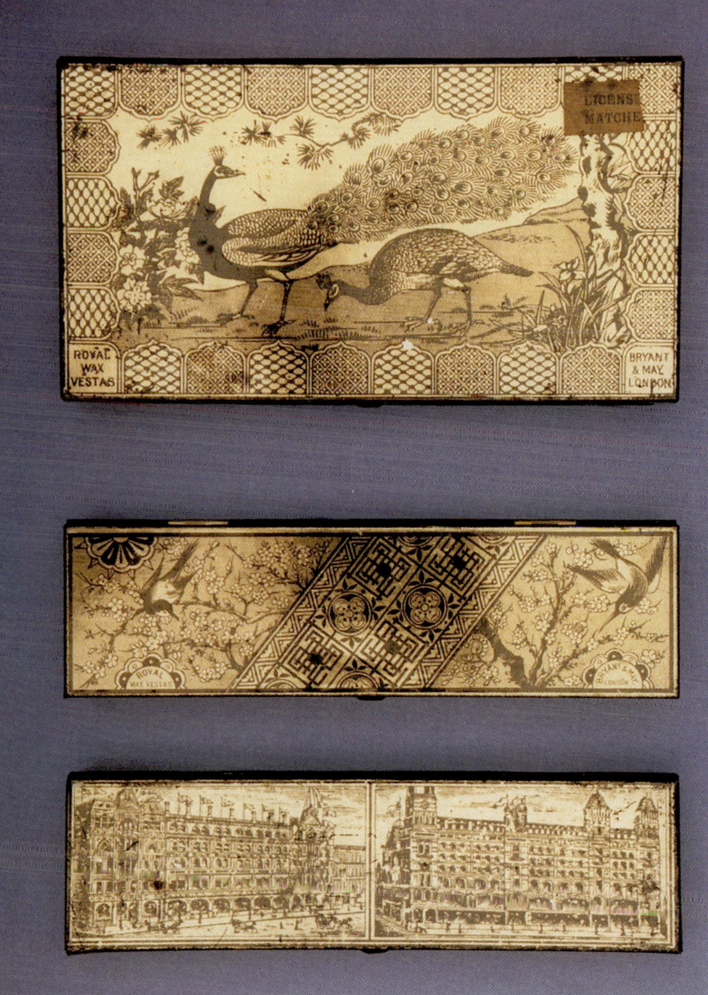

Fig. 416 Britain. Tin plate. Made by Bryant & May. Top: to hold 1000 matches. Centre and lower: to hold 500 matches. From 1873 until c.1895. L - 16cms.

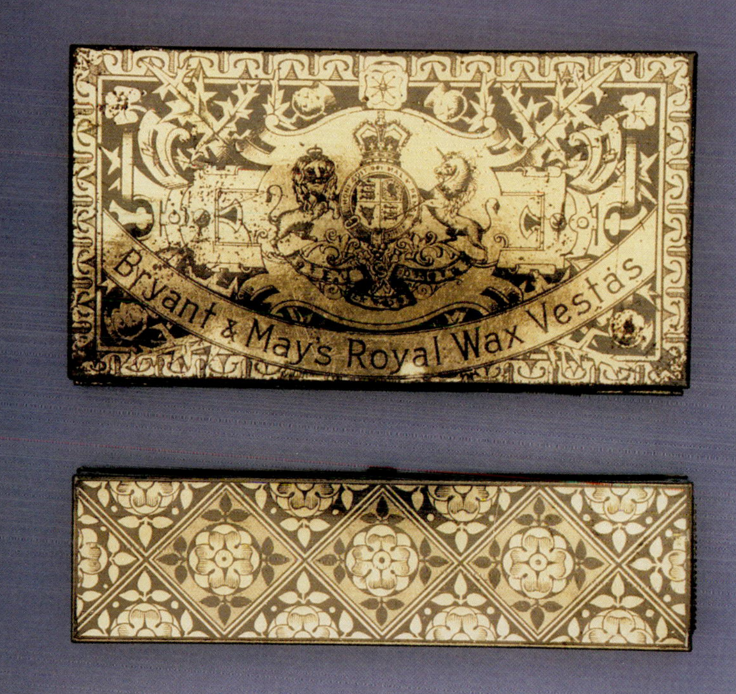

Fig. 417 Reverse sides of Fig. 416 top and centre.

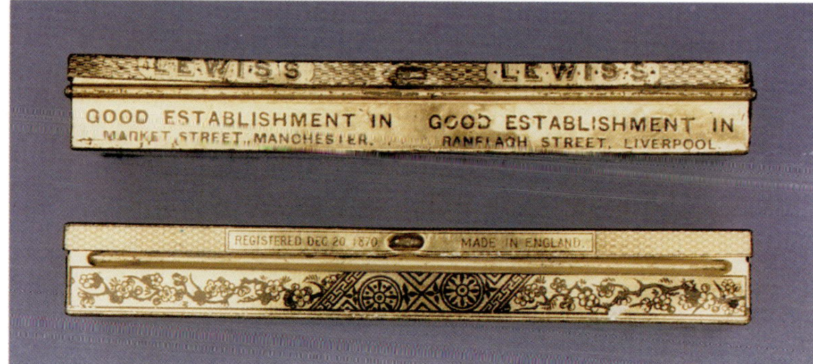

Fig. 418 Front edges of Fig. 416 lower and centre.

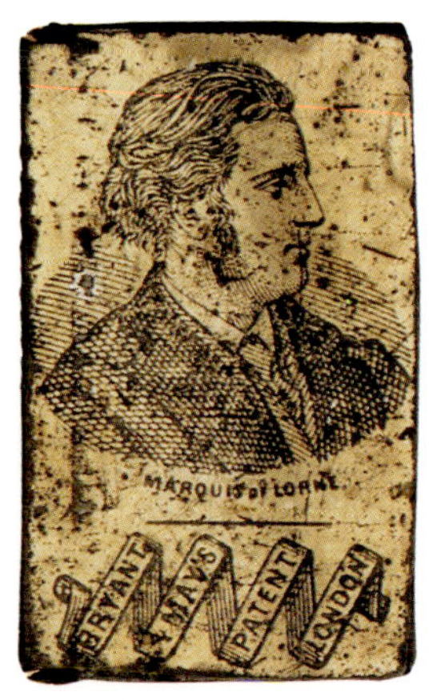

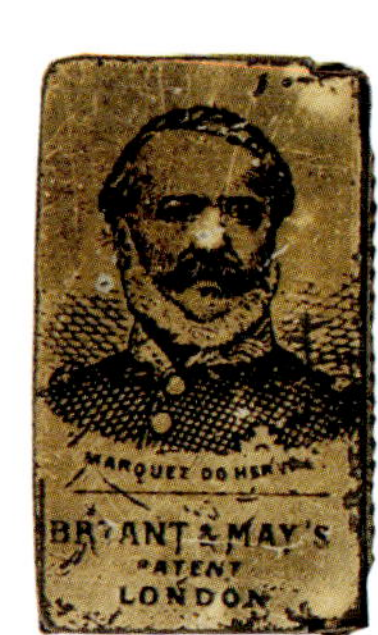

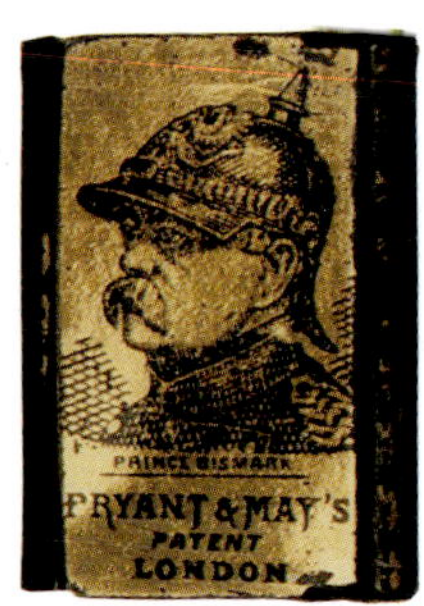

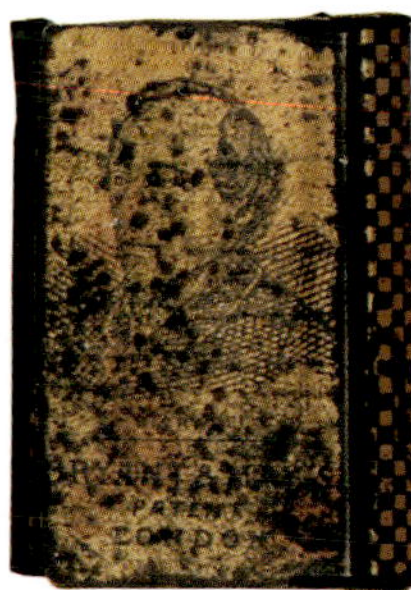

Fig. 419 Britain. Tin plate. Made by Bryant & May. Left: the Marquis of Lorne. 1873. H - 6.3cms. Left centre: The Marquez Do Herval(?). 1871. H - 4.5cms. Right: Prince Bismark and Disraeli. 1874. H - 4.4cms.

In the early 1870s Bryant & May introduced boxes to hold 500 or 1000 wax vesta matches, with black and gold designs. The lids of three examples are shown in **Fig. 416,** with the underside of two in **Fig. 417,** and the front edge of two in **Fig. 418.** The front edges of most of these refer to a Useful Registered Design of 1870 that relates to the catch; the reference is visible in the lower box of Fig. 418.

By 1871 small tin plate boxes in two sizes were being produced with black and gold portraits of famous personages of the day. Over forty portraits are known to have been reproduced, and changes in the box design occurred. **Fig. 419** shows four examples. The box second from the left, hinged on the right, was the first produced. The larger box, hinged on the left, was next. Both boxes had sharp corners, which was hard on pockets, so the shape was changed in 1874 to rounded edges on the box sides and corners of the lids, as seen in the two examples at the right.

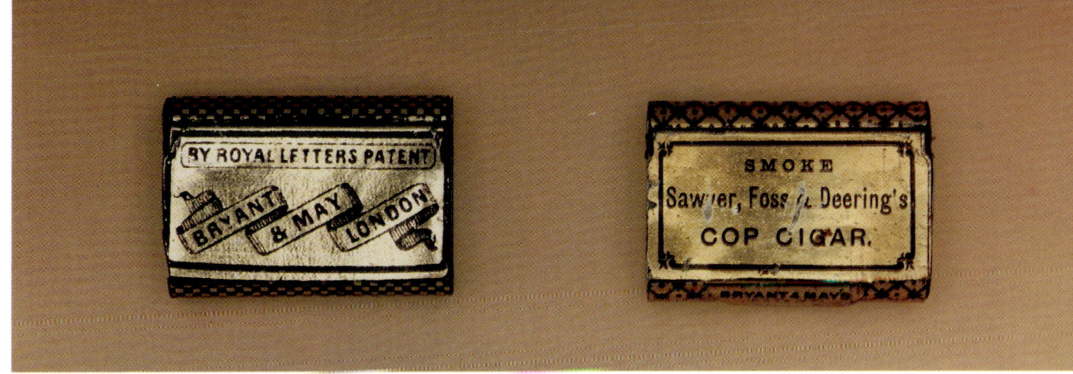

Fig. 420 Britain. Tin plate. Made by Huntley & Bourne for Bryant & May. Left: 1875. Right: 1876. L - 4.4cms.

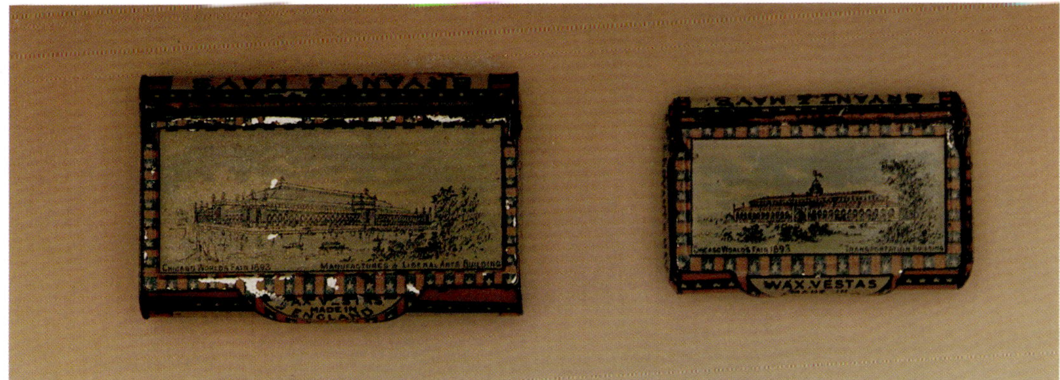

Fig. 421 Britain. Tin plate. Made by Huntley, Boorne & Stevens for Bryant & May. 1893. Left: 5.8cms. Right: to a Registered Design of 1884. L - 4.8cms.

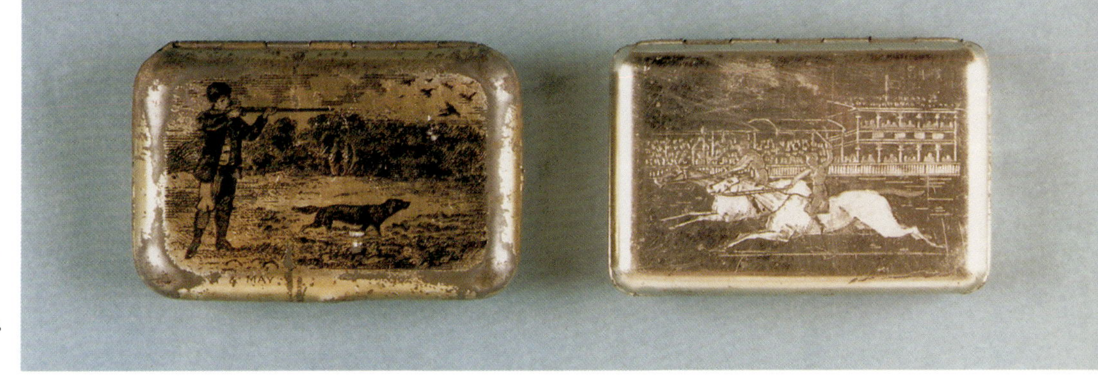

Fig. 422 Britain. Tin plate. Made for Bryant & May. Left: c.1880s. L - 5.8cms. Right: made by Jahncke Ltd. to an Invention Patent of c.1878 and a Registered Design of 1894. c.late 1890s. L - 5.9cms.

Fig. 420 shows two later versions, made after Bryant & May had begun to produce boxes with advertising for other companies. The example at the left dates to 1875, that at the right to 1876, with the front edge of the lid provided with a curved tab. These boxes are known to have been manufactured by Huntley & Boorne (later to become Huntley, Boorne & Stevens) of Reading, Berkshire, with whom Bryant & May had a long association. In 1878 a new method of printing on tin had been devised and Bryant & May acquired the rights to the process, installing the machinery in the Huntley, Boorne & Stevens works.

By about the middle of the 1870s Bryant & May had introduced holders for matchboxes to hang on the wall, and stand-alone types combined with an ash tray. The company had become the leader in its field, with most of its products mass-produced for the less affluent members of society.

It did not confine itself to matchboxes alone, but produced other forms of tin-plate boxes for gloves, tea, handkerchiefs, and other items, which were first filled with its boxes of matches. Its designs drew wide acclaim, eliciting condescension from a prominent arts magazine that said "The patterns are most artistic, indeed, they are almost too good for such low-priced articles."

Bryant & May constantly endeavored to improve upon the design of its boxes, yet at the same time reduce the costs. The next development of the previous boxes shown was to the lid, which was provided with a semi-circular tab on the front edge, and appeared in 1876. Two examples are shown in **Fig. 421,** both made by Huntley, Boorne & Stevens, for the Chicago World's Fair of 1893, at which Bryant & May's exhibited. The smaller of these two boxes has a registration number for 1884, which was for "a box with rounded ends and a spring lid, the back of the box serving as a spring." The larger box has flat ends, but the same lid spring arrangement that was in use in 1876.

The style of the decorative design on the box to the left in **Fig. 422** suggests that the box was made in the early 1880s but its construction is quite different from the most common Bryant & May boxes. Whereas most boxes have the main body made of one piece, bent up to form the ends and sides, this box has a separate base plate which interlocks by means of lugs into the sides, made from a single long length of tin plate with lugs that correspond to the gaps in the base plate. A smaller version of this type of box is shown in **Fig. 423** with an impressed design on the lid.

The more usual form of boxes with rounded edges and corners is shown in **Fig. 422 right,** and is marked on the end "Jahncke's Patent."

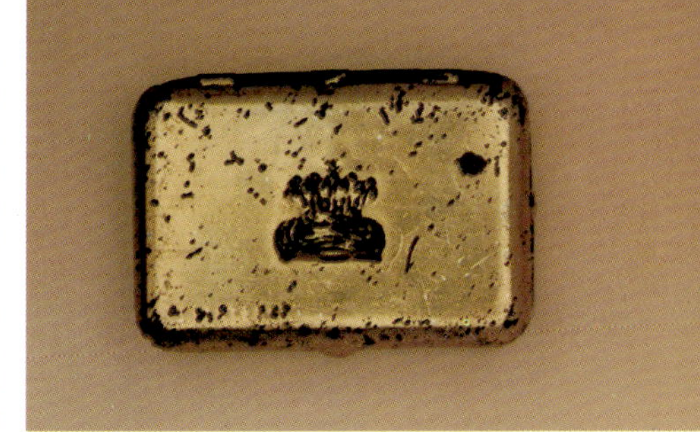

Fig. 423 Britain. Tin plate. Made by, or for, Bryant & May, to same method of Fig. 422 left. c.1880s. L - 4.5cms.

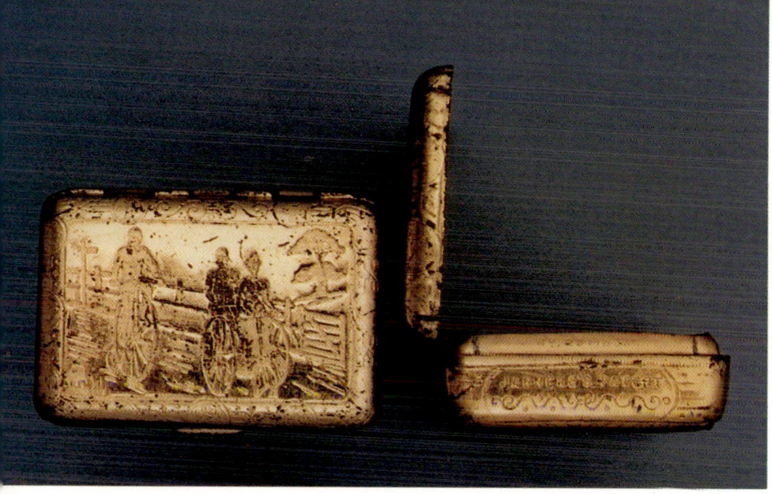

Fig. 424 Britain. Tin plate. Made by Jahncke Ltd. for Bryant & May. Right: showing the Registered Design number, and "Jahnckes Patent". Left. marked as right. L - 4.6cms.

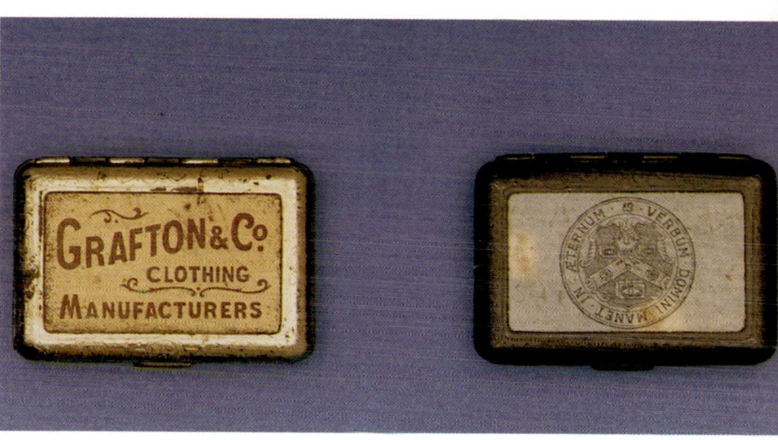

Fig. 427 As Fig. 424 left.

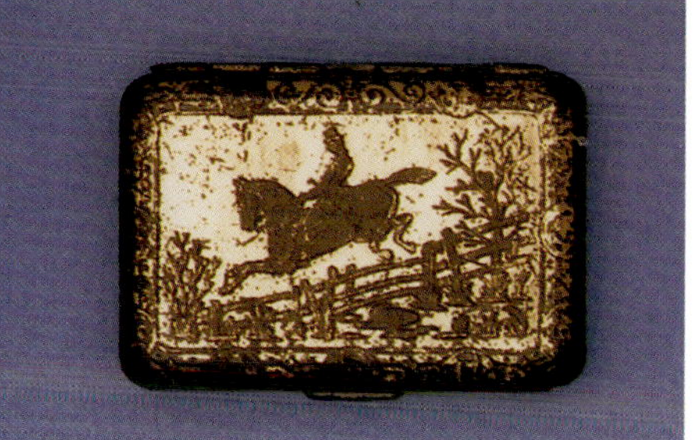

Fig. 425 As Fig. 424 left.

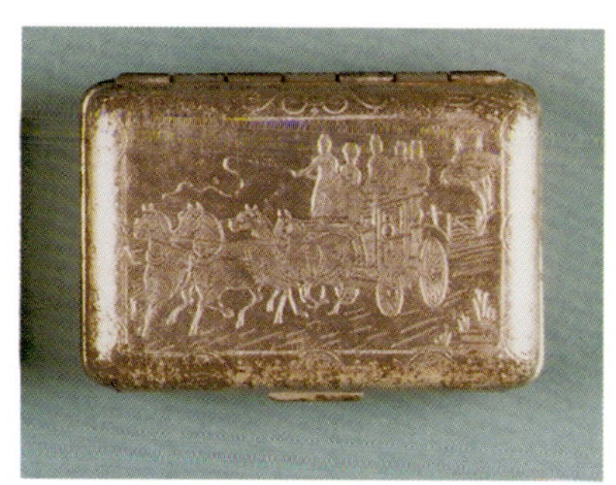

Fig. 426 As Fig. 424 left.

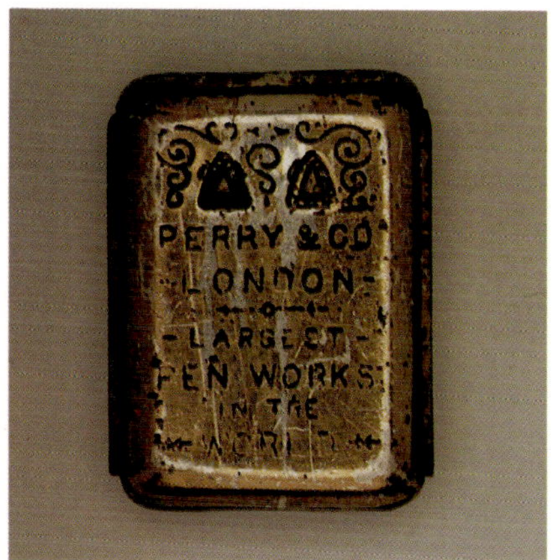

Fig. 429 Britain. Tin plate. Made for Perry & Co. to a United States Invention Patent of 1874 by George Zuchschwerdt. L - 4.4cms.

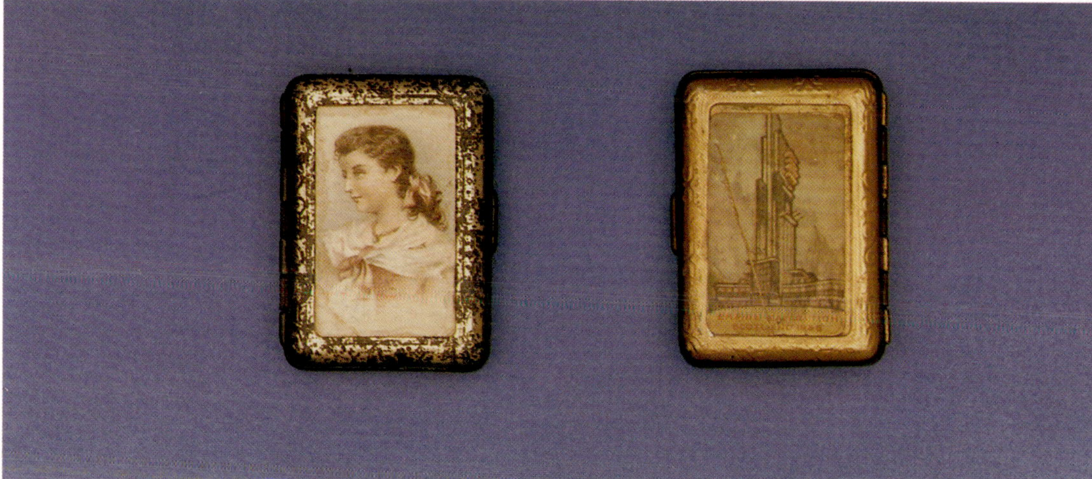

Fig. 428 Left as Fig. 424 left. Right: marked with Registered Design number for 1894, but made in 1938.

Ernst Jahncke was a "Metallic Box Manufacturer" in London who held several Invention Patents and Registered Designs, some in conjunction with Henry Herbst, an engineer. Jahncke went on to produce most of the boxes in **Figs. 424 to 428,** with Bryant & May acquiring a major holding in the company in 1895.

The example in **Fig. 424 right** illustrates the mark "JAHNCKE'S PATENT" on the exposed end of the box, and above it on the bezel "Rd.231183." The patent was probably one issued to Herbst in 1878, for the method of manufacturing the box. The Registered Design was issued to Jahncke in 1894 for the design on the edges, the frame edges of the lids, and the bases of the boxes.

The boxes were supplied with a wide variety of designs on the lids, including gold and silver varnished finishes for hunting, yachting, horse racing, coaching and cycling scenes. Paper labels were glued to the lid, some of which bore advertising for small businesses, others photographs of personalities. There was a series of at least forty International Code of Signals flags used by shipping, and one with an impressed representation of Queen Victoria.

Bryant & May must have produced many thousands, if not hundreds of thousands, of these boxes. The small ones retailed at one penny a box, including the matches, and were supplied with a customer's own name and printed matter. They were still being produced as late as 1938, as is evident from the box in **Fig. 428 right** with a label for the Empire Exhibition held in Scotland that year. The Registered Number was still applied to the bezel of this box, although protection for that number had run out in 1897, and it was illegal to continue to use it after that date!

These boxes were mostly intended to hold wax vesta matches. The bases usually had rectangular striking patches, either in a corrugated form or of the punch-dot grater type, but they are occasionally found with a patch glued to the base for striking safety matches.

By 1876 Bryant & May had introduced a tin plate box with a sliding lid. It was marked "B & M.Pat." However the box shown in **Fig. 429,** which is identical, including the design on the back, is marked with a United States Invention Patent date for 1874, issued to George Zuckschwerdt for an "Improvement in Sheet-Metal Boxes;" his drawings indicate a long narrow box for cigars or pencils. Perhaps Bryant & May acquired the British rights to this patent. The example was made for Perry & Co., London pen makers.

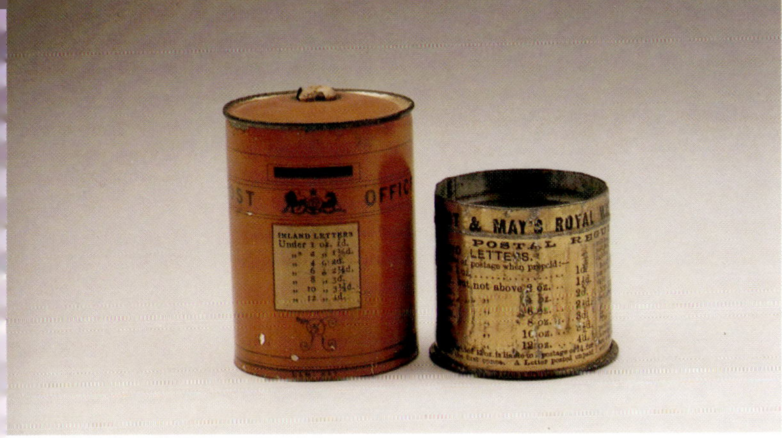

Fig. 430 Britain. Tin plate, bone. Made by or for Bryant & May. From 1876 until post 1906. H - 6.7cms.

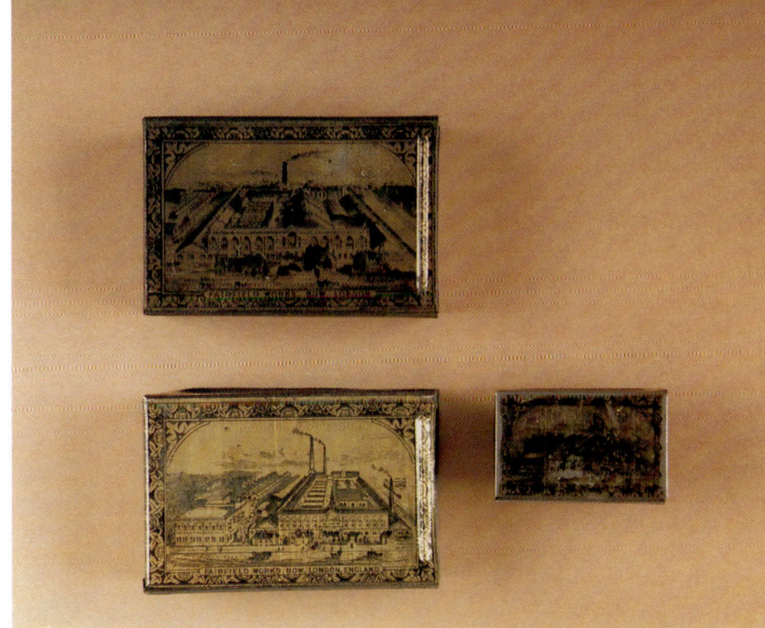

Fig. 432 Britain. Tin plate. Made to a Useful Design of 1873 (shown in Fig. 360). Top left: c.1887. Lower left: c.1890. L -7.5cms. Right: c.1890. L - 4.3cms.

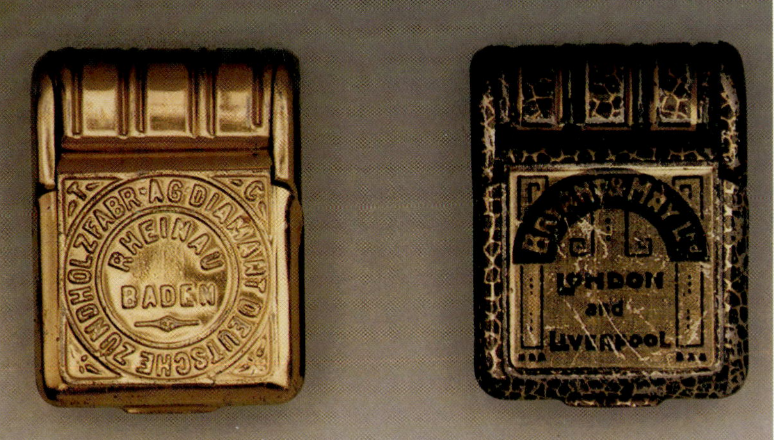

Fig. 431 Britain. Tin plate. Made to an Invention Patent of 1897 by Tito L. Carbone and Edward Cooper. H - 4.7cms.

From 1876 until sometime after 1906, Bryant & May produced a stand-alone novelty box in the form of a Post Office pillar box, an example of which is shown in **Fig. 430.** Made of tin plate, it has a full depth slip-on lid, with a bone match socket set into the top of the lid. These boxes had the current letter rates and other postal regulations printed on the outside of the lid and of the main box body. By 1894 they were being made in three sizes, the largest one with the base marked to serve as a perpetual calendar. Most were packed one dozen to a tinplate handkerchief box.

Fig. 431 shows two match holders commonly referred to as 'knapsack' boxes, for obvious reasons. They were an invention of the fertile mind of Tito Livio Carbone and a partner, Edward Cooper, both resident in Uruguay in 1897, the year of the invention.

Carbone was an Italian engineer who, between 1897 and 1927 (five years after he died), had over ninety patents issued in his name at over twenty patent offices around the world. He lived in Italy, Uruguay, Germany, Switzerland and Britain, claiming Swiss nationality at the time of his death, and had his own companies in Germany and in Manchester, England.

His first patent was for a "Sheet Metal Box"—the knapsack box—which was followed shortly after by a patent for a machine to make these boxes. Both patents were issued in Britain, France, Germany and the United States while he was living in Uruguay.

The first knapsack boxes were probably made in Germany, for the Diamant Deutsche Zundwarenfabr. AG of Rheinau, Baden, as shown at the left in Fig. 431. At about the same time they began to be made for the Diamond Match Co. in Liverpool, England. The initials "T" and "C" were stamped in the top corners of the lid, but inverted on the British boxes.

Shortly after these boxes came on the market, Bryant & May acquired the Diamond Match Co. in Liverpool, eventually replacing its name with their own. The Bryant & May boxes for holding wax vestas and Swan vestas are to be found with impressed marks similar in format to the German box. They later moved to a printed format as shown at the right in Fig. 431, and Carbone's intitials were no longer used.

The Bryant & May Useful Registered Design of 1873 for a match box slide, shown in Fig. 360, was the basis of a product line that the company used until the 1930s. The designs were changed over the years, but the first was printed with a multiple fleur-de-lis design.

By 1887 the company was using an illustration of its factory at Bow. Three examples are shown in **Fig. 432.** The earliest version, shown at the top, has a single smokestack. The later version, below, has three smokestacks and the buildings have been extended at the left. Two smaller versions were made, the smallest shown at the right. The reverse of all of these slides has a design showing ten prize medals awarded at international exhibitions. They were also made with a luminous panel over the factory scene.

Probably from the 1920s is a series of six designs of flowers against a black background, made in two sizes, an example of one shown in **Fig. 433.** In the 1930s themes of the royalty occurred, and there were many other designs.

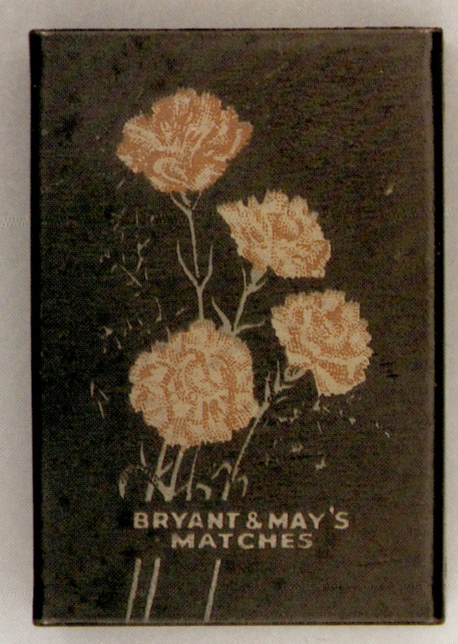

Fig. 433 Britain. Tin plate. Made by or for Bryant & May. c.1920s. L - 7.4cms.

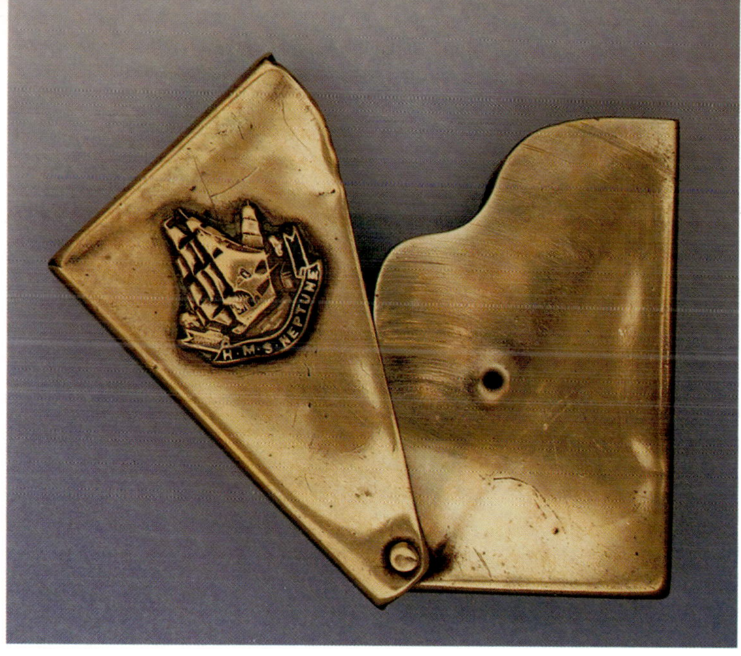

Fig. 434 Britain. Brass. Made for Bryant & May to a Registered Design of 1914 by Alfred Dunhill. H - 6.3cms.

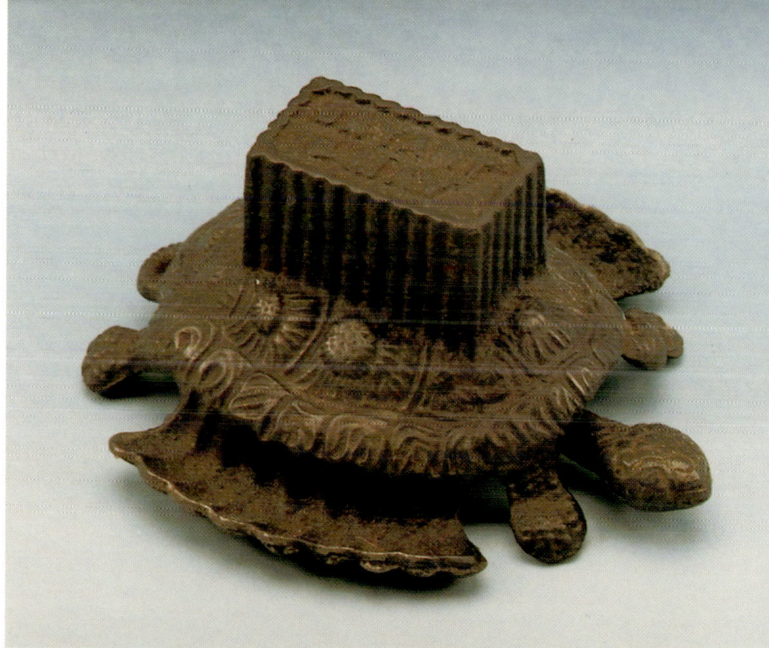

Fig. 436 Britain. Cast iron. Made for Bryant & May by Wright & Butler, to a Registered Design of 1885. L - 11.5cms.

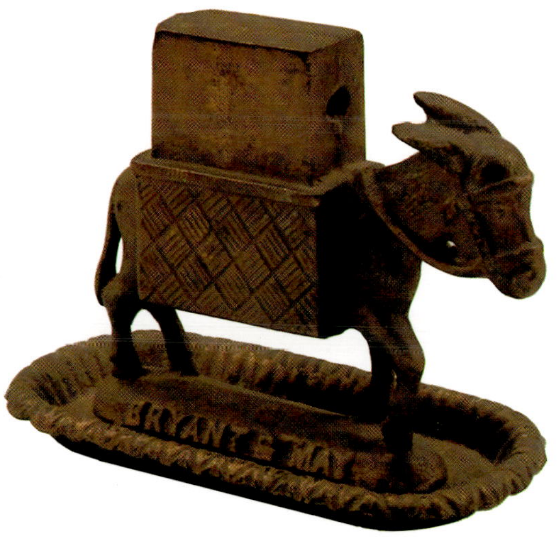

Fig. 435 Britain. Cast iron. Made for Bryant & May by Wright & Butler, to a Registered Design of 1885. H - 10.9cms.

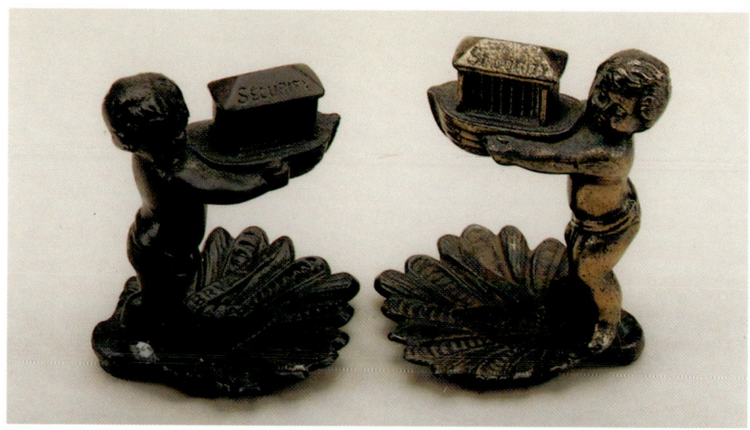

Fig. 437 Britain. Cast iron. Made for Bryant & May. c.1894. H -11.5cms.

From 1914 until 1918 Bryant & May produced the "Service Match Box Cover," shown in **Fig. 434.** This was made to a Registered Design of 1914, issued to Alfred Dunhill, the celebrated London pipe maker. The original holders were plain, with an oxidized, nickel-plated or brass finish; but the addition of regimental or ships' badges soon became popular. Tins of one dozen boxes of Bryant & May's safety matches were specially made to send by parcel post to members of the British Expeditionary Force in France.

Bryant & May did not confine themselves to inexpensive sheet-metal boxes, but marketed a wide variety of match hardware made for them by other companies in cast iron, ceramics, glass, or wood, always with the company name prominently marked upon them. Tartan-decorated cylindrical wooden boxes were probably made by William and Andrew Smith of Mauchline, Scotland, one of Bryant & May's earliest outside contractors.

Wright & Butler, lamp manufacturers of Birmingham, were issued with two Registered Designs in 1885, for cast-iron matchbox holders or stands. The first, shown in **Fig. 435,** was for a donkey; the Bryant & May name appears in raised letters on the ashtray base. The original drawing for this showed an open-topped panier to hold individual matches, later replaced by the block to hold a box of matches. The second, in the form of a turtle, is shown in **Fig. 436,** with the company name on the top of the block. The head is attached to the body by a pair of links, with a counter-balance under the body behind the links, so that the head nods when the figure is moved. The side flanges are intended to hold burnt matches. Both items were given a bronzed finish and were illustrated, in company catalogues and almanacs, with tin match slides with oval luminous tablets. They were apparently last advertised in 1896.

A cast-iron figure of a cherub holding an ark and standing on a shell-like spray of leaves(?) was being produced in 1894. The company name is stamped on the top of the base. The ark, with the word "SECURITY" on it, was the company trademark, which was in use by 1872 and may have been used as early as 1862. The deck structure of the ark acted as a block to hold a box of matches. **Fig. 437** shows two versions. That to the left is believed to be the original version. The example to the right has a gilded finish and may be a later version; it is of poorer quality.

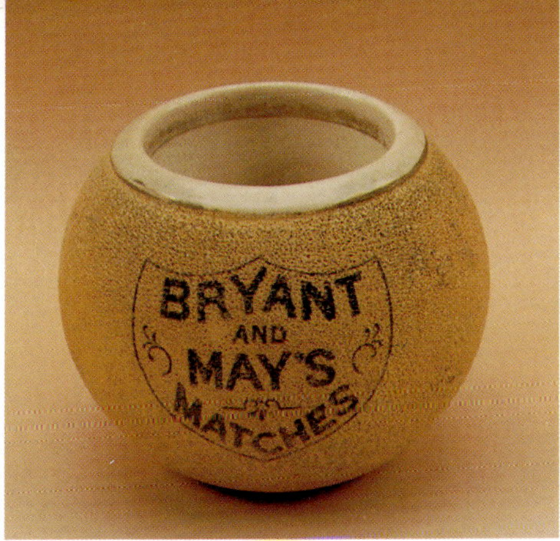

Fig. 438 Britain. Ceramic. Made for Bryant & May. c.1894 to 1914. D - 8.9cms.

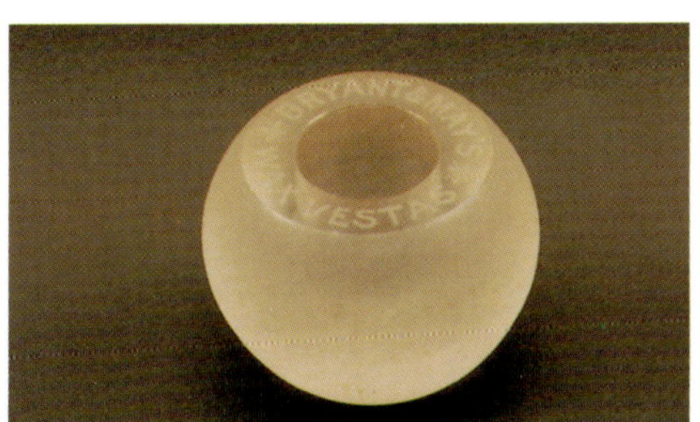

Fig. 439 Britain. Glass. Made for Bryant & May. c.1910. D - 7cms.

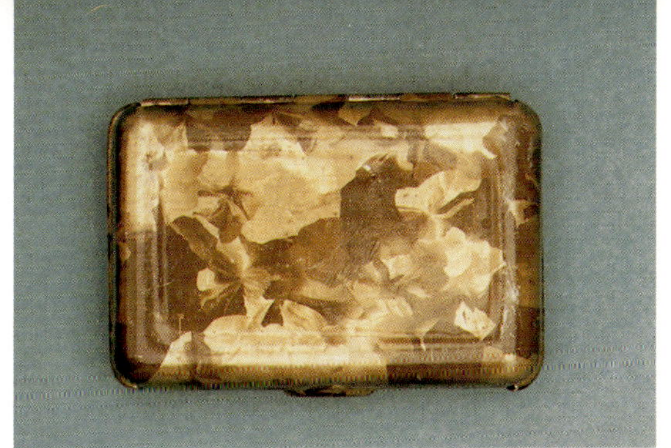

Fig. 440 Britain. Tin plate. Made for the Diamond Match Co. Probably by Jahncke Ltd. c.1895. L - 4.7cms.

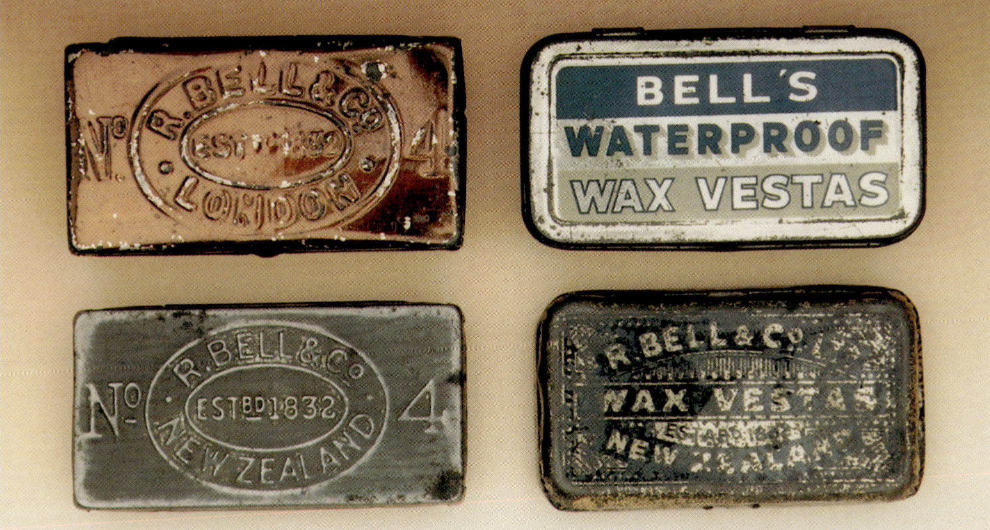

Fig. 441 Probably made in Britain. Tin plate. For R. Bell & Co. c.1870s to 1910. Top right: L - 7.3cms.

A very wide range of ceramic and glass match stands with open tops or a match box block, with and without ashtrays, were made by a number of different companies with the Bryant & May name on them. Advertised as for use in "Clubs, Hotels, Public Institutions, etc.," they were produced from about 1895 until 1920. Not all of the ceramic holders had a maker's mark, for example that in **Fig. 438.** But marks for such well-known potteries as Minton's, J. Macintyre & Co., A. G. Richardson & Co. Ltd., and Wiltshaw & Robinson, among others, are to be found. Glass ball stands are not known to have been marked at all, and the example in **Fig. 439** is no exception. This example has an etched finish so that the rough surface can act as a striker.

The foregoing is but a brief glimpse of the vast range of products put out by, or for, Bryant & May, all designed to put the company name before the public at every opportunity and thereby increase the sales of its matches. This effort probably brought the reward sought, for the company developed into a huge empire, acquiring much of the British and foreign competition.

Many of these products were aimed specifically at the working man, who could not afford better quality items. But at the same time, Bryant & May's products had to be attractive, and a great deal of time was spent in the design stage to develop an item that was cheap to manufacture yet had a good quality decorative appearance.

The company was located in a poor, working-class district of London, which usually experienced a high rate of unemployment. Whereas many local employers took advantage of this situation, however, Bryant & May made a sincere effort to protect the health and welfare of their employees. In spite of this, the women workers at Bryant & May formed the first women's union and promptly went on strike in 1888.

In terms of the company's expansion, its major failure was in the United States, to which it was unable to gain any real access. In l90l it did, however, form a merger with the Diamond Match Co., which was of mutual benefit to both companies, yet permitted them both to retain their independence.

It is probably safe to say that the contribution of Bryant & May to the development of match holders and the proliferation of their use, particularly by the average man, was far greater than that of any other company in the world.

Other companies in Britain used the same manufacturing sources as Bryant & May. The example in **Fig. 440** was made for the Diamond Match Co., obviously by Jahncke, but not marked with his name. It has a gold crystalline finish.

The examples in **Fig. 441** were all made for R. Bell & Co. The upper boxes were for the British market: that to the left probably c. 1870s, that to the right c. 1910. The lower examples were made for the New Zealand branch: that to the left following the early pattern, that to the right a later version constructed in similar manner to the boxes in Figs. 422 and 423, and decorated with similar patterns to Bryant & May boxes in black and gold. The latter pair may have been made after Bryant & May had taken over Bell's, probably around 1915. It seems likely that they were made in Britain. Richard Bell established his company in 1832, it being the first company to manufacture matches as its sole product. He acquired the rights to manufacture wax matches from the patentee William Newton, a patent agent, and was the first to use the name "Vesta" for these matches, in about 1833.

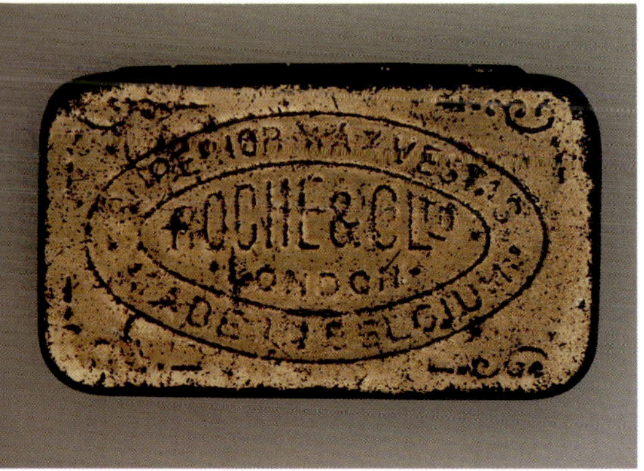

Fig. 442 Belgium. Tin plate. Made for Roche & Co.Ltd. L - 6.1cms.

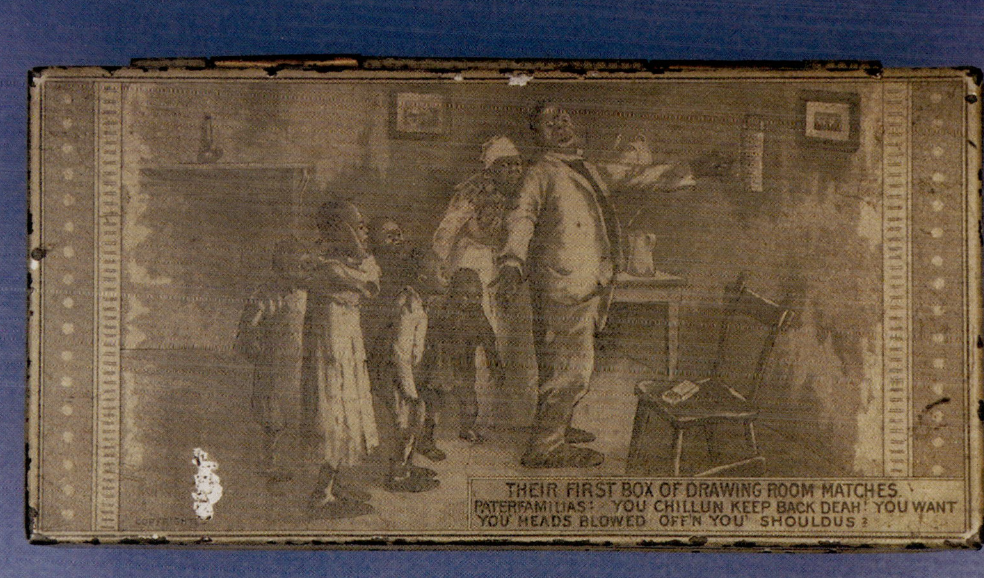

Fig. 443 United States. Tin plate. Made for the Diamond Match Co., by Ginna & Co. Between 1893 and 1901. L - 11.7cms.

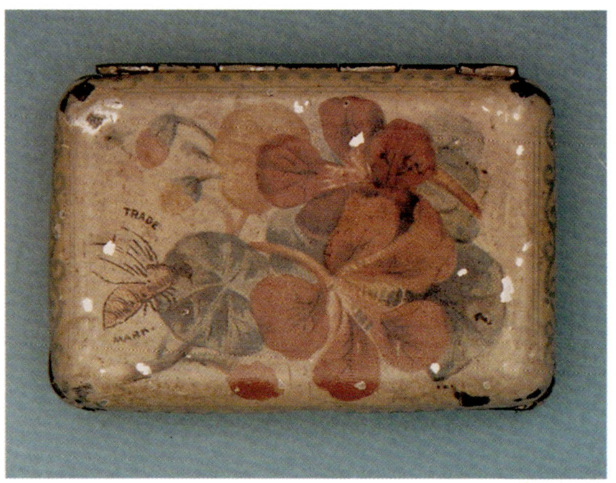

Fig. 444 United States. Tin plate. Made for the Diamond Match Co. by Ginna & Co. pre 1901. L - 5.8cms.

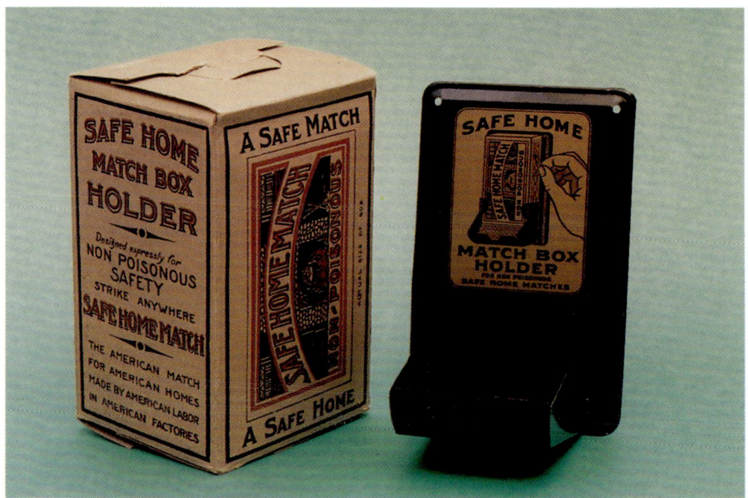

Fig. 445 United States. Tin plate, and cardboard box. Made for the Diamond Match Co. c.1915. H (of holder) - 16cms.

Examples of continental European match holders made for or by the match manufacturers in tin plate appear to be rare. The solitary example shown here in **Fig. 442** was made for Roche & Co.Ltd.—and that for its British market. Roche & Cie. were a French company, with a factory in Belgium and a subsidiary with offices in London from 1901 until 1928.

In the United States it appears as though the Diamond Match Co. was the only company to produce any match hardware of any significance. Its earlier tin-plate boxes were made by Ginna & Co. of New York, which was renowned for its excellence in lithographic design work. Tin-plate boxes marked with its name are not found after 1901, when it merged with sixty other companies to form the American Can Co., although it continued to operate under its own name for a brief period after the merger.

Two examples of Ginna products made for the Diamond Match Co. are shown in **Figs. 443 and 444**. The example in Fig. 443 bears a drawing that first appeared in *Harper's New Monthly Magazine* in January 1893 and was signed "D.New.—N.Y.—92." It is assumed that the Diamond Match Co. acquired the copyright from *Harper's,* for it is marked "Copyright" on the box, which would date the box between 1893 and 1901.

The smaller box in Fig. 444 has the Ginna name on the edge of the base, and that of the Diamond Match Co., along the front edge. The words "Trade" and "Mark" appear above and below the bee on the lid of the box, but the owners of this mark have not yet been traced.

Fig. **445** shows a tin plate wall holder for a box of parlor matches, alongside the original cardboard box in which it was packed and sold in a retail store. It was designed specifically for the "Safe Home Match" which the Diamond Match Co. claims was introduced in 1915. This claim is supported by an invention in 1915 by William A. Fairburn, a Diamond Match Co. employee, for the prevention of afterglow in matches, and which is referred to on the side of the packing box. The design for the cover of the matchbox, using the single word "Home," was registered as a trademark in 1914, with the claim that it had been used "since May, 1913;" this is shown in **Fig. 446**.

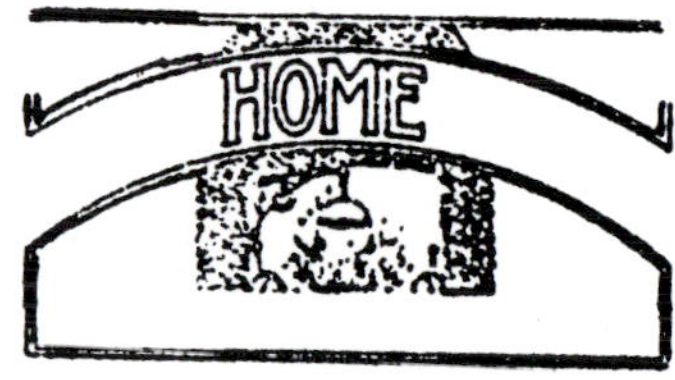

Fig. 446 Registered Trade Mark for the Diamond Match Co. "Safe Home Match" of 1914.

A glass ashtray and book match holder is shown in **Fig. 447**; it is marked underneath "PAT. PENDING. THE DIAMOND MATCH CO." It is believed that "PAT. PENDING" refers to a Design Patent for a "Combined match-holder and ash-receptacle" obtained by Henry C. Traute in 1920; this displays a form of pocket to hold book matches identical to the example. The example was made for the Prince George Hotel, New York.

A second Design Patent of 1920 is shown in **Fig. 448**. This too was issued to Henry C. Traute, as an assignor to The Diamond Match Co., for a "Combined matchholder and ash-receptacle."

The final example in this chapter is a product of Somers Brothers of Brooklyn, New York (another of the companies in the 1901 merger that formed the American Can Co.), shown in **Fig. 449**; it was made for The E. B. Eddy Co. Ltd. of Hull, Quebec. It has been said of Eddy's: "Say 'matches' in Canada and one may as well say 'Eddy'." The company was established in 1851 and is still in business today, although it broke away from the parent company in 1929 and moved to Pembroke, Ontario, to become the Eddy Match Co. The example was made to hold wax vesta matches, for which the Eddy company equipped its factory with new machinery, and in a contemporary advertisement of 1895 claimed to have employed "skilled match-makers from England and the Continent."

Inevitably, other match holders bearing other company names will come to light. But nothing will compare to the significant contribution of Bryant & May.

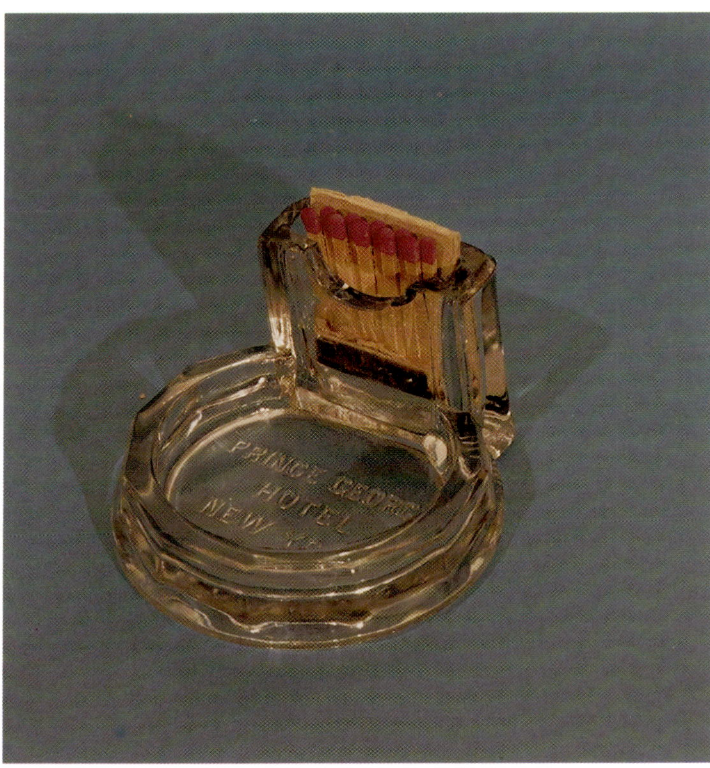

Fig. 447 United States. Glass. Made to a Design Patent of 1920, by Henry C. Traute, assignor to the Diamond Match Co.

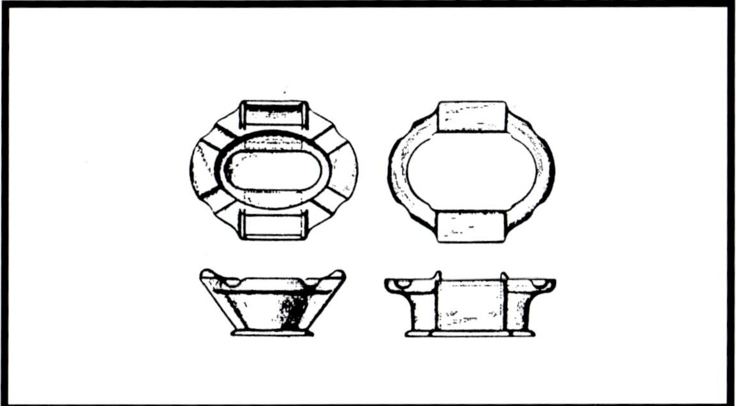

Fig. 448 United States Design Patent of 1920 issued to Henry C. Traute, assignor to the Diamond Match Co..

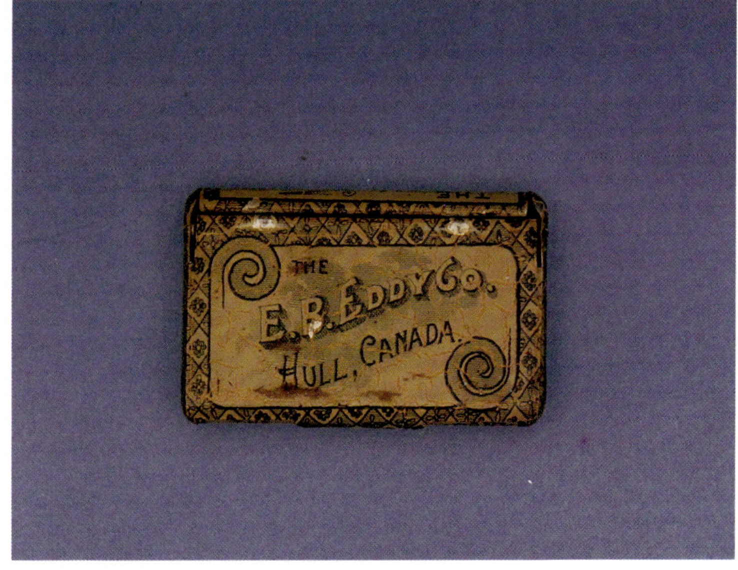

Fig. 449 United States. Tin plate. Made for The E.B. Eddy Co. in Canada by Somers Brothers. Between 1895 and 1901. L - 4.5cms.

Chapter V
Stand-Alone Match Holders

PART 1: INTRODUCTION

Chapter II dealt with early protective match holders, which fall into a period generally regarded as from c. 1830 until c. 1860, when matches were less reliable and too easily subject to accidental ignition. Shaking a box of matches, or leaving it in sunlight, was often sufficient to start a fire within the box that could easily and rapidly spread, leading to major fires in the home or place of business.

Despite this, improvements in manufacturing safer forms of matches did not occur overnight, and there were no government regulations or forms of quality control. Domestic and foreign competition was fierce, labor and materials were cheap, and the conditions were right for the proliferation of unregulated cottage industries in Europe and North America. Consumers purchased their matches from local stores or street-sellers as they needed them, and with no guarantees as to quality or safety.

But improvements did gradually occur as larger businesses began to develop, ultimately taking over the cottage industries or forcing them out of business. To survive, the larger operations had to reduce the risks of fire which would destroy their investment. Furthermore, governments began to regulate labor conditions. These changes led to companies trying to improve the quality of their products, for their own benefit as part of market competition and for public safety.

By 1860 the safety match had been invented, the innocuous red phosphorus had replaced the evil white phosphorus, and the use of sulphur was considerably reduced, particularly in Britain. Matches were far less liable to ignite spontaneously.

Thus the need to make match holders with lids as a means of providing some protection was reduced, which was particularly true with match holders designed to stand on a horizontal surface—the stand-alone types—and those designed to hang on a vertical surface.

As a rule of thumb it is generally believed that all match holders made prior to 1860 were provided with a lid. However, there were exceptions. Open-topped match holders were designed and produced as early as 1851, when an Ornamental Design was registered in Britain by Samuel Messenger of Birmingham; this was in the form of a Cromwellian soldier standing beside a mortar, which was open-topped to hold the matches. There were also a few other designs registered of open-topped holders in the 1850s.

Since holders with lids continued to be made until well after the turn of the century, the presence or absence of a lid is no safe indication of the date of manufacture. However, all of the match holders discussed in this chapter are believed to be post-1860.

The range of materials and shapes used for stand-alone match holders are as varied as those used for the pocket match holders. Metal, wood, ivory, ceramics, and glass were all used to great effect, in simple geometric forms, and a variety of anthropomorphic, zoomorphic and other imaginative forms. Occasionally silver was used, but examples of these are rare. Many holders are unmarked and therefore difficult to date, and their places of origin are also often obscure. For the sake of convenience they have been broken down here by the principal component material.

PART 2: METAL

A series of cast figures that are almost caricatures, with large heads and feet on small bodies, are of unknown origin and date. It has been suggested that they were made in the countries that they represent; however, they include a Chinese person, and China is a very unlikely source. Moreover, the similarities in the representations almost defy coincidence. The most likely source is Germany, and they probably date from between 1850 and 1870.

The example in **Fig. 450** depicts a Grenadier, thought to be from the Hapsburg empire. The head is hinged at the back of the neck to provide access to the matches. His back-pack is roughened for friction. The grounded rifle has the bayonet socket in place, which acts as a match socket, the match completing the bayonet. The piece is made of cast iron, and there are minute traces of black, gold and green paint, suggesting that he was originally brightly painted in the colors of his uniform.

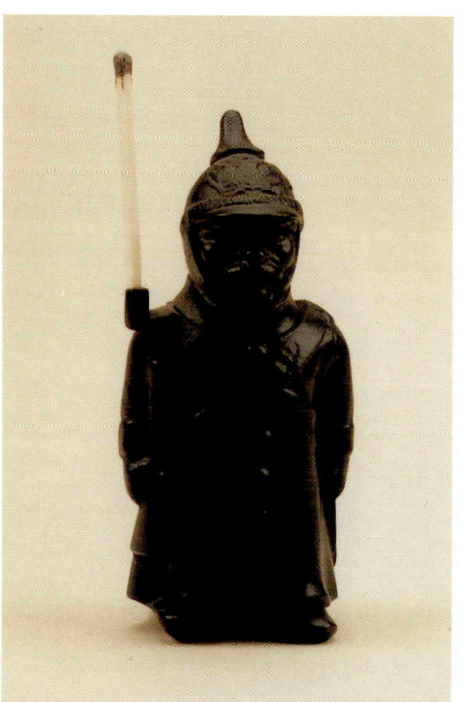

Fig. 450 Probably Germany. Cast iron. Between 1850 and 1870. H -8.6cms.

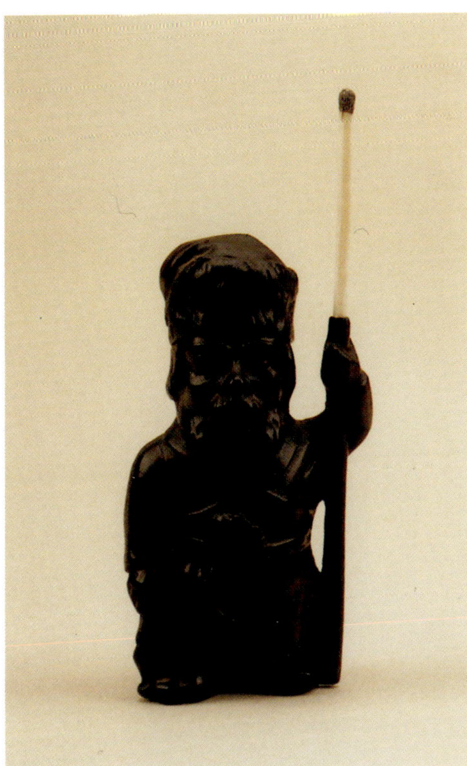

Fig. 451 Probably Germany. Cast iron. Between 1850 and 1870. H -7.7cms.

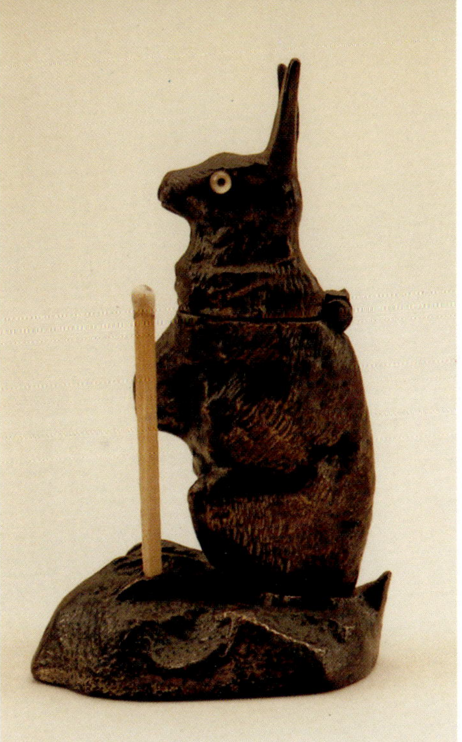

Fig. 452 Europe. Cast brass, glass. c.1890. H - 8.9cms.

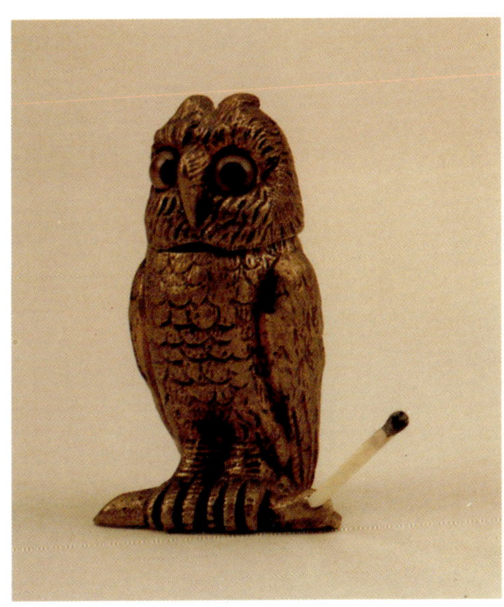

Fig. 453 Europe. Cast brass, glass. c.1890. H - 6.7cms.

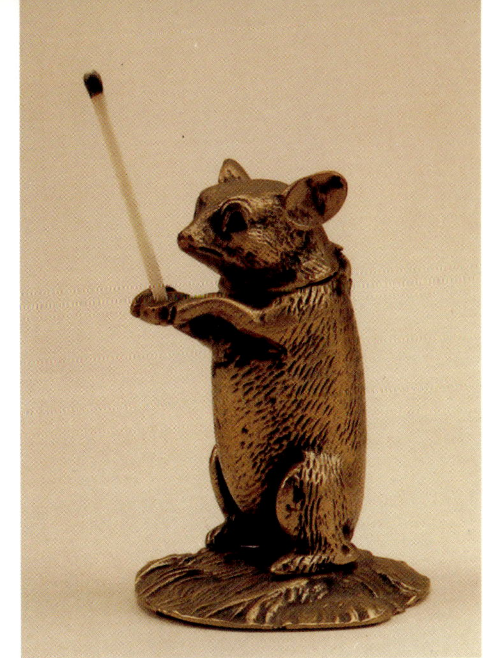

Fig. 454 Europe. Cast brass, glass. c.1890. H - 7cms.

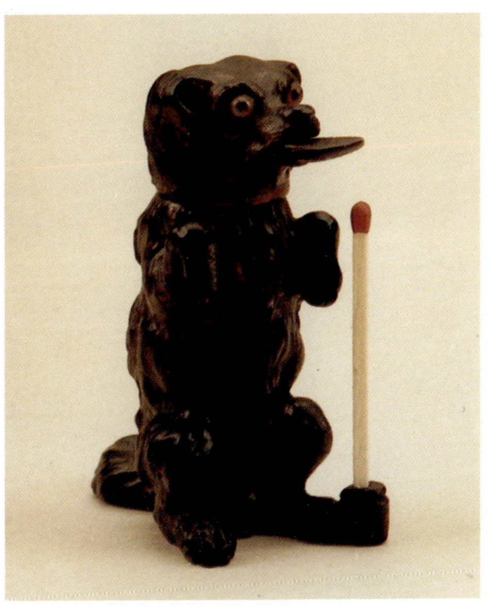

Fig. 455 Europe. Cast brass, glass. c.1890. H - 6.6cms.

Fig. 456 Europe. Cast brass, glass. c.1890. H - 7.1cms.

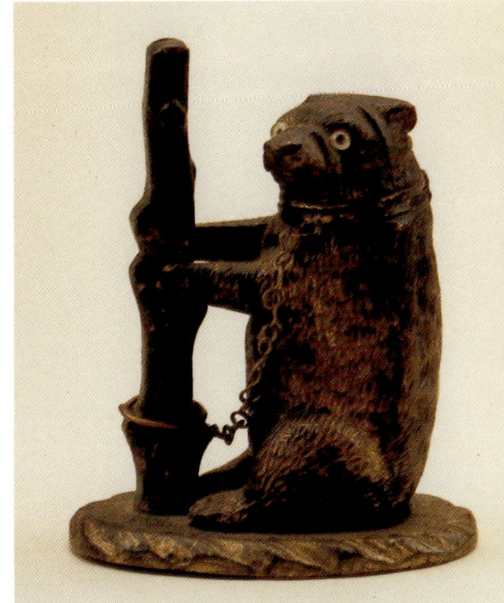

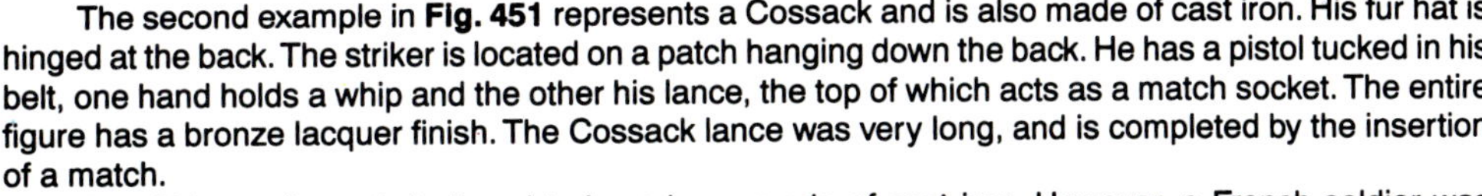

The second example in **Fig. 451** represents a Cossack and is also made of cast iron. His fur hat is hinged at the back. The striker is located on a patch hanging down the back. He has a pistol tucked in his belt, one hand holds a whip and the other his lance, the top of which acts as a match socket. The entire figure has a bronze lacquer finish. The Cossack lance was very long, and is completed by the insertion of a match.

The Chinese figure is believed to have been made of cast iron. However, a French soldier was probably made of white metal and has heen seen with and without a base. A Scottish soldier has also been recorded.

Another series is in the form of animals, all made in cast brass with glass eyes, and all with match sockets. None of them is marked. Their heads are hinged at the neck to give access to the matches. Fur or feathers are rough enough to serve as the match striker. They were made in Europe, but there is little to suggest that any were made by the same company. They probably date to c. 1890.

Of the examples in **Figs. 452 to 456**, all but the dancing bear are shown with the match *in situ* in the socket. The mouse is holding what is assumed to be a piece of cheese. The dog has a begging bowl in his mouth. The dancing bear is chained to a post, a common sight in Europe in the Victorian period; the top of the post serves as the match socket. This figure quite closely resemmbles the 'bear and ragged staff' emblem of the Earls of Warwick.

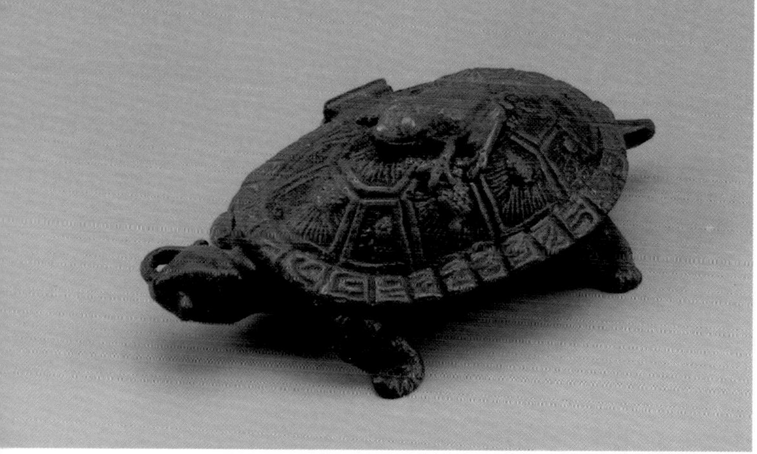

Fig. 457 Europe. White metal. c.1900 to 1920. L - 9.1cms.

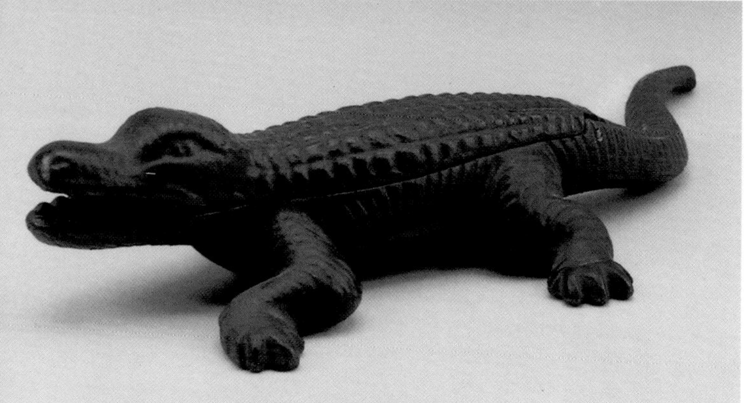

Fig. 458 United States. Cast iron. Made by L. Glow. c.1910. L - 22.1cms.

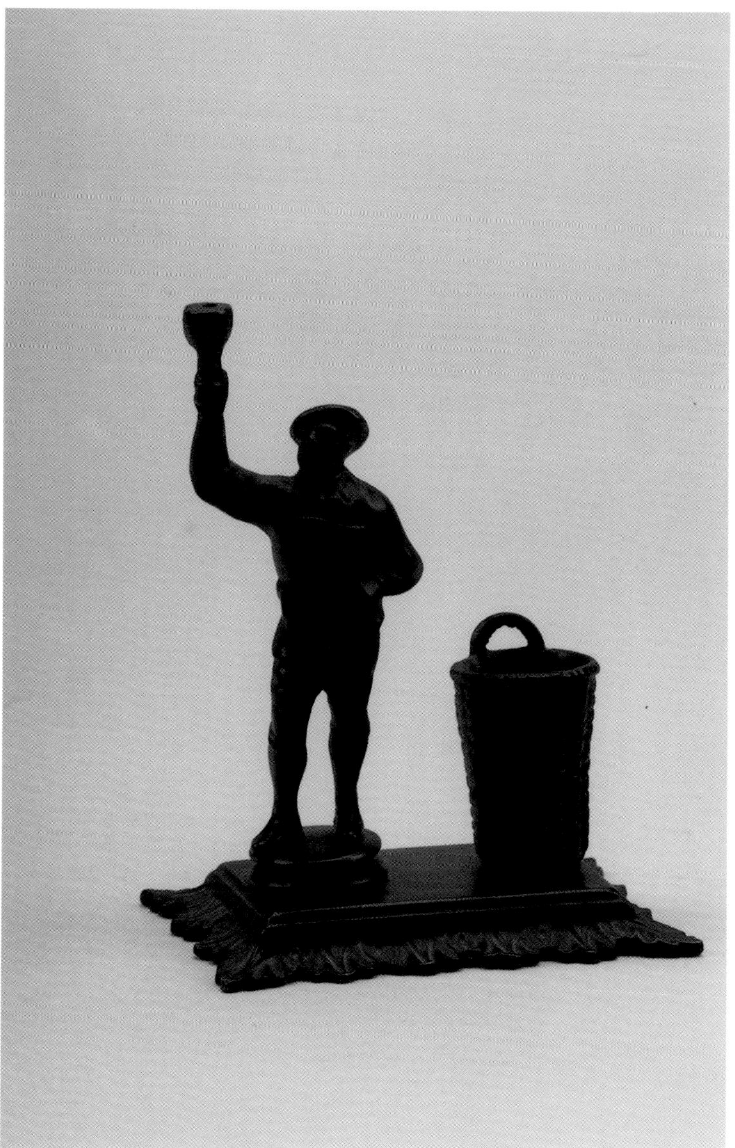

Fig. 459 Europe. Cast iron. c.1860 to 1870. H - 9.6cms.

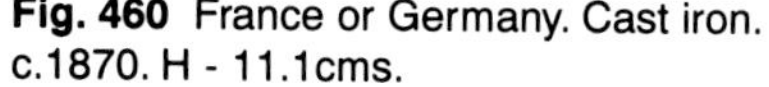

Fig. 460 France or Germany. Cast iron. c.1870. H - 11.1cms.

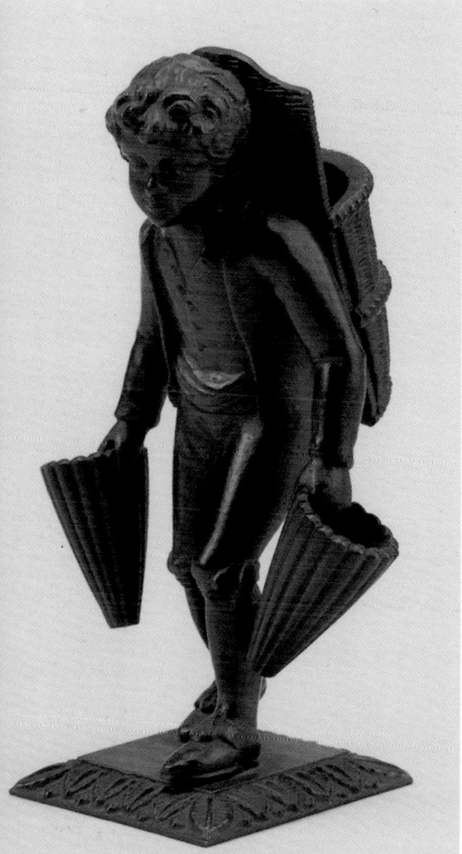

In white metal is a painted tortoise or turtle with a snake in its mouth and a frog on its back, shown in **Fig. 457**. The carapace is hinged to form the lid of the match compartment, with a grooved panel on the underside to form the striker. This was probably made in Europe between 1900 and 1920. Tortoises, frogs and flies were popular subjects, usually found in cast brass or iron.

The earliest recorded example of a fly was made by E.G.Zimmermann of Hanau, Germany around 1860, and was enamelled in bright colors. A frog was the subject of a United States Design Patent issued to Bradley & Hubbard of West Meriden, Connecticut in 1871. The Pearson-Page Co. Ltd. of Birmingham and London were making match holders in 1927 in the form of a tortoise for six shillings, a fly for five shillings and six pence, and a frog for four shillings and six pence; these were exported to North America. They have almost certainly been the subject of recent copies in the past few years: *caveat emptor!*

The cast-iron match holder in the form of an alligator shown in **Fig. 458** has the upper part of the body hinged at the tail for access to the matches. The inside of the lower jaw is roughened for friction. It was made as an advertising piece, and is marked underneath "Compliments of L.Glow. Brass Patterns....ferson." It is assumed that Glow's was the maker, and it was probably made c. 1910.

The figure in **Fig. 459** is one of a series of cast iron figures, probably all made by the same (unidentified) company in Europe between 1860 and 1870. The example represents a woodsman with an axe tucked into his belt adjacent to a bunch of keys. He holds aloft a torch, which also acts as a match socket, and beside him is an open-topped basket for the matches. Other figures in the series are mounted on identical or similar bases, and stand beside an identical basket. The most commonly found piece is in the form of a knight in armor with one fist raised to hold the match.

A very finely modelled figure in cast iron of a young man working at gathering grapes is shown in **Fig. 460**. The detail in the wrapped-weave basket on his back is exceptional, as is the face and hair. It too lacks any marks, but is probably French or German, from c. 1870.

Fig. **462** Europe. Cast brass, stone. c.1870s. H - 11.1cms.

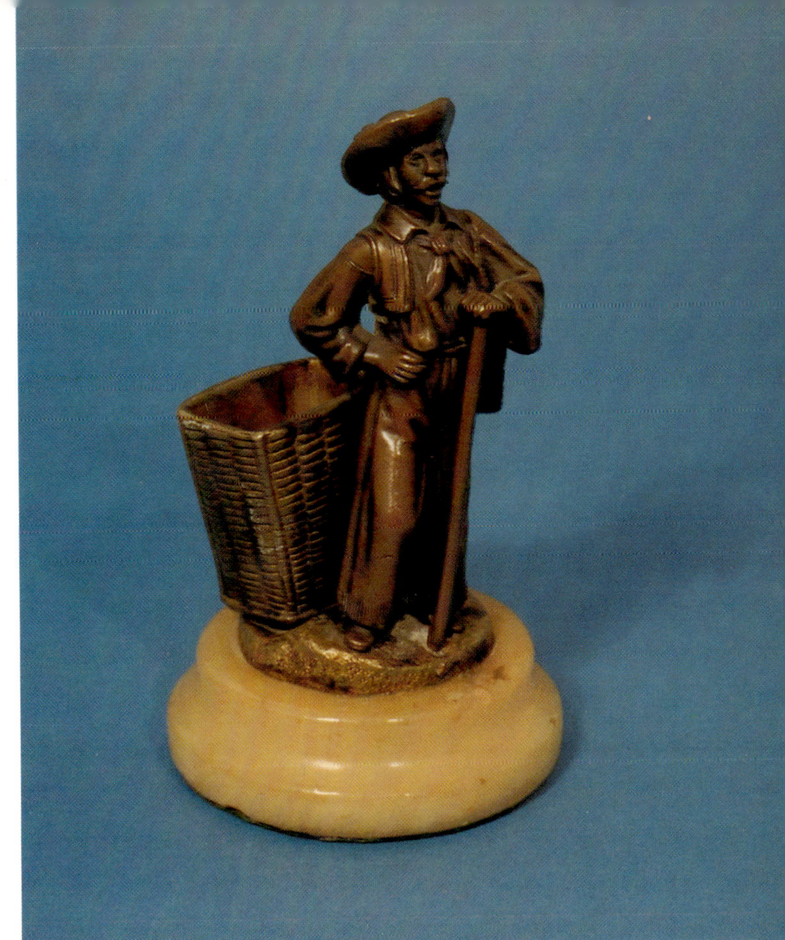

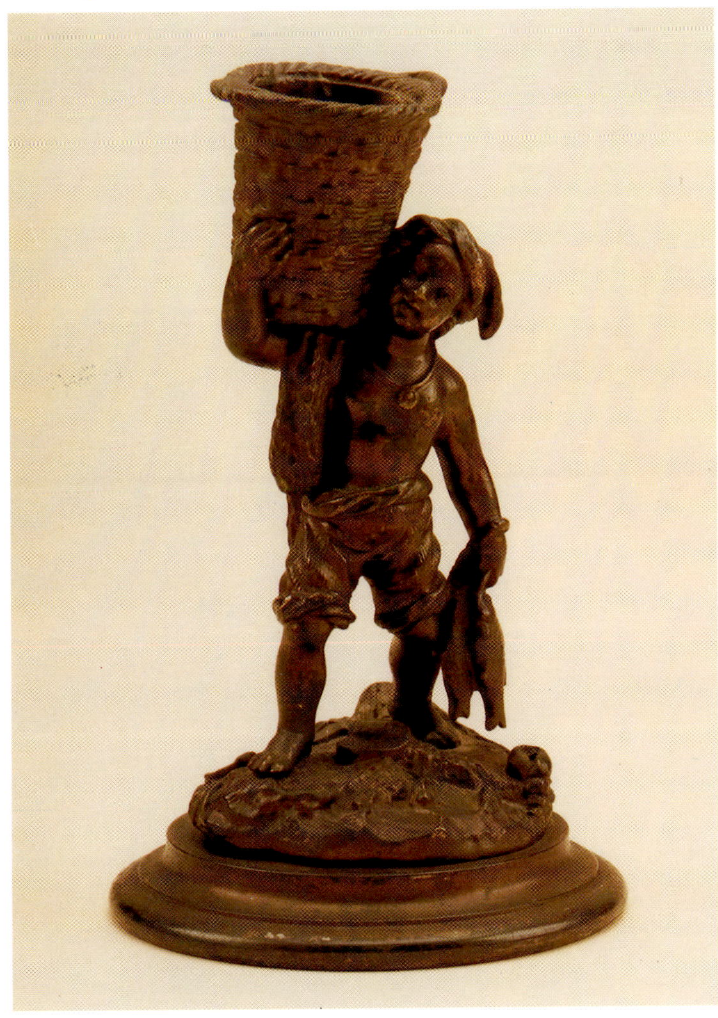

Fig. 461 Probably France. White metal. c.1880. H - 14.6cms.

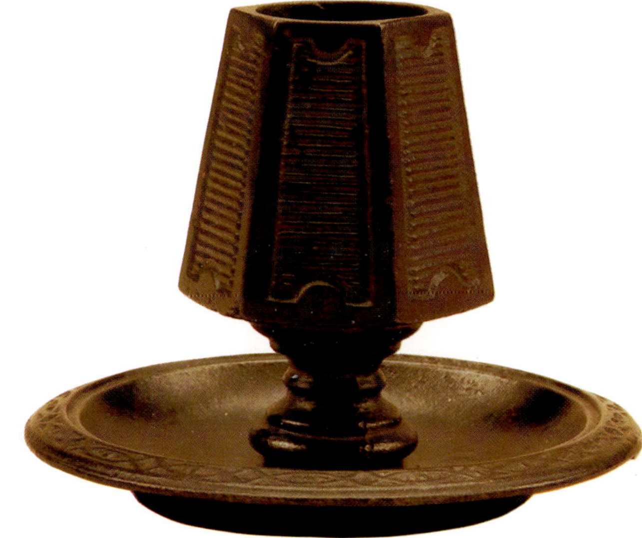

Fig. 463 Germany. Cast iron. Made by E. G. Zimmermann. c.1870. H - 8.8cms

Cast in white metal is a figure of a fisherman with his catch, shown in **Fig. 461**. He carries a net over one shoulder, upon which rests a wicker-weave open-topped basket to hold the matches. He is walking across a beach strewn with shellfish, one of which has a hole for a match socket. The figure was originally gilded; a second piece has been seen with its original gilding and mounted on a black marble base. It is probably French, c. 1880.

The finely modelled figure in **Fig. 462** is made of cast brass with a bronze finish. The open-topped basket behind the figure has shoulder straps, but the character has not been identified as to his origins or profession. He is mounted on a yellow stone base, and is European, probably c. 1880. Somewhat similar figures were the subject of Ornamental Registered Designs in Britain in the mid-1870s.

From E.G.Zimmermann is an open-topped match holder and ash tray in cast iron, shown in **Fig. 463**. It is probably c. 1870, an early example of a holder that was likely made for commercial use in hotels, bars, etc., rather than for domestic use. The hexagonal holder sides all have a striking surface, and the tray has a simple decorative edge. It does not match the high quality of the company's earlier figures.

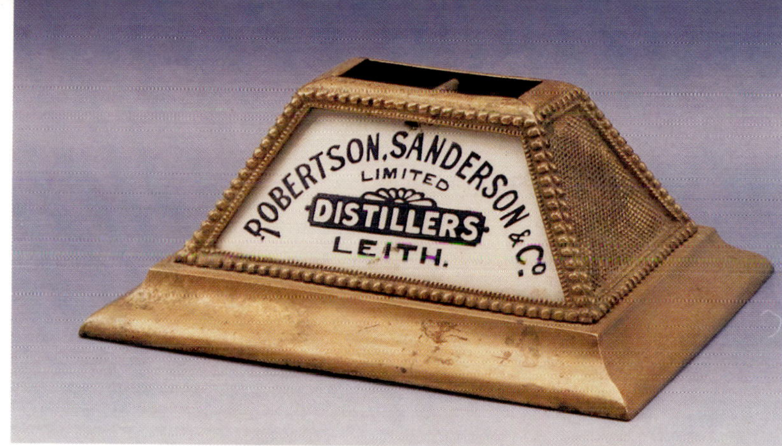

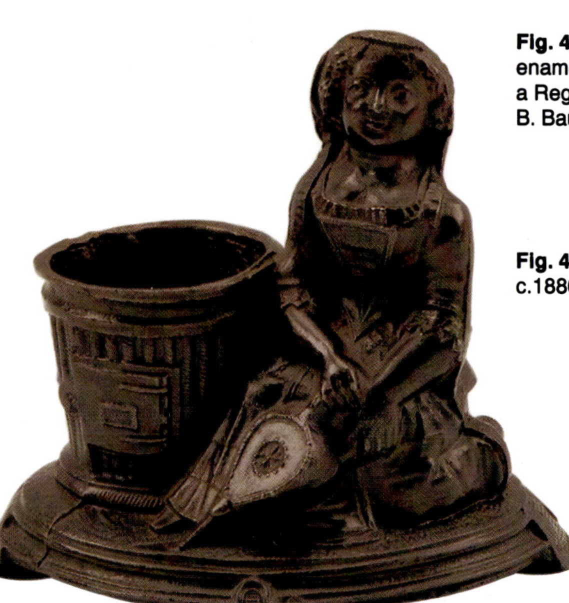

Fig. 464 Britain. Cast brass, steel, enamel. Made by Jenkinson & Co.Ltd. to a Registered Design of 1892 by Rupert B. Baugh. L -15.8cms.

Fig. 466 Germany? White metal. c.1880. H - 9cms.

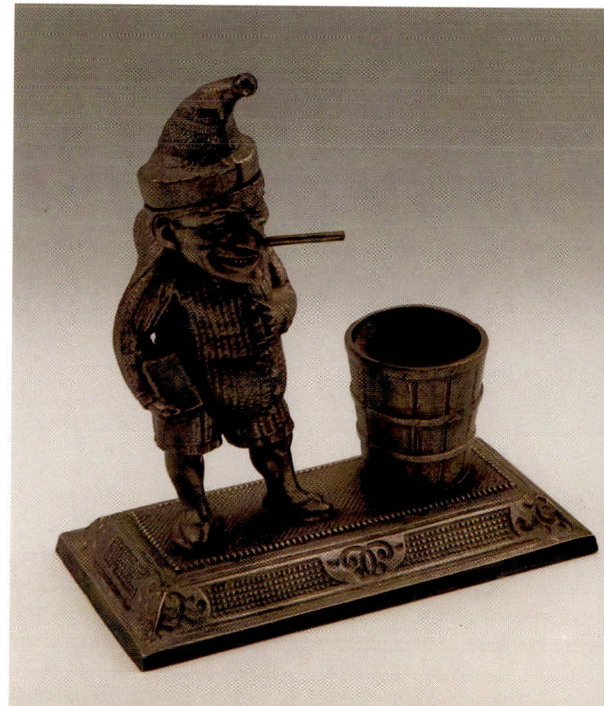

Fig. 467 Probably France. White metal. c.1880s. H - 15.5cms.

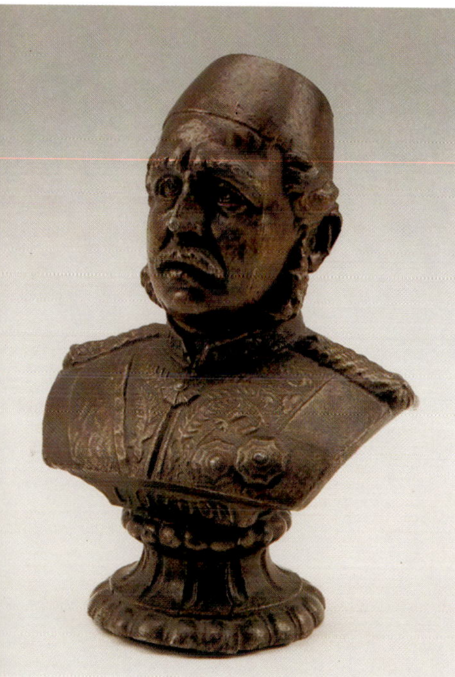

Fig. 465 Britain. White metal. Made by E. Kealing Teale & Co. c.1885. H - 13.4cms.

The open top of the match holder shown in **Fig. 464** is divided into two compartments, probably to keep the matches upright. It is made of cast brass, with steel enamelled plates on both sides bearing advertising. The sloped ends are roughened for friction. On the underside of the base is the raised wording "JENKINSON & CO. LTD. MAKERS. BARTHOLOMEW ROW, BIRMINGHAM" and a Registered Design number for 1892, issued to Rupert Benjamin Baugh of Mosley, near Birmingham. It was intended for distribution to public houses, clubs and restaurants which sold the advertisers' products, to stand on their bar counters and, possibly, table tops.

The cast white metal holder in **Fig. 465** is a bust of General Gordon, who died a hero at the hands of the forces of the Mahdi after holding them at bay for some weeks in Khartoum, in the Sudan, in January 1885. The top of Gordon's fez is open to serve as the match holder, and the back of his shoulders are roughened for friction. It was probably made in 1885 to commemorate Gordon's death. The bust is unmarked, but a similar piece in the form of a bust of "Buffalo Bill" Cody was the subject of a Registered Design in 1887, the year that he toured Europe with his famed "Wild West Show." It was issued to E. Kealing Teale & Co. of London, Art Metal Workers. It seems reasonable to hypothesize that Teale's had produced Gordon's bust previously.

Also in cast white metal, in **Fig. 466**, is a young lady kneeling beside an oven, which may originally have had a loose-fitting lid. She is holding a pair of bellows. The group is mounted on an oval base, marked underneath "Grd.79." This may be the maker's model number, or it may indicate a registered design number of German origin. It is probably c. 1880.

The well-modelled figure of Mr.Punch in **Fig. 467** shows him standing beside a pail-shaped match holder on a rectangular base, the top of which is roughened for friction. Mr. Punch is holding what is probably a box of matches in one hand and he is smoking a cigar. The cigar is hollow and intended to hold a wick that passed through the cigar into the body. The body is hollow and the hat is hinged at the back to permit the body to be filled with some form of inflammable fluid to soak the wick. The hat is by no means airtight. This type of white metal figure was commonly found in France, where they were used as a form of lighter for customers of tobacconists and in some public places. They probably replaced figures with gas burners. Presumably made in France, they were also used in Britain (probably imported from France) around the 1880s.

The United States was late in entering the field of manufacturing match holders of any type, but once its companies had begun they too showed considerable imagination and ingenuity. However, they had a tendency to lay emphasis on reducing production costs, and a high percentage of the invention patents were directed towards permitting the extraction of only one match at a time, almost to the point of being an obsession.

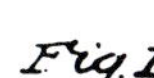

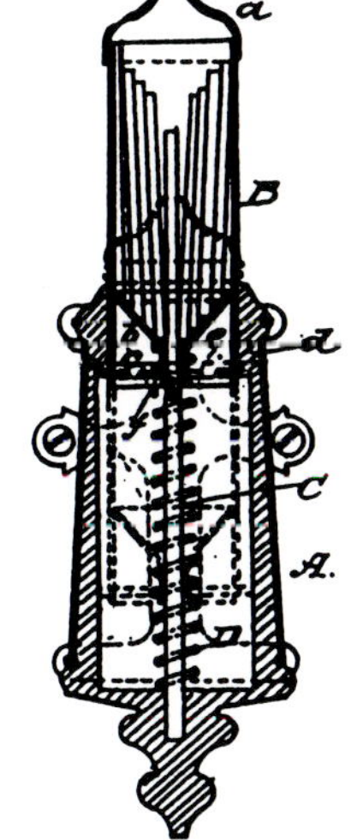

a: push fit lid with knurled sides.

B: brass cylinder to hold matches.

b: sloped sides of inside of B, to guide match onto top of C.

C: rod with concave top to receive the head of the match.

A: main body of box, made of cast iron.

Fig. 469 United States Invention Patent drawing of 1864 by George Snow.

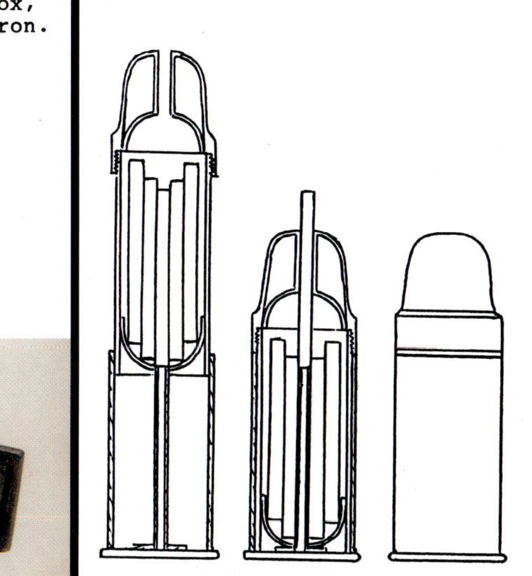

Fig. 470 Britain. Drawings from a Useful Design of 1879 by Edwin Day.

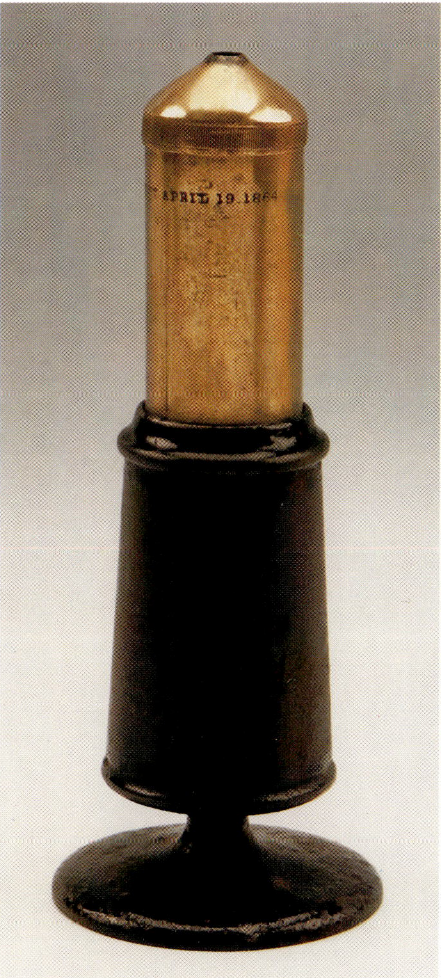

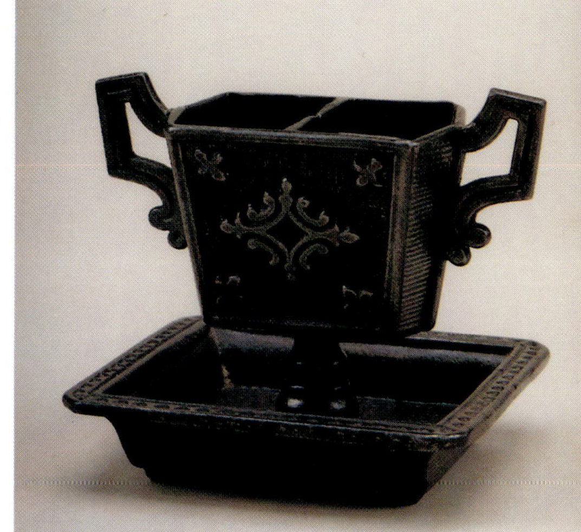

Fig. 471 United States. Cast iron. Made by, and to, an Invention Patent of 1871, by Albert D. Judd. H - 8.8cms.

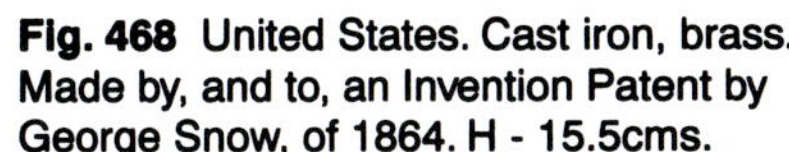

Fig. 468 United States. Cast iron, brass. Made by, and to, an Invention Patent by George Snow, of 1864. H - 15.5cms.

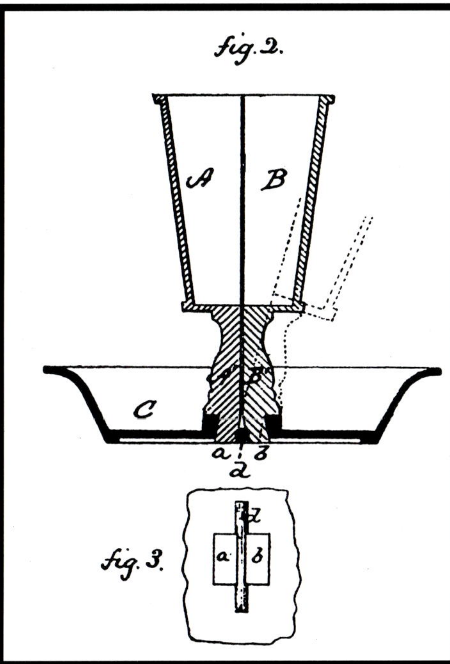

Fig. 472 United States Invention Patent of 1871 by Albert D. Judd.

One of the early U.S.Invention Patents was issued to George Snow of New Haven, Connecticut in 1864; the end product is shown in **Fig. 468**. In his own words, it could be made at "reasonable cost" and "the box may be filled with matches and only one removed from it at once." His patent drawings show a box to be fixed to a wall, as shown in **Fig. 469**, but in his specifications he stated "or it may be secured to a proper base when designed for standing alone and to be removed from place to place as required for use." The main body is made of cast iron and the match receptacle of brass. The theory was that the brass receptacle was pushed down into the body; a match was picked up on the tip of a rod; and this carried it out through the hole in the top of the receptacle, to be removed and ignited. The author's efforts at replicating this practice found it not very effective, except when the receptacle is full. The box is marked with Snow's name and the patent date, and it is assumed that Snow made them.

Fifteen years later exactly the same idea was the subject of a Useful Registered Design in Britain. It was registered by a Birmingham artist, Edwin Day, and he called it ~The Automatic Case for Matches, Needles, &c." The design is shown in **Fig. 470**. No examples of this device have been recorded.

Albert D. Judd of New Haven, Connecticut was a manufacturer of hardware for builders and upholsterers, for ornamental and other uses; his catalogue of 1872 includes nine match holders made of cast iron, all subjects of Invention and Design Patents issued to him. The example in **Fig. 471** was made in two sizes, and in different designs, according to an Invention Patent of 1871, two drawings of which are shown in **Fig. 472**.

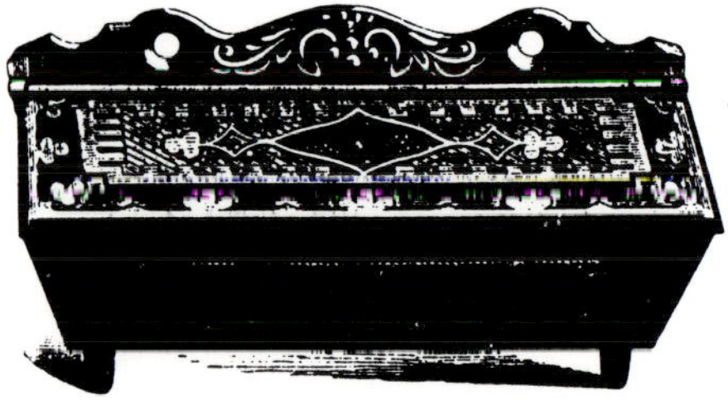

Fig. 473 Illustration from the Judd Mfg.Co., catalogue of 1872 of cast iron match holder made to an Invention Patent of 1872.

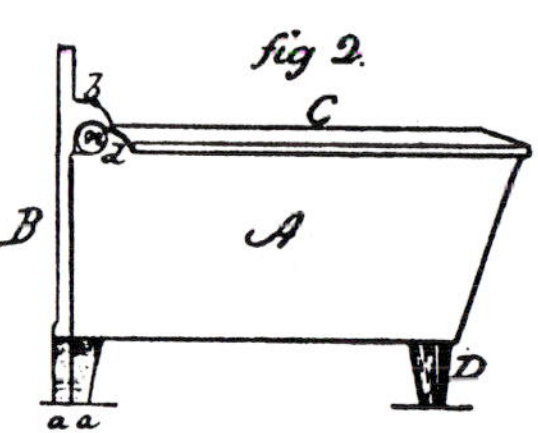

Fig. 474 Drawing from the Invention Patent of 1872 relating to Figs.473 and 475.

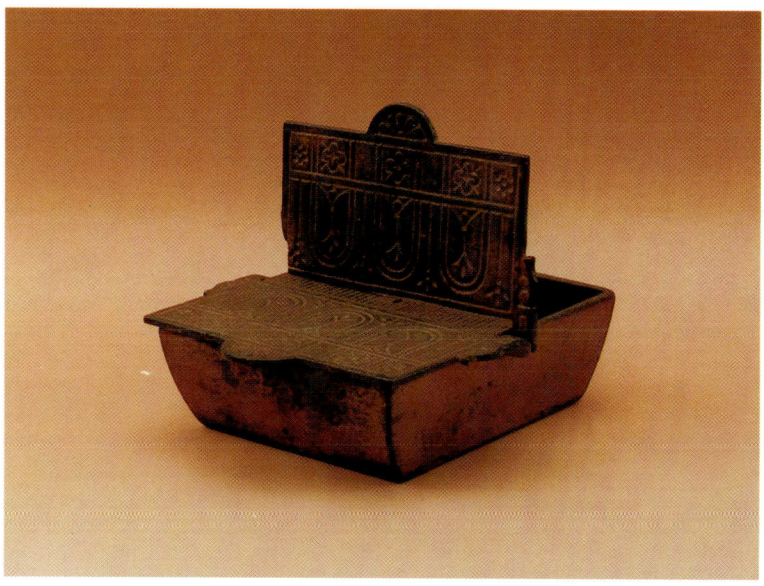

Fig. 475 United States. Cast iron. Double version made to the Invention Patent of 1872 in Fig. 474, by Albert D. Judd. c.1875. L - 12.7cms.

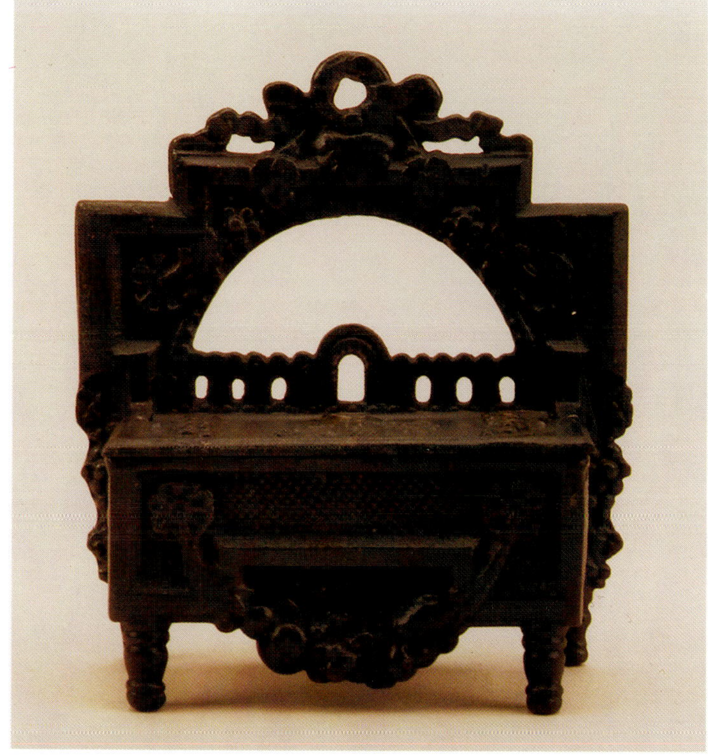

Fig. 476 United States. Cast iron. Made by, and to, a Design Patent of 1871 by Albert D. Judd. H - 10.9cms.

The box body was made in two halves, with the bottom of each half shaped to form part of a dovetail whose inside edges were angled. The two body halves were brought together at the bottom, leaving the tops separated. The dovetail was then pushed into the hole in the base and the tops were pulled together. This left a wedge-shaped gap in the center of the dovetail through which a pin was pushed; the pin locked the two halves in place.

Judd made these holders in three different finishes: the example as shown in maroon, plain at $4.00 per dozen; maroon and "gold bronze" at $4.50 per dozen; and in a bronze finish at $5.00. A second and more ornate version was offered, in cast brass at $9.50 per dozen, and in bronze and silver-plated versions at $10.00 per dozen.

In 1872 Judd was issued with an Invention Patent for a method of hinging the lid of a cast-iron box which eliminated the need for any tool work, other than providing a rivet to hold all the parts together in a single operation. **Fig. 473** shows a copy of his product, as shown in his catalogue, and **Fig. 474** one of the drawings from his patent. The version illustrated came in medium and large sizes and six different finishes, selling from $1.75 to $3.25 per dozen.

A twin-lidded match holder shown in **Fig. 475** has been found bearing the same patent date. But, after an exhaustive search for the patent, it was realised that the construction meets Judd's previous patent. It is assumed that, because the example does not appear in his 1872 catalogue, it was made after that date.

A product based on Judd's only known Design Patent, issued in 1871, is shown in **Fig. 476**. This example is provided with a lid, but he made them in twelve different versions, with or without lids, in brass or cast iron, and in six finishes. They cost from $4.00 to $10.50 per dozen, with the most expensive being a silver-plated version with a lid. Although shown here as a stand-alone, it could also be used as a wall-hanging match holder.

Fig. 478 United States. Brass. c.1880s. L - 14.1cms.

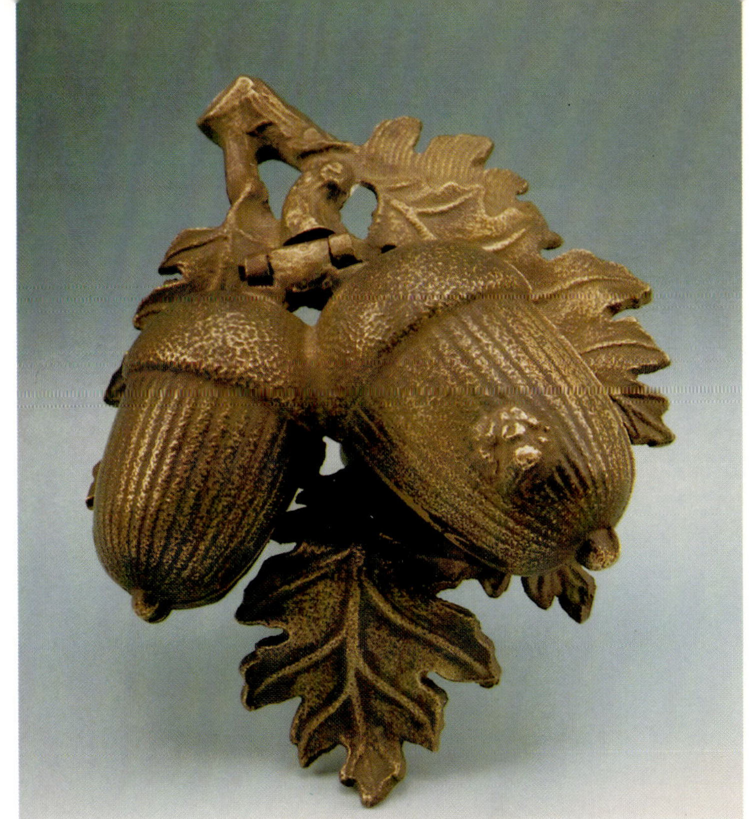

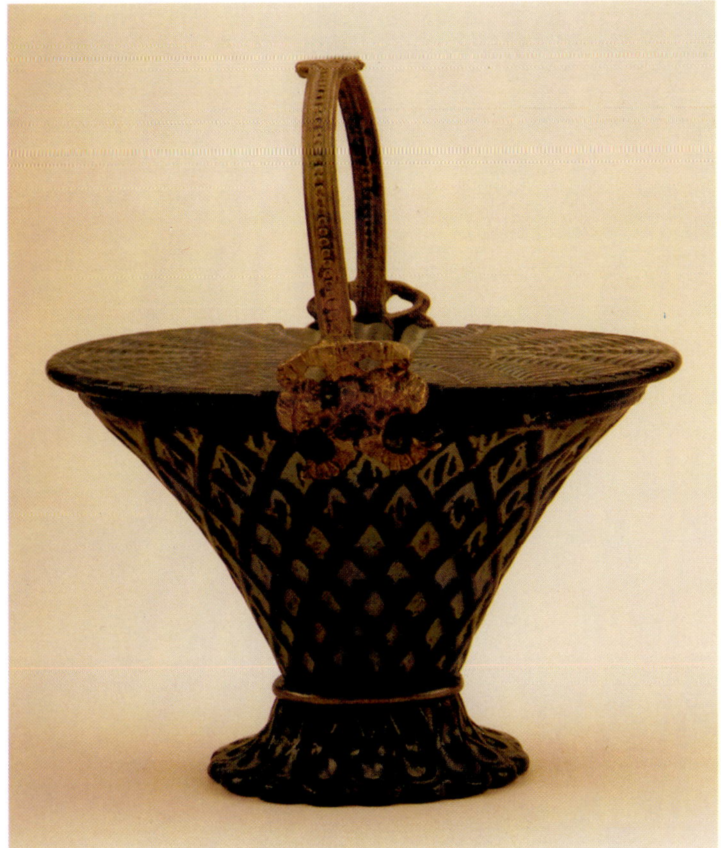

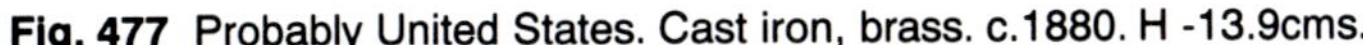

Fig. 477 Probably United States. Cast iron, brass. c.1880. H -13.9cms.

A cast-iron match holder in the form of a basket with a brass handle is shown in **Fig. 477**. The two lids open, and the striker is located between the lids. It is unmarked, but is believed to have been made in the United States, c. 1880.

In the form of two large acorns resting on oak leaves is a double holder made of cast brass, shown in **Fig. 478**. One of the oak leaves is grooved for friction. It is unmarked, but is believed to be from the United States, possibly made by Sargent & Co. of New Haven, Connecticut. This company made at least two wall-hanging match holders in the form of acorns and oak leaves; these were shown in its catalogue of 1884, which is probably about the time that the example was made.

An unusual form of match holder and cigar cutter is shown in **Fig. 479**. It represents a coffee mill, and is made of plated brass with a wooden base. The drawer at the front holds the matches, and there is a corresponding drawer at the back to catch the cigar clippings. The blade of the cigar cutter is located inside the box at the back, and the cigar is inserted through a hole above the drawer; the blade is activated by depressing the handle at the top. The striker is located along one side of the wooden base. The example has no maker's mark or other identifying mark, but a paper label glued to the underside of the base shows that the device came from Nathan Michaels, a tobacconist in Montreal, Quebec, who operated out of three locations. Michaels is listed in the City Directory in those three locations only between 1890 and 1892, although he owned one or two of them before and after those dates. He made and sold his own brands of cigars, and the device no doubt stood on the counter of one of his stores for the use of his customers.

The small cylindrical match holder in **Fig. 480** is of a suitable size to fit in the pocket, yet it has a number of projections that would make it hard on a pocket lining, and the subsequent constant rubbing would erode the fine details. It has therefore been included in this stand-alone section. It is made of bronze, cast by the *cire perdue*, or "lost wax," method. The body sides were probably modelled in wax in the flat, then wrapped around an uneven cylindrical core, and the base added, before it was cast. It depicts a harbour scene with ships and some imposing buildings in the background, and people (fishermen?) and rocks in the foreground. Considerable detail is discernible in the people, none of whom are more than 13 mm high. It is assumed that the scene shows actual buildings in a real location, although it has not been possible to identify either. The lid is hinged where the body join occurs, and bears a finely modelled head of a lion surrounded by twelve raised hemispheres, with a single ball catch at the front edge. It is speculated that it is of Dutch origin, c. 1880.

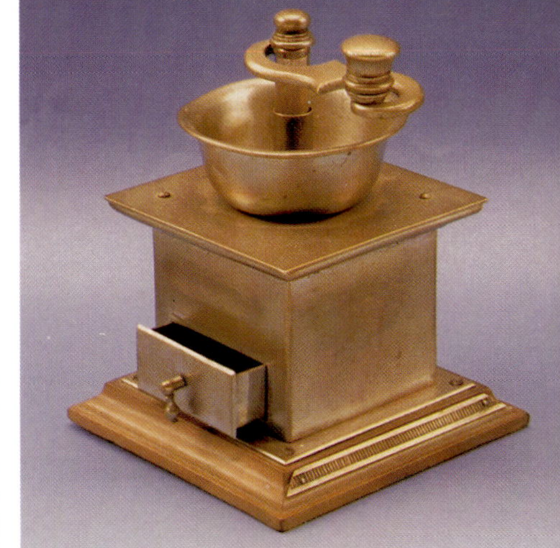

Fig. 479 United States. Plated brass, wood. c.1890 to 1892. H -11.6cms.

Fig. 480 Holland? Cast bronze. c.1880. H - 6.7cms.

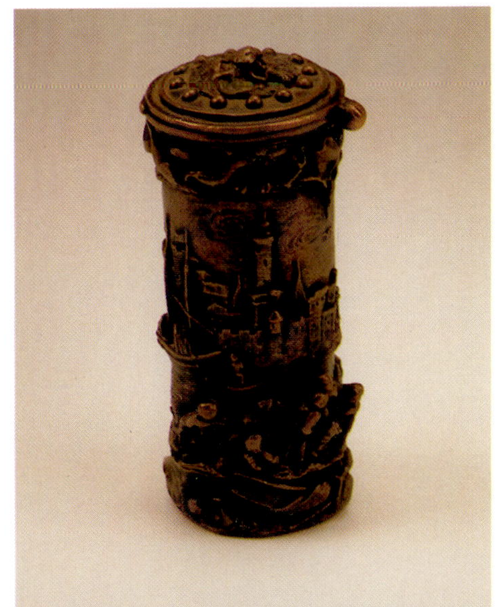

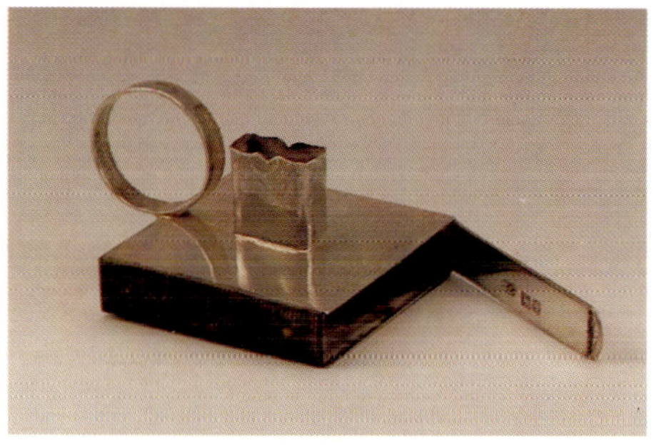

Fig. 481 Britain. Silver, steel. London. Marked "SC". 1902. L -5.5cms.

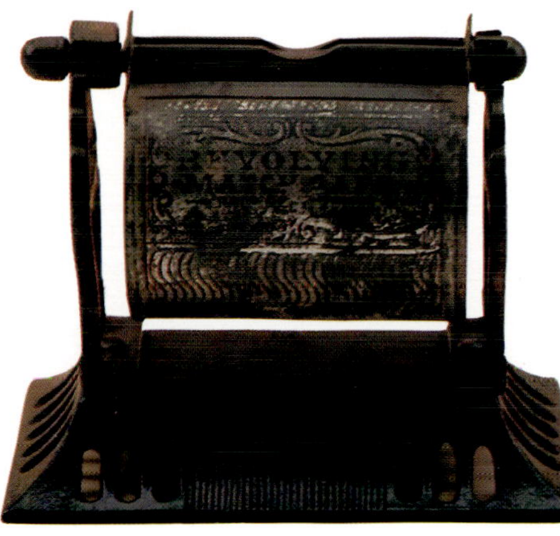

Fig. 485 United States. Cast iron, tin plate. Made to an Invention Patent of 1879 by Adam F. Able. H - 9.8cms.

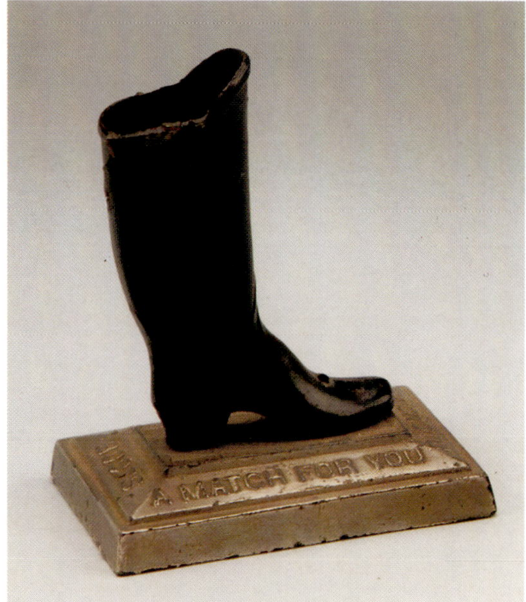

Fig. 486 United States. Cast iron, tin plate, wood. 1890s. H -9.9cms.

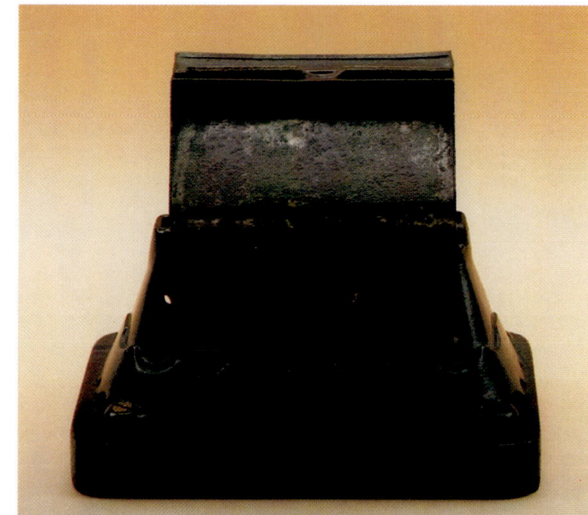

Fig. 482 United States. White metal. c.1890s. H - 8.2cms.

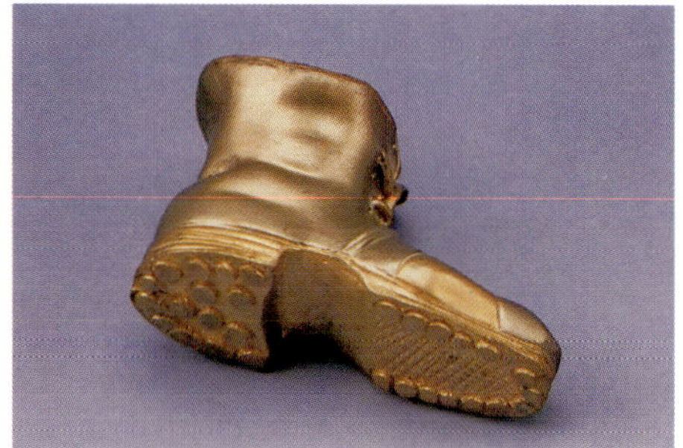

Fig. 483 Probably United States. Cast brass. c.1910. L - 6.3cms.

Fig. 484 Probably Britain. Cast brass. c.1930s. L - 7.8cms.

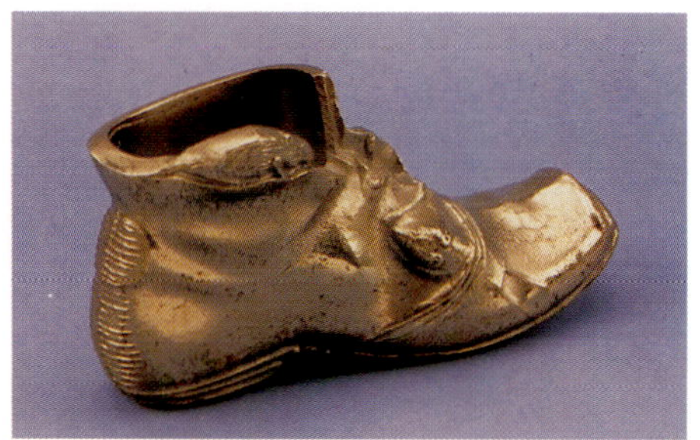

In **Fig. 481** is a silver box with a finger ring and rectangular socket for a stick of sealing wax; it was obviously intended to stand on a desk. One side of the box is hinged for access to the matches and has a steel strip roughened for friction. It is hallmarked for London, 1902, with an unidentified maker's mark of "SC."

The boot mounted on a rectangular base in **Fig. 482** is made of white metal, the boot painted black. On the upper part of the boot is the raised lettering "WOONSOCKET RUBBER CO.," and around the base "A MATCH FOR YOU BUT NONE FOR WOONSOCKET BOOTS." The hollow underside of the base is corrugated for friction. It was probably made in the 1890s. The Woonsocket Rubber Co. of Rhode Island was incorporated in 1867, and acquired by the new corporation of the U.S. Rubber Company in 1893, but continued to operate under its original name until about 1932. At one time it claimed to be the largest rubber company in the world, with an excellent reputation for the quality of its rubber boots and shoes.

Old shoes with open tops were a popular subject. The two following examples are made of cast brass. In **Fig. 483** the battered boot has been painted silver, leaving the sole and patch on the side unpainted. The striker is located on the sole. It is probably c.l910, but its origins are unknown. The example in **Fig. 484** is much more recent, probably from the 1930s. It is being chewed on by two mice. On one side is an enamelled maple leaf with a "ribbon" below with "Calgary" on it, it must have been a souvenir of that Alberta city. The striker is located down the back of the heel. Although unmarked, these have been seen marked "Made in England."

The passion of United States inventors to design match holders that would permit the extraction of only one match at a time was apparently seldom fruitful, in terms of the number of end products that reached the mass production stage. But some were made and are shown here.

Adam F. Able of New Orleans, Louisiana, was successful in 1879, and an example of his invention is shown in **Fig. 485**. The tin plate cylinder that holds the matches is suspended from a bar, around which the cylinder revolves, depositing a single match in a slot in the top of the bar in the process. The bar is supported on a cast-iron stand which is roughened for friction. The cylinder is decorated and bears the words "REVOLVING MATCH SAFE" and the patent date, but no maker's name. It is possible that this piece was made in New Orleans, therefore making it one of the few match holders made outside of New England at that time.

The example shown in **Fig. 486** is in poor condition and no marks are to be found. It has a tin plate match compartment that slides up and down on a wooden panel, all set inside a cast-iron base mounted on a wooden base. When the match compartment is raised, a match falls into a slot in the top of the wooden panel, to be ejected when the compartment is lowered.

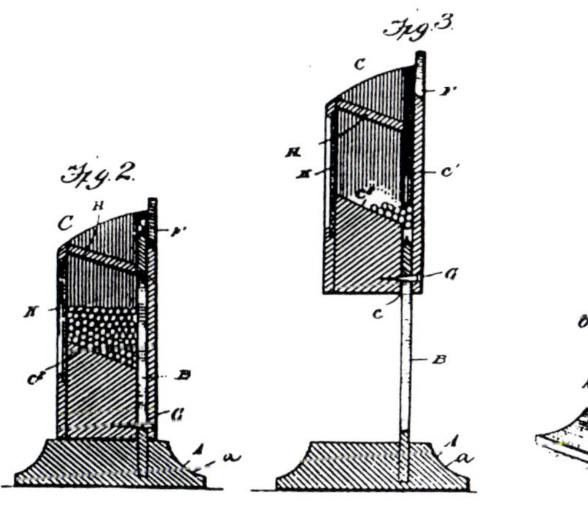

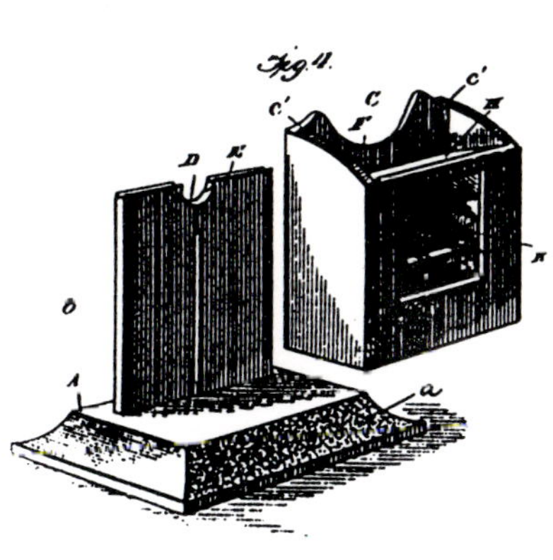

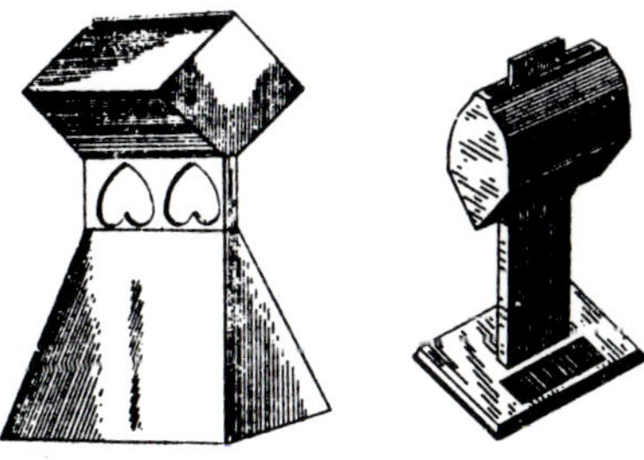

Fig. 488 Design Patents of 1897, showing same type of holder as in Fig. 486.

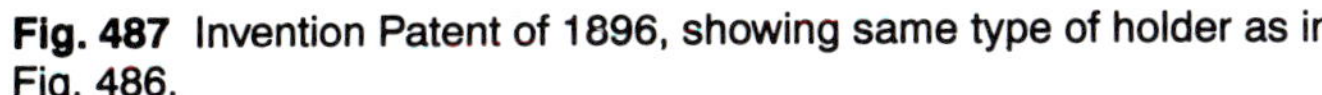

Fig. 487 Invention Patent of 1896, showing same type of holder as in Fig. 486.

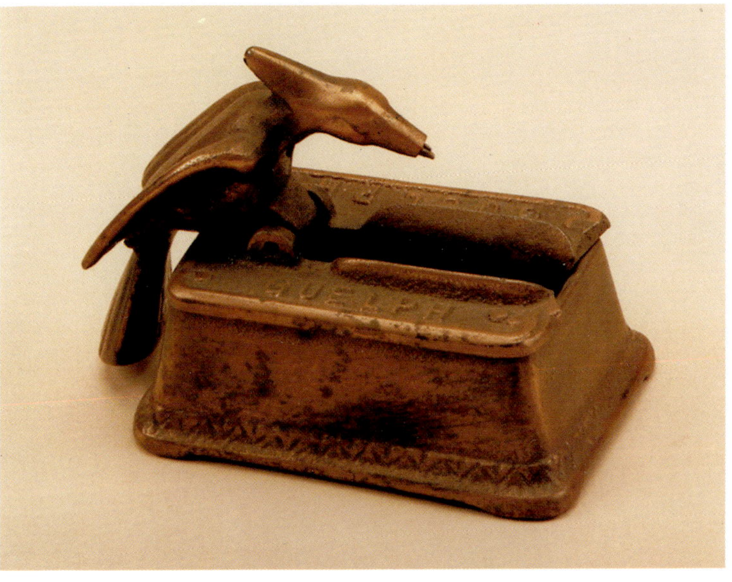

Fig. 490 United States. Cast iron. Date unknown. Possibly a modern copy. L - 11.3cms.

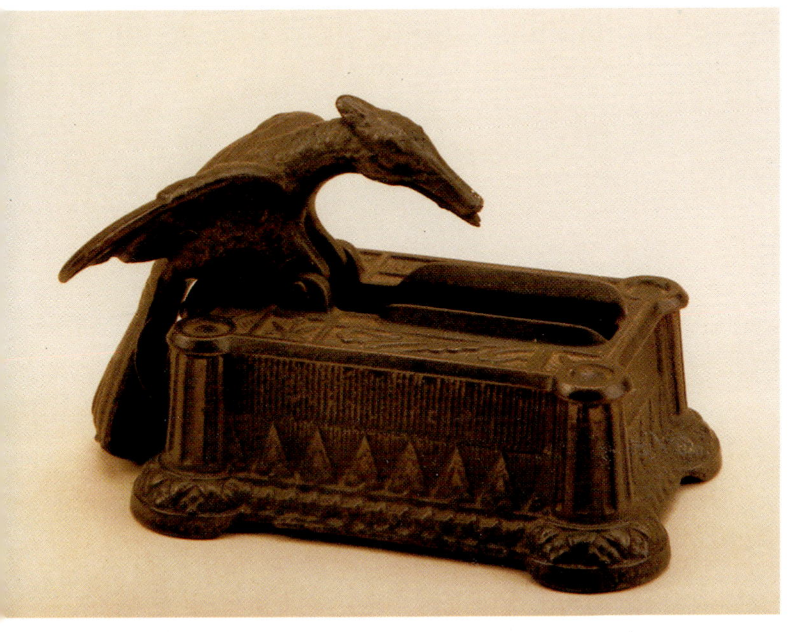

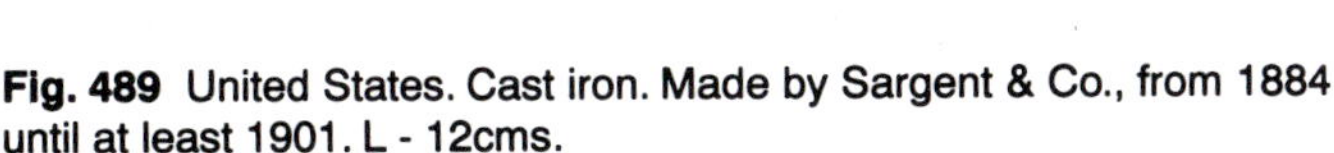

Fig. 489 United States. Cast iron. Made by Sargent & Co., from 1884 until at least 1901. L - 12cms.

This type of match holder was the subject of one Invention Patent in 1896, the drawings shown in **Fig. 487**, and two Design Patents in 1897, shown in **Fig. 488**. That to the left in Fig. 488 most closely resembles the actual example. These patents suggest that the example dates to c. 1897.

The cast iron example in **Fig. 489** incorporates the form of a bird, pivoted so that when its head is thrust downwards the pair of points in the beak spear a match, in the main body of the box, and withdraw the match when the bird returns to its upright position. This example was made by Sargent & Co. of New Haven, Connecticut, and was shown in its 1884 catalogue as "No.60, Bronzed Match Safes, per dozen, $6.00" and in the 1901 catalogue as "No.60, Tuscan Bronzed Match Safes, Eagle Pattern, per dozen, $4.00." "Tuscan" was one of several trade names that the company used.

A second example of the same concept is shown in **Fig. 490**. Also made of cast iron, it has a copper finish; the detailing of the bird and box sides are poorly produced. It has raised letters on both top sides saying "GUELPH." This type of box has been reproduced, and it is possible that this example is a modern reproduction. This form was also found in Europe, and may have been made in Britain. Often it had lugs at the base to screw the device to a bar counter. In Germany a pivoted monkey was used, positioned over a trough mounted on four legs; this is known to have been exported to Canada in the late 1890s.

In the United States, Charles Kitschelt, as assignor to the New York company Nicholas Muller's Sons & Co., was issued with a Design Patent based on the bird concept; the box body, however, was round. This is shown in **Fig. 491**. It is assumed that these were manufactured by Muller's, but no examples have yet been seen. In 1882 George Franke of Baltimore, Maryland was issued with an Invention Patent for an almost identical box; one of the drawings is shown in **Fig. 492**. At the end of his written specifications he states: "I am aware that the box and a pivoted figure for picking up objects placed in a box is old."

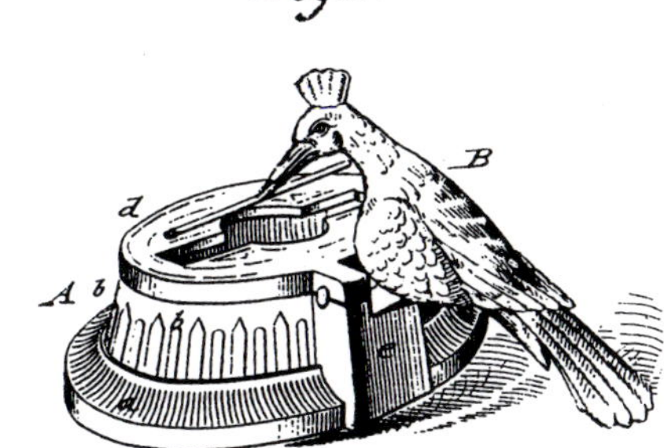

Fig. 491 Design Patent of 1880 by Charles Kitschelt.

Fig. 492 Invention Patent of 1882 b George Franke.

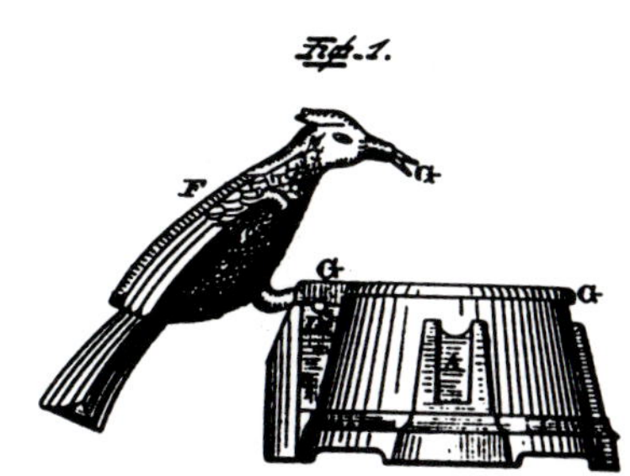

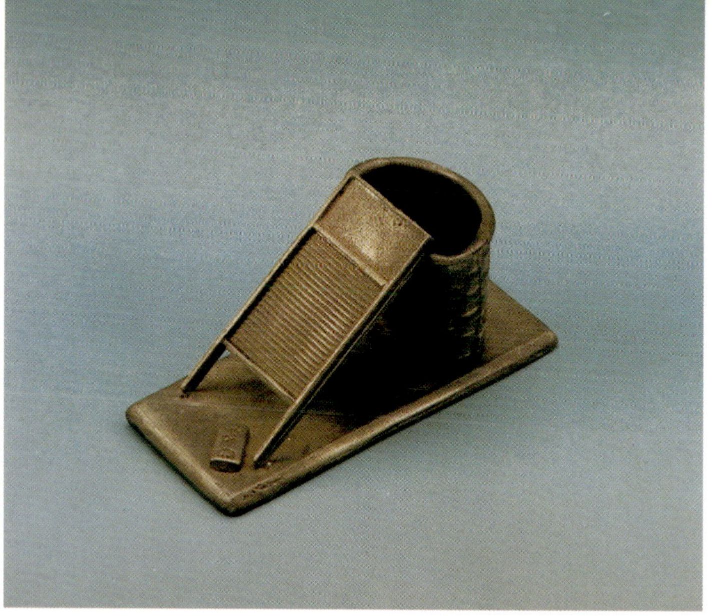

Fig. 493 United States. White metal. Made for Proctor & Gamble. c.1910. L - 7.1cms.

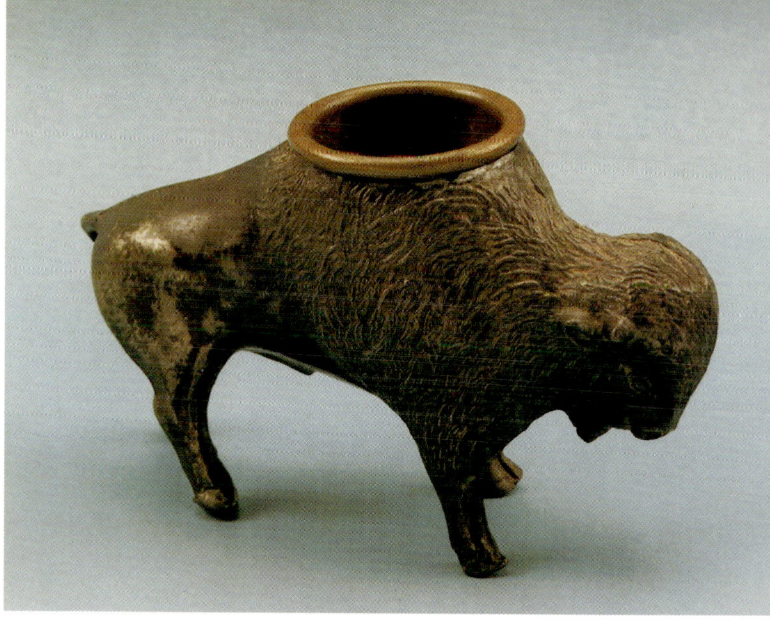

Fig. 495 United States. White metal, brass. c.1930s. L - 9.5cms.

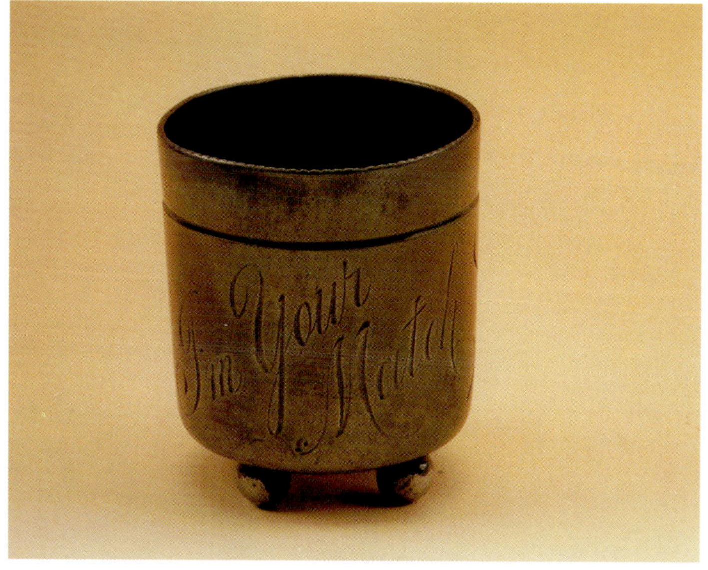

Fig. 494 Canada. Silver plated. Made by the Crown Silver Plate Co.. Between 1909 and 1922. H - 5.3cms.

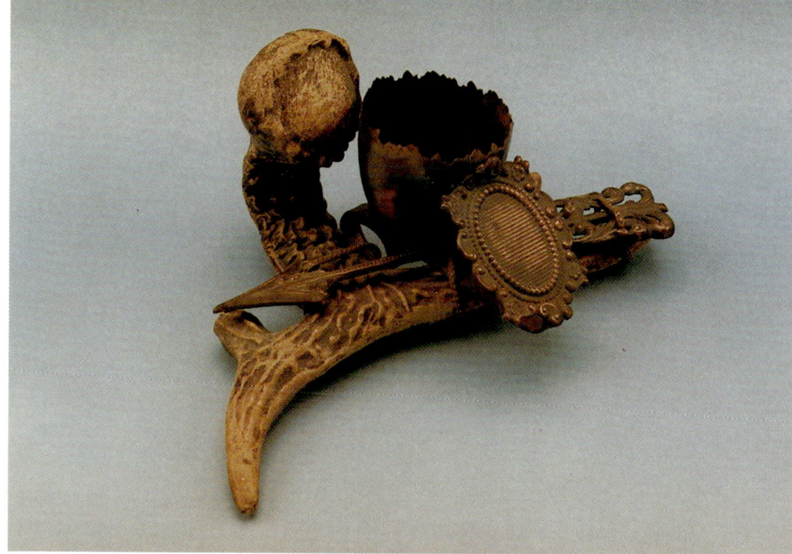

Fig. 496 Possibly United States. Copper, antler. c.1930. L -14.6cms.

The same idea was the subject of a United States Design Patent of 1948 intended for use as a toothpick holder, in the form of a woodpecker seated on a log. This was produced and is quite commonly found.

Made of white metal and shown in **Fig. 493** is an open-topped match holder in the form of a washboard leaning against a wicker-weave basket, with a bar of soap marked "P & G" near the base of one leg of the washboard. This was probably made about 1910 as a promotional gift for users of Proctor & Gamble's soap. It has an indistinct maker's mark on the underside of the base, which may be "DA Co.," and a pattern number "79."

A simple silver-plated cylindrical match holder, lacking a striker, in **Fig. 494**, is inscribed "I'm Your Match." It is mounted upon four ball legs, and marked on the underside "Crown S.P. Co. Triple" and with the pattern number "139." The Crown Silver Plate Co. was located in Toronto, Ontario, and is known to have been in business from 1909 until about 1922.

In the form of a male buffalo made of white metal, with a cylindrical brass well set in the back to hold matches, is an example shown in **Fig. 495**. There were a number of similar animal figures, including the head of a bulldog with brass wells to hold the matches; all were probably produced in the United States by the same unidentified company, and probably date from the 1930s. The strikers were formed by the hair of the animals.

The example shown in **Fig. 496** uses the antler of a deer as a stand to support a copper superstructure of an egg with its top removed (as the match holder), mounted upon an elaborate arrow and bound by three narrow copper strips to the antler. The striker is formed by a frame enclosing an oval center piece. This was probably made by a United States company, c. 1930.

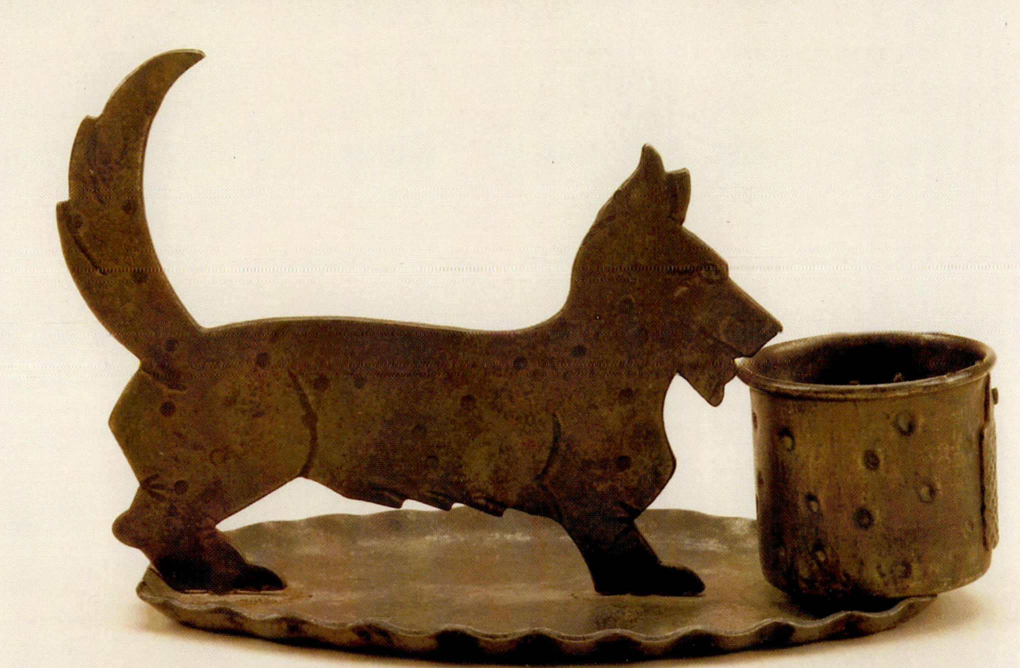

Fig. 497 Probably Germany. Steel. c.1930s. L - 16.2cms.

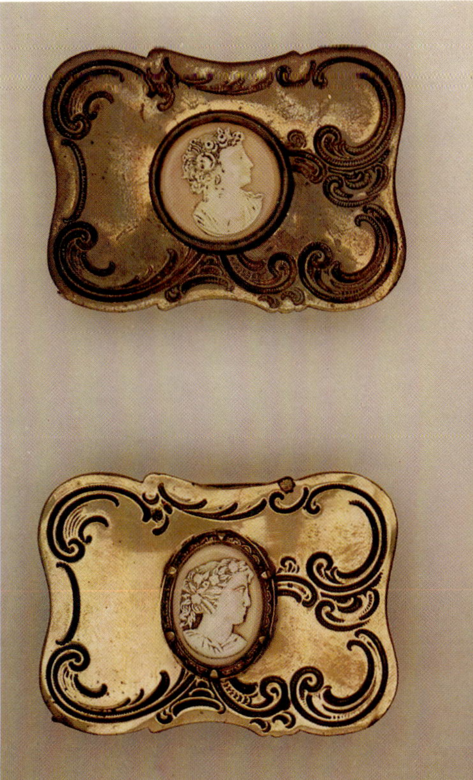

Fig. 498 Britain. Brass, celluloid. c.1875. L - 7.9cms.

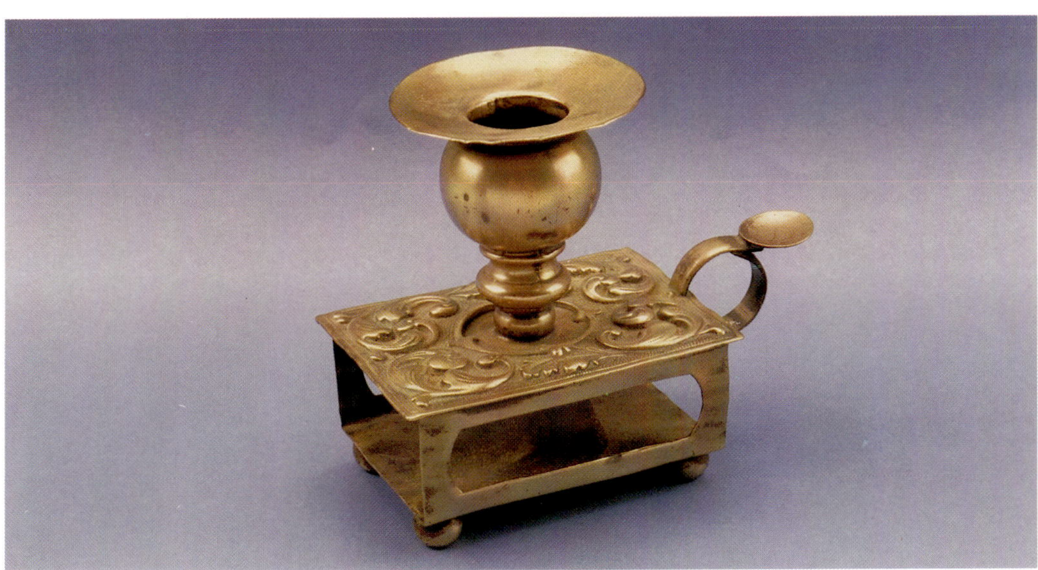

Fig. 499 Britain. Brass. c.1875. H - 9.1cms.

An import into Canada, the example shown in **Fig. 497** is made of sheet steel, in the form of a Scottish Terrier peering into a cylindrical match receptacle. There is a cross-hatched striker plate riveted to the front of the receptacle. It is stamped underneath "COBERG" and has a paper sticker printed "DIRECT IMPORTERS. Herman Bros. MONTREAL." The Herman Bros. company sold china and gifts from 1927 until 1936, when they became Herman Bros. Ltd. The example is of German origin.

Devices for holding a box of matches were common, and began to appear around 1873 when Bryant & May were issued with their Useful Registered Design for a matchbox slide as shown in Fig. 360.

Two slides for larger boxes of matches, shown in Fig. 498, were probably produced specifically to hold Bryant & May safety matches of a size that it is believed were made only between 1862 and 1876. But the boxes were not made for Bryant & May, although they were probably made in Britain. When the author acquired one it contained a Bryant & May matchbox advertising the company's wall holder that was designed in 1874. So it is assumed these slides were made between 1874 and 1876. They are made of brass, the upper one with a bronzed finish, and both provided with a celluloid medallion in a cameo style of classical head, fitted into a frame that is held to the top of the slide by means of lugs.

Fig. 499 shows a combined matchbox holder (for the same size Bryant & May matchbox as in the previous items) and a holder for a large candle. It has a ring for carrying the device from room to room. It is made of brass, with impressed rococo designs on the top, and a ball foot at each corner. This was probably made in Britain between 1874 and 1876.

Undated and unmarked is a slide made of brass with impressed designs of ancient Egyptian forms, shown in **Fig. 500**. It could possibly have been made in Egypt, though a European origin is just as likely; the date is probably c. l900 to 1915.

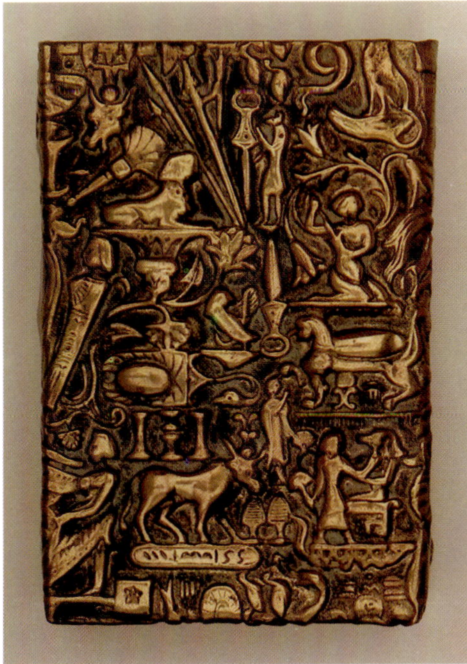

Fig. 500 Europe. Brass. c.1900 to 1915. L - 7.4cms.

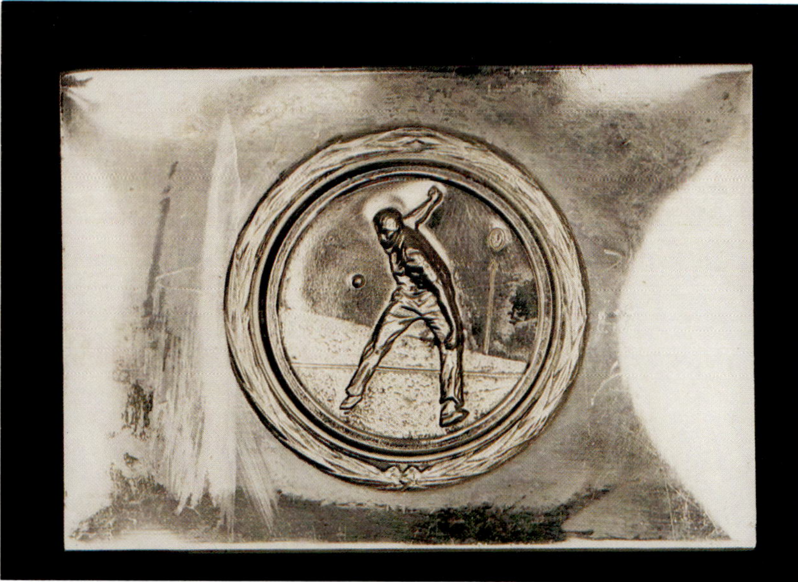

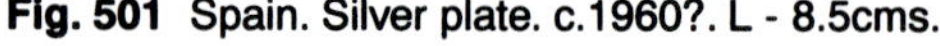

Fig. 501 Spain. Silver plate. c.1960?. L - 8.5cms.

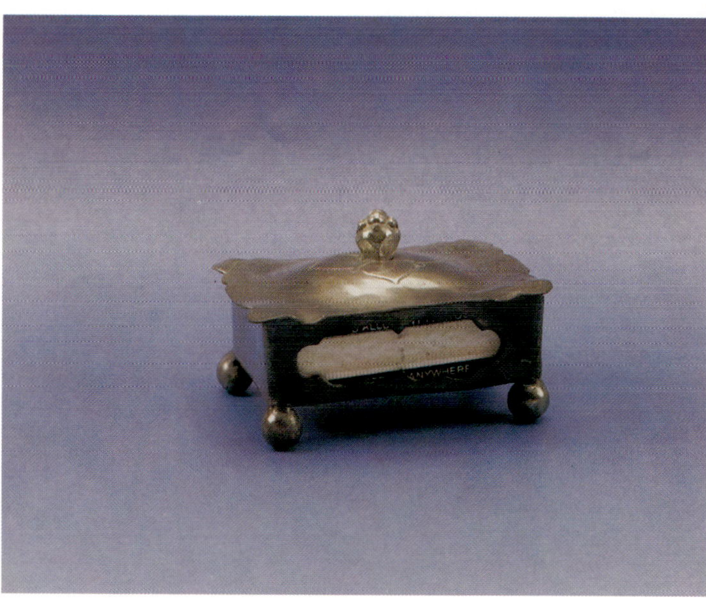

Fig. 502 Origin unknown. Pewter. c.1920s. L - 6.2cms.

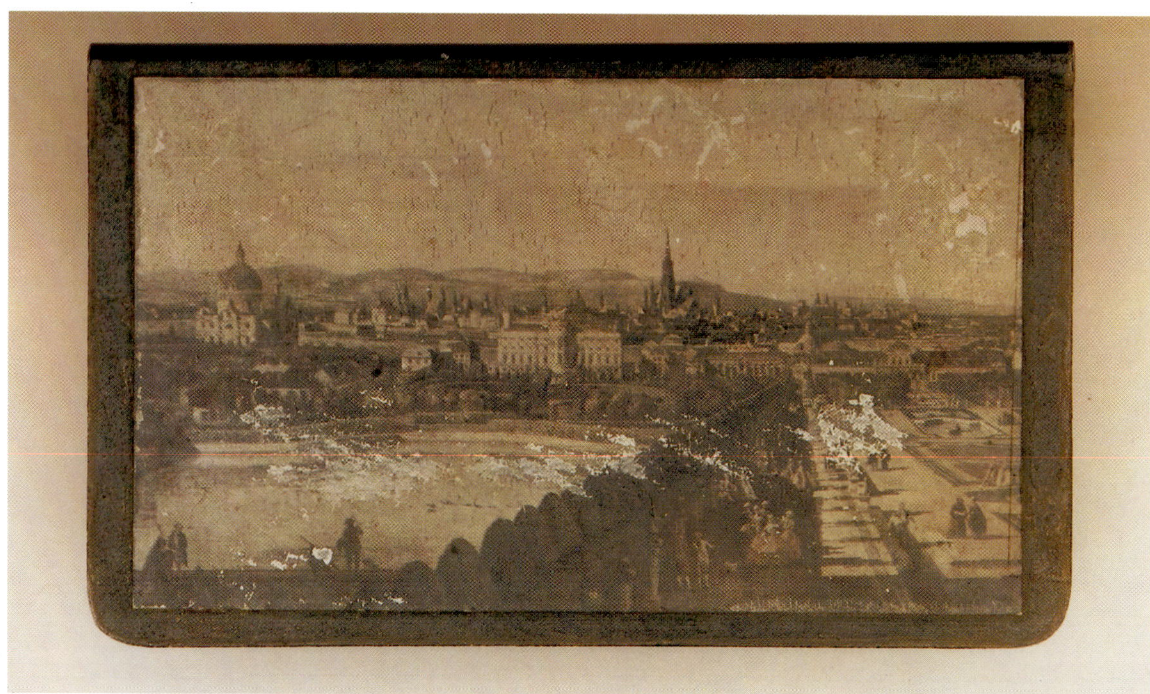

Fig. 503 Probably United States. Tin plate, paper. c.1930s. L -12.1cms.

The top view for a silver plate slide is shown in **Fig. 501**; the item was made in the Basque region of Spain, probably of recent vintage. It was obviously intended to stand on a horizontal surface, having a small domed foot at each corner. The medallion depicts a man playing the Basque national pastime of 'Pilota' (*Pelota* in Spanish), a sport similar to squash, with every village or town having its own court or courts.

In pewter is a casket with a lid hinged longitudinally, shown in **Fig. 502**. It is unmarked, but probably dates from the 1920s, and may have been made in the United States, or possibly Sweden.

For a large box of 200-250 'parlor' type matches is a tin-plate matchbox grip, shown in **Fig. 503**. The tin plate has an antiqued bronze finish, and the top panel an applied paper picture of a late 18th or early l9th century scene of what is believed to be Florence, Italy. It was probably made in the United States, where that size of matchbox was most popular, circa the 1930s.

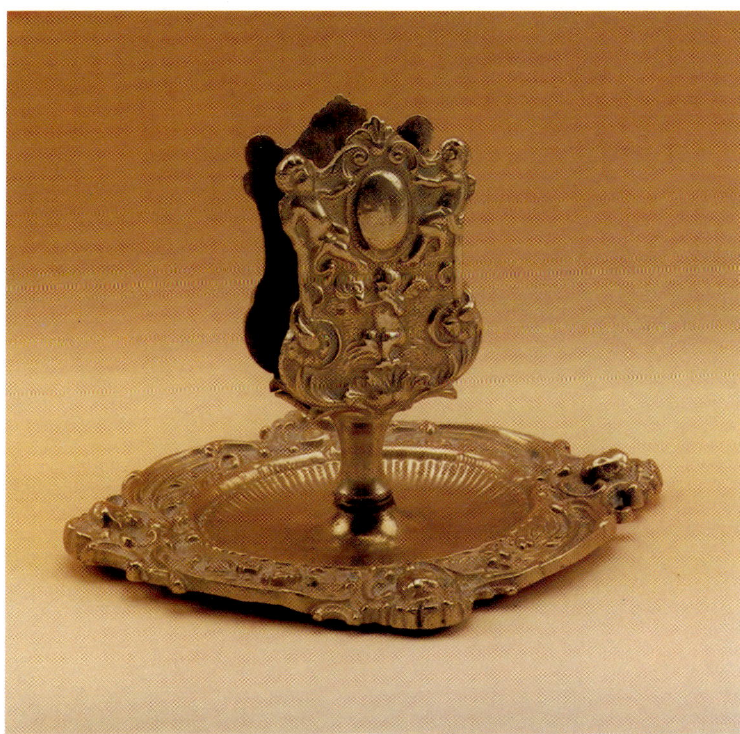

Fig. 504. United States. Cast brass. Made by M. Loewenstein to Design Patents of 1900 shown in Figs. 505 and 506. H - 11cms.

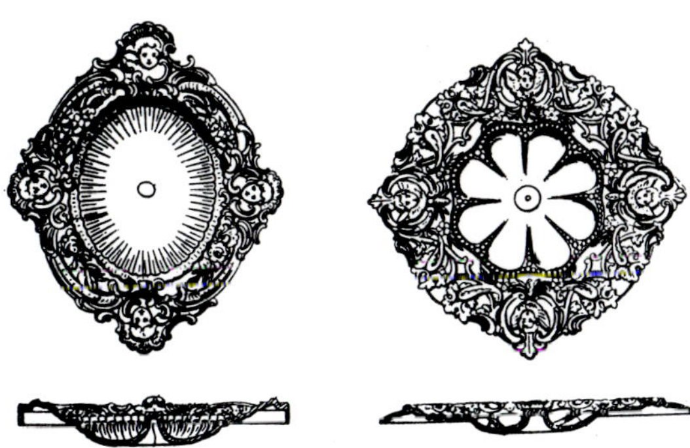

Fig. 506 Design Patent of 1900 by Frank J. Gressly for "Bases for match box holders". One shown in Fig. 504.

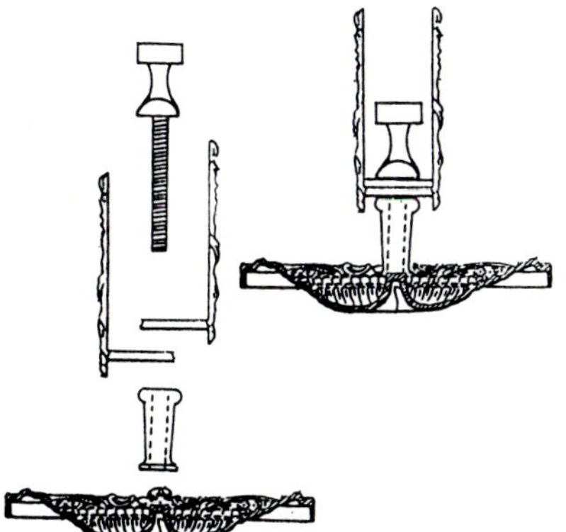

Fig. 507 Details of construction of Fig. 504.

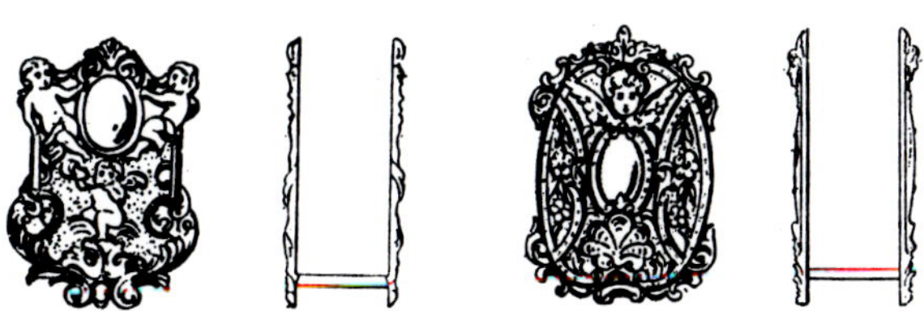

Fig. 505 Design Patent of 1900 by Frank J. Gressly for "Match box holders". One shown in Fig. 504.

Vertical matchbox stands were common in Europe and the United States. The example in **Fig. 504** is made of cast brass. It is marked on the underside of the ashtray "M. LOEWENSTEIN. N.Y.," and with a patent date for 1900 and two numbers. The two numbers and the date were for Design Patents issued to Frank J. Gressly of New York. He had submitted designs for two "Match-Box Holders," shown in **Fig. 505**, and for two "Bases for Match-Box Holders," shown in **Fig. 506**. Either of the two holders could be fixed to either of the two bases. The fact that Loewenstein chose to mark the numbers on the bases is unusual, and is the only example seen to date of the numbers being applied to a match holder. Gressly may have been employed by Loewenstein, but he is not recorded as an assignor to the company. The design did not provide details of how the matchbox holders should be constructed. However, details of the construction are shown in **Fig. 507**; they may have been provided by Gressly, or resolved by the manufacturer.

Matchbox holders of the type shown in **Fig. 508** were made from about 1900 until probably well into the 1940s, in Europe and the United States. The example is made of brass and is weighted at the bottom for stability, but many were quite flimsy. They were also made of other materials, including silver, and are often found attached to a smoker's stand, or combined with an ashtray.

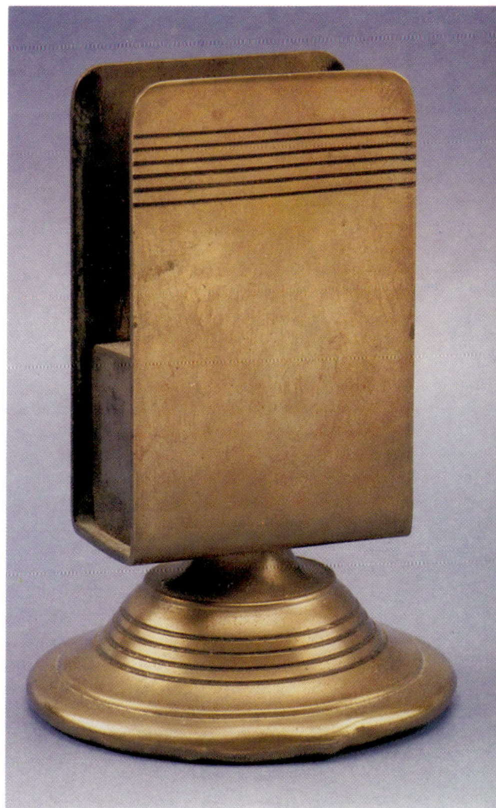

Fig. 508 Origin unknown. Brass, iron. First half of this century. H - 8cms.

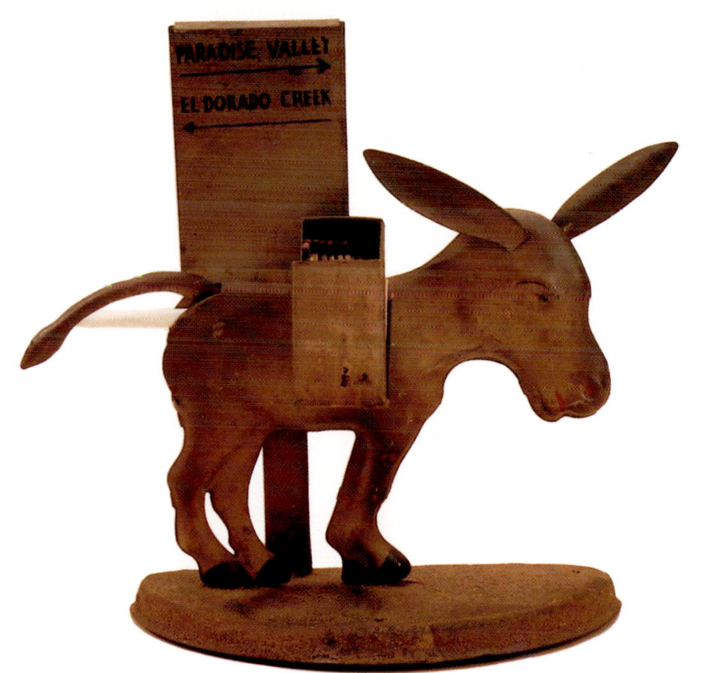

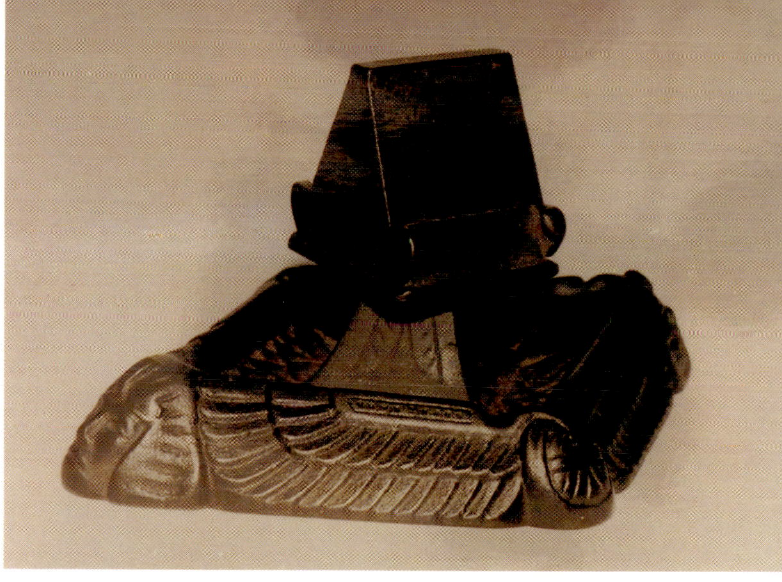

Fig. 510 United States. Cast iron. Made to a Design Patent of 1914 by Edwin A. Merritt. W - 18.7cms.

Fig. 509 United States. Tin plate, wood. c.1930s H - 27.3cms.

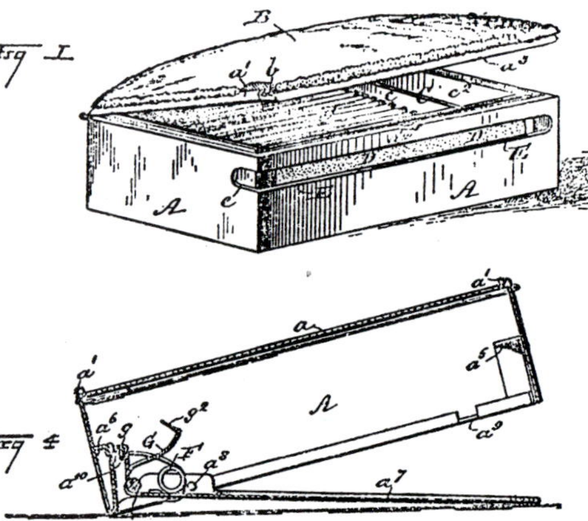

Fig. 511 United States Invention Patent of 1890 for a combined match holder, pin cushion and mouse trap.

Designed to dispense cigarettes and hold a box of matches is an amusing mule shown in **Fig. 509**. The mule stands beside a roadside signboard which acts as a container for about ten cigarettes, loaded from a sliding panel on the front. By pressing the front ear of the mule forwards, its tail is raised and a cigarette is ejected from the bottom of the container out under the tail. Made of tin plate, the matchbox holder takes the form of a panier on the mule. The base is provided with a circular depression for spent matches or ashes. The signboard is supported by a wooden post, and there are three round feet made of wood. The base may have been resurfaced using sand, or this may be original, intended as an additional striking surface. A second version of this piece has been seen painted in bright colors. It is no doubt from the United States, and probably dates from the 1930s.

Stand-alone book match holders are less common. The example in **Fig. 510** is made of cast iron. It was the subject of a Design Patent issued in 1914 to Edwin A. Merritt of New York, as an assignor to the Diamond Match Co., but the example does not bear a maker's name. The design was principally for the the block holding the book matches; the Egyptian style elements around the base were not a part of the original design.

A survey of United States patents suggests that many inventions were not particularly practical, occasionally even bordering on the lunatic fringe. One such invention in 1890 incorporated a match holder with a pin cushion and a mousetrap! Two of the patent drawings are shown in **Fig. 511**. The specifications do not indicate the material to be used, but it was probably intended to be made of metal. The pin cushion was located on top of the lid which, when raised, revealed the match compartment. The base was also hinged, and could be fixed in the open position with a trigger mechanism and hook for bait. The mouse entered the open box, nibbled at the bait which released the body of the box to fall over the mouse and trap it. The box was then taken to a sink and immersed in water until the mouse had drowned. In order to achieve this, the pin cushion and match tray had first to be removed. There seems little connection between the three uses of this device, and it is doubted that it ever reached the production stage.

PART 3: ORGANIC MATERIALS

The range of stand-alone match holders made of organic materials is considerably smaller than those of metals and ceramics. Production methods using wood were generally more labor-intensive and less conducive towards mass production techniques; the increased costs were reflected in the price and resulted in lower sales.

Since metal and ceramics could be fashioned in molds or with dies using mass production processes, the forms were not confined to the vagaries of the material, in contrast to wood, whose grain tends to dictate form. Therefore most wooden forms are either cylindrical and capable of being turned on a lathe, or are rectangular, made from flat slabs.

This did not prevent the production of aesthetically pleasing designs, and even led to some ingenious methods of embellishment. However, there was also the occasional 'clunker'.

Wooden match holders were more common in the period of the early protective match holder, prior to 1860 (as discussed earlier), before mass production methods reduced labor costs. Nonetheless, they continued to be made in later times. The Smiths of Mauchline, Scotland and the Tonbridge workers continued to display considerable ingenuity in producing decorative wooden items until after the turn of the century.

William and Andrew Smith had earlier developed their methods of applying Scottish tartans and black transfer designs. But, as the century progressed, their time-consuming processes became too expensive to compete with other products on the market, and they began to cut corners. This led to a decline in the quality of their products.

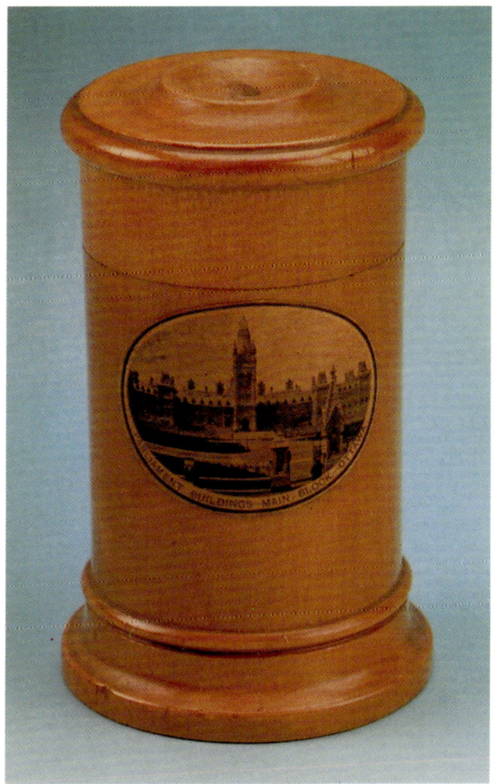

Fig. 512 France? Wood. c.1900. H - 7.9cms.

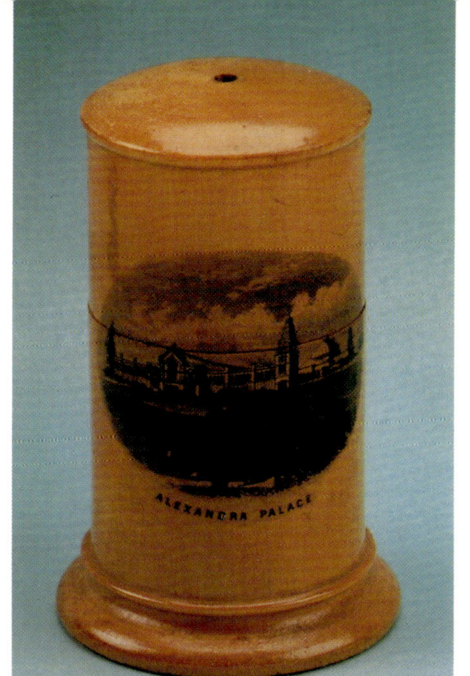

Fig. 513 Scotland. Wood. Probably made by William & Andrew Smith. c.1900. H - 7.6cms.

Fig. 514 Scotland. Wood, Probably made by William & Andrew Smith. c.1910. H - 6.4cms.

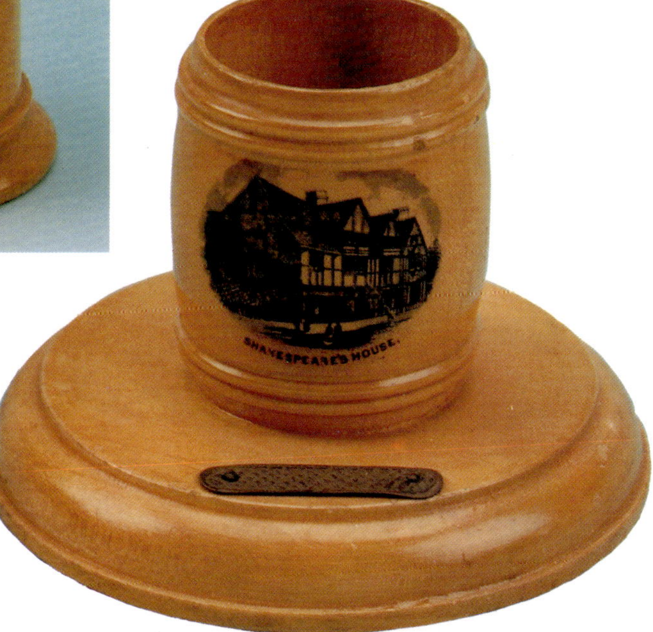

An example of what is probably a competitor's product is shown in **Fig. 512**, with a sepia photograph of the Parliament Buildings in Ottawa, glued to the body. This was probably made in France around 1900, but without the photograph, which was applied in Canada by the importer. The base is furnished with a piece of sandpaper glued into a recess.

At approximately the same time, the Smiths were still using their transfer designs, as may be seen in **Fig. 513**; this transfer is of the Alexandra Palace in North London, which was not completed until 1898. At the back of the cylinder is a paper label, doubtless glued on after the box had left the Smiths, with the wording "A Souvenir From Alexandra Palace." The underside of the base is recessed for a sanded striker, and an ivory match socket, now missing, was set into the top of the lid.

An open-topped match holder is shown in **Fig. 514** with a black transfer design of Shakespeare's house. This is probably from c. 1910 and made by the Smiths, although the lacquer finish is inferior to their earlier work. The striker is in the form of a brass strip nailed to the base.

Around the turn of the century, the Smiths developed another method of decorating their woodenware that led to it becoming known as 'Fernware'. An example is shown in **Fig. 515**. Fern leaves were gathered in the Isle of Arran; they were glued to the box's surface, which was subsequently varnished. The result was an uneven surface. This was later changed, by pinning the leaves to the box, applying a dark varnish over the top, then removing the leaves, filling the pin holes, and applying paint or stain to the exposed wood, before applying a final coat of varnish.

Both processes were laborious. Eventually paper printed with fern designs was applied to articles before the final coat of varnish. These are *usually* distinguishable from the earlier two processes by the join in the paper, yet the example in Fig. 515, which is assumed to be paper-covered, shows no signs of a join. The lid is provided with a bone or ivory match socket, and the underside of the base is recessed for a sanded striker. Fernware continued to be made until well into the 1920s.

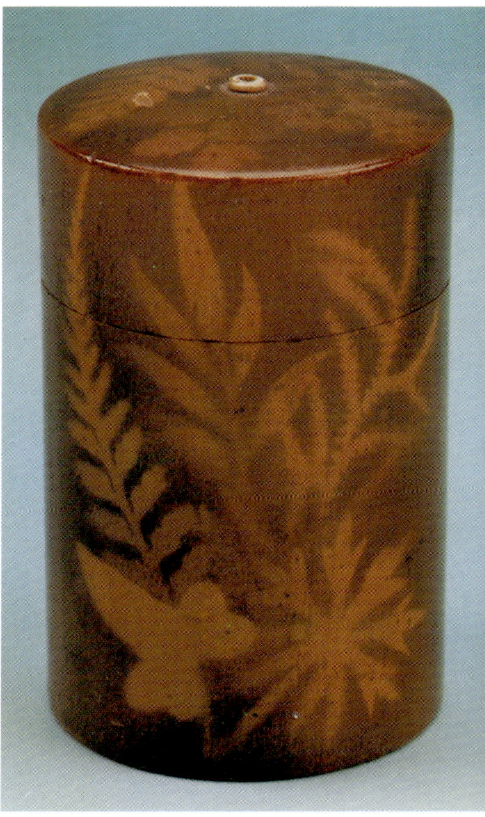

Fig. 515 Scotland. Wood, bone or ivory. Made by William & Andrew Smith. Early 1900s. H - 8.2cms.

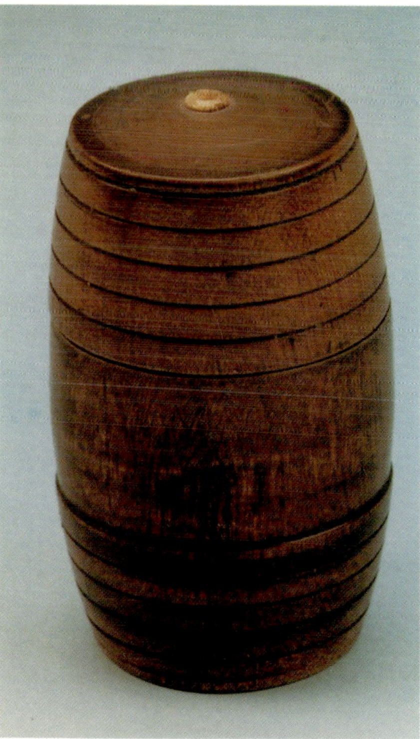

Fig. 516 Europe. Wood, bone or ivory. c.1860s. H - 7.5cms.

Fig. 517 Britain. Ebony, bone or ivory, brass. c.1870. H - 9.1cms.

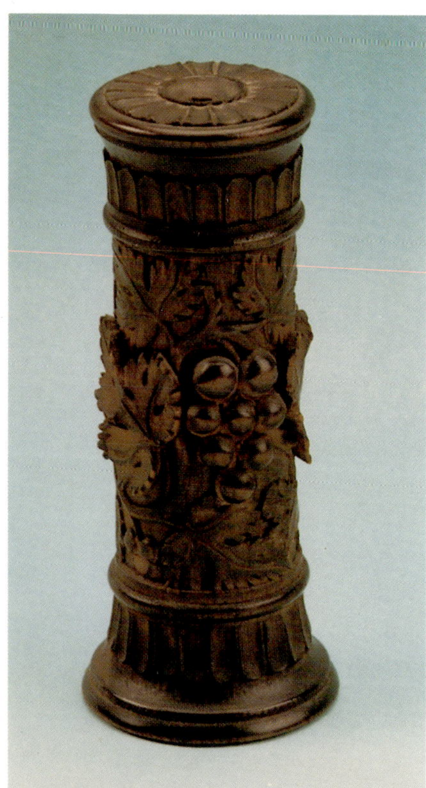

Fig. 518 Possibly France. Wood, ?sand. Match socket missing. c.1860 to 1870. H - 8.6cms.

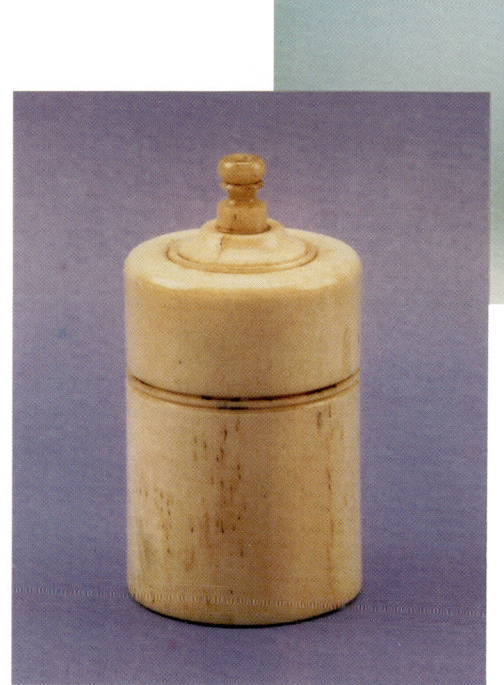

Fig. 519 Probably Britain. Ivory. c.1890. H - 5.5cms.

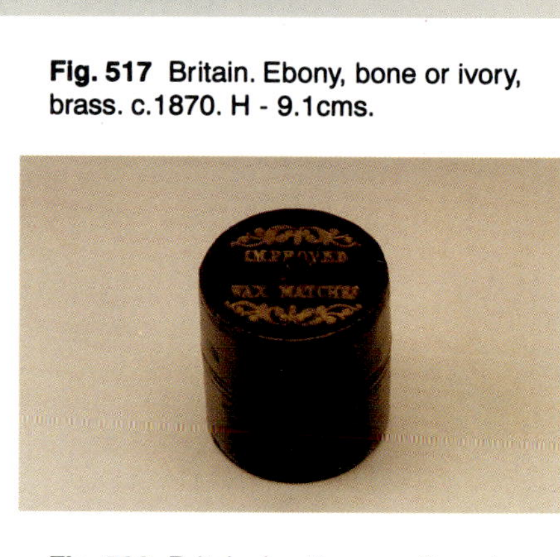

Fig. 520 Britain. Leather, cardboard, brass. c.1860s. H - 4.2cms.

The wooden example in **Fig. 516**, in the form of a barrel, is stained red, probably to simulate mahogany. The lid is supplied with a bone or ivory socket. The base was sanded for friction. It is no doubt of European origin, and dates from about 1860 to 1870.

The open-topped mortar in **Fig. 517** is made of ebony, with a bone or ivory match socket that probably represents the touch hole, and bone or ivory decorative elements fixed by means of brass-domed tacks. The striking patch is made of brass attached to the edge of the base. It is probably British, from c. 1870, and was part of a series of open-topped and lidded match holders with similar forms of applied decoration.

The decorative elements on the holder shown in **Fig. 518** appears at first glance to have been carved from the sides of the cylinder. But, when examined under a magnifying glass, it can be seen that the vine leaves and grapes have been carved separately and glued to a plain cylinder. The same applies to the decorative borders at the top and bottom. However, the top of the slip-on lid *was* carved from the solid wood. The match socket, probably of ivory, is missing, and the striker recessed into the base appears to be a thick layer of sand and glue mixed. The workmanship, extremely fine and delicate, may be of French origin, probably c. 1860 to 1870.

Very simple in design is an ivory cylindrical holder shown in **Fig. 519**, with a screw-on lid surmounted by a match socket. Concentric circles on the base act as the striker. A very similar box was shown in a catalogue of Silber & Fleming of London and Paris, issued between 1884 and 1889. This company made some of the products that it sold, particularly jewelry and gas lighting fixtures. It also imported a wide variety of household goods from around the world, including cast-iron match holders from the United States. It sold these wares wholesale and retail. The example may have been produced in Britain or France.

Marked in gold letters on the top of the lid "IMPROVED WAX MATCHES," the example in **Fig. 520** is made of red leather covering a cardboard body. The base was sanded for friction, and it has a brass match socket set into the lid. It is probably British from c. 1860 to 1870.

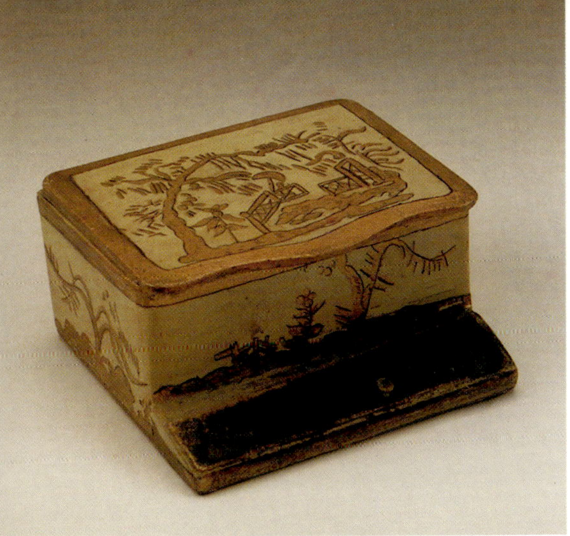

Fig. 521 Britain? Wood. c.1900. L - 8.8cms.

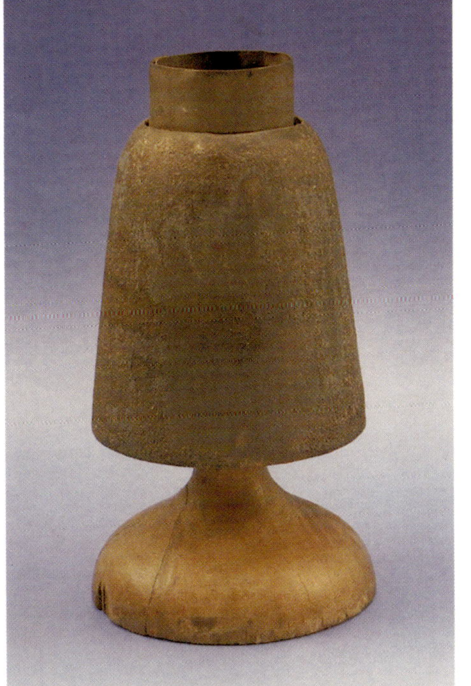

Fig. 522 United States. Wood, tin plate. c.1880s. H - 12.5cms.

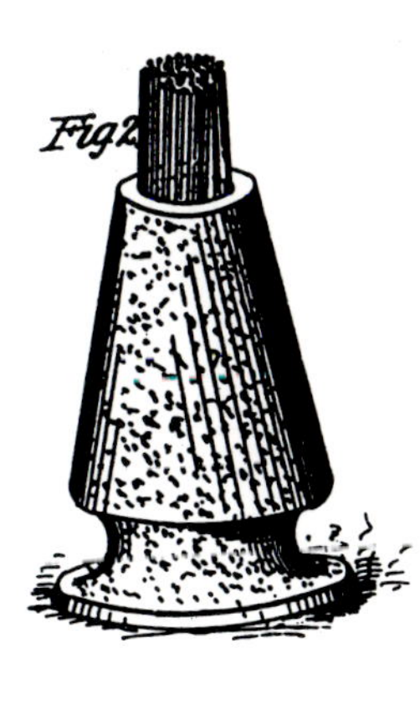

Fig. 523 United States Invention Patent of 1865 by Jason H. Merrill

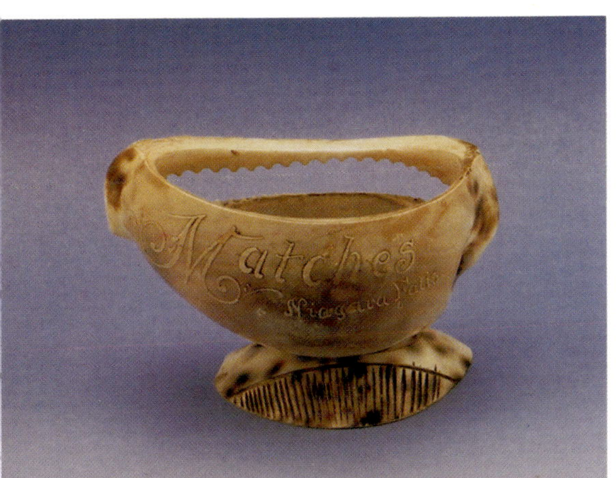

Fig. 524 United States. Tiger cowry. Made to a Design Patent of 1899 by Sigmund M. Rosin. H - 5.8cms.

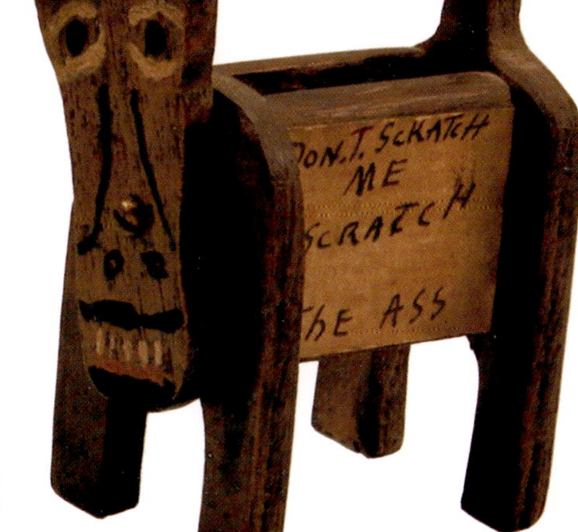

Fig. 525 United States. Wood, paper. c.1920s or 1930s. H -10.2cms.

Of rectangular form, made of wood, and shown in **Fig. 521** is a box on which is painted a crude Japanese-style garden scene; the elements are in gold, outlined in black, against a lime green background. The striker along the ledge at the lower front is a piece of fine emery cloth. The underside is marked by hand, in black ink, "Made in ...," but is unfortunately too indistinct to read. A similar box in far worse condition has been seen, decorated in a Japanese style of a type that is commonly found on papier maché work from the Midlands of Britain. So it may be that the example here is British-made, and dating from about 1900.

United States companies seem to have hardly entered this field, only four examples being attributable to them. The first, shown in **Fig. 522**, is an unmarked open-topped holder turned from a piece of wood, with a tin-plate cylinder fitted into the top, and the sides sanded for friction. A piece of very similar shape was the subject of a United States Invention Patent of 1865, issued to Jason H. Merrill of Norwalk, Connecticut; one of the drawings is shown in **Fig. 523**. The patent was not so much for the shape, but for the material—clay, sand and water—to be baked like pottery, which provided an overall rough surface suitable for igniting matches. It is not suggested that the wooden example is the result of Merrill's patent, but he may have sold the rights to a manufacturer who chose to change the material—a practice apparently quite frequent in the United States.

In 1899 Sigmund M. Rosin of Philadelphia, Pennsylvania, was issued with two Design Patents using a shell, the *Cypraea Tigris*, or tiger cowry. The first patent was for a napkin ring cut from a section of the shell. The second was for a match holder using the entire shell, shown in **Fig. 524**. A section of the shell was cut off, inverted and secured to the main body by means of a nut and bolt, to serve as a base. Part of this base was roughened for friction. The front of the body has raised letters, "Matches. Niagara Falls," probably created by writing the letters on the surface in wax, then removing the background by dipping it in acid. It is assumed that Rosin made the boxes himself, for sale to the souvenir trade.

A homemade match holder is shown in **Fig. 525**, made from odd scraps of wood, and representing an ass. The face is crudely painted, and on the back is a piece of emery cloth as the striker. Glued on one side is a piece of paper with hand-written wording "DON'T SCRATCH ME SCRATCH THE ASS." It was probably made in the 1920s or 1930s.

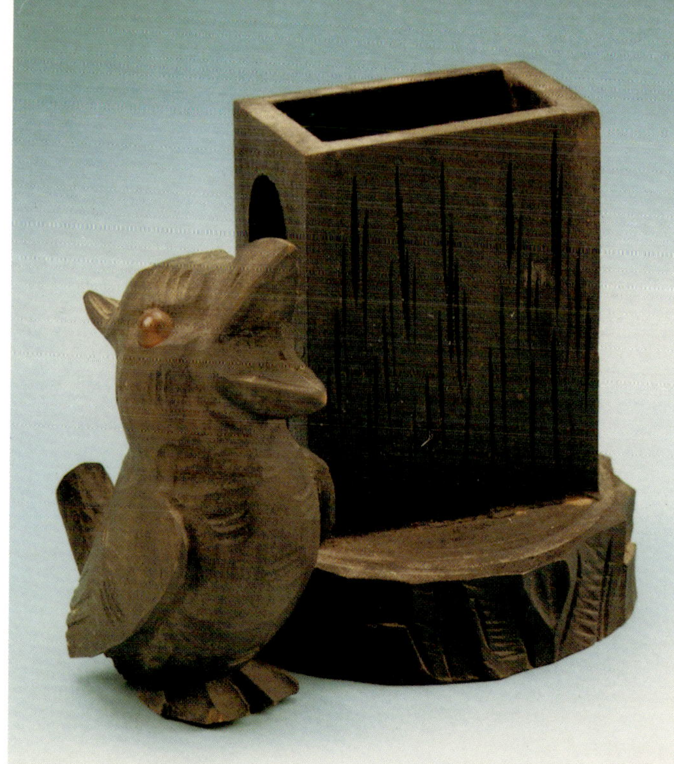

Fig. 526 United States. Wood, glass. c.1940s. H - 7.8cms.

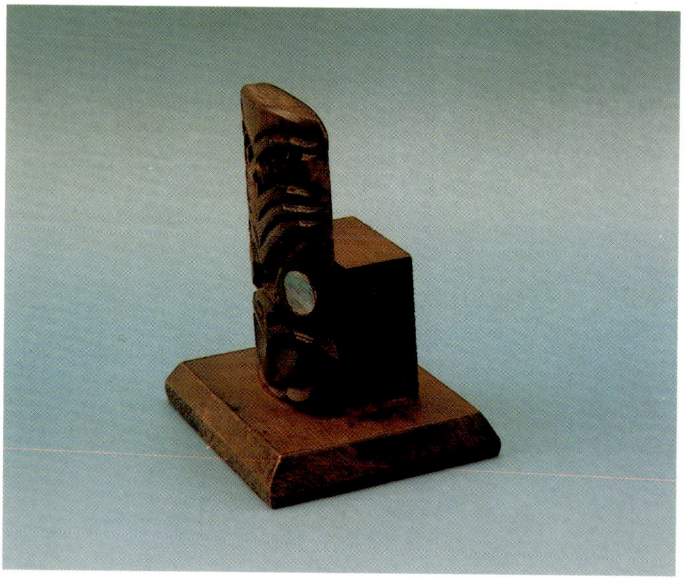

Fig. 527 New Zealand. Wood, shell. c.1960. H - 7.5cms.

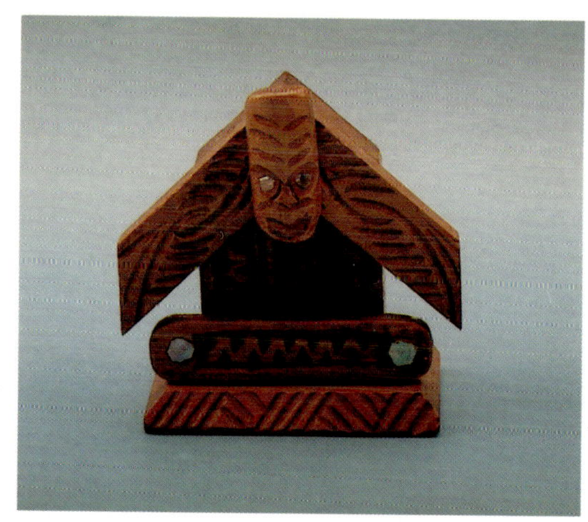

Fig. 528 New Zealand. Wood, shell. c.1960. H - 6.7cms.

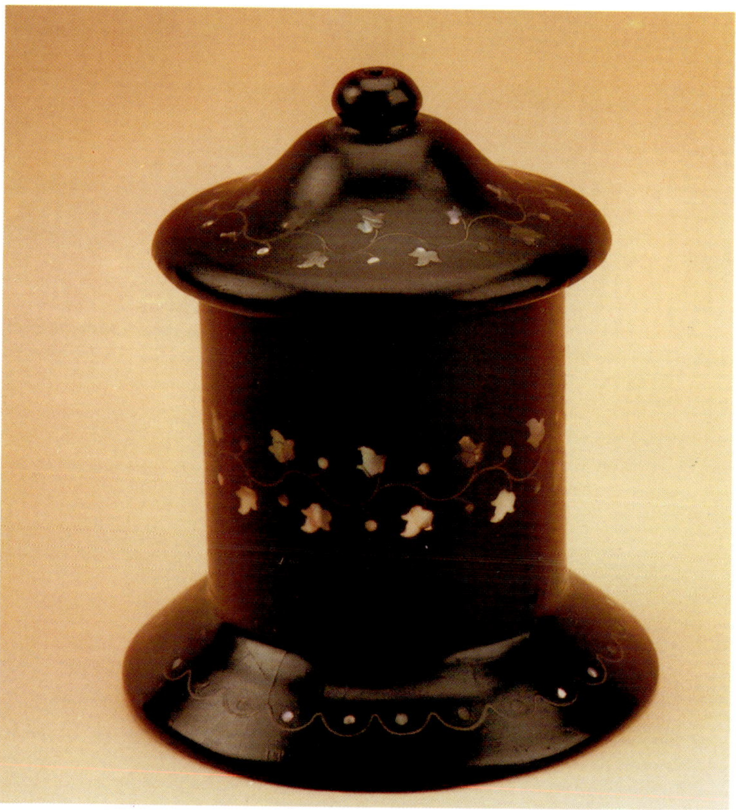

Fig. 529 Britain. Papier mache, pewter, shell. c.1870 to 1890. H - 8cms.

Probably from the 1940s is the matchbox holder shown in **Fig. 526**. The base represents a section of a log, supporting a rectangular cover made from four pieces to hold the matchbox. Attached to the base by means of a dowel is a caricature of a Blue Jay, with glass eyes. The log and box holder are stained black, the bird is dark brown.

From New Zealand are two matchbox stands shown in **Figs. 527 and 528**. They have been carved in forms and designs that loosely represent Maori art styles, and include some inlaid *paua* shell, a local form of abalone shell. They were not carved by the Maori, but were made for tourists about thirty years ago.

Papier maché was used extensively in Britain, Germany and France to make a wide variety of domestic wares, from sizable pieces of furniture to the more humble match holder. Regrettably these match holders were seldom, if ever, marked with a maker's name, which makes positive identification impossible. It is doubtful, however, if match holders were made of this material until close to the end of the papier maché vogue, between c. 1870 and 1890.

Fig. 529 shows one with a shallow, loose-fitting lid, terminating in a match socket, and decorated in typical fashion with abalone shell and very narrow pewter strips, against a black japanned background. The domed underside of the base is sanded for friction. This was probably made in Birmingham or Wolverhampton.

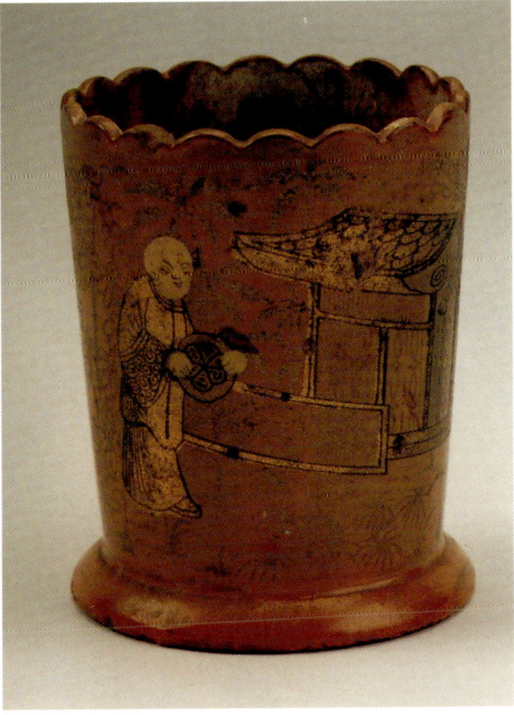

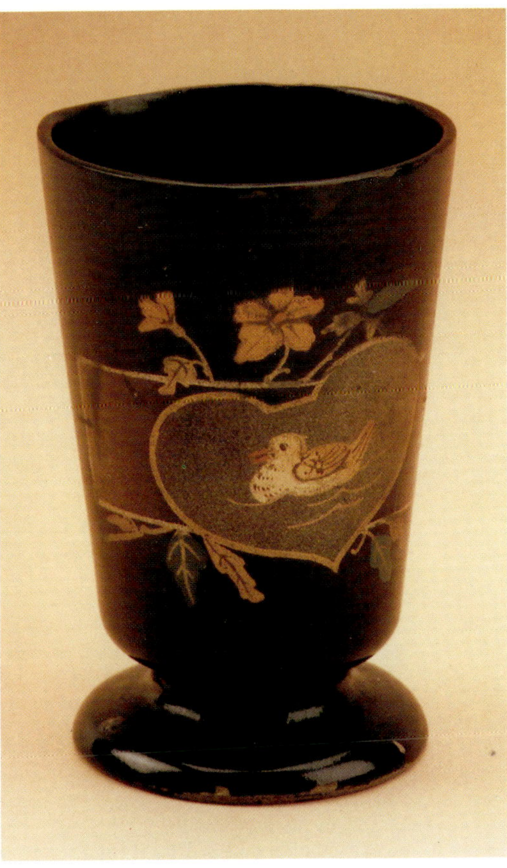

Fig. 531 Probably France. Papier mache. c.1870 to l890. H -8.1cms.

Fig. 530 Britain. Papier mache. c.1870 to 1890. H - 6.4cms.

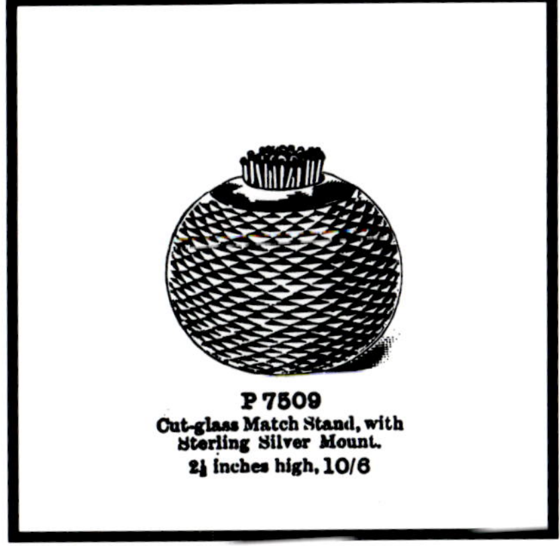

Fig. 532 Britain. An illustration from a catalogue by Mappin & Webb Ltd., of 1900.

The example in **Fig. 530** is an open-topped vase shape with a scalloped rim. It has a typical design depicting Japanese people; their faces are picked out in pink, with the rest of the design work in gold, with black outlines, against an orange background. The underside of the base is sanded for friction. This too is believed to be from Birmingham or Wolverhampton.

The third example is another open-topped vase shape, shown in **Fig. 531**. Against a black japanned finish are some well-executed, colorful designs: a duck, a butterfly and flowers. The underside is sanded for friction. This may be of French origin, but without a mark this is pure speculation.

PART 4: BALL STANDS

Match holders in glass, ceramics, and stone of a globular form were produced in Europe, mostly in Britain. Small versions were made for domestic purposes, and larger versions for use in public places. Bryant & May referred to the larger versions in its catalogue of 1894 as follows: "These stands are specially designed for use in Clubs, Hotels, Public Institutions etc., etc." Examples of ball stands made of pottery and glass for Bryant & May are shown in Figs. 438 and 439.

Varying in diameter from 5 cm up to 11.5 cm, and weighing up to one pound twelve ounces, they were made either as complete spheres, hemispheres, or flattened spheres; some were mounted on an ashtray. They were commonly used as advertising items for the producers of alcoholic beverages. Probably first produced around 1890, some were still being produced into the 1930s.

Most of the spherical glass match stands have parallel, horizontal grooves around the body, referred to by the Harrod's Stores Ltd. (London) in its catalogue of 1895 as a "Threaded Glass Match Stand." However, others in cut glass had multifaceted sides, usually with one or two patches of horizontal ribbing as a striker, or had a coarse-etched overall surface, as shown in Fig. 439.

Many were provided with a silver rim bearing hallmarks, a useful dating mechanism. The Harrod's Stores Ltd. catalogue of 1895 showed silver-rimmed stands in five sizes, from 2" to 4" in diameter, costing from four shillings and six pence to seven shillings and six pence each. Henry Birks & Sons of Montreal, Quebec showed them in 1923 with a silver rim at $1.50, and in 1925 with a silver-plated rim at $3.00 each. In 1932 the Goldsmiths & Silversmiths Co. of London showed one 4" in diameter, with a silver rim, at seventeen shillings and six pence, and a smaller one mounted on a silver ashtray at one pound seven shillings and six pence.

An illustration from the 1900 catalogue of Mappin & Webb Ltd. of London showing a cut glass ball stand is seen in **Fig. 532**, but a striking area is not shown.

Not all of these glass ball match stands had a silver rim. The example in **Fig. 533** has a threaded rib surface. An elliptical panel advertises Schweppes Soda (in red letters), against an etched background.

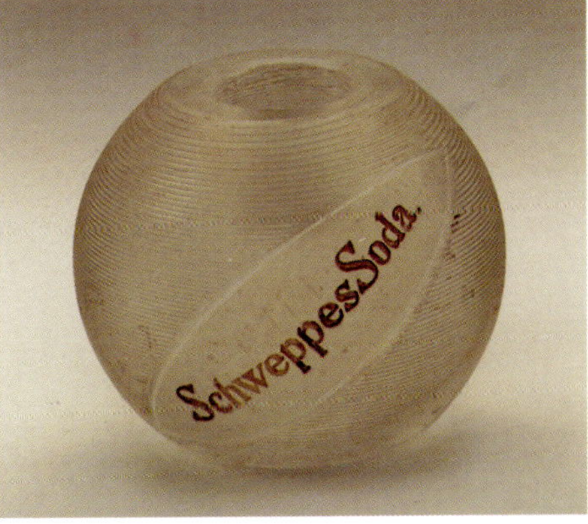

Fig. 533 Britain. Glass. c.1910. D - 9.5cms.

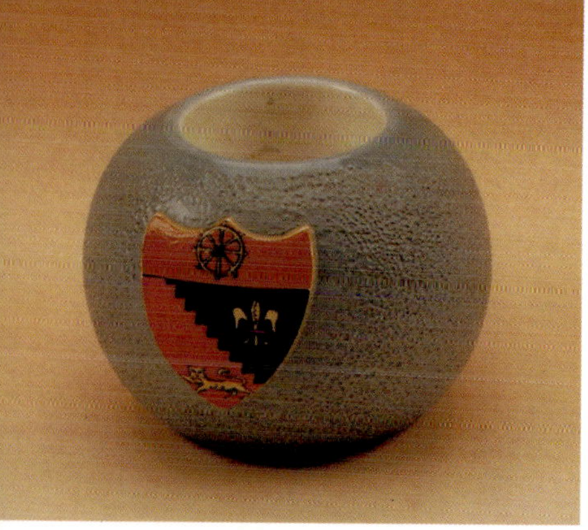

Fig. 534 Britain. Ceramic. Made by Wiltshaw & Robinson. Between 1894 and 1906. D - 8.4cms.

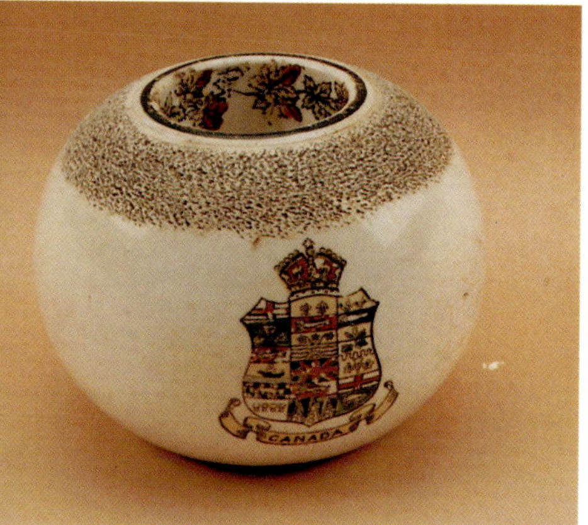

Fig. 535 Britain. Ceramic. Made by Frank Beardmore & Co.. Between 1903 and 1906. D - 9.1cms.

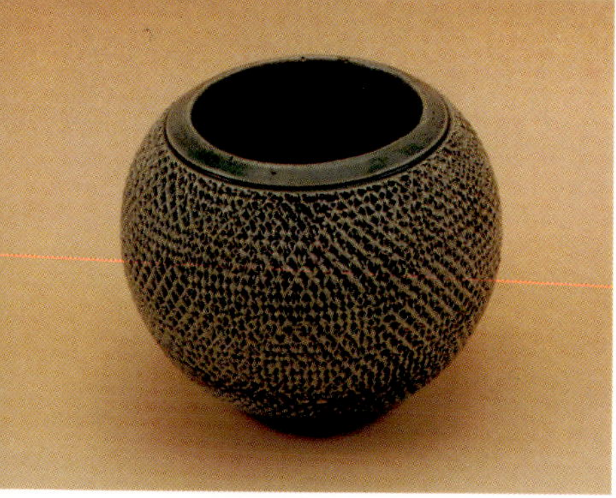

Fig. 536 Britain. Ceramic. Made by the Watcombe Pottery Co.. Pre 1901. D - 6.3cms.

Fig. 537 Britain. Ceramic. Made by Taylor, Tunnicliffe & Co.. Between 1875 and 1898. D - 6.4 cms.

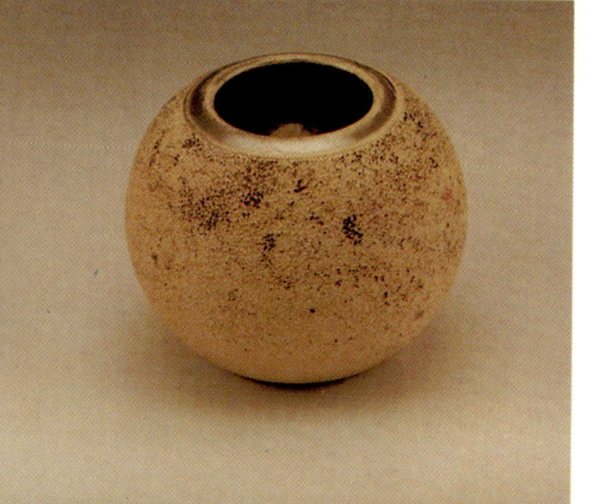

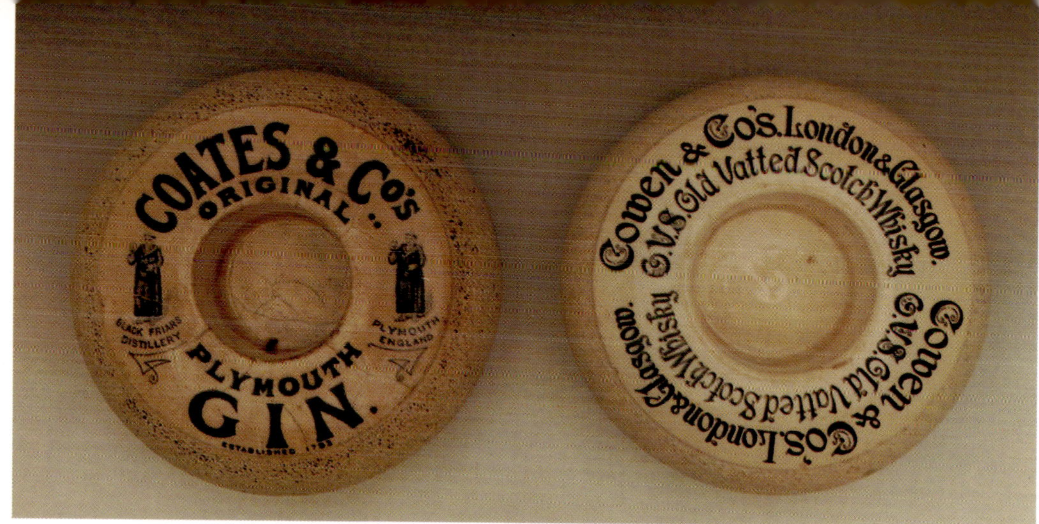

Fig. 538 Britain. Ceramic. Left: marked Wedekind & Co. D -11.6cms. Right: marked Norton & Gregory, D - 11.4cms. c.1900.

Ball match stands made of stone are less common. Two were illustrated in the 1895 Harrod's Stores Ltd. catalogue: a spherical form in "White Stone" in two sizes, and an oval form mounted on an ashtray in "Coloured" stone. These were priced at under one shilling each.

Roger Fresco-Corbu (see Bibliography) refers to another one as made of Connemara Marble, quarried in the Connemara area of County Galway in the Republic of Ireland, where local craftsmen used this apple-green stone to make small souvenirs.

In Germany, E.G. Zimmermann of Hanau (referred to in Chapter II) had added, in about 1850, a marble works to its factory, which was in production as of the 1980s. In its 1929 catalogue were illustrated three ball match stands, each in four different styles and finishes, between 6 cm and 7 cm in diameter, from 3.25 to 14 marks each.

By far the most common form of ball match stand were those made of ceramic material. As with the glass and stone varieties, it seems likely that they began to appear about 1895. Almost inevitably, Bryant & May was among the first to make them available for public consumption, but the company did not manufacture them.

An example by Wiltshaw & Robinson of Stoke-on-Trent is shown in **Fig. 534**. It is marked "Carleton Ware," which was used from c. 1894 until c. 1906, and also has a retailer's mark of Colin Lunn of Cambridge and Oxford. Presumably the shield represents one of the university colleges of these two cities. Except for the shield, the entire surface is roughened for friction.

From 1915 to 1917 Henry Birks & Sons Ltd. was offering a "Combination Match Holder and Ash Bowl in Royal Doulton Ware" for $2.50. The catalogue illustration shows a ball stand with a similar finish to the preceding example, with a separate silver 'well' to fit in the hole in the top of the ceramic stand, to hold the matches. It is assumed that the inside of the ball was hollow to act as an ash bowl, and that the silver match holder would be removed while a cigarette was smoked.

Doulton & Co. of Lambeth, London, produced a wide variety of ball stands from about 1895 until the 1920s. They typically bore fine decorative designs, and many were advertising pieces, usually for breweries. These stands are sometimes marked with the monogram of the artist, which gives an added dimension to identification and research.

The example in **Fig. 535** was made by Frank Beardmore & Co. of Fenton, Staffordshire. This company was in business from 1903 until 1914. The white body has the Canadian crest showing the provinces that existed before Alberta and Saskatchewan became provinces in 1906, so the assumption is that this was made prior to 1907. Around the inside of the rim is a line of maple leaves, and around the outer edge of the rim is a band roughened for friction.

The two preceding examples, in Figs. 534 and 535, are large pieces and were no doubt intended for use in public institutions. The following two examples are smaller, lack advertising or other decorative devices, and were probably for domestic use. The example in **Fig. 536** has a diamond-mesh impressed surface for friction; impressed on the base is "WATCOMBE.TORQUAY." This was the Watcombe Pottery Co., which was in business from 1867 until 1901 before combining with Aller Vale Art Potteries of Newton Abbot, Devonshire, to become the Royal Aller Vale & Watcombe Pottery Co.

The second example in **Fig. 537** has a stippled finish for friction. A printed blue mark on the underside is for Taylor, Tunnicliffe & Co. of Hanley, Staffordshire, and is believed to have been used between c. 1875 and 1898.

In 1908 the Empire Porcelain Co. of Stoke-on-Trent registered a design for a reversible ball stand. Stood one way up it was like the preceding pieces, but when inverted the hole was rectangular, with a block in the center to hold a box of matches.

The next three examples were referred to by Bryant & May as "Squat Stands." There are many examples, all bearing advertising for well-known brands of gin or Scottish whisky, and intended to stand on the bar counters of public houses, clubs, or retail liquor stores. They are all cream in color, with a smooth section around the rim bearing printed advertising, and the sides roughened for friction.

The example at left in **Fig. 538**, advertising Plymouth Gin, has a printed mark on the underside for Wedekind & Co. Wedekind was not the maker, but a London wholesaler who apparently supplied a lot of advertising items to Coates & Co. The Cowen & Co. example, on the right, has a printed mark for Norton & Gregory, London, another wholesaler.

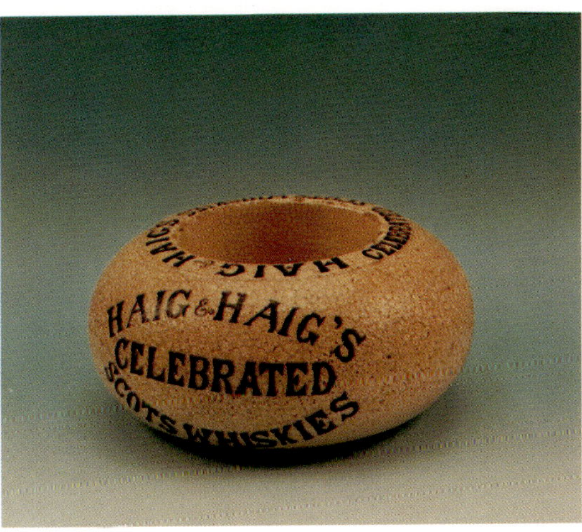

Fig. 539 Britain. Ceramic. Made by R. Hammersley & Son Ltd. Pre 1905. D - 10.5cms.

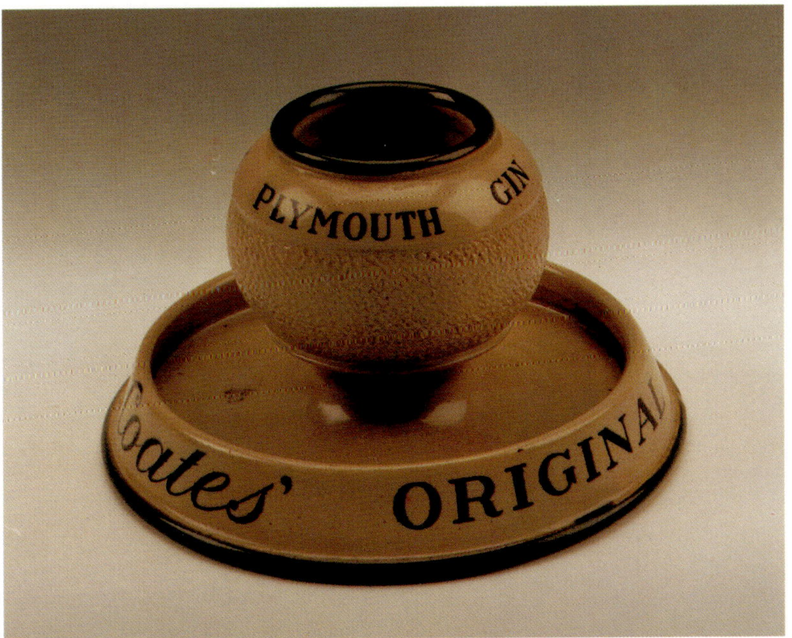

Fig. 541 Britain. Ceramic. Marked Hancock & Corfield. c. 1910. D - 14.8cms.

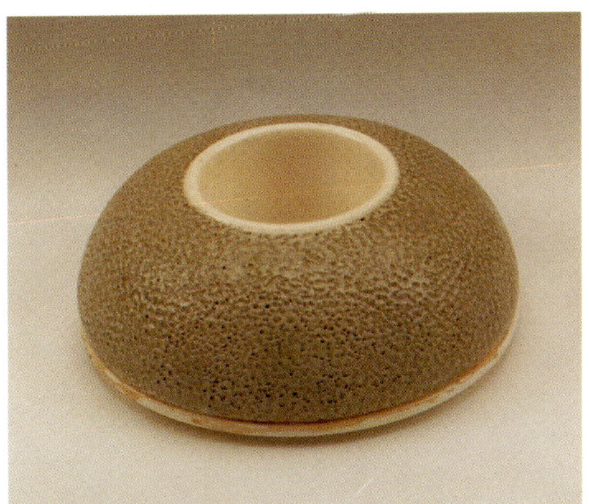

Fig. 540 Britain. Ceramic. Made to a Registered Design of 1901. D - 9.4cms.

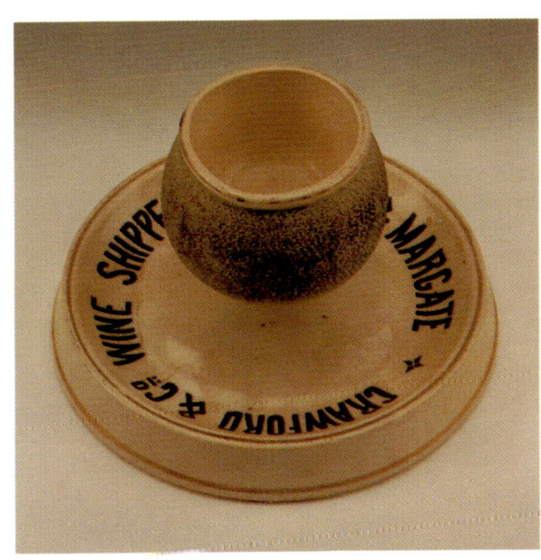

Fig. 542 Britain. Ceramic. Unmarked. c.1910. D - 13.2cms.

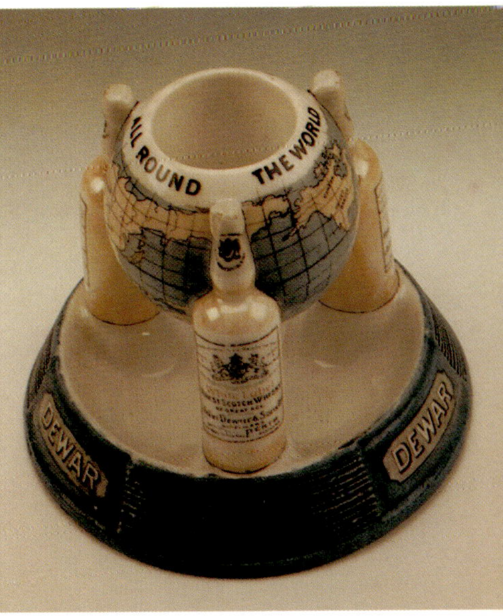

Fig. 543 Britain. Ceramic. Unmarked. c.1910. D - 13.1cms.

The example in **Fig. 539** is a little smaller and bears a maker's mark reading "R.Hammersley & Son Ltd. Burslem," a Staffordshire pottery. This company ceased trading in 1905.

In 1898 Wiltshaw & Robinson registered a design for a hemispherical match holder, which the company apparently made for the Diamond Match Co. Ltd. of Liverpool. The example shown in **Fig. 540** has a registered number for 1901 and is almost identical to the design, except for the depth of the base, which in the earlier version was almost half an inch deep. The base and upper sections of the example appear to have been made as separate parts and glued together.

Ball match stands also came mounted on ashtrays. None of the examples here have maker's marks, although the example in **Fig. 541** has a wholesaler's mark "Hancock & Corfield.Mitcham.," which was located in Surrey; again Coates & Co's famous Plymouth Gin is advertised.

Made for Crawford & Co., wine shippers of London and Margate, Kent, is a slightly more elegant piece shown in **Fig. 542**.

The ball in the example in **Fig. 543** is a somewhat distorted representation of the globe, supported by three facsimiles of Dewar's White Label Scotch Whisky bottles. The side edge of the tray has three sets of alternating bands of ribbed sections (strikers) and smooth sections bearing the printed name of Dewar.

Doulton's made a similar piece for Worthington's Pale Ale, with the globe on two supports, the sides of the supports providing the space for the striking surfaces.

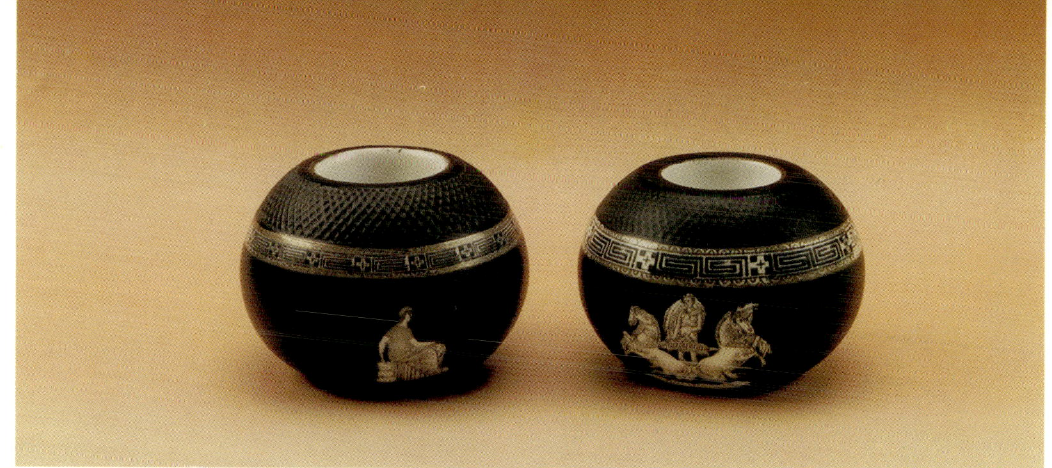

Fig. 544 Germany. Ceramic. Made by Porcelain Factory Tettau. Possibly inkwells. Post 1957. Left: D - 8cms. Right: D - 7.8cms.

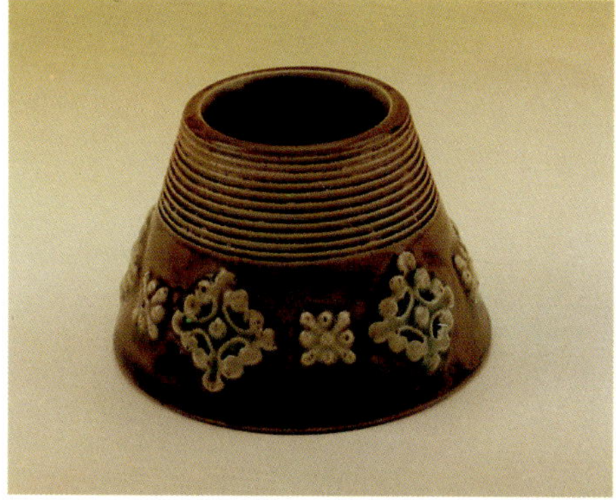

Fig. 545 Britain. Ceramic. Made by Doulton & Co. Lambeth. Between 1891 and c.1920. D - 8.3cms.

A very late aberration of the ball stand, or what I have perceived as a ball match stand, are two pieces shown in **Fig. 544**. They have a printed blue maker's mark of the Royally Privileged Porcelain Factory Tettau, in Bavaria, Germany; this mark is believed to have been used after 1957. They are attractively decorated, and the sides have an indented diamond lattice pattern which would serve quite effectively as a striker. Perhaps, as a collector, I have deluded myself into believing that they were intended as match stands; they might have been intended for some other purpose, such as an inkwell.

PART 5: LOYSEL'S LEGACY.

The drawing for Edward Loysel's patent of 1861, for a ribbed striking surface in ceramics, is shown in Fig. 74. A contemporary illustration of the end product is seen in Fig. 75, and a later example of this type of match holder in Fig. 76. His idea appears to have been pushed into the background soon after the patent date. It did not resurface until 1870, when there was an Ornamental Registered Design by William Thomas Standish of London for an open-topped holder in glass which he called a "Lucifer Stand." This was in the form of a truncated cone that closely resembles the examples in Figs. 546 to 548.

Ceramic versions reappeared about 1875, probably in France initially, then spread around the world to Britain, the United States and Japan. Various styles and forms developed, and there was some overlapping of design ideas between the ball match stands and the ribbed strikers.

The truncated cone version was made in Britain by Doulton's of London; an example is shown in **Fig. 545**. It has the impressed Doulton mark first used c. 1891, a pattern number of 347, and the artist's initials "EG" (yet to be identified). The ribbed striking surface extends less than half way down the body, the lower half having applied decorative elements.

Another version is shown in **Fig. 546**, apparently of British manufacture. There is a printed mark of "GUERNSEY COOKING WARE" around a monogram of "AP" inside a large letter "C." The lettering and body color is reminiscent of products by the Longpark Pottery Co. of Torquay, Devonshire.

A French example, popular in the first decade of this century, is shown in **Fig. 547**. It displays in its form and decoration a certain elegance lacking in some of the other examples. On the underside is a printed mark, "Décor" over "J.P." over "L," the mark for Guérin-Pouyat-Elite Ltd. of Limoges.

The example in **Fig. 548** was made in the United States. It has a printed mark of "KT&K" over "CHINA," for Knowles, Taylor & Knowles of East Liverpool, Ohio. The company is perhaps best known for its "Lotus Ware," a fine, delicate bone china produced from c. 1889 until 1896. Before and after these dates the company was producing a much thicker china ware for the hotel trade, for which the example was no doubt intended.

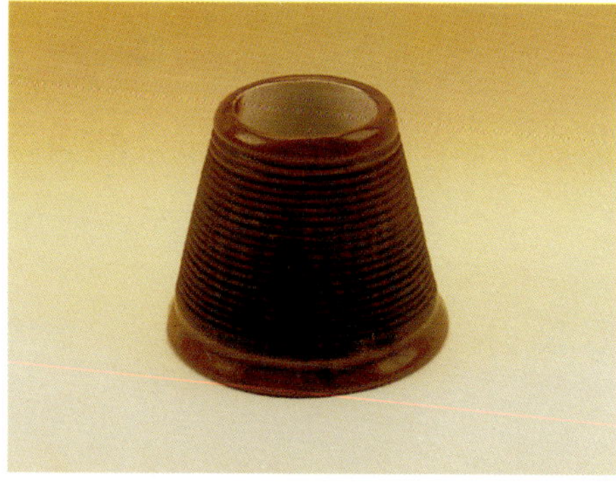

Fig. 546 Britain. Ceramic. Unidentified mark. c.1910. D - 7.2cms.

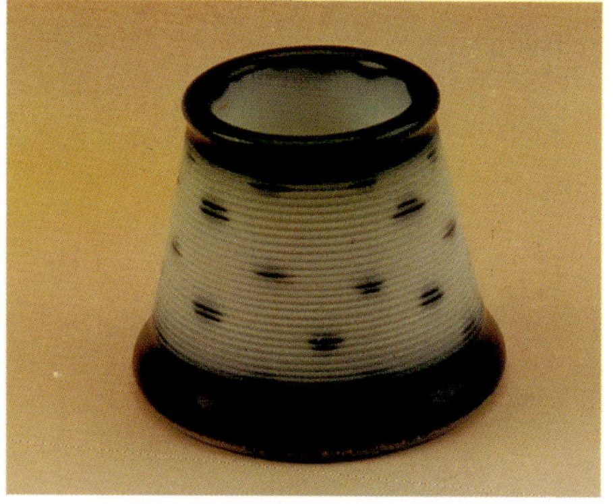

Fig. 547 France. Ceramic. Made by Guerin-Pouyat-Elite Ltd. c.1910. D - 6.8cms.

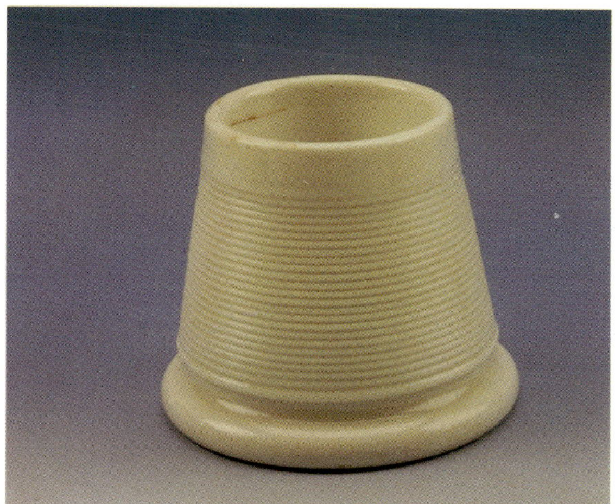

Fig. 548 United States. Ceramic. Made by Knowles, Taylor & Knowles. c.1910. D - 7.9cms.

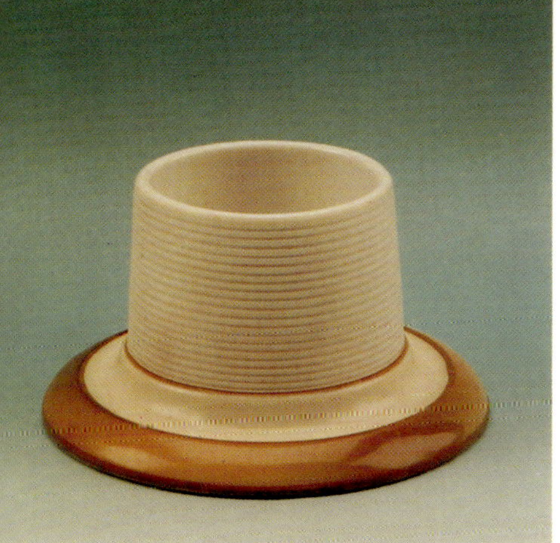

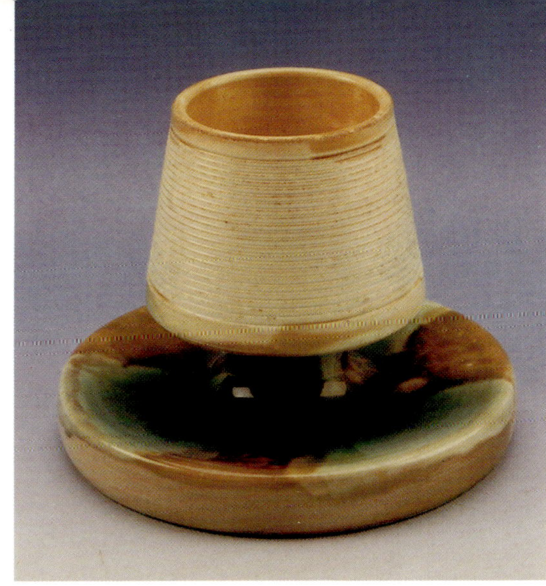

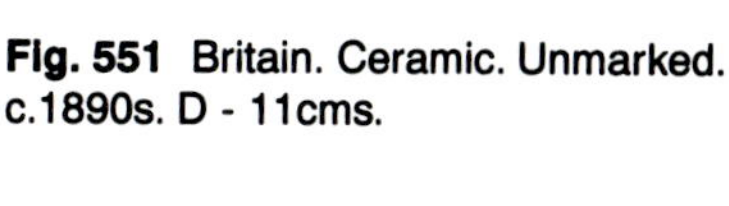

Fig. 551 Britain. Ceramic. Unmarked. c.1890s. D - 11cms.

Fig. 549 Japan. Ceramic. Made by Nippon Kaisha Ltd. Post 1921. D - 9.2cms.

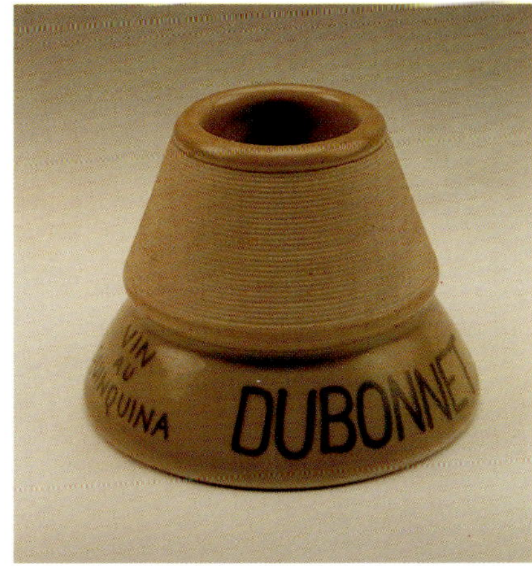

Fig. 553 France. Ceramic. Unmarked. c.1885 to 1910. D - 9.3cms.

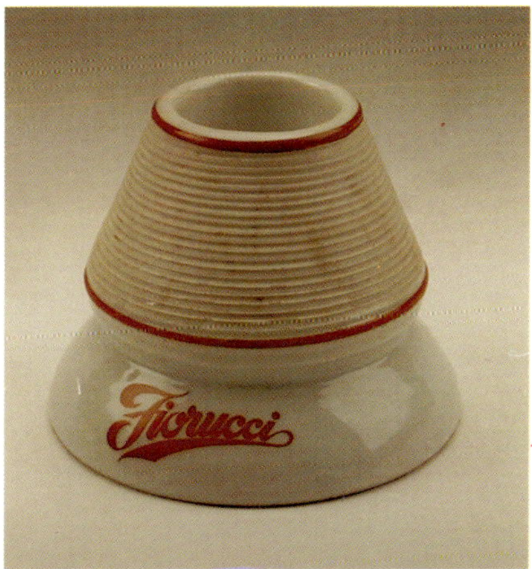

Fig. 550 France or Germany. Ceramic. c.1900. H - 5.7cms.

Fig. 552 United States. Ceramic. Unmarked. c.1910. D - 14.5cms.

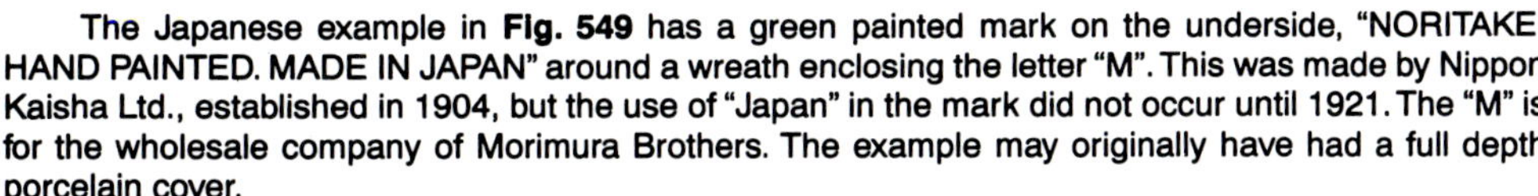

Fig. 554 France. Ceramic. Unmarked. c.1885 to 1910. D - 9.8cms.

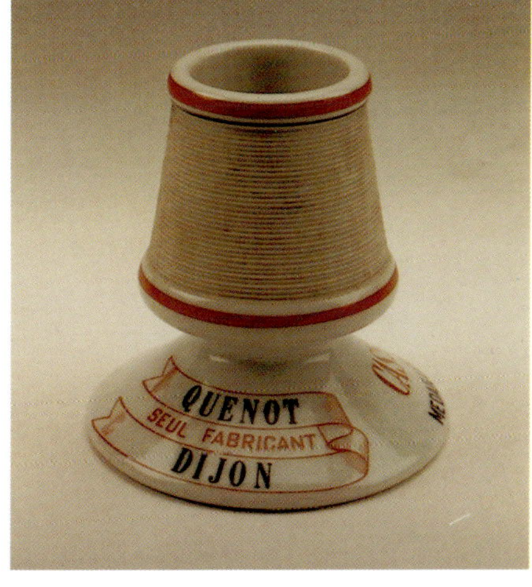

Fig. 555 France. Ceramic. Unmarked. c.1885 to 1910. H - 9.2cms.

The Japanese example in **Fig. 549** has a green painted mark on the underside, "NORITAKE. HAND PAINTED. MADE IN JAPAN" around a wreath enclosing the letter "M". This was made by Nippon Kaisha Ltd., established in 1904, but the use of "Japan" in the mark did not occur until 1921. The "M" is for the wholesale company of Morimura Brothers. The example may originally have had a full depth porcelain cover.

An unmarked example in **Fig. 550** is probably bisque ware, and is not well executed. This may be of French or German origin, intended for the domestic market, c. l900.

The unmarked example in **Fig. 551** is in the form of a truncated cone, mounted on a short column, set on a shallow ashtray. The mottled green and browns on the ashtray, as well as the overall form, suggest this may be of British origin. A very similar piece has been seen with the Wedgwood mark and the date letters for 1878.

"Keen's English Chop House," printed around the ashtray in the example in **Fig. 552**, has not been identified; but it is assumed to have been in the United States, and the holder was probably made there. Raised lettering on the underside says "CUSTOM MADE FOR KEEN'S ENGLISH CHOP HOUSE", and the term "Custom Made" was more commonly used in the United States.

It seems likely that almost every bar and café in France provided its clientele with match holders on the tables. In a painting by Vincent van Gogh entitled "Agostina Segatori: In the Café Le Tambourin" (1888), such a holder is shown on the table in front of the model Agostina, the owner of the Montmartre café. Works by other artists of the same period also show match holders, mostly of a form believed to be almost exclusively French.

The examples in **Figs. 553 to 555** are typical of such items, advertising alcoholic beverages which were popular then (and some remain so today). Glued to the underside of each is a circular patch, treated for striking safety matches. This form was in use from c. 1885 until c. 1910. No doubt they were made in France, but none has been seen with a maker's mark.

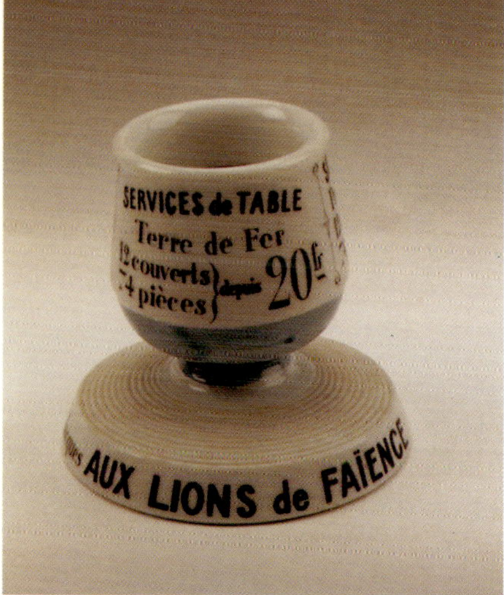

Fig. 556 France. Ceramic. Possibly made by Aux Lions de Faience. c.1885 to 1910. D - 9cms.

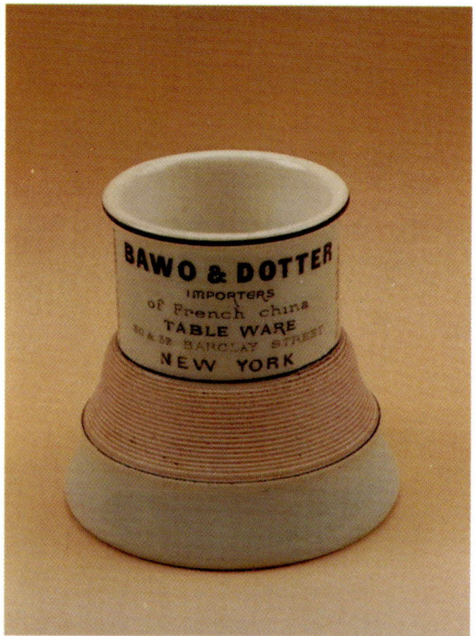

Fig. 557 France. Ceramic. Made for Bawo & Dotter at their factory in Limoges for their headquarters in New York. c.1885 to 1910. D -7.6cms.

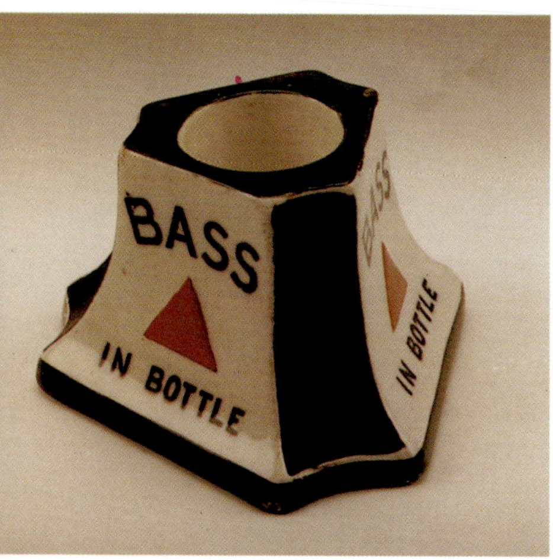

Fig. 558 Britain. Ceramic. Made by Minton's. Between 1895 and 1900. H - 6.5cms.

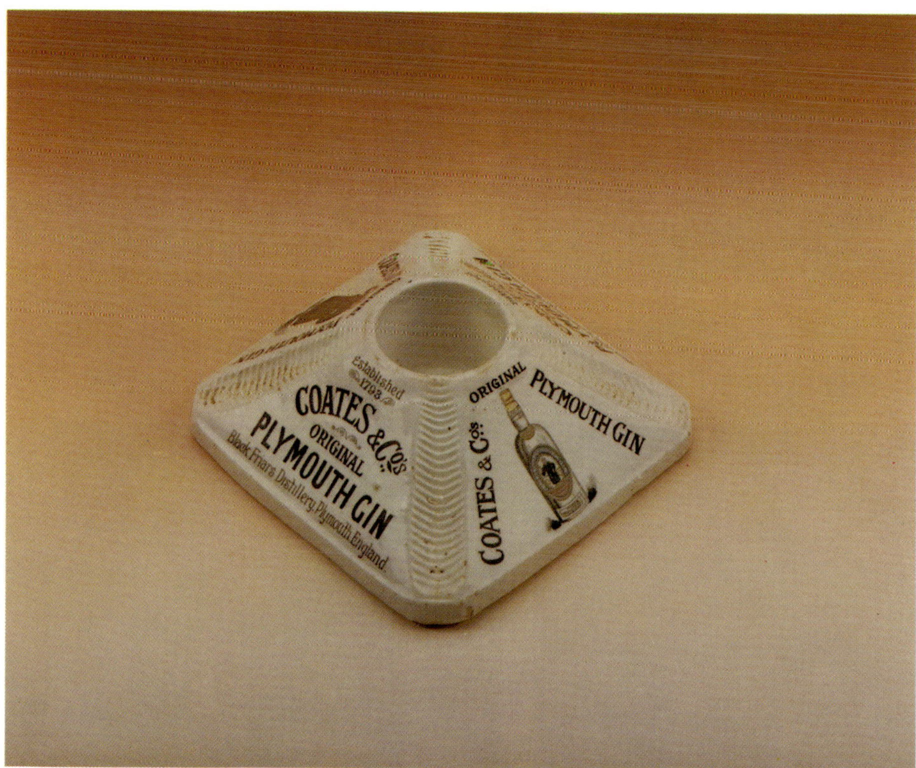

Fig. 559 Britain. Ceramic. Marked Wedekind & Co. c.1900. W - 12.6cms.

Also typically French in form, the example in **Fig. 556** has the striker located on the upper part of the base, and a circular patch underneath for safety matches. The advertising is for Aux Lions de Faience, with a Paris address; this company dealt in porcelain and glass for domestic and commercial consumption. If it was also involved in manufacturing, it may have made the match holder.

The example in **Fig. 557** was made for, and probably by, Bawo & Dotter, which maintained a head office in New York City, and owned factories in Fischern, Bohemia (now Czechoslovakia), and Limoges, France. The reverse side of the match-well shows an illustration of its factory in Limoges, where this example was probably made, and also refers to a Paris address which was presumably an office. The company probably exported the example to its headquarters in New York. It is known to have been in business from 1864 until c. 1914. The striker is the pink band around the central portion, but there is no sign it ever had a safety match pad fixed to the underside of the base.

This type of match holder can be found in metal, usually brass, either polished or nickel plated, in conical forms; they have ribbed surfaces, and are often mounted on an ashtray. Three versions mounted on ashtrays were shown in the 1895 Harrod's Stores catalogue, from one shilling and four pence to nine shillings and six pence each.

The remaining examples are what may loosely be described as developments that grew out of the Loysel ribbed striker legacy, and the ball match stands. They show some elements from one or other form.

The Bass Pale Ale hexagonal match stand shown in **Fig. 558** has the printed mark of Minton's, from Stoke-on-Trent; the word "England" was added under the mark in 1891, and changed to "Made in England" in 1902. In addition there is also a faintly impressed mark of a swan that Minton's used only between 1895 and 1900. The stand also bears the printed mark "THE PROPERTY OF BASS & CO. LTD. BURTON-ON-TRENT," suggesting the probability that the holder was made specifically for Bass to distribute to the public houses that sold its ale. The three narrow, dark, vertical sides are ribbed for friction; they appear to have been treated for the ignition of safety matches, but tests have failed to ignite a safety match. An identical holder was made by Doulton & Co. Ltd., and has a Registered Design number for 1906. It seems odd that Doulton should register a design for a piece previously made by a competitor apparently for some years.

The rectangular, squat form in **Fig. 559** also has the striker areas in troughs running up from the corners. It has a printed mark reading "Wedekind & Co. London," the previously mentioned retailers who supplied a number of advertising items to Coates & Co. This is probably c. 1900.

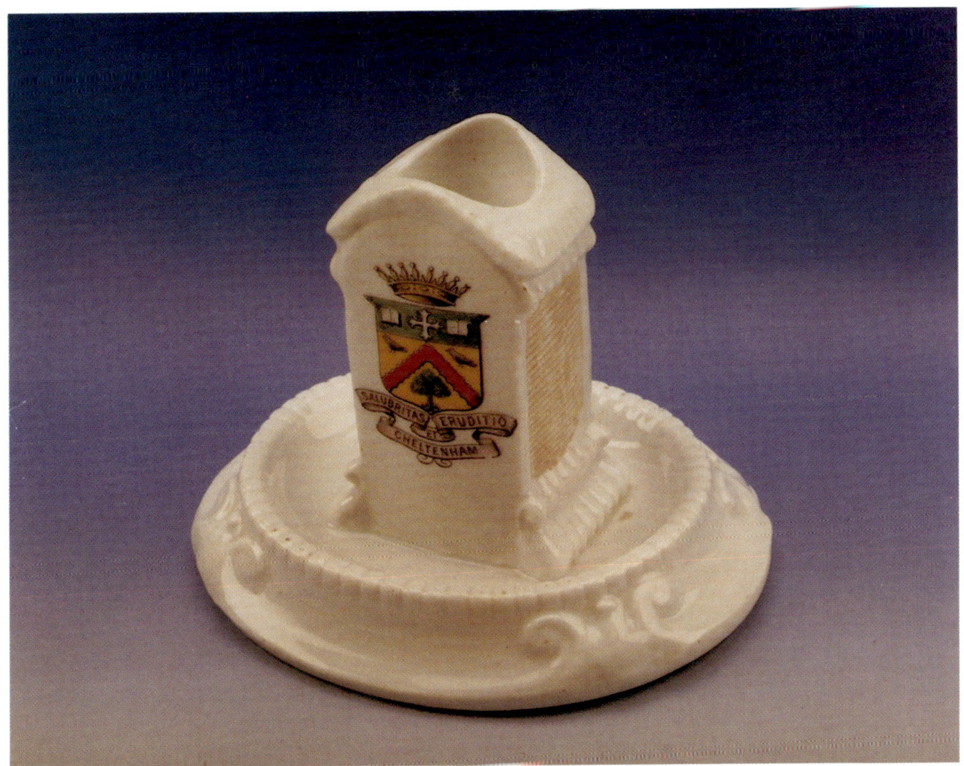

Fig. 560 Austria. Ceramic. Made to a British Registered Design of 1906. H - 12cms.

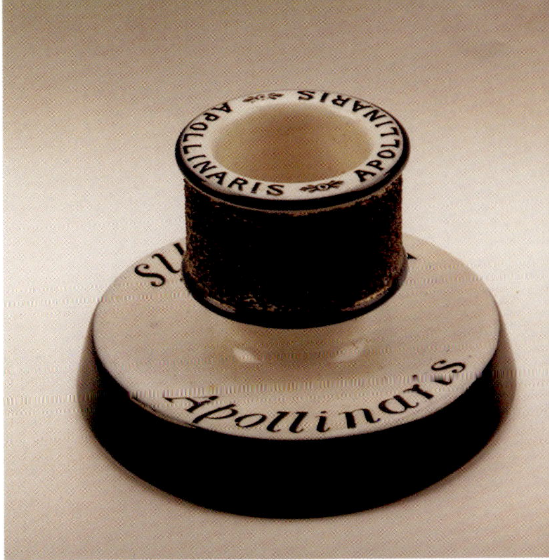

Fig. 561 Britain. Ceramic. Made by W. Wood & Co. Post 1915. D -11.4cms.

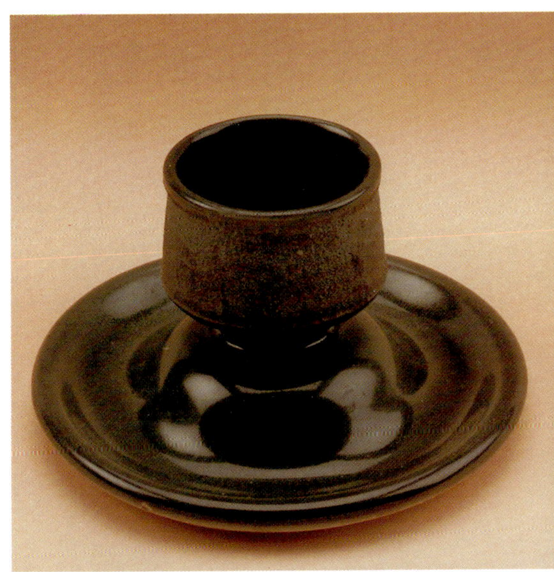

Fig. 562 Britain. Ceramic. Made by Doulton & Co. of Burslem, Staffordshire. Post 1902. D - 12.8cms.

The example in **Fig. 560** is marked "Made In Austria" and has a British Registered Design number for 1906. The registration has not been checked, but it is possible that it was registered to an Austrian company, or it could have been made under license from a British company or designer. The ribbed striking patches are located on opposite sides of the column. Other examples may be found, usually with a design on the front column side only. This example bears the crest of the Gloucestershire town of Cheltenham, but another known example has advertising for "Caley's Table Waters." So they were obviously produced to order as souvenirs and advertising items.

The popular mineral water Apollinaris was exported from Germany throughout Europe and North America from before 1895; it is still produced today. The example in **Fig. 561** advertising that beverage, bears the printed mark of W. Wood & Co. of Burslem, Staffordshire, used between 1915 and 1932, when the company ceased trading. The outside of the cylindrical holder has what appears to be a sanded finish.

The example in **Fig. 562** has a more elegant shape, but a drab finish. There is a sanded striker on the holder section. It bears the printed mark of Doulton & Co. Ltd. of Burslem, Staffordshire, used from 1902 onwards.

In the truncated cone form, made from an unidentified material that *appears* to be a cross between pottery and concrete, is an example shown in **Fig. 563**. The rim and base are trimmed with brass, and the sides sanded for friction. It is unmarked; however, later on the same day I acquired it in Champlain, New York State, I saw a similar piece in northern New Hampshire. This may of course be coincidence, but does suggest the possibility that it came from a local source in that region of the United States.

As in the other sections of this book, the examples shown here only scratch the surface of what there is available to be found. A fascinating collection of this type alone could take a lifetime to put together, provide ample research opportunities, and still not cover all of the possibilities. As reminders of the past, of places, and products long forgotten or even still available, they can provide endless amusement and even education.

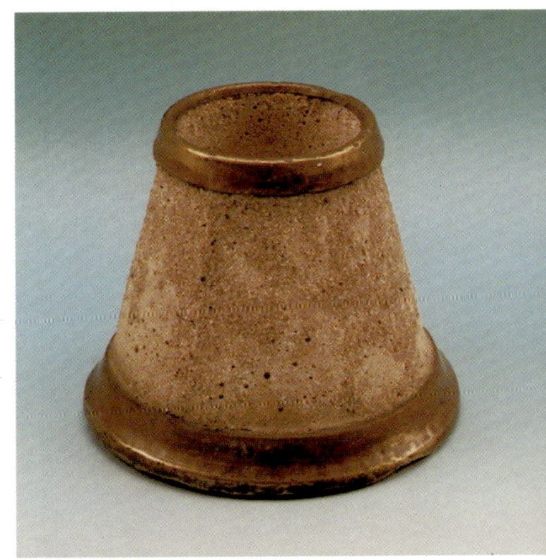

Fig. 563 United States. Ceramic type, brass. Date unknown. D -8.6cms.

PART 6: NOVELTIES AND OTHER CERAMIC FORMS

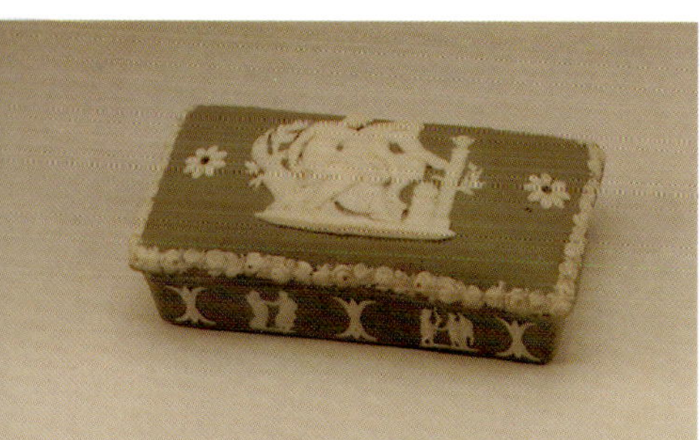

Fig. 564 Britain. Ceramic. Made by Josiah Wedgwood & Sons Ltd. Between 1891 and 1910. L - 9.6cms.

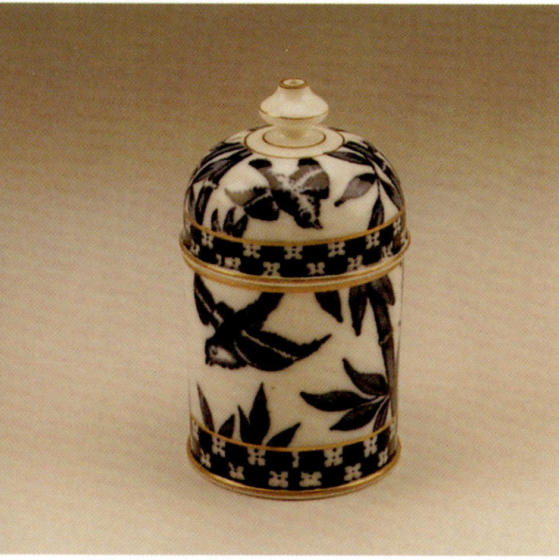

Fig. 565 Britain. Ceramic. Made by Coalport Porcelain Works. Between 1881 and c.1891. H - 8.1cms.

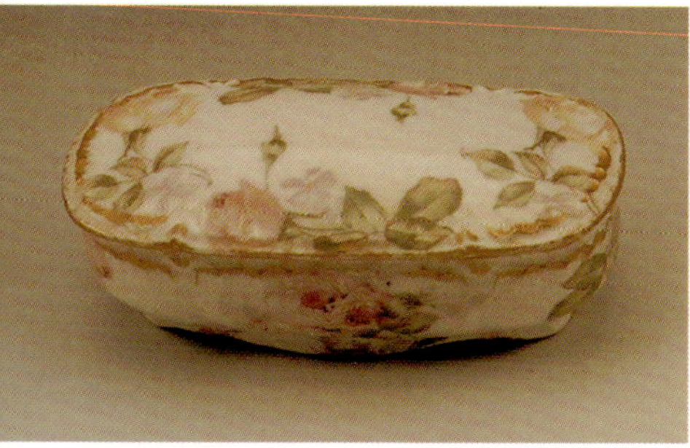

Fig. 566 France. Ceramic. Marked "GDA Limoges". c.1900. L -10.8cms.

Fig. 567 Britain. Ceramic. Made by Wileman & Co. Between c.1911 and c.1923. L - 10.5cms.

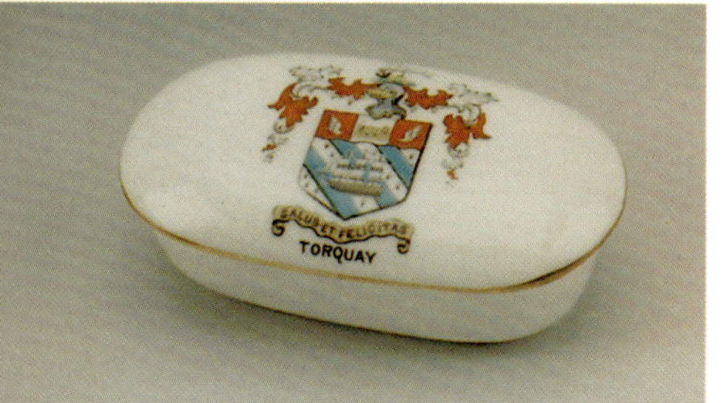

Match holders with lids were less common than those with open tops, and are probably a carry-over from the early protective holders; although the lids helped to disguise the purpose of the object, which may have been an aesthetically desirable factor in some homes. There was a tendency for such forms to exhibit greater sophistication, at a slightly higher purchase price.

Austria, France, Germany, and later Czechoslovakia were the major producers of the open-topped forms, usually very inexpensive and cheerful in appearance. Often sentimental or humorous, they were acquired for ornamental reasons—to add clutter to mantlepieces and other horizontal surfaces in Victorian and Edwardian homes. They were often given as prizes at fairs, leading to the appellation of 'fairings'. They may be charming or gaudy according to personal taste, but they have attracted many collectors, in spite of the fact that many are unmarked or undated.

It is probably fair to say that the better quality pieces were those that were marked. Among the leaders in the field were Conta & Boehme of Possneck in Thuringia, Germany, whose mark was a shield enclosing an arm bent at the elbow, the hand holding a dagger. The company specialized in manufacturing souvenirs, dolls, doll parts, and decorative household items. It also produced a wide range of match holders, two examples of which are shown in this section, while a third example is shown in Chapter VII on wall match holders. The company was established in 1790 and continued operating until the 1930s.

In Britain perhaps the earliest manufacturer of lidded forms was Josiah Wedgwood & Sons Ltd., known to have produced two types, one in the form of a casket and the other a cylinder. They were decorated in his renowned Jasper ware designs, in various shades of blue, light green, and lilac, and bore his impressed mark and quite frequently a date mark, which can be decoded from a number of books on ceramic marks.

The casket type was made in either an oval or a rectangular form, the latter shown in **Fig. 564**. Each had a slightly domed, loose-fitting, lift-off lid, the underside grooved transversely for friction. The top was provided with two small sockets for wax vesta matches, and its white decorative elements were of classical, geometric and floral forms. The example here has the impressed Wedgwood name, along with the word "England," which indicates that the box was made between 1891 and 1910 (when the words "Made in" were added). There is also an impressed letter "P," indicating the Wedgwood Pearl body. There is no date mark, but this type of holder was made from about 1860 until well into the 1930s. In the 1930s the form continued to be made, but without the match sockets and striking patch, offered as "trinket" boxes.

Wedgwood's cylindrical holders were made with a deep slip-on lid. One type had a flat top and a match socket in the center; a second had a domed lid, with a small match socket, or match and candle sockets. These were first made in 1855, continuing until the 1930s.

The example shown in **Fig. 565** is similar in size and shape to the Wedgwood cylindrical types, but has a bolder match socket. On the underside of the lid is the printed mark of the Coalport Porcelain Works of Coalport, Shropshire, used between 1881 and c. 1891. As with the Wedgwood type, the striker is located on the underside of the base in the form of concentric circles.

The oval casket form shown in **Fig. 566** was made in Limoges, France. It bears the underglaze printed green mark of "GDA," as well as a printed orange mark over the glaze reading "GDA" above "LIMOGES" enclosed in a wreath, with the words "HENRY MORGAN & CO. COLONIAL HOUSE, MONTREAL." An oval striking patch is located on the underside of the loose-fitting lid, on which the design is the popular Victorian "Moss Rose." It was probably made about 1900 to a specific order from the Morgan company, but no doubt was also made for more general distribution.

The oval casket in **Fig. 567** was made as a souvenir of Torquay in Devonshire and has a printed mark over the glaze "MANUFACTURED FOR D. I. ALLAMS & SONS, TORQUAY." It has a printed, green underglaze mark for Wileman & Co. of Longton, Staffordshire, used from c. 1911 until c. 1923. These souvenirs were no doubt made with crests of other British towns.

The oval casket form shown in **Fig. 568** is in much thicker china decorated in dark greens with some gold trim; it is less finely detailed than the foregoing examples. It has the impressed mark "EICHWALD," and a pattern number. Eichwald is located in Bohemia, Czechoslovakia (formerly part of the Austro-Hungarian Empire, prior to the Versailles Treaty of 1919). Only one pottery company is listed for that town, B. Bloch & Co., in business from 1871 to 1940. It used various marks, and the mark on this piece is believed to have been one of the earlier ones.

Fig. 568 Bohemia (now Czechoslovakia). Ceramic. Probably made by B. Bloch & Co. c.1890s. L - 9.5cms.

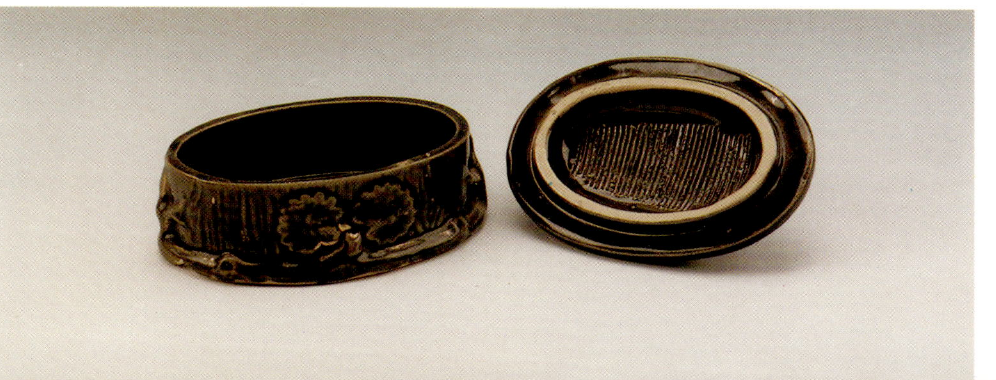

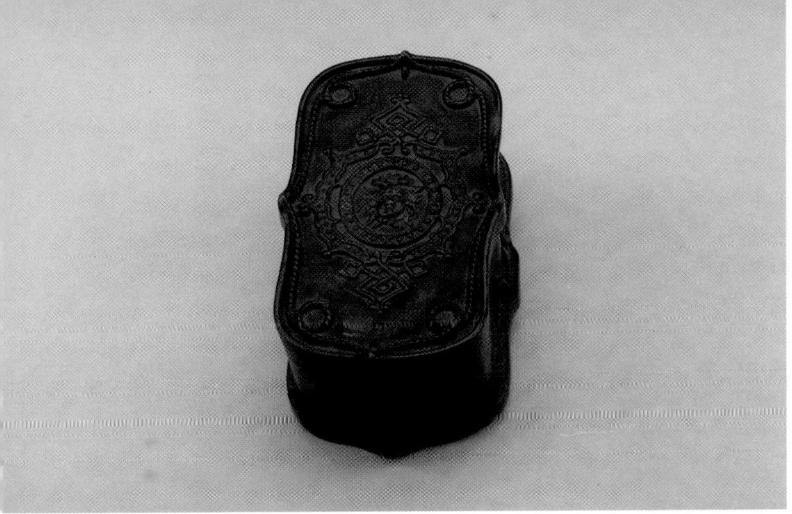

Fig. 569 Bohemia (now Czechoslovakia). Ceramic Made by W. Schiller & Son. c. 1885. L - 12.6cms.

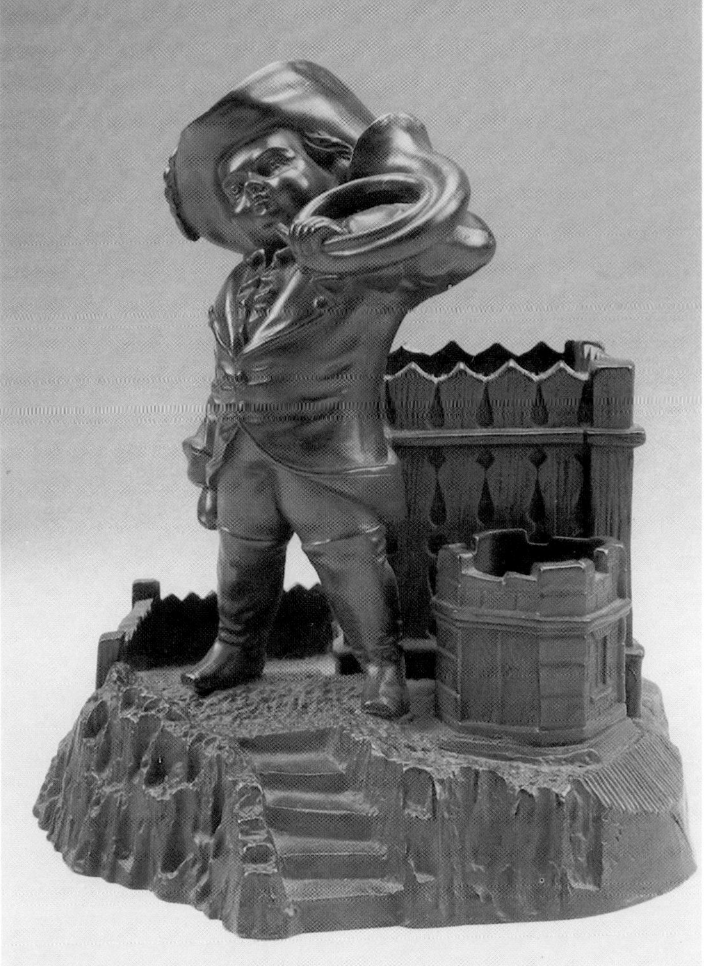

Fig. 570 Bohemia (now Czechoslovakia). Ceramic. Made by W. Schiller & Son. c. 1885. H - 20.8 cms.

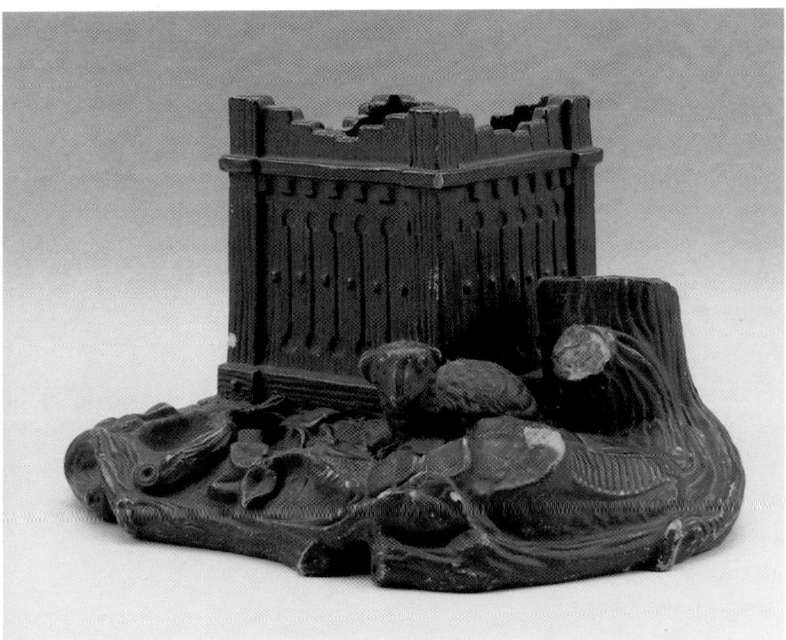

Fig. 571 Bohemia (now Czechoslovakia). Ceramic. Made by W. Schiller & Son. c.1885. W (of base) - 17.8cms.

In a terra-cotta body with dark brown glaze is a casket with a pseudo-classical design and rope-twist borders around the lid and base, shown in **Fig. 569**. It has an impressed mark "WS&S," for W. Schiller & Son of Bodenbach, Bohemia. The company made quite a wide variety of casket forms; the number of examples that have been seen suggests that it was quite prolific in its output and probably exported many to North America.

However, caskets were not Schiller's only products; it produced, also in terra-cotta, an extensive series of combined cigar and match holders in sculptural forms that display considerable imagination. The example in **Fig. 570** shows a young man about to blow his horn (perhaps representing Little Boy Blue), with a fenced compound for the cigars behind him, and a smaller castle-like compartment at his side for the matches. The striker is located just below the match holder to its right. The company mark and pattern number "83" are impressed on a small platform behind the cigar holder.

A second example in this style is shown in **Fig. 571**. The fenced compound acts as the cigar holder, while the hollow tree trunk is to hold the matches. A sheep is nestled down in the foliage behind the striker platform. A depression with a log across it in front of the cigar holder, acts as an ashtray. It has the impressed Schiller mark and the pattern number of "54" on the underside of the base.

In a similar style, but in quite a different body which appears to have used clay made in different colored layers to produce a striated effect, is the example in **Fig. 572**. The taller tree trunk has holes to hold cigars, the match holder is formed by a smaller hollow tree trunk at the left. The two are overlaid with large leaves and branches of oak, including acorns. A fox peeps out from under the roots of the larger tree trunk. The striker is located on a platform at the front edge. There is no maker's mark, but on the underside of the base is the number "136" in an elaborate escutcheon; this is presumably a pattern number. No doubt made in the same region, all of these last three examples probably date to c. 1890.

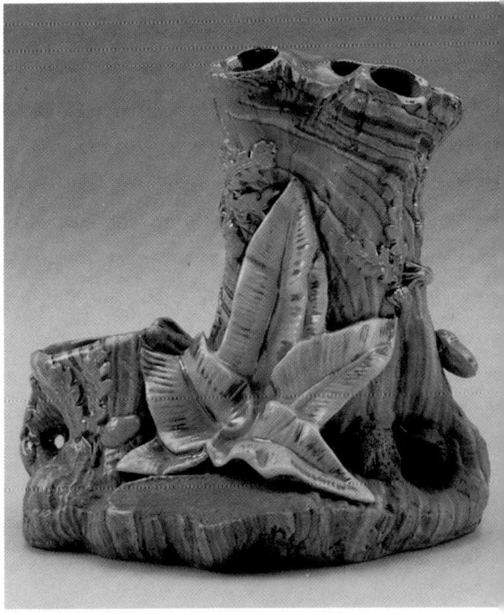

Fig. 572 Europe. Ceramic. c.1885. H - 11.6cms.

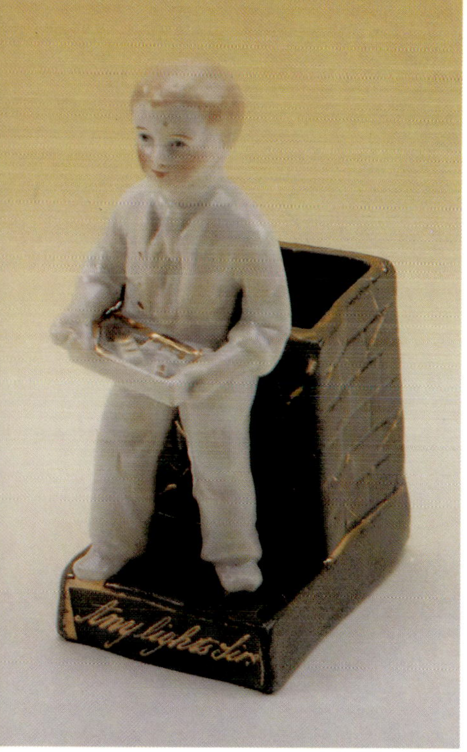

Fig. 573 Germany. Ceramic. Made by Conta & Boehme. Last quarter of 19th century. H - 11.4cms.

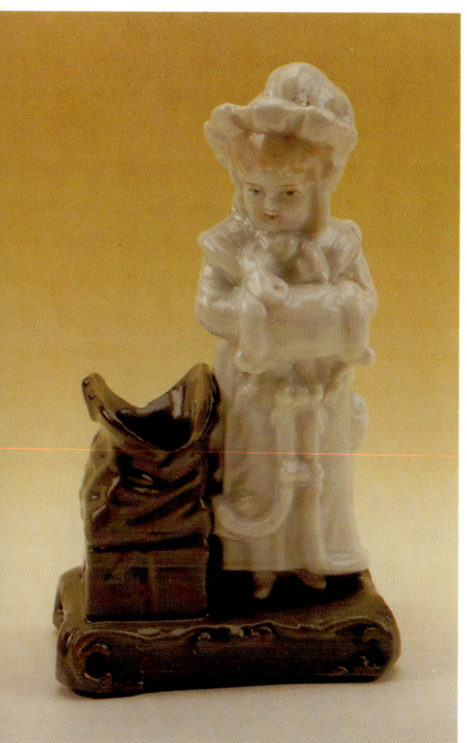

Fig. 574 Germany. Ceramic. Made by Conta & Boehme. Last quarter of l9th century. H - 15cms.

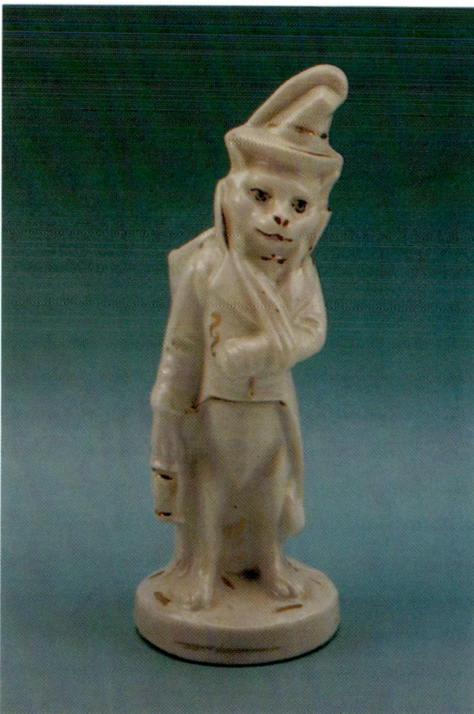

Fig. 575 Europe. Ceramic. Last quarter of 19th century. H - 14cms.

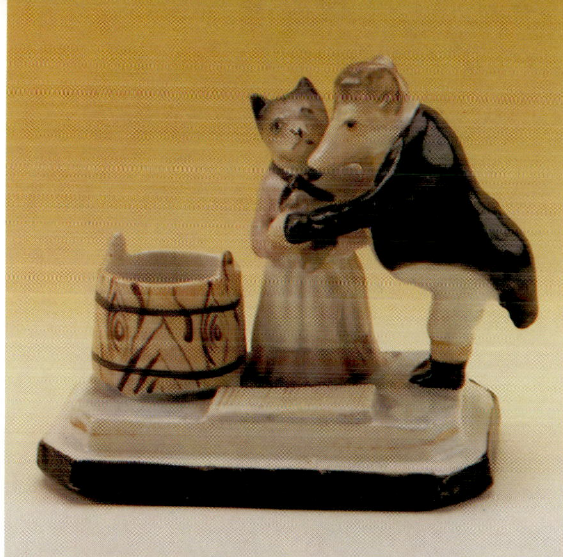

Fig. 576 Europe. Ceramic. Late 19th century. H - 10.7cms.

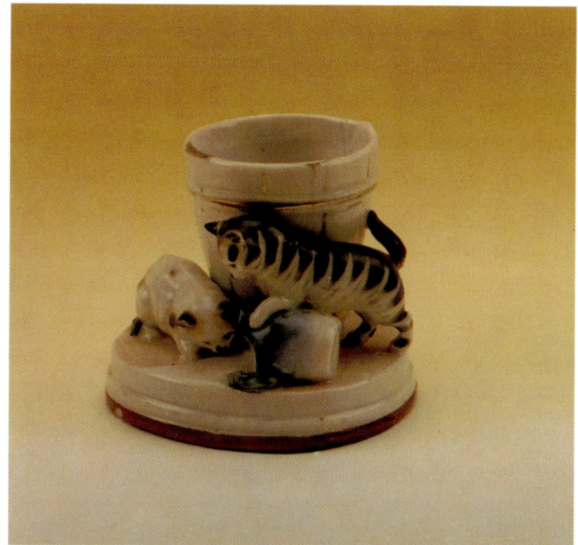

Fig. 577 Europe. Ceramic. Late 19th century. H - 6.5cms.

Probably dating from the last quarter of the l9th century are two examples of Conta & Boehme, shown in **Figs. 573 and 574.** The boy in Fig. 573 is a match seller, and along the front edge of the base in gold lettering, is the inscription "Any lights Sir?". He stands with his back towards a hollow stack of bricks: as the match holder, the back of which is roughened for friction. This was obviously made for the English-speaking market. The young lady in Fig. 574 appears to be waiting for transportation, with her hands tucked into a muff. Beside her is a box tied with string, with an open bag on top to hold the matches. The back of the box is roughened for friction. Both figures have the Conta & Boehme mark and a pattern number impressed on the underside of the base.

Groups, children, animals and domestic scenes were all grist to the Conta & Boehme mill; the company turned such scenes out in profusion. Other companies produced similar examples which were probably inspired by, or even copied from, Conta & Boehme. The three following examples are unmarked and were probably made by contemporary rivals.

Fig. 575 is just recognisable as a cat, which has one front leg in a sling, the other one carrying what is probably a lantern. The basket slung on his back from straps acts as the match holder and the location of the striker. This does not begin to match the quality of Conta & Boehme pieces.

The example in **Fig. 576**, while displaying a certain amusing charm, is again of lower quality. The dancing couple represent a cat with an unidentifiable animal as its partner. However, the example in **Fig. 577** is far better executed. It shows two cats, one of which is lapping the milk from the overturned and broken milk jug, with the milk pail behind them.

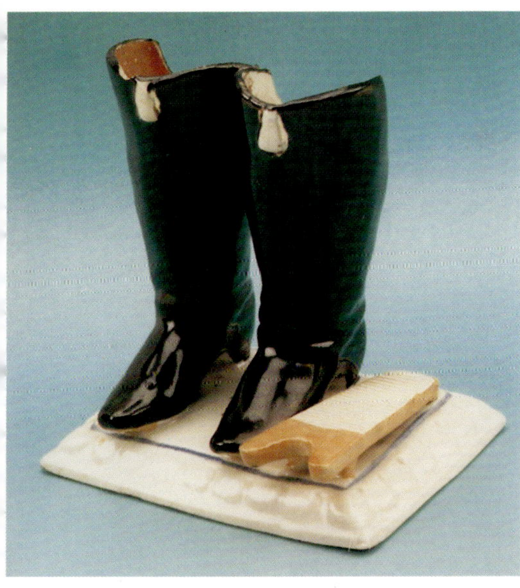

Fig. 578 Europe. Ceramic. Last quarter of 19th century. H - 9 cms.

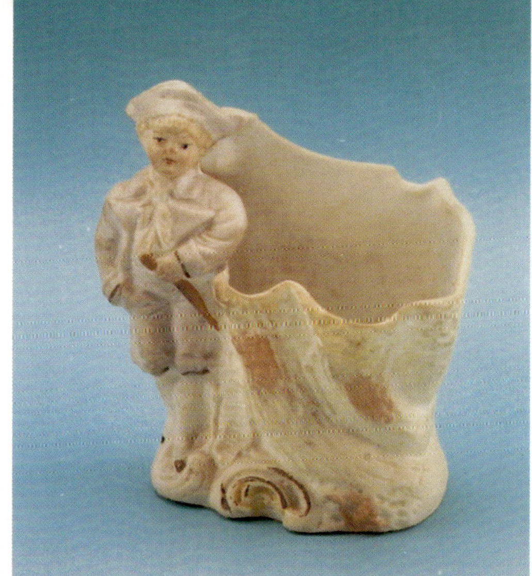

Fig. 580 France? Ceramic. Last quarter of 19th century. H -8.7cms.

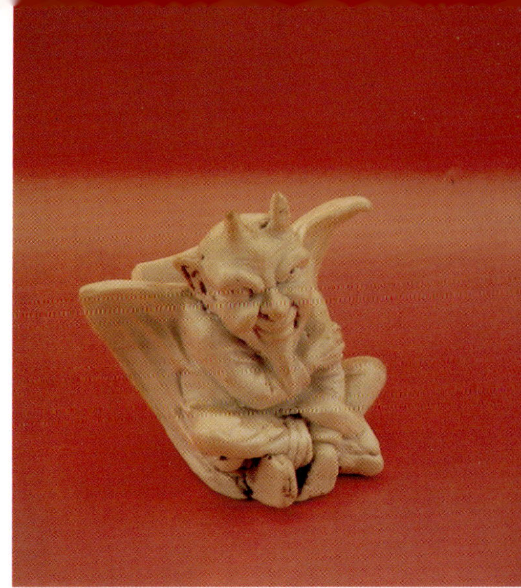

Fig. 581 France? Ceramic. Last quarter of 19th century. H -7.5cms.

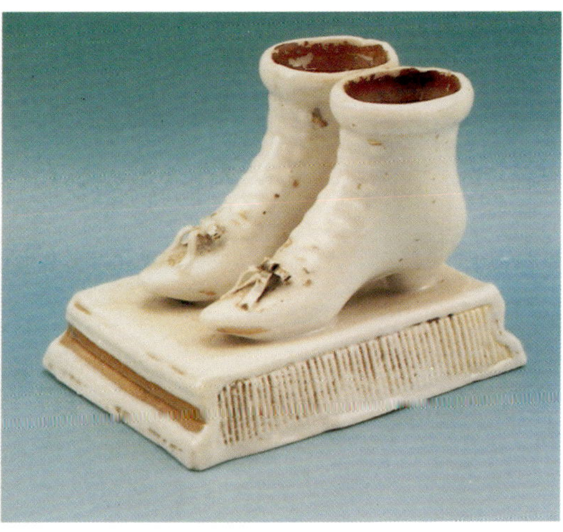

Fig. 579 Europe. Ceramic. Last quarter of 19th century. H -6.1cms.

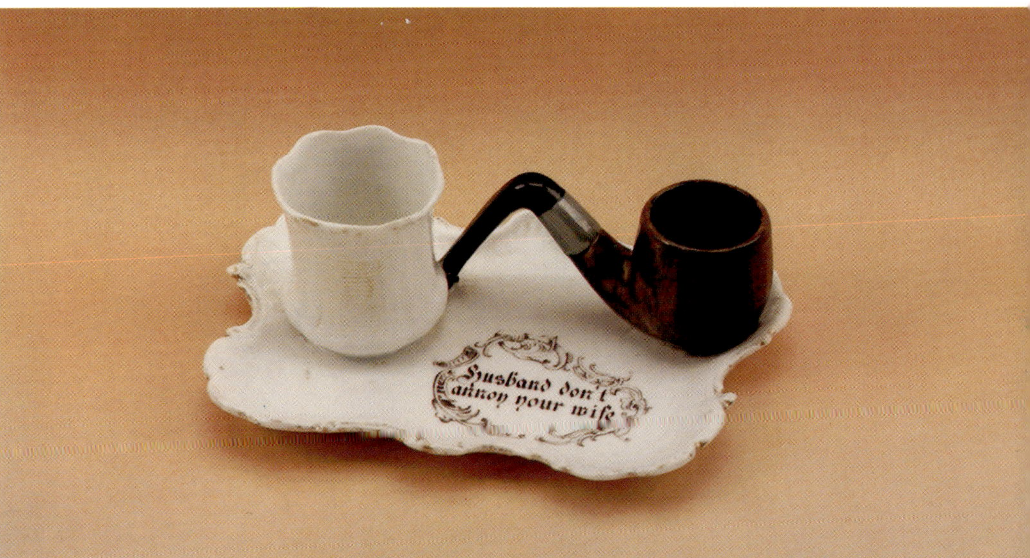

Fig. 582 Bohemia (now Czechoslovakia). Ceramic. Made by Porzellanfabrik "Victoria" Schmidt & Co. c.1900. L - 16cms.

Boots were a popular subject, those of both sexes being represented here. In **Fig. 578** is a pair of gentleman's riding boots beside a boot jack, which is grooved for friction; and in **Fig. 579**, a pair of ladies button boots. Neither example is marked, but they were probably also made in Germany in the last quarter of the 19th century.

Bisque is an unglazed porcelain with a dull surface. It was used fairly extensively to produce a range of inexpensive sculptural forms of match holder. The two examples shown here, in **Figs. 580 and 581**, seem to represent innocence and evil. The young boy leans nonchalantly against an unidentifiable form, the match holder proper, which has the striker on its side. It has an incised number on the back. In the second example, the devil is smiling and seated with his back against a pile of bricks that form the match holder. The body of the devil has been filled, presumably to prevent the matches from falling inside his body and wings. Neither has a maker's mark, but they are probably French, from the last quarter of the 19th century.

The combined ashtray and match holder with the representation of a pipe with a bent stem in **Fig. 582** has the printed blue mark of the Altrohlau, Bohemia company of Porzellanfabrik "Victoria" Schmidt & Co., which traded from 1885 to 1945 and made household, hotel and decorative porcelain. The ash-tray surface has an elaborate printed frame around the words "Husband don't annoy your wife." A striker is located on both sides of the vase match holder, and the pipe bowl could have acted as a second match holder or perhaps as a receptacle for spent matches. This probably dates from around the turn of the l9th century.

Made in Europe, copying the blue Jasper ware of Wedgwood, but of inferior quality, is the example shown in **Fig. 583**. It is an ashtray base of conical form with three holes around the sides; a plated brass well is set into the top to hold matches, with a striker soldered to the rim. It has an impressed pattern number on the underside of the base, and may date from about 1920.

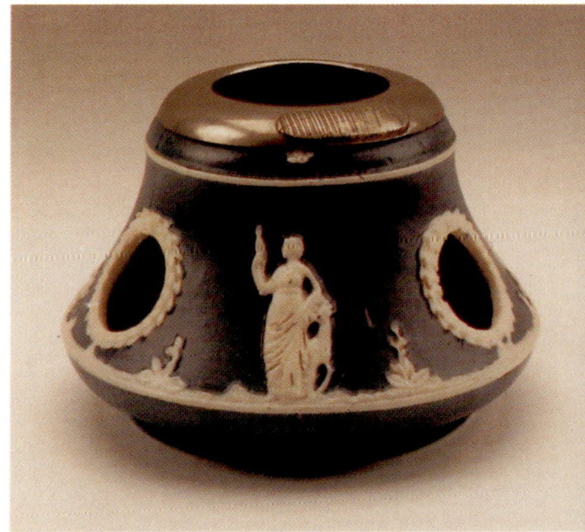

Fig. 583 Europe. Ceramic. plated brass. c.1920. D - 11.3cms.

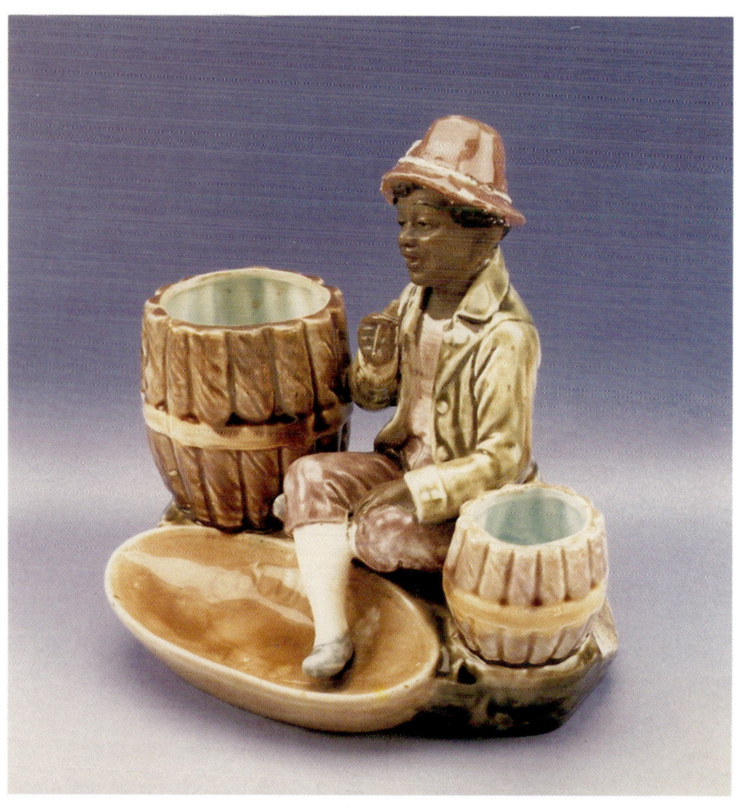

Fig. 584 Europe. Ceramic. c.1900s. H - 16.8cms.

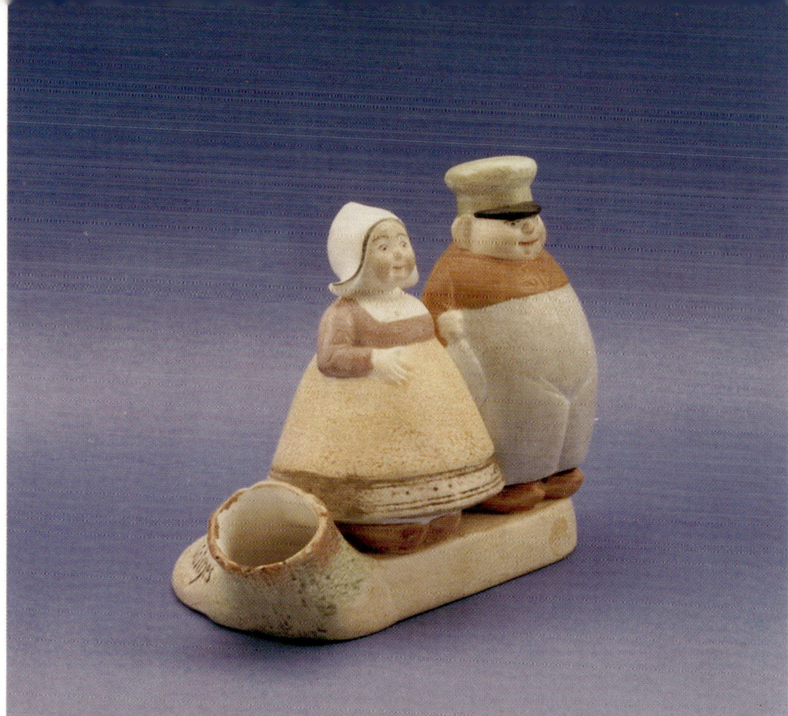

Fig. 586 Germany. Ceramic. Made by Schaffer & Vater Porcelain Factory. c.1910. L - 11.7cms.

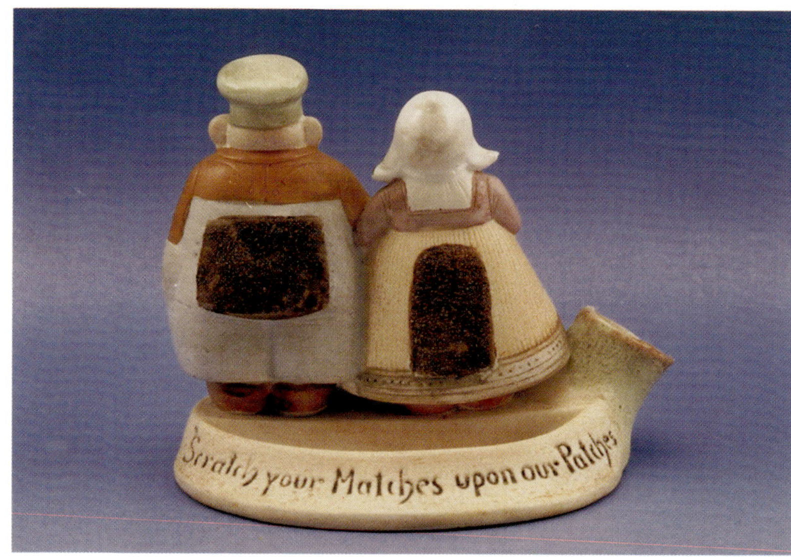

Fig. 587 As Fig. 586.

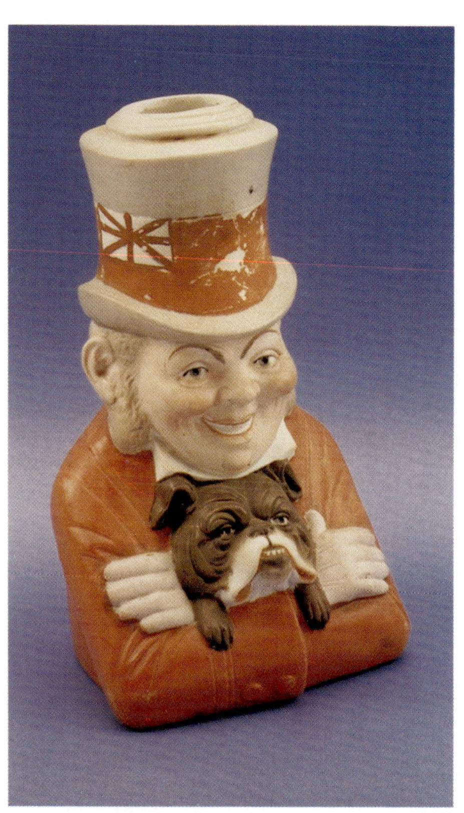

Fig. 585 Germany. Ceramic. Made by Schaffer & Vater Porcelain Factory. c.1910. H - 12.2cms.

A very colorful and finely modeled example, shown in **Fig. 584**, may have been made in Europe for the North American market. The young male negro is savoring a cigar with a smile of contentment upon his face, while seated between two bundles of cigars - one to hold real cigars, the other to hold matches. The trough in front of him has the words "COLUMBIA ALE" in between two oval lines; it is assumed this was made for a United States brewery. The striker is located on the base at the rear. Impressed pattern numbers are to be found on the underside of the base. This may date from the first decade of the 20th century, or possibly a little earlier.

A bust in the form of what is probably John Bull—a hard-drinking, over-eating, typical English gentleman derived from pamphlets written in 1712, popularized by caricaturists in the l9th century—holding a bulldog in his arms, is shown in **Fig. 585**. His top hat serves as the match holder and has an approximation of the Union Jack decorating the band above the brim. There is a hole in the center of the back which serves as access to an ashtray created by the body cavity. It has an impressed mark in the form of a three-pointed crown above a nine-pointed star enclosing the letter "R". This mark was used by the Schaffer & Vater Porcelain Factory of Rudolstadt in Thuringia, Germany, from c. 1896 until c. 1962. This was probably made c. 1910.

Made by the same company, and shown in **Figs. 586 and 587**, is a pair of delightfully rotund Dutch people in traditional dress, including clogs. They stand beside some form of natural growth which acts as the match holder, and with an ashtray behind them. On their backs are the strikers, and around the base of the ashtray the words "Scratch your Matches upon our Patches."

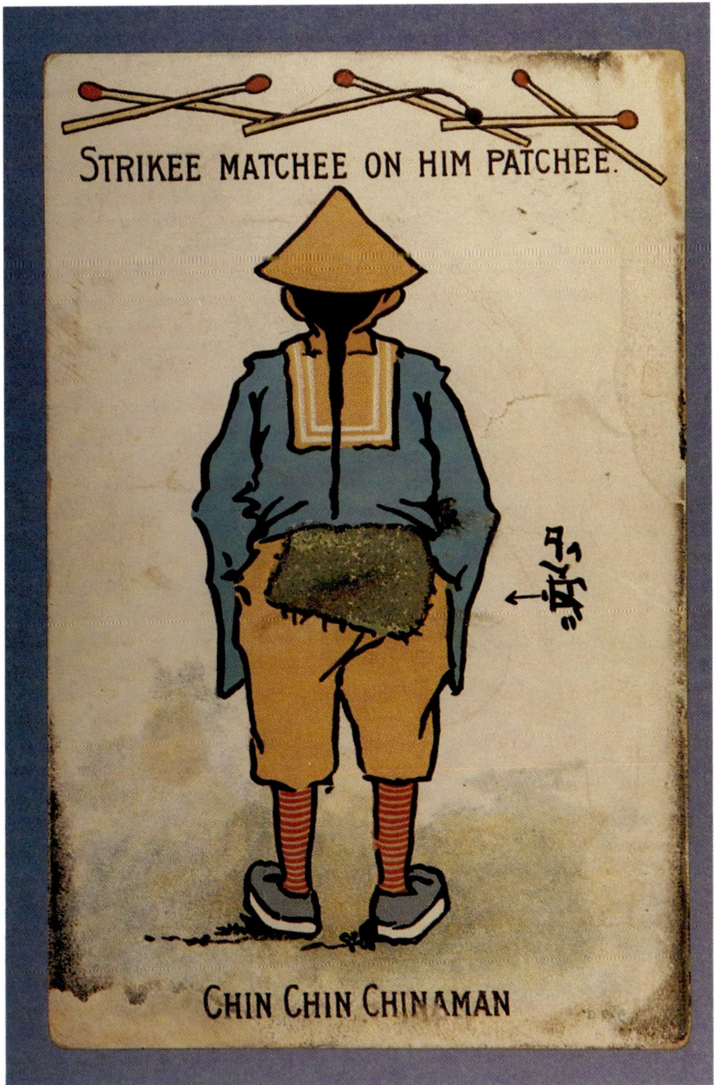

Fig. 588 Britain. Cardboard. Postcard. 1904. Printed by Delittle, Fenwick & Co.

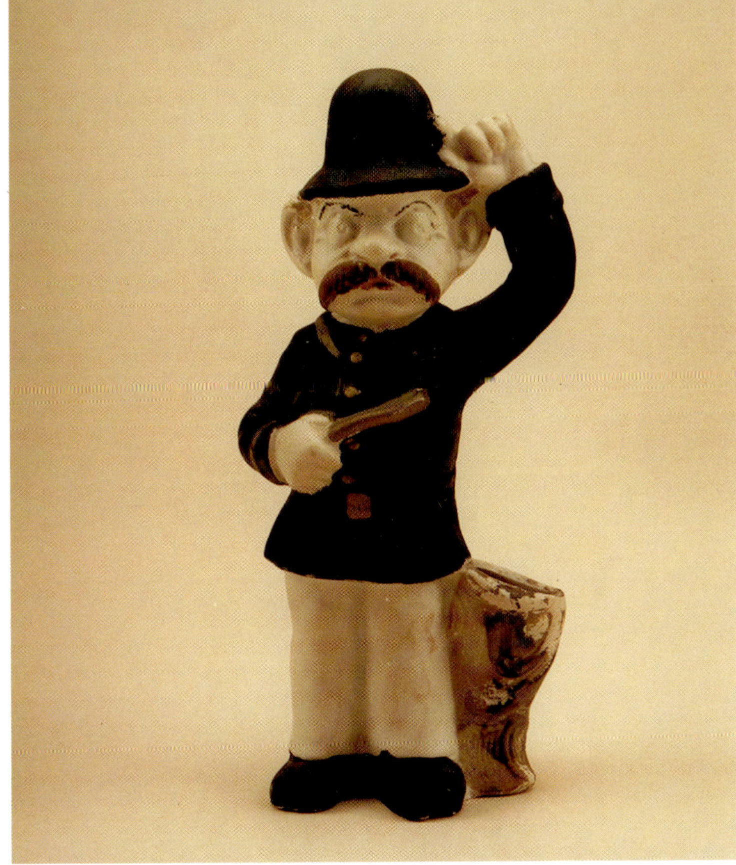

Fig. 589 Europe. Ceramic. c.1900s. H - 20.7cms.

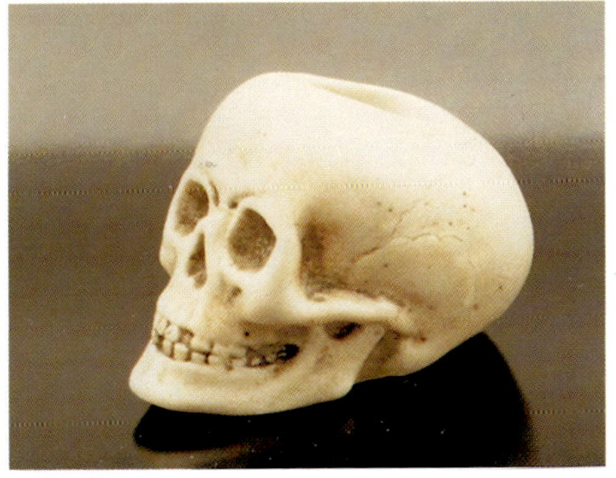

Fig. 590 Germany. Ceramic. Made by Ernst Bohne Sons. c.1900. L -7.3cms.

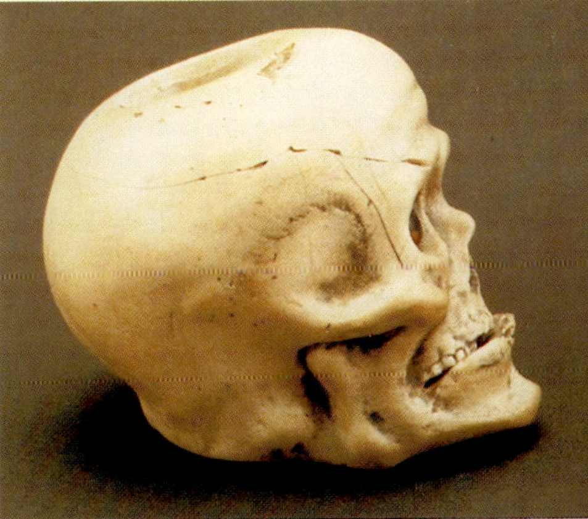

Fig. 591 Germany. Ceramic, glass. Made by Ernst Bohne Sons. c.1900. L - 9cms.

The vogue for what Stanley Aston refers to as "Scratch Mottoes" on ceramic match holders appears to have started in about l909 in Britain, with two registered designs. The first was probably a wall-hanging type with an illustration of a large and a small cat, and the words "Don't Scratch Me Scratch Mother." An almost identical United States Design Patent was issued as late as 1939. The second British Registered Design was for three examples by Max Emanuel & Co., listed as "China and Glassware Manufacturers" of London. Its factory was the Mosanic Pottery Max Emanuel & Co., located in Mitterteich, Bavaria, Germany; the company was trading from c. 1882 to 1918. Two of the Emanuel designs are known to have been produced with the Schaffer & Vater mark.

Other mottoes found on these and other examples are "My word if I catch you bending, I'll strike a match on your ending" and "What if I catch you bending;" and in the United States (an example of which is shown in Fig. 674) "Don't scratch your matches on the walls, Scratch 'em on my overalls!," "Ready for a scratch," "Scratch my back," and "Scratch with us."

The idea, however, may have originated as a postcard with a sanded patch for friction applied to some portion of the illustration, of which there were quite a few. The example in **Fig. 588** would not be acceptable today, but reflects the attitudes of the time that it was postmarked (August 1, 1904). It was printed by Delittle, Fenwick & Co. of York, England.

An unusually large piece in bisque in the form of a comic policeman is shown in **Fig. 589**. The style of the policeman suggests a United States origin, but the match holder located at his side, which bears the striker, has more of a European flavor. It is probably somewhat later than the previous bisque items.

Ernst Bohne Sons of Rudolstadt, Thuringia, Germany was trading from 1854 until c. 1920, producing domestic table wares and figurines. Two examples of the company's work are shown in **Figs. 590 and 591**, in the form of skulls. The striker is located at the back of the skulls, and the larger version in Fig. 591 has glass eyes. Both are marked underneath with a printed blue anchor with a "B" on the stem.

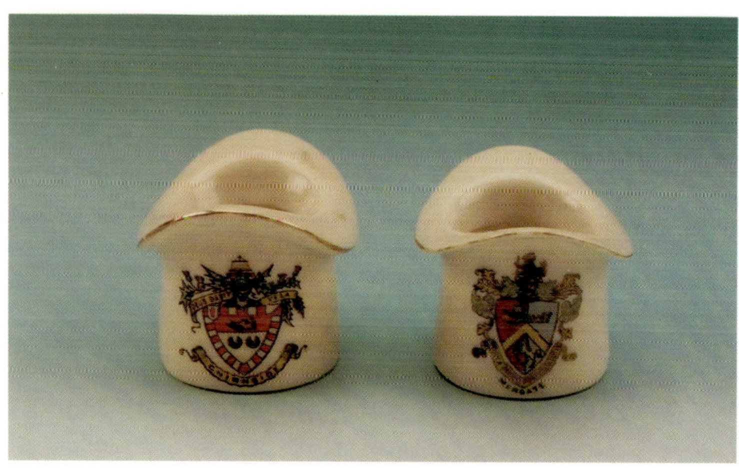

Fig. 592 Europe. Ceramic. Left: made by the Nautilus Porcelain Co. of Glasgow. Between 1896 and 1913. W - 6.5cms. Right: made in Czechoslovakia. After 1919. W - 6.6cms.

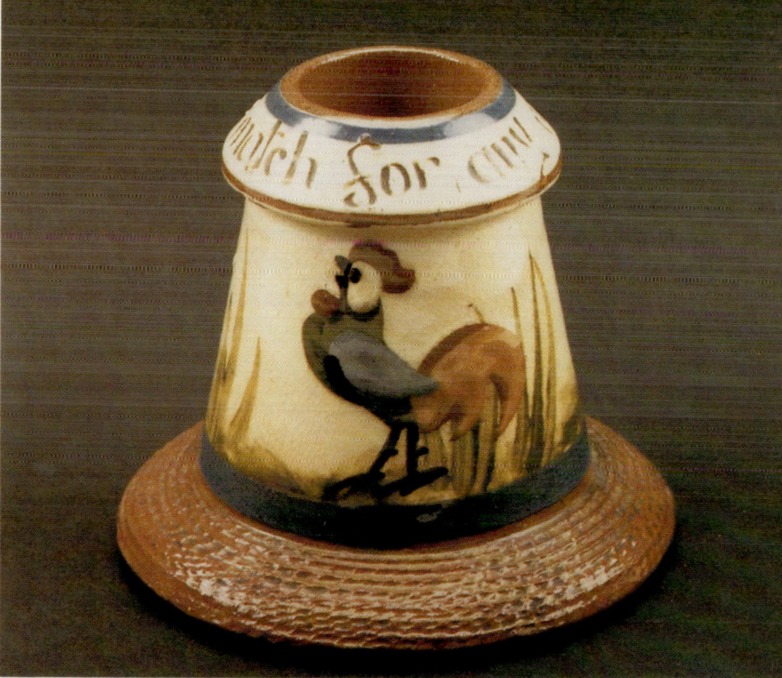

Fig. 594 Britain. Ceramic. Made by Longpark Pottery Co. c.1910. H - 8.1cms.

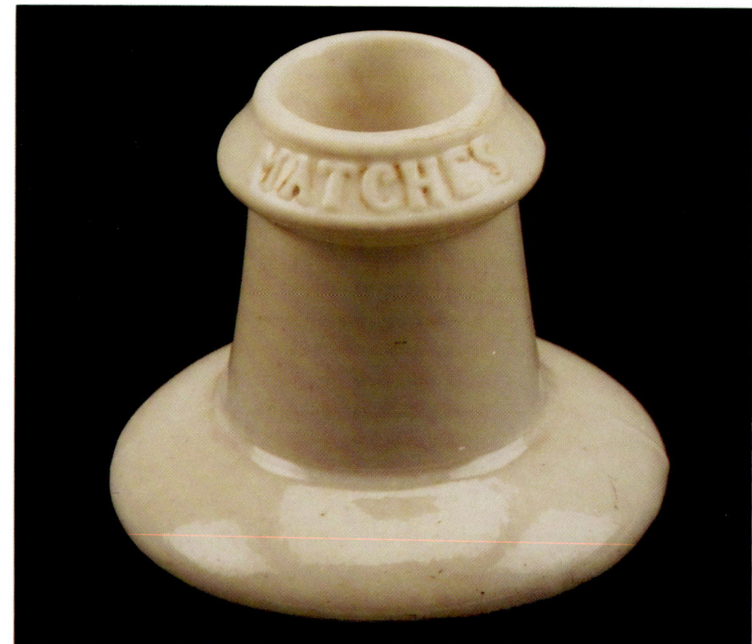

Fig. 595 Britain. Ceramic. Made by Arkinstall & Sons. c.1910. H -6.1cms.

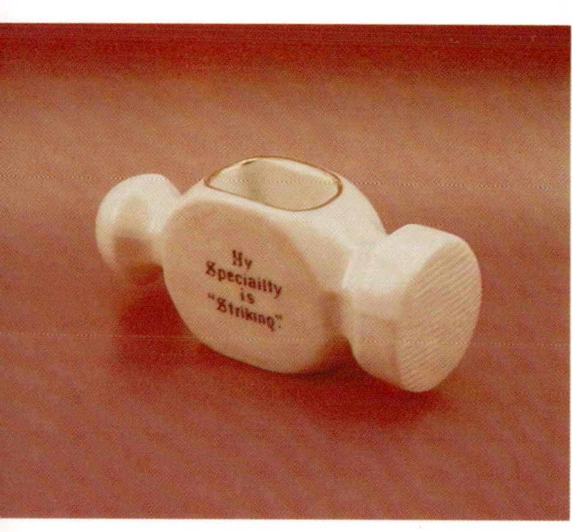

Fig. 593 Europe. Ceramic. c.1920. L - 8.4cms.

Porcelain top hats with crests of British towns are quite common match holders. Two examples are shown in **Fig. 592**. That to the left has the crest of Chirnside, a small town in Scotland, and was made by the Nautilus Porcelain Co. of Glasgow, trading from 1896 until 1913. The hat to the right has the crest of Margate, Kent, a popular seaside resort, and was marked Czechoslovakia; it must therefore be post-l919. The strikers are located on the tops of the hats, which is the underside as the hats sit in the illustration.

The ball-peen hammer head in porcelain shown in **Fig. 593** has the wording on one side "My Speciailty is 'Striking'." On the reverse side is an over-elaborated crest of Guildford, a Surrey town. The surround of the crest is very fanciful and not part of the town crest itself. The word "Specialty" is mis-spelled, which suggests a certain carelessness by the maker, who did not place a mark, although the pattern number is in a European continental style, and it may be from Czechoslovakia.

In most of Britain, sculptured forms of ceramic match holders were not commonly produced beyond the ball and conical match stand versions. In Devonshire, however, a wide range in a distinctive style were produced by several companies. The example in **Fig. 594** is typical, with a motto around the rim "A Match For Any Man." It bears the black printed mark of the Longpark Pottery Co. of Torquay. This type was made in several sizes and variations on the general form, and the most prolific producers were the Aller Vale Art Potteries of Newton Abbott.

In the same form, but lacking any decoration other than the raised letters "MATCHES" around the rim, the example in **Fig. 595** was made by Arkinstall & Sons of Stoke-on-Trent, Staffordshire, which traded from 1904 until 1924.

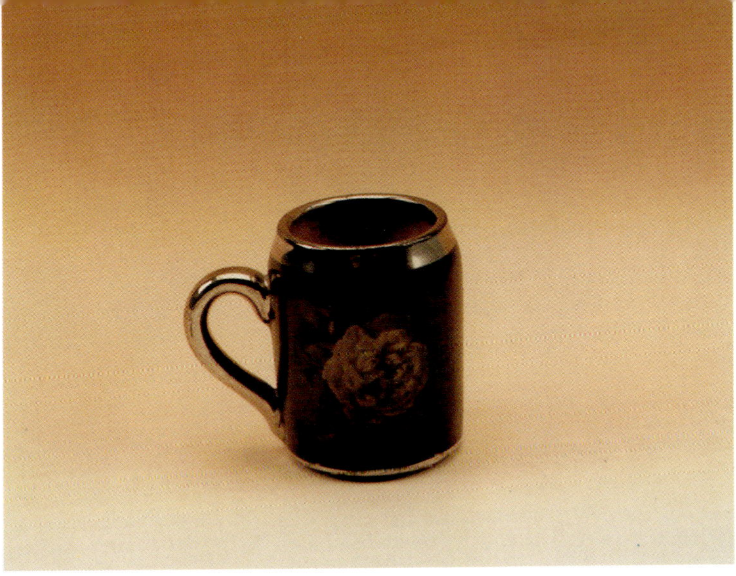

Fig. 596 Britain. Ceramic. Made by Ridgways. Probably between 1910 and 1920. H - 6cms.

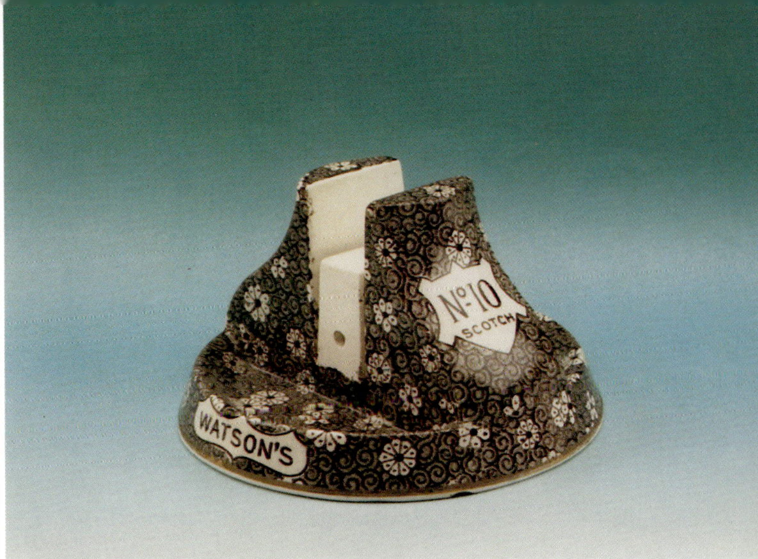

Fig. 598 Britain. Ceramic. Made by Wileman & Co. to a Registered Design of 1913. D - 12cms.

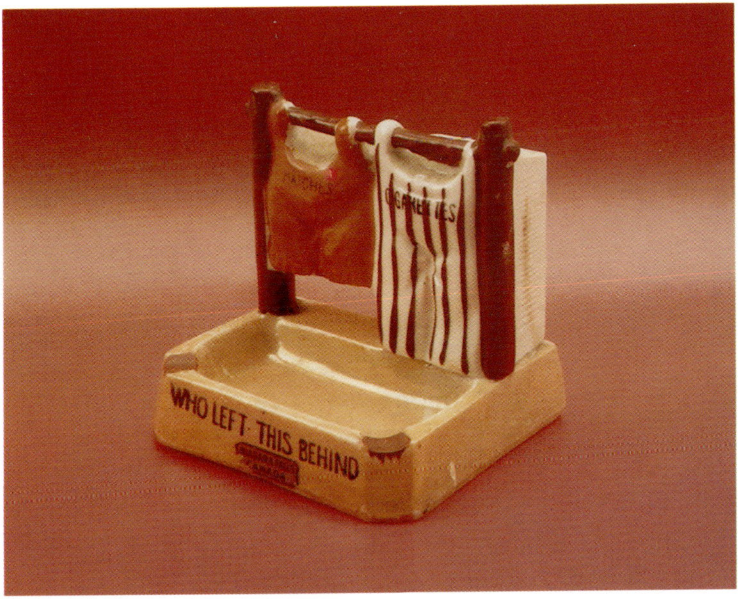

Fig. 597 Japan? Ceramic. c.1930s. H - 8.1cms.

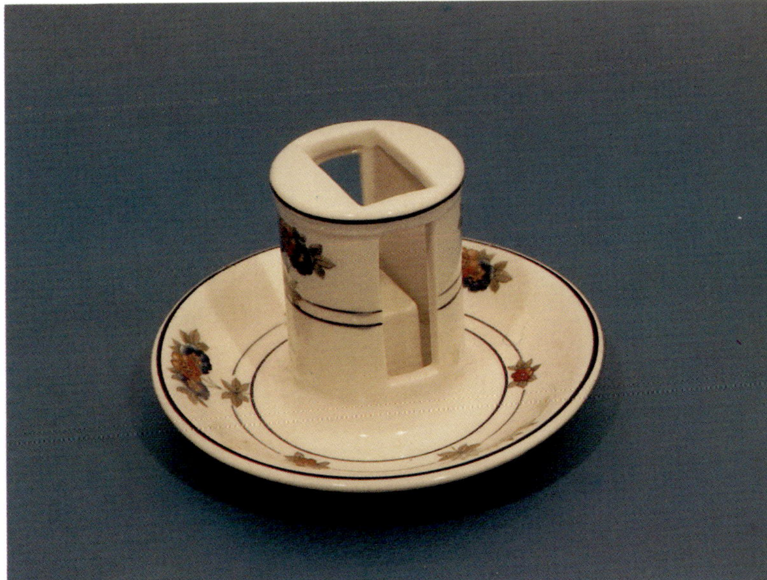

Fig. 599 United States. Ceramic. Made by the Onondaga Pottery Co. 1930s. D - 14cms.

In the form of a small mug, the match holder in **Fig. 596** was apparently a part of a dinner service. When acquired it came with a bowl, a plate, a jug, and a larger mug, in the same colors and with almost identical designs. These had the mark of Ridgways of Hanley, Staffordshire, trading from 1879 to 1920; as well as a mark, in a fancy escutcheon, reading "Royal Vistas Ware. From Paintings by Famous Artists." The underside of the example has concentric circles for a match striker. It was probably made between 1910 and 1920. A similar small mug with striker has been seen with unglazed advertising for Utica, a northern New York State town, and was probably made in the United States.

An inexpensive combination ashtray with match and cigarette holders, shown in **Fig. 597**, was probably made in the 1930s. The example is unmarked, but others have been seen marked "Made in Japan." Under the motto along the front edge a transfer label has been applied for "Niagara Falls, Canada."

Matchbox holders in ceramics were also made. The example in **Fig. 598** has a printed mark over the glaze for J. Watson & Co. Ltd., Distillers of Scotch Whisky in Dundee, Scotland; it is also marked with a Registered Design number for 1913, which was issued to Wileman & Co. of Longton, Staffordshire, who no doubt made the holder. They were probably made for other companies, with different designs and advertising.

The United States apparently produced a very limited number of ceramic match holders. The example in **Fig. 599** is a matchbox holder, made by the Onondaga Pottery Co. of Syracuse, New York. This company used a date mark system on its products, but the mark on the example does not match that system. It is believed to be for July 1934.

The foregoing is but a brief summary of the vast range of what I have loosely termed "sculptural ceramic forms" which were produced to fill the shelves in most Victorian and Edwardian homes with knick-knacks. They represent yet another dimension in the field of match holders.

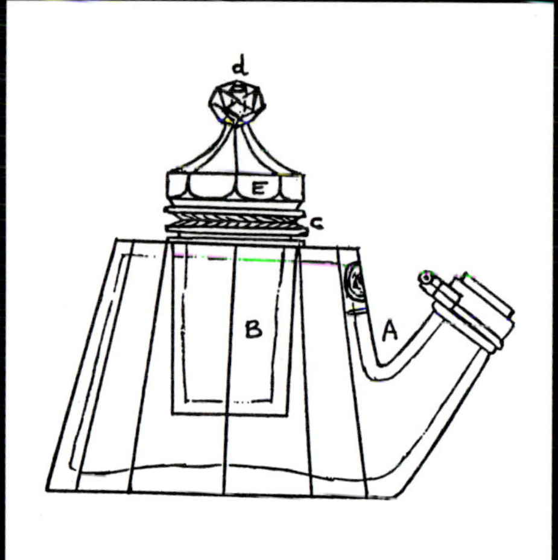

Fig. 600 Illustration from a Registered Design of 1840, by Gabriel Riddle for a glass "Fountain Ink and Taper Light Stand."

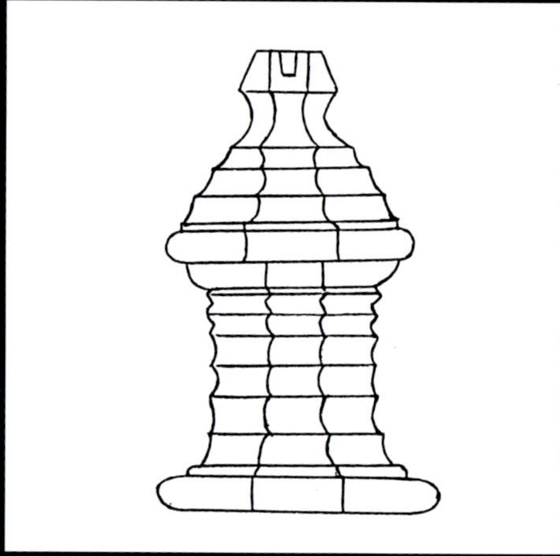

Fig. 601 Ornamental Design registered in 1847 by Percival & Yates for a "Glass Match Box."

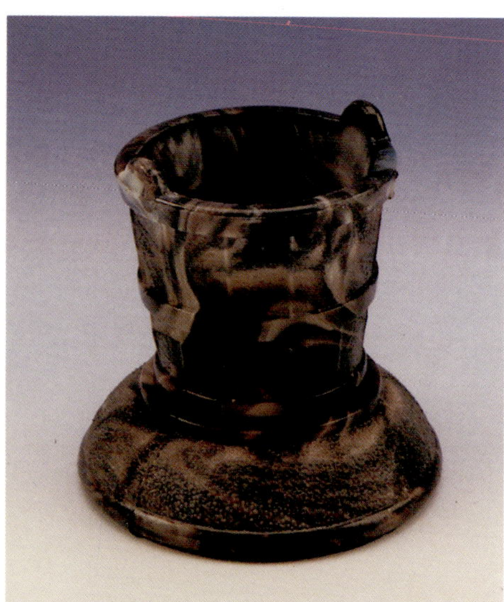

Fig. 602 Britain. Glass. Made by George Davidson & Co. Early 1880s. H - 7.8cms.

PART 7: GLASS

Reference to glass match holders may be found in Chapters II, IV, V Part 4, and VII, but the pieces mentioned there do not constitute the only glass forms to be found. The brief survey that follows attempts to fill some of the gaps.

The first recorded reference to a glass match holder is to be found in Britain, submitted under the Design Copyright Act of 1839. A copy of the design is shown in **Fig. 600**; it was registered on June 18, 1840 by Gabriel Riddle of Southwark, Surrey. It was for a "Fountain Ink and Taper Light Stand" which Riddle described as:

> "consisting of a Glass Fountain inkstand A with a bottle B fixed into the top for containing wax tapers with an inflammable composition, the friction of which upon a rough part C of the cap or cover, causes instant ignition. When the taper is lighted it is to be placed in a hole D at the top of the cover E."

It is believed that this was also the first design that incorporated a match socket, although sockets were in use for some years before. The combination of taper holder and socket with an inkwell at such an early date also supports the argument that the intent behind the match sockets was to aid letter-writing, and not to serve as a night light.

An early Ornamental Design registered under the Designs Act of 1842, which superseded the 1839 act, is shown in **Fig. 601**. This was for a "Glass Match Box"' and was registered in 1847 by Percival & Yates of Manchester, known to have made pressed glass articles. Similar pieces are known to exist, and the glass holder shown in Fig. 63 may possibly have been made by them; but none shows any signs of having been made using the pressed glass technique.

Perhaps the earliest open-topped glass match holder was of the type shown in **Fig. 602**. These were made in northeast England by at least two companies. A design was registered as part of a parcel of twelve designs by Sowerby & Co. of Gateshead-on-Tyne, in 1878. The example here is almost identical, but bears the mark of George Davidson & Co., Sowerby's great rivals in pressed glass from the same town. It was probably made after 1881, when the design protection period had elapsed for Sowerby's. It is made of purple marble slag glass.

Fig. 603 illustrates three trademarks used by Sowerby's, Davidson's, and Greener & Co. of Sunderland, barely ten miles from Gateshead. It is unlikely that the Greener trade mark will be found on match holders, but the mark bears a close resemblance to that of Davidson's and can easily be mistaken for it.

Other match holders of somewhat similar forms in opaque glass, either round or rectangular, were made in Britain, but are seldom marked.

Of later vintage is a transparent glass holder set in an ashtray, shown in **Fig. 604**. The holder has threaded ribbing for the striker, and is fitted with a silver rim, hallmarked for 1915 by H. Bushell & Co. of Birmingham.

Other forms of transparent glass match holders are to be found in the shapes of a boot, a jockey's cap, and a horse's hoof. These were sometimes fitted with a silver rim, the hallmarks of which will provide a date. Usually ribbed for striking, they may also have a frosted finish sufficient to permit ignition of a match. Other registered designs are recorded between 1870 and 1903, including a top hat in 1889, ribbed around the brim, and registered by Edward Moore of the Tyne Flint Glass Works of South Shields, another northeast England glass company.

Toothpick holders are popular collectible items in the United States, and the National Toothpick Holder Collectors' Society has done a great deal towards identifying manufacturers, and assigning names to patterns, often where none existed at the source of manufacture. However, many toothpick holders were also intended for matches, a fact often recorded in the manufacturer's catalogues.

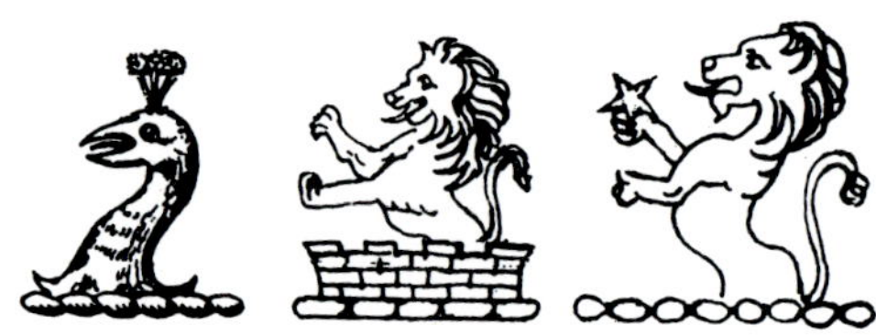

Fig. 603 Trademarks. Left: Sowerby & Co. Centre: George Davidson & Co. Right: Greener & Co.

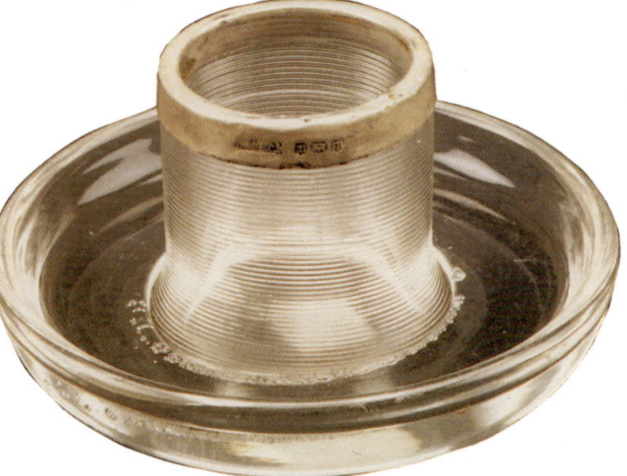

Fig. 604 Britain. Glass, silver. Silver made by H. Bushell & Co. 1915. D - 8.1cms.

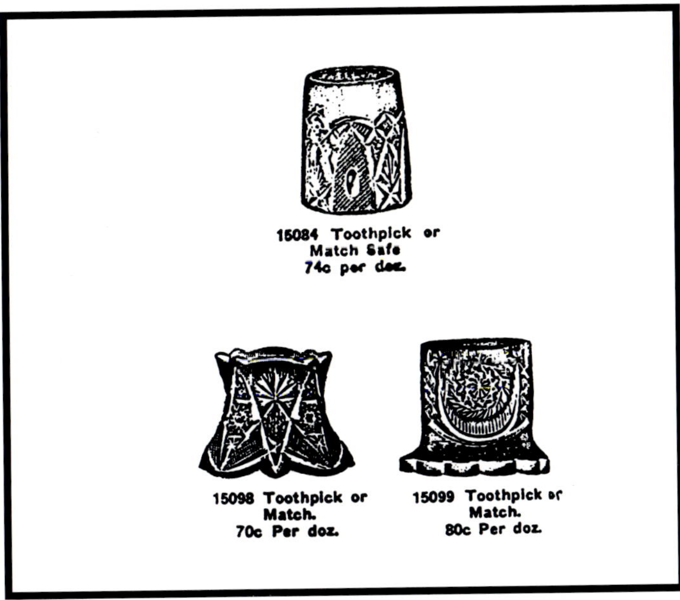
15084 Toothpick or Match Safe 74c per doz.

15098 Toothpick or Match. 70c Per doz.

15099 Toothpick or Match. 80c Per doz.

Fig. 605 Illustrations from a U.S. Glass Co., catalogue of 1909.

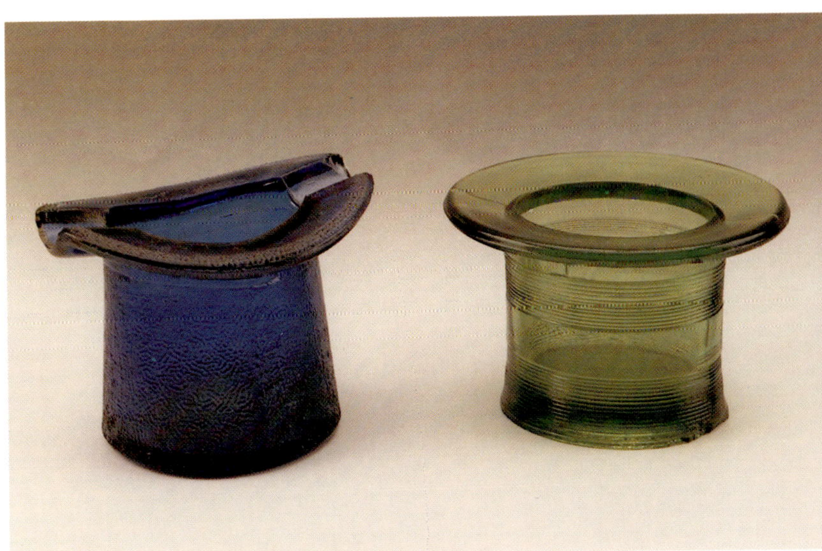

Fig. 606 United States. Glass. Left: c.1930s. H - 6.1cms. Right: c.1910. H - 5.5cms.

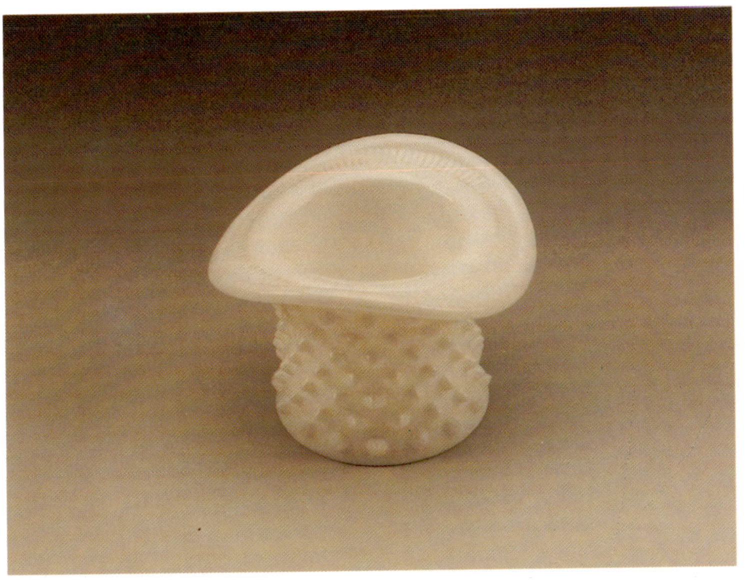

Fig. 607 United States. Glass. First decade of 20th century. H -6.8cms.

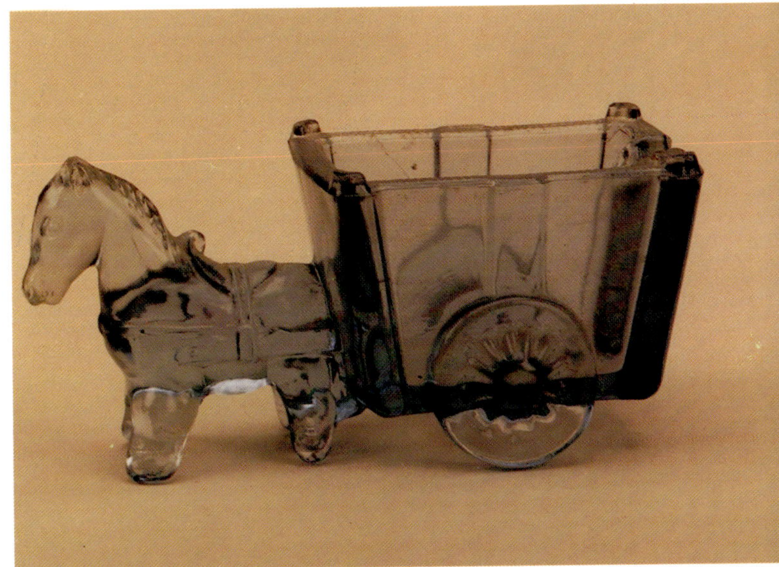

Fig. 608 United States. Glass. c.1930s. L - 11.7cms.

From a U.S. Glass Co. catalogue of 1909, **Fig. 605** shows three illustrations of glass vessels labelled as "Toothpick or Match Safe". The names of the designs for these vessels, recorded elsewhere in the text on the page, were: "15084—New Hampshire; 15098—U.S.Regal; 15099—Spinning Star." A number of other items on the page are labelled for "Toothpicks," but could quite easily be mistaken for, or used as, match holders. The difference is often marginal.

Glass containers shaped as top hats were popular in the United States. Again these could have been used as toothpick holders, or for some other purpose, but the three examples shown here are all provided with what is perceived as being match striking surfaces.

In **Fig. 606**, the example in blue has a striker around the edge of the brim, which also has two depressions in which a cigarette was intended to rest. The sides of the hat could also be used as a striker, and the underside has concentric circles that may have been used for the same purpose. These have been seen with advertising for various companies on them, and probably date from the 1930s. The green example is probably earlier, and is a little more elegant. Its sides have some ribbing, but the base is finely ribbed; both areas may have been used as strikers.

The example in **Fig. 607** is in "milk" glass, with a hobnail pattern. The rim has a band of transverse grooves for a striker. This may be from the first decade of this century.

The novelty form of a horse and cart, in blue, shown in **Fig. 608** is another questionable piece. The rim of the cart has a roughened surface suitable for striking matches, and the back edge has a depression to rest a cigarette. The question is: is it an ashtray or a match holder? This probably dates from the 1930s.

The milk glass bowl with brass chain in **Fig. 609** was intended to hang from a gaslight fixture, thus keeping the matches close to where they would be required. This type of match holder was quite common in the United States, and was available in various shapes, dating from around the turn of the 19th century, or possibly earlier.

Another glass piece intended for the same purpose was in the form of an umbrella. The illustration in **Fig. 610** is from a glass company catalogue of c.1892, and shows a hanging variety and a stand-alone version. These may be hard to find, the handles doubtless being easily broken.

Representations of shoes may commonly be found with a striker down the back of the heel. The illustration in **Fig. 611** is from the same page in the catalogue as the umbrellas, and described simply as a "Slipper," without indication of its intended use. They are frequently found today in antique stores and at shows, but it is suspected that most are reproductions. They seldom show any signs of wear, which would be expected of glass that is close to 100 years old. Again, it is a case of buyer beware.

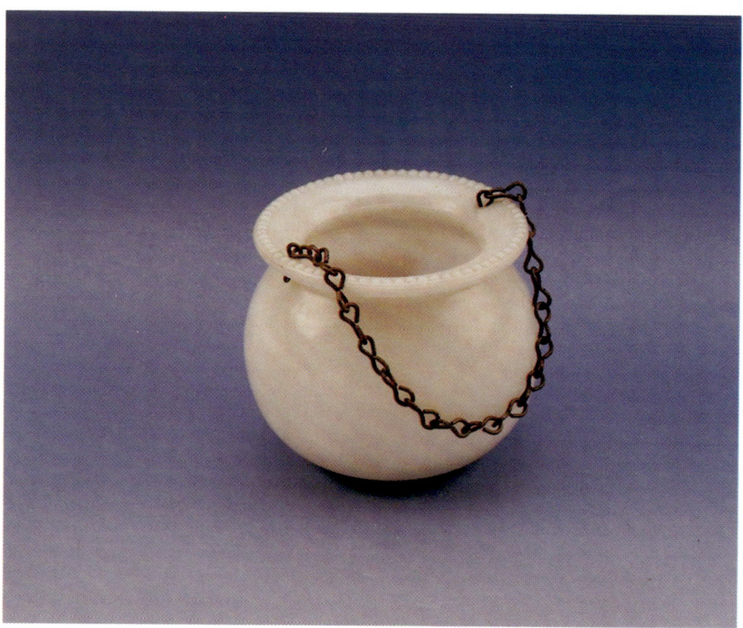

Fig. 609 United States. Glass, brass. D - 7.6cms.

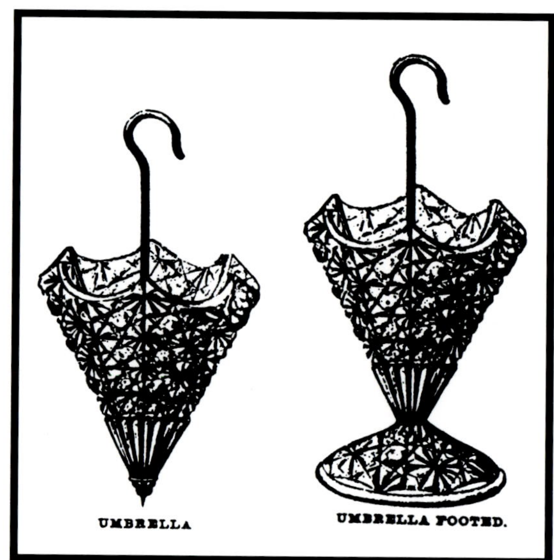

Fig. 610 Illustration from a United States glass company catalogue of c.1892.

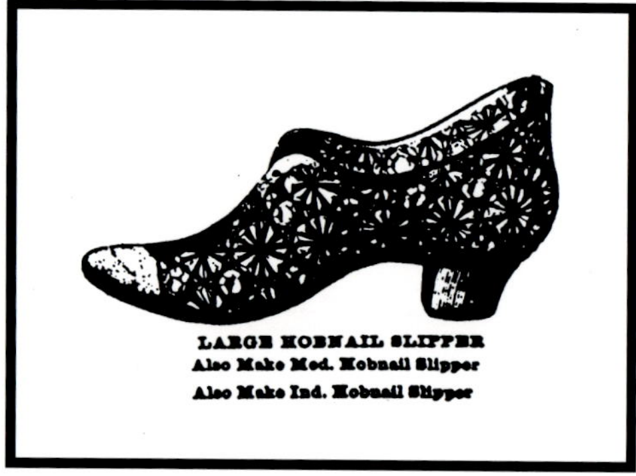

Fig. 611 Illustration from a United States glass company catalogue of c.1892.

Chapter VI
Anomalies in Match Devices

Matches were made in various sizes: from as short as 4 mm, to as long as 70 mm. Many forms of matches came and went on the market. First there was the continuous match, invented in 1860; a length was expelled from a propelling pencil-like device and, when ignited, burned until the exposed portion reached the tip of the device, where it died for lack of oxygen. Another 1860 invention was the repeating match, made in a fashion similar to the strips of caps for repeating toy pistols. In 1922 there was the disc match, made of card and joined like book matches, but in the form of a circular disc.

All of these, and other forms of match, were invented and re-invented in a slightly different fashion, and required special devices or holders to achieve a successful end result; namely, the means of producing a flame. Most were short-lived gimmicks doomed to failure almost from the outset. Perhaps the most unfortunate invention, which did not appear until the 1930s, was the pull match. Pull matches were set in between two pieces of thin card and, when pulled out, ignited on a narrow band of igniting compound inside the cards. This idea worked, and holders for the long strips of "trapped" matches were produced in the late 1930s. But World War II intervened and the idea was abandoned for a variety of reasons.

The term "unique" is often applied to things that are *not* one of a kind. But the next device described here is believed to have been a unique invention, and examples are rare.

A British Invention Patent was issued in 1867 to Bewicke and Alex Bewicke Blackburn of Chelsea, London, for "Improvements in Lucifer Matches or Tapers, and in the Apparatus for Holding and Igniting the same." An example of the device, in the open position, is shown in **Fig. 612**, and in the closed position in **Fig. 613**. Outwardly it has the appearance of an Egyptian oil lamp with twin handles in the form of snakes; the body is made of brass, and the inner works of ferrous metals.

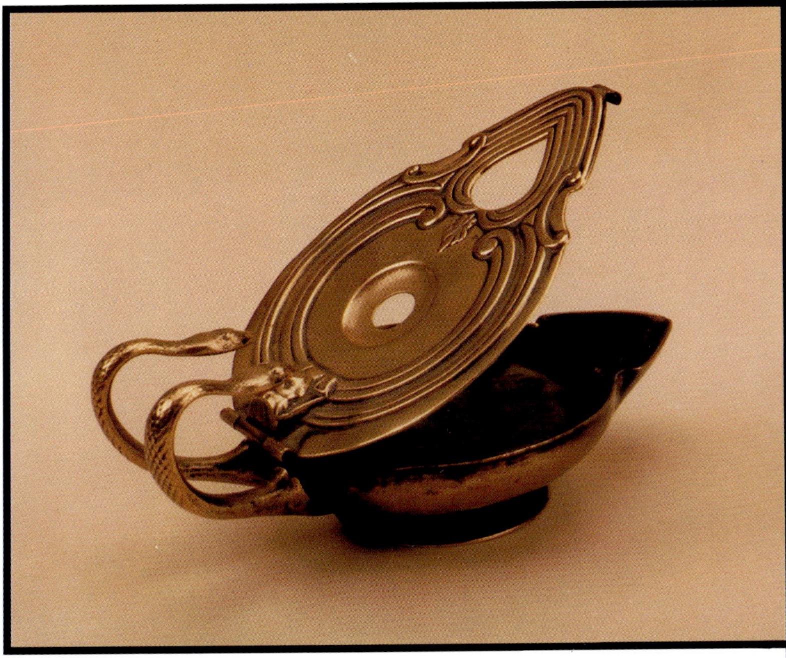

Fig. 612 Britain. Brass, steel. Made to an Invention Patent of 1867 by Bewicke and Alex Bewicke Blackburn. L - 17.7cms.

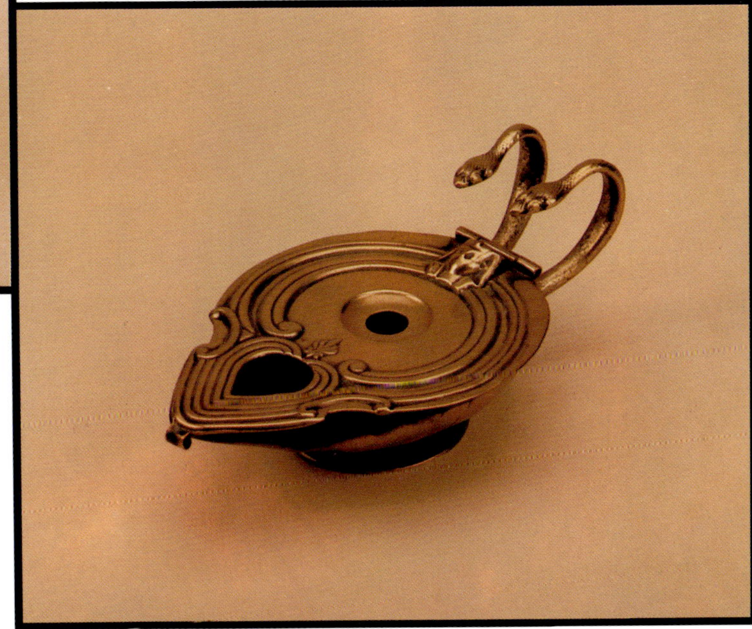

Fig. 613 As Fig. 612.

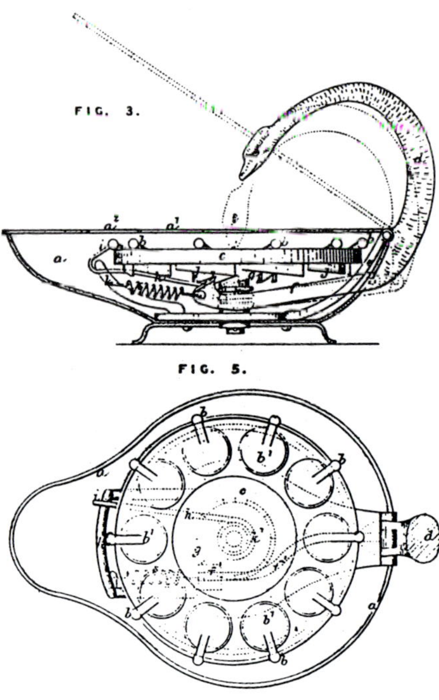

Fig. 614 Drawings from the patent for Figs. 612 and 613.

Fig. 614 shows two of the patent drawings as the invention was originally conceived, and demonstrates how the fairly complex mechanism was intended to work. As may be seen, the original design was for a single arm in the form of a snake, pivoted at the back of the body. When depressed it rotated a steel plate, upon which was mounted a wooden disc with ten match-type heads, each one moving round thirty six degrees to he ignited by a comb-like striker. It produced a flame that eminated from the hole at the front of the lid. The action of the snake-arm was intended to create the illusion that the snake was striking a victim through the hole in the center of the lid, causing the flame to erupt at the front. It is assumed that, in practice, the mechanism failed to work in the desired manner. Consequently the end-product was provided with two snake-arms that operated in a scissors action.

The design of the match for this device consisted of a very short-stemmed wax vesta type match, which would be "inserted in a solid combustible composition, such as wax, tallow, or stearine, which is contained in a small or shallow cup." Ten "cups" were part of a circular wooden disc which was mounted on the steel disc that is visible inside the body in Fig. 612. Although the patent specifications refer to a method of making the matches, they make no reference as to how a purchaser could replace them once the original supply was exhausted. It would have been beyond the capabilities of any householder to undertake making them, without possessing specialized knowledge and the necessary chemicals. It can only be assumed that a replacement supply would have been available at the point of the original purchase.

The object of this invention was "to produce a lighted taper or match which will burn sufficiently long, say five or ten minutes, to admit of sealing two, three, or more letters or parcels." The Blackburns no doubt went back to the drawing board before finally producing the device. At least three others are known to exist, but it is likely that a significant number were produced for a brief period before the invention disappeared from the market.

Another type of match that periodically appeared on the market in one form or another was the pellet match. This was essentially a stemless match. As such it could not be ignited without some special device to hold it, so as to avoiding burning the fingers. In effect, the device was a form of lighter. The earliest known patent for such a device was issued in 1846; at least five others were invented between 1846 and 1886. They were probably all short-lived, and few examples survive; it is doubtful if they were ever popular. The example described here, invented in 1887, was produced only for a few years; further examples of similar devices were invented and produced later in the century and into the 1920s.

On July 19, 1887, James S. Foley of Chicago, Illinois, and Joseph Ruse of Toronto, Ontario, were issued with a Canadian Patent for a pencil-like device for using pellet matches; they called it a "Match Magazine and Lighter." The same patent was issued in Britain in August 1887 and in the United States on October 2, 1888. Two of the drawings for this patent are shown in **Fig. 615**. No examples of these devices have been recorded, and they were probably never manufactured. Foley and Ruse quickly followed these patents with a second version that used two tubes to hold the pellets. This was patented in Canada on October 31, 1887, and in the United States on October 2, 1888 (the same day as the first patent); a patent was taken out in Britain by a Patent Agent on December 5, 1887. Drawings from the Canadian and United States patents are shown in **Fig. 616**; in Britain the same drawings were used but a second, less complex version, shown in **Fig. 617**, was included.

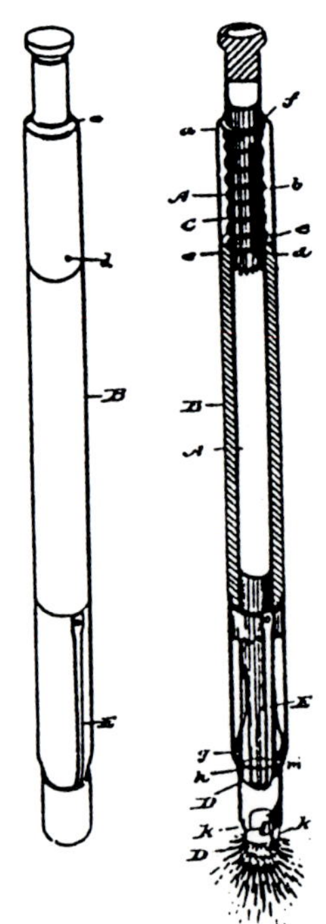

Fig. 615 Drawings from Invention Patents by James S. Foley and Joseph Ruse, issued in 1887 in Britain and Canada, and in 1888 in the United States.

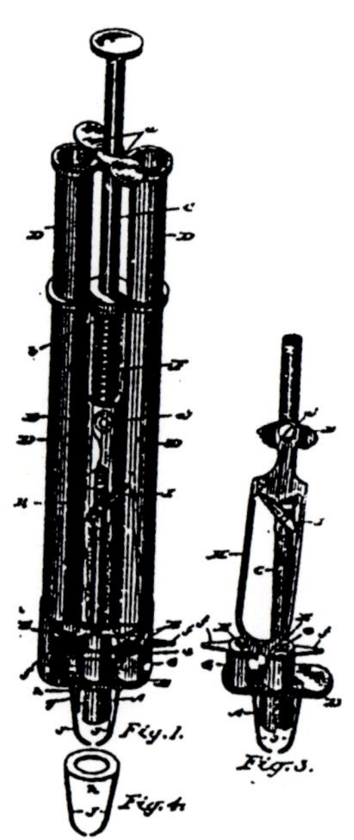

Fig. 616 Drawings from Invention Patents by James S. Foley and Joseph Ruse, issued in Canada and Britain (to a Patent agent) in 1887, and in the United States in in 1888.

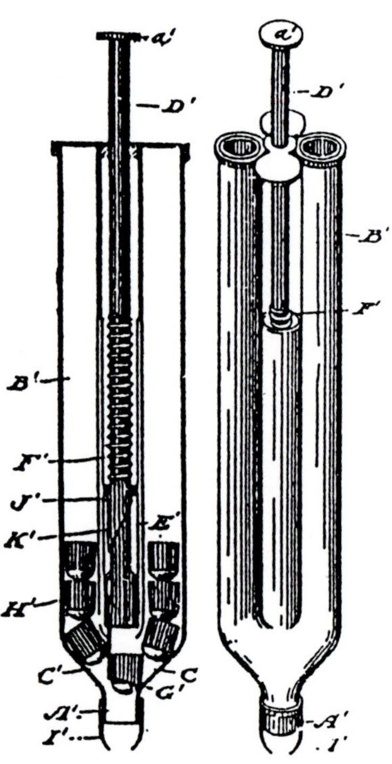

Fig. 617 Drawings from an Invention Patent in Britain, issued to a Patent Agent in 1887, of a second version of the Foley and Ruse patent.

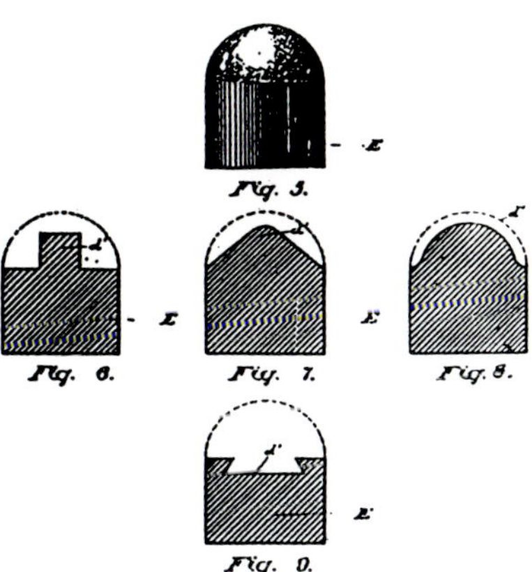

Fig. 618 Drawings of the "pellet matches" that were a part of the Canadian and British Invention Patents, of Foley and Ruse in 1887.

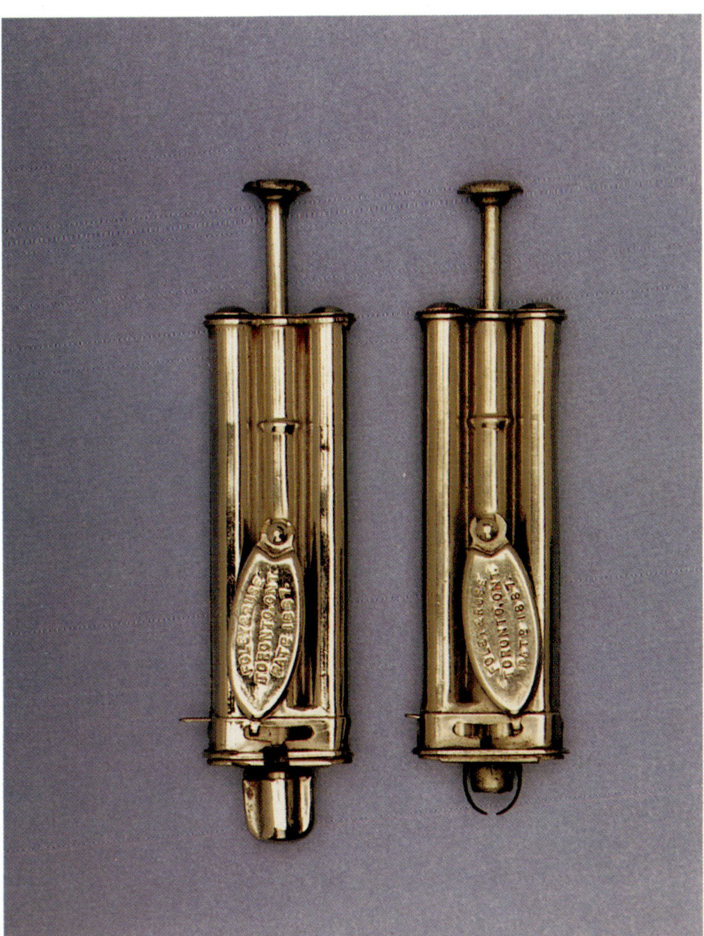

Fig. 619 Canada. Plated brass. Made by Foley & Ruse to an Invention Patent of 1887. L - 8.5cms.

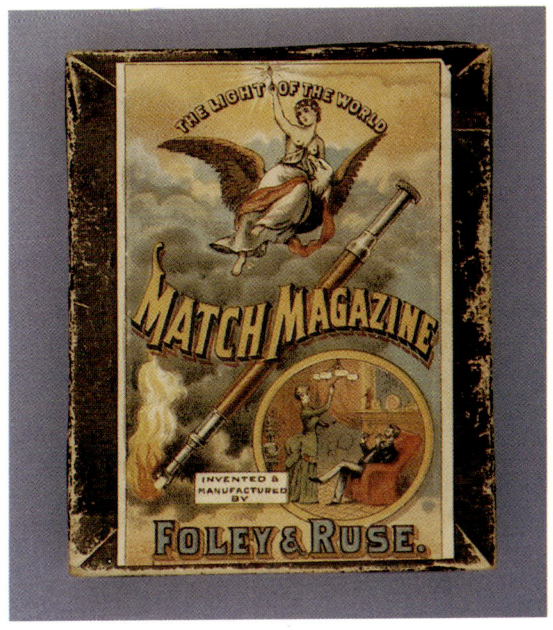

Fig. 620 Canada. Cardboard. Box to hold approximately one dozen Foley & Ruse match magazines as shown in Fig. 619.

The pellet matches themselves were the subject of a separate patent in Canada, issued on December 1, 1887, and were a part of the British patent of December 5, 1887. They are shown in **Fig. 618**. Yet they were apparently not patented in the United States. Essentially, the pellet matches were designed to carry the igniting compound at the tip of what Foley called the 'Stubs', without increasing the diameter of the match. The match was pushed out of a tube through a pair of claws, which created the necessary friction for ignition and then gripped the sides of the 'stub'.

The twin tube device in Fig. 616 was provided with a plunger mechanism located between the two tubes; this served to eject the pellet and also to permit one pellet at a time to drop into position, alternating the feed between the two tubes. The simpler version relied upon gravity to feed the pellets into line with the plunger, but it was probably found that the pellets became jammed at the bottom. Filling the tubes was achieved by rotating about the plunger a plate at its top; this exposed the open ends of the tubes, the claws being protected by a push-on cap.

Foley and Ruse began to manufacture these devices; two examples are shown in **Fig. 619**. The company was listed in the Toronto City Directory of 1889 as "Match Manufacturers" at 60 Adelaide West Street, the only year that they were listed. It seems certain that they made the devices there, the swing plate on the front of the device being marked "FOLEY & RUSE.TORONTO.ONT.PATD.I887". The devices were packed one dozen in a box, an example of which is shown in **Fig. 620**. Curiously, the colorful label shows an example of the first pencil-like patent diagonally across the box, and the figure of Columbia holding another one in her hand instead of the usual torch. In the circular frame at the bottom is a domestic scene of a lady lighting a gas chandelier, and a seated gentleman lighting his cigar, both using the pencil device. The box, however, was too short to hold what would have been a longer device, and was obviously made for the twin tube version. The match magazine was illustrated in George Zorn's catalogue of c. 1892, as shown in **Fig. 621**. From this it is assumed that Foley and Ruse were still making the devices, but perhaps not in Toronto.

In the United States, matches for these devices were made by the Davenport Magazine & Match Co. of Davenport, Iowa, and the label on the box stated "Foley & Ruse's Magazine Matches." In the patents, Foley claimed to be from Chicago, but in the Toronto City Directory of 1889 he was said to be a resident of Davenport. The Davenport City Directory of 1888-89 reveals that Foley was the Superintendent, and Ruse the Manager, of the Davenport Magazine and Match Co., and that both were "boarders" at Kimball House in Davenport. They did not appear in the 1890-91 Davenport City Directory. From this it is assumed that both were operating in Toronto and Davenport at the same time.

In Britain, the devices were made by Perry & Co. Ltd. of Birmingham and London. They were marked "Patent. Perry & Co. London," but it is assumed they were made under license. The matches were made by the Fusee Vesta Co. of Wandsworth, London. A copy of the cover from a box is shown in **Fig. 622**, it was printed "PERRY & CO. PATENT PELLET MATCH", and included instructions on how to use and fill the match magazine.

James S. Foley seems to have been a wanderer, frequently on the move. It may be speculated that he met Joseph Ruse in Toronto, while Ruse was employed by the Dominion Organ & Piano Co. there, and that together they held their first patents for an organ pedal cover, issued in the United States and Germany in 1887. Within a few years Foley had moved to Britain, staying in London for a time, before moving on to Wolverhampton. By 1917 he had applied for over one hundred patents, on such diverse things as typewriter and automobile parts, and had also become a British citizen.

THE · AUTOMATIC · MATCH · MAGAZINE.

Something Entirely New! NO OIL, NO WICK, NO GETTING OUT OF ORDER.

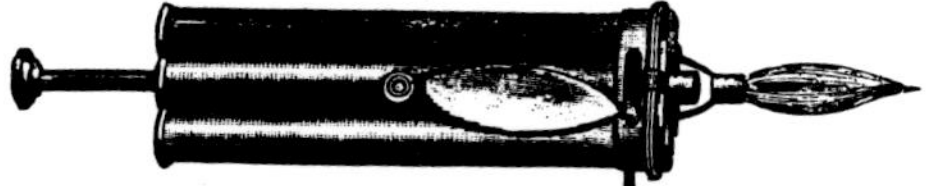

READ THE DIRECTIONS.—Hold Magazine with igniting end downward. Do not place thumb on moveable shield. Open Magazine by turning cover on top end of tubes, and drop the matches in with igniting point downward. Fill both tubes, then replace cover. Remove cap from lighter at lower end, then press quickly on plunger with finger; this will instantly produce light. Magazine should be turned light upwards as soon as match is ignited. When through using, replace cap. The burned match remains, until pushed out by the next match used. As matches by their own weight drop from tubes into carrier, it is absolutely necessary that Magazine should be held with lighter downwards when pressing plunger to ignite match. If Magazine clogs, take off slide at lower end and clean.

Price for Machines, $2.25 per dozen; or $24.00 per gross.
Price for Extra Matches, 15c. per dozen; or $1.50 per gross, (5 dozen matches in box).

Fig. 621 Illustration from a catalogue of c.1892 by George Zorn of the Foley & Ruse Match Magazine.

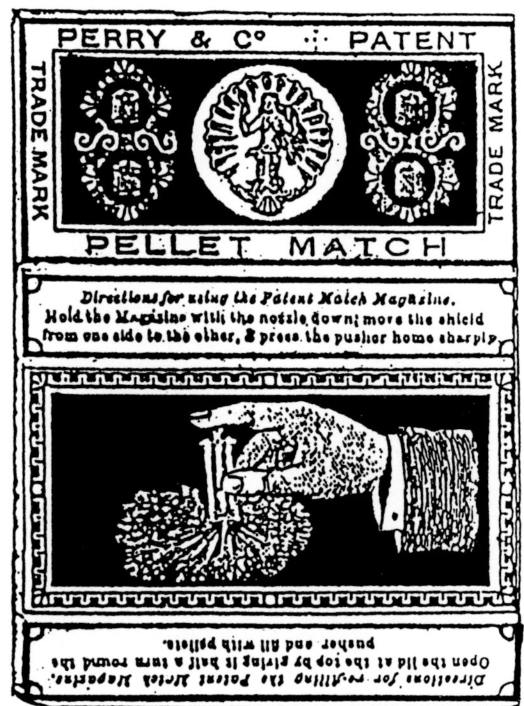

Fig. 622 Illustration of a cover of a box of "Perry & Co., Patent Pellet Matches", made by the Fusee Vesta Co., for the Foley & Ruse type match magazine in Britain.

Chapter VII
Wall-Hanging Match Holders

This form of match holder did not reach the same height of popularity in Europe as it did in the United States. This is evident from a comparison of the number of patents, both invention and design, that may be found in the patent records of Britain and the United States, and from the apparent paucity of examples available in the European antique markets. Still, it must be admitted that *in relative terms* they are also scarce in the North American antique markets, where other types of European match holders are reasonably common.

There is no apparent reason for this difference. It may be speculated that North Americans preferred to have match holders where they could be easily found. If a holder was attached to a wall, adjacent to where it was most frequently required, then it had a fixed location; whereas stand-alone or pocket holders were subject to being moved at the whims of any member of a household. Furthermore, a wall-mounted holder could be located at a point less likely to be reached by small children, which may have been a consideration.

Many North American wall holders were designed for use in the kitchen, where matches were most needed for lighting gas or oil lamps, and kitchen ranges, throughout the entire day; that was also the room where many families tended to congregate. They were also often vehicles for advertising, targeted at the housewife, and it was probahly less acceptable to put up such crass objects in other rooms of the house.

It is perhaps predictable that the European manufacturers of wall-holders were mostly those that have cropped up in relation to the other forms of match holders. In Germany, E. G. Zimmermann of Hanau made wall holders in cast iron, probably around the 1860s. Conta & Boehme of Possneck, Thuringia, made what is believed to be a very rare ceramic form of a Japanese lady with a nodding head, seated and holding a fan; this is shown in **Fig. 623**. Figures with nodding heads are not uncommon, but are believed to be rarely marked, unlike this example, which probably dates from c. 1880.

The origins of the ceramic holder shown in **Fig. 624** are unknown. It lacks the fine finish and detail of the previous example, and it is speculated that it may be European; but there is no conclusive evidence to support such an attribution.

In Britain there was only one Ornamental Design registered between 1843 and 1884. That was to George Benton and James Henry Stone of Birmingham, in 1866, for an open-topped holder to be made of metal. However, there *were* a number of Useful Designs registered in the same period, of which at least two were to Bryant & May. The first Useful Design was in 1864, registered to John Hadley of Norwood, Surrey, and shown in **Fig. 625**. A metal holder, the match compartment at the base was lidded, and a slotted pocket on the back plate was for holding sandpaper.

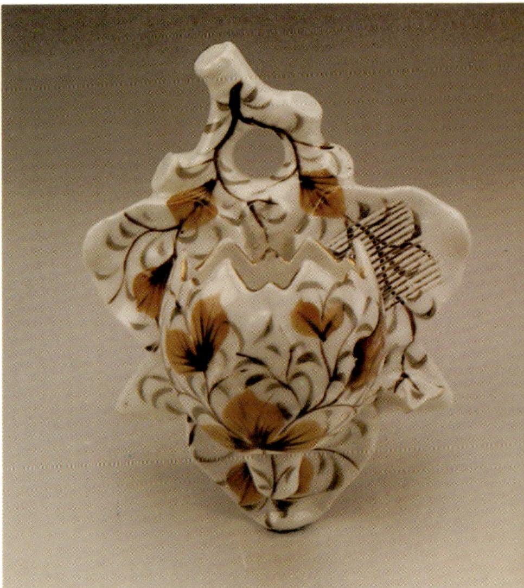

Fig. 624 Europe? Ceramic. H - 13.3cms.

Fig. 623 Germany. Ceramic. Made by Conta & Boehme. With a nodding head. c.1880. H - 18.8cms.

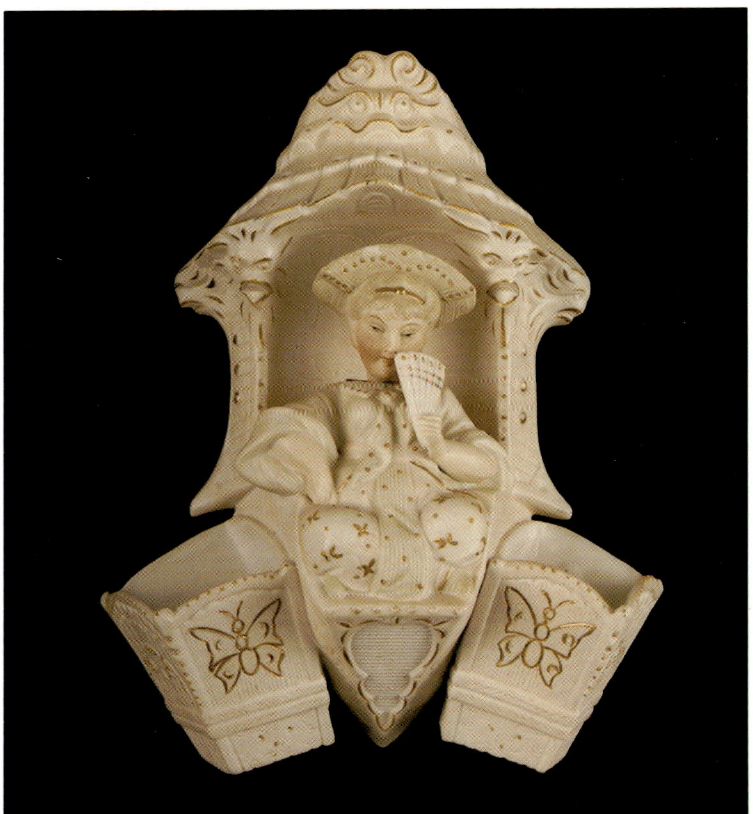

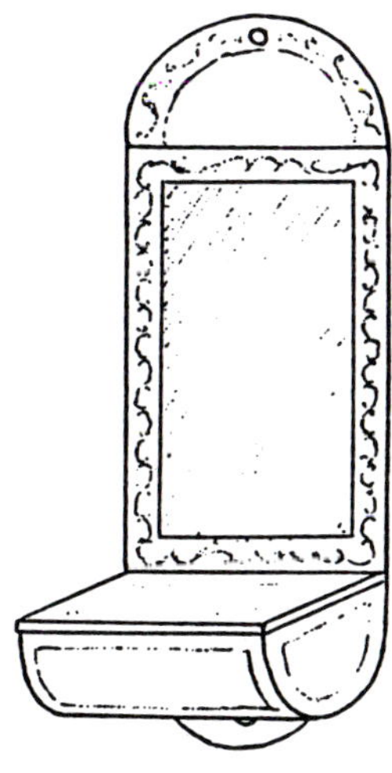

Fig. 625 Britain. Useful Design of 1864 by John Hadley.

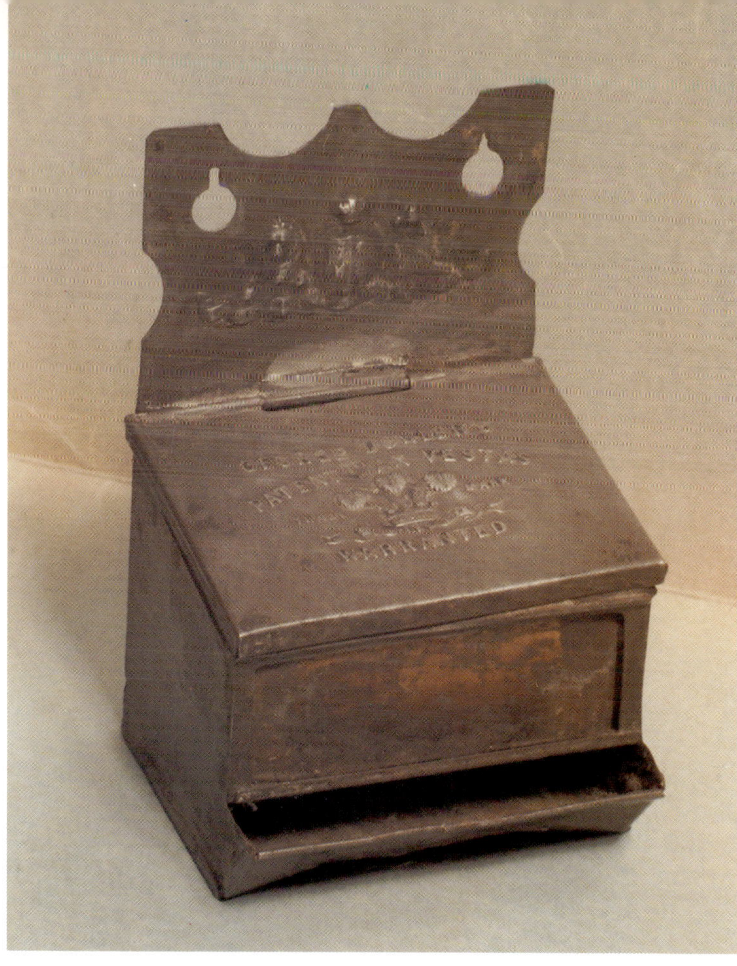

Fig. 626 Britain. Tin plate. Made by George Dowler. c.1860 to 1875. H - 12.3cms.

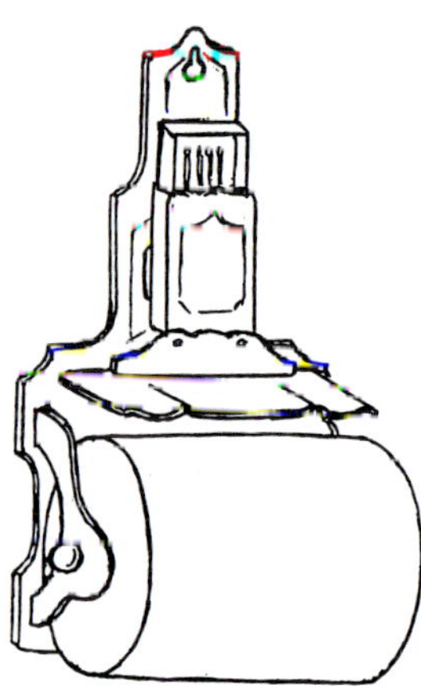

Fig. 629 Britain. Registered Design of 1906 by John Harper & Co. Ltd.

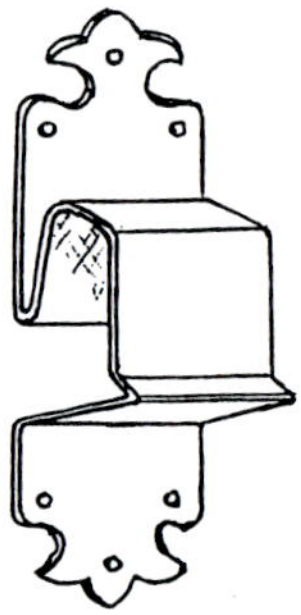

Fig. 630 Britain. Registered Design of 1909 by George Hopkins & Co.

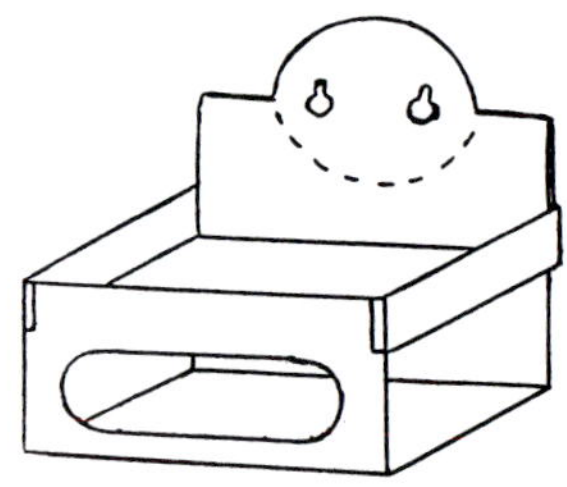

Fig. 627 Britain. Useful Design of 1874 by Bryant & May.

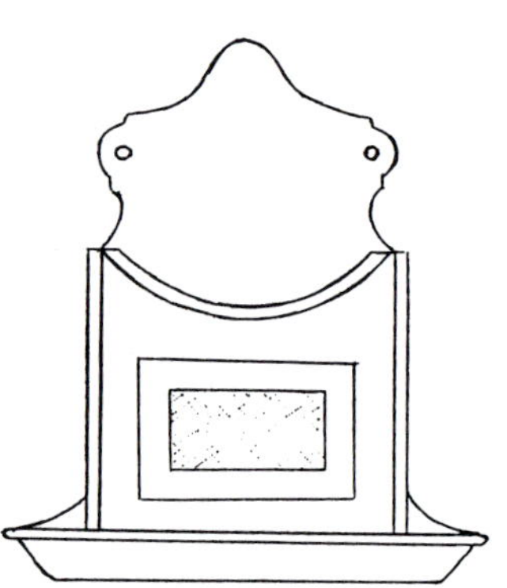

Fig. 628 Britain. Useful Design of 1879 by Bell & Black.

Between 1860 and 1865 George Dowler of Birmingham had begun to make wax vesta matches, retaining his Great Charles Street factory as a brass foundry, and opening a new factory in Nechells, a suburb of Birmingham, which is probably where he made the matches. He also made tin-plate boxes for these matches; the styles were similar to those of Bryant & May, but Dowler was probably making his before Bryant & May. Dowler made small tin-plate pocket boxes and a wall-hanging match holder; an example of the latter is shown in **Fig. 626**. This has the Royal Coat of Arms impressed on the back plate, and on the lid was Dowler's trademark, the Prince of Wales' feathers in a crown. Dowler went out of business between 1870 and 1875, just over a century after the family-run company had started trading.

Bryant & May were making two very similar wall holders in 1873: one for wax vestas, which could be ignited on a roughened area on the holder, and the other for safety matches, which came supplied with a reserve of prepared striking surfaces. The tray at the front was for spent matches. In the company's Diary and Almanac for 1873 it was noted that

> "The Patent Safety Match Holder is specially adapted for use in Nurseries, Kitchens, Bedrooms, Smoking Rooms, Hotels, Banks, Offices, Warehouses, —in fact everywhere. The Patent Safety Match Holder is intended to be nailed up to prevent it being carried about the house, thus saving much loss of time, as it frequently happens that boxes that are not fixed are carried into other rooms, and when it is really of importance to obtain a light quickly, cannot be found."

Some of these holders were later provided with a luminous patch, applied to the back plate, an addition that lasted for a few years. After about 1890 they had postal information printed on the sides.

In 1874 Bryant & May registered a Useful Design for holding a box of safety matches, shown in **Fig. 627**. This holder was made out of a single piece of sheet metal, folded but not soldered. The selling price of four pence included a box of safety matches.

A Useful Design, shown in **Fig. 628**, was registered in 1879 by another London match manufacturer, Bell & Black. It is open-topped, with the striker panel in the back plate and a tray for spent matches at the bottom.

After the new Patents, Design and Trade Marks Act of l883 came into force on January 1, 1884, there were only two designs registered for matchbox holders. The first, shown in **Fig. 629**, was registered in 1906 by John Harper & Co. Ltd. of Willenhall (near Wolverhampton). It is described as a "Combined Toilet Paper Holder and Match Stand" and could have been intended for use in only one room in (or outside!) the house. The matches could also have been useful for lighting a gas-fired water heater in the bathroom. The second Useful Design, shown in **Fig. 630**, was registered in 1909 to George Hopkins & Co., brassfounders of Birmingham. This is perhaps among the simplest and most economical designs of its day, in any field.

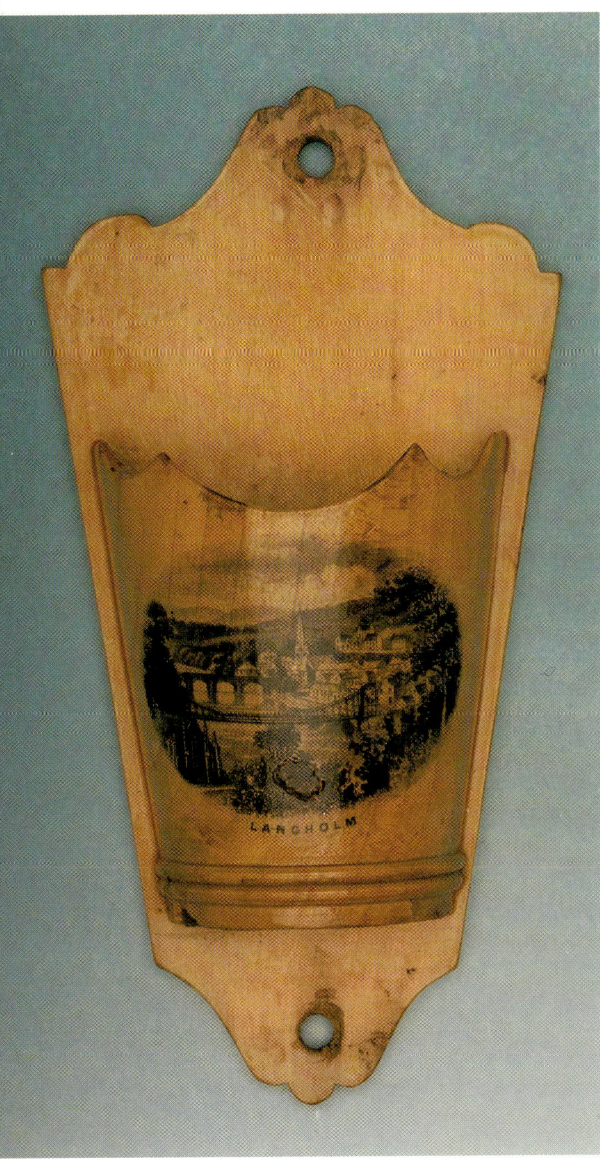

Fig. 631 Scotland. Wood. Probably by William & Andrew Smith. c.1900. H - 13.1cms.

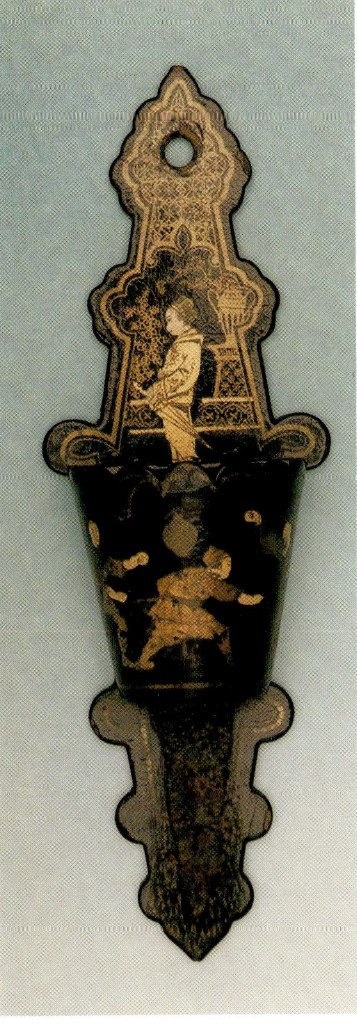

Fig. 632 Britain. Papier maché. c.1870s. H - 20.7cms.

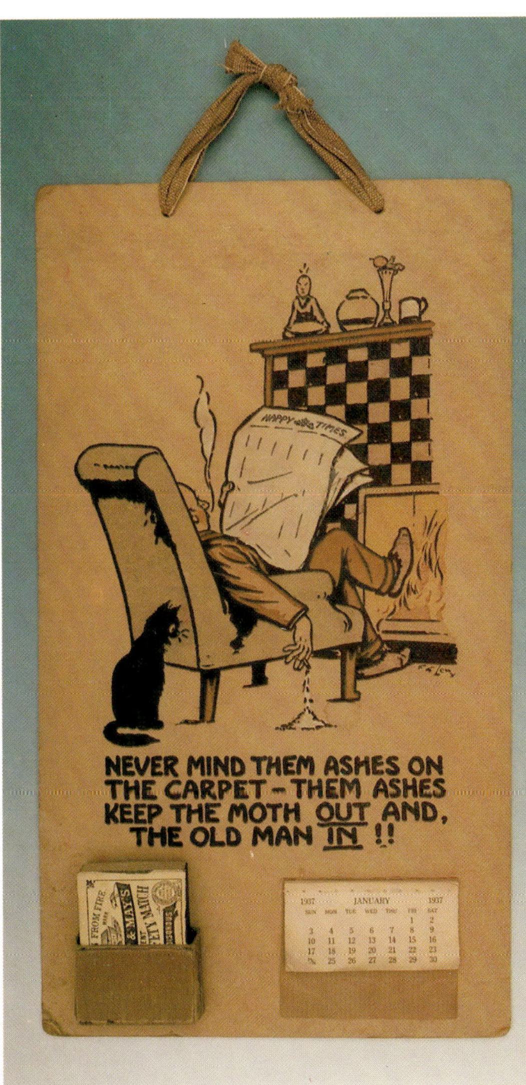

Fig. 633 Britain. Cardboard, paper. Made by Savory Dennison. 1937. H - 31cms.

William & Andrew Smith of Mauchline, Scotland, probably made the example in **Fig. 631** around 1900. The black transfer design is a view of Langholm, in Dumfriesshire, Scotland.

The example in **Fig. 632** is made of papier maché in a typical shape. Examples may be found with a larger match compartment, or two compartments, usually with a fairly elaborately curved back plate. The example here has a Japanese-inspired design, but they may also be found with flowers that resemble marguerites, and with black or orange backgrounds. A major center of production of papier maché was the Birmingham and Wolverhampton area of Britain; this type of match holder is usually attributed to that area, although there is no known evidence to support such an attribution. They were mostly made between c. 1870 and 1890, and there is evidence to show that they were imported into the United States; one of the same shape as the example "in red and black" was illustrated in an 1871 catalogue put out by F. A. Walker & Co. of Boston, Massachusetts. Walker's described themselves as "Importers, Manufacturers, Jobbers, and Retailers," and the catalogue included a number of stand-alone marble match holders that may have been imported from E. G. Zimmermann.

In a typically British vein of humor is the cartoon on the combined calendar and matchbox holder shown in **Fig. 633**. The calendar is for 1932, and on the back is a sticker marked "A Savory Dennison Calender. Made in England."

P. J. Clark of West Meriden, Conn.
Assignor to
S. J. Clark of said West Meriden.
Letters Patent No. 1111. Dated June 28. 1859.

Des. 1111

The schedule referred to in these Letters Patent, and making part of the same.

To all whom it may concern:

Be it known that I, P. J. Clark, of West Meriden, in the County of New Haven, and State of Connecticut, have invented or produced a new and ornamental design for a Match Safe, and I, do hereby declare that the following is a full, clear and exact description of the same, reference being had to the annexed drawings, making a part of this Specification, in which.

Figure 1. is a front or face view of a Match Safe, constructed according to my design.

Figure 2, a plan or top view of ditto.

Similar letters of reference, indicate corresponding parts in the two figures.

This design consists in having the Match receptacles provided with bases in the form of a Scollop Shell. A, represents a plate to which the Match receptacles B, are attached.

The receptacles B, are formed of two longitudinal halves of hollow cylinders or frustums of cones attached vertically to the plate A.

The tops of the receptacles are open to receive the Matches and the lower ends have bases C, of the form of a Scollop Shell made sufficiently convex to conform to the dimensions of the receptacles and fit snugly against the plate A, and form a neat and finished base or lower terminal, adding greatly to the appearance of the match safe.

The bases C, it will be seen do not form a complete shell, the portion that adjoins the joint being removed so as to form a parallel edge a, at the junction of the receptacles and faces and thereby allow the other portion to be adapted to the receptacle and form a finished terminal.

I claim as new and desire to secure by Letters Patent.

The configuration of the bases or lower terminals C, the same being in the form of a Scollop Shell and constituting a new and ornamental device for a Match Safe.

Witnesses,
Hervey Rogers.
George W. Rogers.

500 P. J. Clark.

Exd.
S.M.P.

Fig. 634 Facsimile of a United States Design Patent of 1859 by P. J. Clark.

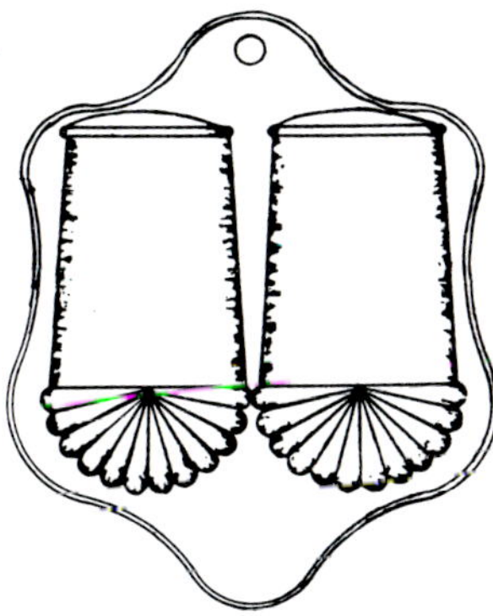

Fig. 635 Drawing from the Design Patent of 1859 by P. J. Clark.

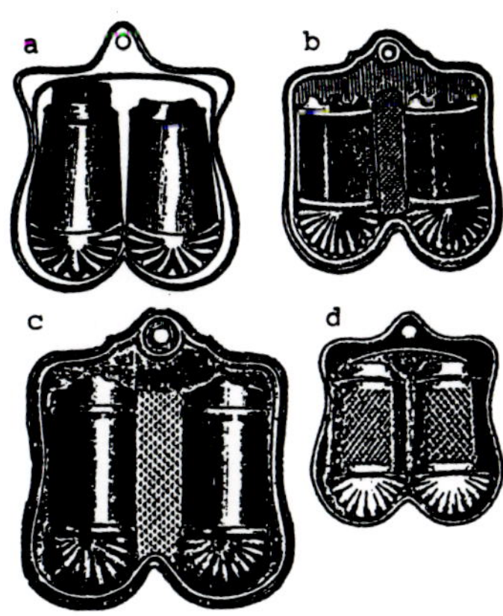

Fig. 636 Illustrations from trade catalogues of the "Twin" match holder. a - Russel & Erwin Mfg. Co. 1865. b - William Frankfurth Hardware Co. 1885. c - Simmons Hardware Co. 1908. d - McLary Mfg. Co. 1910.

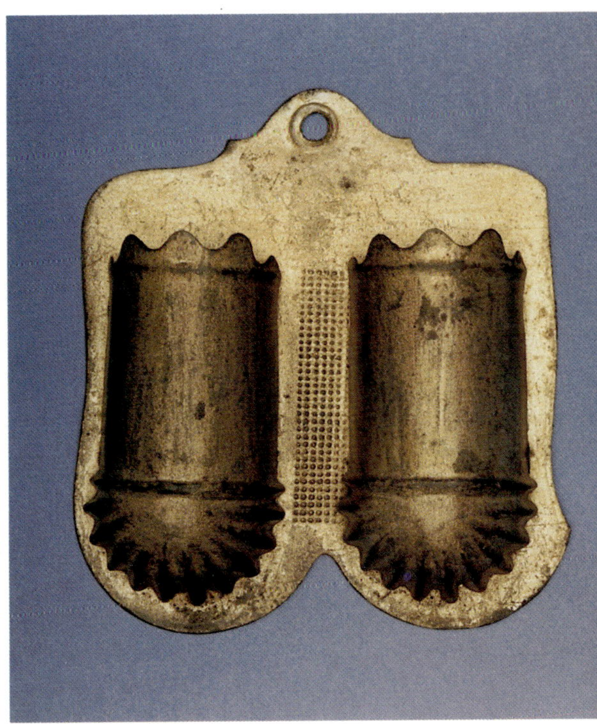

Fig. 637 United States. Tin plate. c.1920. H - 12.8cms.

The first wall match holder known to have been invented in the United States has a quite remarkable history. It was the subject of a Design Patent in 1859; a copy of the handwritten entry is shown in **Fig. 634**, and one of the two drawings in **Fig. 635**. It seems likely that the specifications were written up by the examiner, whose initials appear in the bottom right-hand corner. It was not until about 1867 that Design Patents were published in printed form.

The patent was issued to P. J. Clark, as assignor to S. S. Clark of West Meriden, Connecticut, no doubt a relative. It is possible that the Clarks' made these tinplate holders at first, although there is no recorded evidence to support this. But, over a period of at least sixty-two years they are known to have been made, with minor variations, by several other companies. The essential claim section of the patent refers to the bases of the match receptacles as "Being in the form of a Scallop Shell;" the rest of the holder was non-essential to the patent.

Wherever they have been illustrated by the many hardware companies that made or stocked them, they are referred to as the "Twin," usually under the heading of "'Match Safe." As a match safe, one would expect this holder to be provided with a lid. Yet it is not known to have been made with a lid; considering the early date of the patent, this in itself is surprising.

The illustrations in **Fig. 636**, taken from four different hardware company catalogues, clearly demonstrate the variations - none of which match the original design. Example "a" appeared in the catalogue of the Russell & Erwin Manufacturing Co. of New Britain, Connecticut, in 1865. From the 1885 catalogue of the William Frankfurth Hardware Co. of Milwaukee, Wisconsin, "b" was offered at $l.00 per dozen. Holder "c" was also offered at $1.00 per dozen in 1908, by the Simmons Hardware Co. of Saint Louis, Missouri. The example in "d" is from the McClary Manufacturing Co. of London, Ontario, who was making them by 1910 and impressed its mark on the back plate - the only company yet found to have applied its name. They were offered at 68¢ per dozen. In the 1913 mail order catalogue of Kresge's they were offered at 5¢ each "Finished in blue enamel." The last entry for these holders has been found in a 1921 catalogue of McLennan, McFeely & Co. Ltd. of Vancouver, British Columbia, hardware retailers, at 15¢ each. At least six other entries have been found in various hardware retailers' catalogues in between the dates mentioned above.

The example in **Fig. 637** is yet another variation. Unmarked, it could potentially be dated from anywhere between 1859 and c. 1921. However, the gold painted finish may be original, and there are no signs of corrosion, which suggest that it is probably closer to the 1920s. Without any marks, it is impossible to tell.

This is a long history for such a cheap, but obviously popular and effective device. It is probably only surpassed in longevity of history by Marble's waterproof pocket match holder. The Twin match holder may be commonly found today in antique stores, usually in an advanced stage of corrosion. One has recently been illustrated in a published price guide at the exorbitant price of $250.00, with an annotation that says "1859," but this is almost certainly incorrect.

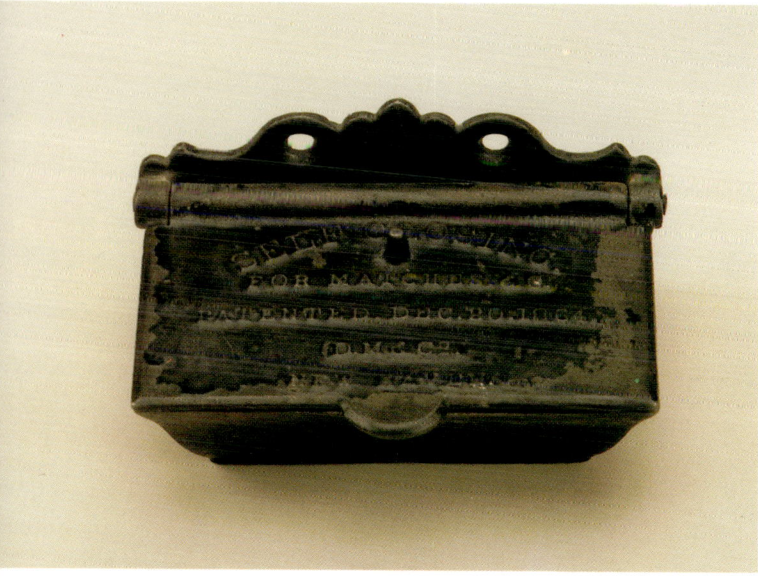

Fig. 638 United States. Cast iron. Made by Mallory, Wheeler & Co., to an Invention Patent of 1864 by William H. Andrews. L - 10.1cms.

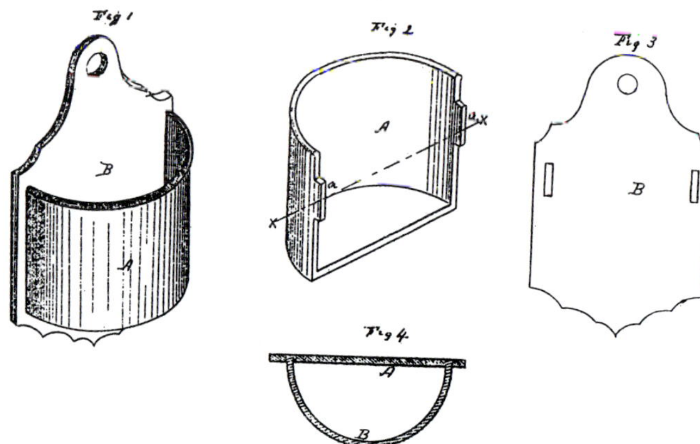

Fig. 640 Drawings from a United States Invention Patent of 1868 by John A. Evarts.

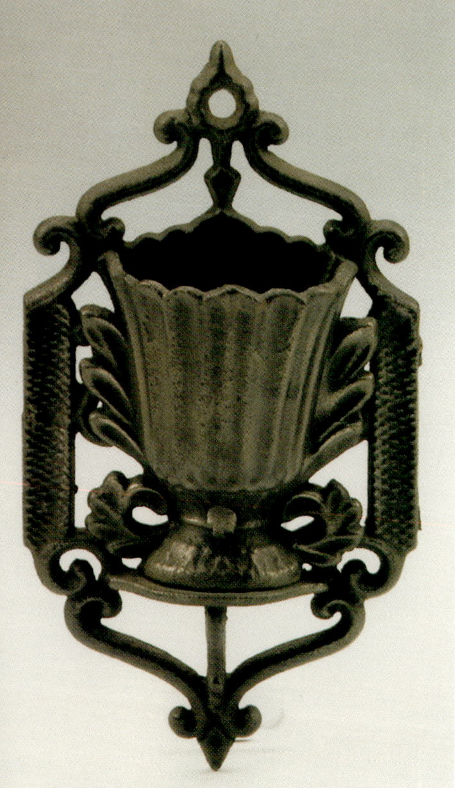

Fig. 639 United States. Cast iron. Made by J. & E. Stevens & Co. to a Design Patent of 1867 by Russel Frisbie. H - 15.7cms.

The cast iron box in **Fig. 638** could be used as a stand-alone holder, but was designed primarily as a wallhanging holder. The lid has raised lettering "SELF CLOSING. FOR MATCHES &C. PATENTED, DEC.20.1864. M.W. & Co. NEW HAVEN". The Invention Patent was issued to William H. Andrews, assignor to Burton Mallory of New Haven, Connecticut, and was essentially for the self-closing lid. In his opening statement Andrews notes the advantage of this invention as:

> "the box cannot, by any accident or carelessness, be left open, and is designed more particularly for use in manufactories, but is applicable to all places and for all purposes of a similar nature."

These boxes may be found not only with the initials "M.W. & Co." but also "D.M. & Co.," with the rest of the wording the same. The answer to this apparent mystery may be found in a trade catalogue of 1871, put out by Mallory, Wheeler & Co., or M. W. & Co., the front cover of which reveals them as "Successors to Davenport, Mallory & Co.", or D. M. & Co.; it also lists the principals as "Burton Mallory, J. Davenport Wheeler and Frederick B. Mallory". Therefore, any examples marked "D. M. & Co." must be pre-1871.

The company mostly made locks and door furniture; the index to the catalogue mentions "match safes," but does not illustrate them. However, they *were* illustrated, in three sizes, by the Dover Stamping Co. of Boston, Massachusetts, in its catalogue of 1869. They are also shown in the 1871 catalogue of F. A. Walker & Co. of Boston, again in three sizes and in two finishes: "Black, Plain" and "Fancy Finish." No prices are given. A plain version has been seen, but it was unmarked.

In 1867 Russel Frisbie was issued with a Design Patent for a "Match Safe" which showed two match compartments; he described it as "a half flower vase, made of suitable material, resting on a shelf supported by brackets fastened to an open work back." These were made with one and two "flower vases," a single vase example being shown in **Fig. 639**. They were produced in cast-iron by J. & E. Stevens & Co. of Cromwell, Connecticut. They have been reproduced in recent years in cast-iron and in cast brass.

John A. Evarts, as assignor to Bradley & Hubbard of West Meriden, Connecticut, was issued with an Invention Patent in 1868 for an "Improvement in Match-Safe." The patent drawings are shown in **Fig. 640**, and the patent was for a method of casting the match safe. The receptacle for the matches was cast first with its lugs, as shown in his Fig. 2. This section was then placed in a new mold with just the lugs exposed, and the back plate, shown in his Fig. 3, was poured so that the receptacle joined to the back plate in the casting process. The end-products were made of cast iron, which is a brittle material. So, with the parts cast separately and fitted together by hammering the lugs, it was no doubt found that many breakages occurred. Furthermore, personal experience as an apprentice in an iron foundry leads me to suspect that other problems would have been encountered by the new patent method: when the molten iron was poured into the mold containing the receptacle, it would be likely to react quite violently when it came in contact with the cold iron part.

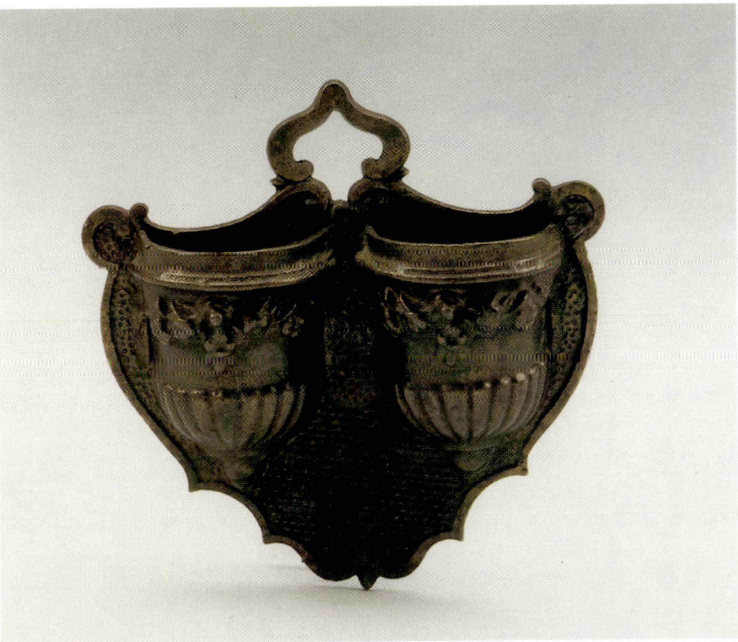

Fig. 641 United States. Cast iron. Made by Bradley & Hubbard to the Invention Patent in Fig. 640. c.1868. H - 10.3cms.

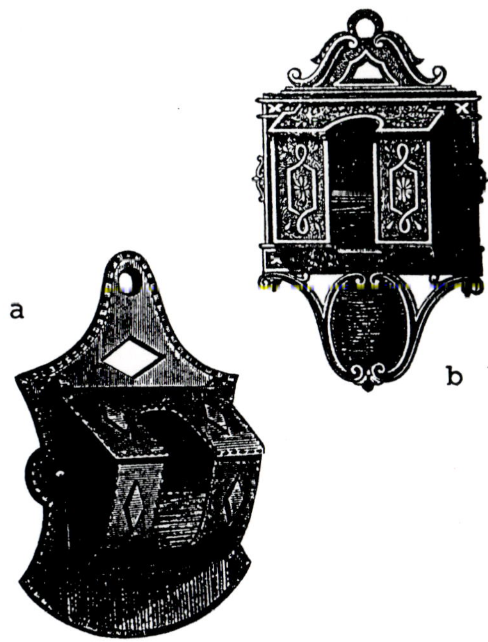

Fig. 642 Illustrations of two wall holders made by the Charles Parker Co. to two Invention Patents of 1868 and 1870. a - from an 1881 catalogue of the Simmons Hardware Co. b - from an 1885 catalogue of the William Frankfurth Hardware Co.

An example is shown in **Fig. 641**. The lugs show no signs of having been hammered to join the two parts, and it is marked with the patent number, which suggests that the method *was* used successfully. As may be seen, the end product was far more elegant than the patent drawings, and was made with two match receptacles. They were shown in the catalogue of the Dover Stamping Co. in 1869, who quoted numbers from 1800 to 1806, which suggests they were made in other sizes and/or finishes. They also appeared in the F. A. Walker & Co. catalogue of 1871 in one size only. Prices were not listed. The illustrated example is marked "1800."

Charles Parker of Meriden, Connecticut was a leader in developing match holders. Discussed elsewhere are his inventions relating to pocket match holders with folded edge seams, and to the three-piece, raised bead pocket boxes. But these were to come later; his earlier inventions were concerned with cast-iron wall holders.

His first invention patent for a wall holder was issued in 1868 to his assignor Hiram Richmond. It showed a lidded box with a slot in the front that continued up into the lid, thus making it easier to insert fingers to remove a match. Two sizes were made as shown in **Fig. 642 A**, taken from an illustration in an 1881 catalogue of the Simmons Hardware Co.: "for Ordinary Matches, at $.20 each," and "for Long Matches at $.25 each." A second version was shown in an 1885 catalogue of the William Frankfurth Hardware Co., (**Fig. 642 B**), where it was described as "No.30, Parker's Berlin Bronzed, Self Closing...per dozen, $1.75." By then it had been redesigned, probably to keep pace with the current decorative trends of the day.

Parker's obviously found the same problems of too many breakages occurring when the two parts of the box were riveted together, for in 1870 George Geer of Parker's was issued with a patent that resolved the problem. The specifications stated:

> "To overcome these difficulties is the object of my invention, which consists in forming ears upon the front edge of the box-part, and corresponding recesses in the rear, so that the ears on the front may, by slightly compressing the two sides, be sprung into the corresponding recesses in the rear, and thus secure the two parts together."

Thereafter, examples of the boxes, as shown in Fig. 642, were marked with both patent dates.

Between the dates of these two patents, in 1869, Richmond had been issued with another patent. This one was for a box with a counterweighted door that could be pushed in with the fingers for retrieving a match; when fingers were removed, the door swung back into the closed position automatically. An example is shown in **Fig. 643**; it is marked with the Richmond 1869 patent date and also that of 1870 by Geer. These too were illustrated in the Simmons Hardware Co. catalogue of 1881, as "Bronzed, for Ordinary Matches at $ .20 each." The box was still being offered in the Simmons catalogue of 1908, apparently little changed, at $2.50 per dozen; but the illustration does not mention the Parker name, and the patent protection had run out by that time. Parker was still very much in business in 1908, however, and may well still have been producing them.

In early 1869, Frank Marquard of Newburyport, Massachusetts, was issued a patent for an "Improved Vulcanizable Compound To Imitate Horn, Hard Rubber, & c." The composition consisted of sawdust, sulphur, a gummy substance such as starch, vegetable gum or gelatine, and a coloring matter. The ingredients were mixed and dried at "a moderate temperature," before being "reduced to a fine powder" and stored ready for use. Placed in a mold and heated to "about 300 degrees Fahrenheit," the powder would "be melted and vulcanized," after which it could be polished. Marquard refers to its potential as a composition for "knife handles, cane and umbrella handles, door-knobs, buttons, and various other useful articles."

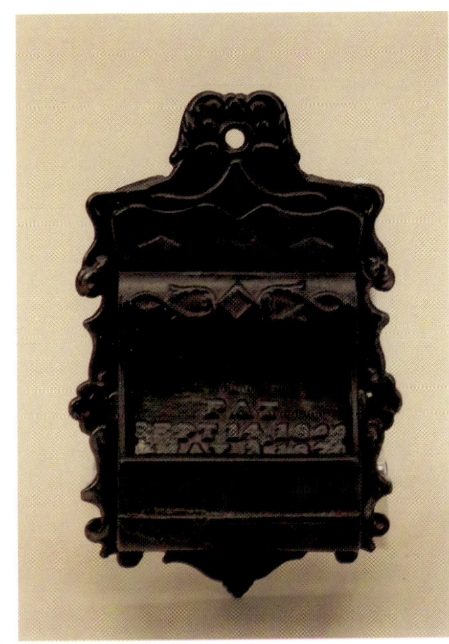

Fig. 643 United States. Cast iron. Made by the Charles Parker Co. to Invention Patents by Hiram Richmond of 1869, and George Geer of 1870. H - 16.2cms.

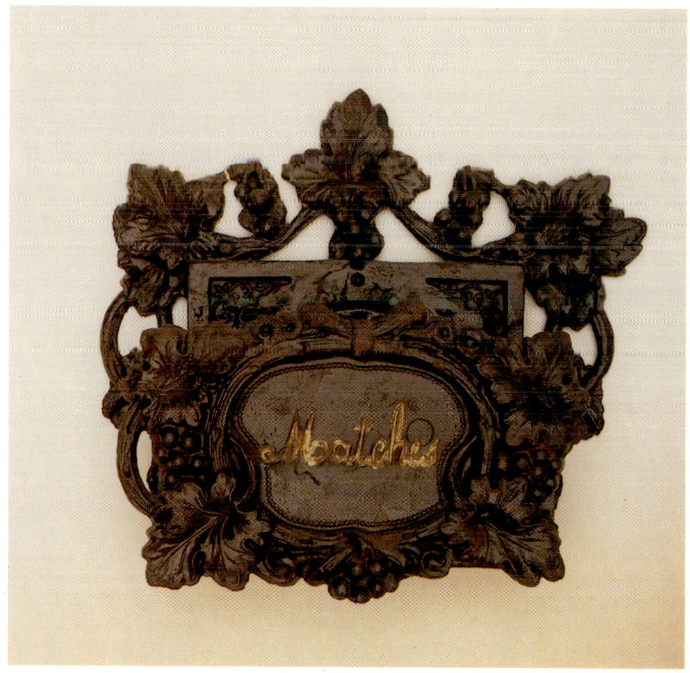

Fig. 644 United States. Vulcanized composition, wood, tin plate. Made by the Vulcanized Wood Co. The composition the subject of an Invention Patent of 1869 by Frank Marquard. W - 15.8cms.

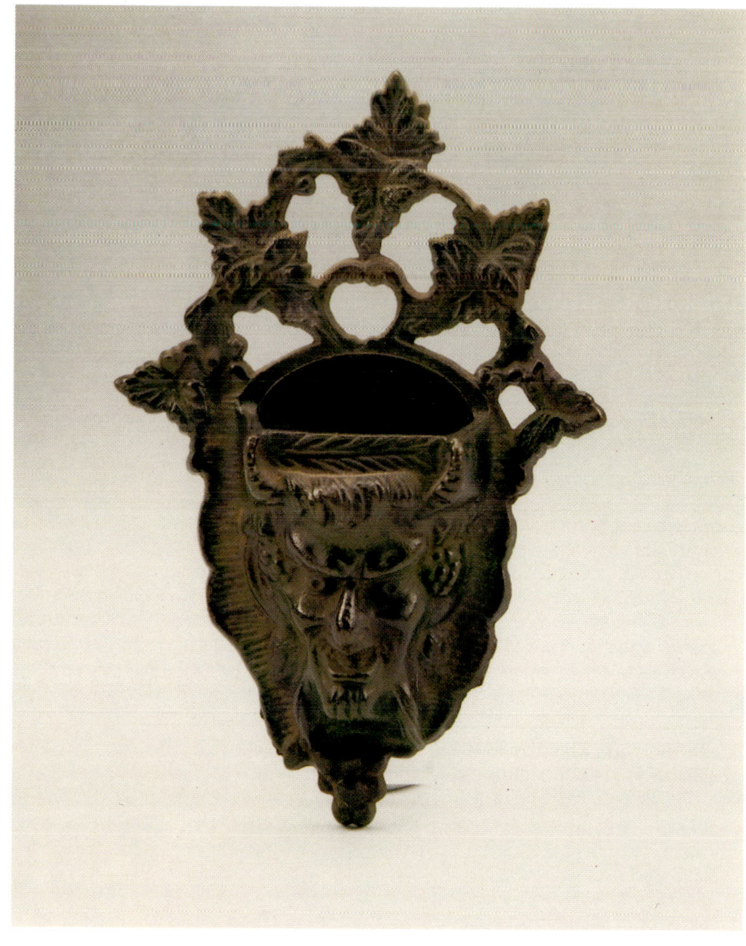

Fig. 647 United States. Cast iron, tin plate. c.1870s. H -15.4cms.

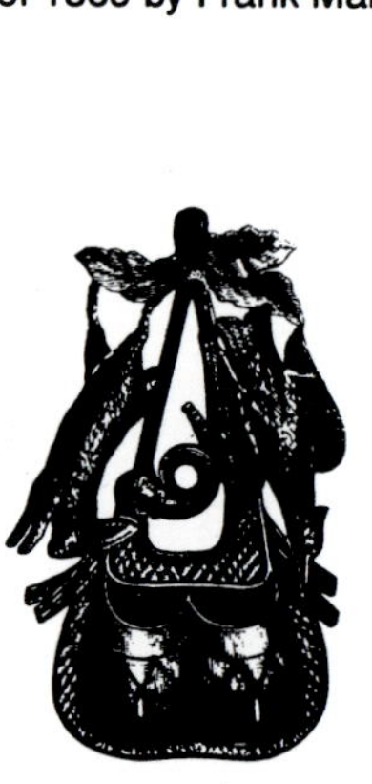

Fig. 645 Drawing from a Design Patent of 1870 by Frederick W. Brockspier.

Marquard was an assignor to the Vulcanized Wood Co., of Newburyport, and probably owned the company. It is not known how many "useful articles" he produced, but a wall-hanging match holder was one such article; an example is shown in **Fig. 644**, marked with the patent date and company name. The front and back panels are molded from the vulcanized material, separated by a pair of open-topped match compartments made of thin wood, lined with sheet tinplate.

Frederick W. Brockspier was issued with Design Patents for wall holders in 1868, 1869 and 1870. He was an assignor to Sargent & Co. of New Haven, Connecticut, who made the end products of his designs in cast-iron. The most popular one was that of 1870, which Brockspier described as:

> "The receiver represents a game-bag, by the strap of which the bag is suspended; upon one side hangs a bird, and upon the other a rabbit".

An illustration of this from Sargent & Co.'s catalogue of 1884 is shown in **Fig. 645**. It was described as "No.37. Game Pattern, per doz., $4.00." It was not shown in the company's 1901 catalogue. This piece has been copied in recent years, usually with poorer workmanship, sometimes with additions or other small changes, and usually with the original patent date. Unscrupulous dealers will provide reasons as to why it is the genuine article. Again, it is a matter of buyer beware.

Several other wall-hanging match holders of about this period (that is, the 1870s) have been reproduced, often with elements of the ornament picked out in bright paints. It is possible in many cases to recognise a modern reproduction quite easily: detail is often quite indistinct, or the metal has run out from edges, but occasionally they have been "aged," and the asking price may be high, even for the genuine article. At a low price they may be acceptable as an inexpensive reproduced example of the type. **Fig. 646** is an example of an inexpensive purchase, which may or may not be genuine.

Also from about the 1870s is another cast-iron holder incorporating the head of the devil, shown in **Fig. 647**. Although unmarked, it is not suspected of being a modern copy, and shows some similarities to pieces designed in 1872 and produced by Stevens & Brown Manufacturing Co. of Cromwell, Connecticut.

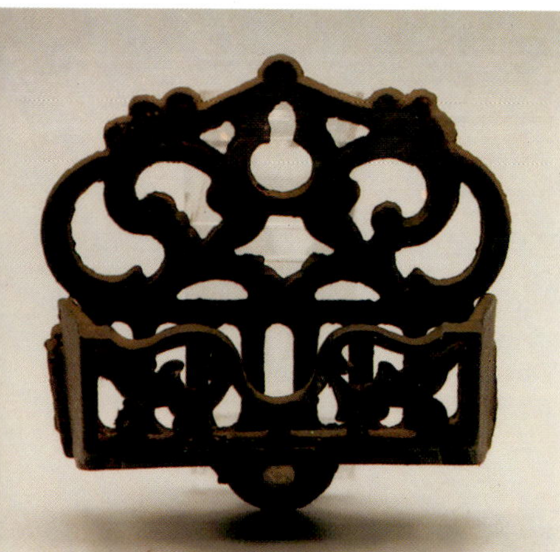

Fig. 646 United States. Cast iron. c.1870s. H - 8.2cms.

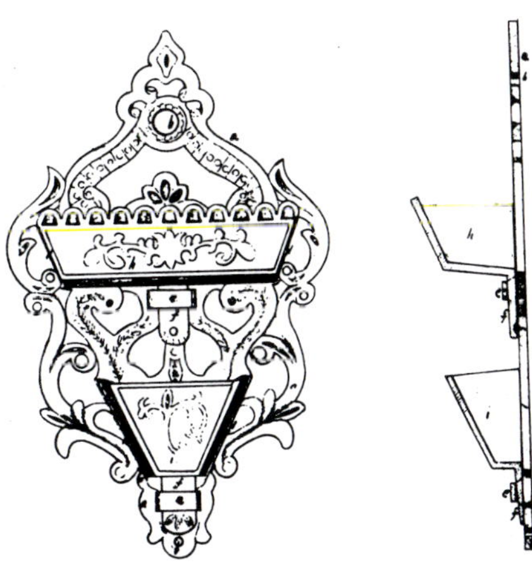

Fig. 648 Drawings from United States Invention Patent of 1870 by Albert D. Judd.

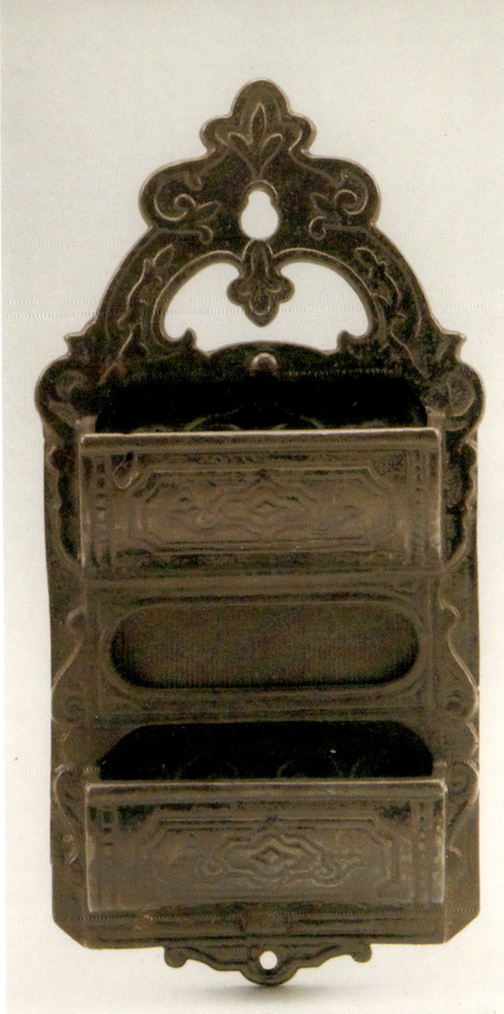

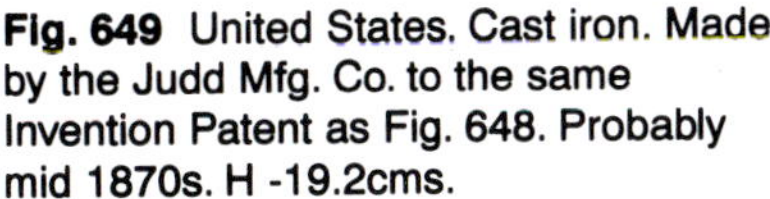

Fig. 649 United States. Cast iron. Made by the Judd Mfg. Co. to the same Invention Patent as Fig. 648. Probably mid 1870s. H -19.2cms.

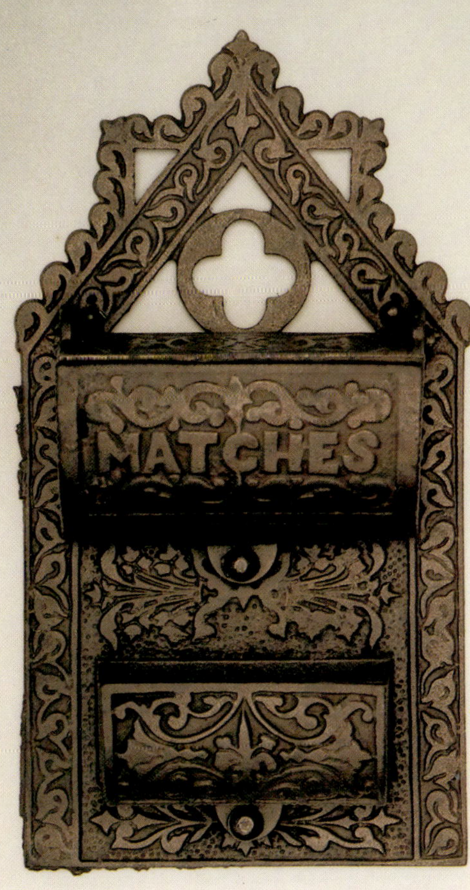

Fig. 650 United States. Cast iron. Made by Hart, Bliven & Mead Mfg. Co. to a Design Patent of 1876 by Otto F. Fogelstrand.

Albert D. Judd of New Haven, Connecticut held several patents, some of which have been discussed in Chapter V Part 2. He was issued with an Invention Patent in 1870 for a wall holder, the drawings of which are shown in **Fig. 648**. His company's catalogue of 1872 shows two versions of the piece illustrated, one with a less elaborate back plate; it also shows a third version which is quite different in appearance but, if examined carefully, meets the same patent claims which relate to the method of fixing the match receptacles to the back plate. The example in **Fig. 649** is marked with the same patent date. In this example Judd has cast a part of the back plate and the match receptacles as one piece; the other part of the back plate has been cast separately, the two parts being joined by means of a lug slipping into a loop, which conforms with the patent. He sold the type shown in the patent drawing for $2.25 per dozen, and the simpler version at $2.00 per dozen. His "Gothic Pattern" version, which more closely resembles the example shown, sold for $3.50 per dozen.

Otto F. Fogelstrand was an assignor to the Hart, Bliven & Mead Manufacturing Co. of Kensington, Connecticut. He was issued with seven Design Patents for match holders between March 1875 and 1877, and also held a number of Design Patents for other forms of hardware. An example of one of his designs of 1876 is shown in **Fig. 650**. When acquired it had been heavily overpainted in bright colors, and not very well at that, much of the detail being lost under the paint. These and other of his designs remained popular for a number of years; the type exemplified was exported to Britain, where it was illustrated in the Silber & Fleming catalogue of 1883. Other designs of his appeared in an 1884 Montgomery Ward & Co. mail-order catalogue from Chicago, and in an 1886 catalogue from Risley & Kerrigan, hardware wholesalers from Toronto, Ontario.

An Invention Patent was issued in 1878 to John Gilbert of Newark, New Jersey, as assignor to James, Aikman & Co., for a match holder in sheet metal. The wording of the opening statement says:

> "My invention relates to an improvement in the construction of match-safes, whereby the cost of manufacture is reduced and an article of convenient shape and tasty appearance produced from a single piece of sheet metal".

The drawing from the patent, showing the outline of the body of the box, is shown in **Fig. 651**. The lid was a separate piece. An example of the end product is shown in **Fig. 652**; the patent date is stamped on the back plate. They were shown in an 1886 catalogue from Hall & Carpenter, tinplate and metals wholesalers of Philadelphia, described as "Self-Closing Match Safes. Decorated." No price was listed. The word "Matches" had been added to the front of the body, but it is not clear if this was painted or impressed.

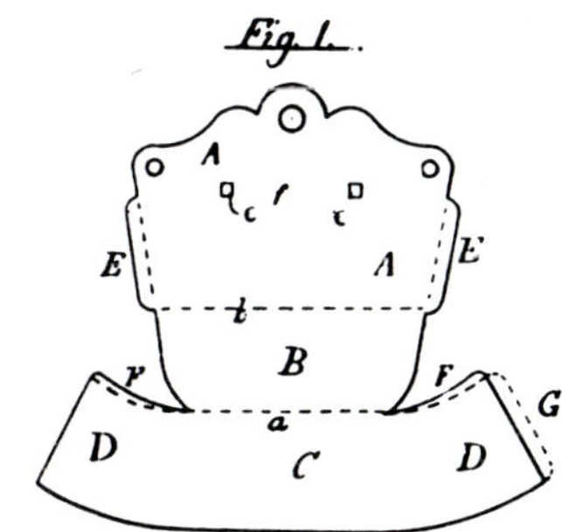

Fig. 651 Drawing from a United States Invention Patent of 1878 by John Gilbert.

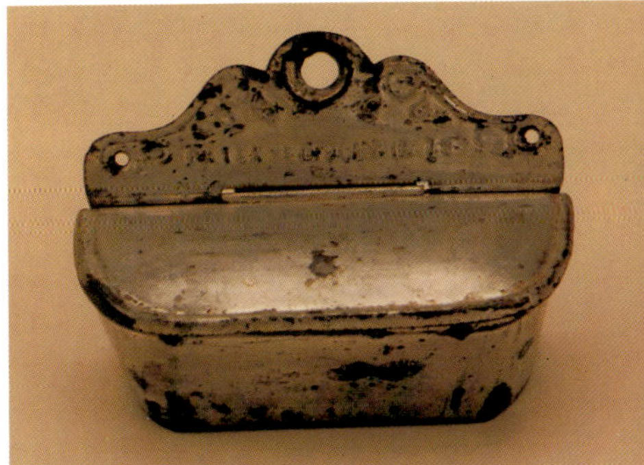

Fig. 652 United States. Tin plate. Made by James, Aikman & Co. to the Invention Patent of 1878 in Fig. 651. W - 11.2cms.

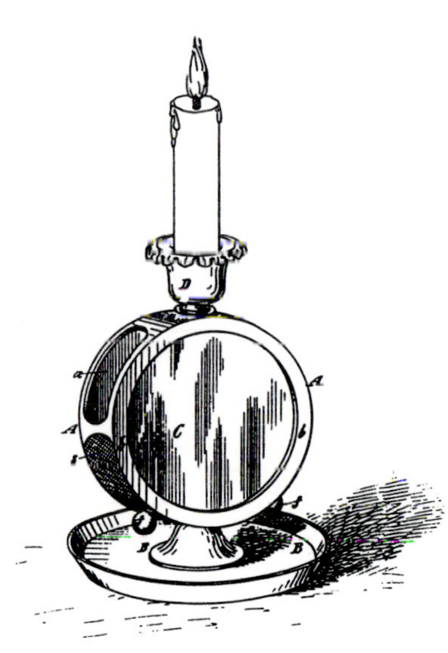

Fig. 653 Drawing from United States Invention Patent of 1882 by William Trotter Jr.

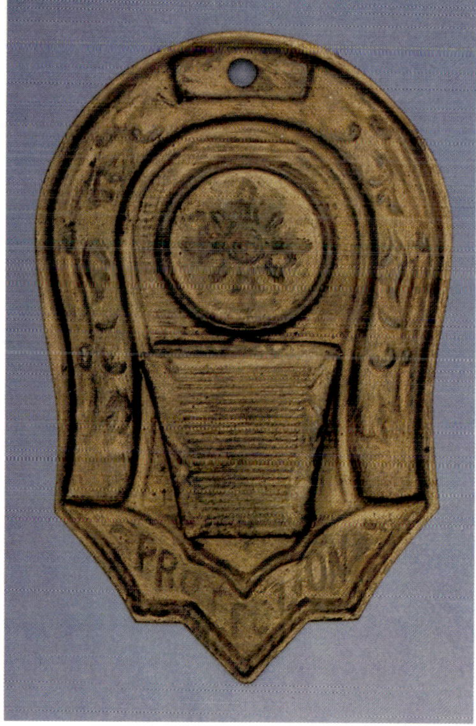

Fig. 656 United States. Tin plate. Made to a Design Patent of 1884, shown in Fig. 657. H - 15.2cms.

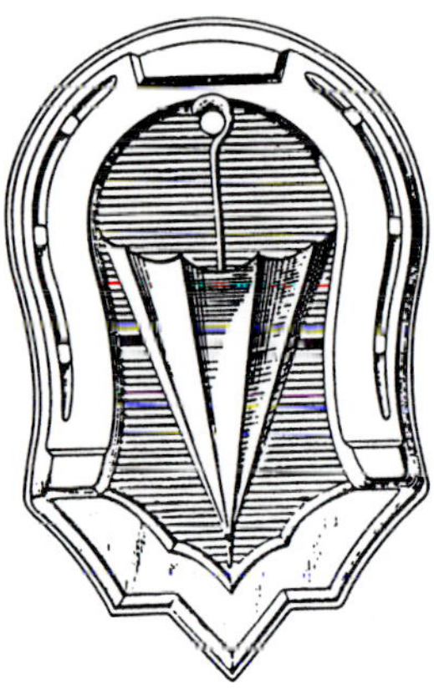

Fig. 657 Drawing from a United States Design Patent of 1884 by James F. Lockwood and Alva Bryant.

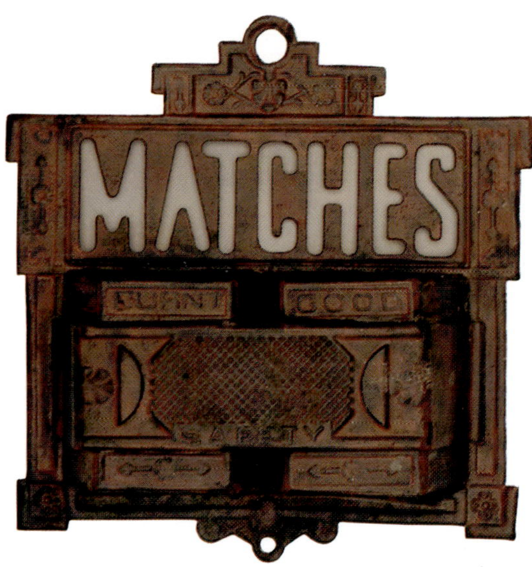

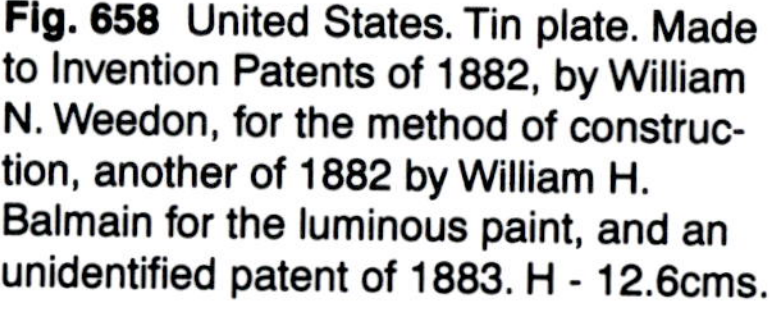

Fig. 658 United States. Tin plate. Made to Invention Patents of 1882, by William N. Weedon, for the method of construction, another of 1882 by William H. Balmain for the luminous paint, and an unidentified patent of 1883. H - 12.6cms.

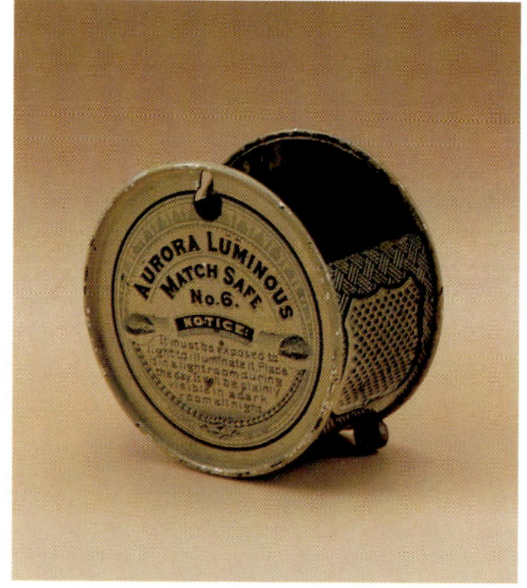

Fig. 654 United States. Tin plate. Made to the Invention Patent in Fig. 653. D - 7.8cms.

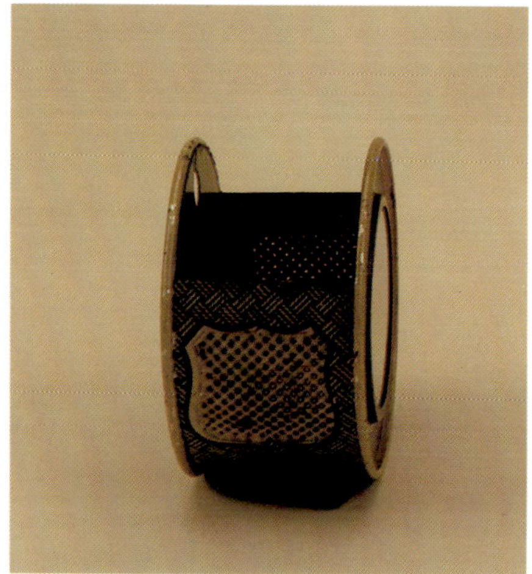

Fig. 655 As Fig. 654.

William Trotter Jr. of Oyster Bay, New York State was issued an Invention Patent for a "Combined Match-Box and Candlestick" in 1882. His patent drawing is shown in **Fig. 653**. The previous year he had been issued with two other patents for match holders that involved the use of luminous paint, both of which were withdrawn and re-issued on December 13, 1881. Trotter may have sold his patents or he may have had his own company. Whichever the case, the example in **Figs. 654 and 655** was produced to his 1882 patent, minus the candlestick and the ashtray. It was marked with the re-issue date of his earlier patents, to which it bears not the slightest resemblance, however. The end product was capable of being used as a stand-alone type, since it had two ball feet to keep it stable, or as a wallhanging type. Unfortunately the maker's name is not recorded on the example. It was illustrated in the Montgomery Ward & Co. mail-order catalogue of 1884 as:

> "Luminous Match Safes, made of brased tin, can be hung up or used on mantle, and plainly visible in a dark room at night. No.6. Each, 20¢, per doz.$2.10."

Immediately following this entry in the Montgomery Ward & Co. catalogue is a second luminous match safe, made of glass, in rectangular form, and referred to as "'No.3." This may have been re-designed from one of Trotter's 1881 patents.

Although unmarked, there is little doubt that the tinplate example in **Fig. 656** was made to an 1884 Design Patent, issued to James F. Lockwood and Alva Bryant of Philadelphia, Pennsylvania; a copy is shown in **Fig. 657**. Some minor changes have occurred between design and production; in particular, the umbrella-shaped holder (of the patent) has been replaced by a more conventional form that appears later on a number of Canadian-made items (see Figs. 661 to 663).

Another tin-plate wall holder was the subject of an Invention Patent issued to William N. Weedon of New Bedford, Massachusetts, in 1882; it is shown in **Fig. 658**. In his specifications he states:

> "The device described consists of but three pieces, each of which may be formed with dies, so as to require no fitting, and the whole easily and quickly combined or separated at any time and by any person. When arranged for use the safe is convenient, efficient, strong, and durable, and in consequence of its construction can be produced at a small cost".

It is not known who made these holders—perhaps Weedon had his own company—but the plate holding the two receptacles had to be amended. A drawing of the plate from his patent is shown at the top in **Fig. 659,** and my own sketch of the amended plate is shown below it. These indicate that the lugs "A" at each end were enlarged and the format changed, to provide an improved fixing; that two lugs at "B" were added and bent inwards to prevent the receptacles from moving laterally; and that two more lugs were included at "C" to hold a piece of safety match igniting strip.

On the back of the example are the remnants of a label which gives the following instructions on how to use it:

> "Hang Safe where the Letters receive and absorb freely either DAYLIGHT or any ARTIFICIAL LIGHT, and they will glow in DARKNESS. When using "SAFETY MATCHES" leave them in the box and tear off the CHEMICAL PAPER from the box and place it under the FRONT of Safe."

The label also had three patent dates: one was Weedon's; one has not been identified; and the third, of 1882, was issued to Harriet Fox, executrix for the deceased William H. Balmain of Ventnor, on Britain's Isle of Wight, for "Self-Luminous Paint." It was first filed in Britain in 1877, and subsequently in eleven other patent offices around the world, before finally being filed in the United States.

These holders were offered by two Canadian companies, both referring to them as luminous. In 1895 and 1896 mail order catalogues from T. Eaton & Co. Ltd. of Toronto, Ontario, they were priced at .15¢ each. Hobbs Hardware of London, Ontario, were wholesalers who in about 1898 priced them at $3.25 per dozen, almost twice the price of Eaton's.

Glass wall-hanging match holders may be found, some probably reproductions, but they are less common than metal types, probably due to the fragility of the material. **Fig. 660** shows an example in gold or amber pressed glass, the holder ribbed as a striker, and a tray included for spent matches below. The back plate has an alternating button and diagonal-cross design, for which glass collectors no doubt have a special name. This is believed to be from the United States, probably from the first decade of this century.

The Thomas Davidson Manufacturing Co. Ltd. of Montreal, Quebec was established in 1860, and by 1901 claimed that its factory had "a floor room of 9 1/2 acres and over 600 employees." In its 1901 catalogue were shown twelve items that were match holders or that incorporated match holders in the design. One was a pocket match holder, two were stand-alones, the others of the wall-hanging type. Among the most popular designs were what they called "Dressing Cases." Two examples are shown in **Figs. 661 and 662**. Two match receptacles are attached to the back plate, with or without a mirror in between, and at the bottom is a tray to hold a comb or hair brush. Some examples also included a whisk holder soldered to the front of the tray. The example in Fig. 661 is made of tin-plate with impressed designs overall; that in Fig. 662 is lithographed, and probably later in date.

The impressed tin-plate type was being made by 1893 and continued to be produced until at least 1911. It may be found in the mail-order catalogues of T. Eaton & Co. throughout that period: in 1893 they were priced at .30¢ each; in 1901 at .15¢ each; and in 1911 at .8¢ each. In the Davidson's catalogue of 1901 they were for sale at $1.50 per dozen, that is 12.5¢ each. In the catalogue of the Hobbs Hardware Co. in about 1898, the same form of Dressing Case was being offered, but the impressed designs on the tin-plate were quite different, and they were being described as "Egyptian Mirror Dressing Cases." It is not known who made them. A very similar version, in mint condition, has been seen recently but is believed to be a reproduction; it showed no traces of wear, corrosion or the accumulated grime that an original would have gathered, even under the most careful storage conditions, over a period of at least eighty years.

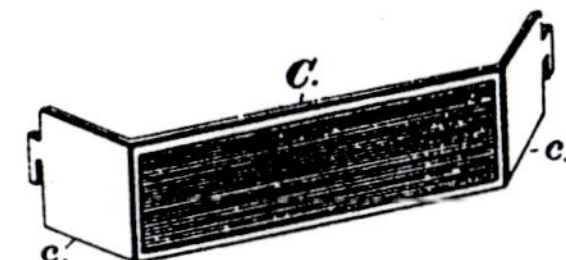

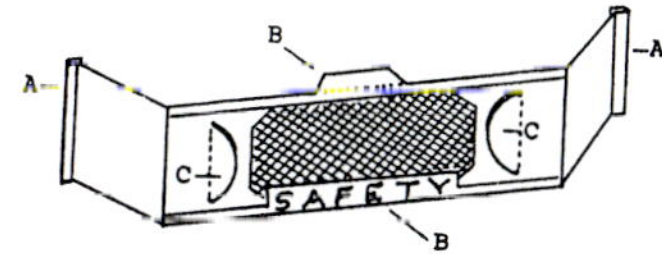

Fig. 659 Drawings of the plate along the front of Fig. 658. Top: from the patent drawings. Lower: sketch of the amended end product.

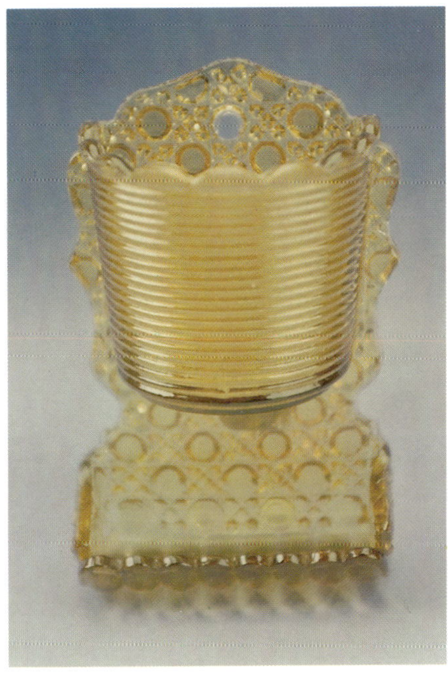

Fig. 660 United States. Glass. c.1910. H - 12.8cms.

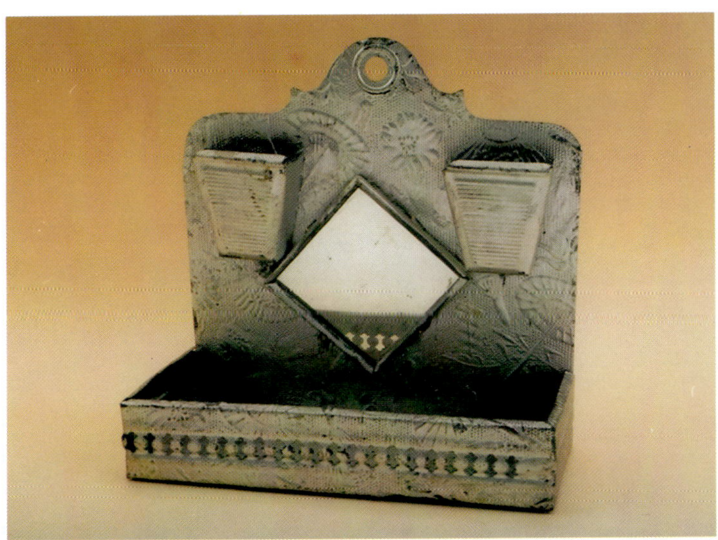

Fig. 661 Canada. Tin plate, glass. "Dressing case". Made by the Thomas Davidson Mfg.Co.Ltd. c.1901. H - 17.8cms.

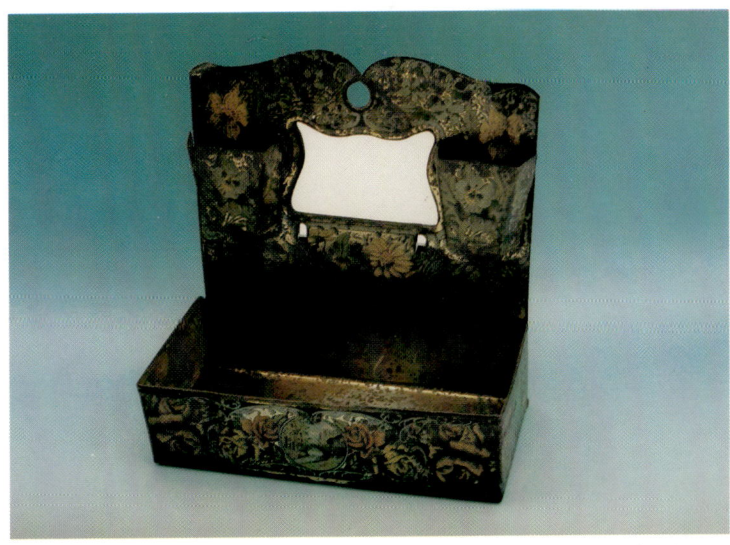

Fig. 662 Canada. Tin plate, glass. "Dressing case". Made by the Thomas Davidson Mfg.Co.Ltd. c.1910. H - 17.6cms.

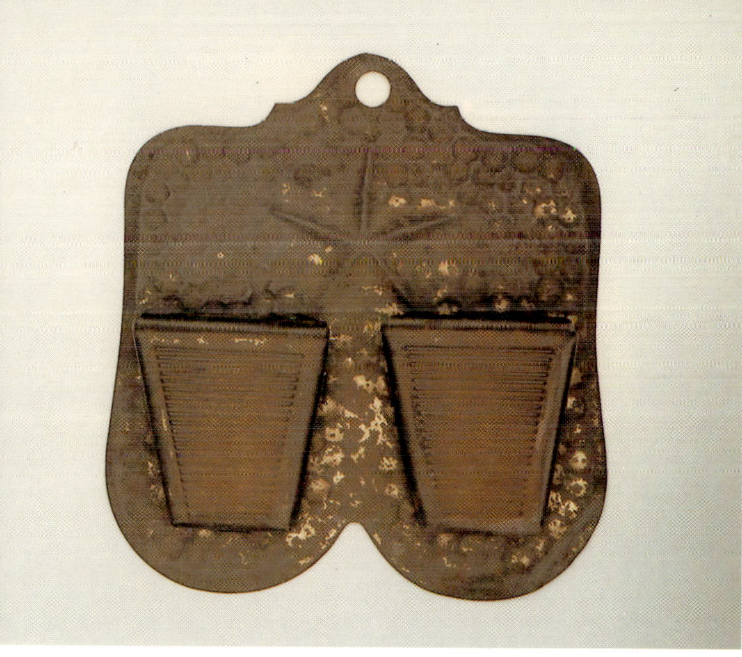

Fig. 663 Canada. Tin plate. Probaby made by the Thomas Davidson Mfg.Co.Ltd. from c.1894 until c.1919. H - 12.6cms.

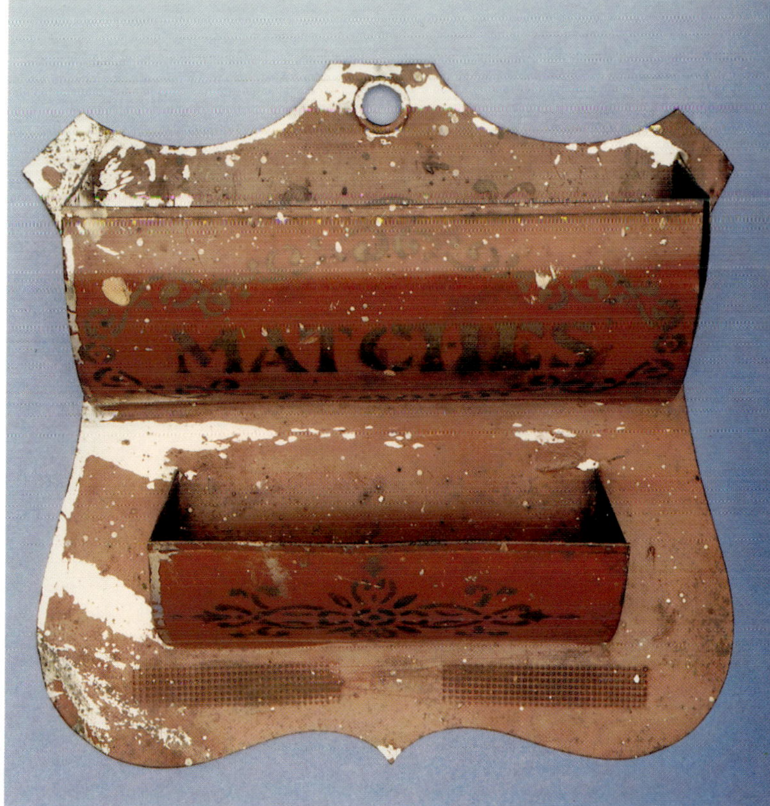

Fig. 664 Canada? Tin plate. c.1910. W - 20.6cms.

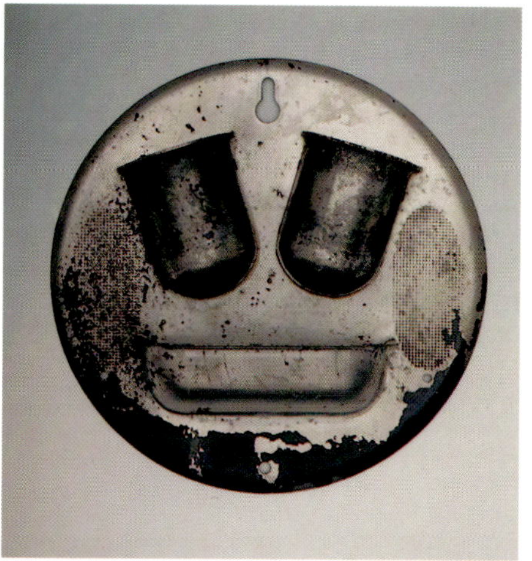

Fig. 665 United States. Tin plate or steel. Made by the Cassidy-Fairbanks Mfg.Co. From 1907 until 1910. D - 14.5cms.

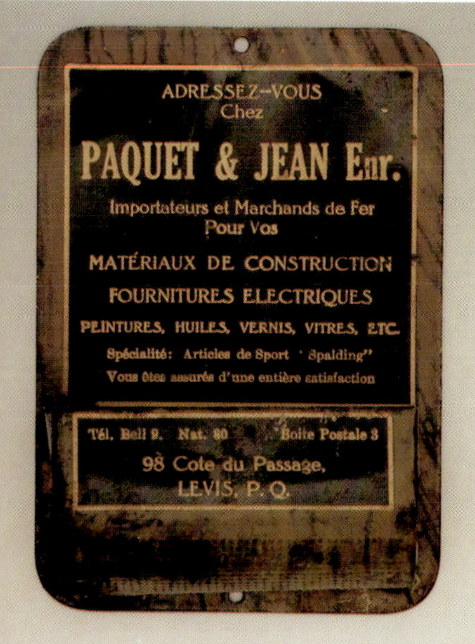

Fig. 666 United States. Tin plate. c.1915. H - 12.4cms.

A version of the "Twin" wall match holder, with a back plate similar to that of the Clark's patent, but incorporating two of the match receptacles of the type used in the preceding examples, is shown in **Fig. 663**. This was illustrated in the T. Eaton & Co. catalogues from 1894 until at least 1919, and in most was said to be "Canadian Made". This may also have been made by the Thomas Davidson Mfg. Co. Eaton's were selling these for 5¢ and 10¢ each in 1895, but without explaining why two prices were quoted. In 1919 they were 8¢ each.

The example in **Fig. 664** probably dates from about 1910, when a similar piece was shown in the T. Eaton & Co. catalogue of that year. It is probably Canadian-made, with the match receptacles soldered to the back plate, rather than using lugs that pass through the back plate to be bent over at the back, as was the more usual and cheaper method of construction. The example was sold at auction in 1983, being a part of the family possessions of Mosom M. Boyd, who started the Boyd Lumber Co. in Bobcageon, Ontario, in 1877.

From 1907 until 1910 another wall holder was illustrated in the T. Eaton & Co. catalogues; this is shown in **Fig. 665**. Made of thick sheet tin plate or steel, with two match receptacles and a trough for spent matches, they were made by the Cassidy-Fairbanks Manufacturing Co. of Chicago, Illinois.

Tin-plate wall holders lent themselves well to advertising. They took printed messages easily and cheaply. The introduction of chromolithography by the early 1890s heralded the beginning of brightly colored tin-ware, and manufacturers were quick to take advantage of the possibilities that the process offered.

The most common form was as shown in **Fig. 666**. The example is particularly dull, bearing only printed information—the name, address and telephone number of a Quebec merchant, and the type of merchandise sold. Still, by far the majority were bright and cheerful, advertising specific products, often utensils for the kitchen (which is where most wall holders were likely to be placed) or other items found in or around the home. Many were given away at the point of sale of the advertised product; or, for four cents in postage stamps, the product companies would send one by mail. They helped take advertising into rural areas where the more sophisticated home wares were not readily available in the small town or village store.

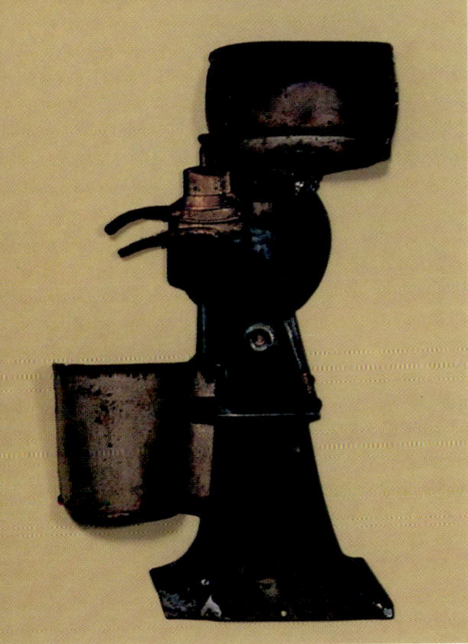

Fig. 667 United States. Tin plate. Made to a Design Patent of 1908 by Linnaeus T. Savage. H - 15.8cms.

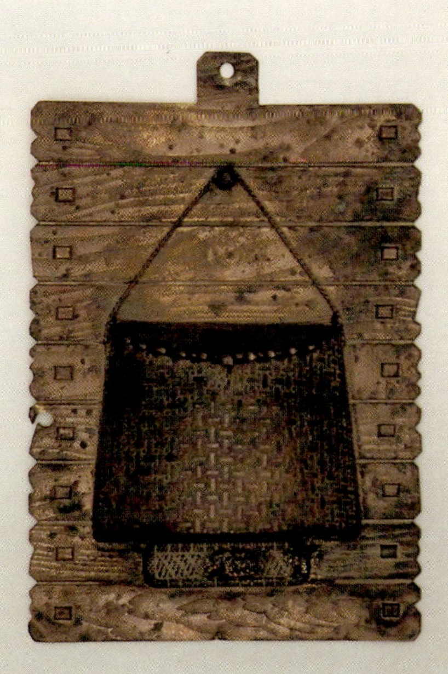

Fig. 669 United States. Brass. c.1910. H - 12.5cms.

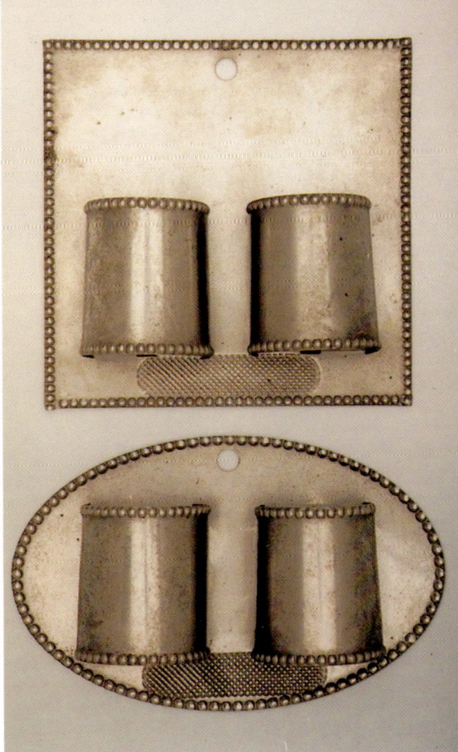

Fig. 670 United States? Plated brass. c.1910. Top: H - 10.6cms. Lower: W - 12.4cms.

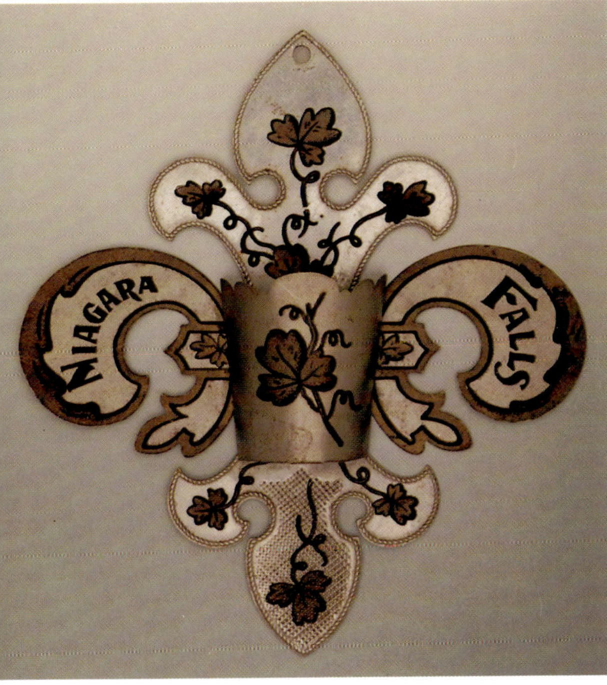

Fig. 668 United States. Aluminum. 1909. H - 14.6cms.

Other forms were made displaying more imagination in the design. Linnaeus T. Savage of New York was issued with two Design Patents for such items. The first was in 1908 for the De Laval Separator Co., and is shown in **Fig. 667**. This was produced in at least three versions, each printed with the number claimed to be in use. The example here claims one million in use; it also includes the patent date and Savage's name.

In aluminum, the example in **Fig. 668** is a souvenir of Niagara Falls. It was almost certainly made in the United States, and it is quite possible that other resort spots had similar pieces. On the back is the date "June 16th 1909", written in pencil, probably contemporary with its manufacture.

Fig. 669 shows a holder made of brass with a copper finish. It represents a fisherman's basketry creel with a hinged lid, hanging on a panel of planks. This is probably c. 1910.

The examples in **Fig. 670** are made of plated brass. The match receptacles are attached to the back plate by means of lugs. They are no doubt of North American manufacture, made by the same company, and probably c. 1910.

The amusing, if not bizarre, example in **Fig. 671** was made from a lobster pincer—*chelae*—by the author in an attempt to reproduce the black and white illustration in a Design Patent of 1910. The Design Patent was issued to Ivory L. Hall of Vinalhaven Island, off the coast of Maine. Vinalhaven was, and still is, a major center for lobstering. Hall was 36 years old in 1910, and had been listed in the 1900 census as a "junk dealer." Inquiries by the Vinalhaven Historical Society have failed to turn up any extant examples based on Hall's patent.

The author's own experiments have shown that the end product leaves something to be desired. The shell of the claw is quite brittle once boiled. In order to remove the meat, it would likely have to be boiled; besides, the subsequent color after boiling is better than the natural color. When the meat is removed, the cartilage that holds the small section of the claw in place has to be retained, or the claw will separate. This cartilage material impedes access for the matches; yet, if it were removed, the matches would drop into the bottom of the claw, which would be a further hindrance. The idea is intriguing, but not very practical, and it is possible that very few were ever produced by Hall, if in fact he sold any.

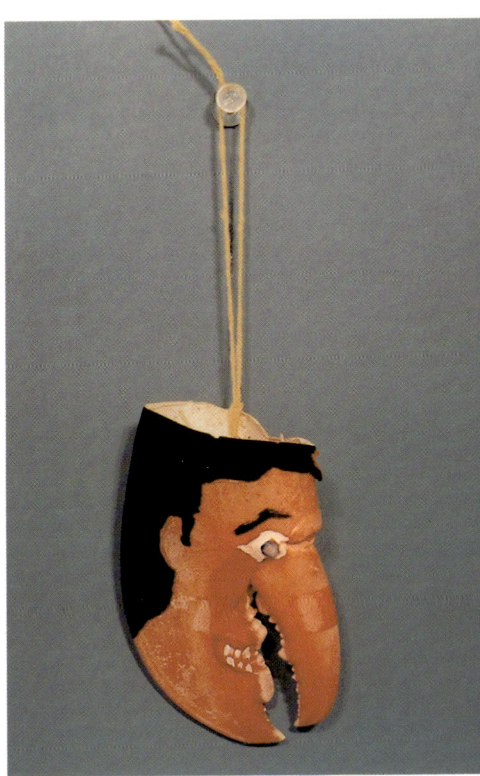

Fig. 671 Lobster pincer. Copied from a United States Design Patent of 1910, by Ivory L. Hall. Reproduction by the author, 1993. H -8.5cms.

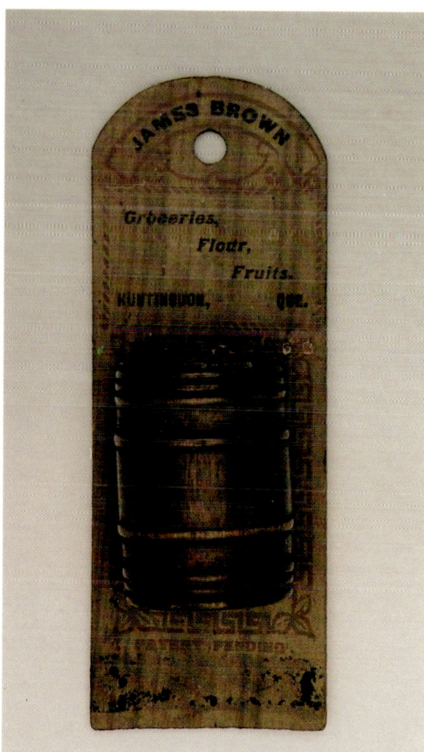

Fig. 672 Canada? Wood. c.1910. H - 15.1cms.

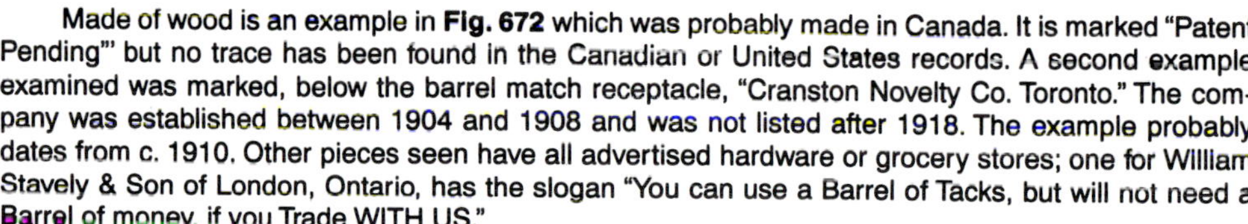

Made of wood is an example in **Fig. 672** which was probably made in Canada. It is marked "Patent Pending"' but no trace has been found in the Canadian or United States records. A second example examined was marked, below the barrel match receptacle, "Cranston Novelty Co. Toronto." The company was established between 1904 and 1908 and was not listed after 1918. The example probably dates from c. 1910. Other pieces seen have all advertised hardware or grocery stores; one for William Stavely & Son of London, Ontario, has the slogan "You can use a Barrel of Tacks, but will not need a Barrel of money, if you Trade WITH US."

The example in **Fig. 673** has two half-cylinders in wood as match receptacles, attached to a thin wood back panel by means of strips of plated brass. It bears advertising for a hardware and tinsmith business that was established in 1895, before finally closing down in about 1939. The holder probably dates from c. 1910. Other wooden match holders in the same general form, often more elegant and intended for use in a formal setting, were also produced about the same period.

Reference has been made, in Chapter V Part 6, to holders with "Scratch Mottoes." The example in **Fig. 674** shows a version made of three-ply wood, with a match receptacle in the form of half a cylinder. Made in the United States, this type became quite common from about 1910 onwards. Several versions may be found in the T. Eaton & Co. mail-order catalogues from 1911 until c. 1914; they were sold for 12 cents each.

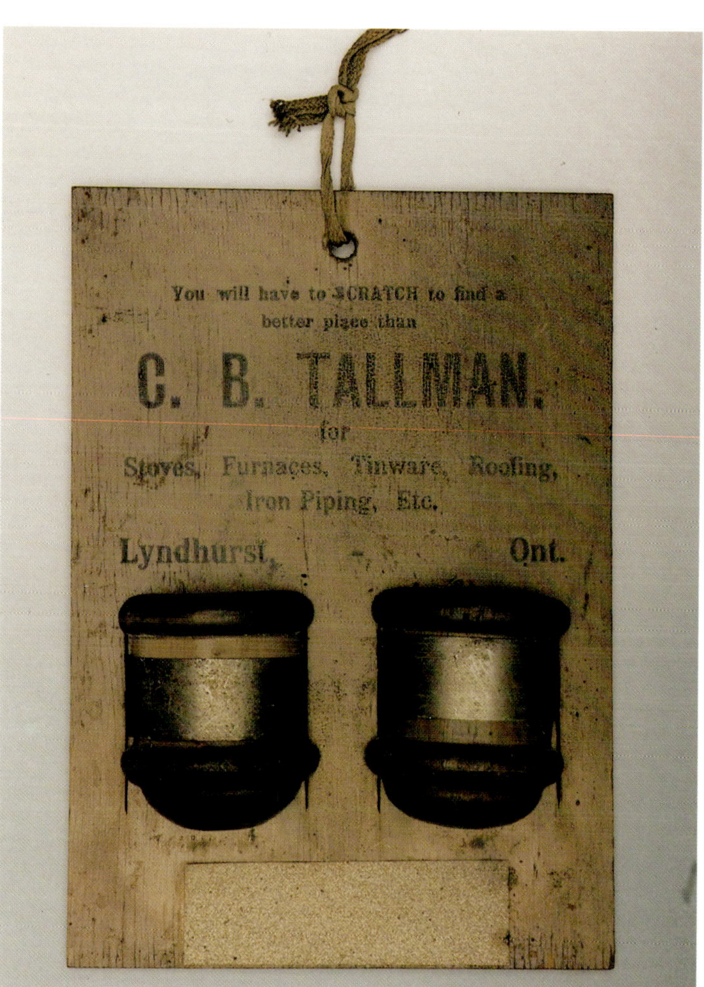

Fig. 673 Canada? Wood, plated brass. c.1910. H - 17.8cms.

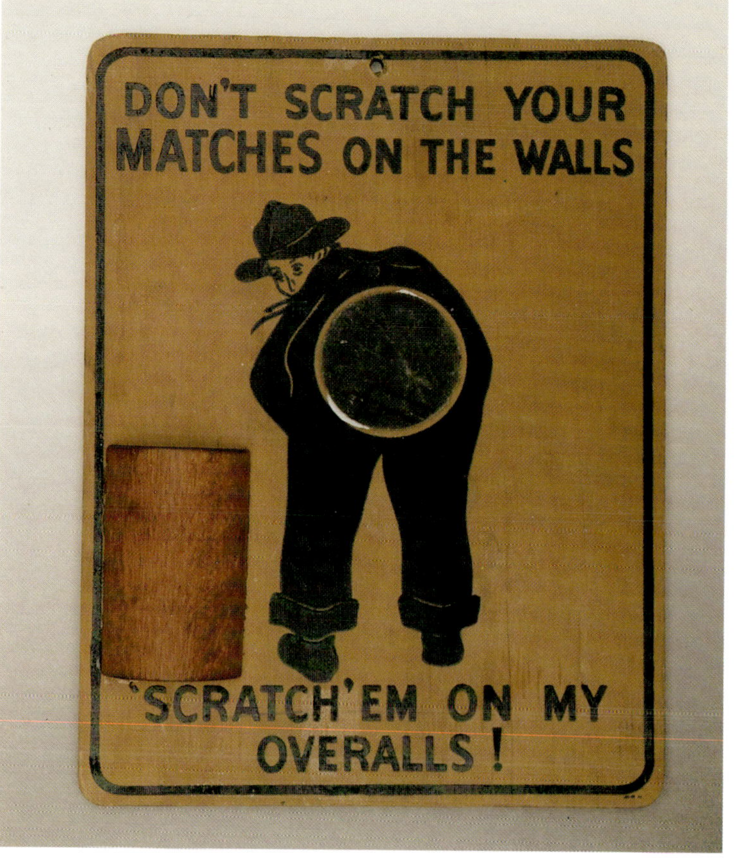

Fig. 674 United States. Wood. c.1910 to 1915. H - 17.7cms.

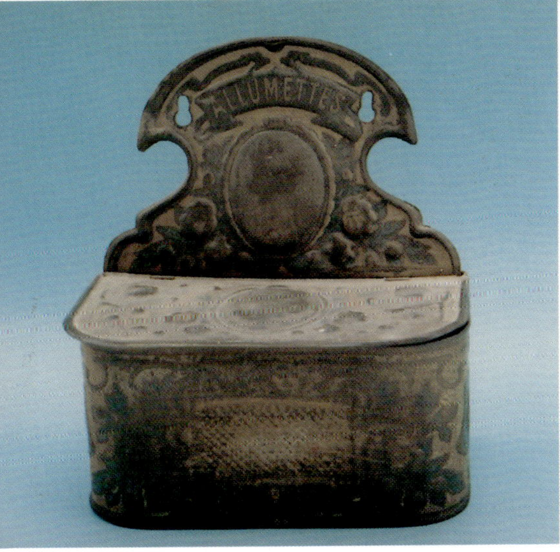

Fig. 675 ?France or the United States. Tin plate. c.1900 to 1910. H - 14.3cms.

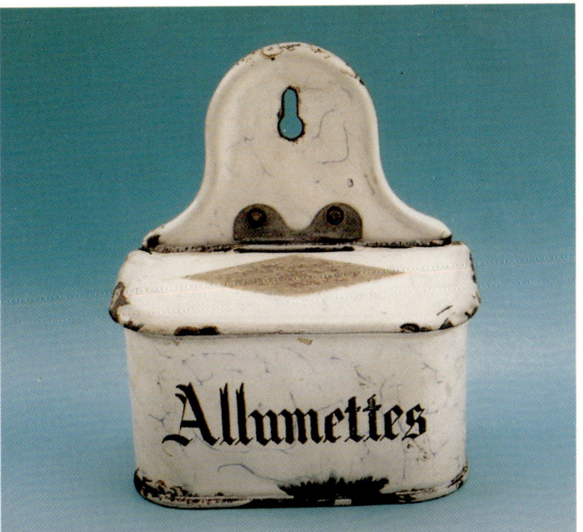

Fig. 676 ?France or the United States. Tin plate, enamelled. c.1900 to 1910. H - 16.7cms.

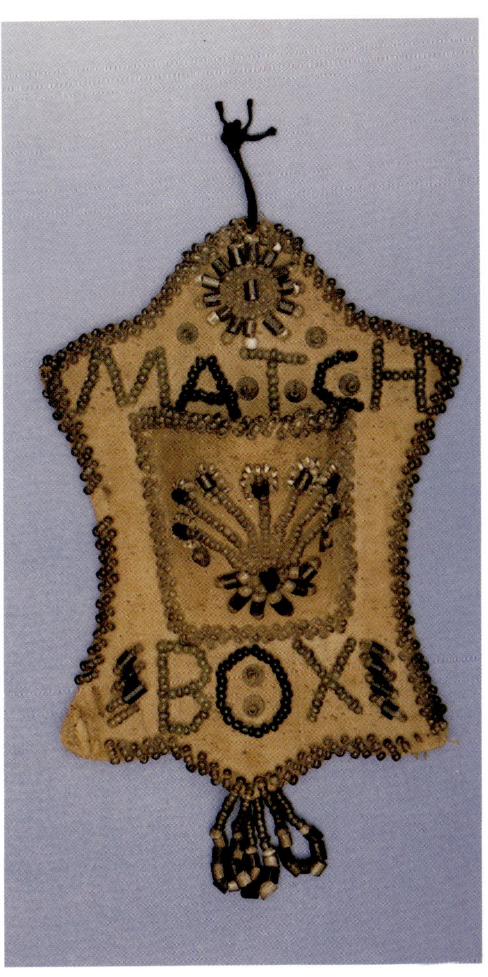

Fig. 677 Canada. Cloth, cardboard, glass. c.1910. H - 20cms.

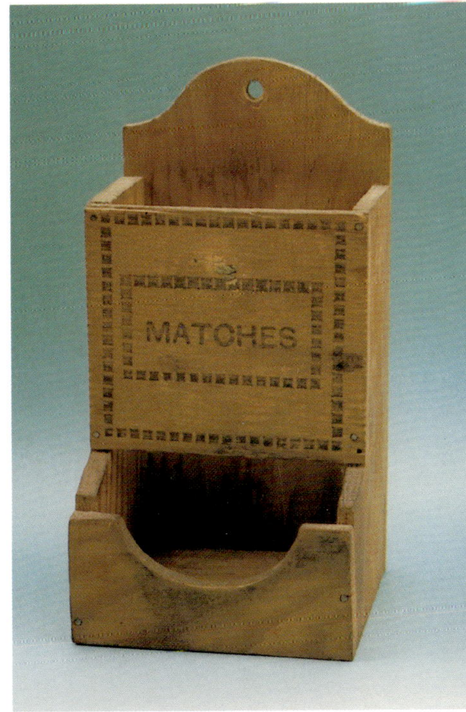

Fig. 678 United States. Wood. Probably post WWII. H - 16.4cms.

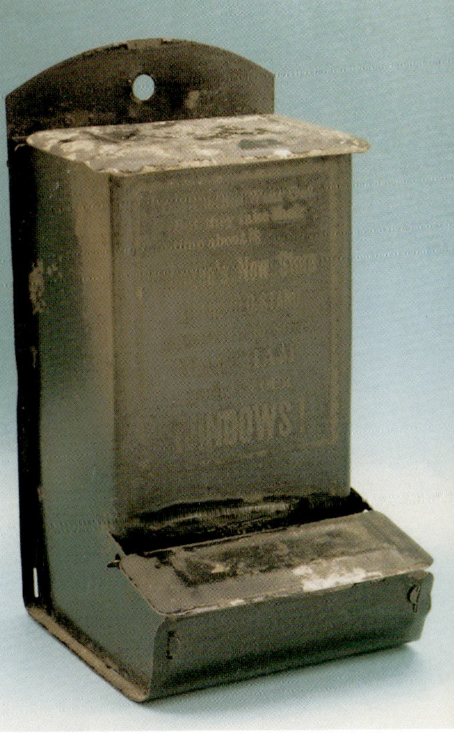

Fig. 679 United States. Tin plate. c.1905 to 1910. H - 15.4cms.

Two examples of wall holders marked "Allumettes" are shown in **Figs. 675 and 676**. These were obviously made either in France or in the United States for the French-speaking market, probably between c. 1900 and 1910. The example in Fig. 675 is made of lithographed tin plate with mostly floral designs. That in Fig. 676 is of sheet iron or tin-plate with an enamelled finish. This is commonly called "graniteware" in North America, though in Britain that term was introduced in about 1840 and refers to a type of ironstone pottery body.

Made of cloth sewn to a cardboard backing, and decorated with glass beads and sequins, the example in **Fig. 677** was made around 1910, probably in the Montreal region of Quebec. It may have been made by women in a small cottage industry, or possibly on one or other of the Indian Reserves in the region for sale to Europeans. Versions of these may be found with two matchbox pockets.

In plywood, the example in **Fig. 678** probably dates from the 1930s, or possibly the 1950s, and was made to hold a large box of 200 or 250 parlor matches. On the back are the remnants of a paper label bearing the name "Woolworths," in a style that suggests the post-World War II period.

Tin plate holders for large boxes of matches began to appear around the turn of the century, and there were a number of Invention and Design Patents. Almost every kitchen in North America had such a holder, and they were still in everyday use until well into the 1950s, when electric ranges began to become more common. The example in **Fig. 679** is black, with a lid on the top and over the well from which the matches were extracted. Strangely, there is no sign of a striker, and no slots in the sides to provide access to the striker on the matchbox. It has advertising on the front as follows: "Our Clothing Wears Out, But they take their time about it. Lanagan's New Store, At THE OLD STAND. 669-671 Main Street, WALTHAM. LOOK IN OUR WINDOWS!" It is assumed that the city is Waltham, Massachusetts. The holder probably dates between c. 1905 and 1910.

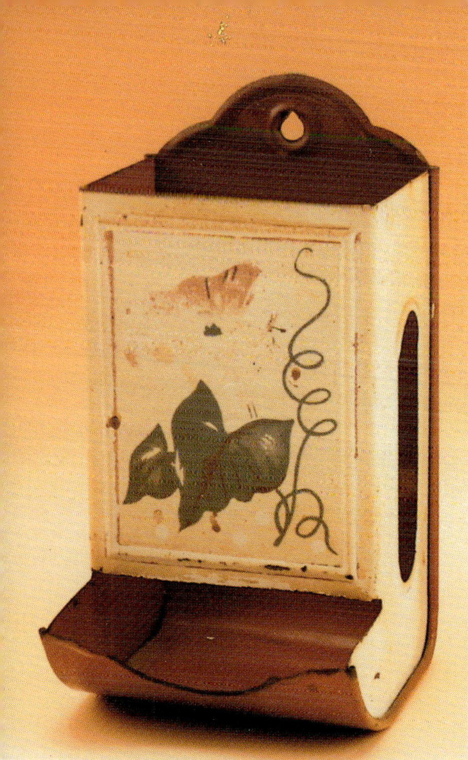

Fig. 680 United States. Tin plate. c.1930s and 1940s. H - 15.4cms.

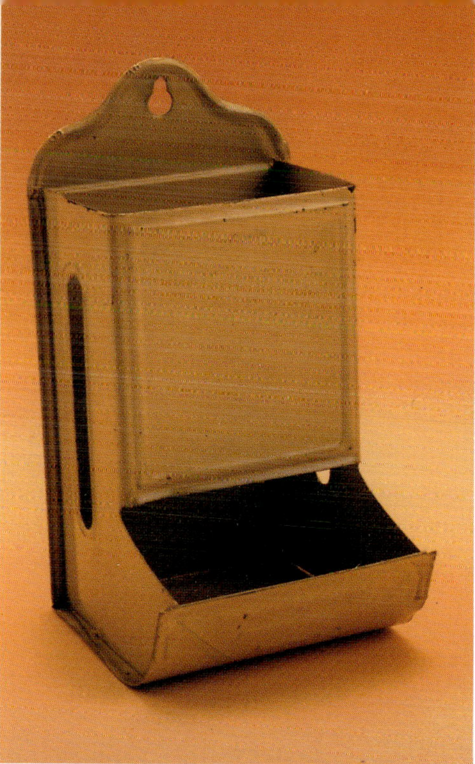

Fig. 681 United States. Tin plate. 1980s. H - 15.3cms.

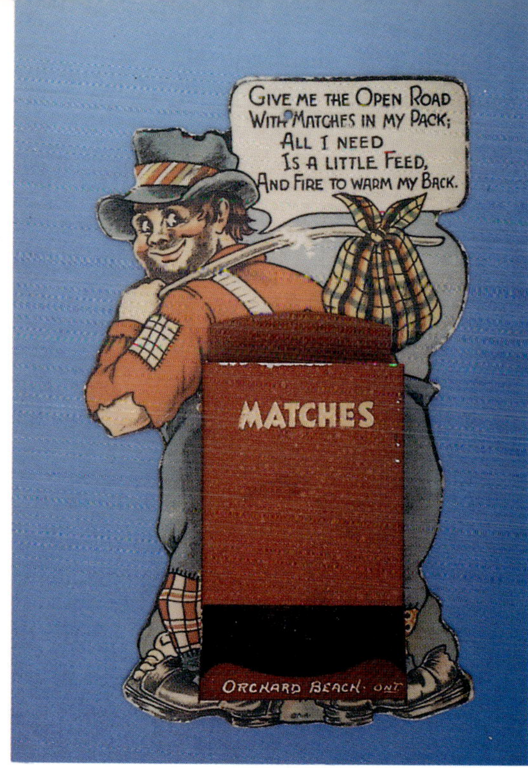

Fig. 682 Canada? Tin plate, cardboard. c.1946 to 1955. H -25.1cms.

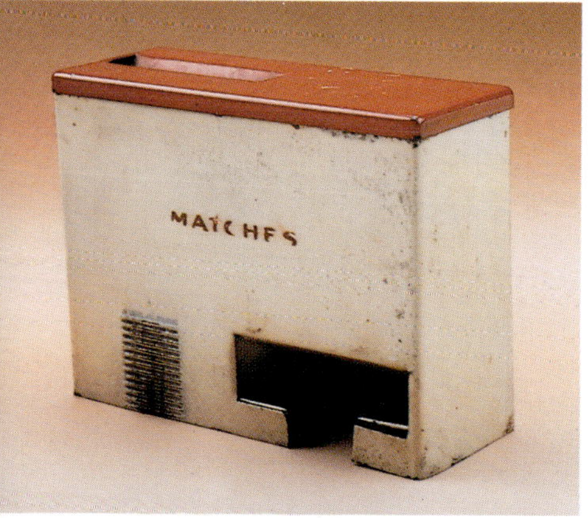

Fig. 683 United States. Tin plate. Made by the Columbus Speciality Co.. Marked with a U.S. Invention Patent of 1935 by Bertis Hamilton, to which it does not conform. W - 14cms.

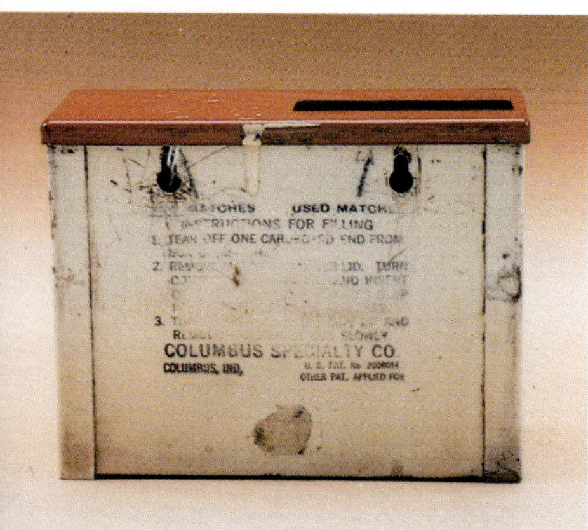

Fig. 684 As Fig. 683.

Variations occurred; some were provided with a tray for spent matches, usually located on the upper part of the front or side panels. By the 1930s this holder was being made in its simplest form: open at the top and at the trough, often with a printed design of flowers (as shown in **Fig. 680**), and with slots on both sides to provide access to the striker on the matchbox. It is common to find these holders overpainted, no doubt to match the kitchen decor. Some have a round mark stamped on the back, "Mafd. By P.N.Co., Fulton, Illinois, U.S.A." They were still being made in the late 1980s, and are possibly still being made today. They are unmarked, and usually undecorated, other than in a plain color, and cost about three or four dollars. The example in **Fig. 681** is one such modern piece.

The example in **Fig. 682** is attached to a cardboard backing cut out in the form of a tramp. It was a souvenir of Orchard Beach, Ontario. This too lacks a striker, although the paint finish would probably be capable of igniting a normal friction match. Although the holder is unmarked, the same tramp has been seen with a pin cushion attached to it, in place of the match holder; this had the name and address of an Ottawa, Ontario, tailor printed on it. The tailor was only at the printed address from 1946 until 1955, which provides the probable date of the match holder version.

Bertis Hamilton of Columbus, Indiana, was issued with an Invention Patent in 1935 for a "Match Container." The second paragraph of his written specifications adequately describes his objectives:

> "In carrying out my invention, I provide a box of incombustible material, such as sheet metal, divided into two compartments by a vertical partition, one of such compartments being intended to contain unused matches and the other burnt matches. Unburnt matches are supported in their compartment by a yielding means which will permit them to be withdrawn from the bottom of the compartment one at a time. The other compartment is provided with a slot in its top through which burnt matches can be dropped. Associated with this opening are baffles which obstruct the ready flow of air through the slot and insure that the match dropped into the burned-match compartment while still ignited will be promptly extinguished for want of oxygen."

The end product was manufactured by the Columbus Speciality Co. of Columbus, Indiana; front and back views are shown in **Figs. 683 and 684**. On the back are printed instructions for filling the device, the maker's name, and the patent number. So it is clearly identified as stemming from the Hamilton patent; but, without that identification it would be impossible to recognize it as Hamilton's. The front view clearly shows a very large opening from which the matches may be extracted, probably as many as half a dozen at a time, should it be so desired. The "baffles" that Hamilton specified and showed in his drawings, do not exist; there is no trace of them ever having been intended for inclusion. But what is perhaps the worst aspect, from the point of view of Hamilton's intentions, is that in the bottom of the "burned-match compartment" there is a 4 mm diameter hole, which would encourage an up, or down, draught, so increasing the oxygen supply to any match that remained ignited.

Thus the intent of Hamilton's invention and his legal claims section were totally ignored; the device in no way meets his specifications or drawings. To compound this apparent folly, the company also made a single compartment version to hold matches only, yet still included the patent number.

In effect, we have come full circle: from the early mistakes made by George Dowler of Birmingham in 1850, in which he was perhaps pardonable for his ignorance and folly, to eighty-five years later, in a far more enlightened society, where ignorance had receded, and folly was far less excusable. On the other hand, in fairness to the Columbus Speciality Co., it probably did not sell its match holder as "fire proof" or "fire resistant". Surely, however, its ethics were questionable.

Chapter VIII
Epilogue

The era of match holders is usually regarded as spanning from about 1830 until about 1930. In fact it began in 1826 with the John Walker tin-plate boxes: the early forms of pocket boxes copied the format of snuff boxes (with the lid hinged longitudinally), then the lid moved to the narrow end of the box and was hinged on the edge. Shortly after the turn of the century, the gas or petrol lighter began its ascent in popularity, many of the early forms copying those of match holders. After World War I, the pocket match holder began to loose ground in popular preference, eventually fading almost to obscurity by the 1930s.

Vestiges of the phenomenon continued to manifest themselves long after 1930 however, and the match itself was still very much in use. Indeed, matches are still made today; although in North America at least, the book match is the most common form to be found. The introduction of cheap throw-away lighters has further severely reduced the production of the original wood-stemmed matches, and the specialty match holders have all but disappeared. But not quite.

Perhaps surprisingly, a survivor in the field is one that first appeared in 1900, patented by Webster Marble, but now made in Hong Kong and imported into North America. The example in **Fig. 685** is identical to the first production run, without modification. This waterproof box is sold locally in Boy Scouts stores or in hunting and camping equipment stores, locked in the inevitable plastic-formed cover with cardboard backing, which frustrates the purchaser tying to separate the box from its wrapper. It still costs only just over three dollars; that is, just over six times its original price. How much has inflation risen in ninety-odd years?

Another waterproof match holder of cylindrical form, shown in **Fig. 686**, is made of a modern plastic. It was being made by 1950, when illustrated in a catalogue of D. H. Howden & Co. Ltd. and H. S. Howland Sons & Co. Ltd. of Toronto and London, Ontario; they called it the "K.M." matchbox, and sold it at $1.48 per dozen. The description includes the remark "fitted with flint strike bar at bottom of case to produce sparks if match supply runs out." The same box is made today and issued to members of the Canadian Armed Forces as part of a survival kit, including the flint.

In Mexico, hand-made glass match holders of the stand-alone type, shown in **Fig. 687**, were still being made in the l990s by Feder's, and imported into Canada and probably the United States. In Canada they were marketed as "The Arafy Collection," in three different forms of "Sculptured Artistic Glass" holders, with a complement of safety matches included.

Mention has already been made, in the previous chapter, of the continued manufacture of tin-plate wall holders to hold a large box of parlor matches. These large boxes are still available, so it is assumed the holders will continue to be made while that continues to be the case.

In 1988-1989 Caesars Atlantic City Hotel Casino provided a small plastic pocket match holder, in limited numbers, to customers. The example in **Fig. 688** contained about thirty safety matches; a strip of striking compound is glued to the underside of the box.

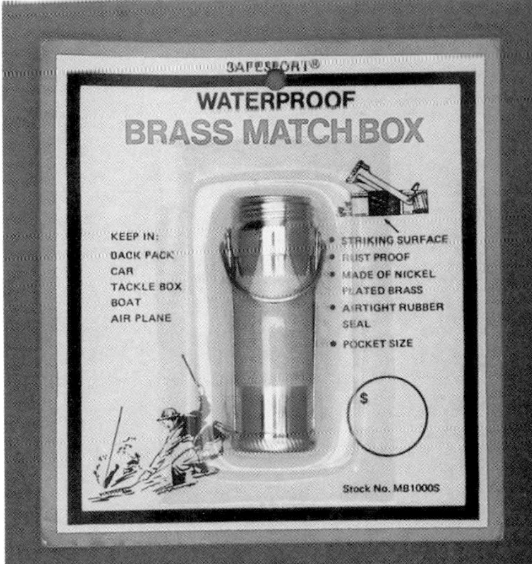

Fig. 685 Hong Kong. Plated brass. Made for the Safesport Mfg. Co. in the United States. 1990s. Originally patented in 1900. See Fig. 175.

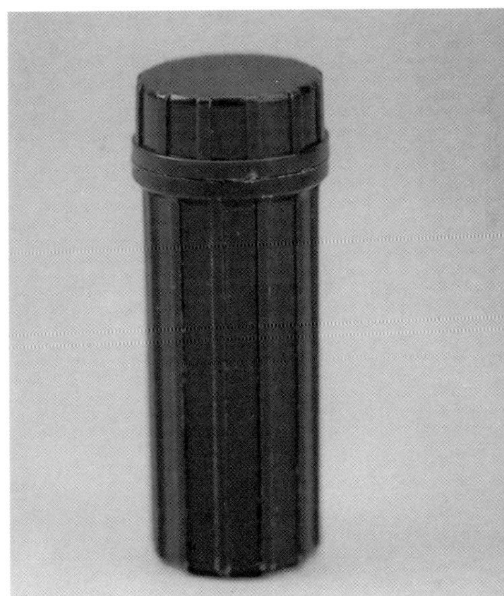

Fig. 686 United States? Plastic. From c.1950 until today. H -7.5cms.

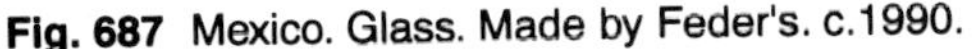

Fig. 687 Mexico. Glass. Made by Feder's. c.1990.

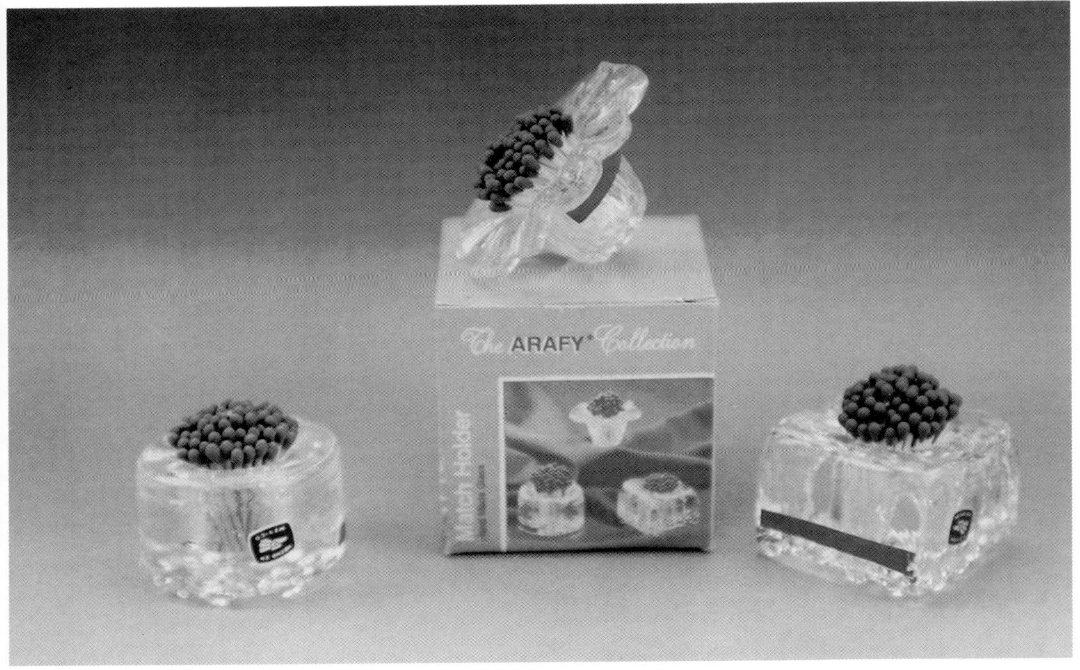

Fig. 688 United States. Plastic. 1992. W - 5.3cms.

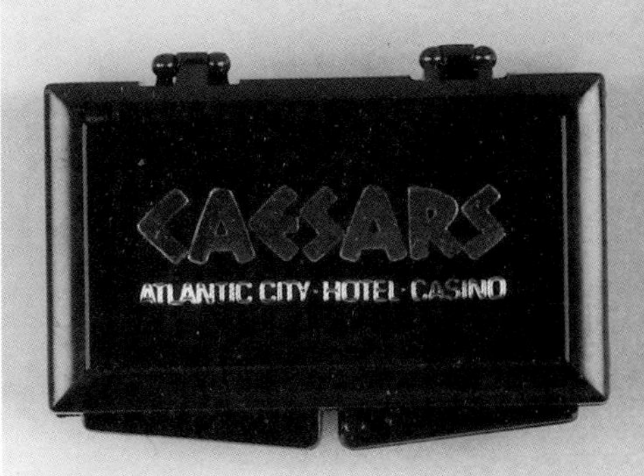

In a similar black plastic material, a series of match holders with slip-on lids has been produced. Twenty examples are shown in **Fig. 689**. They were, and still are, produced by Painting The Town Inc., of New York City, as souvenirs—many for movie films and musical shows. They first appeared in 1981; six were produced in 1992. They sell in souvenir shops from $6.00 to $8.00 each, complete with a complement of safety matches. A strip of striking compound is glued on the back. They register a very colorful and contemporary ending today to a phenomenon that has lasted from 1826 until at least 1993, a period of one hundred and sixty seven years.

To conclude, it should be pointed out that this book is not intended as a definitive work. It is rather an attempt to provide a glimpse into the development of a type of product that was a part of the daily life of most people in the Western world for a century. As has often been said within these covers, this book only scratches the surface! There remains scope for further research, to add to the body of information so far accumulated. It is hoped that this publication will encourage others to add further to our knowledge of this small part of human heritage.

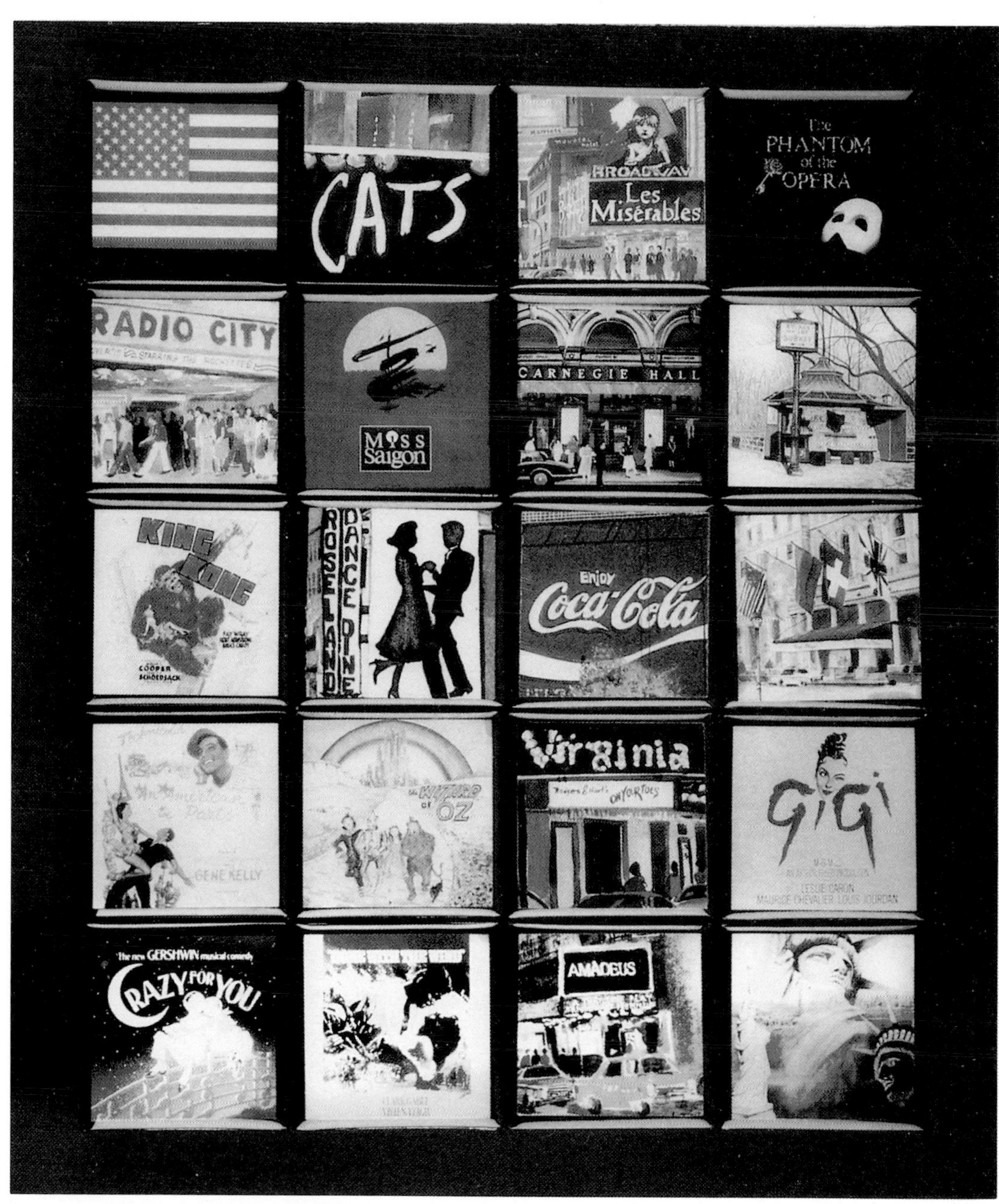

Fig. 689 United States. Plastic. Produced by Painting The Town Inc.. 1981 until today. 5cms square.

Appendix A
Patent Marks

UNITED STATES

Invention Patents were normally granted for a period of fourteen years, and Design Patents for either three and a half, seven, or fourteen years. In the U.S. the period of the grant started on the day of publication, which occurred every other Tuesday, including Christmas Day. In Great Britain and most other countries the period of the grant started on the day of application.

Marks on United States match holders are usually to be found as "PAT.D. 3 JAN '89," or something very similar. The same form of mark is found on both Invention and Design Patents, which may lead to some confusion in a search through the patent volumes.

The indexes for the two forms of patent are published in each volume as separate lists. Both indexes are organized alphabetically under the surname of the inventor, and, in cases where the inventor was an assignor to a company, under the company name with a cross-reference to the inventor. The inventions are also listed alphabetically by type.

This may sound simple enough, but in practice it can be complicated if the search is via the type of invention. Under the heading of "Match" there are several sub-headings, such as "Match box," "Match safe," "Match splint," "Match machine," etc. But the patent may combine a match holder with a cigar cutter, a stamp holder, a candle box, or other form of article. Or the patent may relate to the catch or spring in a box. Or it may be for a chemical formula that has wider applications. Therefore, if the preliminary search does not reveal the patent under "Match," other categories may need to be looked at in the index.

If that strategy lacks success, then a search has to be undertaken of all the patents for the date given. There could be as many as from two to five hundred patents for that one date; this requires a lengthy and patient search, but may eventually lead to success.

An example illustrating this type of problem relates to the Whitehead & Hoag boxes with raised beads. The celluloid covers are marked "Pat.d 6 June, 1905". It was assumed that the patent related to the box; but after extensive searches it was found that the patent was for a method of printing on celluloid.

If the patent cannot be found easily in the Invention Patents indexes, a search of the Design Patents is recommended before a search of every Invention Patent for the marked date.

After about 1930 it is more common to find the Invention Patent Number marked on an item, with the letter "D" preceding a Design Patent number. These things make a search much easier.

GREAT BRITAIN:

(The complex system used for designs is dealt with in Appendix B.)

Invention Patents were granted for a period of seventeen years, starting from the date of application. The indexes are compiled alphabetically only under the inventor's name; since that is seldom marked on an item, the indexes are therefore of very limited help in a search.

The mark on a holder is usually in the form of "Pat.No.1212" (for example), which is also of limited use. A patent number was assigned starting with No.I at the beginning of each year, and going through to several thousand by the end of a year. It may be possible to estimate the approximate date, from the style of an item, and to seek the marked number in the patent volumes for several years either side of the estimated date.

Around the turn of the century the system was broken down into "Classes" of invention, which further complicates a search. It may be possible to search the appropriate "Class" under which a matchbox is supposed to be listed. But what is, to the collector, obviously a matchbox may have been the subject of an invention relating to some other form of box, such as cigarette, or sweetmeat, or stamp box.

A search (assuming the appropriate patent volumes are available), can be frustrating and frequently disappointing. Copies of Invention Patents of the United States, Britain and Canada are available in the national capitals. Copies of United States Design Patents are available in all three capitals. Copies of British Registered Designs and Canadian Design Patents are unique documents available only in the capitals of the originating countries. Some copies of United States patent records may be available in some of the larger city libraries, or possibly university libraries. They are worth checking.

Appendix B

Registered Designs in Great Britain

The Design Copyright Act of 1839 was introduced for "new and original designs for articles of manufacture." These could be submitted to the Office of Registry of Designs, a branch of the British Patent Office. This particular act only survived until 1842, when it was replaced by the Designs Act of 1842; this related to ornamental designs, and was subsequently amended in 1843 to create a parallel series for "non-ornamental or useful designs."

The acts of 1842 and 1843 survived until 1883, when the Patents, Designs and Trade Marks Act replaced them, introducing a simpler single-class system. The rationale for the change was that with the two-fold system it was often difficult to determine to which class a design belonged. These systems offered protection (in theory, at least) for a period of three years, with some exceptions where only a one year period was granted.

Each of the three systems referred to here had different forms of marks, examples of which are shown.

The ornamental designs under the 1842 Act were marked with a diamond-shaped mark, as shown below, which is a form of coding. The diamond mark to the left covered the period from 1842 until 1867; that on the right from 1868 until 1883.

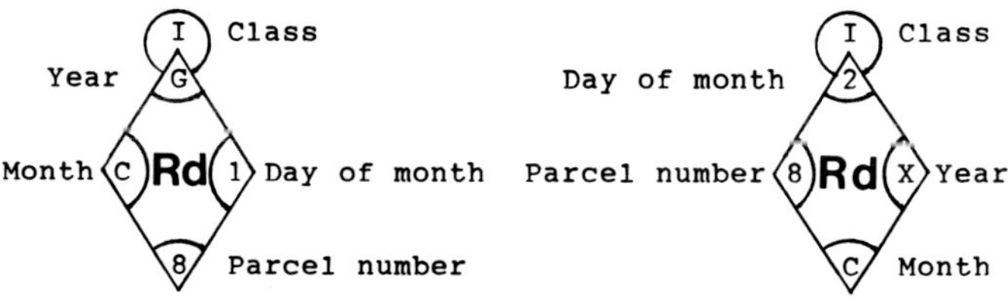

The key to the code is as follows. The external circle at the top remained the same throughout, the Roman numeral(s) within denoting the class of material, of which there were thirteen: class I, as shown, represented metal, IV represented ceramics. In the centre of the diamond was "Rd", denoting Registered. In the corners of the diamond were letters or numbers, which denoted the year, the month, the day of the month, and the parcel number for that day. The relative position of these marks, one to the other, changed in 1868 as may be seen in the diamond mark at the right.

The following table can be used to decipher these marks.

YEARS

1842-67
Year letter
at top

A = 1845	N = 1864
B = 1858	O = 1862
C = 1844	P = 1851
D = 1852	Q = 1866
E = 1855	R = 1861
F = 1847	S = 1849
G = 1863	T = 1867
H = 1843	U = 1848
I = 1846	V = 1850
J = 1854	W = 1865
K = 1857	X = 1842
L = 1856	Y = 1853
M = 1859	Z= 1860

1868-83
Year letter
at right

A = 1871	L = 1882
C = 1870	P = 1877
D = 1878	S = 1875
E = 1881	U = 1874
F = 1873	V = 1876
H = 1869	W = Mar. 1-6, 1878
I = 1872	
J = 1880	X = 1868
K = 1883	Y = 1879

Note the exception for W above.

MONTHS (BOTH PERIODS)

A = December	K = November (and December 1860)
B = October	M = June
C or O = January	R = August (and September 1 to 19, 1857)
D = September	W = March
E = May	
G = February	
H = April	
I = July	

Thus the diamond registration mark at the left gives the date of January 1, 1863, and that to the right the date of January 2, 1868. These are the earliest dates that a piece bearing the mark could have been made. Unfortunately, only by consulting the relevant volumes at the Public Record Office in Kew, London, can the name of the person or company who registered the design be found.

The "Non-Ornamental or Useful Designs" introduced in 1843 used a different marking system. The mark "REGISTERED 20 DEC. 1870" may be seen on the Bryant & May box in Fig. 418; or the number may be included, which occurs on the top of the Dowler box shown in Fig. 27 as "REGISTERED No.2349 - 25TH JUNE 1850".

From January 1884 a new system was introduced, using consecutive numbers, preceded by "Rd" or "Rd. No." The following table gives the years in which these numbers occur, starting in January of each year.

1	- 1884	351202	- 1900	653521	- 1916
19734	- 1885	368154	- 1901	658988	- 1917
40480	- 1886	385180	- 1902	662872	- 1918
64520	- 1887	403200	- 1903	666128	- 1919
90483	- 1888	424400	- 1904	673750	- 1920
116648	- 1889	447800	- 1905	680147	- 1921
141273	- 1890	471860	- 1906	687144	- 1922
163767	- 1891	493900	- 1907	694999	- 1923
185713	- 1892	518640	- 1908	702671	- 1924
205204	- 1893	535170	- 1909	710165	- 1925
224720	- 1894	N.A.	- 1910	718057	- 1926
246975	- 1895	575817	- 1911	726330	- 1927
268392	- 1896	594195	- 1912	734370	- 1928
291241	- 1897	612431	- 1913	742725	- 1929
311658	- 1898	630190	- 1914	751160	- 1930
331707	- 1899	644935	- 1915	760583	- 1931

An example may be seen in the holder in Fig. 138R, marked "Rd.26844," which is for the year 1885.

All of these designs are kept at the Public Records Office at Kew, London. They are a unique set of records that have never been published; indeed, they could not be published because of the nature of the contents, quite apart from the sheer quantity. Each registered design is recorded in two separate volumes. The smaller volume of each pair provides the written information. The second volume has the "representations" in the form of drawings or actual samples, in a format that is up to 24 inches high by 16 inches wide, and up to 10 inches thick. Samples of cloth, some quite large, are glued into the book, as are other flat items of paper. There are some 1,600 volumes.

This is a fantastic record, and the only record, and it can only be seen in London. Some volumes are in poor shape and not available for viewing, but most can be seen if the researcher can supply a valid reason for doing so. Access is restricted and closely supervised. Copies can only be obtained by executing your own pencil sketches; no photocopying is permitted. It may be possible to obtain photographs in some cases, but these would be expensive.

The numerical sequence started in 1884 is still in operation today, but most of the designs are industrial.

Appendix C
Date Marks on the Silver of Great Britain

The hallmark system of marking sterling silver in Great Britain as we know it today started in the 18th century, although marks had been in use from the 12th century. Five marks were used until late in Queen Victoria's reign, one of the marks being the monarch's head. This practise was then abandoned in favor of four marks.

The marks appeared in a set sequence, with the maker's mark first. This was followed by the mark for sterling silver, a lion rampant. Then came the mark of the assay office. The final mark was the date letter, which changed each year.

Here we are concerned mainly with the marks of Birmingham, Chester and London, where most of the sterling silver match holders were made (although a few may be found with marks for other assay offices); and within the period between 1840 and 1940 only.

Below are the assay office marks, followed by the date letter for each year.

BIRMINGHAM:

Assay Office mark:

Date marks:

Year	Date mark
1840	R
1841	S
1842	T
1843	U
1844	V
1845	W
1846	X
1847	Y
1848	Z
1849	A
1850	B
1851	C
1852	D
1853	E
1854	F
1855	G
1856	H
1857	I
1858	J
1859	K
1860	L
1861	M
1862	N
1863	O
1864	P
1865	Q
1866	R
1867	S
1868	T
1869	U
1870	V
1871	W
1872	X
1873	Y
1874	Z
1875	a
1876	b
1877	c
1878	d
1879	e
1880	f
1881	g
1882	h
1883	i
1884	k
1885	l
1886	m
1887	n
1888	o
1889	p
1890	q
1891	r
1892	s
1893	t
1894	u
1895	v
1896	w
1897	x
1898	y
1899	z
1900	a
1901	b
1902	c
1903	d
1904	e
1905	f
1906	g
1907	h
1908	i
1909	k
1910	l
1911	m
1912	n
1913	o
1914	p
1915	q
1916	r
1917	s
1918	t
1919	u
1920	v
1921	w
1922	x
1923	y
1924	z
1925	A
1926	B
1927	C
1928	D
1929	E
1930	F
1931	G
1932	H
1933	J
1934	K
1935	L
1936	M
1937	N
1938	O
1939	P
1940	Q

CHESTER:

Assay Office mark: 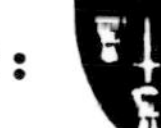

Date marks:

1840	B
1841	C
1842	D
1843	E
1844	F
1845	G
1846	H
1847	I
1848	K
1849	L
1850	M
1851	N
1852	O
1853	P
1854	Q
1855	R
1856	S
1857	T
1858	U
1859	V
1860	W
1861	X
1862	Y
1863	Z
1864	a
1865	b
1866	c
1867	d
1868	e
1869	f
1870	g
1871	h
1872	i
1873	k
1874	l
1875	m
1876	n
1877	o
1878	p
1879	q
1880	r
1881	s
1882	t
1883	u
1884	A
1885	B
1886	C
1887	D
1888	E
1889	F
1890	G
1891	H
1892	I
1893	K
1894	L
1895	M
1896	N
1897	O
1898	P
1899	Q
1900	R
1901	A
1902	B
1903	C
1904	D
1905	E
1906	F
1907	G
1908	H
1909	I
1910	K
1911	L
1912	M
1913	N
1914	O
1915	P
1916	Q
1917	R
1918	S
1919	T
1920	U
1921	V
1922	W
1923	X
1924	Y
1925	Z
1926	A
1927	B
1928	C
1929	D
1930	E
1931	F
1932	G
1933	H
1934	I
1935	K
1936	L
1937	M
1938	N
1939	O
1940	P

LONDON:

Assay Office mark: 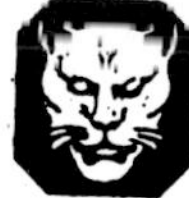

Date marks:

1840	E
1841	F
1842	G
1843	H
1844	I
1845	K
1846	L
1847	M
1848	N
1849	O
1850	P
1851	Q
1852	R
1853	S
1854	T
1855	U
1856	a
1857	b
1858	c
1859	d
1860	e
1861	f
1862	g
1863	h
1864	i
1865	k
1866	l
1867	m
1868	n
1869	o
1870	p
1871	q
1872	r
1873	s
1874	t
1875	u
1876	A
1877	B
1878	C
1879	D
1880	E
1881	F
1882	G
1883	H
1884	I
1885	K
1886	L
1887	M
1888	N
1889	O
1890	P
1891	Q
1892	R
1893	S
1894	T
1895	U
1896	a
1897	b
1898	c
1899	d
1900	e
1901	f
1902	g
1903	h
1904	i
1905	k
1906	l
1907	m
1908	n
1909	o
1910	p
1911	q
1912	r
1913	s
1914	t
1915	u
1916	a
1917	b
1918	c
1919	d
1920	e
1921	f
1922	g
1923	h
1924	i
1925	k
1926	l
1927	m
1928	n
1929	o
1930	p
1931	q
1932	r
1933	s
1934	t
1935	u
1936	A
1937	B
1938	C
1939	D
1940	E

Appendix D
Invention and Design Patent Information

For those readers who may be interested in obtaining their own copies of specific patents or designs, the following provides additional details that will enable them to trace the sources without a search.

In order to identify the type and nationality of the patent, the following abbreviations are used to save space and avoid tedious repetition:

U.S. Invention Patent	- AIP
U.S. Design Patent	- ADP
British Invention Patent	- BIP
British Ornamental Design	- BOD
British Useful Design	- BUD
British Registered Design	- BRD
Canadian Invention Patent	- CIP
Public Records Office Volume (example:)	- BT45/3

Fig.	Type.	Number.	Other information.
24(L)	BOD	37,093	28 Sept.1846. Thomas Wharton, Birmingham. (BT43/4)
24(R)	BUD	446	9 May.1845. Augustus Septimus Braithwaite, London. (BT45/3)
25			As 24(L and R)
26	BUD	2,349	25 June.1850. Thomas Dowler, Birmingham.
28(L)			As 26. (BT45/12)
28(R)	BIP	1,114	28 June.1853. George Dowler, Birmingham.
32	BUD	2,465	4 Oct.1850. Allen & Moore, Bir mingham. (BT45/13)
34(L)	BOD	42	10 Apr.1851. W. & J. Harcourt. Birmingham. (BT47/1)
34(R)	BUD	159	12 Apr.1851. W. & J. Harcourt. Birmingham. (BT47/3)
38	BUD	2,683	l2 Feb.1851. W. & J. Harcourt. Birmingham. (BT45/l4)
40	BIP	429	18 Oct.1852. W. & J. Harcourt. Birmingham.
70	BIP	12,469	12 Feb.1849. Jarvis Palmer. London.
74	BIP	2,821	9 Nov.1861. Edward Loysel. London.
79	AIP	149,194	31 Mar.1874. Chauncey Buckley, assignor to Charles Parker. Meriden, Connecticut.
80	AIP	132,246	15 Oct.1872. As 79.
		147,098	3 Feb.1874. As 79.
		149,194	As 79.
	CIP.	2,808	18 Oct.]873. Charles Parker, assignee of Chauncey Buckley.
82	AIP	228,598	8 June 1880. Chauncey Buckley, assignor to Charles Parker Co. Meriden, Connecticut.
84	ADP	20,200	4 Oct.1890. Adolph Thommen, assignor of one half to Enos Richardson & Co. Newark, New Jersey.
96	ADP	19,177	7 Jan.1890. Harry P. Fairchild. New York.
114	BRD	38,283.	1885. Sampson Mordan. London.
116	BIP	2,205	1902. Albert Barker. London. Abandoned.
126(L)	BRD	124,608	4 May.1889. Jenkins William Evans. Birmingham. (BT51/55)
126(CL)	BRD	172,886	13 June.1891. Frederick W. Tomkinson. Birmingham. (BT51/64)
127	BIP	4,709	29 Mar.1887. F. W. Powell. London.
	BRD	122,107	27 Mar.1889. Albert Lines. Aston. (BT51/5?)
129(C)	BIP	4,709	29 Mar.1887. F. W. Powell. London.
131(C)	BRD	363,510	1900. Charles B. Ketley. Patent Agent. Birmingham. (BT50/401)
136	BRD	603,901	3 July.1912. John Walker & Co. London.
138(C)	BIP	1,212	26 Jan.1887. Samuel Basnett. Hockley.
138(R)	BRD	26,844	1885. Thomas Burns & James Stone Dumbell. Wolverhampton. (BT50/34 & BT51/113)
141	BIP	275,405	23 July.1926. Philip George Marr. London.
	BRD	728,449	1927.
142	BIP	275,405	23 July.1926. Philip George Marr. London.
157	AIP	26,865	17 Jan.1860. Albert M. Smith. New York, New York.
158	AIP	198,692	25 Dec.1877. Charles Scofield. Vineland, New Jersey.
159	AIP	229,101	22 June.1880. Francis S. Dangerfield. Auburn, New York.
160	AIP	256,093	4 Apr.1882. Arthur P. Yates. Syracuse, New York.
161	AIP	323,029	28 July.1885. William M. Ducker. New York, New York.
162(L)	AIP	305,941	30 Sept.1884. John Lines, assignor to the Scovill Mfg.Co. Waterbury, Connecticut.
166	AIP	595,070	7 Dec.1897. Ernest Oldenbusch, assignor to William Schimper & Co. Hoboken, New Jersey.
168	AIP	484,092	11 Oct.1892. August Goertz. Newark, New Jersey.
169	AIP	660,848	30 Oct.1900. Benno vom Eigen, assignor to Aug.Goertz & Co. Newark, New Jersey.
170(T)	AIP	753.381	1 Mar. 1904. Benno vom Eigen, assignor to Aug. Goertz & Co. Newark, New Jersey.
171(L)	AIP	589,921	14 Sept.1897. Richard J. Ashworth, assignor to the Waterbury Mfg.Co. Waterbury, Connecticut.
172(0)	AIP		As 171(L)
174	AIP	199,444	22 Jan.1877. Charles Jacobi. Rantoul, Illinois.
175	AIP	650,944	5 June.l900. Wehster L. Marble, assignor of one half to Frank H. Van Cleve. Gladstone, Michigan. (Cleve was Marble's partner).
177	AIP	640,262	2 Jan.1900. Thomas Addison Bell. Birmingham, Alabama.
217	ADP	21,924	25 Oct.1892. Simon Zinn. New York, New York.
220	ADP	16,983	9 Nov.1886. August H. Wirz. Wallingford, Pennsylvania.
222	AIP	283,238	14 Aug.1883. Edward J. Hauck. Brooklyn, New York.
223	AIP		As 222.
230	BRD	96,937	28 Mar.1888. Jenkin William Evans. Birmingham. (BT50/99 & BT51/47)

231	BRD	105,032	31 July.1888. Frederick Wm.Tomkinson. Birmingham. (BT51/49)
256	BOD	305,221	17 Nov.1876. Buncher & Haseler. Birmingham. (BT44/3 & BT43/41)
257	BIP	1,874	9 Feb.1886. Hezekiah Hewitt. Birmingham.
258	BRD	387,671	24 Feb.1902. Charles E. Brann. London. (BT50/455)
262	BIP	2,870	8 Feb.1899. Gregory Aloyouis Robinson. London.
263	BIP		As 262.
274	BIP	6,056	1895. Thomas Morton. Birmingham. Also: France; No.246,467, 8 Apr.1895.
293(G&H)	AIP	791,503	6 June.1905. (printed on celluloid covers). Richard E. Roehm, assignor to the Whitehead & Hoag Co. Newark, New Jersey.
294(C)	AIP	750,447	26 Jan.1904. Albert F. Fuller, assignor to the J. E. Mergott Co. Newark, New Jersey.
294(B)	AIP	799,844	19 Sept.1905. Albert F. Fuller, assignor to the J. E. Mergott Co. Newark, New Jersey.
295(F)	AIP	956,092	26 Apr.1910 (filed 2 May 1908). Christian Hiering and Albert Fuller, assignors to the J. E. Mergott Co. Newark, New Jersey.
296	AIP	744,074	17 Nov.1903. Christian Hiering, assignor to the J. E. Mergott Co. Newark, New Jersey.
297	AIP	749,479	12 Jan.1904. Benno vom Eigen, assignor to Aug.Goertz & Co. Newark, New Jersey.
298(B-E)			As 297.
301(TR)	BRD	430,409	13 Apr.1904. Charles E. Brann & Co. London. (BT50/455)
304	BIP	15,003	1899. Alfred Pearse. London.
309	BIP	5,104	1896. Frederick M. B. Bertram and Gregory A. Robinson. London.
310	AIP	1,533,402	14 Apr.1925. Alexis F. Gillet, assignor to Jubilee Mfg.Co. Omaha, Nebraska.
311	BIP	28,157	24 Dec.1908. Judah Ahronsberg. Birmingham.
323	AIP	213,406	18 Mar.1879. Francis A. Farrell Brooklyn, New York.
324	AIP	65,142	28 May.1867. John A. Whipple. Cambridge, Massachusetts.
325	AIP	65,445	4 June.1867. Curtis R. Stickney. Hartford, Connecticut.
326	AIP	157,282	1 Dec.1874. Moses Goldman. Syracuse, New York.
360	BUD	5,488	6 Sept.1873. Bryant & May. London. (BT45/27)
381	AIP	749,539	12 Jan.1904. Harold A. Dodge. Elizabeth, New Jersey. Reissued in November 1904.
	ADP	36,783	9 Feb.1904. Mark O. Anthony. New York, New York. Withdrawn in favor of Dodge.
382	AIP	894,256	28 July.1908. Emanuel Ciner. New York, New York. Also incorrectly marked "JAN.12.04.", should be:
	AIP	761,461	31 May.1904. Benno vom Eigen, assignor to Aug.Goertz & Co. Newark, New Jersey.
383	AIP	894,256	As 382.
384	AIP	761,461	As 382.
385	AIP	1,033,240	23 July.1912. Franz A. Fuller, assignor to the J. E. Mergott Co. Newark, New Jersey.
387	ADP	57,632	26 Apr.1921. Franz A. Fuller, assignor to the J. E. Mergott Co. Newark, New Jersey.
390	AIP	1,985,751	25 Dec.1934. Max Vogel. Frankfort-am-Main, Germany.
395	AIP	871,440	19 Nov.1907. James V. Reed, assignor to the J. B. Williams Co. Glastonbury. (For the hinge).
397	AIP	1,209,759	26 Dec.1916. Hans F. Richter, assignor R. J. Reynolds Tobacco Co. Winston Salem, North Carolina.
398	AIP		As 397.

409	BOD	23,618	19 Dec.1844. John Hynam. London. (BT44/1 & BT44/3)
411	BIP	12,146	1848. Alexander S. Stocker. London.
412			As 411.
413	BUD	208	14 May.1851. Provisional registration. James Septimus Cockings. Birmingham. (Patent Agent.) (BT45/15) Transferred to:
		2,956	23 Sept.1851. Full registration. Samuel Alexander Bell & John Black. London. (BT48/3, BT46/1)
414	BUD	2,956	As 413.
416(T&C)	BUD	5,206	20 Dec.1870. Bryant & May. London. (For the catch on the front of the boxes.)
417	BUD	5,206	As 416.
418(B)	BUD	5,206	As 416.
421(R)	BRD	222	12 Jan.1884. Bryant & May. London.
422(R)	BUP	2,145(?)	29 May.1878. Henry William Herbst. London.
	BRD	231,183	1894.
424			As 422(R).
425			As 422(R).
426			As 422(R).
427			As 422(R).
428(L)			As 422(R).
428(R)	BRD	231,183	1894.
429	AIP	150,929	12 May.1874. George Zuckschwerdt. New York, New York.
431	BIP	17,329	22 July.1897. Tito Livio Carbone and Edward Cooper. Monte Video, Uruguay.
432			As 360.
434	BRD	642,237	1914. Alfred Dunhill. London.
435	BRD	22,410	21 Feb.1885. Wright & Butler. Birmingham. (BT51/11 & BT50/29)
436	BRD	32,725	4 Sept.1885. Wright & Butler. Birmingham. (BT50/43)
446			Trademark: Ser.No.80,151. Filed 29 July.1914. The Diamond Match Co. Chicago, Illinois. "Claims use since May,1913."
447	ADP	54,567	2 Mar.1920. Henry C. Traute, assignor to The Diamond Match Co. Chicago, Illinois.
448	ADP	56,039	10 Aug.1920. Henry C. Traute, assignor to The Diamond Match Co. Chicago, Illinois.
464	BRD	196,556	9 Aug.1892. Rupert Benjamin Baugh, Birmingham. (BT51/69)
468	AIP	42,414	19 Apr.1864. George H. Snow. New Haven, Connecticut.
469			As 468.
470	BUD	3,206	4 Sept.1879. Edwin Day, Birmingham. (BT47/9)
471	AIP	121,788	12 Dec.1871. Albert D. Judd. New Haven, Connecticut.
472			As 471.
473	AIP	122,836	16 Jan.1872. Albert D. Judd. New Haven, Connecticut.
474			As 473.
475			As 473.
476	ADP	4,630	7 Feb.1871. Albert D. Judd. New Haven, Connecticut.
485	AIP	219,135	2 Sept.1879. Adam F. Able. New Orleans, Louisiana.
487	AIP	567,369	8 Sept.1896. Friedrich Aleith, assignor of one half to J. M. Alieth. Casselton, North Dakota.
488(L)	ADP	26,703	2 Mar.1897. Nicholas Altmyer. Coggon, Iowa.
488(R)	ADP	27,776	26 Oct.1897. Matthias T. La Rouche and Frank S. Baker. Utica, New York.
491	ADP	11,863	13 July.1880. Charles Kitschelt, assignor to Nicholas Muller's Sons & Co. New York, New York.
492	AIP	260,187	27 June.1882. George Franke. Baltimore, Maryland.
504	ADPs	32,734	Match box holder.As 505L.
		32,736	Base. As 506L.
505(L)	ADP	32,734.	29 May.1900. Frank J. Gressly. New York, New York.
505(R)	ADP	32,735	As 505(L).
506(L)	ADP	32,736	As 505(L).

506(R)	ADP	32,737	As 505(L).
510	ADP	46,055	7 July.1914. Edwin A. Merritt, of New York, assignor to The Diamond Match Co. Chicago, IL.
511	AIP	439,467	28 Oct.1890. H. Brandt.
523	AIP	49,542	22 Aug.1865. Jason H. Merrill. Norwalk, Connecticut.
524	ADP	31,851	21 Nov.1899. Sigmund M. Rosin. Philadelphia, Pennsylvania.
540	BRD	370,813	1901.
[illegible]	BRD	470,[illegible]	1906.
598	BRD	652,614	24 Sept.1913. Wileman & Co. Longton, Staffordshire.
600	BUD	337	18 June.1840. Gabriel Riddle. London. (BT42/2)
601	BOD	?	5 Nov.1847. Percival & Yates. Manchester. (BT43/60)
612	BIP	2,662	21 Sept.1867. Bewicke Blackburn and Alexander Bewicke Blackburn . London .
613			As 612.
614			As 612.
615	BIP	10,729	4 Aug.1887. James S. Foley, Chicago, Illinois, and Joseph Ruse, Toronto, Ontario.
	CIP	27,206	19 July.1887. As BIP 10,729.
	AIP	390,467	2 Oct.1888. As BIP 10,729.
616	CIP	33,222	31 Oct.1887. James S. Foley, Chicago, Illinois, and Joseph Ruse, Toronto, Ontario.
	BIP	16,703	5 Dec.1887. Alfred Julius Boult (Patent Agent).
	AIP	390,468	2 Oct.1888. As CIP 33.222.
617	BIP		As BIP 16,703.
618	CIP	28,695	21 Oct.1887. As CIP 33,222.
619			As 616.
625	BUD	4,640	2 July.1864. John Hadley, Norwood, Surrey. (BT45/64)
627	BUD	5,610	3 Oct.1874. Bryant & May. London. (BT45/28)
628	BUD	6,144	18 Feb.1879. Bell & Black. London. (BT45/29)
629	BRD	484,541	7 Aug.1906. John Harper & Co.Ltd. Willenhall, Staffordshire. (BT50/650)
630	BRD	544,082	17 June.1909. George Hopkins & Co. Birmingham. (BT52/41)
634	ADP	1,111	28 June.1859. P. J. Clark, as signor to S. S. Clark, West Meriden, Connecticut.
635	ADP	1,111	As 634.
638	AIP	45,554	20 Dec.1864. William H. Andrews, assignor to Burton Mallory of New Haven, Connecticut.
639	ADP	2,553	15 Jan.1867. Russel Frisbie, assignor to J. and E. Stevens & Co. Cromwell, Connecticut.
640	AIP	73,706	28 Jan.1868. John A. Evarts, assignor to Bradley & Hubbard, West Meriden, Connecticut.
641	AIP		As 640.
642	AIP	[illegible]	[illegible] Oct.[illegible]. Hiram Richmond, assignor to Charles Parker, West Meriden, Connecticut.
	AIP	102,676	2 May.1870. George Geer, as signor to Charles Parker, West Meriden, Connecticut.
643	AIP	94,775	14 Sept.1869. Hiram Richmond, assignor to Charles Parker, West Meriden, Connecticut.
	AIP	102,676	As 642.
644	AIP	85,945	19 Jan.1869. Frank Marquard, assignor to Vulcanized Wood Co. Newburyport, Massachusetts.
645	ADP	4,428	25 Oct.1870. F. W. Brocksieper, assignor to Sargent & Co. New Haven, Connecticut.
648	AIP	102,828	10 May.1870. Albert D. Judd. New Haven, Connecticut.
649	AIP		As 648.
650	ADP	9,619	14 Nov.1876. Otto F. Fogelstrand, assignor to Hart, Bliven & Mead Mfg. Co. Kensington, Connecticut.
651	AIP	205,954	16 July.1878. John Gilbert, as signor to James, Aikman & Co. Newark, New Jersey.
652	AIP		As 651.
653	AIP	262,514	8 Aug.1882. William Trotter Jr. Oyster Bay, New York.
654	AIP		As 653.
655	AIP		As 653.
657	ADP	15,518	4 Nov.1884. James F. Lockwood and Alva Bryant. Philadelphia, Pennsylvania.
658	AIP	268,760	5 Dec.1882. William N. Weedon. New Bedford, Massachusetts.
	AIP	264,918	26 Sept.1882. William H. Balmain. Ventnor, Isle of Wight, Hampshire. (for luminous paint.)
659(T)	AIP	268,918	From 658.
667	ADP	39,434	28 July.1908. Linnaeus T. Savage. New York, New York.
671	ADP	40,477	1 Feb.1910. Ivory L. Hall. Vinal Haven, Maine.
683	AIP	2,008,016	16 July.1935. Bertis Hamilton. Columbus, Indiana.

Bibliography

Aston, Stanley G. *Newsletter of the British Matchbox Label & Booklet Society.*
Vol.30. pp.6694-6699. Design Registrations. Pt .I.
Vol.30. pp.6727-6730. Design Registrations. Pt.2.
Vol.30. pp.6762-6765. Design Registrations. Pt.3.
Vol.30. pp.6800-6803. Design Registrations. Pt.4.
Vol.30. pp.6822-6827. Design Registrations. Pt.5.
Vol.31. pp.6893-6897. Design Registrations. Pt.6.
Vol.31. pp.6922-6927. Design Registrations. Pt.7.
Vol.31. pp.6961-6964. Design Registrations. Pt.8.
Vol.31. pp.7000-7004. Design Registrations. Pt.9.
Vol.31. pp.7021-7025. Design Registrations. Pt.10.
Vol.32. pp.7060-7064. Design Registrations. Pt. 11.
Vol.32. pp.7090-7094. Design Registrations. Pt.12.
Vol.32. pp.7123-7127. Design Registrations. Pt.13.
Vol.32. pp.7158-7162. Design Registrations. Pt.14.
Vol.32. pp.7193-7197. Design Registrations. Pt.15.
Vol.30. pp.6673-6674. Lithophane match holders.
Vol.31. pp.6854-6858. Disc matches.
Vol.32. pp.7244-7246. The Automaton pocket vesta box.
Vol.33. pp.7265-7269. Match barrels & other souvenirs from ships.
Vol.33. pp.7301-7305. Pellet Matches. Part 1.
Vol.33. pp.7337-7342. Pellet Matches. Part 2.
Vol.33. p.7409. Pellet Matches - a P.S.
Vol.33. pp.7373-7376. Match barrels & other souvenirs from famous ships.
Vol.33. pp.7450-7453. Patented Puzzle Boxes. Part 1.
Vol.34 pp.7482-7485. Patented Puzzle Boxes. Part 2.
Vol.34 p.7488. The Automaton pocket vesta box. A second postscript.
Vol.34 pp.7628-7633. Continuous matches and repeating matches.
Vol.34 pp.7670-7673. Pocket boxes by Henry Roman.
Vol.35 pp.7753-7756. Pocket matchboxes patented by Abraham Martin.

Beaver, Patrick. *The Match Makers.* Henry Melland, London. 1985.

Christy, Miller. *The Bryant and May Museum of Fire-Making Appliances* - Catalogue of the Exhibits. Simpkin, Marshall, Hamilton, Kent & Co.Ltd. 1926; and Supplement 1928.

Cooper-Hewitt Museum. *Matchsafes in the Collection of the Cooper-Hewitt Museum.* Smithsonian Institution. 1981.

Cushion.J.P. *Handbook of Pottery and Porcelain Marks.* 4th Edition (revised and expanded). Faber & Faber . London . 1980.

Fresco-Corbu, Roger. *Vesta Boxes. Antique Pocket Guides.* Lutterworth Press. Guildford, Surrey. 1983.

Fresco-Corbu, Roger. *Newsletter of the British Matchbox Label & Booklet Society.*
Vol.20. pp.4738-4739. Hardware fakes.
Vol.31. pp.6990-6991. Trade tins with strikers.
Vol.31. pp.7028-7029. Ne Plus Extra matchbox.
Vol.32. pp.7072-7073.Book-shaped metal vesta boxes.
Vol.32 pp.7104-7105. Metal vesta boxes modelling advertised goods.
Vol.32. pp.7134-7135. Wedgwood Jasperware match containers.
Vol.32. pp.7234-7236. Grotesque china match stands.
Vol.33. pp.7278-7279. Doulton match holders.
Vol.33. pp.7312-7313. Match related Scottish souvenir woodware.
Vol.33. pp.7365-7367. Stone match containers.
Vol.33. pp.7395-7396. Papier-Mache hardware.
Vol.33. pp.7416-7417. Crested china match holders.
Vol.33. pp.7474-7475. Glass match-holders.

Godden, Geoffrey A. *Encyclopaedia of British Pottery and Porcelain Marks.* Bonanza Books, New York.1964.

Hoffman, Professor Lewis. *Puzzles Old and New.* Frederick Warne & Co., London. 1893.

Jakovsky, Anatole. *L'Epopée du Tabac.* Editions D'Art et Industrie. Max Fourny. Paris. 1971.

Jones, Kenneth Crisp, ed. *The Silversmiths of Birmingham and Their Marks, 1750 - 1980.* N.A.G. Press Ltd. London. 1981.

Jung, S.Paul,Jr. *Reprint of George Zorn & Co.,* Fifth Edition Catalogue of Pipes and Smokers Articles, Etc., Etc.. c.1892. Privately printed. 1989.

Luker, J.H. *Hardware: Bryant & May. World Matchbox Label Series.* Vesta Publications. 1982.

Mactaggart, Peter and Ann. "Tunbridge End Grain Mosaic: A Misnomer." *The Chronicle of the Early American Industries Association,* vol.36, no.2, (June 1983), pp.32-36.

McKinstry, E. Richard. *Trade Catalogues at Winterthur. A Guide to the Literature of Merchandising. 1750 to 1980.* Garland Publishing, Inc., New York. 1984. (The 1,885 trade catalogues listed in this book are available on microfiche from Clearwater Publishing Co., New York.)

Petsche, Jerome E. *The Steamboat Bertrand.* Publications in Archeology 11. U.S. Department of the Interior, National Park Service, Washington. 1974.

Pinto, Edward and Eva. *Tunbridge and Scottish Souvenir Woodware.* G.Bell & Sons, London. 1970.

Rainwater, Dorothy T. *Encyclopedia of American Silver Manufacturers.* Third Edition Revised. Schiffer Publishing Ltd., Atglen, Pennsylvania. 1986.

Rontgen, Robert E. *Marks on German, Bohemian and Austrian Porcelain, 1710 to the Present.* Schiffer Publishing Ltd. Atglen, Pennsylvania. 1981.

Sparacio, George. New & reproduced Matchsafes. *Antique & Collectors Reproduction News.* Oct.1992. pp.8 - 10.

Sullivan, Audrey G. *A History of Match Safes in the United States.* Riverside Press, Ft.Lauderdale, Florida. 1978.

Tardy. *International Hallmarks on Silver Collected by Tardy.* Tardy, Paris. 1981.

Index of Manufacturers, Wholesalers, Retailers, Inventors and Designers

Price Guide

The prices quoted represent the highs and lows that would be expected to-be asked in north eastern North America for items in good condition. Items in near mint condition may be higher, in poorer condition the price may be lower. Within the price ranges quoted is what is believed to be reasonable. Below the lower price may be regarded as a potential bargain, and above the higher price should be cause for second thoughts.

Prices are likely to be higher in New York, London, and in the California area, and lower in New Zealand. Other markets have not been experienced.

This price guide is therefore only very superficial, based upon limited experience in the wider field.

A serious collector will base the price to be paid upon what the significance of the item is to the collection. If the item contributes towards filling a gap or providing additional information for other parts of a collection that enhances the overall historic and/or scientific value, then the price is a secondary consideration. Historic and scientific information is not measurable fiscally, but a serious collector may regard this aspect of greater importance than aesthetic appearance.

The quoted prices are in U.S. dollars. The average value of a piece based upon the figures provided is between $55.00 and $80.00. But other sources of prices have been quoted as high as $2,000.00, and the collection here only includes one gold item and no finely enamelled items, which may range from $600.00 to $1,500.00 each.

Fig.#	Price	Fig.#	Price.	Fig.#	Price.
1	80-120	83	450-500	133	30-40
2	60-100	84	500-700	134	75-100
3	80-120	87	200-300	135	120-150
4	40-80	88	140-180	136	60-80
5	30-50	90	80-120	137	50-75
6	50-80	91	80-120	138L	30-40
7	200-250	92	100-140	138C	60-80
8	200-250	94	80-120	138R	40-60
9	140-200	95	100-140	139	75-100
10	200-280	96	80-120	[illegible]	75-100
11	200-280	97	80-120	141	40-60
12	200-280	98	80-120	143	30-40
13	200-280	99	80-120	144L	40-60
14	200-280	100TL	100-140	144R	50-75
17	60-100	100TR	60-80	145	40-50
18	60-100	100B	60-80	146	75-100
19	50-80	101	75-100	147T	75-100
20	180-240	103	75-100	147B	25-30
22	120-150	104	75-100	148	300-350
23	200-300	105	75-100	150	40-60
25	100- 150	106	75 - 100	151	50-75
26	120-180	107	80-120	152	60-80
29	60-100	108	150-200	153	80-120
35	200-250	109	75-100	154	30-40
36	50-80	110	75-100	155	60-80
37	60-80	111	120-150	156	40-60
39	80-120	112	700-800	157	50-75
41	80-120	113	80-120	158	40-60
42	80-120	114	1200-1400	159	40-60
43	250-350	115	80-120	160	50-75
44	60-80	116	100-140	161	30-40
45	60-80	117	120-150	162	30-40
47	75-100	118	650-750	163L	30-45
48	140-180	119L	120-150	163R	40-60
49	60-80	119R	80-120	164	30-40
50	60-80	120	100-140	165	30-40
51	80-120	121	80-120	166L	60-80
52	60-80	122	50-75	166C	40-60
53	60-80	123	80-120	166R	60-80
54	60-80	124	80-120	167	50-75
55	80-100	125	70-100	168	50-75
56	50-80	126	60-80	169	60-80
57	50-80	127	80-120	170TL	80-120
58	50-80	128L	80-120	170TR	60-80
60	80-120	128C	75-100	170BL	50-75
63	120-150	128R	60-80	170BR	40-60
64	140-180	129L	50-75	171L	30-50
65	50-75	129C	75-100	171R	25-30
71	120-150	129R	50-75	173	25-35
72	120-150	130	80-120	174	40-60
76	60-80	131	40-60	175	30-40
80	40-60	132	30-50	176	30-40

Fig.#	Price.
177	40-60
178	30-40
179	40-60
180	40-60
181TL	60-80
181TC	40-60
181TR	30-40
181B	60-80
182L	25-30
182R	40-60
183	25-30
184	25-30
185	30-40
186	30-40
187	25-30
188L	50-75
188R	60-80
189	50-75
190	60-80
191	50-75
192	60-80
193	80-120
194	50-75
195T	60-80
195B	50-75
196	60-80
197	60-80
198	60-80
199	100-150
200	60-80
201	100-125
203	30-40
204	50-75
205	60-80
206	60-80
207	60-80
208T	30-40
208B	40-60
209T	30-40
209B	25-35
210	100-120
211	50-75
212	10-20
216	100-150
217	100-150
218L	40-50
218R	40-60
219	50-75
220	80-120
221	80-100
222L	50-75
222R	40-60

Fig.#	Price.
224	60-80
226	100-150
227	100-150
228	60-80
229	100-150
230	100-150
231	100-150
233	100-150
234	40-60
235	100-150
236	100-150
237	100-150
238	100-150
239	100-150
240T	80-120
240B	100-150
241	125-175
242	100-150
243	100-150
244	100-150
245	100-150
246L	100-150
246TR	100-150
246BR	80-120
247L	100-150
247R	80-120
248	100-150
249	100-150
250	100-150
251	100-150
252	100-150
253	100-150
254	80-120
255TL	80-120
255TC	80-120
255TR	60-80
255BL	50-75
255BC	50-75
255BR	80-120
256	60-80
257	60-80
258	75-100
259	50-75
260L	80-120
260R	100-150
261	100-150
262	150-200
264	100-150
265	100-150
266	150-200
267	100-150
268	100-150

Fig.#	Price.
269	80-120
270	100-150
271	125-175
272	100-150
273L	80-120
273C	60-80
273R	40-60
274	100-150
275	100-150
276	80-120
277	100-150
278	80-120
279	100-150
280	150-200
281L	100-150
281R	60-80
282	100-150
283	100-150
284	150-200
286	400-450
287	150-200
288	400-450
289	400-450
291	40-50
293	30-50
295	30-50
296	40-60
298	30-50
299	40-60
300	30-50
301	30-50
302	40-60
303L	25-35
303C	25-35
303R	20-30
305	75-100
307	50-60
308	40-60
311	100-150
312	60-80
313	60-80
314	50-75
316	50-75
317	60-80
318	50-75
319	50-75
320	100-150
321	75-100
322	20-30
323	40-60
327	80-100
329	35-50

Fig.#	Price.	Fig.#	Price.	Fig.#	Price.
330	100-125	395	10-15	456	125-150
332	80-100	396	20-30	457	30-40
333	80-120	398	10-15	458	30-40
337	50-75	399	5-10	459	100-125
338	30-50	400	10-15	460	150-200
339	80-100	401	10-15	461	150-200
341	30-50	402	15-25	462	100-150
342	25-40	403	10-15	463	75-100
343	60-80	404	15-25	464	100-150
344	30-50	405	15-25	465	100-150
345	80-100	406	15-25	466	60-80
346	60-80	407	10-15	467	150-200
347	80-100	408	10-15	468	75-100
349	60-80	409	60-80	471	75-100
350	75-100	410	60-80	475	60-80
352	40-60	411	60-80	476	60-80
353	50-75	414	60-80	477	50-75
354T	40-60	415	20-30	478	40-60
354B	30-50	416	30-40	479	75-100
355	30-50	419	20-30	480	200-250
356	40-60	420	20-30	481	100-150
357	30-40	421	30-40	482	30-50
358	40-60	422	20-30	483	30-40
359	20-30	423	20-30	484	15-20
361	20-30	424	20-30	485	60-80
362	15-25	425	20-30	486	60-80
363	40-60	426	20-30	489	100-150
364	10-20	427	20-30	490	75-100
365	15-25	428	20-30	493	40-50
368	10-20	429	20-30	494	20-30
369T	20-30	430	50-75	495	30-40
369B	40-60	431	20-30	496	40-50
371	15-25	432	20-30	497	25-35
372	15-25	433	20-30	498	30-50
373	15-25	434	30-40	499	60-80
374	15-25	435	75-100	500	20-40
376	15-25	436	75-100	501	30-50
377	5-10	437	75-100	502	20-30
378	5-10	438	30-50	503	15-25
379	5-10	439	30-50	504	60-80
380	20-30	440	20-30	508	10-20
381	15-25	441	20-30	509	75-100
382	20-30	442	20-30	510	40-60
385	25-35	443	150-200	512	60-80
386	40-60	444	40-50	513	60-80
387	20-30	449	40-50	514	50-70
388	20-30	450	150-200	515	75-100
389	15-25	451	150-200	516	60-80
390	5-10	452	125-150	517	60-80
391	5-10	453	125-150	518	100-150
392	2-4	454	125-150	519	75-100
393	8-15	455	125-150	520	30-40

Fig.#	Price.
521	40-50
522	20-30
524	40-50
525	10-20
526	15-25
527	10-15
528	10-15
529	60-80
530	40-60
531	50-75
533	50-75
534	50-75
535	50-75
536	40-50
537	40-50
538	60-80
539	60-80
540	60-80
541	60-80
542	60-80
543	75-100
544	20-30
545	50-75
546	30-40
547	40-60
548	40-60
549	30-40
550	25-35
551	50-75
552	60-80
553	50-75
554	50-75
555	50-75
556	50-75
557	50-75
558	75-100
559	60-80
560	60-80
561	60-80
562	80-100
563	25-35
564	50-75
565	80-120
566	40-60
567	40-60
568	25-30
569	40-60
570	80-120
571	60-80
572	50-75
573	50-75
574	50-75

Fig.#	Price.
575	40-50
576	40-50
577	40-50
578	30-40
579	30-40
580	30-40
581	30-40
582	40-60
583	30-40
584	80-120
585	50-75
586	80-120
589	30-40
590	30-40
591	40-50
592	20-30
593	30-40
594	40-50
595	30-40
596	10-15
597	20-30
598	40-50
599	30-40
602	60-80
604	40-60
606	20-30
607	20-30
608	20-30
609	30-40
612	100-150
619	50-60
623	350-450
624	30-40
626	80-100
631	40-50
632	40-50
633	20-30
637	20-30
638	50-75
639	40-60
641	50-75
643	60-80
644	40-50
646	25-35
647	30-40
649	60-80
650	60-80
652	30-40
654	30-40
656	25-35
658	40-50
660	40-50

Fig.#	Price.
661	30-40
662	30-40
663	15-25
664	30-40
665	20-30
666	40-60
667	80-100
668	20-30
669	20-30
670	15-25
672	20-30
673	20-30
674	20-30
675	20-30
676	20-30
677	20-30
678	15-25
679	40-50
680	20-30
681	10-15
682	30-40
683	30-40
685	10-20
686	5-10
687	10-15
688	6-8
689	6-8

Additional Prices

16L	200-280
16R	200-250
445	40-60
447	20-30
448	30-40